The Giant Book of
Unsolved Crimes

The Giant Book of Unsolved Crimes

Edited by Roger Wilkes

Magpie Books, London

Constable & Robinson Ltd
3 The Lanchesters
162 Fulham Palace Road
London W6 9ER
www.constablerobinson.com

First published in the UK as
The Mammoth Book of Unsolved Crimes by Robinson,
an imprint of Constable & Robinson Ltd 1999

This edition published by Magpie Books,
an imprint of Constable & Robinson Ltd 2005

loguing in Publication Data is available
British Library

·84529-206-5

bound in the EU

9 10 8 6 4 2

CONTENTS

INTRODUCTION

Some years ago, I disturbed the bones of an old murder case. It was unsolved: a man had been convicted but then freed on appeal, and no one else had subsequently been brought to book. Back in 1931, the hot-from-the-hob headlines had blazed the tale. An insurance agent called Wallace had murdered his drab little wife, beating out her brains in their cluttered front parlour in Liverpool with such unclerkly ferocity that the walls were streaked, spattered and flecked as high as the picture-rail. Wallace was accused of having devised an alibi of consummate cunning, involving the critical synchromesh of logged telephone calls, word-of-mouth messages, at least three tram timetables and a bogus appointment. Picking it over for a radio programme half a century later, a panel of experts agreed that Wallace did not murder his wife—indeed, could not have done so. Moreover, newly uncovered testimony suggested a different solution and buttressed the case against a different suspect, a much younger man who boasted secret CID connections, a propensity to steal and to dissemble, and who nursed a grudge against Wallace. Yet amid the excitement of discovery, we discerned an unexpected note of melancholy. It now seemed a shame to spoil a perfectly good whodunnit. We had, in a sense, performed the reverse of alchemy and transmuted the burnished gold of mystery into dross. Solving the riddle had diminished the story, reduced it to a commonplace. Everyone loves a good murder, but especially a murder that defies solution, that continues to frustrate and ultimately defeat our forensic skills and the constructs of logic. We'd rather our unsolved crimes remain unsolved. What draws us is the magnetic field of mystery.

Why is this so? The poet W.H. Auden, a self-confessed addict of detective fiction, viewed the popularity of the whodunnit as a substitute for religious patterns of certainty, the dialectic of innocence and guilt. But Auden was anxious to dignify the genre. He described the *noir* tales of the American Raymond Chandler, a writer of the hard-boiled school, as serious studies of a criminal *milieu*, to be read and judged, not as escape literature, but as works of art. And yet, in the end, detective fiction is imprisoned within a basic formula. It is a ritual, as Auden himself reminds us: "a murder occurs; many are suspected; all but one suspect, who is the murderer, are eliminated; the murderer is arrested or dies."* The connoisseur of real-life crime is affronted by this comfortable and threadbare format. He knows that in the real world, not every crime mystery is solved by the arrival of the detective, the furrowing of brows and the application of improbable powers of deduction. Murder is always mysterious. Here are crimes so puzzling, sometimes clueless, often motiveless, that we can only guess at the truth of them.

The history of unsolved crime is as old as the history of crime itself, but it has only been documented in any coherent form for the last 200 years or so. One of the earliest recorded cases of unsolved murder in London dates from 1678 when Sir Edmund Berry Godfrey, politician, magistrate and woodmonger, was found dead in a ditch. The crime remains one of the most celebrated of historical British mysteries. Sir Edmund was the magistrate before whom Titus Oates swore the existence of a Popish Plot, by which English Protestants would be massacred, the King assassinated and a Catholic ministry installed in his place. The "plot" was Oates's invention, but Godfrey's murder ensured that the tale gained widespread currency. Whoever did the murder was supposed to have dripped blobs of wax on to the body, possibly in an effort to throw suspicion on to the priests from the popish Queen's Chapel. Three Catholic suspects were duly arrested, tried and hanged for the murder, but the trial was a travesty and the part played by this

---

* W.H. Auden, *The Guilty Vicarage*, reprinted in *The Dyer's Hand* (Faber & Faber, London, 1948)

wretched trio in Godfrey's demise (if any) remains hidden. The great essayist in black humour Thomas de Quincey (1785–1859), applying the principles of aesthetic criticism to murder ("as one of the fine arts"), judged Sir Edmund's assassination "the finest work of the seventeenth century" precisely because no one knew who had done it. "In the grand feature of *mystery*, which in some shape or other ought to colour every judicious attempt at murder, it is excellent," de Quincey declared, "for the mystery is not yet dispersed".*

Another early unsolved case occurred in Bristol in the middle of the eighteenth century, de Quincey's Augustan age of murder, a double killing he applauded for its "originality of design, boldness and depth of style". This was the shocking case of a Mrs Ruscombe, who lived in College Green with a single maidservant. Some suspicion arising, neighbours broke into the house and found Mrs Ruscombe murdered in her bedroom and the servant murdered on the stairs. The case was never officially solved, although suspicion fell on several local tradesmen including a baker and a chimney-sweep. Some fifty years later, de Quincey himself claimed to have learned the real murderer's identity: a notorious Lancashire highwayman who concealed his profession by drawing woollen stockings over his horse's legs to muffle the clatter of its hooves. Such exceptional murders aside, crime chronicles from the pre-industrialized age disclose few cases that were unresolved or that proved insoluble; indeed, there was an underlying assumption that although the mills of justice may have ground slow and exceeding small, at least they ground passably true. Justice always got it right. Forces of law and order, including those predating the modern police, were deemed incorruptible and all-knowing, incapable of making mistakes. Virtually every suspect fed into the machinery of the courts emerged at the other end bearing the brand of guilt and often doomed to die. Acquittals were rare. A more brutal public appetite demanded vengeance. It would not do to have crimes left unsolved, loose ends trailing. Fortunately, when cases fell short of a conviction, few people came to hear about it.

The spread of literacy in the early nineteenth century put a brake on such ignorance. In Britain, a series of sensational murders (the Thurtell–Hunt case, the crimes of the bodysnatchers Burke and

* Thomas de Quincey, "On Murder Considered as one of the Fine Arts" (*Blackwood's Magazine*, London, 1827)

Hare, and the murder by William Corder of Maria Marten in the Red Barn) excited the interest of an embryonic popular press, and the die was cast. Indeed, in 1824 the trial of Thurtell and Hunt, a couple of Regency conmen who bludgeoned their victim, shot him and finally slit his throat, was the first "trial by newspaper". But all these cases ended with the snap of the hangman's trap that was richly deserved, and the day of the unsolved crime as an identifiable genre had not yet dawned.

Murder was a favourite topic of popular literature in England as early as Elizabethan times, and accounts of occasional homicides "pathetic or merely horrifying" appeared in seventeenth- and eighteenth-century broadsheets. Shakespeare read about real-life murder, and so, in a later age, did Dickens. In his day, an eager reading public drawn from the literate (and, by definition, "respectable") section of the population devoured the accounts of crimes and criminals pulled together and published by the hacks of Grub Street. Detective fiction, too, was putting down roots, with Edgar Allan Poe's "tales of ratiocination" of the 1840s establishing a format that would reach its apotheosis nearly a century later. Fashionable ladies dispatched their servants to purchase the most celebrated of Grub Street compilations, the *Newgate Calendar*. In the 1870s their daughters and granddaughters "over-jewelled and over-victualled on champagne" thronged the Old Bailey for the trial of the Stauntons, the flinty-hearted family accused in the so-called Penge Mystery. One of the lawyers recalled those "well-dressed women, favoured occupants of the choicest seats [who] stared through lorgnettes and opera-glasses at the four pale and weary creatures who came to their places in the dock"* and who "skimmed the pages of *Punch* when the interest flagged".†

The lower orders, meanwhile, devoured their news of crimes and criminals from cheap broadsheets printed and hawked about the streets by entrepreneurs such as James "Jemmy" Catnach (1792–1841). At the time of the Thurtell–Hunt case, Catnach alone, operating four presses day and night, produced a quarter of a million such broadsheets; when the trial began he hired two extra printers and turned out half a million copies of the proceedings. They

* Sir Edward Clarke KC, *The Story of My Life* (John Murray, London, 1918)

† J.B. Atlay (ed.), *The Trial of the Stauntons* (Wm Hodge, Edinburgh, 1911)

were crude and flimsy productions, but they had an immediate mass appeal. Few survive. Like those observed in London as early as the 1680s by the poet John Dryden, these sordid and often scandalous sheets were not designed for posterity. Most were passed roughly from hand to hand, or pasted to walls before becoming, in Dryden's lapidary phrase, "martyrs of pies, and relics of the bum."*

But it was the yellow press, launched in the middle of the nineteenth century, that offered its army of semi-literate readers a large weekly helping of crime that became as much an essential ingredient of the dreary British Sunday as roast beef and Yorkshire pudding. By the 1830s, *The Observer* was proclaiming twenty columns of crime a week, a level of coverage only matched by the *News of the World*, making its debut in 1843. By the 1870s, the *Daily Telegraph*, founded in 1855 as the first penny daily, was able to boast the biggest circulation in the world (200,000 copies a day), and to attribute its success chiefly to its comprehensive coverage of crime. At last, the British middle classes were becoming (respectably) crime-conscious.

Murder was also a staple of popular Victorian popular fiction. The gothic novels of the late eighteenth century had spawned a low-life offspring, the crude genre known as the penny dreadful (and its collateral, the shilling shocker). More uplifting than either, Charles Dickens also helped to raise Victorian awareness of criminality, since most of his novels features murder, robbery, rape, incest, arson or some assorted villainy. Dickens, an experienced journalist, published his early works in weekly parts and recognized the cliffhanging possibilities of crime-based plots. After his death in 1870, other writers like Wilkie Collins seized the flame and forged ahead. Collins's novel *The Moonstone* contains echoes of real-life Victorian cases, while the now-forgotten *Chetwynd Calverley* by William Harrison Ainsworth contains a poisoning case squarely based on the notorious Bravo mystery at Balham in 1876, one of the earliest "unsolved" crimes in the age of mass literacy.

I have surveyed the landscape of unsolved crime with a wide-angle lens. Every crime included in this collection is (or was) "unsolved" in one way or another, but in staking out the limits of my territory I have stretched the definition of that word in order to accommodate as wide a range of cases as possible. At the core of these cases are those real-life mysteries that are as perplexing now as they ever were:

---

* John Dryden (1631–1700), *Mac Flecknoe* (1684)

they encompass murders by person or persons unknown, crimes that
resulted in no criminal charge, or where (demonstrably) the wrong
person was accused or (again, demonstrably) the right person was
not. Pre-eminent among these puzzlements are the crimes of Jack
the Ripper in the East End of London in the so-called autumn of
terror in 1888.

The Ripper killings remain shrouded in a fog of absurd claims
and improbable culprits. No one will ever know the Ripper's identity
for certain, which is why the mystery still supports an annual crop of
new books, articles, films, videos and websites, not to mention an
entire society of Ripperologists, complete with official newsletter and
merchandise. Among these seekers after truth are numbered some of
the true crime industry's most distinguished and talented, along with
the daftest and most dismal. Happily and harmlessly, each keeps the
other entertained. In 1998 Colin Wilson calculated that no fewer
than fifty books had appeared on the case since Leonard Matters
first proposed a certain Dr Stanley as the Ripper in a book published
in 1929. And yet behind the terrifying and unstoppable juggernaut of
Ripper writing, there is little that encapsulates the facts, the theories
and the evidence in the digestible, if not bite-sized, form sought by
the anthologist. Here, for the first time, Philip Sugden, historian,
teacher and cool-headed Yorkshireman, fills that void.

The Victorian Ripper was the progenitor of the modern Mr X,
that shadowy wraith responsible for countless unsolved crimes of
the twentieth century. He and his kind were the people who
killed Hilda Murrell, the British anti-nuclear campaigner; who
slew Elizabeth Short, the American floozy known as the Black
Dahlia; who murdered and mutilated heaven-knows-who in the
Brighton Trunk Crime Number One; who spirited Shergar away
in the mists of an Irish dawn. There is the Mr X who snuffed out
Mary Rogers in Edgar Allan Poe's New York, and the one who
plugged Jake Lingle in the Chicago of booze and bullets. There is
his more contemporary counterpart, the Mr X who masqueraded
as the Zodiac killer in 1960s California. We meet them all here,
through a glass darkly, but not yet face to face. Irving Wallace,
Colin Wilson and Jonathan Goodman are among those making
the introductions.

This collection conducts us through the ranks of the acquitted,
men and women who have placed themselves on a jury of their
peers and received deliverance, but who have left a thousand
questions unanswered. Eric Ambler ponders the case of Dr John

Bodkin Adams in an essay seeing the light of day for the first time in nearly forty years. The American humorist James Thurber wryly recalls the classic Hall–Mills affair from the 1920s. Then there are classic puzzles from Britain between the wars, such as the case of the spinsterly wan Annie Hearn and her salmon sandwiches—retold by the ebullient Daniel Farson—and that of Ronald Light and his infamously abandoned green bicycle, related by the American master, Edmund Pearson.

These were cases in which the jury were agreed that the evidence against the accused was wanting. There are others where juries have returned guilty verdicts, only to have those verdicts overturned by a higher court. Of these, the case of William Herbert Wallace from 1931 remains pre-eminent, the *ne plus ultra* of murder mysteries. The trial jury's verdict of guilty was speedily reversed on appeal, and Wallace went free, only to die within two years of a chronic kidney ailment. It was a nightmare of a case, straight from the pages of Kafka or Poe. Raymond Chandler reckoned it would "always be unbeatable". In 1940, the *doyenne* of criminologists, Fryn Tennyson Jesse, drove around Liverpool on a crime-crawl. "We found the little house," she wrote to her friend and fellow murder-fancier Alexander Woollcott, "and it was occupied". Without knocking, Miss Jesse peered in from the street. "The windows were so thickly shrouded with swathings of Nottingham lace curtains that it was impossible to get a glimpse of the rooms within," she reported. Her view may have been obscured, but not her insight. Miss Jesse's estimation of the Wallace case, dating from the early 1950s, differs from mine, but here it is, appearing in print for the first time.

Some crimes continue to be contested not in courts of law but in the tribunal of public opinion. In Britain, of all murder case verdicts to be disputed since the second World War, that against James Hanratty remains one of the most difficult and unsettling. Hanratty, a twenty-five-year-old petty crook, was hanged in 1962 for murdering Michael Gregsten in a lay-by at Deadman's Hill on the A6 near Bedford. Gregsten and his mistress, Valerie Storie, were hijacked at gunpoint while parked in a lonely cornfield. After shooting Gregsten dead, the gunman raped Miss Storie and shot her too, leaving her paralysed for life. Journalist Paul Foot concluded in his book on the case that "I am as sure as it is possible to be that James Hanratty did not commit the A6 murder". Nearly forty years after the case, Paul Foot is as certain as ever that, in Hanratty's case, Britain hanged an innocent man.

This miscellany also covers cases in which, although crime was committed, no one was subsequently charged. The American, Dorothy Dunbar, puzzles over a *cause célèbre* from the London of the nineteenth century, the Bravo mystery at Balham.

There is a small category of cases which remain unsolved because of outbreaks of judicial foot-in-mouth disease. These are instances in which those who were thought to have been responsible for crimes have subsequently been not only exonerated but officially pardoned. I have excluded the ordeal of Timothy Evans, hanged in 1950 for the murder of his wife and baby daughter at 10 Rillington Place, west London. Although Evans was eventually pardoned, the solution to the mystery seemed clear: Mrs Evans and her child had been murdered, along with others, by another resident at 10 Rillington Place, John Reginald Halliday Christie. We can be much less certain, however, about what really happened in a handful of other cases, including those of Sacco and Vanzetti in 1920. The American anarchists Sacco and Vanzetti were officially exonerated by the Governor of Massachusetts in 1977, fifty years after they were executed by electric chair.

Sometimes, juries are unable to agree on the question of culpability, and the legal process becomes deadlocked. The result can be that the accused goes free, leaving the question of guilt unresolved, as happened in two cases in different continents in the first decade of the twentieth century. In New York, Nan Patterson, the girl from the *Florodora* chorus, left little by way of a mystery when she emerged from her third trial to public acclaim in 1906, but the story comes up fresh at the hands of Alexander Woollcott and one is inclined to excuse him if his exuberance betrays a ring of invention. More soberly, as befits an English barrister, Jack Smith-Hughes is altogether less tolerant of black-bearded Willie Gardiner. The Methodist elder of piratical aspect seems to have bamboozled the juries at both his trials.

Was it murder? The question invites us to consider another selection of cases in which the evidence is just so intractable as to leave us at best doubtful and at worst openly sceptical. For nearly forty years, the debate over how Marilyn Monroe really met her death has spiralled this way and that, conspiracy theorists have laid siege to the facts, and the entire case has been sucked down into the black holes of the Kennedy assassinations. Kirk Wilson pulls together what is known about the death of Hollywood's most potent female icon. From an earlier age and landscape, the Scottish criminologist William Roughead throws the tragedy of Ireland's Eye into the sharpest relief, and explains that although the accused man Kirwan was convicted of murder and punished with a life sentence, subsequent medical opinion suggests that Kirwan's wife probably died of natural causes, and that in fact there was no murder. In the Maybrick poisoning case of 1889, it is equally likely that no murder was done, and that the victim (the drug-driven cotton man James Maybrick) succumbed to his self-administered nostrums without the help of his neglected wife Florence. Arrested and tried for murder, but in reality convicted for the unpardonable sin of adultery, Mrs Maybrick's martyrdom grinds the gears of modern manners. At Liverpool prison, she lay in the condemned cell listening to her own scaffold being erected, but at least her deliverance was at hand, and a reprieve (the mob, for once, clamouring for mercy) snatched her from the brink.

No such respite was afforded the young Elizabeth Fenning, the servant accused in the year of Waterloo of trying to poison the family she worked for in London. She evidently belongs in that hapless band of the wrongly accused, those who (it seems) have been falsely arraigned for the crimes of others or for crimes that were never even committed. Numbered with her we find the medieval Frenchman Martin Guerre, whose story has recently been revived in a London West End musical. The mystery of Guerre's disappearance and his unexpected return years later is certainly the stuff of legend, but whether the man dangling at the end of the tale was an wronged innocent or a guilty imposter seems a very close call indeed.

Crime and its insolubility has hooked and held a surprisingly distinguished crop of writers. Well into middle age, Rebecca West, hailed at the halfway point of the twentieth century as the best writer in the English language, suddenly turned her talent to crime reporting. In December 1949 she addressed the case of Donald Hume, accused of the murder of the shady car dealer Stanley Setty. Her impressions at Hume's trial, one of which is included here, were published in the newspapers before being reworked into her full-scale and haunting study *Mr Setty and Mr Hume* which appeared a few years later. Hume was acquitted of murder, and Miss West thought it likely that Setty's murder was likely to rank as one of the great unsolved mysteries. "The possibility that Hume murdered Mr Setty can definitely be excluded," she wrote. "But who murdered Mr Setty, and how, and where, is known to nobody but the murderer. Not for lack of evidence. That is piled sky-high. There is so much that whatever theory the mind may base on that evidence, there exists some fact which disproves it."* She was wrong. Hume had pleaded guilty to being an accessory to Setty's murder, and served eight years of a twelve-year sentence. But on his release, he went to a Sunday newspaper and confessed to murdering Stanley Setty. In fact, Hume went on to murder again and was sentenced to life imprisonment, spending nearly thirty years in Broadmoor.

Like Rebecca West, the critic Alexander Woollcott enjoyed a lifelong fascination with murder, and was one of the first to strike a distinctively American tone in writing about crime. The British may have the best mysteries, but by and large the Americans infuse the histories of crime with greater fizz. It was an American, Truman Capote, who in the 1960s invented a completely new genre, the non-fiction novel, and with the publication of *In Cold Blood* raised the true crime book to the level of literature. In the thirties, Woollcott relished the retelling of old murders in what he self-deprecatingly dismissed as "a grab-bag of twice-told tales". He was living in a less sophisticated age than our own, in which the incidence of unsolved crime (or, at any rate, murder) is statistically rare. Of the 681 homicides reported in England and Wales in 1996, for example, only forty-six remained unsolved a year later, a clear-up rate of ninety-three per cent. Improved detection and scientific techniques are responsible, methodology that would have been unrecognizable (indeed, unimaginable) to the fictional 1940s detectives of the Department of Dead Ends, a non-existent branch of Scotland Yard, invented by writer Roy Vickers,† in which details of all unsolved murders were stored. But in spite of such giant strides, unsolved murders will never be killed off altogether. Consigning mystery to history is not a realistic option. The American crime writer Ed McBain believes people like mysteries because they can come close to the violence without being part of it, and can be sure that "the people who are doing the violence at the end of it are going to be caught". But the stories that follow have no ending, for they finish curled up in a question-mark; we are drawn closer to them because the mystery is not yet dispersed.

* Rebecca West *Mr Setty and Mr Hume* in *A Train of Powder* (Macmillan, London 1955)
† Educated at Charterhouse and Oxford, Vickers (1888–1965) was a journalist and author of more than seventy novels.

EVIDENCE BY ENTRAPMENT

(Rachel Nickell, 1992)

Brian Masters

In Britain, the most notoriously unsolved murder of the 1990s was that of Rachel Nickell on Wimbledon Common. Her killing, witnessed by her little son on a summer's morning, provoked a national clamour. Detectives eventually arrested Colin Stagg, an out-of-work loner who lived nearby. But he was freed by a judge at the Old Bailey when it was revealed that police had tried to snare their suspect into confessing by the use of a so-called "honeytrap," a woman police officer who, operating undercover and using the name "Lizzie James", had befriended Colin Stagg and sought to establish a relationship with him. The judge, Mr Justice Ognall, ruled that evidence from such a witness was inadmissible. The prosecution dropped the case, and Colin Stagg was cleared of murder. The case also raised questions about the use of psychological profiling, and it was this contentious aspect of the investigation that concerned the British author Brian Masters (b. 1939). He has written about many controversial murder cases in Europe and America since his classic study of the mass murderer Dennis Nilsen appeared in 1985.

Rachel Nickell was an enchanting, pretty, ebullient girl, described by her father as "a bright star" whose "happiness was so real you could touch it". On 13 July 1992, she went bouncing out for a

walk on Wimbledon Common with her two-year-old son Alex,
arriving there at ten a.m. Thirty-five minutes later she was dead,
viciously stabbed forty-nine times in a random, motiveless murder
which bore all the signs of psychopathic disorder. It had taken three
minutes to dispatch Rachel and leave her little boy, bathed in her
blood, clinging to her body and pleading for her to get up. No
wonder the nation was overwhelmed with pity. And no wonder
Mrs Nickell shed tears in court last week when the case against
the man accused of killing her daughter was not even allowed to
go to trial. I do not know the Nickell family, but having spent
many weeks with Bruce and Pat Cottrill, whose daughter Fiona
Jones was slaughtered by a stranger in France, I think I know
something of their anguish. Being cheated of an answer, a result
proclaimed in court, makes it seem that Rachel's death did not
matter.

But it was not the fault of the court that there was no evidence
to connect Colin Stagg to the crime. It was the fault of naïve
and increasingly desperate police methods born of understandable
frustration. The murderer left no tangible clues. Police had mounted
the biggest murder hunt in London's history. They interviewed
hundreds of people, drew up a list of over 500 suspects, cautioned
scores, actually arrested and released thirty-two men. One of these
had been Stagg, who had been interrogated for three days from
18 September 1992; he had co-operated fully and given a reliable
account of his movements. They searched his flat and found nothing
of any relevance. Nevertheless, they did not forget him.

It was not entirely a mistake for police to seek the guidance of
an "offender profiler" to describe the sort of man they should be
looking for, but it was, perhaps, foolish to attach importance to
what can only be intelligent conjecture. Anyway, they had nothing
else, so they turned to Paul Britton, a psychologist who works in
Leicester and who had helped on other investigations. Offender
profiling is not a science; it relies upon the merging of experience
with intuition, and was first developed by the National Centre for
the Analysis of Violent Crime, a division of the FBI at Quantico,
Virginia, as a tool to assist traditional detection. The acknowledged
expert there is Robert Ressler, who is frequently called upon to
offer an opinion, although the judge at the trial of Jeffrey Dahmer
in Milwaukee declined to allow Mr Ressler to testify in court.
When American judges have permitted an "offender profile" to
be presented in evidence, they have regretted it. Convictions have

been secured on seventeen occasions, and all of them have been overturned by a higher court.

The trouble is, "offender profiling" is an infant art. It is experimental and haphazard. Professor David Canter has written about the "shadow" left by the criminal of himself at the scene of crime, which is a striking image, but he has more reliably concentrated on the clues he might find as to methods rather than as to personality. It is when one starts postulating the personality of an unknown killer that the "shadow" becomes really insubstantial, and this is what happened, sadly, to the Wimbledon inquiry.

The FBI's Behavioural Science Unit, where psychological profiling originated as an aid to the analysis of violent crime, was based precisely upon this idea that behaviour *always* reflects personality. Therefore, if you can see how the murderer behaved towards his victim, you can work out what kind of man he is. To this end, a team of FBI agents conducted extensive interviews with thirty-six convicted sex murderers between 1979 and 1983 in order to discover what they had in common, and use the results to make a composite picture of the typical offender. They found, for example, that nearly half of them had been sexually abused in childhood and most of the rest at a later stage. Seventy per cent of them had problems functioning as sexual adults and had to use pornography as a stimulus. They enjoy watching somebody look terrified, and had a compulsive itch to dominate and control somebody else. Pornography, the FBI concluded, was never the cause of the murder, but the fuel of a unrealized fantasy which might include murder. When inhibiting factors were weak, the fantasy might explode, so it was another characteristic of these men that they had little capacity for self-restraint and poor self-esteem.

(Incidentally, the film *Silence of the Lambs* purported to show an FBI agent interviewing serial killer Hannibal Lecter. Just one of the fraudulent aspects of that film was that agents always operate in twos when in close contact with a dangerous convict).

The value of the psychological profile is debatable. It is obviously useful in eliminating suspects who might be happily married clergymen or clubbable classical lexicographers, but the rather general characteristics which are left can cover an awful lot of people. Ted Bundy, the plausible good-looking young man who killed and disfigured several girls in various of the United States in the 1970s, was not caught by the FBI's profile but because he fired on a traffic policeman who gave chase when he was driving a stolen car. He had killed for years undetected. Once in custody, however, he was identified with the help of the profile, which for the defenders of this method is sufficient justification. For its critics, there is just too much reliance placed on hunches, which can often be quite unsupported.

Paul Britton said the murderer of Rachel Nickell would have a strong inclination to sexual fantasy, would seek a young submissive adult woman for sexual gratification, would seek to dominate and control her and would be excited by her fear. More specifically, he would look for buggery as well as vaginal intercourse. All this was, frankly, fairly commonplace, in so far as this kind of murderer is always an isolated fantasist, inadequate on a social level and dangerous only when the fantasies are unleashed into the real world. Britton suggested that the use of a knife indicated that the murderer belonged to a very small category of sexual sadists, and he was probably thinking of those described by (his almost namesake) Robert Brittain in *Medicine, Science and the Law* in 1970. But again, he went further in proposing that Rachel's killer would be interested in so-called satanic rituals. It is difficult to see why that should be so, except as a wild idea.

So the police had to find somebody whose sexual fantasies were rather less innocuous than yours or mine—not an easy task given that fantasies are necessarily private. By a lucky chance, they were approached by a girl called Julie Pine who had been in correspondence with a man contacted through a lonely hearts column. This man's third letter was so disgusting that she thought the police ought to know. His name was Colin Stagg, unemployed, thirty years old and still a virgin. His file was brought out again, and it revealed that his bedroom was painted black and he possessed some books on cult subjects. (So do I, and my room was painted blood-red thirty years ago, but never mind.)

Investigators then instigated the undercover operation designed to elicit a confession from Stagg. A woman police officer, using the fictitious name of Lizzie James, wrote to Stagg on 19 January 1993, posing as a friend of Miss Pine and presenting herself as attractive and much more broadminded than the other woman. She said her favourite record was "Walk on the Wild Side", a blatant come-on. Britton predicted that Stagg would respond and would gradually ease his way through confidence to confession. It should take at least two weeks, but no more than sixteen. Throughout, Britton would control the content of WPC James's letters and monitor Stagg's replies.

The first reply came immediately, with an admission from Stagg that "I do sometimes get painfully lonely". He said his only friend was his dog Brandy, whom he walked on the common every day. On instruction, "Lizzie" picked up the theme of loneliness and revealed: "I haven't had a relationship with a man for a very long time, and I sometimes long for company, of the kind only a man can give." She gave the impression, too, that she would not object to a sexual fantasy as Julie had. Stagg was being enticed from the very beginning by what amounted to an *agent provocateur*.

He told her that he had never had a sex life, that women didn't want to know, and included the fantasy letter she had asked for, telling of sex in the dark. She then put herself forward as a woman of experience, and encouraged him to fantasize further. "There's more to you than meets the eye," she wrote, "I'm sure your fantasies know no bounds . . . you're a brilliant story-teller . . . I'm working myself up." She sent him a picture of herself. "You've certainly brightened up my life," he told her. "Nothing like this has ever happened to me before. It's like a dream come true. I have never been attractive to women, that's why I have so many fantasies." She commiserated with a mixture of sympathy and seduction. "I understand exactly how you feel. Your honesty is so refreshing. I do hope we will always be honest with each other, as being betrayed and let down is so difficult to get over . . . Don't worry, you won't be lonely much longer. Each time you write, I know we get closer and closer. There are secrets about me that I long to share with someone. I've got things to tell that you won't believe."

Colin Stagg was an obliging, enthusiastic correspondent, but annoyingly slow in fitting the profile Mr Britton had devised. He was supposed to be keen on anal sex, so Lizzie introduced the subject, archly rather than directly. "I hope I'm not sounding unnatural," she wrote, using a word obviously planted, "but there's so much more to explore than just straight sex." He did not seem to realize what she meant. Again, the prediction was that he would want to dominate, so she offered herself to him. "You've taken charge, you're so powerful. I want to feel you all-powerful and overwhelming. I want you to burst." Throughout the correspondence, she urged him to write ever bolder fantasy letters, and responded immediately to these, withholding her reply if he failed to include a fantasy or came up with a tame one.

There is no doubt that Stagg liked to write exciting sexual fiction, but the content of his letters was being dictated and shaped by Lizzie. As Mr Justice Ognall said last week, the fantasies he expressed during the first two weeks of the correspondence were such as might occur to any heterosexual and inexperienced young man. These were not good enough, so he had to be encouraged in the invention of more outrageous scenes. At one point, she sent him a tape-recording which Mr William Clegg, in his submission to the court for the defence, described as "the most hard-core pornography one could imagine . . . an extraordinary document for a working police officer to send to a suspect in a murder investigation . . . without precedent". The paradox in this sorry tale seems to be that the more kinky prose came from Paul Britton, via the police officer.

When Lizzie begged Stagg to reveal something terrible in his past, because she could never be comfortable with a normal man, the best he could come up with was mutual masturbation with a boy when he was seventeen. ("That must have been a disappointment," murmured someone in court.) He wondered whether she might be a journalist in disguise, but he was by this time so bewitched by her that he would do anything to keep the relationship going, especially since she held out the prospect of meeting and, eventually, settling down together. The tenor of his replies was often domestic, romantic, hopeful. He spoke of redecorating his flat and of their cooking dinner together. But she wanted more pornography, so he supplied it rather than lose her. At one point he showed apprehension about the effect his stories might have. "Don't worry," he wrote. "No harm will come to you. I don't want to upset you." Prosecuting counsel John Nutting said this demonstrated that he was anxious not to go too far. More likely, surely, that he did not know how far to go. A psychotic fantasist has no such scruples, because he is indifferent to and ignorant of the effect of his imaginings. Nor, and this is very important, does he share them with anyone else. It could be argued that Stagg effectively excluded himself as a suspect by divulging these fantasies. "I now have some idea of what you want," he wrote before one exotic tale.

After five months, the undercover operation had got nowhere. Colin Stagg simply was not matching up to expectations, was not delivering according to the theoretic "profile". WPC James, knowing that he was hard up, offered him money, but he would not accept. She promised they would go on holiday together, at the same time making it clear that he was not all that she had hoped for. If he wanted her, he must come up to her level. She introduced the theme of hurting people, not in fiction but in fact, inviting him to respond. "I do not understand," he wrote. "Do you mean physically, mentally, or emotionally? I lead a very quiet life." She then hinted at a dark secret. "Can you imagine what I have done?" she asked, to which he made the obtuse reply, "You haven't given me any real clues. What do you mean?"

The policewoman finally went to the point, saying that she had participated in a ritual murder and had personally cut the throat of a young woman and her child, after which she had had the best sexual experience of her life. He decided to match this by confessing to a murder in the New Forest with his cousin when he was thirteen years old. As everyone in court subsequently agreed, this was an invention; no such event had occurred. They talked about the killing of Rachel Nickell, and he admitted that thinking about it turned him on. He liked the idea of the knife. It looked as if the investigation was getting closer to its aim. She intimated that it would be "great" if he had done it, and "I wish you had". He would then be worthy of her, and they could live together for ever. "It wouldn't matter to me if you had murdered her. I'm not bothered," she wrote. "If I didn't like you so much I could lie to you and say I did do it, just to keep you," he said. Mr Justice Ognall intervened to point out that this would seem to indicate that he would not confess despite the most powerful inducement.

Colin Stagg and "Lizzie" met four times. They continued to discuss Rachel's murder, which he described inaccurately. He said she had been raped. She had not. He misidentified where she had been found. And on their last encounter, he described the position of her body, with a crucial detail relating to the position of her hands which, though still inaccurate, the police construed as a confession. It had taken seven months. The next time the two met, "Lizzie" was in her true colours, in uniform. The judge commented wrily that this must have been a traumatic experience for them both.

The Crown admitted that the operation had necessarily been deceitful but that "more serious offences do justify more unusual methods of investigation". While the law permits evidence obtained by clandestine means to be given in evidence in certain circumstances, it stipulates that the information so obtained must be other than that discoverable by question and answer, in order to uphold the centuries-old common law which protects an individual from incriminating himself. In the Stagg/James relationship there was, however, no difference between asking questions and eliciting material designed to build up an incriminating psychological profile. Had the 700 pages of transcripted conversations and correspondence been allowed in evidence, it would have been the first time such evidence was presented in British criminal history. We now know that the judge did not allow it, because the suspect had clearly been manipulated with a view to inculpating himself, and that exculpatory material had been set aside. Mr Justice Ognall, a deeply experienced and splendidly sane Yorkshireman, is no friend to villains, but is even less an ally to subterfuge. The overriding demands of fairness in the justice system must prevail.

What case did the Crown hope to present against Colin Stagg? There was no murder weapon, no motive, no evidence of previous personality disorder apart from one instance of indecent exposure, no forensic evidence to link him to the brutal murder of Rachel Nickell. The prosecution had three planks. First, Stagg had been on Wimbledon Common at the time of the offence (along with 500 other people). Second, that he had described the position of Rachel's body (not accurately, as it turned out). Third, that his fantasies matched those to be expected according to the predictions of Paul Britton. When this last plank was disallowed, the first two diminished to invisibility, and the Crown had to concede they had no evidence at all. Hence the formal verdict of Not Guilty.

Colin Stagg is perhaps a flawed character. He had some timid pornography in his flat, of the sort you may find on the top shelf at your newsagent's, and he has a minor conviction on his record. But we must all, I think, be glad that he was not tried on evidence obtained by underhand methods, for it is a fundamental safeguard of the citizen against the State that such citizen retains the right not to incriminate himself. It is a basic right, at the very heart of our criminal justice system, and if it were diluted we should all have reason to feel less safe.

This was the burden of the judge's ruling. There was an additional danger to which he referred obliquely as "an even higher mountain to climb", and that was the reliability of the "offender profile" which started it all. Had the police evidence been admitted before a jury, could not the defence have objected to Mr Britton's inclusion as an "expert" witness in any case? Mr Justice Ognall gave several indications that he thought as much. He referred to the undercover operation as "fishing" for specific characteristics listed in Mr Britton's "profile", and depicted him at one point as the "puppet-master". It was significant, he hinted, that little or no attention was paid to other letters which Stagg had written to a third woman, because they contained nothing to coincide with the personality postulated in the profile. Hence Mr Britton's portrait of the hypothetical person responsible for Rachel's murder took precedence over all else. If anything like this managed to seep into the system, any one of us facing charges might find ourselves judged according to the unsupported opinion of a person we had never met, and our denials held to corroborate our guilt (Britton had predicted that it would be part of the suspect's personality to deny involvement with the crime).

Mr Clegg submitted to the court that Britton's technique was "inherently prone to error and had not been accepted by the scientific community". Expert evidence is only heard in our courts if the expert is accepted as such by his peers and has been exposed to critical scientific scrutiny, the results of that scrutiny having been published. Mr Clegg pointed out that Britton's offender profile was speculative, intuitive and therefore unreliable; that the principles upon which it was based were not identified; that there was no means of knowing how he arrived at his conclusions; and that his assessment of the suspect took no account of the fact that his fantasy letters were written to satisfy the demands of the undercover agent.

The judge referred to a ruling by the Supreme Court of the United States (Daubert v. Merrell Dow Pharmaceuticals, 28 June 1993) in which it was stated that a trial judge, before admitting expert scientific testimony, should make a preliminary assessment as to whether the methodology underlying such testimony was scientifically valid and tested.

In England, there is also the long-established rule (in *Phipson on Evidence*) regarding evidence as to propensity. Evidence may not be given that the defendant "has a disposition to commit crimes of that kind", in other words that he is the sort of man who might have been capable of committing the crime with which he is charged.

It is doubtful whether Mr Britton would have been called to give evidence. Britton's contribution to the search for the killers of little James Bulger in Bootle consisted, according to the police, in assuring them that no adult was involved in the murder. He proved to be right. But since no adult, except a retarded one, would have covered the body with bricks or stuffed batteries in the boy's mouth, the reasoning that children might be responsible was not a complicated one.

THE SHORT, SWEET MARTYRDOM OF JAKE LINGLE

(Jake Lingle, 1930)

Kenneth Allsop

No one knows who shot "Jake" Lingle dead. But there were strong suspicions that Chicago's supreme ganglord Al Capone ordered Lingle's murder. Lingle followed the hazardous calling of crime reporter, covering the Chicago gang wars that disfigured the Prohibition years of the late 1920s. His assassination, on a summer's day in 1930, was bruited as an outrage even in a city accustomed to violent death. At first, the killing was written off as an act of retaliation by gangsters against an honest $65-a-week reporter. But when investigators scrutinized Lingle's lifestyle, they found evidence linking him to both the city's police chief and Capone himself. Federal agents probing Capone's tax affairs discovered that Lingle's annual income amounted to some $60,000, and that the humble journalistic drudge was living the life of a millionaire, complete with holiday homes, chauffeured limousine and a permanent suite at a Chicago hotel. Investigators had made an appointment to interview Lingle the day after the murder. One theory holds that Capone feared Lingle might betray him to the tax agents, since (not being a gangster himself) he did not consider himself bound by the underworld's code of silence. Kenneth Allsop (1920–73) unravels the mystery in his panoramic *survey of Chicago's bootleggers. A prolific writer, Allsop was best known in Britain as a television journalist. In the 1960s he was a reporter on the BBC's* Tonight *programme, and regularly anchored the nightly current affairs show* 24 Hours.

On Monday, 9 June 1930 Alfred J. ("Jake") Lingle, a thirty-eight-year-old crime reporter on the Chicago *Tribune*, was shot to death while walking, smoking a cigar and reading the racing news in a crowded underpass at Randolph and Michigan during the lunch hour. A noteworthy detail in the plot was that one of Lingle's killers was apparently dressed as a parson.

His death created a furore, the parallel of which it is difficult to imagine in Britain. An American reporter—that is, a reporter on the general news-gathering staff, a position which has a different connotation from the British title, for the American reporter may be merely a leg-man, a fact-gatherer who telephones in his information to a desk re-write man—is not startlingly well paid. Yet he has a place in public regard, a compound of glamour, respect and authority, that has no counterpart in Britain. The murder of Lingle instantly assumed the importance and gravity that had attached to the murder of McSwiggin and other police and Federal officials—and, as in the case of McSwiggin, it was an uprush of moral indignation that plunged in as precipitous a slump of disillusionment.

Lingle's duties on the police beat for the *Tribune* earned him sixty-five dollars a week, a poor sum. He had never had a by-line in the paper; his name was unknown to its readers. Posthumously, when his name was famous (and fast becoming notorious), he was revealed to have had an income of $60,000 a year. He owned a chauffeur-driven Lincoln limousine. He had just bought a $16,000 house at Long Beach, on the Michigan Riviera, where his wife and two children, Buddy (six) and Pansy (five) were to spend the summer months. He had recently taken a suite of rooms at the Stevens, one of Chicago's most stylish hotels. He was an addicted gambler at horse and greyhound tracks. All this was known in a general manner among his colleagues, and the discrepancy between his meagre newspaper salary and his lavish spending was understood to be possible because of a big legacy he had received.

On the day of his death he was on the way to the races. He left his wife packing for her departure to the lake. He himself was that afternoon to go to the meeting at Washington Park, Homewood. Another significant point about that day, 9 June, was that the Sheridan Wave Tournament Club, a society gambling parlour at 621 Waveland Avenue, where the champagne, whisky and food was distributed with the managements's compliments during play, was to reopen that evening, an event of some interest to Lingle.

Retrospectively, it seems certain that Lingle knew he was in trouble. Attorney Louis B. Piquett, former City Prosecutor, later volunteered to tell the police that twenty-four hours before Lingle's death he had met Lingle in the Loop. They stood on Randolph Street talking of the discovery of Red McLaughlin's body from the canal. Lingle was giving Piquett his theory of the killing when "a blue sedan with two men in it stopped at the kerb alongside us. Lingle stopped in the middle of a sentence, looked up at the two men in a startled way and they looked back at him. He apparently had forgotten what he had been saying for he turned suddenly, walked back the way he had come, hurriedly said 'Good-bye', and entered a store as quickly as he could." And again on the day of his murder, after lunching at the Sherman Hotel he met Sergeant Thomas Alcock, of the Detective Bureau, in the lobby and told him: "I'm being tailed."

He was. After buying cigars at the Sherman kiosk, he walked the four blocks to Michigan Avenue to catch the one-thirty p.m. train for the Washington Park race-track, and descended the pedestrian subway to enter the Illinois Central suburban electric railway in Grant Park. At any time of day the subway is as busy a channel as the killers could have chosen, and at lunchtime on this Monday it was swirling with two opposite streams of shoppers and office workers.

A strange aspect of what followed is Lingle's apparent unconcern. He knew he was being followed, and a man of his experience must have known that there was only one purpose in that. Yet, on the evidence of witnesses, he arrived at the entrance to the subway walking between two men. One had blond hair and wore a straw boater and a grey suit. The other was dark in a blue suit. At the entrance Lingle paused and bought a racing edition of an evening paper, and as he did so a roadster swung into the kerb on the south side of Randolph Street and blew its horn to attract Lingle's attention. One of the men in the car called out: "Play Hy Schneider in the third!" According to Armour Lapansee, a Yellow Cab superintendent who overheard the exchange, Lingle grinned, waved his hand and called back "I've got him".

Lingle walked on into the subway. He was seen by Dr Joseph Springer, a former coroner's physician and a long-standing acquaintance. "Lingle didn't see me," Springer stated. "He was reading the race information. He was holding it before him with both hands and smoking a cigar."

Lingle had almost reached the end of the subway. He came abreast of the newsstand twenty-five feet short of the east exit, and the dark man who had been walking at his side diverted as if to buy a paper. As he did, the blond man dropped behind Lingle, levelled his left hand which held a snub-barrelled .38 Colt—known, cosily, among police and mobsters as a belly-gun—and fired a single bullet upward into Lingle's neck, which penetrated the brain and left the forehead. He fell forward, cigar still clenched between his teeth, newspaper still in his hands.

Throwing away the gun, the blond killer ran forward into the crowds, then doubled back past Lingle's body and out up the eastern staircase. He jumped a fence, changed his mind again, ran west into Randolph Street, through a passage—where he threw away a left-hand silk glove presumably worn to guard against fingerprints—and, pursued by a policeman, ran into Wabash Avenue, where he escaped into the crowds.

Meanwhile in the subway, a Mr Patrick Campbell saw the dark-haired accomplice hurrying towards the west exit. He went to intercept him, but his movement was blocked by a priest who bumped into him. Campbell said: "What's the matter?" and the priest replied: "I think someone has been shot. I'm getting out of here."

Later Lieutenant William Cusick, of the Detective Bureau, commented brusquely: "He was no priest. A priest would never do that. He would have gone to the side of the stricken person."

The pattern pieced together. It seemed clear that Lingle had walked into a trap formed by perhaps a dozen men. But what was never put forward as a theory, and which seems the likeliest explanation of his meek and unhesitating advance into the trap, was that, during his progress along the pavement, down the stairs and along the subway between two men, he was being nudged along by a gun hidden in a jacket pocket, under orders to walk naturally and keep reading the paper.

That evening Colonel Robert R. McCormick, proprietor of the Chicago *Tribune*, summoned his news staff together and addressed them on the death of a reporter whom he had never seen and whose

name he had never before heard. Pasley, who was there, says he
talked for forty-five minutes and pledged himself to solve the crime.
Next morning the front page scowled with an eight-column banner
headline announcing the sudden end of Lingle. The story read:
"Alfred J. Lingle, better known in his world of newspaper work
as Jake Lingle, and for the last eighteen years a reporter on the
Tribune, was shot to death yesterday in the Illinois Central subway
at the east side of Michigan Boulevard, at Randolph Street.

"The *Tribune* offers $25,000 as a reward for information which
will lead to the conviction of the slayer or slayers. An additional
reward of $5,000 was announced by *The Chicago Evening Post*,
making a total of $30,000."

Next morning the Hearst Chicago *Herald and Examiner* also
offered a $25,000 reward, bringing up the total to $55,000.

McCormick continued to take Lingle's death as an affront to
him personally and a smack at the press which transcended in
seriousness all the other hundreds of cases of physical violence and
the network of nefariousness. Two days later the *Tribune* carried an
editorial headed "THE CHALLENGE" which read:

"The meaning of this murder is plain. It was committed in
reprisal and in attempt at intimidation. Mr Lingle was a police
reporter and an exceptionally well-informed one. His personal
friendships included the highest police officials and the contacts
of his work made him familiar to most of the big and little fellows
of gangland. What made him valuable to his newspaper marked
him as dangerous to the killers.

"It was very foolish ever to think that assassination would be
confined to the gangs who have fought each other for the profits
of crime in Chicago. The immunity from punishment after gang
murders would be assumed to cover the committing of others.
Citizens who interfered with the criminals were no better protected
than the gangmen who fought each other for the revenue from liquor
selling, coercion of labour and trade, brothel-house keeping and
gambling.

"There have been eleven gang murders in ten days. That has
become the accepted course of crime in its natural stride, but
to the list of Colosimo, O'Banion, the Gennas, Murphy, Weiss,
Lombardo, Esposito, the seven who were killed in the St Valentine's
Day massacre, the name is added of a man whose business was to
expose the work of the killers.

"The *Tribune* accepts this challenge. It is war. There will be casualties, but that is to be expected, it being war. The *Tribune* has the support of all the other Chicago newspapers . . . The challenge of crime to the community must be accepted. It has been given with bravado. It is accepted and we'll see what the consequences are to be. Justice will make a fight of it or it will abdicate."

Police Commissioner Russell was galvanized into at least making a statement. It went colourfully: "I have given orders to the five Deputy Police Commissioners to make this town so quiet that you will be able to hear a consumptive canary cough," but he added, as a preliminary explanation for any further action: "Of course, most of the underworld has scuttled off to hiding-places. It will be hard to find them, but we will never rest until the criminals are caught and Chicago is free of them for ever." An editorial next day remarked bleakly: "These gangs have run the town for many months and have strewn the streets with the lacerated bodies of their victims. Commissioner Russell and Deputy-Commissioner Stege have had their opportunity to break up these criminal gangs, who make the streets hideous with bleeding corpses. They have failed." Instantly Russell replied: "My conscience is clear. All I ask is that the city will sit tight and see what is going to happen."

All that actually happened was that Russell and Stege, in the words of a newspaper, "staged a mock heroic battle with crime by arresting every dirty-necked ragamuffin on the street corners, but carefully abstained from taking into custody any of the men who matter". Meanwhile some of the blanks that until now had remained gaping oddly in the accounts of Lingle's character and circumstances began to be sketched in.

It is fair to infer that up to then the *Tribune* management was genuinely unaware of them. Some of the facts that had so far remained unmentioned were that he had been tagged the "unofficial Chief of Police"; that he had himself hinted that it was he who had fixed the price of beer in Chicago; that he was an intimate friend of Capone and had stayed with him at his Florida estate; that when he died he was wearing one of Capone's gift diamond-studded belts, which had come to be accepted as the insignia of the Knights of the Round Table of that place and period; that he was improbably maty, for a newspaperman of his lowly status, with millionaire businessmen, judges and county and city officials; that he spent golfing holidays and shared stock market ventures with the Commissioner of Police.

By the time a week had passed certain reservations were beginning

to temper the *Tribune*'s anger. It is apparent that more details of
Lingle's extramural life were emerging. On 18 June there appeared
another leading article, entitled "THE LINGLE INVESTIGATION GOES
ON". In this the *Tribune* betrayed a flicker of uneasiness about the
character of its martyr. "We do not know why this reporter was
killed," it admitted, "but we are engaged in finding out and we
expect to be successful. It may take time; the quicker the better, but
this enlistment is for duration. It may require long, patient efforts,
but the *Tribune* is prepared for that, and hopes that some lasting
results will be obtained which will stamp justice on the face of the
crime." To endorse its new crusading resolution, two days later the
Tribune added to its Platform for Chicagoland on the masthead of
its centre page "END THE REIGN OF GANGDOM". Appended was an
explanatory editorial: "The killers, the racketeers who exact tribute
from businessmen and union labour, the politicians who use and
shield the racketeers, the policemen and judges who have been
prostituted by politicians, all must go."

Ten days elapsed, and there had obviously been some concentrated rethinking by McCormick and his editorial executives. The
word-of-mouth buzz about Lingle's background and liaisons that
was meanwhile racing around Chicago, supported by somewhat
less reverent stories in other newspapers, evidently induced the
Tribune to take a revised, frank, let's-face-it attitude. On 30 June
a column-and-a-half editorial was published. Under the heading
"THE LINGLE MURDER", it read: "When Alfred Lingle was murdered
the motive seemed to be apparent . . . His newspaper saw no other
explanation than that his killers either thought he was close to
information dangerous to them or intended the murder as notice
given the newspapers that crime was ruler in Chicago. It could be
both, a murder to prevent a disclosure and to give warning against
attempts at others.

"It had been expected that in due time the reprisals which have
killed gangster after gangster in the city would be attempted against
any other persons or agencies which undertook to interfere with the
incredibly profitable criminality. No one had been punished for any
of these murders. They have been bizarre beyond belief, and, being
undetected, have been assumed, not least by their perpetrators, to
be undetectable—at least not to be punishable.

"When, then, Lingle was shot by an assassin the *Tribune* assumed
that the criminals had taken the next logical step and were beginning
their attack upon newspaper exposure. The *Herald and Examiner*

and the *Chicago Evening Post* joined the *Tribune* in offering rewards for evidence which would lead to conviction of the murderers. The newspaper publishers met and made a common cause against the new tactics of gangland. The preliminary investigation has modified some of the first assumptions, although it has not given the situation a different essence.

"Alfred Lingle now takes a different character, one in which he was unknown to the management of the *Tribune* when he was alive. He is dead and cannot defend himself, but many facts now revealed must be accepted as eloquent against him. He was not, and he could not have been a great reporter. His ability did not contain these possibilities. He did not write stories, but he could get information in police circles. He was not and he could not be influential in the acts of his newspaper, but he could be useful and honest, and that is what the *Tribune* management took him to be. His salary was commensurate with his work. The reasonable appearance against Lingle now is that he was accepted in the world of politics and crime for something undreamed of in his office, and that he used this in his undertakings which made him money and brought him to his death . . .

"There are weak men on other newspapers and in other professions, in positions of trust and responsibility greater than that of Alfred Lingle. The *Tribune*, although naturally disturbed by the discovery that this reporter was engaged in practices contrary to the code of its honest reporters and abhorred by the policy of the newspaper, does not find that the main objectives of the inquiry have been much altered. The crime and the criminals remain, and they are the concern of the *Tribune* as they are of the decent elements in Chicago . . .

"If the *Tribune* was concerned when it thought that an attack had been made upon it because it was inimical to crime, it is doubly concerned if it be the fact that crime had made a connexion in its own office . . . That Alfred Lingle is not a soldier dead in the discharge of duty is unfortunate considering that he is dead. It is of no consequence to an inquiry determined to discover why he was killed, by whom he was killed and with what attendant circumstances. *Tribune* readers may be assured that their newspaper has no intention of concealing the least fact of this murder and its consequences and meanings. The purpose is to catch the murderers . . .

"The murder of this reporter, even for racketeering reasons, as the evidence indicates it might have been, made a breach in the wall which criminality has so long maintained about its operations here. Some time, somewhere there will be a hole found or made and the Lingle murder may prove to be it. The *Tribune* will work at its case upon this presumption and with this hope. It has gone into the cause in this fashion and its notice to gangland is that it is in for duration. Kismet."

Kismet, indeed. For during this revisionary interim McCormick's investigators and the police had uncovered transactions of a ramification that could not have been anticipated in the affairs of a slum-boy baseball semi-professional who had wormed his way into bottom grade journalism. Lingle's biography, in fact, accords with the career of any under-privileged opportunist who finds in the gang a reward for endeavour. His first job after leaving a West Jackson Boulevard elementary school was as office boy in a surgical supply house, from where, in 1912, he went as office boy at the *Tribune*. He was at the same time playing semi-professional baseball, and met at the games Bill Russell, a police patrolman, with whom he struck up a friendship, and who, as he progressed through a sergeantcy upward to deputy commissionership, was a valuable aid to Lingle in the police-beat feed work he was now doing for the *Tribune*. Pasley, who worked on the *Tribune* with him during the twenties, has described Lingle's relationship with the police and the underworld: "His right hand would go up to the left breast pocket of his coat for a cigar. There was a cigar for every greeting. They were a two-for-a-nickel brand and Lingle smoked them himself. He knew all the coppers by their first names. He spent his spare time among them. He went to their wakes and funerals; their weddings and christenings. They were his heroes. A lawyer explained him: 'As a kid he was cop struck, as another kid might be stage struck.' The police station was his prep school and college. He matured, and his point of view developed, in the stodgy, fetid atmosphere of the cell block and the squad-room. Chicago's forty-one police stations are vile places, considered either aesthetically or hygienically. I doubt if a modern farmer would use the majority of them for cow-sheds. Yet the civic patriots put their fledgling blue-coats in them, and expect them to preserve their self-respect and departmental morale.

"In this prep school and college, Lingle learned a great deal the ordinary citizen may, or may not, suspect. He learned that sergeants, lieutenants, and captains know every hand-book, every gambling den, every dive, every beer flat and saloon on their districts, that a word from the captain when the heat is on will close any district tighter than a Scotsman's pocket in five minutes, that they know which joint owners have 'a friend in the hall or county', and which haven't. Few haven't. He learned that the Chicago police department is politics-ridden."

Pasley's view is that Lingle's undoing was gambling—"he was a gambling fool". He never bet less than $100 on a horse, and often $1,000. In 1921, when he was earning only fifty dollars a week, he took a trip to Cuba and came back loaded with gifts for his friends and colleagues, including egret plumes then coveted by women for hat decorations. His big spending and general prodigal way of life began to attract comment, and he gave it to be understood that he had just inherited $50,000 under his father's will (examination of the probate court records in June 1930 showed that the estate was valued at $500). Later he invented a couple of munificent rich uncles. Pasley's deduction is that it was in 1921 that Lingle "began living a lie, leading a dual life", that the course of his income was not at this time Capone but possibly someone in the Torrio ring—gambling rake-off, slot-machines or police graft. Additional information about his life after office hours was given by John T. Rogers in a St Louis *Post-Dispatch* series. Pointing to the "mysterious sources of the large sums of money that passed with regularity through his bank account", Rogers wrote: "If Lingle had any legitimate income beyond his sixty-five dollars a week as a reporter it has not been discovered . . . He lived at one of the best hotels in Chicago, spent nearly all his afternoons at race-tracks and some of his winters at Miami or on the Gulf Coast . . . At his hotel he was on the 'private register'. His room was No. 2706 and you could not call it unless your name had been designated by Lingle as a favoured one . . . All inquiries for Lingle were referred to the house detective. 'Sure, he was on the private register,' the house officer said. 'How could he get any sleep if he wasn't? His telephone would be going all night. He would get in around two or three and wanted rest.' 'Who would be telephoning him at that hour?' the writer inquired. This question seemed to amaze the house officer. 'Why!' he exclaimed, 'policemen calling up to have Jake get them transferred or promoted, or politicians wanting the fix put in for somebody. Jake could do it. He had a lot of power. I've known him twenty years. He was up there among the big boys and had a lot of responsibilities. A big man like that needs rest." '

This sketch of Lingle's function seemed to be confirmed by a check made of outgoing telephone calls from his suite. They were mostly to officials in the Federal and city buildings, and in city hall.

That Lingle had operated as liaison officer between the underworld and the political machine was the conclusion of Attorney Donald R. Richberg, who said in a public address: "The close relationship between Jake Lingle and the police department has been published in the Chicago papers. Out of town newspapers describe Lingle even more bluntly as having been 'the unofficial Chief of Police'. But Lingle was also strangely intimate with Al Capone, our most notorious gangster. Surely all Chicago knows that Samuel A. Ettelson,* Mr Insull's political lawyer, who is corporation counsel for Chicago, is also chief operator of the city government. Thompson is only a figurehead. Are we to believe that there existed an unofficial chief of police associating with the most vicious gang in Chicago, without the knowledge of Mr Ettelson—who is neither deaf nor blind but on the contrary has a reputation for knowing everything worth knowing about city hall affairs?"

That he had been on intimate terms with Lingle, that Lingle was "among the big boys", was readily conceded by Capone himself. He was interviewed on the subject at Palm Island by Henry T. Brundidge of the St Louis *Star*, who on 18 July 1930 published this report of their conversation:

"Was Jake your friend?"

"Yes, up to the very day he died."

"Did you have a row with him?"

"Absolutely not."

"If you did not have a row with Lingle, why did you refuse to see him upon your release from the workhouse in Philadelphia?"

"Who said I didn't see him?"

"The Chicago newspapers."

"Well, if Jake failed to say I saw him—then I didn't see him."

Asked about the diamond-studded belt Lingle was wearing, Capone explained: "A Christmas present. Jake was a dear friend of mine." And he added: "The Chicago police know who killed him."

* Who wrote the lyrics of Thompson's campaign song "Big Bill the Builder".

Who in fact had killed Lingle? That aspect of the case seemed to have been temporarily shelved while the fascinating data of his financial state was, bit by bit, exposed for examination. By 30 June 1929 two-and-a-half years of business with the Lake Shore Trust and Savings Bank was on the public record. In that period he had deposited $63,900. But, obviously, many of his deals had been in cash, for only one cheque for $6,000 related to the purchase of his $16,000 house. He also carried a large amount of cash on his person—he had had $9,000 in bills in his pocket when he was killed. In March 1930 he paid insurance premiums on jewellery valued at $12,000, which was never located. During that two-and-a-half years he drew cheques for the sum of $17,400 for horse-track and dog-track betting.

Another interesting branch of his activities that came to light were his "loans" from gamblers, politicians and businessmen. He had "borrowed" $2,000 from Jimmy Mondi, once a Mont Tennes handbookman, who had become a Capone gambling operator in Cicero and the Loop—a loan, the report read, which had not been paid back. He had $5,000 from Alderman Berthold A. Cronson, nephew of Ettelson, who stated that the loan was "a pure friendship proposition"; it had not been repaid. He had $5,000 from Ettelson himself, who could not be reached but who sent word that he had never loaned Lingle anything at any time, although he "had a custom of giving Lingle some small remembrance at Christmas time, like a box of cigars". He had a loan of $2,500 from Major Carlos Ames, president of the Civil Service Commission, and Ames stated that this loan "was a purely personal affair needed to cover market losses". He had $300 from Police Lieutenant Thomas McFarland. "A purely personal affair," declared McFarland, as he had been "a close personal friend of Lingle's for many years". Additionally it was alleged that Sam Hare, roadhouse and gambling-parlour proprietor, had loaned Lingle $20,000. Hare denied it.

Yet further enlightenment thrown by the investigation upon the private operations of Lingle was that he had been in investment partnership with Police Commissioner Russell, one of his five separate accounts for stock-market speculations. This particular one was opened in November 1928 with a $20,000 deposit, and was carried anonymously in the broker's ledger as Number 49 Account. On 20 September 1929—preceding the market crash in October 1929—their joint paper profits were $23,696; later, a loss of $50,850 was shown. On all his five accounts his paper profits at their peak were $85,000; with the crash these were converted into a loss of $75,000. Russell's losses were variously reported as $100,000 and $250,000.

"As to the source of the moneys put up by Lingle in these stock accounts and deposited by him in his bank account," the report commented with grim formality, "we have thus far been able to come to no conclusion."

But the Press and the public had come to conclusions—and they were the drearily obvious ones, the ones that again confirmed that they were the inhabitants of a city that lived by spoliation, that they were governed by dishonourable leaders and venal petty officials. As had happened so monotonously before, the dead hero changed into a monster in this fairy-story in reverse. The newspapers continued to theorize why Lingle had been eliminated, and the public were, flaccidly, interested to know; but the fervour, the righteous wrath, had waned. Both the most likely theories identified Lingle as a favour-seller, and both circumstantially indicated Capone's opposition, the Moran and Aiello merger. One story which had percolated through from the underworld was that Lingle had been given $50,000 to secure protection for a West Side dog-track, that he had failed—and kept the money. Another implicated him in the reopening of the Sheridan Wave Tournament Club which had been operated by the Weiss–Moran gang, but which, after the St Valentine's Day massacre, and the fragmentation of the gang, had closed. After recouping, Moran had for eighteen months been trying to muster official help for a reopening. It had been in charge of Joe Josephs and Julian Potatoes Kaufman. It was stated that Kaufman, an old friend of Lingle, had approached him and asked him to use his influence to persuade the police to switch on the green light. The Chicago *Daily News* alleged that then, Boss McLaughlin—who on another occasion had threatened Lingle for refusing to intercede in obtaining police permission for the operation of another gambling house—was commissioned by Moran to make direct contact with the State's Attorney's Office. Kaufman and Josephs separately approached a police official, who agreed to let the Sheridan Wave Tournament open, if Lingle was cut in.

Following this, according to the report, Lingle called on Josephs and Kaufman and demanded fifty per cent of the profits. Kaufman abusively refused. So the club remained closed.

Another newspaper, the Chicago *Herald and Examiner*, carried a similar story. According to their version Lingle demanded

$15,000 cash from Josephs and Kaufman, and when this was refused, retorted: "If this joint is opened up, you'll see more squad cars in front ready to raid it than you ever saw in your life before."

Three days before Lingle was killed, State's Attorney Swanson's staff of detectives, on the orders of Chief Investigator Pat Roche, raided a gambling house in the Aiello territory, the Biltmore Athletic Club on West Division Street. Within an hour after the raid, Lingle was repeatedly telephoning Roche, who refused to talk to him. Next day Lingle accosted him in person and said: "You've put me in a terrible jam. I told that outfit they could run, but I didn't know they were going to go with such a bang."

Meanwhile, Kaufman and Josephs had made up their minds— doubtless after consultation with Moran—to restart the Sheridan Wave Tournament Club in defiance of Lingle. It was widely advertised that it would be opening on the night of 9 June—the day on which Lingle set out for the races for the last time.

An equally plausible theory was that he had got too deeply tangled up in the struggle for money and power in the gambling syndicate. For years there had been bitter war between Mont Tennes's General News Bureau, a racing news wire service which functioned entirely for the purposes of betting, and the independent news services. As an appointed intermediary, in January 1930 Lingle brought the two opposed factions together and a two-year tru.e was agreed upon. The truce may not have extended to Lingle whose services perhaps did not satisfy all the parties.

Possibly all are true: it was simply that Lingle, like so many before him, had gone too far out in these barracuda waters of gang-business.

MISTRESS AND MAID

(Eliza Fenning, 1815)

George A. Birmingham

*Someone seems to have tried to poison the Turner family, but who? From
the moment their cook, young Eliza (or Elizabeth) Fenning, was first
accused, she never faltered in her denials and she continued to declare
her innocence until she was hanged on a summer's morning in 1815 at
the age of twenty-one. Police had to quell the mob that assembled outside
the Turner family's house where Eliza Fenning had prepared the suspect
dumplings. A public subscription raised money for the girl's stricken
parents, who had refused to pay the executioner's fees of fourteen shillings
and sixpence (72½ p). Certainly, on the evidence before us here, there
seems little in the way of a case against this unfortunate young woman.
The affair of the poisoned dumplings is one of the few cases featured in
the Victorian anthology* Chronicles of Crime *where doubt is expressed
about the outcome. This is a twentieth-century account by the prolific
George A. Birmingham. He wrote more than forty books, including some
thirty-four novels, but he was also a full-time clergyman whose real name
was the Rev Canon James Hannay (1865–1950). Before his retirement
he was vicar of Holy Trinity, Kensington Gore, in west London.*

Two coal merchants, two gentlemen, a hatter, a mercer, a vintner,
a cutler, a pawnbroker, a huckster and a bottle-dealer, made up

the jury which, on 11 April 1815, found Eliza Fenning guilty of intent to murder her employer, his wife and his father. There is this much to be said for the bottle-dealer. He was stone deaf. The rest of the jury had not even that excuse. Here is the story.

William Fenning was a private soldier in the 15th regiment of Foot, which in 1790 or thereabouts was stationed in Cork. There he met an Irish girl called Mary Swayne, and married her. She bore him ten children, of whom only one, a daughter, Eliza, lived to grow up. But Mrs Fenning was not fortunate enough to bear all her ten children in Cork. Soon after her marriage the regiment was ordered to Dominica. One hundred and two wives followed their husbands there. Of these Mary Fenning was one. Seven of them returned to England, when the regiment returned—only seven. Mary Fenning was one of these too.

Eliza was born in Dominica, and one story of her childhood there survives. When she was about eighteen months old she pulled down the rushlight which stood beside the bed in which she and her mother were sleeping. She set fire to the bed-clothes, and was only saved from a very painful death by her mother's promptitude in waking up and quenching the flames. The story is common-place and would not be worth repeating if it were not that it was retold afterwards, when Eliza's name was somewhat blown upon. It was retold, and so changed in the retelling that she appeared as a callous, unnatural child who tried to burn her mother alive in bed.

Fenning was a good soldier, and in due time he rose to be a sergeant. He also became Master of the regimental band. After twenty years' service he was discharged with a good character. He settled in Holborn, and got a job under a potato dealer.

The Fennings were not rich, and when she was only fourteen years old Eliza went out to service. She passed from one situation to another, generally with credit. In 1815 she was a pretty, lively girl of twenty-one years of age, and it was then that she went as cook to Mr Robert Gregson Turner. Mr Turner was a law stationer of Chancery Lane. He had a wife, but no children. He had a father, Mr Orlibar Turner, who often visited his house and dined there. He had a mother, Mrs Turner, who took an interest in the young people's affairs. He kept two apprentices, one called Gadsden and the other called King. They were seventeen and eighteen years of age and King was the elder. Besides a cook he kept a housemaid, whose name was Sarah Peer.

Eliza had not been long in the service of the Turners before she got into trouble. One night she went into the apprentices' bedroom, which she certainly ought not to have done. She had very few clothes on at the time, and that made things worse. Mrs Turner saw her coming out, and the only defence that Eliza was able to make was that she had gone there to look for a candle. Mrs Turner could scarcely be expected to accept that as a sufficient excuse for her conduct. According to her own account, Mrs Turner's account, she "reproved her severely". She probably scolded the girl sharply. She also gave her notice to leave. Eliza apologized. Eliza cried. And Eliza promised never to do it again. Old Mrs Turner, who perhaps understood better than her daughter-in-law the difficulty of getting cooks, interceded on her behalf. Mrs Turner forgave her and allowed her to stay on.

Now we come to a conflict of evidence. Eliza herself said that she was very happy at the Turners', more comfortable than she had ever been in any of her previous situations, and that she wanted to stay there. Mrs Turner said that she "appeared very sullen. She failed in the respect that she before paid me." Sarah Peer, the house-maid, said that she had heard Eliza say that she would never like Mr and Mrs Turner any more. It is impossible to know for certain what the truth was, but we can guess. Eliza was almost certainly vexed at being scolded. Mrs Turner probably thought the girl was sullen when she was only frightened. Sarah Peer may have heard Eliza speak as she said, but she may not. Sarah Peer was a nasty little liar.

Whatever Eliza's manners may have been, she remained just as keen as she had ever been on her cooking. She did what only the very best cooks can be persuaded to do. She suggested dishes to her mistress. She constantly asked, for instance, to be allowed to make yeast dumplings, and professed to be able to make them very well. She was evidently eager to show what she could do in this way, for she ordered some yeast from the brewer, apparently on her own account. On Monday, 20 March, she went into the dining-room and announced to her mistress that the yeast had come. Mrs Turner was not pleased about this, and said so. If she got yeast at all, she preferred to get it from the baker.

That evening Eliza made some yeast dumplings, for herself, her fellow-servant and the two apprentices. They were excellent dumplings, and all four enjoyed them greatly and felt no ill-effects after eating them. Next morning Mrs Turner, who had perhaps heard from Sarah Peer how good the dumplings were, ordered some for her own dinner. Mr Orlibar Turner, the father-in-law, was dining in the house that day, and she may have wanted to give the old gentleman a little treat. But like John Gilpin's wife, she had a frugal mind, and yeast dumplings are an expensive form of food. She ordered Eliza to make a beefsteak pie for her own dinner and the apprentices'. Afterwards she should make the yeast dumplings for the party upstairs. Eliza made the beefsteak pie and then took it out to the baker's to have it baked. Then she made the dough for the dumplings, put the yeast into it and set it before the fire to rise. Mrs Turner was certain that there was nobody in the kitchen at the time except Eliza herself. Eliza was equally certain that King, the elder of the two apprentices, was there, at least part of the time. What King had to say in the matter will never be known, for he was never asked whether he was in the kitchen or not. Sarah Peer, according to Mrs Turner, was certainly not in the kitchen. She had been sent up to a bedroom to mend a counterpane. According to Eliza, Sarah Peer passed in and out of the kitchen at least twice, when she went out to fetch a ha'porth of milk to make sauce for the dumplings and when she came back. According to Mrs Turner, Eliza was not only alone in the kitchen, but she was in the kitchen the whole time that the dough was rising and the dumplings were being made. Eliza herself says that she went out of the kitchen at one time to see that the coal merchant's carter deposited the coal which had been ordered in the proper cellar. Mrs Turner says that no coal was ordered and none came that day. But Eliza was right and Mrs Turner was wrong. The coal merchant's delivery note was produced, and showed that his man had left coal at the Turners' house on that day. A coal merchant's bill at that date is an interesting document. Here it is.

March 21, 1 Cauldron Coals, at 65/- . £3–5.
Meting 1/6 Shooting 4/3 . 5/9.

Mrs Turner herself was in and out of the kitchen all the morning. She was fussy about the dough, and Eliza seems to have been a little irritated by her fussiness. Mrs Turner asked why the dough did not rise. Eliza replied that it would rise before she was ready for it. Eliza was right. The dough did rise, but not in a satisfactory manner. The dumplings were not nearly as good as those which she had made the night before. They were black and heavy, and dumplings of that kind cannot be regarded as satisfactory food. Nevertheless, she served them up at three o'clock, and the party of three in the dining-room sat down to them. There were six dumplings in the dish. Mrs Turner helped the two men and took one herself. Then the trouble began.

"I found myself affected in a very few minutes after I had eaten," said Mrs Turner. "I did not eat a quarter of a dumpling. I felt myself very faint, and an excruciating pain, an extreme, violent pain, which increased every minute. It came so bad I was obliged to leave the table. I went upstairs."

Mrs Turner went upstairs at about half-past three o'clock and she remained very ill until nine. A doctor attended her.

The next to fall a victim to the dumplings was Mr Turner, Mr Robert Turner. He also left the table and was very sick. His father followed him and observed that his eyes were swollen, very much swollen indeed. He thought his son's condition was extraordinary. But he had not much time to comment on it. For "I was taken ill myself in less than three minutes afterwards". Both men were downstairs, but Eliza did not come to their assistance. Mr Orlibar Turner thought this strange. It was not really very strange, for Eliza had eaten some of the dumplings too and was just as sick as anybody else.

Gadsden, the younger apprentice, was hanging about the kitchen while his master was dining upstairs. He had had his share of the beefsteak pie, but that does not seem to have stayed his appetite. He wanted some dumpling too. On a plate in the kitchen was a dumpling and a half, and Gadsden was inclined to fall to. Eliza warned him. She knew what these dumplings were like. "Gadsden," she said, "do not eat that. It is cold and heavy. It will do you no good." Nevertheless Gadsden did eat, but not much. He ate a bit about the size of a walnut. Then he took the remains of the milk sauce and ate all of that. Ten minutes later he was taken ill, but not very ill. He was not so ill as to be unable to go to his master when he was called. He was sent at once to fetch old Mrs Turner, the mother of Robert and the wife of Orlibar. On the way to her house he became so sick that he thought he was going to die.

So far the history of the dumplings. Of the household in Chancery Lane only Sarah Peer and King the elder apprentice appear to have escaped. King had perhaps gone out after eating his beefsteak pie. Sarah Peer was in the house. While Eliza was in the throes of her sickness her father, ex-Sergeant Fenning, called to see her. Sarah went to the door and told Mr Fenning that his daughter was out, having been sent on a message by Mrs Turner. Sarah Peer seems to have been one of those people who lie merely for the love of lying, without any object. She knew perfectly well that Eliza was sick in the kitchen, and yet she told Mr Fenning that she was out on a message.

In the Turners' house was a room called the office, in which the two apprentices worked at whatever apprentices of law stationers do work at. In the office table was a drawer, and the contents of that drawer were very curious. It was used as a waste-paper basket and to it the maids went when they wanted paper with which to light the fire. It was also used as a kind of medicine chest, for in it Mr Turner kept a parcel of arsenic. Gadsden, the younger apprentice, said that Eliza often went to the drawer and took from it what paper she wanted, as she had a perfect right to do. Eliza said that she never took any paper out of the drawer at all, that she always asked King to give it to her when she wanted any. Here again it would be very interesting to know what King had to say about the matter, but, as in the case of his presence in the kitchen, King was not asked.

The packet of arsenic was certainly in the drawer on 7 March. Mr Orlibar Turner, the one man in this case who seems to have been thoroughly reliable, saw it there. He heard, but did not know of his own knowledge, that it had disappeared from the drawer soon after 7 March. It had certainly disappeared by 21 March, but what happened to it we do not know. The drawer, being a waste-paper basket as well as a medicine chest, was never kept locked. Anyone might have taken the arsenic.

The next morning Mr Orlibar Turner, having more or less recovered from his sickness, thought he would like to investigate the dumplings. He went into the kitchen and found the pan in which they had been cooked. Eliza, surely a little remiss in her duties, had not washed it up. Perhaps she was too sick to do so. At all events it had the remains of the dough sticking to it. Mr Orlibar Turner filled the pan with water and stirred it. He found that a white powder settled in the bottom of it. He locked it up at once until he had an opportunity of handing it over to Mr Marston, the doctor who had attended them all in their sickness. Mr Orlibar Turner's investigations did not stop with the pan. The knives with which the dumplings had been cut had not been cleaned. He took a look at them and found that they had all turned black. He put two of them into his pocket and kept them for Mr Marston, the surgeon. Then he tackled Eliza and asked her what she had put into the dumplings "that had been so prejudicial to us all"? She said there was nothing the matter with the dumplings, but that the trouble came from the sauce made of the milk which Sarah Peer had brought in. She stuck to that story when old Mrs Turner, who was looking after the family, came into the kitchen.

"Oh, those devilish dumplings!" said the old lady. "Supposing they had done the mischief."

"Not the dumplings, but the milk, madam," said Eliza.

"What milk?" asked old Mrs Turner.

"The halfpennyworth of milk which Sally brought to make the sauce," said Eliza.

And she had some reason for the opinion which she held. The apprentice Gadsden, as she pointed out to Mrs Turner, only ate a very little bit of dumpling, "not bigger than a nut, but licked up three parts of a bowl of sauce with a bit of bread." And he was very sick.

On the other hand, Mr Robert Turner had eaten a dumpling and a half, but took no sauce at all, and he was the most violently sick of the whole party.

The doctor took the pan and the knives, which Orlibar Turner had given him, and examined them. But his examination appears to have been the most superficial imaginable. He found, he says, half a teaspoonful of white powder in the pan, and adds, "I decidedly found it to be arsenic." For all the tests he applied to it, it might just as well have been salt. All he did was to wash the pan round with water, stir it, pour off the water, and look at the powder. He looked at the knives too, and decided that arsenic had stained them black. His mind appears to have been made up long before he saw the pan or the knives that the whole family was suffering from arsenical poisoning.

"All the symptoms attending the family," he said, "were produced by arsenic. I have no doubt of it by the symptoms."

Eliza Fenning was arrested and tried, on the charge of attempting to poison the Turner family, before the Recorder of London, Sir John Sylvester. She was tried at the Old Bailey. One after another the witnesses for the prosecution came forward. Mr and Mrs Turner, Mr and Mrs Orlibar Turner, the doctor, the apprentice Gadsden and Sarah Peer. They told their stories very much as I have set them down, and Sarah Peer as usual lied. Her evidence, so far as it was worth anything, went against Eliza, but she admitted that she was not on very good terms with Eliza. There had been a quarrel between the girls because, as she said, Eliza "had taken something out of my drawer for a duster". Just the sort of thing maids still quarrel about.

The prisoner made some attempt to defend herself. The lawyer who ought to have been doing it was either extraordinarily inefficient or totally uninterested in the case.

"I am truly innocent of the whole charge," she said. "I am innocent. Indeed I am. I liked my place. I was very comfortable. As to my master saying I did not assist him, I was too ill. I had no concern with that drawer at all. When I wanted a piece of paper I always asked for it."

Then she asked that the apprentice should give evidence, and when Gadsden came up to the witness-box again she exclaimed:

"No, my lord, it's not that apprentice boy. It's not the younger apprentice that I want. It's Thomas King that I want, the elder apprentice who knows that I never went to the drawer in my life, for when I asked for paper he always gave it to me, and if he was here, he dare not deny the truth to my face and I wish him sent for."

But he was not sent for.

"You should have had him here before," said the Recorder.

"My lord," said Eliza, "I desired him to be brought and I wish him to be sent for now."

To which the Recorder replied:

"No. It's too late now. I cannot hear you."

The Recorder appears to have been rather a "Harbitrary gent". But he was quite willing to receive Gadsden's evidence.

"The prisoner lit the fire in the office?" he asked, and Gadsden replied:

"Yes. I and my fellow apprentice have seen her go to that drawer many times."

William Fenning, the prisoner's father, came forward and asked to be allowed to give evidence. What he wanted to say we do not know, for the Recorder would not listen to him.

"It's too late," he said. "You must go down."

Then he proceeded to sum up and to charge the jury. He said it had been fully proved that four persons were poisoned, that the poison was in the dough of the dumplings, that it was arsenic and that it was not in the flour, the yeast, or the milk. It was in the dumplings alone, which no person except the prisoner had touched.

After that charge the jury had little choice about their verdict. They found Eliza Fenning guilty. The Recorder passed sentence of death and "the miserable girl was carried from the bar convulsed with agony and uttering fearful screams".

A good many people appear to have been dissatisfied with the trial and the verdict. There was a doctor, for instance, who became interested in the case from a scientific point of view. He wanted to know whether arsenic really does blacken knives or not. He found out by experiment that it does not. He wanted to know whether arsenic, sprinkled on dough, prevents the dough from rising. He found that it does not. Dough covered with arsenic will rise just as well and form just as airy dumplings as dough without any arsenic in it. Having made these two discoveries, which, one might imagine, the doctor who gave evidence might have made for himself, this gentleman sent his results to the Home Secretary. Then he went to the Turners, hoping to be able to induce them to sign a petition for Eliza's reprieve.

Robert Turner was in the house when this doctor called. So was Mr Orlibar Turner, his father. They took a look at the dumpling on which arsenic had been sprinkled and were forced to admit that the poison had not prevented the dough from rising. Then their family doctor, the gentleman who had given evidence at the trial, came in. He was shown the dumplings and he was told about the knives which had been treated with arsenic without turning black. He said that the experiments were ingenious "and tended to operate in the girl's favour". Having made this remark, he evidently thought he had done all that could be required of him. He hurried away, perhaps to try some experiments of his own with dumplings and knives and arsenic. Then the doctor with the taste for experiment pleaded with the Turners, and tried to persuade them that the girl was perhaps innocent. He produced some effect on their minds.

"If there is anything which I can do for her," said Mr Orlibar Turner, "I'll go to the top of the ladder to do it."

"Well then, sir," said the doctor, "you will sign a petition for the remission of her sentence."

"I will with pleasure," said Mr Orlibar Turner.

"And so will I," said his son.

And so perhaps they would, but as ill-luck would have it the Recorder, the Sir John Sylvester who had tried the case, was shown into the room at that minute. He was evidently a friend of the Turners, which was perhaps natural enough. He was a lawyer and they were law stationers. They must have come into frequent contact with each other. On seeing the Recorder the doctor produced his dumplings again and explained all about his experiments. Then he went on to tell the Recorder that he had "stated at the trial two things that were erroneous". Arsenic does not prevent dough from rising, and arsenic does not blacken knives. The Recorder could scarcely be expected to stand that. He showed his opinion of this man of science by saying, after listening to all that was told him about the experiments, that he would go home and inquire of his cook what she thought about the matter. He was evidently in a hurry to do this, for he went away at once. Mr Robert Turner saw him to the door.

Mr Robert Turner came back and he said to his father:

"The Recorder says you must not sign any petition, for if you do it will throw suspicion on the rest of your family."

The petition went forward to the Home Secretary, or whoever received it, without the signatures of the two Turners.

The next person who interested himself in the case of Eliza Fenning was a prominent member of the Society of Friends. He approached the Recorder in order to secure a short reprieve for Eliza in order that the evidence against her might be more fully inquired into. He was an eminently respectable gentleman, as all prominent Quakers were then and still are. After his interview with the Recorder he wrote a letter to a friend:

"The Recorder then said . . . 'that the reason we felt so much interest about her (Eliza) was only because she was a pretty woman, and he felt so perfectly satisfied of her guilt (there never being a clearer case) that he knew no possible reason for delaying the execution.' "

That settled the Quaker. No man, especially a man who occupies a position like his, can afford to be accused of being particularly interested in pretty servant girls.

But one more effort was made to save Eliza. On the morning before she was hanged the Recorder was asked "whether any alteration could be formed in the opinion respecting the propriety of her execution if satisfactory evidence were adduced that there was an insane person in the Turners' house who had declared that he would poison the family."

"The Recorder," wrote the gentleman who approached him this

time, "assured me that the production of such evidence would be
wholly useless."

This "insane person" was Robert Turner. It appeared that he had,
in September or October, rushed into the house of a Mr Gibson, of
the firm of Corbyn & Co., Chemists and Druggists, and, according
to a statement made by Gibson, appeared "in a wild and deranged
state". Mr Gibson took him into the counting-house and kept him
there while he sent hastily for his father. While he waited Robert
Turner said:

"My dear Gibson, do, for God's sake, get me secured or confined,
for, if I am at liberty, I shall do some mischief. I shall destroy myself
and my wife. I must and shall do it, unless all means of destruction
are removed out of my way. Do, my good friend, have me put under
some restraint. Something from above tells me I must do it, and
unless I am prevented, I certainly shall do it."

Mr Gibson also stated that before the trial he had called on Mr
Turner and urged "the impropriety of proceeding with the trial,"
considering his son's state of mind. He even, backed by mutual
friends of his own and the Turners', mentioned "the impropriety
of Mr Robert Turner's being at large under the circumstances with
which he was afflicted".

These hints of the state of mind of the younger Turner are a
clue to an alternative theory as to how the arsenic got into the
dumplings, if it was not put in by the girl who mixed and kneaded
the dough and who was hanged for the crime. It is conceivable that,
in a dark hour of insanity, with the stealth and cunning of the mad,
Robert Turner put the arsenic on the waiting dough, and afterwards,
with mind cleared again and oblivious of its clouded moment, ate
of the food with which he himself had planned to kill his wife and
household. It would be interesting to know where Robert Turner
spent the morning of 21 March, and if he could have been, even
for a moment of it, in his own kitchen.

There is no doubt, as far as one can judge from the accounts
which survive 100 years after the event, that the evidence on which
the unfortunate Eliza was condemned to death is unconvincing.
The first thing which strikes the unbiased reader is the total lack
of motive for the crime. It is clear that Eliza not only tolerated but
liked being with the Turners. She had been reproved by her mistress
three weeks before the dumplings were made. But why, if she really
bore her mistress a grudge for this, which seems improbable, did
she not put the poison in any of the many kinds of food and drink

which she must have prepared for her during those three weeks? According to Mr Turner's evidence, the arsenic had been missed a fortnight before it had turned up again in the dumplings. If Eliza had it she could have used it any day—why wait a fortnight? If, on the other hand, anybody else had taken it, with the intention of putting it in the Turners' food, he might have had to wait a fortnight before he got the opportunity, and the dough, lying unguarded by the kitchen fire while the cook cleaned knives in the scullery, might have been that opportunity. Thomas King, the second apprentice, is the dark horse of the trial. Why was he not called as a witness? What was he doing in the front kitchen while Eliza cleaned knives in the back? Had he any grudge against the Turner family? Why was Eliza so anxious that he should give evidence? These things we shall never know. But we do know that, except Sarah Peer who was out, Thomas King was the only member of the household who did not eat the fatal dumplings. Is it possible that Thomas, a mischievous, high-spirited lad, who had thoroughly enjoyed Eliza's dumplings the night before and listened for rather longer than interested him to her telling Sarah Peer exactly how she made them with so light a hand, thought he would play a joke on Eliza and at the same time inconvenience the employers he may possibly have regarded as pompous and tiresome? Could he, in a spirit of malicious mischief, have crept into the kitchen and sprinkled on the dough a handful of the powder he knew was kept for poisoning mice? He may well have thought it would be amusing to listen to Eliza explaining to an irate mistress why the dumplings she prided herself on making so well had made everybody ill. It is even possible that he would have considered it amusing to watch the Messrs Turner retiring precipitately from the office, with the hope that they would not return for the afternoon. When he realized the results of his prank, he may have preferred to let Eliza suffer than to put his own neck into the noose.

Had Eliza put the poison in the food it is hardly conceivable that she would have eaten it herself. But she did eat it, for, according to the evidence of Robert Turner's mother—not a witness likely to have been biased in her favour—she was afterwards very ill. In fact, she spent the first few days after her arrest in the prison hospital. Eliza was a light-hearted girl, even described by a former employer as "giddy", and not at all likely to want to commit suicide. But if she did put arsenic in the dough, and in a fit of remorse subsequently eat it, she surely would have taken the precaution of washing up the dish she made it in. One hopes, for Eliza's honour as a cook, that it was merely because she was ill that she had not washed up that dish—but even if she had been suffering the agonies of the damned surely if she had put the arsenic in it she would not have failed to wash it out.

Her demeanour from the moment she was suspected was, we read, open and frank. She never attempted to deny that she had made the dumplings unaided. She never failed, to the very end, to affirm her innocence. Before her trial, while she was waiting for it in Clerkenwell Prison, she wrote to her young man, one Edward P—.

Dear Edward,—

You may be truly surprised at me for not writing or sending to you; but no doubt you have heard what has happened to me, for I now lay ill at the infirmary sick ward at the New Clerkenwell Prison; for on last Tuesday week I had some yeast dumplings to make, and there was something in them which I can't answer for, and they made four of us, including myself, dangerously ill; and because I made them, they suspect me that I have put something in them, which I assure you that I am innocent of; but I expect that I shall be cleared on Thursday, if in case I can attend . . . Edward, I shall never be right or happy again, to think that I ever was in prison . . ."

This strikes one as being the letter of an innocent woman, who explains her situation quite simply, and does not even realize its seriousness. She evidently never contemplated anything but acquittal. The one thing that troubled her was "to think that I ever was in prison".

Later she wrote again, annoyed because she had heard that her Edward had gone to a ball with "another".

"If you were in my case," she wrote, "I think I should spend my time a little better than going to such diversions."

A guilty woman, mad with anxiety as to her fate and oppressed by the sin on her conscience, would hardly have cared if her young man was going about with another girl.

Just before her trial she wrote:

"Thank God I shall stand my trial at the Old Bailey, where I shall have a counsellor to plead for me; so I have nothing to fear, as my conscience tells me that I am not guilty."

Poor Eliza's touching faith in her counsel was but ill-repaid. After the trial was over she seemed dumb-founded by the verdict, and even still incapable of believing that she was doomed to die.

"I attended my trial on Tuesday, and they have, which is the most cruellest thing in this world, brought me in guilty, because I had the fire to light in the office where the arsenic was kept, and my master said that I went often into the office for things and so, on that account, they suppose that I must have taken the arsenic out of the drawer, which is the most horrid thing I ever can think of; for was I to die this instant, I am sure I should be happy in thinking I am innocent . . .

"I shall never think of marrying any person excepting yourself; but I must for ever give up any thought of such, as it may hurt your character . . .

"Don't think that I shall be denied of seeing you, though I may be confined most likely six months at least; but perhaps it is all for the best, for I am confident that it will make me both steady and penitent the rest of my life . . ."

The only reason Eliza saw to prevent her marrying Edward was that the alliance might "hurt his character", and she evidently did not contemplate more than six months in prison. It is sad to think that Edward's affection did not stand the strain of the verdict. Eliza's last letters to him are full of reproach for the times he promised to come and see her and did not come. And, a month before her death, she ceased to write to him, after a last letter in which she prayed that he might never "feel the pangs of a broken heart".

Eliza herself was not, apparently, the only person who did not realize the seriousness of the charge against her. When she came up for her preliminary examination before a magistrate he offered to let her out on bail—an offer which was only declined because her parents were too poor to produce the required sum.

"An impartial trial," wrote Lord Erskine, "is the first and dearest privilege of every Englishman". It was too dear for Eliza. She had no money with which to pay for legal aid. Her parents did manage to scrape together five pounds, of which two guineas were paid to her very inadequate counsel, and the rest to a low-class solicitor who made a living by preparing briefs for the very poor prisoners at the Old Bailey who could afford no better advice.

Rumours of Eliza's ingrained wickedness and stories of her depravity naturally arose immediately after she was condemned to death. The tale of her early attempt to burn her mother to death was freely circulated, and stories that she had put poison in a tea-kettle at another place where she was employed, and that she had attempted to cut the throat of a former mistress, were rife. A disinterested person, perhaps the same person who made experiments with yeast dumplings on Eliza's behalf, traced two of these stories to their source and gives an interesting account of their origin. The tea-kettle story was pursued through a Mr C— to a Mrs B—, thence to a dyer's shop assistant, who had heard it from an oil-man, who denied knowing anything about it, but was able to give the name of the family Eliza was reputed to have tried to poison—that of a grocer called Mr Hardy of Lincoln's Inn Fields. Mr Hardy, while interviewed as he weighed out the tea behind the counter of his shop, said Eliza was "a bold, sly, artful, designing girl . . . a hoity-toity, wild, unsettled sort of girl". He refused to say anything about her having poisoned a tea-kettle, but Mrs Hardy was more communicative. She said:

"One day I went into the parlour, and the tea-kettle was upon the fire, and I see the tea-kettle a-frothing at the mouth. With that I says to myself, Lord bless me, says I, what can make the tea-kettle froth at the mouth? Thinks I to myself, I've heard of poison being put into tea-kettles; and still the tea-kettle kept on frothing at the mouth. With that I takes me the tea-kettle off the fire, and goes into the yard and empties it; and then I wrenches it out with cold water, and wrenches it again and again, and fills it with clean water; and then I comes in again and puts the tea-kettle upon the fire."

Asked what, after these highly dramatic proceedings, she said to Eliza, Mrs Hardy replied.

"Lord bless me! I don't say it was Eliza as did it. It might have been her or it might not. I don't know if she lived with us at the time. She might or she might not. I'm sure I can't say."

Mr Hardy continued to reiterate that Eliza was "a sly, quick, clever, artful girl, as sharp as a needle". He had, however, no definite complaint to make about her, except that she read books, and "he never knew no good come of servants reading".

This pretty well disposed of the tea-kettle story.

When Mrs Williams of Gray's Inn, whose throat Eliza was reputed to have attempted to cut, was finally, after some difficulty, traced, she said that Eliza had never been her servant;

she had never seen her, and no one had ever attempted to cut her throat.

Eliza Fenning was executed on 27 July 1815. We have a very full contemporary account of the execution, from which I quote. The fact that she slept soundly the night before her execution, from nine o'clock till four in the morning, might be taken as an indication of her innocence by those who hold that a guilty conscience is a bar to sleep. At four o'clock she arose and washed and dressed, and soon afterwards the chaplain came to her.

"She was seated on the bench, against the partition of her cell, with her elbow on the table, and her head reclining on her hand, exceedingly dejected, and unable to speak."

"Applicable passages from the book of Job" were read to her till seven.

"Whilst in prayer, the Ordinary entered, and on its conclusion, he by kind language endeavoured to get her to speak, but she was faint and exhausted. About seven she said 'she was bewildered, and that it all appeared like a dream to her'.

"She was now left to be dressed in the clothes she was to suffer in."

Some women like to go well dressed to the grave. Eliza for her execution was neatly dressed in a white muslin worked gown, and worked muslin cap, bound with white satin ribbon. She wore a white ribbon round her waist and pale lilac boots laced in front.

"On being re-visited, in about half an hour, her dejection had diminished, and she seemed resigned. Mr— prayed fervently, and she clasped her hands and looked upwards: not having done so before, he exhorted her to pray. 'I cannot speak, sir,' said she, 'but I pray from my heart.' Her countenance became tranquil and serene, and she observed, 'I wish to leave the world—it is all vanity and vexation of spirit. But it is a cruel thing to die innocently: yet I freely forgive every one, and die in charity with all the world, but cannot forget my injured innocence.'

"The clock struck eight. Mr— suggested prayer for the last time. She anxiously asked, 'We have not time, sir, have we?' Before she knelt she deliberately removed her gown that it might not be soiled. During prayer the officer tapped at the door; she approached him smiling, and inquired if he was ready. As she departed she lifted up the sash of the window, and looking through upon the prisoners, who remained locked in their cells, but who had mounted up to their different windows to see her go out to die, she kissed her hand to them, and said cheerfully, 'Good-bye, good-bye to all of you.' She leaned on Mr —'s arm, and for a moment he perceived that the weakness of human nature prevailed—she staggered, but recovered instantly, and passed on to where the criminals are bound . . .

"Elizabeth Fenning walked to the spot steadily. The officers of the Sheriff and the prison, and several spectators, were awaiting her appearance. Oldfield, who was to suffer with her, was already there. He had, two months before, written her a letter of solemn exhortation and fervent piety. When she saw him, she exclaimed, 'Oh, Oldfield, you are going to heaven.' The hangman approached her: he bound her arms, by the elbows, to her body, and tied her hands together in front—she stood erect and unmoved: he then wound her halter round her waist. At this ceremony her fortitude was astonishing, even to those who had been accustomed to witness these appalling preparations of the living for premature death. No tear started from her eye; her lip did not quiver for an instant; not a feature changed; not a muscle of her countenance moved.

"Mr— then, in the hearing of all present, addressed her in these words: 'Elizabeth, I most solemnly adjure you, in the name of that God before whose presence you are to appear, if you know anything of the crime for which you are about to suffer, make it known.' She replied in these words, distinctly and clearly, 'Before God, then, I die innocent.'

"The cavalcade then, preceded by the Sheriffs and their officers, with Lord Yarmouth and the other spectators, moved slowly through the dark passage, the walls reverberating the Ordinary's distinct enunciation of the words, 'I am the resurrection and the life, saith the Lord,' and other portions of the burial service appointed to be said. When he pronounced, 'I know that my Redeemer liveth,' Oldfield exclaimed, 'So do I.' Mr— inquired if she too believed it: she replied, 'Yes, and I feel happy.'

"She walked with a steady and firm step to the awful platform, at the door of which Mr— stopped her, and again addressed her in the same words that he used when she was bound; observing that it was the last moment they should be together: she replied:

" 'I am going to die, and as a dying person, I declare to that God before whom I shall appear very shortly, I die innocent; and, mark my words, sir, God will convince you by a circumstance this day.'

" 'What circumstance?' said Mr—.

" 'By a circumstance today, sir,' she answered, 'God will convince you I die innocent.'

" 'How do you know,' Mr— again said to her, 'that God will convince us today by a circumstance?'

" 'I hope God will do it, sir,' she replied.

"The whole of the conversation lasted not more than two minutes. Then Mr— bade her an eternal farewell.

"She ascended the scaffold with firmness and even energy, and was the first of the three unfortunate convicts that appeared.

"She seemed in earnest and solemn devotion as she passed on to the further end of the scaffold. Her step was rather quick, but not hurried—it was the pace of a person walking in abstracted thought among a crowd. She stood still with her face towards Ludgate Hill; the Ordinary stood opposite to her, with a book. The hangman, standing behind her, took a white cotton night-cap from his pocket, and attempted to draw it over her face, but it was too small, as were two others which he also tried. He then tied a white muslin handkerchief over her face; but not considering this to be sufficient covering he produced a pocket-handkerchief which had evidently been used. She disliked this, and desired it might not be put on. She cried, 'Pray do not put it on—pray do not—pray do not let them put it on.' The Rev. Mr Vazie, who was with her on the scaffold, suggested to Mr Cotton that 'the man had better not put on that dirty pocket-handkerchief, as the poor creature's sense of cleanliness was offended by it.' 'Pray,' said she, 'Mr Cotton, do not let him put it on—pray let him take it off—pray do, Mr Cotton.' Mr Cotton replied, 'My dear, it must be on—he must put it on.' She was very dissatisfied with it and felt much uneasiness; but it was, nevertheless, tied across her eyes by the hangman. He then placed the cord round her neck, and ascending a pair of steps, threw the other end of it over the beam, and made it fast with several knots. During this time Mr Vazie stood by her on the scaffold, and when the duty of the Ordinary required his attention to the other convicts, this gentleman supplied his place.

"The scene was now particularly affecting. Oldfield, who had obtained permission in the press yard to die next to Elizabeth Fenning, ascended the scaffold with a cheerful countenance. He walked up to her immediately, and smiling, conjured her to maintain her firmness, and not to let the last moment of life escape her without revealing whatever she might have on her mind. She expressed the composed state of her thoughts, and repeated her innocence with extraordinary fortitude of manner. Mr Vazie took occasion most earnestly to entreat her confession. She solemnly, and with wonderful energy, protested her innocence.

"The unhappy girl herself being of short stature, Mr Vazie, who was tall, and stood fronting her, rather towards her right hand, stooped to converse with her. She spoke through the linen coverings which concealed her face—their conversation was earnest—when she spoke his left ear was directed to her face. He addressed her repeatedly, and earnestly enforced what he said by rapid movements of his right arm and hand . . . Mr Vazie had made a last vain effort to obtain an acknowledgment of her having committed the crime for which she suffered; and he then exhorted her to confess what other sins she had committed, enforcing on her the certainty that sins which were apparently slight to man were heinous in the sight of the Almighty. She answered him that 'for what she was about to suffer she had not committed; she was wholly innocent; and that her other sins she had confessed to God. He knew them and she hoped for His forgiveness and pardon.' The Ordinary, when disengaged from the two poor creatures who were about to die with her, earnestly entreated her for the last time . . . She expressed her firm assurance of happiness hereafter—denied that she was guilty—and resolutely persisted in her innocence. The platform fell: she raised her arms, and dropped them immediately. Her last words were, 'I am innocent.' She died without a struggle."

A hundred years ago the bodies of persons hanged for murder were not hastened underground in secrecy, so Eliza's parents were allowed to take away her dead body—but not for nothing.

"After my child was cut down," said her father, "and she was put into the dead house, I was obliged to pay fourteen shillings and sixpence before I was permitted to take her away. I had no money. I went and borrowed the money and paid it, and had the body delivered to me."

This is a copy of the receipt for the money.

For Elizabeth Fenning.

"1815.
July 26th. Executioner's fees, &c.,
          Striping, use of shell. £0 14 6
          Settled. C. Gale, Junior.

After the execution, all day, hostile demonstrations were going on outside the Turners' house, and there was even an attempt to set it on fire.

Meanwhile Eliza's body was lying in her father's kitchen, and crowds of people had the intense satisfaction of staring at it—actually eyeing the remains of a young and pretty woman who had been hanged for murder. Happy was the lot of the crowd of 100 years ago which did not have to vent its morbid curiosities on the corpses of mere film stars.

"An immense crowd was attracted to see the body," reported *The Observer* of 30 July 1815, "which, to use an Irish expression, was 'waking' in all due form, being placed in the kitchen of the house, and dressed out in ribbons, flowers, etc."

THE REAL MARIE ROGET

(Mary Rogers, 1841)

Irving Wallace

The murder of an obscure New York shopgirl, Mary Cecilia Rogers, in 1841 would have been long forgotten but for her fleeting acquaintance with one of America's most brilliant nineteenth-century writers, Edgar Allan Poe (1809–49). The reckless and gifted Poe based his Gothic tale The Mystery of Marie Roget *on her case. Irving Wallace (1916–90) was a American magazine writer in the 1930s and 1940s, before turning to screenwriting and fiction. Since publishing his first novel in 1959, Wallace has become one of America's most popular and successful writers. However, his first book was not a novel at all, but a survey of the "lives of extraordinary people who inspired memorable characters in fiction," published in 1955 as* The Fabulous Originals. *In it, Wallace related the true stories of the real people who became immortalized in nineteenth- and twentieth-century fiction, such as Dr Joseph Bell (whose life inspired Conan Doyle to create Sherlock Holmes) and Deacon Brodie (Robert Louis Stevenson's inspiration for Dr Henry Jekyll and Mr Edward Hyde). Edgar Allan Poe made no secret of the source of his fictional character Marie Roget; he wrote to friends that his creation was inspired by the unsolved murder of Mary Rogers.*

*"People begin to see that something more goes to the composition
of a fine murder than two blockheads to kill and be killed—a
knife—a purse—and a dark lane. "*

Thomas de Quincey

For eighteen months during 1837 and 1838, Edgar Allan Poe,
after being fired as editor of a Richmond literary magazine for
excessive drinking, was a resident of New York City. He dwelt,
with his pale, somewhat retarded child-bride, Virginia, and his
matronly, possessive aunt and mother-in-law, Maria Clemm, in
a cheap apartment on Sixth Avenue.

Poe, trying unsuccessfully to freelance for magazines, often
restless with despair, became a familiar figure on Broadway.
Few persons who saw him forgot him. In his neat, shabby, black
swallow-tail coat and mended military cape, striding nervously,
briskly along, he had the look of a neurotic peacock. His head,
set large on a slender frame, seemed always in the clouds. His hair
and scrub moustache were dark brown, his eyes sad and grey, and
it was remarked that he had "hands like bird claws".

His destination in many of these walks, as a few would remember
after his death, was John Anderson's tobacco shop at 319 Broadway,
near Thomas Street. This small store was a popular hangout for
famous authors like James Fenimore Cooper, as well as for magazine
editors, newspaper reporters, and gamblers employed in the vicinity.
And here Poe came for gossip and stimulation, and certainly for
contacts.

When he had money, which was not often, Poe brought cigars
or plugs of tobacco from the beautiful salesgirl behind the counter.
She was employed, largely because of her vivacity and comeliness,
as a full-time clerk, and her name was Mary Cecilia Rogers. It may
be assumed that Poe, through the frequency of his visits and small
purchases, knew her fairly well. He could not know, however, how
soon Miss Rogers would serve him in another capacity.

By early 1839 the strange, eloquent, self-styled "magazinist"
was no longer a regular customer of John Anderson, tobacconist.
Poe was established at $800 a year salary—the greatest sum he
would ever earn in his life, and considerably more than his total
income from the ten books he would write—as managing editor
of a periodical in near-by Philadelphia. The periodical was owned
by a reformed comedian named William Burton, who eventually
sold it to George Graham, a cabinet-maker turned publisher.

Poe was retained as editor of *Graham's Magazine*, and he worked doggedly in a third-floor cubicle shared with a Swedish assistant, reading and purchasing manuscripts, laying out new issues, and writing criticism and fiction. In short months his industry and ability helped boom the circulation of *Graham's* from 5,000 to 37,000. Occasionally, as his duties demanded it, he made the uncomfortable six-hour train trip to New York City. It may be assumed that on these short visits he looked in on John Anderson's tobacco shop and renewed his acquaintance with Mary Rogers, the attractive clerk behind the counter.

We do not know the date when Edgar Allan Poe last laid eyes on Mary Rogers. But we do know, approximately, the date when he first saw her name in print. Poe was a habitual reader of the sensational penny papers. Some of his finest fiction was culled from seemingly insignificant news items. Only months before, having read of an escaped ourang-outang, he had conceived the world's first detective story and published it in *Graham's* as "The Murders in the Rue Morgue". Thus it was, in early August of 1841, that Poe consulted his latest batch of New York newspapers and stumbled upon the familiar name of Mary Rogers.

He came across the bald news item on the second page of the *New York Sunday Mercury* for August 1. Since it was often filled with errors, he consulted the other papers. James Gordon Bennett's gaudy *New York Herald* for August 5 fully substantiated the *Mercury's* story. We can believe that what Poe read grieved him deeply. For what he read told him that the pretty girl who so often sold him tobacco in the shop on Broadway had been brutally murdered. According to both accounts, Mary Cecilia Rogers was found floating in the Hudson River off Hoboken on Wednesday, 28 July 1841. She had been beaten and strangled, and was quite dead when fished out of the water.

Poe's reaction to the crime was no different from that of most decent New Yorkers. True, they were used to murder. Only five years before, at a time when most newspapers thought crime an improper subject to report, James Gordon Bennett, that brash and colourful cross-eyed Scot, had given the *New York Herald* a circulation of 50,000 with his reporting of the Ellen Jewett case. Miss Jewett, an attractive prostitute, had been bloodily dispatched in a house of ill-fame, and Mr Bennett broke a tradition of journalistic silence on such matters by having a look at the corpse and reporting to all and sundry: "The body looked as white, as full, as polished as the purest Parian marble. The perfect figure, the exquisite limbs, the fine face, the full arms, the beautiful bust, all, all surpassed in every respect the Venus de Medici." This story broke the ice, and thereafter the constant reader had gore delivered daily at his breakfast.

Yet, despite this saturation of homicide, the murder of young Mary Rogers affected the citizenry with a shock of dismay. Miss Rogers was not just another anonymous victim. She had been, the woodcuts and columns made plain, a Grecian beauty endowed with every virtue—and virginity besides. She had worked honestly for a living. She had been adored and respected by customers of consequence. She had been the kind of woman one married, or had for sister or daughter. She had been a girl to whom half of New York could be likened. Now she was dead—killed with ferocity, in secret—and now no one was safe.

We have, fortunately, the typical reaction of a New Yorker of the period. Philip Hone, a cultured, wealthy citizen who dabbled in politics and kept voluminous diaries, read the accounts of Miss Rogers's slaying about the same time as Poe did, and recorded his feelings:

"Friday, 6 Aug—Shocking Murder. The body of a young female named Mary Cecilia Rogers was found on Thursday last in the river near Hoboken, with horrid marks of violation and violence on her person. She was a beautiful girl, an attendant in the cigar shop of John Anderson in Broadway. She left home for a walk on the Sunday previous and was seen near Barclay Street in company with a young man, as if on an excursion to Hoboken; since which no trace of her was found, until the dreadful discovery on Thursday.

"She is said to have been a girl of exceeding good character and behaviour, engaged to be married, and has no doubt fallen victim to the brutal lust of some of the gang of banditti that walk unscathed and violate the laws with impunity in this moral and religious city. No discoveries have yet been made."

The mystery of Mary Rogers was a nine-week wonder. The leading Manhattan journals, the *Herald*, the *Commercial Advertiser*, the *Courier and Enquirer*, the *Tribune*, inspired by the possibilities of record circulation, and the underpaid metropolitan police, inspired by offers of rewards amounting to the unheard-of figure of $1,195, kept the case boiling. Dozens of suspects, including two of Mary's suitors, a sailor, two abortionists, a wood-engraver, and several Bowery gangs, were closely questioned. Every suspect and every clue led to a dead end. By mid-October another murder, equally savage, had taken over the headlines and the attention of the law, and the hunt for the killer of Mary Rogers was actually, if not technically, abandoned.

But if Mary Rogers was forgotten in New York, she was not forgotten in Philadelphia. From that first day when he had read of Mary's death, Poe followed every new development in the case. He read as many papers as he could find, but principally a periodical called *Brother Jonathan*, which gave the case the most complete coverage and often condensed the accounts of rival sheets. Poe's later knowledge of the details of the crime makes it quite apparent that he filed away every clipping relating to Mary's death and also made copious notes on the theories prevailing.

The murder fascinated Poe for reasons other than his personal knowledge of the victim. Undoubtedly the crime had particular appeal to Poe because it remained unsolved. This untidy fact made it a puzzle. Quite plainly, the pieces were all there. But they had not been properly put together. Poe was, as we know, a fanatic about puzzles. He enjoyed nothing more than to match his mentality against the most difficult cryptograms, codes, riddles, enigmas. Mary Rogers was such a challenge to his intellect.

He toyed with the idea of a story based on Mary Rogers, but he did not write it for fully six months after news of the crime had died down. When he finally did convert it into his second detective tale, it was created less out of an inner compulsion than out of an outer need for additional finances. Indirectly, it was Virginia Poe who was responsible for Mary Rogers being put to paper.

The weeks when Poe had been following the crime were, relatively, the most peaceful and secure of his entire life. In all the years before, he had never known normality. Orphaned by his actor parents at the age of two, he had spent five years in England with his guardian, a Scotch merchant. Entering the University of Virginia, he caroused and ran up gambling debts amounting to $2,500, and was withdrawn after less than a year's attendance. Poe enlisted in the army as a private, was bought out by his guardian, then sent to West Point, where he was promptly court-martialled for neglecting roll calls and disobeying his superiors. On a visit to Baltimore, he met his father's youngest sister, Maria Clemm, and his cousin, a frail child named Virginia, and thereafter he was never apart from them.

When Poe was twenty-four, he married Virginia, who was

thirteen. It is thought that their marriage of twelve years was never consummated. We know that Maria Clemm encouraged the marriage. Whether it was because she wanted a provider, as some critics have insisted, or because she wanted a son, we shall never be certain. Of Poe's union with Virginia, Montagu Slater has observed: "He married Virginia and lived under Maria Clemm's apron because for some reason he dare not live with a normal woman, he was afraid of sex and afraid of life. Why? Oscar Wilde included him in a list of celebrated homosexuals."

Poe's sex life, or rather his lack of it, as well as his excessive drinking, made him a cadaver upon which psychiatric amateurs, and professionals as well, have fed since the advent of Freud. Since no analyst ever met or treated him, there is no means by which the accuracy of their guesses may be estimated. One analyst, Marie Bonaparte, who put the known facts of Poe's life on the literary couch some years ago, thought he drank "to fly from the dire and unconscious temptations evoked in him by the dying Virginia". Other psychiatrists have concluded that he loved Virginia and hated her, that he wanted her dead and feared she would die. Whatever his real torments and fears about facing reality, his admirer Baudelaire sensed that his greatest torture was that he had to make money—in a world for which he was unequipped.

But in 1842, in Philadelphia, Poe was briefly making his way for the first time. He was not drinking, and he was less moody than ever. To supplement his meagre earnings on *Graham's* he often wrote stories at night in the downstairs front parlour of the three-storey brick house he had rented on the Schuylkill River. Life was difficult but well knit when suddenly, during an evening in January 1842, the whole thing unravelled—for ever.

On that fateful evening Virginia was playing the harp and singing. Suddenly she "ruptured a blood-vessel". From that moment until her death five years later, she was an invalid, consumptive and haemorrhaging. And Poe came apart. He drank and he took opium and he destroyed every small opportunity. In four months he was finished as editor of *Graham's*.

Soon his financial situation became desperate. He tried to obtain a federal job in Washington, but ruined the chance when he made his appearance drunk and wearing his clothes inside out. In Philadelphia every new day was a threat. Maria Clemm, though she pawned Poe's books, had only molasses and bread to serve for meals. The ailing Virginia kept warm in bed by encouraging her pet cat, Catarina,

to curl upon her bosom. In desperation, Poe turned his torn brain
back to the subject of free-lance fiction. And at once he remembered
Mary Cecilia Rogers.

He wrote her story in May of 1842, seated before the cold fireplace
of his Philadelphia parlour, scribbling steadily "on rolls of blue
paper meticulously pasted together". He employed, for reference,
the clippings he had saved on the actual crime, and his thinly
fictionalized story quoted many of the Mary Rogers news stories
word for word. " 'The Mystery of Marie Roget' was composed
at a distance from the scene of the atrocity," he explained later,
"and with no other means of investigation than the newspapers
afforded. Thus much escaped the writer of which he could have
availed himself had he been upon the spot and visited the localities."
The manuscript, completed, ran to over twenty thousand words in
length.

On 4 June 1842, Poe wrote an inquiry to George Roberts, editor
of the popular *Boston Times* and *Notion Magazine*:

My Dear Sir.

It is just possible that you may have seen a tale of mine
entitled "The Murders in the Rue Morgue" and published,
originally, in "Graham's Magazine" for April, 1841. Its *theme*
was the exercise of ingenuity in the detection of a murderer.
I have just completed a similar article, which I shall entitle
"The Mystery of Marie Roget—a Sequel to the Murders in
the Rue Morgue."

The story is based upon the assassination of Mary Cecilia
Rogers, which created so vast an excitement, some months
ago, in New York. I have, however, handled my design in a
manner altogether *novel* in literature. I have imagined a series
of nearly exact *coincidences* occurring in Paris. A young grisette,
one Marie Roget, had been murdered under precisely similar
circumstances with Mary Rogers. Thus, under pretence of
showing how Dupin (the hero of The Rue Morgue) unravelled
the mystery of Marie's assassination, I, in reality enter into a
very long and rigorous analysis of the New York tragedy. No
point is omitted. I examine, each by each, the opinions and
arguments of the press upon the subject, and show that this
subject has been, hitherto, *unapproached*. In fact, I believe
not only that I have demonstrated the fallacy of the general
idea—that the girl was the victim of a gang of ruffians—but

have *indicated the assassin* in a manner which will give renewed impetus to investigation.

My main object, nevertheless, as you will readily understand, is an analysis of the true principles which should direct inquiry in similar cases. From the nature of the subject, I feel convinced that the article will excite attention, and it has occurred to me that you would be willing to purchase it for the forthcoming Mammoth Notion. It will make 25 pages of Graham's Magazine; and, at the usual price, would be worth to me $100. For reasons, however, which I need not specify, I am desirous of having this tale printed in Boston, and, if you like it, I will say $50. Will you please write me upon this point?—by return mail, if possible.

Yours very truly,
Edgar A. Poe

Having completed this letter, Poe wrote two more, with similar contents, to other editors. One was to a friend, Dr Joseph Evans Snodgrass, of the *Baltimore Sunday Visitor*. In this letter Poe said: "I am desirous of publishing it *in Baltimore*. . . . Of course I could not afford to make you an absolute present of it—but if you are willing to take it, I will say $40." The third letter was to T.W. White, editor of the *Southern Literary Messenger* in Richmond.

All three editors turned down the suggested story. Poe then sold it to the most unlikely market of all—*Snowden's Ladies' Companion* of New York, a periodical which the author contemptuously regarded as "the ne plus ultra of ill-taste, impudence and vulgar humbuggery". *Snowden's* ran "The Mystery of Marie Roget" as a three-part serial in their issues of November and December 1842 and February 1843.

In the very opening paragraphs Poe gives full credit to Mary Rogers for inspiring the creation of Marie Roget. Then, for the second time in his fiction, Poe introduces the world's first imaginary detective, the eccentric Chevalier C. Auguste Dupin who dwells in the Faubourg Saint-Germain with his friend, companion, and sounding-board, the unnamed narrator of the story. Ever since his solution of the killing of a mother and daughter at the hands of an ape in a sealed room in the Rue Morgue, Dupin has "relapsed into his old habits of moody revery". In fact, he is so deeply "engaged in researches" that he has not left his shuttered rooms for a month, and is therefore unaware of a murder that is creating great agitation throughout Paris.

The body of Marie Roget has been found floating in the Seine. Though the Sûreté has offered a reward of thirty thousand francs, there has been no break in the case. At last, in desperation, Prefect G of the Sûreté calls upon Dupin and offers him a proposition (presumably a sum of cash) if he will undertake the case and save the Prefect's reputation. Dupin agrees to investigate.

After obtaining the Sûreté evidence and back copies of the Paris newspapers, Dupin expounds on all the theories extant. Some sources believe Marie Roget is still alive; others, that she was killed by one of her suitors, Jacques St. Eustache or Beauvais, or by a gang. Dupin rejects all these theories, demolishing each with logic. He feels that the real murderer can be found by a closer study of "the public prints". After a week he has six newspaper "extracts" that indicate the killer. These reveal that, three and a half years before, Marie Roget mysteriously left her job at Le Blanc's perfumery and was thought to have eloped with a young naval officer "much noted for his debaucheries". Dupin reasons that this naval officer returned, made love to Marie, and when she became pregnant he murdered her or saw her die under an abortionist's instrument. He then disposed of her body in the Seine.

Dupin points to the clues that will expose the killer. Letters to the press, trying to throw suspicion on others, must be compared with those written by the naval officer. The abortionist, Mme Deluc, and others, must be questioned. The boat which the officer used to dispose of Marie's body must be found. "This boat shall guide us," says Dupin, "with a rapidity which will surprise even ourselves, to him who employed it in the midnight of the fatal Sabbath. Corroboration will rise upon corroboration, and the murderer will be traced."

But in concluding his story Poe neglects to show Dupin catching and exposing the murderer. Instead, Poe concludes abruptly, using the trick of an inserted editorial note which announces: "We feel it advisable only to state, in brief, that the result desired was brought to pass; and that the Prefect fulfilled punctually, although with reluctance, the terms of his compact with the Chevalier."

There was no immediate discernible reaction to the magazine publication of "The Mystery of Marie Roget". It was not until almost four years later, when the story appeared again as part of a collection of Poe's fiction, that it made any impression at all.

In July 1845 the publishing firm of Wiley and Putnam selected "Marie Roget" and eleven others of Poe's narratives, out of the seventy-two he had written, for reprinting in book form. Before publication, however, Poe took great care to revise this story, as well as several others.

In a series of factual footnotes Poe explained that "the lapse of several years since the tragedy upon which the tale is based" made the notes and revisions necessary. "A young girl, Mary Cecilia Rogers, was murdered in the vicinity of New York," he explained, "and although her death occasioned an intense and long-enduring excitement, the mystery attending it had remained unsolved at the period when the present paper was written and published (November 1842). Herein, under pretence of relating the fate of a Parisian grisette, the author has followed, in minute detail, the essential, while merely parallelling the inessential facts of the real murder of Mary Rogers. Thus all argument founded upon the fiction is applicable to the truth: and the investigation of the truth was the object. . . . The confessions of two persons (one of them Madame Deluc of the narrative) made, at different periods, long subsequent to the publication, confirmed, in full, not only the general conclusion, but absolutely all the chief hypothetical details by which that conclusion was attained."

Wiley and Putnam's 228-page pamphlet *Tales by Edgar A. Poe* appeared as Number XI of the firm's Library of American Books, priced at fifty cents per copy, of which eight cents went in royalties to the impoverished author. Upon its appearance in the bookshops, it was heavily outsold by two competing imports from abroad: *The Count of Monte Cristo*, by Alexander Dumas, and *The Wandering Jew*, by Eugène Sue. Nevertheless, it did attain a moderate sale.

The real success of the *Tales*, on the heels of "The Raven", which had been published six months earlier, was not financial but critical. The *Boston Courier* pronounced it "thrilling" and the *New York Post* recommended it as "a rare treat". In London, the *Literary Gazette* considered its author a genius, and in Paris, Baudelaire was honoured to translate it into French. Of the twelve tales, "Marie Roget" created the greatest divergence of opinion. And, in the century since, the novelette has continued to divide its readers. Edmund Pearson thought it "rather tedious" and Howard Haycraft felt that it had "no life-blood". Russel Crouse disagreed. "It is a brilliant study in the repudiation of false clues," he said, "a fascinating document in the field of pseudo-criminology."

Whatever its actual literary merit, "The Mystery of Marie Roget" attained early immortality as one of the three tales—preceded by "The Rue Morgue" in 1841 and followed by "The Purloined Letter" in 1844—responsible for the founding of the modern detective story. Scholars have variously credited Herodotus, the Bible, and the *Arabian Nights* with this honour. Their erudition must be rejected as utter nonsense. As George Bates has remarked: "The cause of Chaucer's silence on the subject of aeroplanes was because he had never seen one. You cannot write about policemen before policemen exist to be written of."

Organized crime-detection was in its infancy when Edgar Allan Poe created the character of Dupin. The mystery story was an unheard-of art form when Poe became, in the words of Willard Huntington Wright, "the authentic father of the detective novel as we know it to-day". In "Marie Roget", and in his two other crime stories, Poe prepared the mould for the first eccentric amateur sleuth and his thick-witted foil, a mould which a thousand authors have used in the years since. In these stories, too, Poe introduced the first of a legion of stupid police officers, red herrings, perfect crimes, and psychological deductions.

After Poe, of course, came the deluge. But in his lifetime he had no idea of what he had wrought. His detective tales, as startling innovations, profited him little. With Virginia's death, he buried Dupin. He dwelt in an alcoholic daze. He became engaged to several wealthy women, but married none. In Baltimore, bleary with drink, drugs, and insanity, he stumbled into the chaos of a Congressional election and was led by hoodlums from poll to poll to vote over and over again as a repeater. Left in a gutter without his clothes or his senses, he was taken to the Washington College Hospital, where he groaned: "I wish to God somebody would blow my damned brains out." It was on a Sunday's dawn that he died murmuring: "God help my poor soul."

But seven years before, when he first wrote "Marie Roget", he saw himself as something better. The character of C. Auguste Dupin was Poe's idealization of himself, "a cool, infallible thinking machine that brought the power of reason to bear on all of life's problems". The name Dupin he had found in an article on the French Sûreté in *Burton's Magazine*. This was probably André Dupin, a French politician who wrote on criminal procedures and died in 1865.

The character of the blundering Prefect G was undoubtedly drawn from the very real, if quite improbable, François Vidocq, a French baker's son who was sent to the galleys for thievery, and who later served as head of the Sûreté for eighteen years. Poe read Vidocq's fanciful four-volume *Mémoires*, which contained the detective's boast that he had placed twenty thousand criminals in jail. Poe was not impressed. He thought Vidocq "a good guesser" and a man who "erred continually by the very intensity of his investigations. He impaired his vision by holding the object too close."

But the most important character in "The Mystery of Marie Roget" was the unhappy victim. And she, as Poe had told us, was Mary Cecilia Rogers.

Despite her subsequent notoriety, Mary Rogers's beginnings remain as enigmatic as her sudden end. For all the columns of copy published in the days following her death, Mary Rogers continues a shadowy, forever tantalizing figure of a young woman. She was born in New York City during 1820. There was, apparently, an older brother, who went to sea in his youth and engaged in a variety of speculative enterprises abroad. We know nothing of Mary's father, except what Poe wrote of her fictional counterpart, Marie Roget: "The father had died during the child's infancy, and from the period of his death . . . the mother and daughter had dwelt together." As Mary grew up, her widowed mother, ill, nervous, harried by debt, sought some means of making a livelihood. This problem was solved by Mary's seafaring brother, who returned from South America with profits gained from an obscure business venture. He presented a portion of these profits to mother and sister, then signed on a ship and sailed out of our story.

Mrs Rogers wisely invested her windfall in a boarding-house at 126 Nassau Street in New York City. While the house gave Mary and her mother a roof over their heads, it gave them little else. At no time did it entertain more than two or three male boarders, and these were usually struggling clerks or labourers.

To supplement the meagre income of the boarding-house, Mary Rogers decided to seek outside employment. This was in 1837, when she was seventeen. All accounts agree that she was beautiful. Crude contemporary prints depict her as a dark-eyed brunette, who wore her hair fashionably bunned. She had a complexion without blemish and an aquiline nose, and was much admired for her "dark smile". She was favoured, too, with a full, firm bosom, a slender figure, and a manner of great vivacity. She did not have to look far for employment. Her beauty came to the attention of one John Anderson, a snuff-manufacturer who ran a tobacco shop at 319

Broadway, near Thomas Street. Aware that "her good looks and vivacity" would be an asset to a business which catered to male trade, Anderson installed Mary behind his counter. The store was already a popular hangout for gamblers, sporty bachelors, newspaper reporters, and magazine editors. With the appearance of Mary Rogers, the clientèle grew and improved.

We know that during 1837 and 1838 Edgar Allan Poe frequented the tobacconist's and was impressed with Mary Rogers. But there were other author customers, more prosperous and better known, who were equally impressed. Fitz-Greene Halleck, the somewhat forbidding, partially deaf, middle-aged poet, who had once served as secretary to John Jacob Astor, often appeared carrying his familiar green cotton umbrella. He was, it is said, sufficiently enchanted by Mary to write a poem rhapsodizing her beauty.

James Fenimore Cooper, on his frequent trips to New York from Cooperstown, was another regular at John Anderson's. He was a breezy, frank, pugnacious man, who had already published *The Spy* and spent a fortune instigating libel suits against reviewers who called his writings "garbage". Cooper was uninhibited in his opinions, and highly vocal, and there can be little doubt he often sounded off to Mary on the money-madness of America and the provincialism of New York.

The most famous customer, however, was fifty-four-year-old Washington Irving. He dwelt alone in a small stone Dutch cottage on the Hudson, and was known everywhere for his creation of Ichabod Crane and Rip Van Winkle. A stout, genial, unaffected man, Irving must have entranced Mary Rogers with anecdotes of his youth. As a lawyer he had helped defend Aaron Burr. And he counted among his friends Dolly Madison, John Howard Payne, and Mary Godwin Shelley.

Few of the customers attended Mary Rogers after shop hours. At her mother's insistence, the proprietor, when he could, escorted her home at dusk. For New York was shot through with rowdyism. At nightfall the gangs, the Bowery Boys and the Dead Rabbits, rose out of the slums to molest, to maim, and to murder with butcher knives. It was estimated that in the waterfront area alone over fifteen thousand sailors were robbed of two million dollars in a single year.

Though there was much that was unlovely in New York—Dickens disliked the spittoons as much as the slums, and Cooper objected to the pigs in the red-brick streets—there was also much that held attraction for a young lady. There were beer gardens that seated a thousand persons, and behind the wrought-iron fences of the great homes couples danced the polka and the waltz, and to the north of the city were vast green picnic grounds and glistening ponds for boating. There is every reason to believe that Mary Rogers enjoyed these pleasures.

While she may not have dated her customers, there is evidence that Mary Rogers was a gay girl. After her death, much was made of her chastity. Dr Richard Cook, of Hoboken, who performed the autopsy, announced that Mary had been "a good girl". He reaffirmed to the *New York Herald* "that previous to this shocking outrage, she had evidently been a person of chastity and correct habits". Surely the good doctor's diagnosis was more sentimental than scientific. From the number and variety of the young men who were interrogated after her death and who seemed to know her intimately, it is unlikely that Mary Rogers was a virgin.

Especially she seemed to have great affection for numerous of her mother's boarding-house guests. William Keekuck, a young sailor who had boarded with Mrs Rogers in 1840, had occasionally dated Mary, as had his older brother before him. Alfred Crommelin, for whom she left a rose on the last day of her life, was a handsome boarder characterized by the press as her "former suitor". Daniel Payne, a cork-cutter and an alcoholic, lived under the same roof as Mary, dated her regularly, and intended to marry her. These were three escorts known by name. There were probably many more. In the light of her environment, it is surprising that Mary's reputation was not worse. She had grown to maturity without paternal discipline, without family life, without security. Her beauty had marked her as a perpetual target for adventurous men-about-town. Her job, in a shop patronized solely by males, made her sophisticated beyond her years. Her oppressive financial status and her confinement to a rundown boarding-house, coupled with a lively personality, encouraged her to accept nocturnal escape with any attractive gallant.

In October of 1838, when she was only eighteen, there occurred a curious interlude in the life of Mary Rogers. On the morning of Thursday, 4 October, she failed to appear for work at the cigar store. The same day, her distressed mother found a note from Mary on her bedroom table. The contents of the note, which Mrs Rogers turned over to the city coroner's office, were never divulged. Three and a half years later, at the time of her death, the *New York*

Herald told its readers: "This young girl, Mary Rogers, was missing from Anderson's store . . . for two weeks. It is asserted that she was then seduced by an officer of the US Navy, and kept at Hoboken for two weeks. His name is well known on board his ship."

The reporters who frequented the cigar store, and knew Mary, quickly filed stories on her disappearance. With one exception, they all suspected foul play. The one exception was an anonymous cynic on the *Commercial Advertiser* who thought that the young lady had gone "into concealment that it might be believed she had been abducted, in order to help the sale of the goods of her employer".

After two weeks the erratic Mary returned to her mother and her job. She had no explanation to offer, beyond remarking that she had "felt tired" and gone to rest with some friends in Brooklyn. When she was shown a copy of the *Commercial Advertiser*, with its snide suspicions of hoax, she became furious. "She felt so annoyed at such a report having got abroad during her temporary absence on a country excursion," said the *Journal of Commerce*, "that she positively refused ever to return to the store." It is not known for certain, however, if she actually left John Anderson's because her honesty was impugned by the customers, or if she left simply because her mother, ailing and infirm, required her assistance to help maintain the boarding-house. But leave she did, in 1839, some months after returning from her mysterious holiday.

Her activities in the three years following are unknown. It is to be presumed that she spent her days cleaning and cooking in her mother's boarding-house, and her nights supplying diversion for her mother's paid-up roomers. We know that one boarder, Alfred Crommelin, ardently pursued her and was rejected. Her lack of interest determined him to remove his person from the boarding-house. However, he made it clear that if she had a change of heart, he might still be available. Another roomer, the convivial cork-cutter Daniel Payne, had more success. Though a man of limited means, he found ways to entertain Mary and became her most frequent escort. They soon reached an understanding, and Mary began to refuse all outside engagements. Payne was under the impression that they were engaged to be married. But before a date could be determined, another date occurred of more historic importance in the annals of crime.

Sometime on Saturday morning, 24 July 1841, Mary Rogers visited the office of her rejected suitor, Alfred Crommelin. He was out to an early lunch and his business quarters were closed. From his door, as was the custom, he had hung a slate for messages. On this slate Mary engimatically scribbled her mother's name. Then she inserted a rose in the keyhole of the door and departed. Crommelin discovered both the signature on the slate and the red rose shortly after lunch, but, as far as we know, did nothing about them. Perhaps he was occupied with his business. Perhaps he was not satisfied with the show of affection. Or perhaps he visited her after all and never confessed it.

The following morning—the now famous morning of Sunday, 25 July 1841—broke hot and humid. It was, the press duly reported, ninety-three degrees in the shade. Many New Yorkers went to church. Many more New Yorkers fled the furnace of the metropolis for the greener pastures of New Jersey and Connecticut. Mary Rogers, too, decided to escape the heat of the city's centre. It was ten o'clock in the morning when she rapped on Daniel Payne's bedroom door. He was busy shaving. She called to him that she was going to spend the day at the home of a cousin, Mrs Downing, whom she frequently visited. Payne, occupied with his beard, called back that he would meet her when she descended from the stage at Broadway and Ann Street at seven o'clock that evening. This was agreeable to Mary, and she promptly left for her cousin's residence on Jane Street two miles away.

Late in the afternoon Payne bestirred himself, went into the city, and dallied at several grog shops where he was well known. When he emerged shortly before seven to keep his rendezvous, he noticed that heavy clouds hung low overhead. There were rumblings of thunder and flashes of lightning. Certain that rain was in store, and aware of Mary's habits, he decided that she would probably spend the night with her relative. He did not bother to go to Broadway and Ann Street. Instead, he returned directly to Mrs Rogers's boarding-house and went to bed.

When Payne came down to breakfast in the morning, Mary had not yet appeared. Since it had poured the night before, and since the hour was still early, her absence was not unusual. But when Payne made his way back to the house for lunch and found that Mary had still not appeared, he was disturbed. Mrs Rogers was also disturbed. She was heard by her coloured maid to remark that "she feared she would never see Mary again".

Immediately after lunch Payne set out for Mrs Downing's place in Jane Street. Upon his arrival he was surprised and agitated to learn that Mary was not there. Nor had she been there the previous day. She had been expected, but had not appeared. Mrs Downing had not seen her for over a week.

By nightfall Payne and Mrs Rogers had contacted all of Mary's relatives and friends in the vicinity. None had seen her. None had heard from her. She had disappeared completely. Payne and Mrs Rogers were now sufficiently alarmed to try other means of inquiry. Payne went to the offices of the *New York Sun*, the most widely read of the cheaper newspapers, and placed an advertisement asking for information about Mary Cecilia Rogers.

The advertisement appeared in the *Sun* on 27 July. Among its many readers was Alfred Crommelin, the rejected suitor who had so recently received a rose from Mary. He, too, was troubled by her curious disappearance, her second such in three and a half years. Crommelin promptly appointed himself a search party of one. He assumed that Payne and Mrs Rogers had thoroughly scoured the city. He determined to try the outskirts. On Wednesday morning he made his way towards Hoboken, New Jersey. What sent him so far afield, yet with such unerring accuracy, we must deduce for ourselves.

It was a sweltering morning when Crommelin reached Hoboken. He was about to make inquiries after Mary, when he noticed a group of people gathering on the Hudson at a site where spring water was sold for a penny a glass. This site, a cool retreat on the water, was known as Sybil's Cave. Crommelin joined the crowd, and then became aware for the first time of what they were watching. All eyes were on a rowing-boat, manned by two men, being pulled towards the shore, dragging behind it a body attached to a rope.

What had occurred, only minutes before, was that two sight-seers, James M. Boulard and Henry Mallin, while strolling beside the water, had noticed a human form floating in midstream. The pair had immediately requisitioned the rowing-boat and headed for the body. Almost simultaneously three men in a sailing-boat, John Bertram, William Waller, and someone named Luther, had also seen the body, which they had at first thought to be a bag of clothing, and started towards it. The rowing-boat got there first. The body was that of a disfigured, fully dressed young female. Boulard and Mallin hastily secured a rope to her and pulled her in.

When the unfortunate female at last lay on the beach, Crommelin pressed forward with the others for a better view. Crommelin recognized the corpse at once. "It's Mary Rogers!" he exclaimed. "This blow may kill her mother!"

She was still wearing the costume she had worn four days earlier—flowered bonnet, its ribbon tied under her chin, blue dress, petticoat, pantalettes, stockings, and garters. Her face had been badly bashed, and her body bore bruises of violence. From the condition of her corpse, there was every evidence of foul play. Mary's wrists were tightly tied with hemp, and about her throat was wound a strip of lace torn from her petticoat. Edgar Allan Poe, in his graphic account, made it clear that death was caused by strangulation, not by drowning. "The flesh of the neck was much swollen," he wrote. "There were no cuts apparent, or bruises which appeared the effect of blows. A piece of lace was found tied so tightly round the neck as to be hidden from sight; it was completely buried in the flesh. . . . The knot by which the strings of the bonnet were fastened was not a lady's, but a slip or sailor's knot."

Upon the arrival of the Hudson County authorities, the body was promptly transferred from the beach to the small village of Hoboken. There, Dr Richard F. Cook, serving as county coroner, hastily performed the autopsy. By nine o'clock that evening the formal inquest began. Crommelin once more identified the corpse as that of Mary Rogers. He spoke of her reputation for "truthfulness, and modesty and discretion", and theorized that she had probably been lured to the Hoboken area by some man. Dr Cook then testified as to the results of his autopsy. She had been murdered, he stated. She had also been subjected to sexual intercourse, most likely raped, possibly once, possibly many times.

When the witnesses at the inquest had concluded their testimony, the coroner's jury deliberated briefly, then announced that the victim's death had been caused by "violence committed by some person or persons". And thus the mystery of Mary Rogers was officially embarked upon its journey into history.

Mary's mother and Daniel Payne had been notified of the tragedy earlier in the day. The news was brought to them by the man named Luther, who had witnessed from his sailing-boat the recovery of the body. The day following the inquest, Alfred Crommelin appeared at the boarding-house to confirm the identification of Mary. He had secured from the Hoboken morgue a flower from Mary's hat, a curl from her hair, a strip of her pantalettes, and a garter. These he displayed to the bereaved mother. Mary had been buried hours before. The speedy interment was made necessary by the rapid decomposition of her body due to excessive exposure to water and hot weather.

Though Mary Rogers had vanished on 25 July 1841, and had been found on 28 July, no New York newspaper mentioned her murder until 1 August. After that, for more than two months she was rarely off the front pages of the popular press.

The sensational publicity accorded the case created wide and feverish interest. Despite this, the police made only desultory efforts to solve it. There was an immediate dispute over the matter of jurisdiction. New Jersey authorities tried to lay the investigation in the lap of the New York police, arguing that Mary had been killed in New York and dumped into the Hudson, and had drifted into the New Jersey area by sheerest accident. The New York police, on the other hand, replied that Mary had been slain off Hoboken, had been discovered near that community and buried there, and that therefore the problem was plainly a responsibility of the New Jersey authorities.

While both states wrangled, the Manhattan press helped resolve the issue by accusing the New York police of shirking their duty, pointing out that Mary Rogers, no matter where she was killed, had been a resident and citizen of New York. At last New York City officialdom bowed to this pressure and reluctantly undertook the case. On Wednesday, 11 August, Mary Rogers was exhumed from her Hoboken grave and removed to the Dead House at City Hall Park in New York City. Mrs Rogers and several relatives were brought to the Dead House, where they positively identified various articles of clothing that had belonged to Mary.

The New York police now had the enigma in their hands. They were neither equipped to solve it, nor, it must be admitted, were they terribly interested. The High Constable of the force, a squat, bald-headed old man named Jacob Hays, was capable enough. He had solved many crimes during his career, and had introduced the techniques of shadowing and the third degree to America. But at the time he was handed the portfolio of the Mary Rogers case he was sixty-nine years old and approaching retirement. Hays, therefore, turned the case over to his handfull of Leatherheads—so-called after the heavy leather helmets they wore—and assigned its perusal to a Sergeant McArdel.

The Leatherheads, who wore no uniforms and carried no firearms, were divided into two groups. The daytime force consisted of two constables from each city ward and a half-dozen marshals. The night force, called the Night Watch, consisted of 146 men. The latter group worked as labourers during the day, then supplemented their salaries by becoming policemen at night. Their pay, as part-time law-enforcement officers, was eighty-seven cents an evening.

Naturally, since they were overworked and underpaid, the Leatherheads had little interest in any new crime that might require extra exertion. Furthermore, many resented any intrusion upon their routine activities, which had been so organized as to give them bonuses above their meager police pay. For, since the city would not raise their wages, a great number of police bolstered their incomes by secretly allying themselves with professional criminals. The standard practice was for thieves to ransack a shop while the Leatherheads turned their backs. Then, when the shopkeepers offered cash rewards for the return of their merchandise, the Leatherheads miraculously recovered the loot, though rarely the looters. Upon collecting the rewards, the Leatherheads split the money with the criminals. Theft was a paying business; murder, unless there was a reward involved, was not. The Mary Rogers case, then, was little more than an unprofitable nuisance.

For almost two weeks after the murder, the police remained inert, while the press fumed and the public boiled. On the day Mary Rogers's corpse was transferred to New York, a committee of angry citizens acted. They sponsored an open meeting and collected $455, to be given as a reward to anyone who apprehended the killer. Shortly after, Governor Seward of New York added an official reward of $750, and the guarantee of a full pardon to any accomplice willing to turn informant.

Now, at last, there was sufficient bounty to spur Sergeant McArdel and his Leatherheads into action. Quickly a long list of suspects was summoned to police headquarters and interrogated. Foremost among these was Daniel Payne. He had known Mary Rogers best, and spoken to her last, before her disappearance. It was felt that he had acted in a suspiciously "unloverlike" manner, presumably because he had not troubled to wait for her at Broadway and Ann Street as he had promised. The police theorized that she might have left him for another, and that he, in a drunken rage, might have killed her out of jealousy. But Payne, in a detailed statement, was able to account for every hour of the critical Sunday.

Alfred Crommelin was the next to be questioned. The police, remembering the rose in the keyhole, felt that "there was still some slight tendresse betwixt him and the young lady".

Also, Crommelin had been curiously anxious to halt the police investigation. Earlier, he had begged McArdel to drop the case, since a continued inquiry, with its attendant notoriety, might be seriously damaging to Mrs Rogers's health. Yet Crommelin, like Payne, had an acceptable alibi.

Another of Mrs Rogers's boarders remained suspect. Dr Cook had indicated that the bonnet string about Mary's chin had been tied in a sailor's knot, and that there was a sailor's hitch behind her dress, by means of which she had been lifted and dropped into the Hudson. It appeared that, the year before, a young man named William Keekuck had roomed with Mrs Rogers. Keekuck was now an ordinary sailor in the United States Navy. He was at sea, on the USS *North Carolina* when the authorities sent for him. The moment his ship docked at Norfolk, Virginia, Keekuck was taken off and hustled to New York for cross-examination. There was indeed some evidence against the frightened sailor. He had boarded his vessel in a great hurry, and very late, the night of 25 July. His trousers had been stained, though it was no longer possible to prove that these had been bloodstains. Keekuck admitted that he had dwelt with Mrs Rogers, and had known Mary, but insisted that he had been only an acquaintance. It was his brother who had been a suitor. Though in New York City on shore leave during 25 July, he had not seen Mary Rogers. In fact, he had not seen her since 3 July, and was able to substantiate this to the temporary satisfaction of the police; but before he was finally dismissed William Keekuck was three times hauled off the *North Carolina* for questioning.

Meanwhile, the police were bringing in other promising suspects. Great hopes were held, briefly, over the apprehension of one Joseph M. Morse, a rotund and bewhiskered wood-engraver, who lived in Nassau Street near Mrs Rogers's boarding-house. On the Sunday of Mary Rogers's disappearance, Morse had been seen travelling to Staten Island with an attractive young lady who was not his wife. On the morning Mary was removed from the Hudson, Morse heard about it, left his business at midday, returned home in a frenzied state, had an argument with his wife, beat her up, and departed the metropolis for parts unknown. The authorities were swiftly on his trail. They found him in Worcester, Massachusetts. He had shaved off his beard, purposely lost weight, and was hiding under an assumed name. His prospects, to say the least, were dismal.

Morse was brought back to New York City under guard. There were street mutterings of lynching. Morse quickly admitted that he had picked up a comely young lady on the Sunday in question and escorted her to Staten Island. His purpose was not homicidal, but carnal. He had, in fact, shown some ingenuity. He had set his watch back in order to miss the last ferry home. The ruse was successful. Morse then suggested to the young lady that they adjourn to a hotel. She proved amenable. They rented rooms, whereupon Morse made amorous advances, as planned. These advances, he remarked unhappily, were rejected. He slept the night alone, and returned on the morning ferry to his family hearth and his wood-engraving business. Shortly after, he heard from neighbours of Mary Rogers's Sunday disappearance and death. At once he worried that his attractive companion might have been Mary Rogers. Though he had left her defiant and healthy, he realized that she might have been murdered after his departure, and that he would be discovered and blamed. Without further ado, he fled the suddenly oppressive climate of New York City for Massachusetts.

While the police weighed the veracity of Mr Morse's little adventure, the penny press publicized it. And luckily for Mr Morse. For, shortly after, the young lady Morse had abandoned on Staten Island came forward to identify herself and to corroborate his story and her own virginity. The police promptly turned the Sunday Lothario over to the custody and further cross-examination of his waiting spouse.

But the mystery of Mary Rogers still remained unsolved. McArdel and his Leatherheads now abandoned Mrs Rogers's boarders and the other obvious suspects to concentrate on a line of investigation that had been too long neglected. The police asked themselves the following questions: What had been Mary Rogers's movements after she left the boarding-house for her cousin's residence? Since she had left at ten o'clock in the morning, while church was out and the streets were filled, who had seen her? And whom had she been seen with? In what direction was she headed? And by what means of transport? These questions, much to the gratification of McArdel, speedily produced an entirely new net of suspects and theories.

A stage-driver named Adam Wall was found who thought he had picked up Mary Rogers at the Bull's Head ferry and driven her to a picnic area near Hoboken. Wall said she was accompanied by "a tall dark man", perhaps twenty-six years of age.

Others quickly appeared to support the assumption that Mary

had visited Hoboken with a stranger or strangers. In fact, two men told the authorities that they had been walking along the shore, approaching Sybil's Cave, on 25 July, when they observed a rowing-boat with six young males and a girl. The girl was attractive enough to hold their attention. Minutes after the girl ran off into the near-by woods with her bevy of admirers, another rowing-boat, containing three anxious gentlemen, drew up. Its occupants inquired of the two visitors if they had seen six men and a girl in the vicinity. When the visitors admitted they had seen just such a group head into the woods, the occupants of the rowing-boat inquired if the girl had gone willingly or by force. Upon learning that she had gone willingly, the occupants took to their oars and slid away.

Next, several witnesses came forward with the recollection of seeing Mary strolling that Sunday morning towards Barclay Street in Manhattan. At Theatre Alley, a short lane off Ann Street which once led to the stage door of the Park Theatre, she had been met by a young man "with whom she was apparently acquainted". From the direction she took thereafter, it was thought she could have gone to the Hoboken ferry—or entered the infamous residence of Mrs Ann Lohman, a notorious and busy abortionist who was known to the carriage trade as Mme Restell.

Actually, there was no direct evidence to connect Mary Rogers's murder with Mme Restell's illegal practices. But whenever there occurred an untimely death in New York, especially one involving a fashionable or beautiful female, there were immediate whisperings against the portly and wealthy English-born Madame. Her record, to be sure, was unsavory. She had been an immigrant dressmaker, had wedded a dispenser of quack medicines named Lohman, and, it was thought, had disposed of him for the inheritance. Thereafter she had lent her talents to birth-control.

Mme Restell's mansion of Greenwich Street was visited by a steady stream of unmarried expectant women, many the mistresses of millionaires and Congressman. At the time of Mary Rogers's death, the Madame's shuttered establishment, nick-named "the mansion built on baby skulls", had netted her earnings upwards of one million dollars. Shortly after Mary's burial, public feeling against Mme Restell ran so high that crowds gathered about her doorway shouting: "Haul her out! Where's the thousand children murdered in this house? Who murdered Mary Rogers?" On that occasion, violence was prevented only by the quick intervention of the police, who undoubtedly found the mammoth Madame too lucrative a source of income to trouble with such trifles as the corpse of a onetime cigar-counter employee.

The police had just about exhausted their inquiry into Mary Rogers's movements when a new and sensational bit of evidence suddenly came to light. Two young men, the sons of a Mrs Frederica Loss, who kept a public inn a mile above Hoboken, were beating about the bush near Weehawken on 25 August. In the thicket they found a small opening that led into a cramped tunnel or cave. They explored further, and discovered inside the cave four stones built into a seat. Draped on and about the seat were a silk scarf, a white petticoat, a parasol, a pocket-book, a pair of gloves, and a mildewed linen handkerchief initialled in silk "M.R.".

Mrs Loss's sons immediately gathered up the feminine apparel and brought the find to their mother. She went directly to the Hoboken police, who excitedly contacted their colleagues in New York City. At once the press was filled with woodcuts and stories of Mrs Loss, her inn, and two of her three sons who had made the discovery, and the opening in the thicket near the cliffs of Weehawken.

This publicity flushed forth a new witness. A stage-driver came forward. He dimly remembered transporting a girl of Mary Rogers's description and a tall "swarthy" man to Mrs Loss's inn on 25 July. This recollection succeeded in stirring Mrs Loss's own memory. She vaguely remembered the couple. They had had cakes and drinks. Then Mary, or someone like her, and the "swarthy" man had gone off together into the near-by woods overlooking the river. Some minutes later Mrs Loss had heard a woman's scream from the vicinity of the woods. She had paid no attention. On Sundays the area was filled with gangs of rowdies and loose young ladies who were often vocal.

With the find at Weehawken, all the tangible clues were in. Since the case had not been broken in fact, it could only be solved on paper. Police authorities and amateur sleuths of the city room were soon busy formulating and publishing theories. The overwhelming majority were in accord on Weehawken as the site of the crime. But on the subject of the criminal's identity there was a great passionate diversity of opinion.

Who killed Mary Rogers? In the months after her death, almost every literature contemporary was certain he knew. The authorities seemed to lean towards Mrs Loss and her three sons. Justice Gilbert Merritt, of New Jersey, devoted much time to questioning Mrs Loss.

He believed that she practised abortion, or permitted her inn to be
employed by physicians for that purpose and that Mary Rogers had
died during an operation in one of her back rooms and had been
disposed of in the Hudson by her sons. The effects in the thicket,
he felt, were only a red herring to divert suspicion. "The murder of
the said Mary C. Rogers was perpetrated in a house at Weehawken,"
Justice Merritt announced, "then kept by one Frederica Loss, alias
Kellenbarack, and her three sons, all three of whom this deponent
has reason to believe are worthless and profligate characters."

Sergeant McArdel, of the New York Leatherheads, interrogated
only the three sons, and found them as undelightful as had Justice
Merritt. They were sullen and they were contradictory. But they
steadfastly denied that their mother had practised abortion. When
one of them was asked if visitors ever paid their mother fifty dollars
for any purpose, he replied: "I never have known any sick person
brought to my mother's house to be attended upon." McArdel, too,
concluded that Mrs Loss was guilty of manslaughter, and that her
sons were her accomplices in removing the body.

Of all the authorities, Dr Richard F. Cook held most heartily to
his original theory that Mary had been gang-raped and then brutally
killed. Again and again he told the press that he was "confident" she
had been "violated by six, or possibly eight ruffians; of that fact, he
had ocular proof, but which is unfit for publication."

The majority on newspaper row supported Dr Cook's theory.
Murder after murder had been committed by roving bands of
rowdies in the New York metropolitan area and among the
outing-sites of New Jersey. The weekly *Saturday Evening Post*
saw signs of gang violence in the disorder of the thicket, and
the *Journal of Commerce* saw the handiwork of street ruffians in
the fact that no men's handkerchiefs had been used to strangle
Mary. "A piece of one of the unfortunate girl's petticoats was torn
out and tied under her chin, and around the back of her head,
probably to prevent screams," remarked the *Journal of Commerce*.
"This was done by fellows who had no pocket-handkerchiefs."

For weeks the *New York Herald*, which had been crusading against
vandals and butcher boys, also championed the gang-rape notion.
The *Herald* theorized that Mary and her "swarthy" escort had indeed
visited Mrs Loss's inn for refreshment, and then proceeded to the
woods for further refreshment. In the brush they had been set
upon by a waiting gang of roughnecks. Mary's escort had been
assassinated immediately, and Mary herself slain after she had

been attacked. Then both bodies had been shoved into the river. But if this held any probability, what happened to the remains of the "swarthy" escort? As a matter of fact, the body of an unidentified man was found floating in the Hudson five days after Mary's body was recovered. But the man was neither tall nor dark.

The *New York Herald* flirted with one other intriguing possibility. It recalled Mary's first disappearance, three and a half years before the murder. "It is well known that, during the week of her absence . . . she was in the company of a young naval officer much noted for his debaucheries. A quarrel, it is supposed, providentially led to her return home. We have the name of the Lothario in question . . . but for obvious reasons forbear to make it public." The *New York Herald* was suspecting someone Mary had met through young Keekuck, possibly a superior on the USS *North Carolina*. Or possibly it was still making allusions to Keekuck himself.

Brother Jonathan was the first of several journals to subscribe to the idea that Mary Rogers had not been murdered at all. Its editors argued that a body in the water only three days, or less, would not be "so soon afloat" and that it would not be "so far decomposed". The corpse fished out of the Hudson at Sybil's Cave must have been in the water "not three days merely, but, at least, five times three days". Therefore, the body could not have been that of Mary Rogers.

On the other hand, if the body had actually been that of Mary Rogers, then *Brother Jonathan*'s choice for the murderer was Alfred Crommelin. "For some reason," said the journal, "he determined that nobody shall have anything to do with the proceedings but himself, and he has elbowed the male relatives out of the way, according to their representations, in a very singular manner. He seems to have been very much averse to permitting the relatives to see the body."

Daniel Payne fared better than his rival boarder. While there were murmurings about his motives, and about his addiction to drink, all sources agreed that his affidavit concerning his activities on the fateful Sunday was foolproof. Though, as a matter of fact, no original suspect completely escaped judgment in the press. Even the unlucky Joseph Morse, wood-engraver and commuter to Staten Island, had his backers. The *New York Courier and Inquirer* had received anonymous letters which made its editors regard Morse as quite capable of "the late atrocity".

Only one publication advocated Mme Restell as a candidate

for the Tombs. The *National Police Gazette* doggedly waged a campaign against her. As late as February 1846 the *Police Gazette* was editorializing: "The wretched girl was last seen in the direction of Madame Restell's house. The dreadfully lacerated body at Weehawken Bluff bore the marks of no ordinary violation. The hat found near the spot, the day after the location of the body, was dry though it had rained the night before! These are strange but strong facts, and when taken in consideration with the other fact that the recently convicted Madame Costello kept an abortion house in Hoboken at that very time, and was acting as an agent of Restell, it challenges our minds for the most horrible suspicions."

There was yet one more theory to be put forth. And this, appearing more than a year after the crime, proved to be the most widely publicized and controversial of them all. It was, of course, the theory advanced by Edgar Allan Poe in "The Mystery of Marie Roget," which he expected would give "renewed impetus to investigation".

In his thinly disguised novelette—he used French names in the body of the story, but identified each character, newspaper, and site with factual footnotes relating to the Mary Rogers case—Poe began by attempting to demolish the pet theories promoted by his predecessors. "Our first step should be the determination of the identity of the corpse," Poe stated, obviously referring to *Brother Jonathan*'s conjecture that Mary Rogers still lived. At great length, and with questionable scientific accuracy, Poe pointed out that a body immersed in water less than three days could still float. "It may be said that very few human bodies will sink at all, even in fresh water, of their own accord." As to the impossibility of decomposition in less than three days: "All experience does *not* show that 'drowned bodies' require from six to ten days for sufficient decomposition to take place." In short, Poe had no doubt that the body recovered at Sybil's Cave was that of Mary Cecilia Rogers.

However, as to the exact scene of the crime Poe was less certain. That the thicket at Weehawken "was the scene, I may or I may not believe—but there was excellent reason for doubt". Poe set down his doubts in detail. If the articles of clothing had been in the thicket the entire four weeks after the murder, they would have been discovered earlier. The mildew on the parasol and handkerchief could have appeared on the objects overnight. Most important, "Let me beg your notice to the highly artificial arrangement of the articles. On the upper stone lay a white petticoat; on the second, a silk scarf; scattered around, were a parasol, gloves, and a pocket-handkerchief. . . . Here is just such an arrangement as would naturally be made by a not-over-acute person wishing to dispose the articles naturally. But it is by no means a really natural arrangement. I should rather have looked to see the things all lying on the ground and trampled under foot. In the narrow limits of that bower, it would have been scarcely possible that the petticoat and scarf should have retained a position upon the stones, when subjected to the brushing to and fro of many struggling persons." Yet, after all these observations against the Weehawken thicket as the scene of the crime, Poe, in the end, concluded that Mary Rogers must have met her end there, after all.

In studying the roll of suspects, Poe felt that there was no evidence whatsoever against Mme Restell or against Morse. He felt that Daniel Payne's deposition to the police vindicated him entirely. As to Crommelin: "He is a busybody, with much of romance and little of wit. Any one so constituted will readily so conduct himself, upon occasion of real excitement, as to render himself liable to suspicion." *Brother Jonathan*'s editors had selected Crommelin as the murderer, said Poe, because, resenting their implications that he had not properly identified the corpse, Crommelin had gone in and brashly insulted the journal's editors. Mrs Loss was a possibility, but, from her actions, Poe felt that she had played oₐly a secondary part in the crime.

Poe refuted most strongly the popular theory of gang murder. The thicket displayed signs of violent struggle, yet several men would have overcome a frail girl quickly and without struggle. There were evidences that the body had been dragged to the river. One killer might have dragged Mary's corpse, but for several, it would have been easier and quicker to carry her. Nor would a number of assailants have overlooked an initialled handkerchief. Finally: "I shall add but one to the arguments against a gang; but this one has, to my own understanding at least, a weight altogether irresistible. Under the circumstances of large reward offered, and full pardon to any king's evidence, it is not to be imagined for a moment, that some member of a gang of low ruffians, or of any body of men, would not long ago have betrayed his accomplices. . . . That the secret has not been divulged is the very best proof that it is, in fact, a secret. The horrors of this dark deed are known only to one."

This, then, was the essence of Poe's theory. The crime, he insisted, had been committed by a single individual in the thicket at Weehawken. Carefully he reconstructed the murder:

"An individual has committed the murder. He is alone with the ghost of the departed. He is appalled by what lies motionless before him. The fury of his passion is over, and there is abundant room in his heart for the natural awe of the deed. His is none of that confidence which the presence of numbers inevitably inspires. He is *alone* with the dead. He trembles and is bewildered. Yet there is a necessity for disposing of the corpse. He bears it to the river, and leaves behind him the other evidences of his guilt; for it is difficult, if not impossible to carry all the burthen at once, and it will be easy to return for what is left. But in his toilsome journey to the water his fears redouble within him. The sounds of life encompass his path. A dozen times he hears or fancies he hears the step of an observer. Even the very lights from the city bewilder him. Yet, in time, and by long and frequent pauses of deep agony, he reaches the river's brink, and disposes of his ghastly charge—perhaps through the medium of a boat. But now what treasure does the world hold—what threat of vengeance could it hold out—which would have power to urge the return of that lonely murderer over that toilsome and perilous path, to the thicket and its blood-chilling recollections? He returns not, let the consequences be what they may."

And who was this murderer?

He was, Poe decided, an earlier lover. He was the young man who had eloped with Mary Rogers on her first disappearance from the cigar store. Three and a half years later he returned and proposed again. "And here let me call your attention to the fact, that the time elapsing between the first ascertained and the second supposed elopement is a few months more than the general period of the cruises of our men-of-war." He was, then, a navy man on shore leave, the very officer the *New York Herald* stated she had gone off with. When he came back to New York, he interrupted Mary's engagement to Payne. She began to see him secretly. But why did he kill her? Possibly he seduced her and she became pregnant. He took her to Mrs Loss's for an abortion, and she died accidentally. Or possibly he failed to seduce her, and, on an outing to Weehawken, he finally raped her. Then, fearing the consequences of the act, he was forced to kill. At any rate, concluded Poe: "This associate is of swarthy complexion. This complexion, the 'hitch' in the bandage, and the 'sailor's knot' with which the bonnet-ribbon is tied, point to a seaman. His companionship with the deceased—a gay but not an abject young girl—designates him as above the grade of the common sailor."

Poe, like the *New York Herald* before him, claimed to know the name of this navy officer. On 4 January 1848, in a letter to an admirer, a young medical student in Maine named George Eveleth, Poe disclosed: "Nothing was omitted in 'Marie Roget' but what I omitted myself—all that is mystification. The story was originally published in *Snowden's Ladies' Companion*. The 'naval officer' who committed the murder (or rather the accidental death arising from an attempt at abortion) confessed it, and the whole matter is now well understood—but, for the sake of relatives, this is a topic on which I must not speak further."

In 1880 John H. Ingram published a biography of Poe. In it he revealed the name of Poe's suspected "naval officer". The name of the murderer, said Ingram, was Spencer. He did not know his first name, or explain where he had learned his second name. Based on this bit of name-dropping, William Kurtz Wimsatt, Jr, of Yale University, in an investigation of Poe's deductive prowess, attempted to track down the elusive Spencer. He learned that at the time of Mary Rogers's death in 1841 there were only three officers in the United States Navy named Spencer. One was in Ohio at the time Mary vanished in New York; another was infirm; the third was active, and a definite and fascinating possibility. He was eighteen-year-old Philip Spencer, the problem son of Secretary of War John Canfield Spencer. In short, his family was sufficiently influential to hush up any bit of unpremeditated homicide and sufficiently impressive to make Poe admit that "for the sake of relatives, this is a topic on which I must not speak further". Philip Spencer, it might be added, was quite capable of carrying on an affair with Mary and seeing her to an abortionist, or of killing her under different circumstances. Three months before the murder he had been expelled from his third school, Geneva College (now Hobart College), for "moral delinquency". He drank too much and he absented himself from classes too often. Where did he spend his time of truancy? In New York, and with Mary? We do not know. But we do know that in the year following her death he was caught and convicted of planning, and almost executing, the only mutiny in American naval history. Returning from a training cruise to Africa aboard the brig *Somers*, Acting Midshipman Philip Spencer chafed at the conditions on the vessel. He conspired with two subordinates,

Boatswain's Mate Samuel Cromwell and Seaman Elisha Small, to
kill his superiors and convert the *Somers* into a pirate ship. His
plot—though the seriousness of his intention later became a matter
of great controversy—was exposed in time by Captain Alexander
Mackenzie, and young Spencer, hooded and manacled, was hanged
from the main yard-arm with his unfortunate companions.

While the publication of Poe's "The Mystery of Marie Roget"
created a brief flurry of interest in Mary Rogers, it must be remarked
that this interest was confined largely to readers of *Snowden's Ladies'
Companion*. By 1842 the Leatherheads had given up their hope of
obtaining the cash reward and had reverted to their old, less complex
practice of restoring stolen merchandise. By 1844 the Leatherheads
had been replaced by the more efficient, better-paid Municipal
Police, and High Constable Jacob Hays was in retirement. As
for the press, it had turned to matters of more topical interest.
With each passing month, as the Mary Rogers case receded in
time, the chances for its solution became more difficult. For one
thing, popular interest, always fickle, had subsided, and with it the
pressure that stimulated police activity. For another, the mortality
rate among the suspects had mounted in rapidity—and violence.

On Friday, 8 October 1841, Daniel Payne followed his betrothed
to an early grave. On that morning a boatman, walking down a path
to the Hudson River at Weehawken, passed the much-publicized
thicket. He saw a man stretched on the ground. The man was
Daniel Payne. Beside him was an empty bottle of laudanum. He
was alive when the boatman reached him, but lapsed unconscious
and never recovered. Two days later a coroner's jury agreed that
he had committed suicide, but decided that his death might also be
attributed to "congestion of the brain, brought about by irregular
living, exposure, aberration of the mind". His friends announced
that from the day he learned of Mary's death Payne had lived
almost exclusively on a diet of rum, and had probably drunk
himself to death.

A month later Mrs Loss was also dead. One of her sons had been
tampering with a loaded gun, when it accidentally discharged. The
bullet struck her. As she lay dying, she summoned Justice Gilbert
Merritt. She said she had a statement to make concerning the fate
of Mary Rogers. According to the *New York Tribune*, Mrs Loss had
the following deathbed confession:

"On the Sunday of Miss Rogers's disappearance she came to
her house from this city in company with a young physician, who

undertook to procure for her a premature delivery. While in the hands of the physician she died, and a consultation was then held as to the disposal of her body. It was finally taken at night by the son of Mrs Loss and sunk in the river. . . . Her clothes were first tied up in a bundle and sunk in a pond . . . but it was afterwards thought that they were not safe there, and they were accordingly taken and scattered through the woods as they were found."

After Mrs Loss's death, her sons were closely questioned. They refused to confirm their mother's confession. The authorities also discredited it, and it was soon forgotten.

On April Fool's Day 1878 Mme Restell, hounded by Anthony Comstock and fearing a jail sentence (she had once served a year on Blackwell's Island), donned a diamond-studded nightgown and stepped into her bathtub. Minutes later she was dead by her own hand. She had cut her throat. "A bloody ending to a bloody life," was Comstock's epitaph. The *Police Gazette* only regretted that she had expired without a word about Mary Rogers.

In the more than one hundred years that have passed since the death of Mary Rogers, every other suspect went to his grave in silence. Yet no one was permitted to rest in peace. For the mystery of Mary Rogers provided too fascinating and gruesome a game to be affected by any time limit. Though the $1,195 cash reward may have long since expired, the pursuit of a solution continued to hold rewards of its own. The reason is plain: a solved crime is a mere spectator sport, but an unsolved one remains an invitation to participate.

"There is no more stimulating activity than that of the mind, and there is no more exciting adventure than that of the intellect," Willard Huntington Wright once remarked. "Mankind has always received keen enjoyment from the mental gymnastics required in solving a riddle." Few unsolved crimes, it is true, have possessed those elements of murder most foul, yet complex, with clues and suspects sufficient, yet bizarre and simple, to provide riddles of enduring quality. But there have been a handful that managed to meet all specifications. The destruction of Andrew and Abby Borden, in Fall River, Massachusetts, was such a riddle. The shooting of Joseph Bowne Elwell, the bridge expert, in his New York apartment, was another. The discovery of Starr Faithfull on a Long Island beach fulfilled the stringent requirements. And certainly the savage slaying of Julia Wallace in a Liverpool suburb while her husband, William Herbert Wallace, searched, or pretended to search, for an insurance prospect at the non-existent Menlovc Gardens East has, in a few decades, become "the perfect scientific puzzle".

However, the mystery of Mary Rogers, more than most, has stood the test of time as a mental exercise because it offers a challenge provided by only a few other unsolved murders. While it had the standard ingredients—the beautiful victim known to celebrities, the provocative clues from sailor's knot to the arrangement of apparel at Weehawken, the colourful collection of suspects ranging from lovers to abortionists—it also had the genius of Edgar Allan Poe. Thus, when we transport ourselves in time back to that sweltering July morning in 1841 and begin the game and the hunt, we not only compete with the police and press of the period, but we challenge the analysis and deduction of the world's first great detective-story writer. In short, we have the added excitement of pitting ourselves against Poe.

Ever since Poe's death in 1849, armchair amateurs at detection have begun the game by attempting to discredit the master's theories before proceeding with their own. Will M. Clemens, who visited Sybil's Cave and the Weehawken thicket in 1904 for *Era Magazine*, decided that "the confessions mentioned by Poe are of doubtful authenticity". Edmund Pearson after studying contemporary accounts, concluded that "Poe, in writing fiction about the case, was in the position of being able to depart from fact when he liked, and adhere to it when it suited his purpose; that he was first and last a romancer, and a devotee of the hoax; and that the theory that he actually solved the mystery of the death of the real Mary Rogers is not proven, and is very doubtful." Russel Crouse, after pondering "The Mystery of Marie Roget", stated: "As an actual aid in the solution of the crime it is of no more use than the less literary contributions of the stupid and bungling police of the day. For Poe's ratiocination stems from untrustworthy and highly controvertible rumour rather than from fact."

Several other commentators on crime have been less harsh with Poe. They have seen some merit in his deductions, and allowed for the possibility of his being proved right in the future. A quarter of a century ago Winthrop D. Lane reopened the case for *Collier's* magazine. He announced that if Mrs Loss's deathbed confession was correct, it vindicated Poe completely. "He absolved Payne and Crommelin of complicity," said Lane. "He said no gang did the murder. He advanced the idea of a fatal accident under

Mrs Loss's roof (though he had no idea of the nature of the accident)—and here he made an extraordinarily shrewd guess. He thought the articles of clothing might have been placed in the thicket to divert attention from the real scene—and here he was exactly and uncannily correct."

William Kurtz Wimsatt, Jr, after his own probings into the case, doubted that it would ever be solved. But he had no doubt that if new evidence were uncovered, it would be evidence generally in support of Poe's theories. "We shall know the truth only if it was somewhat as Poe and Ingram say, if there was a confession by a man of influential family, if this was known as an inside story, and if someone on the inside wrote the secret down in a document which survives and is to come to light." If this document revealed the murderer as a naval officer, possibly the son of a Secretary of War, then Poe would have triumphed entirely over his critics. "For all his idle argument about bodies in the water," wrote Wimsatt, "his laboured inconsistency about the thicket and the gang, for all his borrowing of newspaper ideas, or (where it suited him) indifference to newspaper evidence, despite the fact that he was so largely wrong and had to change his mind, he did fasten on the naval officer."

But if not Poe's naval officer, then who else?

As early as 1869 a mystic and lecturer, Andrew Jackson Davis, who had been acquainted with Poe, presented his own solution to the Mary Rogers case in the form of a novel called *Tale of a Physician*. Davis thought Mary had become pregnant by a wealthy lover, who then took her to a New York City abortionist, probably Mme Restell. When Mary died on the table, the lover paid off and fled to Texas.

In 1904 Will M. Clemens still had the opportunity to interview several of Mary's contemporaries about Hoboken. Most of these elders felt that Mary and her "swarthy" escort had both been murdered inside Mrs Loss's inn by her three unrestrained sons, for purposes of either rape or robbery. In 1927 Allan Nevins thought that the responsibility for the death of Mary Rogers "was not the work of Payne but of another lover". Nevins believed that Mary had been seduced, and had died of an illegal operation. In 1930 Winthrop D. Lane discovered the original records of Mary Rogers's inquest in the dusty basement of the Hudson County Courthouse. After reading these and pursuing other evidence, Lane pointed the finger of guilt at Mrs Loss. He regarded her dying confession of the crime as the truth.

"Mrs Loss's confession," wrote Lane, "has had a curious history. It seems to have failed to get itself accepted as the truthful explanation of the affair . . . And yet it is the most likely explanation. Why should she make such a confession if it were not true? She was on her deathbed—and had nothing to gain unless it was a clear conscience. A mother is not likely to implicate her son in so serious an affair unless there is some powerful reason. It is less likely that she lied than that the others, for reasons entirely unknown to us, failed to make use of the confession."

The reason, perhaps, that the confession was not fully acted upon was that its existence was of doubtful authenticity. After the *New York Tribune* reported Mrs Loss's dying statement to Justice Merritt, the Justice promptly wrote an open letter to the *Courier and Enquirer* denying the confession and stating that the *Tribune's* story was "entirely incorrect, as no such examination took place, nor could it, from the deranged state of Mrs Loss's mind". The *Tribune* replied that it had obtained its story from two of Justice Merritt's magistrates. The *Herald* challenged the *Tribune* to print the names of the magistrates. The *Tribune* retreated into hurt silence.

Like all the others who have studied the facts of the case, I, too, have played the game. Among the major suspects, my choice for the most suspicious is Alfred Crommelin. I believe that Mary Rogers was his mistress at the time she was engaged to marry Payne. Why, then, the rose in his keyhole? Because she wished to tell him, before aborting his child, that she still loved him. And how, then, his fortuitous arrival at Sybil's Cave? Because he knew where her body had been disposed of by the abortionist, and he knew where it might be found, and wished to be immediately on hand to identify it and see that it received Christian burial. But how, then, did Crommelin have an alibi for the Sunday? Quite logically because he was not present when Mary died, but with friends, who established his alibi.

To my mind, the most stimulating aspect of the Mary Rogers affair is the broad scope of possible suspicion. A damaging indictment can be constructed against almost anyone remotely connected with Mary Rogers. There is no limit to the boundaries of one's fancy or surmise. Consider the oft-overlooked John Anderson, tobacconist, who was Mary's employer. He was beside her for long hours each day. He walked her home. He had, surely, an eye for a well-turned ankle. It was thought, on newspaper row, that he had encouraged her first disappearance. Had he perhaps encouraged her second also?

In 1887 the *New York Tribune* reported that John Anderson had hired Edgar Allan Poe, whom he had long known as a customer, to write "The Mystery of Marie Roget" in order to divert suspicion from himself. While this titbit opens up delightful possibilities, its veracity is certainly to be questioned. It appears that Anderson lived on to a senile old age. After his death in 1881, his will was contested on the grounds of legal insanity. The fight was still in the New York courts during 1901, when Mary Rogers made a ghostly appearance before the bar. In the tug-of-war involving Appleton *v.* New York Life Insurance Company, it was revealed that old Anderson had claimed he knew who killed Mary Rogers. He knew, he told relatives, because she told him. She had often appeared before him as a nightly apparition, and during one such nocturnal tête-à-tête she had revealed the name of her murderer. Unfortunately, Anderson kept the name "a spiritual secret".

Among other peripheral suspects, in a category with the Broadway tobacconist, I would be inclined to include the seemingly harassed Mrs Rogers, proprietress of the historic rooming house on Nassau Street. An impoverished old woman, to be sure, and ailing, of course. Yet how did she manage to maintain her house? The boarders seem to have been so very few and far between. Certainly there must have been another steady source of income. The son in South America? Possibly. Or Mary?

Does it strike a blow at motherhood and country to suggest that Mrs Rogers, out of fear of bankruptcy, employed the beautiful cigar girl for the pleasure of her guests—and of visitors to her vacant rooms? Assuming this premise, it is not beyond the realm of possibility that Mary was trapped in pregnancy, and that her mother took her to an abortionist, under whose instruments Mary expired. Then it would have been Mrs Rogers, grief-stricken, who disposed of the body with the aid of Crommelin or another.

Or was the secret murderer of Mary Cecilia Rogers one of the most illustrious names in literature? Was the murderer Edgar Allan Poe himself?

Poe knew Mary Rogers when he dwelt in New York City, and in the half-year before her death he frequently travelled from Philadelphia to New York. Might he not have seen her again? Not at the boarding-house, not he, a married man. But at cafés or hotels—or on outings to New Jersey. She was beautiful and gay, and would have served as a welcome escape from the neuter Virginia and the dominating Maria Clemm and the hounding Graham. And of course he would have attracted her. He had some social station; he was published; he was brooding and brilliant.

Might not Poe have been the "swarthy" gentleman who accompanied Mary to Weehawken? And there, in the thicket, in one of his drunken, narcotic rages, might he not impotently have attempted rape, or even actually raped her, and then been forced to silence her forever? His record of alcoholic rage with women is well known. It is a fact that in July 1842, bleary with drink, he took a ferry to New Jersey to see his old Baltimore sweetheart, Mary Devereaux, who was then a married woman. Poe, his eyes bloodshot, his stock under his ear, was already in Mary Devereaux's house, waiting, when she returned from a shopping-trip with her sister—most fortunately with her sister. Poe fell upon her, screaming: "So you have married that cursed——! Do you love him truly! Did you marry him for love?"

Mary Devereaux held firm. "That's nobody's business; that is between my husband and myself."

But Poe pressed after her. "You don't love him. You do love me. You know you do."

While, on this occasion, Poe was finally pacified and sent packing, he may not have left Mary Rogers so easily.

But all of this, I confess, is speculation. As to actual evidence that Edgar Allan Poe murdered Mary Rogers? I can only repeat once more that we are playing a game . . .

After Mary Cecilia Rogers was removed from the Dead House in mid-August of 1841, she was buried in the New York City metropolitan area. No one knows to-day the exact position of her final resting-place—except that she may be found still in the pages of "The Mystery of Marie Roget".

CHECKMATE

(Julia Wallace, 1931)

F. Tennyson Jesse

The Wallace case of 1931 is regarded as the classic English whodunnit, a labyrinth of clues and false trails leading everywhere except, it seems, to the identity of the murderer. It remains, in many ways, a nightmare of a case: every shred of evidence seems to invite equal and opposite meaning, and critics have praised its chess-like qualities. The setting is wintrily provincial, the milieu lower middle-class, the style threadbare domestic. J B Priestley's fog-filled Liverpool remembrance of "trams going whining down long sad roads" is the quintessence of it. Events turn tantalizingly on finical questions of time and distance; knuckle-headed police jostle with whistling street urchins for star billing, while at the centre of the drama stands the scrawny, inscrutable figure of the accused man, William Herbert Wallace, the Man From The Pru. Wallace's wife Julia has been found murdered on her front parlour rug, and the killer has made a mysterious telephone call, but was it Wallace himself fashioning an alibi or an unknown man in the shadows?

F(ryniwyd) Tennyson Jesse (1888–1958), great niece of Tennyson, the Victorian Poet Laureate, was a novelist and criminologist who edited six volumes of Notable British Trials. *Her best-known novel,* A Pin To See The Peepshow (1934), *is based on the Thompson–Bywaters murder case of 1922. Miss Jesse's short essay on the Wallace case, written in 1953, appears here for the first time.*

William Herbert Wallace was an insurance agent employed by the Prudential Insurance Company and he lived alone with his wife Julia in a small modest street of grey two-storey houses at Anfield, Liverpool. He was a quiet and studious man of rather frail appearance and he customarily wore steel-rimmed spectacles. He may have taken undue pride in his fine bushy mustache but that we shall never know. He was fond of intellectual pursuits and his behaviour was gentle, considerate and sweet-tempered. Julia was a delicate fluttery little woman of his own age—they were both fifty-two—who painted graceful water-colours and appears to have shared her husband's intellectual pretensions. She took no part in the local activities, such as they may have been, but was content to listen to her husband's views on the new atomic science and on his stoic philosophy, and pleased to give an accomplished if somewhat rusty accompaniment on the piano to her husband's earnest efforts on the violin. He, on the other hand, was a chess-player of no mean order and several evenings a week he would set out for his Club at the City Café to join his fellow addicts. Monday was competition night so, whatever mutual arrangements he might make with Julia on other nights for music practice or reading aloud, on Mondays he invariably went to his Chess Club. For eighteen years he and his wife had lived amicably, even affectionately, together, with never a harsh word, and for the last sixteen years they had shared this humdrum routine under the humdrum roof of No. 29 Wolverton Street. They were childless but whether from choice or cruel chance is not known. No other man, no other woman, seems to have disturbed emotionally the domestic peace of this fond couple.

At about seven-fifteen on the evening of Monday 19 January 1931, a telephone message for Wallace was taken by Mr Beattie, the Captain of the Chess Club. Wallace was expected there for an important competition game but had not yet arrived, so Mr Beattie wrote the gist of the conversation down and passed it on to Wallace later in the evening when taking a look at the competition in progress. It was to the purport that a man of the name of Mr R.M. Qualtrough wanted to have a talk with Wallace "in the nature of your business"; he was in the throes of a twenty-first birthday party for his daughter and didn't want the bother of ringing again but would Wallace be good enough to call at his house No. 25 Menlove Gardens East at half-past-seven the following evening. Wallace was playing an excellent game, which

he won, but he allowed himself to be weaned from it long enough
to make a careful note of the message and to murmur as he did so
that he had never heard of the gentleman, nor of Menlove Gardens
East, and wasn't sure that he would go. After the match, pleased
with his success and feeling expansive, he reverted to the subject
of Qualtrough's request and curious name and asked the advice
of several members on how they would make the journey. Nobody
had actually been there and after belabouring the question Wallace
left the Club for home still dubious. However, business is business
and on the next evening when the normal work of the day was over
he must have decided to keep the appointment.

Now, according to Wallace, just after six o'clock on Tuesday
20 January he had tea with his wife in the kitchen-living-room as
usual—they only used the front-parlour for music or for their rare
guests—and at six forty-five he left the little grey house to embark
on the complicated series of trams which should bring him to the
district where he hoped to find Menlove Gardens East. It cannot
have been much later than six-fifty for at seven-ten he was on a
tram quarter of an hour's journey from Wolverton Street asking
his way of the tram conductor with fussy insistence. It is a curious
fact that although there is a Menlove Avenue, a Menlove Gardens
South, a Menlove Gardens North and a Menlove Gardens West,
there is no Menlove Gardens East. It is not surprising then that
nobody could help him, but Wallace was a conscientious man to
whom insurance commission was important and having come so
far he wanted to make very sure. He questioned the conductor
of his second tram also and was put down amiably at Menlove
Gardens West where he quartered the area without success, asking
an occasional passer-by and presenting himself hopefully to the lady
of No. 25 Menlove Gardens West. Crestfallen he then inquired of
a policeman who told him firmly there was no street of that name,
but Wallace, remarking that it was still only quarter-to-eight, asked
him if there was a post-office or newsagent open nearby where he
might look up a directory. There he was finally convinced that
the place did not exist, and he said so to the manageress who
had helped him. As it was now after eight o'clock he hurried
home, fitting in his trams like a jigsaw puzzle, feeling foolish,
frustrated and vaguely uneasy. On reaching home he tried his key
in the front door as he normally did but for once it seemed to be
bolted. There is an alley-way running parallel to the street at the
back of this row of houses leading to each of the back entries and

very frequently used by all the occupiers, so he went round to the back which has a solid dark-green painted door giving on a little yard. He could not open that either and, more uneasy now since he could see no slit of light issuing from the back kitchen through the scullery window, he began to knock. Then he thought perhaps his wife, who had a bad cold, must have gone to bed, so he went round and tried the front again as he knew it had a troublesome lock that was apt to stick. Here he had no better success and he was returning to the back entry for a further onslaught when he met his next door neighbours Mr and Mrs Johnston coming out of their own back entry into the alley-way.

Up to this point Wallace's version of how he had spent the evening could only be corroborated intermittently by those strangers of whom he had happened to ask the way but from now on his story has the staunch backing of the Johnstons. He asked them if they had heard anything unusual, saying he could not understand why both doors seemed to be locked against him and he was unable to get any response to his knocking. Mr Johnston said "No" but suggested that Wallace should have another try at the back while he waited. At the door Wallace called back on a note of surprise: "It opens now" and went in to the scullery and through the kitchen where he had left Julia mending his clothes and nursing her cold by the fire. He continued straight upstairs, the Johnstons patiently and anxiously watching his movements by the lights he turned on for there had been a few burglaries recently. There was no sign of his wife so he retreated down the staircase and peeped into the front parlour which was only dimly lighted from the kitchen. He struck a match. Now indeed a shocking sight met his eyes and, his heart thumping, he lit the gas. Mrs Wallace was lying in a pool of blood. Blood had spurted on to the furniture and on to the walls. Her head was most brutally battered in and bone and brain were exposed. She was lying huddled up in front of the gas fire; it was now turned out but her skirt was scorched. Her shoulder rested against his own rolled-up raincoat which was partly burned and copiously stained with blood—as indeed was the whole room including those spurts which can only be arterial. After a few seconds of stunned horror, in the greatest agitation Wallace rushed to the back, calling and signalling to the Johnstons who followed him into the house. He showed them the pitiful body of his wife; then he showed them the kitchen-cabinet with its door wrenched off and his Insurance Company's cashbox from which a few pounds were missing. Without touching anything in the front room they all looked distractedly for some explanation of the calamity but there was nothing to help them, not even a weapon. While Mr Johnston hastened off for the police Wallace broke down and wept, but he pulled himself together before their arrival and remained very calm through the further ordeal of replying to questions; smoking rather heavily and, it has even been said, stroking the cat upon his knee. His statement to the police was clear for he was a clearheaded man; the Johnstons supported him in everything that concerned them. There was no sign of a forced entry; both back and front doors were apt to stick it is true but Wallace said he was almost certain he had unbolted the front door in order to let the police in. He explained that normally when he went out leaving his wife alone in the house she would accompany him to the back door so that she could bolt it behind him and he would return the front way using his key. On this occasion she had said goodbye to him at the back door but he had no means of knowing whether or not she had bolted it; he only knew of his fruitless efforts with the front-door key and his eventual success soon after meeting the Johnstons at eight forty-five in pushing open the door at the back. He explained also that when he and his wife went out together they always took the contents of the cashbox with them and any personal money too but if one of them was in they did not bother. He said that he usually banked his takings for the Insurance Company on a Wednesday and that Tuesday would therefore be the most tempting day for somebody who happened to know this habit, but on this particular week, owing to the payment of benefits, he had much less in the house than other weeks so it was a very small sum that was missing. Since there would surely be some sign of breaking in had the intruder been an ordinary burglar, he could only suppose that somebody, desperate for money, knowing his habits and having watched him leave the house, had presented himself at the door as a client, and that Mrs Wallace had trustingly let him in; that she had taken him to the parlour and had prepared to light the gas fire when he struck her. There were eleven deep wounds in the skull, of which the first smashing blow alone would have caused her death; the other ten had been added with frenzied ferocity when her head was already on the floor. Wallace could then make no suggestion that might point to anyone of his acquaintance who might have conceived this project. After the statements had been taken and he had been searched and closely examined without a trace of blood being found on his person, the weary and heart-broken man was sent off in a car to spend the night at his brother's house some distance away.

Every endeavour to find the weapon proved futile and in fact no weapon was ever found, though a poker and an iron bar which was kept in the parlour grate to clean under the gas fire were missing from the house. Outside the room in which the poor woman lay there was hardly a trace of blood; only a small clot which proved to be hers in the pan of the water-closet upstairs and a little stain on one of a sheaf of banknotes which were sticking up in a vase on the mantlepiece of the Wallace's own bedroom. There was no blood on the staircase and none in the kitchen. The towel in the bathroom was dry and there was nothing to indicate that someone had had a recent bath.

Further investigations showed that Wallace had something over £150 in his personal Bank account and there was no confusion whatever in his accounts with the Prudential. Julia's life had been insured, but for the trifling sum of twenty pounds, so plainly Wallace did not stand to gain financially by his wife's death. Mrs Wallace was last seen alive at about six-thirty on the evening of Tuesday 20 January by the milk-boy making his late delivery; she had spoken to him at the front door. But milk-boys are not prone to wear wrist-watches, they go upon their whistling way taking little heed of the passing hours; some confirmation had to be sought for this testimony. A teenage girl, delivering newspapers at No. 27, estimated that it was nearer twenty-to-seven than half-past-six that she had seen the milkboy at the adjoining house. When the police surgeon examined the body of Mrs Wallace at ten o'clock that night he judged the time of death to have been approximately four hours earlier. This could not be so, as she had been seen alive at or after six-thirty but it did establish that her death must have taken place either immediately before or immediately after Wallace set off on his expedition to Menlove Gardens East. The telephone call of the Monday evening taken by Mr Beattie the captain of the Chess Club, which decoyed Wallace from his house on the night of the attack, was traced to a public call-box a bare four hundred yards from the house in the direction of the City Café for which he was bound. Mr Qualtrough could not be found, but the telephone operator and the chess captain were unanimous in that the caller had a strong gruff voice, and Mr Beattie asserted that with no stretch of the imagination could he say that it was like that of Wallace whose voice he knew well. True, Wallace could have made the call at that time and place on his way to the Club—but so could someone watching to see him go out, someone who particularly did not want to speak to him directly in case his voice were recognized. Such a person could have watched again the next night till he saw that Wallace had taken the bait and was safely out of the way on his wild goose chase; he could have knocked at the door, and obtained entry under pretence of business, and been taken to the parlour to await Wallace's return without arousing any suspicion. Perhaps he had no intention of anything beyond rifling the cashbox. Why then did he do murder? And if he did, how did he first contrive to get into Wallace's mackintosh which ordinarily hung in the little hall and which had obviously received a drenching spray of blood from the first blow? And why should he take away the weapon and embarrass himself with the disposal of it when he had only to wipe it off on the mackintosh and leave it where he had found it? If he were desperate for money and the yield had been so disappointingly small, why did he not take the bank-notes from the bedroom mantelpiece?—he must have known they were there for her blood was on one of them. Though he could not expect that Wallace would be away the whole of two hours, from six forty-five to eight forty-five, he would have known that he had ample time to do what had to be done, especially if robbery alone was his intention. Even if he had meant to kill there was time for everything, for he had at least an hour to devote to it before his host could make the return journey. When Mrs Wallace fell against the gas-fire, as seems probable, and her clothing caught fire, he could have slipped the mackintosh off and drawn her clear with it and beaten out the flames, before with mounting urgency he bolted the front door, broke open the cashbox, and made his way out through the back entry. The great question was, who could this hypothetical assailant be? The game did not appear to be worth the candle for any common burglar, who could just as easily have overpowered the frail little woman and got away with clean hands. Wallace was doing everything he could to help the police but nothing in his or his wife's history accounted for an implacable enemy who might wish to bring utter desolation on them. He had originally given no indication of any personal or mutual acquaintance who might have been admitted by Mrs Wallace in all good faith, but a day or two later he produced quite a list of people, for the most part employees or ex-employees of the Prudential whom he knew to be in financial difficulties with the Company and who might have thought of this desperate way of putting their affairs in order. Somehow it was not convincing that anybody in that position should go to such lengths. Wallace also interrogated the captain of the Chess Club minutely on the matter of the telephone message, saying: "The police have cleared me". As he had not been treated in any way as a suspect the police thought this odd of him.

It is a sad reflection on marriage that where a wife has been violently killed her husband is ordinarily the first to be suspected, but in this case there was no discoverable motive of any kind and such an act was entirely contrary to his nature and interests. Moreover, if Wallace were the murderer he must have acted with astonishing speed to achieve it between the milk-boy's visit and his own departure. The gap was narrow and he must have struck with frantic eagerness almost before the milk-boy's footsteps had receded along the pavement so as to get everything done and be on his way. From seven ten when he boarded the tram till eight forty-five when he met the Johnstons at the back entry every moment was vouched for, and not alone by casual passers-by who might not be reliable even if found, but by officials whose evidence could be checked and counter-checked by time-tables all along his route. Even his half-reluctant purpose to go across Liverpool discussed the night before could be vouched for, and by nearly every member of the Club who attended on the Monday. If Wallace were the murderer then this elaborate excursion of his must be nothing but a prefabricated smoke-screen to hide the preceding *mauvais quart d'heure*; he must have known exactly what he meant to do all the time he sat winning his competition game of chess. If Wallace was the murderer then Wallace was Qualtrough. It remained to be seen whether the reverse could be proved, but on 2 February Wallace was arrested and charged with the murder of his wife. He denied it then and always. He was eventually committed to take his trial at the Liverpool Assizes and the trial took place on Wednesday 22 April 1931 and occupied the three succeeding days.

The little grey house in Wolverton Street may have been dull enough but at the Liverpool Assizes there was a panoply of grandeur. That excellent judge Mr Justice Wright, later Lord Justice Wright, presided. Mr E.G. Hemmerde, K C, Recorder of Liverpool and as deadly a man as the Crown could have, took charge of the prosecution. Mr Roland Oliver, K C, then a very able Counsel and now an extremely good judge, threw himself heart and soul into the defence.

Witness followed witness. The Johnstons, simple, honest people, described Mr and Mrs Wallace as a happy and very loving couple; they had never heard any quarrelling from the house next door—but then there are people who never make a noise in any circumstances. The captain of the Chess Club, no doubt occupied by more complicated things such as the Knight's move, was unable to be more precise about the time of the telephone call but testified that the voice speaking in the name of Mr Qualtrough and the voice of Wallace were not in the least similar—but naturally Wallace would not have been such a fool as to speak in his normal voice. According to the prosecution witnesses Wallace had from half-past-six until nearly seven o'clock in which to accomplish the work—the defence narrowed it to a little over five minutes. The tram-conductors, the policeman, the lady at No. 25 Menlove Gardens West, the manageress of the newsagent, all confirmed the peregrinations that had occupied two full hours of Wallace's time—but while this was in complete accordance with the defence it also supported the theory that it was all part of a deep-laid scheme to establish an alibi. Gradually the case began to assume the unique character for which it is famous; it was not so much that the weight of the evidence swung evenly from one side to the other, it was that the entire evidence pointed equally convincingly in both directions. The police surgeon who was called for the prosecution, an experienced witness, transparently honest and objective, was finally driven by Mr Oliver to give evidence which directly supported the defence; he was compelled to agree that he would expect the assailant of Mrs Wallace to have been saturated with blood to an extent that would make it necessary for him to take a bath or such a thorough wash as Wallace had not time for. His contention too that the blows were struck in a state of maniacal frenzy, while it accounted for the lack of motive, was hard to correlate with the premeditated strategy employed. A woman who from time to time acted as a cleaner in the Wallace's house, and was asked by the prosecution to see if there was anything missing from there, reported that the kitchen poker and the iron bar that had been kept under the gas-fire in the front room had both disappeared—whoever the murderer might be this unaccountable removal would have caused him unnecessary risk.

Wallace elected to go into the box where his manner was mild and composed and his replies reasonable and lucid during the three hours of the ordeal. Mr Qualtrough was the only important character apparently who remained as invisible in the box as he had been throughout the drama in which he played a leading part. All the evidence was circumstantial and on certain vital issues there was no evidence at all; whoever had used the call-box on Monday evening had not been seen by anybody; neither did anybody come forward who had observed Wallace leaving his home on Tuesday. And at the end of it all only one thing was conclusive, either Wallace had done it or he had not.

The judge summed up for an acquittal. He left no doubt that he thought it would be improper to convict. Just over an hour later the jury brought in their verdict of Guilty. I had just come back from foreign parts, where I had been reading the trial, and saw the verdict with astonishment. "But it's against the weight of the evidence" I said. I was soon to realize why. Factually Wallace had been able to stand up to the prosecution's allegations and produce reasonable explanations to refute them; humanly he had not. With the strictly fair judge, the deadly Counsel for the Crown, and the brilliance of Mr Oliver's defence, there was not enough to secure a conviction if Wallace had not gone into the box. People of unpleasing personality, especially if they are guilty, should be advised never to go into the witness box. The jury did not like the man, or his manner which could have been either stoicism or callousness. They did not understand his lack of expression of any kind and they knew that it hid something. It could have hidden sorrow or guilt and they made their choice.

Mr Oliver brought an appeal and won it for his client. The verdict of the jury was set aside as being not in accordance with the evidence. The Prudential Assurance Company magnanimously took him back but he was looked at askance wherever he went. Though he was considerately reinstated in an indoor capacity the suspicion and distrust of neighbours and business associates soon showed him it was hopeless to attempt to continue to earn a living in Liverpool. He was driven to retire to a cottage in the country before the middle of the year, where he died at the beginning of 1933 of what had been for a long time an incurable cancer of the kidneys.

It will be observed that I consider Wallace guilty. I do, for when I read the case I recalled the words of the great Lord Chief Justice, Lord Reading, who was unendingly good to me when I was a young girl in pointing out matters of law. There had been an unimportant murder, in some little suburban house, for no imaginable reason, and I said: "Lord Reading, but why do people like that kill each other, for nothing at all?" and he answered me in what I shall always consider these memorable words: "My child, it is impossible to tell how hardly the presence of one person in a house may bear upon another." For eighteen years Wallace had borne the presence of this little undistinguished water-colourist and accompanist, always there in the only place he had to go to at night except when he went to his Chess Club. Men marry when they are very young for various reasons, and they find themselves tied for life to a person who gets on their nerves. A kind of affection may still exist, but it is difficult to gauge what affection means in someone conceited and pretentious; and Wallace was both. Wishing ardently for respectability, this vain man had had to remain by the side of a woman he considered his inferior in every way, and when at last he broke out it was with extravagant violence. One, two, three . . . how many blows? It does not matter. It is my belief that Wallace came downstairs naked under his mackintosh, murdered his wife with this urgency upon him, tucked his mackintosh under her shoulder, washed himself in the kitchen, and set off into the dark January evening methodically to execute the remainder of what I hope chess players will forgive me for calling essentially a chess-player's crime. Every move and its consequences were planned in advance. He was a punctual man of precise habits and every action was timed. As to the weapon used neither poker nor iron bar was ever found, though all drain-pipes and gratings had been diligently searched by the police. Later, when I had the pleasure of meeting Mr Hemmerde and the disposal of the weapon was discussed he smiled a little grimly and without a word picked up a ruler which lay upon his desk and slipped it up his sleeve. Perhaps early in the grey Liverpool dawn, before any suspicion rested on him, Wallace took a long walk by the river bank—but that is only supposition. If Wallace and Qualtrough were one and the same, ringing up the Chess Club the night before because he had reached a point when he could not support the pressure of a delicate inadequate wife any longer, then there is no doubt he was guilty. The only other possibility is that there was an airy-fairy Qualtrough whom nobody has ever seen. It is a name that comes from the Isle of Man. Did Wallace and his Julia once remark upon the oddness of that name while on a holiday on the island? Who can tell? When he died Wallace left behind him in the cottage a private diary containing a great many very highfalutin' remarks about his beloved Julia . . . "If only she were still with me how lovingly she would have tended the garden . . .", but this of course proves nothing. They were in execrable literary taste but to write badly is not enough, unfortunately, to prove a man a murderer.

Just before the war, my husband and I went to Liverpool to stay with the architect Professor Holford, now Sir William Holford, and on the Sunday afternoon I proposed going to see the Wallace house. Needless to say the men slumbered, but we women set off in search of the little grey house. We found the mean street—and streets, though perfectly respectable and not slums, can be very mean and grey in Liverpool—we found the house. It was occupied, and evidently by people who were houseproud. The front windows were shrouded thickly in white Nottingham lace curtains; surely more thickly than the windows of any other house in the district. We went round to the back entry to see the door that Wallace professed to have found closed against him that night so many years ago. The door was neatly painted in dark green, but on it, crudely chalked in white and quite newly done, was the figure of a hanging man. The unfortunate tenants of the house may have spent the greater part of their days trying to keep the back door free of such disfigurement but the legend of Wallace had not died. It had torn Liverpool in two; half of the great town had been for him and half had been against him; passions had run high. Grown-ups talk in front of children and children sort out for themselves as best they can the truth of what those extraordinary beings say. For all I know, though there have been worse monsters since, a hanging man in chalk may still be decorating from time to time the back door of that little drab house in Liverpool. Children collect legends and keep them long.

Many modern theorists disagree with Miss Jesse's conclusion that Wallace murdered his wife. Three years after starting to research the case, Jonathan Goodman published The Killing of Julia Wallace *(Harrap, London 1969) which suggested that not only did Wallace not murder his wife, but that the real culprit got away with it. At the time, "Mr X" (as Jonathan Goodman was legally obliged to call him) was living in south London. But in 1981, on the fiftieth anniversary of the killing, a Liverpool radio station, Radio City, broadcast a drama-documentary that unmasked "Mr X" (who had died the year before), naming him as Richard Gordon Parry. Parry, a petty thief, had worked alongside Wallace in his insurance business. Gordon Parry had a grudge against Wallace for reporting various minor defalcations to the Prudential, and* there was a hint of curious sexual shenanigans between Parry, twenty-two at the time of the murder, and Julia Wallace, a post-menopausal thirty years older. The radio researchers also discovered that Parry's uncle, Liverpool's city librarian, was uniquely placed to get his hands on the levers of the investigation; quite apart from his exalted position with the Corporation, Parry's uncle employed a secretary whose father was the city's top detective and the man in charge of the Wallace inquiry. Wallace had given Parry's name to the police within thirty-six hours of the murder, but they had seemed satisfied with the young man's alibi that he had spent the evening with his girlfriend. The radio team tracked down this woman, who disclosed that Parry was not, in fact, with her at the crucial hour of Mrs Wallace's death.

A few weeks after the programme, an old man called John Parkes was interviewed. His extraordinary testimony (pooh-poohed by the anti-Wallace police in 1931) seemed to clinch the case against Parry. On the murder night, John Parkes was working as a car cleaner at a Liverpool garage. According to Parkes, Gordon Parry (whom he knew) turned up at the garage demanding to have his car washed, inside and out. Inside the car Parkes found a bloodstained glove. Parry snatched it from him, exclaiming: "If the police found that, it would hang me!"

A CASE THAT ROCKED THE WORLD

(Sacco and Vanzetti, 1920)

Louis Stark

The case of Nicola Sacco and Bartolomeo Vanzetti, two anarchists accused of murder in the course of an armed payroll robbery, convulsed the American political and penal systems during the 1920s. The two men, Italian immigrants drawn together by their radical politics, were indicted as members of a gang of five who killed the paymaster and guard of a shoe factory in South Braintree, Massachusetts, in April 1920, escaping with nearly $16,000 in wages. Identification evidence was strong, but the prosecution argued for a conviction mainly on the two men's "consciousness of guilt". Defence lawyers for Sacco and Vanzetti countered that Attorney General Mitchell Palmer campaigned for the deportation of alien radicals during 1920–21 and argued that their clients' "consciousness of guilt" related to politics and not armed robbery. The case became entangled in political as well as legal issues. After a lengthy trial, both men were convicted of first-degree murder, but the verdict triggered an unprecedented campaign to establish their innocence. Among those signing petitions for clemency were the British playwright George Bernard Shaw, Albert Einstein and the authors H.G. Wells and John Galsworthy. A review of the case ordered by the state governor pointed to grave political bias on the part of the trial judge, but failed to question the verdict. Accordingly, in 1927,

Sacco and Vanzetti went to the electric chair. Doubts about their guilt continued to rankle, and half a century later their names were cleared in a special proclamation signed by the governor of Massachusetts. The author, Louis Stark, was a young reporter on the New York Times *at the time of the Sacco–Vanzetti trial and later became the paper's labour correspondent.*

"What do you know about the Sacco–Vanzetti case?"

This question was addressed to me one evening in February 1922, by Ralph Graves, then Sunday editor of *The New York Times*.

I said I had read a few newspaper articles on the case.

"Are the men guilty?" asked Mr Graves.

"I don't know," was my reply.

"You're just the man I want," he said. "Take a week off, go to Boston, get both sides of the case and then write a piece giving the facts in impartial review. We want the pros and cons and let the reader make his own decision."

That was my introduction to the celebrated case which rocked the world and whose echoes still reverberate every August upon the anniversary of the execution of the two Italians in Charlestown State Prison.

I went to Boston. In due time a 4,000-word summary appeared in the *Times*. Five years later I was in Boston again for the final three weeks of the case, weeks marked by riots all over the world, picketing of the State House, scores of arrests, feverish investigations, desperate eleventh-hour moves on behalf of the two men. All elements of drama were present. Condemnation, suspense, last-minute reprieve, more suspense, appeals, uncertainty, doubts. Then the seven-year climax—execution!

The Sacco–Vanzetti case!

Never had there been one like it in the annals of American jurisprudence, possibly excepting the Mooney case. A seven-year Golgotha for the fish peddler and the shoe worker. The focal point of world-wide discussion of "American justice"; agitation and propaganda that flared into extraordinary demonstrations at home and abroad, all to one purpose, stay of execution, mercy.

The Sacco–Vanzetti case!

The "American Dreyfus" affair in which the sympathies of

eminent men from Europe to Asia were enlisted. Anatole France, H. G. Wells, George Bernard Shaw, Romain Rolland.

The Sacco–Vanzetti case!

A judicial drama enacted in the golden-domed State House in Boston, in the severely plain Dedham courthouse, in Harvard's august halls, in jails, on street corners, in the streets of London, Paris, Berlin, Warsaw, Buenos Aires.

The characters—humble working people, labourers, shoemakers, railroad workers, storekeepers, salesmen, lawyers, doctors, pistol experts, prosecutors, judges, jailers, Harvard professors. All interested in the two principals—those philosophical anarchists, draft dodgers, convicted murderers, two humble Italians, one a shoe worker who had scarcely missed a working day in seven years, thrifty, home-loving; the other a gentle man, loved by children and neighbours.

What was the Sacco–Vanzetti case?

On 15 April 1920, Frederick Parmenter, a paymaster, and Alexander Berardelli, his guard, were fired upon and killed on the main street of South Braintree, Massachusetts, and the payroll of Slater and Morrill's shoe factory, amounting to $15,776.51, was stolen. The two murderers threw the payroll boxes into a car which contained several other men and were driven off at breakneck speed.

At that time the police were on the lookout for men who had taken part in an unsuccessful payroll holdup in Bridgewater on the previous 24 December. Suspicion rested on Italians, as eyewitnesses told the police the holdup men seemed to be of that race. The Morelli gang of Providence was suspected.

On 5 May 1920, Nicola Sacco, steadily employed as an edge trimmer in a shoe factory, and Bartolomeo Vanzetti, a fish peddler, self-employed, were arrested. They were not questioned concerning the two holdups for several days. The "Red raids" instigated by Attorney General A. Mitchell Palmer had created a stir against radicals and the men were cross-examined as to their political beliefs. They were charged with carrying weapons unlawfully, pistols having been found on them, and they offered certain explanations for the weapons.

The arrest of the men, caught in a dragnet for radicals, placed their feet on the road which led to the electric chair seven years later. Vanzetti was a philosophical anarchist, dreamy and contemplative.

He had assisted in some strikes. So had Sacco, whose radical beliefs were vague but socialistic.

Vanzetti was a friend of Salsedo, a follower of Galleani, well known among Massachusetts anarchists. Salsedo, under arrest by agents of the Department of Justice in the Red dragnet and held incommunicado on the fourteenth floor of the Park Row Building in New York was found dead on the pavement below, on 3 May, two days before the arrest of Sacco and Vanzetti. Vanzetti had interested himself in the Salsedo case and had gone to New York late in April to consult Salsedo's counsel. In New York Vanzetti was told that more government raids might be expected and to hide all radical literature possessed by him and his friends. It was while on that mission that he and Sacco were arrested.

Both the Bridgewater and South Braintree crimes were charged to the two men. Sacco proved a time-clock alibi for the first holdup. Vanzetti was indicted, tried for the Bridgewater holdup, and convicted on 22 June, before Superior Court Justice Webster Thayer who sentenced him to twelve to fifteen years in prison. It was later shown that defense counsel bungled the case miserably.

The trial on the lesser charge was in contrast to the usual legal procedure and was obviously part of a "build-up" against both men, for some of the stigma of the Vanzetti conviction spilled over against Sacco when the two were tried together.

On 11 September, 1920, the two were indicted for the South Braintree crime and tried before Judge Thayer the following May. They were convicted of murder in the first degree on 14 July. Eight appeals for a new trial followed, as new evidence was uncovered year after year, and the case became a *cause célèbre*. Men of intellectual probity and all shades of political belief in many nations, convinced of the innocence of Sacco and Vanzetti, enlisted in what became a great army, whose tramping feet were heard in all the capitals of the world. Sacco and Vanzetti became symbols, beliefs, almost a religion—and a crusade for their release swept the earth; a crusade which gained in intensity as the two men neared the shadow of the chair seven years after the shoemaker and the peddler were first arrested as dangerous "Reds".

During my week's investigation in 1922 of the background of the Sacco–Vanzetti trial, I saw the men of the defense committee who had already set the world-wide army on the march. Three men were the leaders in this vast movement. One was Aldino Felicani,

Italian journalist and printer, who, almost single-handed, began the agitation. Felicani was a linotype operator at the time on *La Notizia*, an Italian daily in Boston and he began the publicity by pouring forth dozens of letters to Boston newspapers. He had once been a close associate of Mussolini in the days when Il Duce was a Social Radical and had spent six months in the same Italian jail with him when both paid that penalty for their radical activities. A second chief figure was Frank Lopez, a jovial, thickset young man who became secretary of the Sacco–Vanzetti Defense Committee in Boston. It was from this bare Hanover Street office of the committee that the pamphlets and circulars and letters emanated that gained almost immediate world-wide repercussions, some not at all to the liking of members of the committee who believed that bomb explosions and riots would not help their cause.

The publicity was handled by Morris Gebelow, a slender, dark-haired student who wrote under the pen name of Eugene Lyons and who later went to Soviet Russia as correspondent for the United Press.

I also talked to newspapermen who had covered the case, impartial observers, state officials who had taken part in the trial, and Judge Thayer. It was my purpose to review the evidence on both sides.

The newspapermen, I found, with one exception, felt that the trial had been unfair because of the atmosphere surrounding the case. The men were tried in a steel cage, part of the equipment of Massachusetts courts. An unnecessary show of police force was exhibited when they were led to and from the courtroom. There were needless "searchings" of those entering the courtroom. Newspapermen were "patted" for weapons. The newspapers printed stories of threatening letters sent to the court and the jury. It had been difficult to get jurymen to serve because of the atmosphere of hysteria that preceded the trial. Frank P. Sibley, dean of Boston newspapermen who covered the trial, told me he had never seen anything like it. Four years later he put this in the form of an affidavit in which he told how Judge Thayer had solicited the attention of reporters during the trial, had discussed the case against Sacco and Vanzetti freely, and had even asked Sibley to print a story that he was conducting the trial fairly and impartially.

Sibley's standing in the newspaper fraternity was so high that it was presumed that his affidavit would carry considerable weight. Well over six feet, Sibley, with his sombrero type hat and his flowing Windsor tie, was an outstanding figure wherever he went. As war correspondent with the Yankee Division in France he chronicled the deeds of the New Englanders and their commander in their history-making moments.

From the beginning of the Sacco–Vanzetti trial Sibley saw the gratuitous injection of "patriotism" in the case by the presiding judge and state attorneys. The *Globe*, for which he worked, was one of the most influential of New England's dailies, and its management strongly opposed the idea that their star reporter make an affidavit as to his observations. Sibley, too, was reluctant to take himself out of the role of disinterested spectator and align himself on one side of the case. His perplexities on the ethics of such action tormented him for a long time but finally he felt that in signing the affidavit he was yielding to the highest sentiment of justice and fair play. Incidentally, this star reporter found himself covering trivial assignments such as flower shows for some time after he had made the affidavit.

"What impressed me more than anything else was his [Judge Thayer's] manner," said Sibley. "It is nothing you can read of in the record. In my thirty-five years I never saw anything like it . . . His whole manner, attitude, seemed to be that the jurors were there to convict the men."

After I had had an opportunity to acquaint myself with the facts in the case and the testimony for and against the two Italians, I wired Judge Thayer for an appointment. He replied on 22 February, and a few days later I called on him at his home, 180 Institute Road, Worcester. After greeting me cordially the Judge said, "I hope *The New York Times* is not going to take the side of these anarchists." He pronounced the first syllable of the word "anarchist" as if it were spelled "on".

While I was rather taken aback that he should think the *Times* would be interested in "crusading" for two convicted radicals, I soon realized his remark was merely an introduction to a denunciation of all radicals. My reply to his question was that the *Times* was not concerned with taking either side of the case but that it was interested in having prepared a fair and impartial summary of the evidence on which the convictions were returned.

Judge Thayer then launched into a detailed discussion of the case, making no attempt to conceal his aversion for economic and political dissenters and particularly foreigners. His lips trembled with emotion and his yellow and deeply wrinkled face darkened as he spoke of the need for the defense of American institutions.

It was obvious that to him a philosophical anarchist was the same as a murderer. He went on in this way for an hour, jumping from the trial testimony to criticism of aliens, anarchists, and radicals. They all seemed to be lumped together in his mind.

The Judge stipulated that I was not to quote him. But the measure of his extraordinary prejudice against Sacco and Vanzetti was obvious.

When I left Judge Thayer that night I was deeply discouraged. To witness at firsthand such expressions of antipathy for aliens and radicals as a group, from one who was called upon to judge his fellow man was disheartening. But Judge Thayer's attitude was quite mild compared to that of citizens of Boston five years later when I covered the events of the three weeks leading up to the execution of Sacco and Vanzetti.

The next five years were marked by a quickening of interest in the case due to the publicity that followed every attempt to obtain a new trial and to the propaganda of the little group of men and women who assisted the defense committee.

New evidence was uncovered year after year to prove that the two men were innocent, to prove that they had not had a fair trial, that Judge Thayer had denounced them as "bastards" and anarchists in conversation outside the courtroom. The Judge was begged to allow another member of the Supreme Court to pass on appeals since he was charged with prejudice. He ruled that he was not prejudiced. Affidavits to prove that important witnesses whose testimony helped convict the men had lied were submitted to Judge Thayer. He turned them down. The head of the State Police, who had told the jury that one of the fatal bullets was "consistent" with being fired from Sacco's pistol, said that the question which elicited this answer had been framed by him and the prosecutor but that if he had been asked directly if the so-called mortal bullet had passed through Sacco's pistol, "I should have answered then, as I do now without hesitation, in the negative."

Celestino Madeiros, a young Portuguese, convicted of the murder of a Wrentham bank cashier and confined in the same jail as Sacco in 1925, signed a "confession" that he had taken part in the South Braintree killing and that Sacco was innocent. In further questioning by the defense he made some admissions that implicated the Morelli gang, well known for freight-car robberies and holdups, but Judge Thayer also rejected this "confession" as ground for a new trial.

To hear these various motions, sentence was postponed from time to time but finally, on 9 April 1927, Judge Thayer announced that the two men would "suffer the punishment of death by the passage of a current of electricity through" their bodies.

Asked by the court clerk whether they had "anything to say why sentence of death should not be passed," the two men addressed the court, and protested their innocence. Sacco spoke briefly, preferring to have Vanzetti, whose English was better, speak for him. Vanzetti, a vibrant figure with drooping walrus mustaches, reviewed the case. His words stirred the courtroom—and the world.

"I am not only not guilty of these two crimes," he said in conclusion, "but I never commit a crime in my life. I have never steal and I have never kill and I have never spilt blood and I have fought against the crime and I have fought and I have sacrificed myself even to eliminate the crimes that the law and the church legitimate and sanctify.

"This is what I say: I would not wish to a dog or to a snake, to the most low and misfortunate creature of the earth—I would not wish to any of them what I have had to suffer for things that I am not guilty of. But my conviction is that I have suffered for things that I am guilty of. I am suffering because I am a radical and indeed I am a radical; I have suffered because I was an Italian and indeed I am an Italian; I have suffered more for my family and for my beloved than for myself; but I am so convinced to be right that if you could execute me two times and if I could be reborn two other times I would live again to do what I have done already."

Later he dictated this statement:

"If it had not been for these things, I might have live out my life talking at street corner to scorning men. I might have die unmarked, unknown, a failure. Now we are not a failure. This is our career and our triumph. Never in our full life could we hope to do such work for tolerance, for justice, for man's understanding of men as now we do by accident. Our words—our lives—our pains—nothing! The taking of our lives—lives of a good shoemaker and a poor fish peddler—all! That last moment belongs to us—that agony is our triumph."

The sentencing of the men called for another review of the case, and I wrote a piece for the Sunday section bringing the facts up to date. It was published on 27 April 1927. Fabian Franklin, formerly an associate editor of *The New York Evening Post* and ex-contributing editor to *The Independent*, a man of conservative views, read my article and wrote a letter to the *Times* commenting on it. He was "forced to the conclusion", he wrote, that the men were convicted "upon utterly inadequate evidence, that this result was brought about in large part by deliberate exploitation of the anti-radical passions dominant at the time . . . That the conduct of the trial in many respects violated the first principles of justice and that in denying a new trial when new evidence of a most vital and substantial nature was offered, Judge Thayer failed to live up to the duty of a just and impartial judge."

Mr Franklin was not alone in his doubts of the way the case was handled. As the days went by the doubts grew. The force of these doubts compelled Governor Fuller to appoint a commission headed by President A. Lawrence Lowell of Harvard University and comprising former Probate Judge Robert Grant and Dr Samuel Stratton, President of the Massachusetts Institute of Technology.

Many questions have been asked concerning President Lowell's part in the case. Some have been addressed to him directly but he has made no answers to any of the queries.

During the Sacco–Vanzetti hysteria, alumni and other potential contributors to the Harvard Law School Endowment Fund were refusing to make contributions because of Professor Felix Frankfurter's written defense of the two radicals in his widely read book, *The Case of Sacco and Vanzetti*. It was reported that an offer of $100,000 had been made to the fund on condition that Mr Frankfurter resign.

Why did Mr Lowell accept the appointment at the hands of Governor Fuller when he knew the strong feeling against Sacco and Vanzetti by many potential contributors? Was he willing, for the sake of truth and justice, to take the risk of jeopardizing these contributions if he found the two men innocent? If that is so, how could he have failed to be impressed by those of his associates who denounced Mr Frankfurter for what they considered the effect of the latter's writings on the endowment fund?

Is it possible that in Dr Lowell's mind the convicted men were intertwined with their defender of his Law School faculty and that his feeling against the latter somehow overflowed into the Sacco–Vanzetti case?

Judge McAnarney, one of the original defense attorneys, told the Lowell Commission that Joe Rossi, Italian interpreter at the trial, had made incorrect translations. The defense attorneys did not know Italian, and Vanzetti occasionally caught one of the mistranslations, but his command of English was such that he hesitated to pick up Rossi every time.

Before the Lowell Commission Judge McAnarney, discussing this phase of the case, said that Vanzetti accused the Italian interpreter of helping the government by his misinterpretations.

President Lowell, at this juncture, said that Rossi had been "pretty careless". However, he added that Rossi's attention was usually called to his misinterpretations.

"I couldn't see that it did any harm to anybody," he said; he wasn't helping the government "very much".

Yet at least one of these "slips" was concerned with Sacco's alibi which was obviously of great importance, and in 1926 Rossi was convicted of larceny and also pleaded guilty to an attempt to bribe a judge.

During the trial Rossi frequently drove Judge Thayer in and out of Dedham in his car. The Judge was on very familiar terms with him, calling him "Joe" and telling the District Attorney that he was "going riding with Joe today".

Rossi named one of his children Webster Thayer Rossi, and District Attorney Katzmann, who prosecuted Sacco and Vanzetti, acted as godfather.

The Lowell Commission explored the trial events and the post-trial developments. In considering a motion for a new trial based on a statement of one Gould, bystander at the scene of the South Braintree crime, who was within a few feet of one of the bandits and whose coat was pierced by one of the gunman's bullets, the Commission discarded Gould's testimony as "merely cumulative".

Now Gould positively declared that Sacco had not fired the shot. He had had an excellent opportunity to view the man with the weapon. Even the Lowell Commission said that Gould "certainly had an unusually good position to observe the men in the car".

Yet the Commission discarded this affidavit because it was "merely cumulative". How did they know what the effect of such testimony would have been at the trial? Gould had not been called as a witness, though he had given his name to a police officer and the officer had passed on the name to the State Police. The defense found him after the trial.

In considering the Gould affidavit filed in connection with the motion for a new trial, the Lowell Commission did a strange thing. It said, "There seems to be no reason to think that the statement of Gould would have had any effect in changing the mind of the jury."

Such omniscience calls for no comment.

A witness, Daly, swore that Ripley, the jury foreman, had said, prior to being called as a juror:

"Damn them, they ought to hang anyway."

The Commission said: "Daly must have misunderstood him [Ripley] or his recollection is at fault."

To supplement the Lowell Committee's report, the Governor also made a personal investigation of the case. In this connection the dramatic and significant incident of the "eel" story is worth telling.

The Governor closed his inquiry on 1 August 1927. The last witnesses were Gardner Jackson and Aldino Felicani of the Defense Committee.

"If all the witnesses in the case had been as honest as you two gentlemen are there would have been no trouble in settling it," he told them. "I know you have been telling the truth."

Jackson and Felicani almost leaped with joy as they heard these words. The Governor shook them by the hand and as they turned to go he said to Jackson, "You know I'm a businessman and I'm used to having documentary evidence. You have never produced any paper proving that Vanzetti was selling eels on the day of the Bridgewater crime."

The visitors' hearts fell. Jackson argued that eighteen witnesses had testified that Vanzetti had sold them eels on 24 December 1919. Eels are an Italian delicacy for consumption on the day before Christmas, and the witnesses remembered the man who sold the eels that day, continued Jackson, but the Governor waved aside this testimony with the words, "Oh, but Mr Jackson, they were all Italians," and asked for documentary proof.

The Governor wanted "a paper" before he could believe Vanzetti's alibi that he was selling eels on the day of the Bridgewater holdup. The defense felt it would be impossible to obtain such proof. But perhaps a receipt could be found for the eels. The next day, 2 August, Herbert H. Ehrmann, associate counsel for the defense, and Felicani combed the fish concerns on Atlantic Avenue for record of a shipment of eels to Vanzetti. It was like looking for the proverbial needle in a haystack. All day they rummaged through old and frayed papers in cellars, garrets, and lofts. But life is sometimes stranger than fiction. If this were a short story I would have them find the receipt, rush to the Governor in triumph, and then be rewarded with a new trial or commutation of sentence. Strangely enough, part of this actually happened. The receipt was actually found, almost eight years after it had been filled out, showing a shipment of eels by the American Express to Vanzetti on 20 December 1919. These were the eels he received two days later, prepared and sold the day before Christmas. It is on record that the receipt was found in a box of old papers in the wholesale fish market of the Corsoa and Gambino Company, 112 Atlantic Avenue.

Elated with the find, Ehrmann, Felicani, and Jackson rushed the receipt to the Governor's office. They embraced each other with joy. This would be the proof demanded by the Governor. Surely he would see that the alibi witnesses were not liars.

On the day Governor Fuller closed his private inquiry in the case, I went to Boston to cover the story. The Governor was due to give out the result of his inquiry and that of the Lowell Commission on 3 August 1927.

Albert J. Gordon, for years a reporter on *The Boston Herald*, was assigned to assist me because of his knowledge of the city and its leading personalities. Later, when so many angles developed that we required help, Jonathan Eddy, then a reporter on the *Times* and now secretary of the American Newspaper Guild, was sent to assist us.

In Boston we found newspapermen from all parts of the country. The Sacco–Vanzetti drama was about to reach a climax. Wherever you went there was but one topic of conversation, the Sacco–Vanzetti case. What would Governor Fuller do? The air was electric with excitement. On the streets, in restaurants and shops—wherever men gathered—they talked of the two Italians.

Boston three weeks before the execution of Sacco and Vanzetti was a vast whispering gallery. All sorts of rumors were afloat.

The subject was discussed in Boston's clubs, where the overwhelming judgment was that the men should be executed. In the east end, where the poor people lived, the prayer was for clemency. "Hope clemency" was the cable received by the Governor from Robert Underwood Johnson, former American ambassador to Italy.

Gordon and I canvassed the situation. We spoke to nearly everyone available to discuss the case intelligently, secretaries to the Governor, the lawyers in the case, state officials in a position to know what was going on, newspaper editors close to the Governor and to his associates. As a result we came to a conclusion which we embodied in a dispatch to the *Times* on 2 August. This is what we said in part:

"Nicola Sacco and Bartolomeo Vanzetti will not die in the electric chair on the date set. Neither will they be pardoned. Further reprieve pending steps by the Massachusetts Legislature looking to a new trial was indicated at the State House today as the solution of the historic case of the Italian radicals which Gov. Fuller will place before the Executive Council when it meets tomorrow. The Governor will make known the decision tomorrow night . . .

"Since yesterday the idea of a further reprieve and action by the Legislature in January has gained ground, according to information available in authentic quarters. No details are revealed but the meager news that has leaked out is to the effect that Gov. Fuller will propose to the Council that the Legislature be requested to pass an enabling act permitting a new trial for the condemned men. In the meantime they would be reprieved."

On the same day *The Boston Herald* said the indications were that Sacco and Vanzetti would not die and that the Governor would ask his Council to approve another respite "in order that the doubts which still remain after his exhaustive inquiry may be removed." It began to look as if the men's long fight was won; that the tramp of the marching armies had been heard in the Massachusetts State House.

On 3 August, Boston was restless. The air was charged with suppressed excitement. The guards at the State House seemed uneasy. Everybody knew that the Governor would announce his fateful decision in the evening. The city was a vast guessing contest. Rumors, whispers, hints, doubts, hopes.

The Governor's offices opened at nine o'clock. An army of newspapermen greeted Secretary Herman A. MacDonald on his arrival. MacDonald picked up some papers and went to see the Governor at a near-by hotel.

By noon the Executive Offices were filled with reporters, officials, curiosity seekers, and hangers-on. Mr Jackson, secretary of the defense committee, appeared later with an account of the detailed expenditure of $325,000 in seven years to gain freedom for the convicted men.

Elaborate preparations were made for sending out the decision. The press gallery in the House of Representatives, a floor above the Executive Offices, was converted into a telegraph room. Direct connections were established with newspaper offices.

The afternoon passed slowly. At the Charlestown State Prison where the convicted men were confined additional police took up their grim task of patrolling the prison. Mrs Rose Sacco visited her husband during the morning but for the nineteenth day he refused food and insisted on continuing his hunger strike. Vanzetti appeared a little more cheerful but ate nothing after breakfast. The homes of Governor Fuller in Boston and at Rye, New Hampshire, of Chief Justice Arthur P. Rugg, and of Justice Thayer were put under guard. Luigia Vanzetti, sister of the convicted fish peddler, left Italy for the United States, having been delayed ten days before she could obtain a passport. Judge Thayer played eighteen holes of golf in 84 at the Cliff County Club in Ogunquit, Maine, where he was summering.

Crowds waited restlessly before newspaper bulletin boards. But the reporters were just as restless. We gathered at the State House early in the evening but there was a hitch. Finally, sheet by sheet the Governor's decision was rushed to him for inspection and revision and then rushed back for mimeographing.

Governor Fuller arrived at the State House at eight twenty-five and was surrounded by reporters. He promised to give us a fifteen-minute interview. Half an hour later he emerged, pale and drawn. Instead of making the expected announcement he read from an envelope on which he had scribbled these words:

"I am very sorry not to oblige you with an interview. I can truthfully say that I am very tired and I trust the report will speak for itself. I would prefer not to indulge in any supplementary statement at this time."

He promised to have the decision in our hands at nine-thirty, well in time for most of our deadlines. But last-minute changes were made and nine-thirty came and went. We walked restlessly up and down the corridors, talking, smoking, nervous, quite different from the picture of gay, nonchalant reporters shown on the screen.

At the bare defense-committee offices on Hanover Street a group of men sat on rickety chairs, tables, boxes, and bundles of pamphlets. Professor Frankfurter was there in his shirt sleeves. The night was warm. Over and over again, the visitors read the posters on the walls. One, urging clemency, was signed by members of the French Cabinet. A Mexican poster read "Liberty and Justice". Alongside it was a manifesto by a former member of the Italian

Parliament. The telephone bell rang incessantly. Was there news? No. When would the decision be given out? Soon, maybe. Hurried telephoning to the Executive Offices. No news. Gardner Jackson was everywhere, at the State House, one minute, dashing to the Hanover Street offices the next.

Outside Governor Fuller's office the suspense was painful. We paced the corridors like wolves. Hours went by. Then, shortly before eleven-thirty, attendants appeared with copies of the decision. Two copies were placed in each envelope. The name of each newspaper or press association was on the outside of each envelope. We crowded around Secretary MacDonald like animals. As our papers were called we snatched the envelopes and ran down the long corridor. We tore the envelopes open as we ran, dashing up a flight of marble stairs to our wires. I had five minutes to make the deadline, yet I did not know what the decision was as I ran. As I reached the telegraph operator who had the wire open into the *Times* office I flung the Governor's decision open to the last page and gathered its import.

"Bulletin," I shouted to the operator. "They die!"

The news was flashed to the *Times* by one of the speediest telegraph operators I have ever known. Only a few minutes remained to get a crisp lead into the paper, and I had no time to write it. Glancing hurriedly over the report, I dictated to the operator a lead of about 250 words. I had sent 400–500 words earlier that had already been set in type. A three-column heading was written in the New York office in short order and a previously prepared 1,500-word summary of the case was rushed into the paper.

By this time the press gallery was a veritable madhouse. Reporters were pounding their typewriters like demons. Telegraph operators, peering over the reporters' shoulders, clicked the stories out without waiting for the sheets to be placed before them.

"They die," was the verdict that flashed to all corners of the globe. Street crowds in New York, Philadelphia, Chicago, and scores of cities caught the flash. Cable-office operators in Tokyo and London, Shanghai and Paris caught the electrical impulses that winged under the ocean beds. Messengers dashed in and out of the press gallery. For me there was little time for reflection as I had to begin immediately on a more comprehensive story of the decision for the later editions. Gordon ran to the office of *The Boston Herald* with the second copy of the decision, and the full text was transmitted to the *Times* from that office.

"God save the Commonwealth of Massachusetts!" cried Felicani on hearing the verdict.

Orders from the *Times* office were to give everything we had. We did. Gordon returned to the State House from *The Boston Herald* office, and we sent a complete story of the Governor's decision and of the unanimous verdict of the Lowell Commission against the men for the later editions. About two o'clock in the morning, we left the building, completely fagged out. Boston Common was dark and forbidding. A few homeless men skulked about. On the way back to the Statler Hotel where we were staying we talked of the Fuller decision. Had we been too optimistic? What had happened? Had the Governor changed his mind in a few hours after the news came from South Dakota?

The next day the decision was the only topic of conversation in Boston. We talked it over with Robert Lincoln O'Brien, with Frank Buxton, his associate, and with all our other sources of information. My dispatch to the *Times* that day read: "The decision announced late last night stirred certain important men in Boston to private discussion of the case. These men, it may be stated on excellent authority, wcre taken into the Governor's confidence. They are declaring emphatically tonight that the Governor gave them every indication that he would pardon Sacco and Vanzetti or extend clemency to them . . . They put the change in the Governor's decision as apparently made between three p.m. Tuesday and that midnight."

Between three p.m. Tuesday and midnight Calvin Coolidge, President of the United States, vacationing in South Dakota, had handed out slips of paper to newspaper correspondents on which were typed these words: "I do not choose to run for President in 1928."

Was there a connection between the two stories? Did Governor Fuller change his mind at the last minute when he learned that President Coolidge would not run for office again? That the Governor had high political ambitions everybody knew. The Boston police strike had catapulted Governor Calvin Coolidge into the Vice-Presidency and the death of President Harding had landed him in the White House. Governor Coolidge's issue was "law and order". The Boston police strike was the peg on which he hung the issue. The strike had made the Governor of Massachusetts a national figure.

Whether or not Governor Fuller made a *volte-face* when he

learned of the news from Rapid City is a secret still locked in his breast. Two facts are known, however.

(One). Persons close to the Governor expected clemency up to the last minute. One of these was Robert Lincoln O'Brien, until recently Chairman of the United States Tariff Commission, then editor of *The Boston Herald* and friend of Governor Fuller. Another was a secretary to the Governor who told the same story to Mr Gordon, my associate.

Before me is Mr O'Brien's letter to Mr Gordon, which says in part:

". . . I expected clemency, probably in the shape of a pardon, up to the last minute, and thought I had reason for this belief from what Gov. Fuller himself had voluntarily told me. I sat next to him at the dinner of Boston University commencement, on the day when we both received honorary degrees. What the Governor told me then I repeated in confidence to a former attorney-general of the State who said it was compatible with no other theory than that of clemency; the governor said the lodgment of responsibility in one judge was 'abhorrent' to him. I carefully noted the word 'abhorrent' and told him this was Bentley W. Warren's argument.

"He told me that a son of one of the leading witnesses for the prosecution had been to him to tell him that his mother was utterly irresponsible and mentally incapable of telling the truth. Fuller said I would be surprised at the way much of the testimony collapsed. He led me out to the elevator, delayed its movement, to explain to me that he was going to settle this case in such a way that he could live with his own conscience. He did say that he took no stock in the Madeiros confession and that he was not impressed with the flowing necktie of Frank Sibley. But aside from these two observations his point of view was wholly on the clemency side. I continued to hear things pointing in the same direction although it is fair to say not from the Governor . . ."

(Two). Friends and political associates of Governor Fuller did use the "law and order" argument at a Republican convention conference in Kansas City in the following June of 1928, to push his candidacy for the vice-presidency. But his aspirations were killed by Senator Borah, who announced he proposed to fight Fuller's nomination to the limit.

Senator Borah voiced his views at a conference in the suite of Secretary of the Treasury Mellon in the Muelbach Hotel. A drive was on to nominate former Governor Channing H. Cox of

Massachusetts, but Cox took the position that if any Massachusetts man was to go on the ballot it should be Governor Fuller. At the Bay State caucus Fuller was favoured by a powerful group including Chairman William M. Butler of the Republican National Committee, Louis K. Liggett, and Senator Frederick H. Gillet. It was unanimously voted to enter Fuller's name in the convention and to support him as a unit, and former Speaker Benjamin Loring Young was chosen to make the nominating speech.

John Richardson of Boston, Hoover manager for Massachusetts, had been in favor of Fuller, and Mr Liggett, the new National Committeeman, was also a Fuller supporter. So well did the Fuller boom go that Chairman Butler wired the Governor concerning the situation. Later, at another conference in the Mellon suite, Senator Borah said that he would not stand for Fuller, and that the party could not afford to go to the country on the Sacco–Vanzetti case as an issue, as it would be a false issue. He had nothing against Fuller personally but felt he would be a political liability. Not only would the party be burdened by the platform's plank on the equalization-fee program, but it would have to assume the burden of defending Fuller's action in the Sacco–Vanzetti case, which was "political dynamite", the Idaho Senator argued. He had doubts about the guilt of the two Italians.

Borah went so far as to declare that he would take the convention floor on a point of personal privilege if Fuller's name was placed before the delegates. This was an unprecedented course that the leaders were hardly prepared to face. Congressman Theodore E. Burton of Ohio attacked Fuller's Congressional record and spoke of his unpopularity with his Congressional associates. This determined attack completely eliminated the Bay State executive.

But we did not know these things on that August day in 1927, and the apparent change of mind by Governor Fuller became the more mysterious as we made further inquiries. We learned that not only had the Governor told confidants that the idea of sending the men to the electric chair on "flimsy" evidence was "abhorrent" to him, but he also said he did not approve of having one judge as the sole arbiter of the men's destinies.

A day or two later indication that the Governor might be groomed for Presidency appeared in *The Malden News*, published in Mr Fuller's home town. This editorial stated that "the effect of the decision upon the political fortunes of His Excellency will be to make him the most talked-of man in our country for the President of the United States. The decision, in our judgment, surpasses that of Governor Coolidge in the Boston police strike. No other man mentioned for the Presidency has any such record for courageous public service and for sustaining law and order."

The Governor received messages hoping he would "choose to run" for high office in 1928.

When Gordon and I saw Defence Counsel Thompson the next day he told us that after four years he and Mr Ehrmann were stepping out of the case, which "is now remitted to the judgment of mankind". Their efforts had come to naught. They had been unable to break through the secrecy with which the Governor had conducted his star-chamber inquiry.

They had not been permitted to be present, they told us, during the examination of all witnesses. In the Lowell Commission hearing defense counsel were not allowed to hear the testimony of Judge Thayer or Chief Judge Hall of the Superior Court, and they were excluded during part of the examination of District Attorney Fred Katzmann. What took place at these sessions was not made known to them, and they had no opportunity for cross-examining these witnesses. Counsel for the convicted men were handicapped in being ignorant of what Judge Thayer said in defending himself against the charge that he was prejudiced. Nor could counsel inquire of the jurors the effect on them of the Judge's attitude.

It was too much for Mr Thompson, former president of the Massachusetts Bar Association and head of its grievance committee. He had sacrificed a lucrative private practice to handle the case and now his practice was gone; he was socially ostracized by Boston's "Cabots" and "Lodges" and even by old associates, and his health was impaired. But not his faith in the innocence of Sacco and Vanzetti.

Arthur D. Hill, former District Attorney of Suffolk County and a distinguished member of the Boston Bar, succeeded Mr Thompson as chief counsel. The new legal pilot was assisted among others by Francis D. Sayre, son-in-law of President Wilson, and a new phase of the case was opened—the last battle to free the Italian radicals.

By this time the world-wide interest in the case was unprecedented. On 5 August, twelve Paris dailies devoted four times as much space to the Sacco–Vanzetti case as to the breakup of the Geneva Naval Conference. From the Royalist *Action Française* on the Right, to the Communist *Humanité* on the Left, there were pleas for clemency.

When the cables carried messages from abroad we would go to the State House for some word of the next possible move. In Governor Fuller's entourage the pleas made by Romain Rolland, H. G. Wells, George Bernard Shaw, and other distinguished men and women in Europe and America were regarded as "unwarranted interference". This view was expressed to us without reservation by State officials and by "substantial citizens". The atmosphere became murky indeed. Knots of men gathered on the Common, and Sacco–Vanzetti sympathizers never failed to evoke hostile remarks from those who damned the Italians as "anarchists and foreigners".

Staid Boston flinched whenever anybody suggested that "Massachusetts justice was on trial". Bomb explosions in New York, Baltimore, and abroad heightened the tension in Boston. We could almost feel the wave of local resentment that flared up so swiftly against the doomed men when the reports of violence were published. The pleas for mercy by distinguished men were resented.

We were enveloped in a miasma of hate, fear, suspicion.

Boston in August 1927 was seized with mass hysteria. It was a witch-hunter's paradise.

But doubts arose and would not down. Then the Lowell Committee published its report. The prestige of this committee was so enormous that its "thumbs down" verdict was accepted virtually as gospel by vast numbers, particularly of middle-class groups.

The Lowell report was regarded by most newspapers as final. But upon review by eminent lawyers, there were "indications of error." Some of these were pointed out by Charles C. Burlingham, distinguished member of the New York bar, in *The New York Times*.

Walter Lippmann, editor of the New York *World* and a Harvard alumnus, had at first taken the Lowell report as "the last word". In common with so many others, he had not analysed it critically, but had accepted the judgment and decision of those holding high position. It took a great deal of persuading by Felix Frankfurter, Charles Merz (then an associate on *The World*), and Mr Burlingham to make him analyse the report to its roots. When he did so, he took the entire editorial page of *The World* on 19 August for a strong editorial on "Doubts That Will Not Down", which discussed at great length discrepancies in the testimony and the doubts that still remained.

Even as late as 1936, during the Harvard Tercentenary Celebration, a group of Harvard alumni published a pamphlet—*Walled in This Tomb*—comprising "questions left unanswered by the Lowell Committee and their pertinence in understanding the conflicts sweeping the world at this hour".

Were the distinguished members of the Lowell Committee so unaware of their own bias that they unconsciously permitted it to dictate what they should believe and what they should not believe? What would explain the otherwise inexplicable omissions and commissions of this committee? Was it class feeling, instinctive distrust of a certain class of "foreigners", lack of sympathy with working-class types represented by Sacco and Vanzetti, their natural antipathy as "patriots" to draft dodgers?

The committee members had enormous prestige yet—

(1) They believed a woman whom they said was "eccentric" and "not unimpeachable in conduct", whom the Commonwealth had refused to call because she was unreliable, whose testimony Governor Fuller rejected, whose son said she was not to be believed, whom a police chief—he had known her all his life—said was "crazy, imagines things—has pipe dreams . . ."

(2) They believed that a rent in a cap, alleged to be Sacco's and found near the scene of the South Braintree crime, was a "trifling matter" and did not warrant a new trial. Yet, Judge Thayer had denied motion for a new trial on the ground that the rent was a vital part of the proof against Sacco. This, too, in the face of new testimony by the Braintree Chief of Police, who told the committee that he had made the rent in trying to find a name inside the cap.

(3) They omitted all reference to the important "eel" testimony and the receipt that tended to exculpate Vanzetti. (Nor was there any reference to this important incident in the Governor's report.)

We followed the new counsel Mr Hill from one legal step to another in his attempt to save the men from death in the electric chair, set for 10 August. The Supreme Judicial Court of Massachusetts refused a writ of error. The day before the date set for the execution, Mr Hill, in one of the frankest statements ever made in the State courts, told Judge Thayer in open court that because of prejudice he could not fairly decide the motions before him. He pleaded that Thayer withdraw to allow another judge to be appointed for the final appeal. He pointed out that even the Lowell Committee had found Thayer guilty of a "grave breach of official decorum" in speaking of the case off the bench. He urged that it was an insuperable task to try a case under such circumstances.

Hill filed a new affidavit of a witness who saw the South Braintree shooting and who told the police Sacco and Vanzetti were not in the murder party but who had not been called at the trial.

Hill's appeal was rejected. It was the eighth time in six years that Judge Thayer had denied a new trial.

Judge Thayer completely lacked judicial temperament in this case. His prejudice overflowed to reporters, acquaintances, and friends whom he sought out during lunch, whom he invited to his chambers. In a Boston club, on the golf links, wherever he went, something impelled him to denounce the prisoners before him. He sought to sway an observer for the Boston Federation of Churches to disbelieve Sacco's employer, who had given him a fine character.

Robert Benchley, then dramatic editor of *Life*, whose family knew the Judge well, said that in the summer of 1921 his friend Loring Coes told him "that Web [Thayer] has been saying that these bastards down in Boston were trying to intimidate him. He would show them that they could not and that he would like to get a few of those Reds and hang them too."

The judge was unable to keep his violent language out of the record of the trial. In his charge he went out of the way to compare the duty of the jurors with that of our soldiers in France.

His lack of restraint and judicial temper even led him to exclaim to a friend after he had turned down a plea for a new trial:

"Did you see what I did to those anarchist bastards?"

What drove this New England judge to such extraordinary breaches of judicial decorum? Apparently, his obsession against "Reds" completely deprived him of all unbiased consideration of the case and led him to hang onto it with bulldog insistence, through eight appeals in six years, even going so far as to be a judge of his own prejudice and ruling that he had had none.

While the argument was under way, the American flag was burned in front of our consulate in Casablanca, Communists called a protest strike in Prague, British labor leaders cabled appeals to Governor Fuller, and President William Green of the American Federation of Labor asked for commutation of sentence.

August 9 was to have been the last day of life for Sacco and Vanzetti. The execution hour was set for three minutes after midnight, 10 August. That morning Boston was the center of an influx of radicals, trade-union leaders, liberals, and sympathizers from all over the country. We spent hours watching them try to picket the State House. They wore mourning bands on their sleeves. As rapidly as they appeared they were arrested.

Extraordinary police arrangements were made for the execution. Eight hundred armed men guarded Charlestown State Prison. They were prison police, State Police, and Metropolitan Boston and Cambridge police..

Gas and tear-gas squads were held inside the prison gates. A machine-gun detachment was stationed near the gates.

The nerves of Bostonians were "jumpy". They called up the police and complained of the activities of "foreign-looking men".

On Boston Common I ran into Michael Angelo Musmanno, a vivacious young man with flowing brown hair and streaming black Windsor tie. Musmanno, who had been sent from Pittsburgh to Boston by the Sons of Italy to present to the Governor a resolution expressing that organization's doubts about the case and voicing the hope for some form of clemency, was on his way to get Sacco and Vanzetti's signature to an appeal. We rode to the prison in a taxicab and I waited for Musmanno. When he reappeared I asked Musmanno how Vanzetti felt about the day that was to end with the short walk to the electric chair.

This is what I wrote at the time:

"VANZETTI: Ah, Musmanno, the trouble with the world is that there is no responsibility. You see it is this way. In the court the District Attorney says it is not his fault that we are there. He is paid to prosecute men and he can't help himself. The judge says he has nothing to do with the case except to charge the jury on the law. He says the jury brings in the verdict. The jury says it looks to the judge for guidance so they are not responsible. Then you ask the governor and he says it is up to the Advisory Committee. But the committee says it is the witnesses that make the case. The witnesses say they couldn't help being where they are. They didn't ask to be called. And then there are the guards before our cells. They say they are sorry for us but they can't do anything about it. Then, when they come to strap us in the chair they will say they had nothing to do with it as that is how they earn their living. Well, Musmanno [with a smile], I guess only Nick and I are responsible."

Sacco, who was on the twenty-fifth day of his hunger strike, would not sign the appeal paper placed before him by Musmanno. Vanzetti did so on condition that it cover both cases. Vanzetti autographed Charles A. Beard's *The Rise of American Civilization* for Musmanno and wrote a farewell message on a flyleaf. Musmanno refused to take the two volumes with him at the time as that would mean he had given up hope.

Mr Hill appealed to the governor for a stay of execution pending a final appeal to the full bench of the Supreme Judicial Court. The governor called a special meeting of his Council. He asked seven of the eight living attorneys general to help him consider the request for a respite.

While these meetings were in progress in the State House Mr Hill sped to the home of Supreme Court Justice Oliver Wendell Holmes at Beverly Farms, thirty miles away. The justice held he could not stay the execution as he had no jurisdiction in the case.

In the last desperate days a second appeal was made to Justice Holmes. Those who undertook this mission were Mr Thompson and John Finerty, a Washington lawyer. They talked to him on the porch of his Beverly Farms home. The jurist was deeply moved by the lawyers' recital and told them that there was nothing he would rather do than to grant their request, but he saw no legal way in which he could act.

"You don't have to convince me that the atmosphere in which these men were tried precluded a fair trial," said Justice Holmes. "But that is not enough to give me, as a Federal judge, jurisdiction.

"If I listened to you any more I would do it," he continued. "I must not do it."

He turned on his heel and went into the house.

To Justice Holmes preservation of the fabric of Federal–State relations was a principle higher than life. It was what he had fought for as a lad in the Civil War.

Mr Hill flung himself into his car and hurried to Circuit Court Justice George W. Anderson, who also found he could not intervene. There was but one hope for a stay, that was Governor Fuller. At eight-thirty p.m. Mr Hill poured his appeal before the governor and the Council. They were reluctant to act. Hill argued and pleaded, summoning every argument he had. His effort was successful and a respite for ten days was granted at eleven-twelve p.m., less than an hour before the men were to have met their death.

Captain Charles R. Beaupre of the State Police rushed the reprieve to the Charlestown State Prison.

It was at eleven-forty that Warden William Hendry, the reprieve in his hand and a smile on his face, walked down the long cement corridor leading to the death house. Sacco, Vanzetti, and Madeiros had been prepared for the electric chair.

"It's all off, boys," the warden sang out as he approached the three cells. The men slowly rose from their cots. Vanzetti gripped the bars of his cell. "I'm damn glad of that," he said, "I'd like to see my sister before I die." Sacco and Madeiros made no comment.

The warden returned to his office, passed around cigars to the reporters and witnesses, and smiled with satisfaction as an assistant read the respite with all the "whereases" and "know ye alls".

Now began the ten last days of mental torture for the convicted men and their friends. Robert Morss Lovett, of the University of Chicago, formed a Citizens' National Committee. Glenn Frank, President of the University of Wisconsin, Dr Felix Adler, of the Society for Ethical Culture, and many well-known men and women accepted membership on the committee.

The police refused to allow Sacco–Vanzetti meetings on Boston Common. Powers Hapgood, nephew of Norman Hapgood, tried to make a "free speech" test and was sent to the psychopathic ward for observation.

A week after the reprieve the full bench of the Supreme Judicial Court of Massachusetts heard the last appeal in the case. The same day a bomb explosion wrecked the home of Lewis McHardy, who had been a juror in the case six years previously. This and other events fanned Massachusetts opinion to fever heat. Sacco, under threat of forcible feeding, broke his self-imposed fast on the thirtieth day, six days before he was to die. Four days later he bade a pathetic farewell to his fourteen-year-old son Dante.

August 19. The State Judicial Court denied the final appeal. Preparations were made for an appeal to the Federal courts.

From Cotuit President Lowell told *The New York Times* he would not discuss the case and declined to say why he would not make public the record of examination of witnesses.

Extra police were placed on duty to protect all public officials and public property.

Luigia Vanzetti, in a faded travelling cloak and grasping in her hand a gold medallion of the Madonna, stepped off the *Aquitania* in New York in time to hear that the highest legal tribunal in Massachusetts had shut the door against hope for the brother whom she had not seen in nineteen years.

August 20. Luigia arrived in Boston at four-thirty a.m. At eleven-thirty Mrs Sacco took her to Charlestown State Prison. Every day for a week Mrs Sacco had passed the electric chair on the way to visit her husband in the death house. This day she tried to save Luigia from the gruesome sight by appealing to Warden Hendry. The bluff Scot who had come to respect his two prisoners yielded, and the women were permitted to enter the death cells from another direction.

The warden opened the door for Miss Vanzetti.

"Barto," she murmured, sinking into her brother's arms.

The defence suffered three setbacks in the Federal courts.

Behind the scenes strong pressure was exerted to have the Department of Justice's files opened. Affidavits of former Department of Justice agents indicated that the state and the Federal governments had exchanged information on the case and that the Federal authorities were certain that Sacco and Vanzetti were radicals but not murderers.

August 21. Governor Fuller remained silent on the request that he ask for the Federal files. The acting attorney general had announced he would submit the files if the governor made the request.

Justice Brandeis declined to intervene, as members of his family had been personally interested in the case. (Mrs Sacco had lived in a house in Dedham placed at her disposal by the Brandeis family, and Mrs Brandeis and her daughter Susan had become interested in the case.) They also discussed it with Mrs Elizabeth Glendower Evans of Boston, who assisted the defence committee.

Large crowds gathered near the State House and police stopped a parade of pickets, forbidding all public demonstrations. They called it a "death watch". More than 150 persons were arrested for picketing, including Edna St Vincent Millay, Lola Ridge, John Dos Passos, Professor Ellen Hayes of Wellesley, John Howard Lawson, and "Mother" Ella Reeve Bloor.

Paula Halliday, who used to manage "Polly's" restaurant in Greenwich Village, walked on the Common wearing a red slicker. On her back in black paint were the words: "Save Sacco and Vanzetti. Is Justice dead?"

Police dragged her to the nearest patrol wagon.

Musmanno returned from Washington where he had filed papers for a writ of certiorari, which could not be argued until October.

Lawyers, in a final desperate attempt, dashed off to call on Supreme Court Justice Stone, vacationing on rock-bound Isle au Haut, off the Maine coast.

A telegram imploring Justice Taft to confer on American soil with counsel was sent to him at Point au Pic, Quebec.

Senator Borah, from Portland, Oregon, wired that he would volunteer his legal services if a new trial were obtained.

August 22. Turmoil and street fighting in Paris such as had not been witnessed since the World War. Hundreds arrested and scores hurt.

Forty hurt in a Sacco–Vanzetti demonstration in London.

A riotous demonstration before the American Consulate in Geneva.

Delegations of citizens visited Governor Fuller all day. Frank P. Walsh and Arthur Garfield Hays of New York, and Francis Fisher Kane, former US Attorney in Philadelphia, begged for a respite pending examination of the Department of Justice files.

They said that Acting Attorney General Farnum had at last agreed to have the files opened, and pleaded with the governor not to rush Sacco and Vanzetti to the chair in "indecent haste" while the files were still locked.

Mr Hill begged the Governor to delay the case until the appeal, docketed in the Supreme Court, had been argued.

Congressman LaGuardia flew to Boston to see the Governor and emerged saying the condemned men had one chance in a thousand.

Justices Taft and Stone refused to intervene.

Again Sacco and Vanzetti were prepared for the short walk to the electric chair.

Boston was in a veritable state of siege. Police precautions of 10 August were augmented. Three hundred policemen were thrown around the State House, while pickets marched up to the front door only to be bundled into patrol wagons. Legionnaires shouted and hooted and sang "The Star-Spangled Banner".

A New York labor group headed by Julius Hochman, Luigi Antonini, A. I. Shiplacoff and Judge Jacob Panken saw the Governor. President Green wired again asking for commutation.

The governor received 900 telegrams during the day. Two-thirds asked for clemency.

A group of liberals added their appeals. I watched them leave the governor's office without hope. It was no use, they said. They felt an air of unreality about the whole thing. Never have I seen a more dejected lot. Among them were John F. Moors, a member of the Harvard Corporation; Paul Kellogg, of *The Survey*; Waldo Cook, of *The Springfield Republican*; Dr John Lovejoy Elliott, and Dr Alice Hamilton.

Police charged a crowd near the Bunker Hill Monument. The prison area was an armed camp. Searchlights swept glaring fingers over rooftops, revealing whole families gazing at the prison. All streets leading to the prison zone. Police horses stamped restlessly in the yellow glare of street lamps.

Mrs Sacco and Miss Vanzetti paid three visits to the prison on the last day and made their final appeal to the governor in the evening.

Reporters were given special passes to the prison. Those of us who were to do the execution story were asked to present ourselves at the prison by ten o'clock if possible. Eddy remained on the streets observing the police and the crowds, and Gordon covered the last hours at the State House.

When I arrived at the prison, I found that telegraph wires had again been strung into the Prison Officers' Club. From ten o'clock we filed details of the preparations for the execution. The windows had been nailed down by a nervous policeman "because somebody might throw something in". The shades were drawn. The room was stuffy, and in an hour the heat was unbearable. We took off our coats, rolled up our shirt sleeves, and tried to be comfortable. The Morse operators were the coolest of the fifty men and women in the room. The noise of the typewriters and telegraph instruments made an awful din. Our nerves were stretched to the breaking-point. Had there not been a last minute reprieve on 10 August? Might there not be one now? We knew of the personal appeal then being made by Mrs Sacco and Miss Vanzetti to the governor.

W. G. Thompson, counsel for the two men, saw them for the last time. In an extraordinarily moving account of his final talks, later published in *The Atlantic Monthly*, Thompson described the attitude of the two Italians, their calmness in the face of death, their sincerity, their firm belief in their ideals:

"I told Vanzetti that although my belief in his innocence had all the time been strengthened both by my study of the evidence and by my increasing knowledge of his personality, yet there was a chance, however remote, that I might be mistaken; and that I thought he ought for my sake, in the closing hour of his life when nothing could save him, to give me his most solemn reassurance, both with respect to himself and with respect to Sacco. Vanzetti then told me quietly and calmly, and with a sincerity which I could not doubt, that I need have no anxiety about this matter; that both he and Sacco were absolutely innocent of the South Braintree crime and that he [Vanzetti] was equally innocent of the Bridgewater crime; that while, looking back, he now realized more clearly than he ever had the grounds of the suspicion against him and Sacco, he felt that no allowance had been made for his ignorance of American points of view and habits of thought, or for his fear as a radical and almost as an outlaw, and that in reality he was convicted on evidence which would not have convicted him had he not been an anarchist, so that he was in a very real sense dying for his cause. He said it was a cause for which he was prepared to die. He said it was the cause of the upward progress of humanity and the elimination of force from the world. He spoke with calmness, knowledge, and deep feeling.

"I was impressed by the strength of Vanzetti's mind, and by the extent of his reading and knowledge. He did not talk like a fanatic. Although intensely convinced of the truth of his own views, he was still able to listen with calmness and with understanding to the expression of views with which he did not agree. In this closing scene the impression of him which had been gaining ground in my mind for three years was deepened and confirmed—that he was a man of powerful mind, of unselfish disposition, of seasoned character and of devotion to high ideals. There was no sign of breaking down or of terror at approaching death. At parting he gave me a firm clasp of the hand and a steady glance, which revealed unmistakably the depth of his feeling and the firmness of his self-control . . .

"My conversation with Sacco was very brief. He showed no sign of fear, shook hands with me firmly and bade me good-bye. His manner also was one of absolute sincerity."

At quarter past eleven, Musmanno burst into Warden Hendry's office with a plea for a last talk with Vanzetti. The warden, whose heart was touched by the young lawyer, had to refuse. It was too close to the hour set for the three executions.

Musmanno was on the verge of collapse.

"I want to tell them there is more mercy in their hearts than in the hearts of many who profess orthodox religion," he said. "I want to tell them I know they are innocent and all the gallows and electric chairs cannot change that knowledge. I want to tell them they are two of the kindest and tenderest men I have ever known."

At the State House in the meantime, Governor Fuller talked with Mrs Sacco, Miss Vanzetti, Dr Edith B. Jackson and her brother Gardner, and Aldino Felicani of the Defense Committee.

The governor was sorry. Everything had been done, the evidence had been carefully sifted. To prove it he called in State Attorney General Arthur K. Reading, whose legal explanations were lost on the three women. Reluctantly they left the governor. Hope vanished.

Shortly after midnight, Warden Hendry rapped on the door leading to the interior of the prison and the death house. Musmanno, still in the warden's office, laid a hand on Hendry's arm. "Please, one last request."

"No, no."

Hendry, followed by the official witnesses, solemnly filed into the death chamber. The only reporter present at the execution was W. E. Playfair of the Associated Press. The rules limited the Press to one representative, and Mr Playfair had been handed the assignment when the men were convicted in 1921.

Madeiros was the first to go. His cell was the nearest the chair. A messenger hurried to us with a bulletin.

Sacco walked the seventeen steps from his cell to the execution chamber slowly between two guards. He was calm.

"Long live anarchy," he cried in Italian as he was strapped in the chair.

In English: "Farewell my wife and child and all my friends."

This was a slip probably due to his imperfect command of English. He had two children: Dante, fourteen, and Inez, six.

"Good evening, gentlemen," he said.

Then his last words.

"Farewell, Mother."

Vanzetti was the last to die. He shook hands with the two guards.

To Warden Hendry, he said, speaking slowly and distinctly: "I want to thank you for everything you have done for me, Warden. I wish to tell you that I am innocent and that I have never committed any crime but sometimes some sin. [Almost the same words he had used when sentenced by Judge Thayer the previous April.] I thank you for everything you have done for me. I am innocent of all crime not only of this, but all. I am an innocent man."

A pause.

"I wish to forgive some people for what they are now doing to me."

The warden was overcome. The current was turned on, and when Vanzetti was pronounced dead Hendry could scarcely whisper the formula required by law—"Under the law I now pronounce you dead, the sentence of the court having been carried out."

Mr Playfair lived up to his name. He dashed into our room with all the details of the last Sacco–Vanzetti story most of us were to write.

Governor Fuller remained at the State House until twelve minutes past twelve, a minute after Executioner Elliott had thrown the switch that ended the earthly existence of Sacco. Until a few minutes before midnight, Francis Fisher Kane had begged Governor Fuller for a respite. Thompson, former attorney in the case, remained with the governor until eleven forty five, making his final heart-rending plea for mercy.

When the governor left the State House he knew that the Supreme Court had, on 22 August, docketed two appeals for writs of certiorari. He had a request pending before him that alienists be permitted to examine Sacco and Vanzetti, that execution be delayed until the matter of the Department of Justice's files had been cleared up. He had before him five new affidavits made by new witnesses found by the defense in the closing days. He had, or was presumed to have received from his secretary, the receipt for the eels which Vanzetti had purchased.

So that when the two men died in the electric chair the legal battle to save them was still under way and there was, in the opinion of many of the best minds in America, more than a "reasonable doubt". In the last hour a three-or four-hour reprieve was asked by Defense Attorney Hill so that he could fly to Williamstown in a chartered plane to consult Circuit Court Judge Anderson again.

At the naval airport Hill tried to get in touch with the governor or the attorney general, but without success. When a naval officer found out who Hill and his companions were, he ordered them off the grounds and told William Schuyler Jackson, a former New York attorney general, that "it would give me pleasure to shoot you". Finally a reporter at the State House told them over the telephone that Sacco was in the death chamber. The long battle had ended.

On the way back to the Statler Hotel after the execution, Gordon, Eddy, and I picked up a copy of *The Boston Herald*. BACK TO NORMALCY the leading editorial was captioned. "The chapter is closed," it said. "The die is cast. The arrow has flown. Now, let us go forward to our duties and responsibilities of the common day with a renewed determination to maintain our present system of government and our existing social order."

The Italians were presumed to have been done to death by the State for murder. Yet, in their death, as at their trial, they had been bound up with their radicalism. Divesting the men of their radicalism and their foreign birth, their innocence of the murders would have been shown to the world, in the opinion of many capable lawyers and common-sense laymen. Therefore, in a real sense the men gave up their lives for their beliefs. They were foreigners, slackers, and radicals, and were thus stigmatized during the unfortunate, hysteric days of their arrest.

Many thousands followed the bodies of the two men to Forest Hills Crematory on 27 August. The rain poured on the funeral throng, and when it was all over a policeman wiped his brow and remarked with a sigh, "Well, I hope to Christ it's over now."

But it was not over.

A year later a committee of lawyers (John W. Davis, Elihu Root, Bernard Flexner, Charles C. Burlingham, Newton D. Baker) sponsored publication of the legal records in the case. A cryptic reference in the Lowell Committee's report led the lawyers to ask both President Lowell and the defense counsel for an explanation. It was disclosed that the Lowell Committee, by private inquiry, had convinced itself that it had destroyed Sacco's alibi, which was that he was in Boston applying for a passport to Italy on the day of the South Braintree crime. Witnesses recalled seeing him because on that day an Italian group gave a dinner to Editor Williams of the *Transcript*. The Lowell Committee insisted that the dinner date was 13 May. When a file of *La Notizia* showed that the witnesses were correct, and it transpired that Williams had been tendered dinners on both dates, the Lowell Committee omitted reference to the rehabilitation of the Sacco alibi, though the thirty-two pages of examination apparently demolishing it remained. President Lowell privately apologized to the witnesses. He refused, however, to permit them to publish the incident in *La Notizia*. No mention of this incident appears in the Lowell record, but the defence counsel's version has never been disputed. The only reference that appears is the cryptic statement which mystified the lawyers' committee sponsoring the record, that those present "look in the books produced by the witness".

This incident is one of the high watermarks of the entire case. In fact, when President Lowell said he had ascertained that Mr Williams had been tendered a dinner on 13 May and not on the Sacco alibi date, Attorney Thompson threw up his hands. His dejection was complete, but it was then suggested that the witnesses bring the *La Notizia* files to Thompson's office. This was done, and Thompson with his own eyes read the account of the Williams banquet on 15 April. From the depths of despair Thompson's spirits rose to transports of ecstasy. His witnesses were telling the truth! The Sacco alibi, apparently so important when destroyed by President Lowell, would surely now be equally important to the defense, for it had been rehabilitated by the newspaper item.

Why was this important alibi testimony omitted?

The stenographer said that Dr Lowell had instructed him not to take colloquies.

This interesting correspondence may be found as an appendix on page 5256a of *The Sacco–Vanzetti Case*, published by Henry Holt and Company. President Lowell's reply is there given to Mr Flexner. He says that the files of *La Notizia* showed that the Italians had tendered a luncheon to Mr Williams on 15 April (the date of the South Braintree murders), and that the Committee subsequently assumed in its deliberations there had been two affairs for Williams.

When the record was printed and the correspondence made public many newspapers referred to it editorially and *The New York World*, *The Springfield Republican*, and *The Baltimore Sun* regarded the correspondence as disquieting. They viewed it as a challenge to Dr Lowell. *The Springfield Republican* of March 2, 1929, ended its editorial with these words:

"To this day Mr Lowell has taken no action whatever to clarify his attitude in dealing with the Sacco alibi and he leaves the public in the face of the record as now amplified, to wonder how he could have viewed the alibi as 'serious' when he thought he had destroyed it, but apparently as not 'serious' after it had been rehabilitated."

An interesting and hitherto unpublished sidelight on developments subsequent to the execution was concerned with an inquiry
into the relation of the Morelli gang of Providence, freight-car
thieves and bandits, to the South Braintree robbery. Madeiros had
"confessed" that he had been with the gang that did the South
Braintree job. There was reason to believe that it was the work
of the Morellis. An enormous amount of material was gathered
by the defense on this phase of the situation. In 1929 a meeting
of liberals was held in the New York home of Oswald Garrison
Villard, and $40,000 was pledged to pursue this inquiry. One of
the Morellis appeared to be willing to make a clean breast of the
case. It was planned to drain the pond where the holdup men were
supposed to have thrown the empty money boxes. But the stock
market crash came and pledges were not collected; the pond was
never drained.

"Doubt that will not down," said Walter Lippmann in his
full-page editorial in the New York *World* on 19 August 1927.

On each anniversary of the execution of the two men these
doubts arise again—they are rehearsed at the meetings in Boston
where those who believe Sacco and Vanzetti innocent gather
once a year.

A bronze plaque sculptured by Gutzon Borglum, bearing the
images of Sacco and Vanzetti, was offered to the State of
Massachusetts on 22 August 1937, ten years after their death. The
offer kicked up a row, and Governor Charles F. Hurley, Democrat,
rejected the plaque which bore these words of Vanzetti:

"What I wish more than all in this last hour of agony is that
our case and our fate may be understood in their real being and
serve as a tremendous lesson to the forces of freedom so that our
suffering and death will not have been in vain."

The tragedy of the Sacco–Vanzetti case is the tragedy of three
men—Judge Thayer, Governor Fuller, and President Lowell—and
their inability to rise above the obscene battle that raged for
seven long years around the heads of the shoemaker and the
fish peddler.

THE A6 MURDER

(James Hanratty, 1961)

Paul Foot

Perhaps the most haunting and troublesome British murder case from the early 1960s, before the abolition of capital punishment. James Hanratty, a petty crook from north London, was executed for a cold-blooded shooting in a lay-by on the main A6 road in Bedfordshire, at a spot known as Deadman's Hill. The gunman claimed two victims: Michael Gregsten, the murdered man, and Valerie Storie, his mistress, who was raped, shot and left for dead. Paul Foot, the campaigning journalist, believes that Hanratty was not the A6 killer, and that his execution was a miscarriage of justice. If so, Hanratty himself was the third victim. This account of the case, and Paul Foot's role in its aftermath, appeared at the end of 1997.

Hanratty! The name which has haunted the British criminal justice system for a generation is about to hit the headlines again. Some time in the next few weeks Baden Henry Skitt, former Scotland Yard Commander and Chief Constable of Hertfordshire, now a chief investigator for the Criminal Cases Review Commission, will draft a public statement on the A6 murder, for which James Hanratty was hanged in 1962. The Commission chairman, Sir Frederick Crawford, has hinted to the

House of Commons Home Affairs Committee that the statement will be sensational.

The Hanratty case has intrigued and obsessed me for almost all my adult life. In 1966, when I was twenty-eight, the news editor of the *Sunday Telegraph* sent me to cover an unusual burial. What were purported to be the remains of James Hanratty had been packed into a coffin at Bedford prison and brought to North London. Capital punishment had been abolished the previous year. The Home Secretary, Roy Jenkins, had decreed that convicted murderers, whose bodies had by ancient barbarian law been consigned to quicklime in the prison yard, could be buried in consecrated ground. "There may be trouble there," the news editor beamed. "This chap Alphon may cause a fuss." I had no idea who Alphon was, and after the burial in Wembley, I was none the wiser. There was nothing to report, so I gladly accepted the invitation of James and Mary Hanratty to join the wake for their son in their council house in Kingsbury. The Hanrattys were warm, gentle, determined people, unlikely parents of a man who had been convicted of shooting Michael Gregsten dead in a lay-by off the A6, raping his girlfriend Valerie Storie and then shooting her, leaving her for dead before driving off in the couple's car. Among the guests at the wake were Jean Justice, who told me he was a (rather elderly) law student, and his friend, a barrister called Jeremy Fox. I listened entranced to their assurances not only that Jimmy Hanratty had nothing to do with the A6 murder, but that they had been on intimate terms with the real killer: Peter Alphon.

I was hooked on the case that gloomy February afternoon and, nearly thirty-two years later, I still am. Bob Woffinden's *Hanratty: The Final Verdict* (Macmillan, London 1997) has revived the intoxicating mixture of anguish and curiosity with which Jean Justice inspired me all those years ago. Since that time I have been, as I still am, quite certain that Hanratty was in Rhyl when the couple were shot near Bedford 250 miles away. A few months after the Wembley burial, I went with Jo Mennel, who was directing a film on the A6 case for BBC's *Panorama* (editor, Jeremy Isaacs), to the guest-house in Rhyl where Hanratty said he'd stayed. The landlady, Mrs Grace Jones, was not at all diverted by the pulverising she'd got from the prosecution at the trial. She was more sure than ever that Hanratty had stayed in her house on the night of the murder, 22 August 1961. She was backed up by Terry Evans, whom Hanratty had met in Rhyl some months before the murder.

Evans had not been in Rhyl on 22 August but he had heard later from several people that a young Londoner had been looking for him that night. Could he find any of these people, we asked? Yes, he would try. The following week Jo Mennel and John Morgan, the reporter, went back to interview the Rhyl witnesses on camera. Over a cup of tea in a café, Terry Evans gave them the disappointing news that he could not find the main man he was looking for, a newspaper-seller called Charlie Jones. As the journalists stared morosely into their tea, Charlie Jones came into the café. When questioned about Hanratty, Jones remembered at once the smartly dressed young Londoner who had come off a bus and asked the way to the fairground. The reporters recorded the newspaper-seller, and the "new witness" to the Rhyl alibi was *Panorama's* big scoop.

Not very big, you might think, and you would be right, but as so often in these cases, television publicity about a small matter shook the tree, and big plums started to fall. Lots of other people had seen Hanratty in Rhyl, in much more convincing circumstances. Margaret Walker, who lived in the street behind the guest-house, had made a statement to the police during the trial but had not been called to give evidence. She was absolutely certain that on the evening of 22 August a young man looking like Hanratty had come to her house hoping to find lodgings. Christopher Larman had gone to the police when he saw Hanratty's picture in the paper, certain that this was the man he had directed to Mrs Jones's on a summer evening in 1961, the night before he left for London. When I finally tracked Larman down in Southall in September 1968, he produced an old diary in which he had jotted down the day he had left for London, 23 August 1961.

I became completely certain of the Rhyl alibi over the Whitsun weekend of 1968, when the newly formed A6 Murder Committee, consisting of Justice, Fox, James and Mary Hanratty, their son Michael and me, booked in (at Fox's considerable expense) to the Westminster Hotel, Rhyl. We had advertised in the local press for new witnesses. Trevor Dutton, a farmer from Abergele, came to see us. He said he had come into Rhyl to go to the bank in August 1961, and had been approached in the street by a young man wearing a herringbone suit who tried to sell him a gold watch. Hanratty had said he had gone to Rhyl to try to sell a gold watch, wearing his herringbone suit. When Trevor Dutton produced his bank book, and showed us the stamped date on the counterfoil, 23.8.1961, it suddenly seemed impossible that all these new witnesses could be confirming Hanratty's story so precisely unless he had been there. Yet two secret police inquiries under a Manchester detective chief superintendent managed to conclude that the alibi was a fake. The Labour Home Office Ministers, Jenkins and Dick Taverne, dismissed the case.

In 1969, I got a call at *Private Eye* from a man who said he was John Lennon. I was busy, and snapped away at the caller until I realized he *was* John Lennon. I met him in a Soho restaurant, the staff visibly swooning. He said he was worried about the growing demand for a return to capital punishment, and wanted to publicize the Hanratty case. For a time he financed the campaign of the A6 Murder Committee. Every Sunday, old Jim Hanratty mounted his platform in Hyde Park. "My son said to me: 'Dad, I didn't do it.' That was enough for me." We held huge meetings, filmed at John Lennon's expense, in Watford, Bedford and Wembley.

My book on the case was published in the spring of 1971. One hundred and forty MPs signed a motion calling for a public inquiry. They were curtly rebuffed by the Home Secretary, Reginald Maudling. Three years later, a newly-elected Labour government set up another secret inquiry by a barrister, Lewis Hawser QC. Hawser did for James Hanratty what another barrister, Scott Henderson, had done for Timothy Evans, who was wrongly convicted of the murder of his child. By concentrating on minute differences of detail in witness statements, he managed to dispense with all the people in Rhyl who quite plainly saw James Hanratty on the night of the murder. The Labour Government delightedly accepted the report and washed its hands of the case.

Old Jim Hanratty died of cancer in 1978. On his deathbed, he mourned the failure of the A6 campaign and urged me to continue with it. In truth, though, his death knocked the heart out of the committee. It seemed that every possible effort had been made to right this injustice, without success. Jean Justice kept on chipping away at journalists and lawyers until he, too, died in 1990. That really seemed the end of the matter.

New hope sprang from an unlikely source. In 1992, Bob Woffinden and Ros Franey made a Yorkshire Television programme on the A6 murder to mark the thirtieth anniversary of Hanratty's execution. In 1994, Woffinden and the Hanrattys' lawyer, Geoffrey Bindman, sent a dossier on the case to the Home Office. The outcome seemed depressingly certain: another official brush-off. The man appointed for the whitewash was Det. Chief

Supt Roger Matthews of Scotland Yard. Before long Matthews was shocked to discover that a clear case existed for Hanratty's innocence. His report, to the horror of the Home Secretary Michael Howard, recommended the immediate re-opening of the case. There was only one thing for it: procrastination. After nearly a year's dither, Howard passed the buck to the newly formed Criminal Cases Review Commission and ex-Commander Skitt.

Skitt, of course, is concerned only with Hanratty's guilt. Quite properly, he will have nothing to say about the man who has claimed he did the murder: Peter Alphon. In the years I was preparing my book, I tried to concentrate on the evidence which exculpated Hanratty. I was constantly diverted by interminable phone calls from Peter Alphon. Alphon has many times convincingly confessed to the murder. ("I killed Gregsten and the establishment murdered Hanratty.") He has also, less convincingly, retracted his confessions. He is linked to the murder by a long series of coincidences. He was the first police suspect. He was released only after Valerie Storie failed to pick him out in an identity parade (she later identified Hanratty). Alphon has claimed that he was part of a conspiracy, and was assigned to hold up the couple in the car with a gun. His story endlessly shifted. Whenever it seemed that he was going to produce definite proof of his complicity, he veered away. At the end of my book, I said of Alphon: "Either he committed the A6 murder, or he has been leading all of us, and me in particular, a fantastic dance. I tend, perhaps naturally, to the former view, but I have not the power to find the facts finally to prove or disprove it." Bob Woffinden, by contrast, boldly sets out a scenario which names Alphon as the murderer and explains the conspiracy which led him to the couple in the car, tracing his steps exactly, both in the run-up to the crime and the aftermath. The scenario is tempting, but far from conclusive.

My own feelings about Alphon have changed a little as a result of two recent meetings with him. I arranged the meetings in 1994 when, to my astonishment, I was approached by Janet Gregsten, whose husband was murdered on the A6. I had always assumed that she, perhaps unwittingly, had something to do with the murder, given that her husband was having an affair with Valerie Storie. I had three long meetings with Mrs Gregsten, two of them in Penzance, where she lived. Very quickly she convinced me she had nothing to do with the murder and had no idea who had. She had, however, grown increasingly uncertain about Hanratty's guilt. I found her impressive, quite unlike the jealous demon of my imagination. In January 1995, while we were still discussing how to take the matter further, she died of a heart attack. My brief relationship with her was a warning against jumping to hasty conclusions, in particular about Peter Alphon.

When I arrived at her Penzance flat on 30 December 1994, she waved contemptuously towards a letter written in the familiar and careful handwriting of Peter Alphon. The letter was an invitation to her to spend a few days with Alphon and Jeremy Fox at a luxury hotel near Dublin. Alphon offered her £2,000 if she accepted the invitation. Janet Gregsten was disgusted by the letter. Alphon explained to me later that he wanted to interrogate her about the A6 murder. When I said I had been convinced that she had nothing to do with it, Alphon scoffed: "You've been duped." He was "sure" she had been involved, but not so sure that he could prove it. When I played him part of Mrs Gregsten's taped conversation with me, Alphon seemed perplexed. It occurred to me, watching him carefully, that he really didn't know as much as he pretended. He certainly didn't know what he alleged—that Mrs Gregsten was the prime mover in commissioning the murderer. I started to wonder whether perhaps, if Alphon was the murderer, he had no idea who commissioned him; or even whether he had not done the murder himself, but had become involved in it in some other way.

Fortunately, such speculations are gloriously irrelevant. If James Hanratty is finally cleared of the A6 murder, as we all hope, then Peter Alphon, murderer or not, has, in his own macabre way, helped to keep the case alive all these years.

FLORENCE MAYBRICK

(James Maybrick, 1889)

Edgar Lustgarten

Florence Maybrick was an American abroad, and Americans in particular are fascinated by her ordeal, accused of the cruellest of murders in the bombazine bosom of Victorian England. With her melting blue eyes, voluptuous figure and golden ringlets, she was considered the most beautiful woman in Liverpool. But her feckless upbringing as a southern belle and coquettish drawl affronted provincial hypocrisies and pretensions and damned her as a scarlet adulteress. A nosy children's nanny intercepted a letter from Florence to her lover. Another servant at Mrs Maybrick's house witnessed her mistress soaking flypapers in water, a time-honoured way of obtaining arsenic. Shortly after this, her drug-popping husband James, twenty-three years her senior, died, evidently of arsenical poisoning. Florence Maybrick's trial for murder and subsequent sentence of death (commuted at the last moment to life imprisonment) quickly became an international cause célebre. Some modern commentators have called it the English Dreyfus case. Of it, Raymond Chandler wrote: "The question will never be settled . . . It's just too damned difficult." The question remains: Was it murder? Was Florence a cunning and determined poisoner who persisted in her efforts to dispose of her husband despite the hourly surveillance of a suspicious and hostile family circle? Or was she the grand victim of Victorian hypocrisies, so acutely personified in her dead husband? Of the many treatments of the Maybrick case, this from 1949 by Edgar Lustgarten (1907–78) is among the most attractive. Rattled out in his characteristic staccato, it succeeds in making sense of a notoriously dense and complex case, and creates courtroom vignettes of extraordinary power and vividness. Remembered by many as the inscrutable host of dozens of black-and-white films and television programmes on crime and the law, Lustgarten, a qualified barrister, became a full-time writer and broadcaster after the Second World War.

1

Planned, deliberate killing is no drawing-room accomplishment. It needs callousness of heart, insensitivity of mind, indifference to suffering and contempt for human life. These are grim qualities; repulsive in a man, in a woman against nature. The calculating murderer is vile but comprehensible; the calculating murderess is an enigmatic paradox.

Hence the compelling fascination of those cases where a woman stands charged with a premeditated murder. Reasoning and logic no longer seem sufficient. The onlooker is swayed by imponderable factors: imagination, instinct, the gulf of incongruity between the crime and the accused. He gazes on the figure in the dock; he notes the slight form, the gentle manner, the appealing face. Is it *possible*, he asks himself, that the Crown case is well-founded? Did Edith Thompson *really* instigate that crime and lead her victim, unsuspecting, to the appointed place of death? Did Lizzie Borden *really* slay her stepmother with a hatchet and then calmly wait her chance to slay her father likewise? Was Florence Maybrick *really* a systematic poisoner who did her beastly work for weeks and watched her husband die?

Mrs Thompson, Miss Borden, Mrs Maybrick: in the same dread setting, for the same dread reason, their names have achieved unenviable immortality. And indeed, though widely separated by both time and space, the three women have many things in common. Up to a point, their stories coincide: the charge of murder, the long dramatic trial, a verdict ever after in dispute. Up to a point, their backgrounds coincide: the quiet home, the decent upbringing, the orderly, respectable routine. Up to a point, their very natures coincide: each had a strong and forceful personality, determined to preserve its independence, and rebelling, in one form or another, against the bondage of domestic life.

Only in the last analysis do the three part company, but this final break is radical and sharp. Edith Thompson had passion but no breeding. Lizzie Borden had breeding but no passion. Florence Maybrick had both and therein lies her own peculiar and poignant tragedy.

2

The Maybrick story, with its disastrous denouement, opens in America in 1881.

In that year Mr James Maybrick, a Liverpool cotton broker, paid a business visit to the United States. He was in his early forties; a well-to-do bachelor of vigorous physique and sporting inclinations. In the course of his travels he met Miss Florence Chandler, the daughter of a substantial Alabama banker. Florence Chandler was then only eighteen; vivacious, handsome and sexually magnetic. James Maybrick promptly lost his heart and when he returned to England she came with him as his wife.

The couple ultimately settled down at Aigburth, where they lived in conditions of considerable affluence. They had a fine large house; they maintained several servants; nothing was wanting for their two children or themselves. On the surface, at any rate, the union seemed happy and the Maybrick ménage, like a million others, firmly based upon mutual content.

Then, in the early part of 1889, Mrs Maybrick embarked on an intrigue.

She had formed an attachment to a man named Brierley, and for a time there is no doubt she supposed herself in love. Brierley's attractions are a matter for conjecture; he hovers in the shadows of the case, represented only by a chilly, frightened note written some weeks after his conquest was complete. ("We had perhaps better not meet until late in the autumn.") But the simple fact remains: having given her husband a plausible excuse—an aunt, she said, was to undergo an operation—on 21 March Mrs Maybrick went to London, where she stayed with Brierley for three nights at an hotel.

It should be recalled—for enlightenment, not in extenuation—that her husband was now fifty and she was twenty-six.

There are strong grounds for believing that James Maybrick had preceded her in a marital offence. But the 1880s were the heyday of the sacred Single Standard and his lapse—if lapse there was—passed straight into oblivion. Hers, when it came to light, outraged the prim Victorian conscience and seriously prejudiced her chances when she came to be tried by a jury of her peers.

Mrs Maybrick in due course returned from London and resumed her place as the lady of the house. Mr Maybrick still did not know of her daring escapade. It is doubtful whether he ever did, although Mrs Maybrick later said that, on the day before his death, she made "full confession" and received "entire forgiveness". These expressions, however, are ambiguous.

But if there were gaps in Mr Maybrick's knowledge, he was well aware that Brierley paid attention to his wife. Moreover he resented it, and on 31 March he upbraided Mrs Maybrick in very bitter terms. A violent quarrel followed, in the course of which it seems he struck her more than once and gave her a black eye. Mrs Maybrick was indignant and distressed; she threatened to leave home, but there were the children to consider, and, through the family doctor's tactful mediation, the discord was resolved and the partners reconciled.

Less than a month later—on 27 April—Maybrick showed the first signs of an illness that proved fatal . . .

From that point the scenes flicker like an early film, gathering evil momentum as they pass. Maybrick stricken with vomiting and pain; Maybrick better; Maybrick ill again; Mrs Maybrick nursing him herself; doctors; more doctors; an uncertain diagnosis; Maybrick worse; Maybrick better; Maybrick worse than he had ever been; trained nurses summoned; Maybrick's brother arriving down from London; Maybrick sinking; Maybrick dying; Maybrick dead.

And then—the searching of the house and the discovery of arsenic; in jars, in packets, in tumblers, in pans, in bottles, on garments, on rags, on pocket handkerchiefs. This sinister search assumed still graver significance when a quantity of arsenic was found in Maybrick's corpse.

Maybrick had died on Saturday, 11 May. The postmortem took place on Monday, 13 May. On Tuesday, 14 May, Mrs Maybrick was arrested.

3

The accused's reaction to a charge of murder largely depends on the individual temperament. Some are goaded to hysterical activity, some are incredulous, some are stunned.

It makes no difference in a prison cell. There is nothing you can do except rely on those outside. Relatives and friends must rally to your cause; organizing sympathy, combating rumour, giving reassurance and preparing your defence.

Mrs Maybrick was devoid of such support. Her relatives were in a distant land, and those whom she had counted among her English friends were mostly nosing round in search of evidence against her. Sympathy was scant, rumour raged unchecked, and no one was at hand to offer comfort or advice.

In her extremity Mrs Maybrick wrote to Brierley. "I am writing to you", she said, "to give me every assistance in your power in my present fearful trouble. I am in custody without any of my family with me and without money."

This letter found its way not to Brierley but to the police. Forsaken and alone Mrs Maybrick remained until Messrs Cleaver, a firm of Liverpool solicitors, took up the defence of the unhappy lady and briefed Sir Charles Russell to appear on her behalf.

Russell was, by common consent, the greatest advocate of his generation. One is tempted to go further and roundly declare that the Bar has never known his equal. But in advocacy, as in acting, it is hard to measure the giants of the past. You can read descriptions of a dead actor, but that is not the same as seeing him on the stage. You can read the speeches of a dead advocate, but that is not the same as hearing him in court. The force of a character, the magic of a presence, cannot be distilled at second hand.

Irving or Garrick? Russell or Erskine? No reply can ever be conclusive. But of Russell at least this much may be said. There have been those who, as young men, saw Russell in action and who haunted the courts thereafter for another fifty years. They thus covered what I once heard Quintin Hogg describe as the Golden Age of the English Bar. And though many remarkable counsel followed—Carson, Isaacs and F. E. Smith among them—more often than not the veterans would agree that Russell was the greatest of them all.

He was an able but not outstanding lawyer; as Lord Chief Justice—an office he accepted six years after his defence of Mrs

Maybrick—he had only mild success. But then Russell's disposition was the converse of judicial. By nature he was a fighter, who loved battling for a cause, and no forensic fighter ever carried stronger weapons. Here was no smooth charmer, trading in fair words, and seeking victory by ingratiation. Russell's gift was *power*: the overwhelming influence of a giant personality. One judge called him "an elemental force", and he must often have appeared to his opponents in this guise. His bearing was fearless, his oratory direct, his cross-examination raking and implacable. "He was no respecter of persons," says his biographer, Barry O'Brien. "His blows fell indiscriminately on leaders and on juniors, and even, when the occasion warranted it, on judges. There was a bigness about the man that all appreciated."

Russell was not primarily a criminal defender. His path had lain more among the fashionable "society" suits which were such a signal feature of his time. But in any kind of court this masterful advocate was equally at home. His enlistment on the side of Mrs Maybrick accorded her the champion of whom she stood in need.

4

The coroner's inquest and the hearing by the Bench poured fuel upon the rising flames of local indignation. Mrs Maybrick's lapse with Brierley was the chief talk of the town and coloured every comment on the murder charge itself. She was a loose, foreign woman who had betrayed her English husband; who could be surprised that she had poisoned him as well?

Few were disposed to wait for the full facts. Rigid in righteousness and fierce with hate, Liverpool made up its mind. It did not trouble to conceal this prejudging of the issue. At the police court Mrs Maybrick was hissed by a gathering of ladies who, in dignity and moral sense and delicacy of taste, must be historically regarded as rivals of the harlots who danced in the streets at the trial of Oscar Wilde.

The English law, to guard against such fits of mass hysteria, permits a trial to be transferred from the area of prejudice. The merits of this course were carefully weighed by Mrs Maybrick's lawyers. She herself was clear upon the point; she wanted to be tried in London. "I should receive an impartial verdict there," she wrote, "which I cannot expect from a jury in Liverpool." But after due deliberation the lawyers recommended otherwise and Mrs Maybrick yielded to their view.

Russell was to mention this matter in his final speech. "This lady," he said, "has elected to take her trial in Liverpool before a Liverpool jury, in the community with which her husband lived, in which he was known, and in which upon a bare recital of the supposed facts of this case it was inevitable that, to ill-informed and imperfectly informed minds, great and serious prejudice must have been caused. If she had desired to shrink from meeting a jury drawn from this community she would not have had any difficulty interposed by those who represent the Crown. But she comes before you, asking from you nothing, save that you will willingly grant a careful, an attentive, and a sympathetic hearing to her case."

She might ask, but would she get it? Were the twelve men of the neighbourhood who formed the jury—three plumbers, two farmers, a wood-turner, a baker, a painter, a grocer, a provision merchant, a milliner and an ironmonger—likely to be capable of putting from their minds the campaign of denigration amid which they had been living?

Russell, notwithstanding, began the case with confidence. As he walked to the court on the first morning, he met a friend and entered into conversation. Not unnaturally he was asked what he thought about his chances. "She'll be acquitted," Russell said.

5

The trial of Florence Maybrick opened at Liverpool Assizes on 31 July 1889. The court was packed with an intently listening crowd, and, far beyond the confines of the court-house and the city, millions followed the proceedings as if personally concerned. Seldom has the battle for an individual's life been fought out in an atmosphere of such continuous tension.

Leading counsel for the Crown was Mr Addison, QC. He was a popular Northern Circuit silk; not in the highest flight perhaps, but a thoroughly sound advocate of ripe experience. If he could not match Russell's stature, at least he was not the man to be put off or overawed. Through the five days of conflict that went before the summing-up, Addison never failed to make a valid point.

It early became apparent that, though there was much detailed evidence in prospect, the prosecution rested on three main pillars. There were the fly-papers, there was the meat-juice, and there was a letter written by the prisoner to Brierley only three days before her husband died.

In his opening, Addison dealt with each in turn and explained the interpretation placed upon them by the Crown.

The fly-papers—and, be it noted, the fly-papers alone—were put forward as the source from which the prisoner procured arsenic. On 24 April Mrs Maybrick had bought a dozen; on the 29th, from a different chemist, she had bought two dozen more. Some were seen by servants in the Maybricks' bedroom, soaking in a basin which was covered by a towel.

Addison linked these purchases with James Maybrick's illness which, he recalled, began on 27 April. Maybrick was very bad indeed that day and the day following, but on the 29th he was considerably better. "It is an extraordinary thing", Addison remarked, "that when her husband was just recovering she should have bought these further fly-papers."

That was the extent of the evidence on the fly-papers. It showed that Mrs Maybrick had had them in her possession; it gave ground for suspicion that she had tried to extract arsenic; but there was nothing to prove that any arsenic *was* extracted, or for what purpose any such arsenic had been used.

The evidence on the meat-juice went a good deal further.

During the greater part of his illness, as Addison pointed out, Mrs Maybrick had "regulated" all her husband's medicines. Then in the closing stage the trained nurses appeared. One of these asserted that she saw Mrs Maybrick tamper with a meat-juice bottle before a dose was due. The nurse took care not to give it to the patient and it was subsequently found to contain half a grain of arsenic. This Addison described, with laudable moderation, as "one of the serious features of the case".

Although, in kind and sequel, this was the gravest charge of "tampering", it is necessary to add that it did not stand alone. According to the nurses and to Mr Maybrick's brother, Mrs Maybrick's conduct was generally suspicious. She didn't behave "openly", she changed the contents of the bottles, she caused the dying man to say she was giving him wrong medicines.

The prosecution's third prop, Mrs Maybrick's letter to Brierley of 8 May, worked up into a major issue of the trial. Dashed off hurriedly by a tired and harassed woman, it was examined at the time and has been debated since with a meticulous precision more appropriate to a statute.

This letter (like the other previously mentioned) never arrived at its intended destination. Mrs Maybrick, tied to the sick room, handed it for posting to a servant, Alice Yapp. Yapp, by her own account, dropped it on the ground and opened it, intending to replace the dirty envelope. But having opened it, she read it; having read it, she retained it; and subsequently she passed it to Mr Maybrick's brother, with consequences that cannot be computed even now. Russell went so far as to declare that, but for this letter, no charge would have been made.

Dearest, [it ran] Your letter under cover to John K. came to hand just after I had written to you on Monday. I did not expect to hear from you so soon, and had delayed in giving him the necessary instructions. Since my return I have been nursing M. day and night. He is sick unto death. The doctors held a consultation yesterday, and now all depends upon how long his strength will hold out. Both my brothers-in-law are here, and we are terribly anxious. I cannot answer your letter fully today, my darling, but relieve your mind of all fear of discovery now and in the future. M. has been delirious since Sunday, and I know now that he is perfectly ignorant of everything, even of the name of the street, and also that he has not been making any inquiries whatever. The tale he told me was a pure fabrication, and only intended to frighten the truth out of me. In fact he believes my statement, although he will not admit it. You need not therefore go abroad on that account, dearest; but, in any case, please don't leave England until I have seen you once again. You must feel that those two letters of mine were written under circumstances which must even excuse their injustice in your eyes. Do you suppose that I could act as I am doing if I really felt and meant what I inferred then? If you wish to write to me about anything do so now, as all the letters pass through my hands at present. Excuse this scrawl, my own darling, but I dare not leave the room for a moment, and I do not know when I shall be able to write to you again. In haste, yours ever,

FLORIE

No question but that this gave indications of misconduct. Did it go further and breathe a hint of murder? So the prosecution claimed, laying special stress upon the passage: "He is sick unto death. The doctors held a consultation yesterday and now all depends upon how long his strength can hold out."

It is perfectly true that, at the time this note was written, the doctors did not take a pessimistic view. They thought James Maybrick was seriously ill; they did not think he was at all likely to die.

"On 7 May", said one of them in the box, "I formed a hopeful prognosis and thought he would soon recover. On the 8th I found him better."

"His condition was still as hopeful?" inquired counsel.

"Yes."

"Did you say to Mrs Maybrick or use any words to the effect that all depended on how long he could hold out?"

"No."

"Did you say that he was sick unto death or any words to that effect?"

"No."

"Had he been in any way delirious since the Sunday?"

"No."

So the Crown could and did legitimately argue that, whatever prompted Mrs Maybrick's dire forebodings, it was not the opinions of her medical advisers.

These, then, were the questions confronting the defence. Why did Mrs Maybrick buy and soak the fly-papers? How did arsenic get into the meat-juice? What was the foundation for the statement in her letter that on 8 May her husband was sick unto death?

Here, in fine and stripped of inessentials, was the case on which the Crown relied to send her to the gallows.

6

In his opening Addison refrained from lengthy comment and contented himself for the most part with a recital of the facts. Occasionally Russell growled out a correction. For the rest, he sat as he always did when not himself in action—stern, glowering, infinitely formidable . . .

The first witness was Michael Maybrick, brother of the deceased, who had arrived from London on the fateful 8 May. In his own words, he was "dissatisfied with the case", and he criticised the treatment that his brother had received. In fact, Michael Maybrick had promptly made up his mind that his brother was being poisoned and that it was Mrs Maybrick who was poisoning him.

One can understand, if not excuse, this precipitate conclusion. Minds, too, can be poisoned, and events had conspired to work on Michael Maybrick's. He had been summoned by a telegram that said "strange things are happening". He had heard about the fly-papers in the cab going out to Aigburth. He had seen the captured letter as he stepped inside the house. Add to all this the shock of his brother's serious illness, and it may well be that his state of mind did not conduce to calm assessment.

Certain it is that he engendered among the nurses grave suspicions that did not exist before.

Russell brought this out in a sharp cross-examination.

"Had you from the first a strong suspicion in the case?"

"I had."

"And you expressed this suspicion openly to Mrs Maybrick and the nurses?"

"Not to the nurses."

"Did you not, sir?" The ring of Russell's voice echoes down the years. "Did you not, sir? Are you not aware that instructions were given to the nurses?"

Michael Maybrick fenced.

"Oh, you mean the hospital nurses."

(There were no others, bar the children's nurse, inquisitive Alice Yapp.)

"I said, the nurses."

"Yes, I was aware that they had been given instructions."

"Instructions which would convey the idea that there was felt, by those interested in the case, considerable suspicion?"

"Yes," admitted Michael Maybrick, "that is so."

Russell was not merely attacking Michael Maybrick. He was undermining in advance the evidence of other witnesses: those who "saw" Mrs Maybrick "tampering" with bottles. It is notorious that people see what they expect to see; primed observers are as dubious as spies.

7

Having thus set the stage Russell got to grips with the fundamental questions. Presently he was driving hard and deep into the prosecution's case.

The second witness was a Dr Hopper; he had not attended Maybrick during his last illness but had treated him on and off for many years. (It was Hopper, incidentally, who had acted as peacemaker between Maybrick and his wife.)

"When did you first attend Mr Maybrick?" Russell asked.

"As far back as 1882."

"Were his complaints always the same?"

"Generally."

"To do with the liver and digestive organs?"

"Yes."

"Was he given to dosing himself?"

"Yes, he was."

"Had he a habit of taking larger doses than were prescribed?"

"Yes."

"Did he know arsenic as a nerve tonic?"

"I believe so."

"Did he tell you that he had taken arsenic when he was in America?"

"I gathered as much from his conversation."

"As early as June 1888 did Mrs Maybrick speak to you about certain habits of her husband's?"

"In June or September."

"What did she say to you?"

"She told me Mr Maybrick was in the habit of taking some very strong medicine which had a bad influence on him, for he always seemed worse after each dose. She wished me to see him about it."

"To remonstrate with him?"

"Yes."

Here was laid down the foundation of a substantive defence which Russell built up, brick by brick, as opportunity arose. Here was a plausible alternative explanation of the presence of arsenic in James Maybrick's body. Here too—though not so instantly apparent—was a plausible explanation of its presence in the meat-juice. (In cross-examination Russell never denied that it *was* Mrs Maybrick who had put arsenic in the meat-juice. This

meant that she herself did not deny it. The question therefore
was: in what circumstances and with what motive was it done?
The defence at a later stage tendered an explanation with which
James Maybrick's habit was intimately linked.)

There was no dramatic set-piece on the first day of the trial, no
outstanding single coup in cross-examination. But as one Crown
witness followed on another, Russell kept extracting valuable
admissions. It was agreed by the chemist who sold the first lot
of fly-papers that he lived near Mrs Maybrick and knew her very
well. It was agreed by the chemist who sold the second lot of
fly-papers that Mrs Maybrick had an account running at his shop.
It was agreed by this same gentleman that arsenic is used in many
cosmetic preparations. It was agreed by Edwin Maybrick, another
of James's brothers, that on 30 April he took Mrs Maybrick to a ball.
(This statement, seemingly so trivial, was to grow in importance as
the case developed.)

When Russell left the court at the end of the first day, he could
look with satisfaction on the progress so far made. He had proved
out of the mouths of prosecution witnesses that suspicion had been
planted and Mrs Maybrick's guilt assumed; that the purchase of the
fly-papers was frank and above board; that arsenic was a common
constituent of cosmetics; and that Maybrick was accustomed to eat
arsenic himself.

An effective defence had started to take shape.

8

The most sensational event in the second day's hearing was Russell's
cross-examination of the nursemaid Alice Yapp.

In one sense, Russell was on very sure ground. Yapp's story as
it stood did her the minimum of credit. She sought to justify her
act in opening the letter by a tale which would strain the belief
of the most credulous. Without colourable excuse she had read
the letter's contents—a mean form of prying that invited strong
contempt. By any standard, her behaviour was despicable. She
may have felt sorry for it by the time Russell had done.

Before coming to the letter, he questioned Yapp about the soaking
of the fly-papers.

"Did the housemaid tell you she had seen them in the
morning?"

"Yes."

"And you went into the room after dinner was over?"

"It was about two hours after when I went into the room."

"Out of curiosity?"

"Yes."

"You had no business in the room?"

"No."

"You found them still there as the housemaid had described them?"

"Yes."

"Where were they?"

"On the wash-stand."

"In the principal bedroom?"

"Yes."

"In the bedroom which is directly approached from the landing?"

"Yes."

"Could you see this wash-stand on entering the door?"

"Yes."

"These fly-papers were reported to you as having been there early in the morning, and you have no reason to suppose that they didn't continue there the whole day until you saw them?"

"No."

So the soaking of the fly-papers was as open as their purchase. No need to stress it further. Having elicited from Yapp one more important fact—that Maybrick had got wet on the day he first took ill—Russell switched to the vulnerable flank.

"Now," he said slowly, "with regard to this letter."

Alice Yapp must have been waiting for this moment; waiting with dread for the impending storm to break. She had doubtless heard a great deal about Charles Russell and his tearing asunder of shufflers and knaves. Not that she, Alice Yapp, was to be bracketed with these, but still . . . a clever lawyer might present her in that light. Small wonder if her heart quailed as she gazed on the spectacle: the judge aloft in scarlet, the rows of enthralled onlookers, the terrifying Russell standing there below.

He lost no time in striking at the heart.

"With regard to this letter. Why did you open it?"

Alice Yapp hesitated.

"Because Mrs Maybrick wished that it should go by that post."

"Why did you open it?"

Alice Yapp had made one nebulous reply. Now she stood tongue-tied and made no reply at all.

The judge intervened.

"Did anything happen to the letter?"

"Yes," said Alice Yapp, "it fell in the dirt."

"Why did you open it?" Russell thundered.

"To put it in a clean envelope."

"Why didn't you put it in a clean envelope without opening it?"

This was a poser. Alice Yapp said nothing.

"Was it a wet day?"

"It was showery."

"Are you sure of that?"

"Yes."

"Will you undertake to say that?" It was like a warning bell. "I ask you to consider. Was it a wet day?"

Again Alice Yapp said nothing.

"Aye or no?"

Silence.

"Was it a wet or a dry day?"

Silence.

"Will you swear that it was showery?"

"I cannot say positively."

It was now apparent that Yapp could not remember and was unwilling to commit herself. And it was equally apparent that if the ground was dry there could not have been much dirt for the letter to be dropped in.

"Let me see the letter," Russell said. He turned it over, examining it closely. "Where was it dropped?"

"By the post-office."

"Then you picked it up?"

"Yes."

"And saw this mark on it, did you?"

"Yes."

"Usher; give the letter to the witness." The envelope, with its pathetic inscription, was passed across the court. "Just take it in your hand. Is the direction clear enough?"

Alice Yapp reflected.

"It was very much dirtier at the time."

"It has not obscured the direction?"

"No."

"You didn't rub the mud off?"

"No."

"What did you do?"

"I went into the post-office and asked for a clean envelope to re-address it. I opened it as I was going in."

"There is no running of the ink?"

"No."

Russell glared at her, his underlip thrust forward.

"Can you suggest how there can be any damp or wet without causing some running of the ink?"

"I cannot."

"On your oath, girl, did you not manufacture that stain as an excuse for opening your mistress's letter?"

"I did not."

"Have you any explanation to offer about the running of the ink?"

"I have not."

Russell sat down and Alice Yapp thankfully vanished from the scene. Her public humiliation was thorough and deserved.

But where exactly did this cross-examination lead? Alice Yapp had been demolished; the letter remained with its detrimental phrases. "He is sick unto death." "All depends on how long his strength can hold out."

Later Russell pleaded that the servants and the nurses, together with certain visiting friends, had formed a gloomier view of Maybrick's illness than the doctors and that Mrs Maybrick was influenced by them. "That letter—take it, read it, scan it as you will—is it the letter of a guilty woman who is planning the murder of her husband?"

Maybe, maybe not. But the letter was the one item in the Crown's evidence that retained its early force unimpaired right till the end.

9

Thus far the trial had proceeded on the footing that there was only one question for the jury to decide: did Mrs Maybrick wilfully administer the quantities of arsenic that caused her husband's death? "There is no reason to doubt," Addison had said, "what the doctors will swear—that Maybrick died by arsenic."

But now Russell was to challenge this assumption. He was to bring into discussion a second vital question: did Maybrick die by arsenic at all?

This new factor was impressively introduced just before the court rose on the second afternoon. The three other servants had followed Alice Yapp, and now Dr Humphreys occupied the box. He was the first Crown witness—there were several more to come—who supported Addison's statement on the cause of Maybrick's death. "He died", said Humphreys, "from arsenical poisoning."

The interrogation by prosecuting counsel had concluded, and Humphreys turned a little to face Russell. It was getting very late. There was only just sufficient time to start the cross-examination—a state of affairs which every advocate dislikes. Too often the choice lies between a premature disclosure of one's hand and the undignified expedient of "playing out time."

Russell did neither. With consummate skill he turned the situation to his favour. Altogether that evening he put about a dozen questions. The last five (and the replies they drew) were these.

"Had you ever before assisted at a post-mortem examination of any persons supposed to have died from arsenical poisoning?"

"No."

"Had you ever before assisted at a post-mortem where it was alleged that death was due to irritant poisoning?"

"No."

"Up to the time that the communication was made to you which suggested that there might be foul play, did it in any way occur to you that there were symptoms present of arsenical poisoning?"

"No."

"When was it that the idea was first suggested to you?"

"On Thursday or Wednesday night."

"By Mr Michael Maybrick?"

"Yes."

The court adjourned in excitement. That last few minutes had achieved a transformation. An astonishing possibility now loomed on the horizon—that the doctors would never have bethought themselves of poisoning if Michael Maybrick hadn't put the idea into their heads.

That night the jurymen had something to think over.

Next day—the third of Mrs Maybrick's trial—Russell resumed his questioning of Humphreys with the satisfying certainty that he held the initiative. The doctor was placed on the defensive from the start and, despite his struggles, beat retreat after retreat.

Over Reinsch's test he had a specially rough passage. This test is designed to detect metallic irritants; a sample of excreta is boiled under specified conditions, and if the irritant is present it should show as a deposit.

Dr Humphreys had carried out this test on Maybrick forty-eight hours before the latter died. There had been no deposit, as he honestly confessed. He tried very hard, but not very successfully, to reconcile this illuminating fact with the theory of poisoning to which he now subscribed.

The exchanges on this matter are worth reporting fully. They show what can happen when a witness seeks to temporise under the guns of a first-class cross-examiner.

"So the test was negative?" said Russell, after Humphreys had described it.

"No," Humphreys said. "Not of necessity."

"Why not?"

Doctor Humphreys made a most ingenuous reply.

"Because the quantity I used was so small, and the time I boiled it so short that there might not have been time for any deposit to take place. Further I am not skilled in the details of testing and my test might have been inefficient."

"That is candid, doctor." No doubt Russell's acknowledgment was genuine but he knew that Humphreys had played into his hands. "That is candid. Then you mean to say that although you tried this experiment, you were not able to conduct it successfully?"

A nasty question for a medical man. But Humphreys resolutely spurned the bait.

"I do not pretend to have any skill in these matters."

"It is not a difficult test?"

"No."

"And if there is arsenic it is supposed to make a deposit?"

"Yes, if it is boiled long enough."

"How long did you boil it?"

"About two minutes."

"What quantity did you take?"

"About an ounce."

"Was this quantity sufficient?"

"Quite sufficient."

"So I should have thought. Did you not at that time think your experiment was properly conducted?"

Humphreys floundered.

"I really couldn't tell."

"Dr Humphreys, you were making the experiment with some object?"

"Yes."

"Were you satisfied at the time that it was properly conducted?"

"At the time I had no books to refer to."

"When you came to refresh your memory from books were you satisfied there was nothing you omitted?"

"Yes." Whichever way he turned the doctor found escape shut off. He made another desperate bid. "I don't know whether the instruments were absolutely pure."

"But see, Dr Humphreys, if they were not pure, would you not get a greater amount of deposit?"

"It depends on what the impurity was."

"What impurity do you suggest may have existed?"

"Arsenic."

"If there was arsenic, would it not make it more certain you would get a deposit?"

"Yes."

"Did you find any?"

"I found none."

After that, Russell moved in to the kill.

"Had it not been for the suggestion of arsenic by Michael Maybrick, were you prepared to give a death certificate if James had died on Wednesday?"

"Yes."

"With what cause of death?"

"Gastro-enteritis."

It was a tremendous, breath-taking admission. The judge wanted to make absolutely sure.

"If nothing about poisoning had been suggested to you, you would have certified that he died of gastro-enteritis?"

"Yes, my lord."

The judge wrote solemnly in his book. There was not much left of Dr Humphreys now, but Russell fired one final telling shot.

"Can you mention any post-mortem symptom which is distinctive of arsenical poisoning and not also distinctive of gastro-enteritis?"
The witness thought.
"No," he said, "I can't give you any."
This triumphant climax shook the whole fabric of the prosecution's case. All that day and half the next they tried to shore it up while Russell tenaciously clung to his advantage. In vain for Dr Carter, who had been called in for consultations, to add *his* opinion that death was due to arsenical poisoning; he had to admit that the symptoms caused by arsenic might equally be caused by impure food. In vain for Dr Stevenson, the Home Office toxicologist, to throw his reputation and prestige into the scale; exceptional experience made him a subtler duellist, but he also gave ground to Russell in the end.
"Will you indicate any one symptom," Russell asked him, "which you say is distinctly an arsenical poisoning symptom and which is not to be found in cases of gastro-enteritis?"
"I would form no opinion from one single symptom."
"What do you mean by that answer? That you cannot point to any distinct symptom of arsenical poisoning differentiating it from gastro-enteritis?"
Dr Stevenson had to face it.
"There is no distinctive diagnostic symptom of arsenical poisoning," he said. "*The diagnostic thing is finding the arsenic.*"
Which, of course, was precisely Russell's point. They found some arsenic, so they called it arsenic poisoning. If they had not found arsenic, they would have called it something else. And Russell had shown how the arsenic might have come there: in a series of self-administered, non-fatal doses, unconnected with the ailment from which Maybrick really died.
There was in fact *no murder at all*; the chronic arsenic eater had met his death from natural causes. That, in a nutshell, was the case for the defence.

10

When the Crown case closed at the end of the fourth morning, the defence held a position of considerable strength. Measures were now taken to render it still stronger. Russell in his turn called three distinguished doctors; each affirmed that the cause of death was gastro-enteritis. A whole series of witnesses, from England and abroad, cast further light on Maybrick's arsenic addiction. One, Sir James Poole, a former Mayor of the city, said that Maybrick once had "blurted out" his taste for poisonous medicines. Sir James had been horrified and given him a lecture. ("The more you take, the more you will require; you will go on till they carry you off.")

The Crown, it should be noted, did not dispute this evidence.

Viewed broadly then, the prisoner's case was powerful and imposing. But two important points remained that needed clearing up.

Still those fly-papers—why had Mrs Maybrick soaked the fly-papers? The ground had been admirably prepared for an answer, but the answer itself had not yet been forthcoming. Still, that meat-juice—what on earth had happened to that meat-juice? Here was a wide gap in the walls of the defence.

These matters still urgently called for explanation, and the fact was that only Mrs Maybrick could explain them. Only she could account for her own conduct. Only she could relate what she had done.

Had Mrs Maybrick's trial been taking place today, as a matter of course she would have gone into the box. But sixty years ago, before the Criminal Evidence Act, no prisoner could testify on his own behalf. By leave, an unsworn statement might be delivered from the dock.

Such statements laboured under heavy handicap. They lacked the sanction which attaches to the oath. They lacked the logical development imposed by guiding questions. They could not be made the subject of cross-examination, but even this rule had a double-edged effect.

Should Mrs Maybrick make such a statement? She herself was willing but on Russell lay the burden of decision. The problem must have exercised him greatly. The risks would be acute, the strain almost intolerable but—how else to close that catastrophic gap . . . ?

As the last of his witnesses departed from the box, Russell turned to his client, sitting in the dock behind him. They spoke briefly in undertones; then Russell faced the judge.

"My lord," he said, "I wish to tell you what has taken place. I asked Mrs Maybrick if it was her wish to make a statement. She said yes. I asked her if it was written. She said no."

11

She stood up in the dock, hands trembling but head erect. It was the worst moment of all. Agony enough to sit silent hour by hour while the crowds in court eyed you and whispered. Worse agony by far to lose the shield of counsel, and yourself speak the words on which the verdict might depend. This was the ordeal of young Mrs Maybrick on the fifth successive day of the trial for her life.

At first she faltered, and the sentences came stumbling. "My lord, I wish to make a statement, as well as I can, to you—a few facts in connection with this dreadfully crushing charge." But her voice soon steadied, she kept her nerves under control and, whatever its faults, her statement was relevant and apt.

She explained first how the fly-papers were bought for a cosmetic. She had lost, she said, an American prescription containing arsenic and, having a slight skin eruption, tried to concoct a substitute. She was particularly concerned to get rid of this eruption before 3 April when she was going to a ball.

There had been numerous signposts to this part of her story. On the subject of the meat-juice she sprang more of a surprise.

Maybrick, she said, had complained of being depressed; he had pointed out a powder which he referred to as harmless and implored Mrs Maybrick to put it in his food. "I was overwrought, terribly anxious, miserably unhappy, and his evident distress entirely unnerved me. I consented. My lord, I had not one true or honest friend in that house; I had no one to consult and no one to advise me."

The statement lasted five torturing minutes—torturing to speaker and to listeners alike. At last it was over and she sank back in her chair.

Russell, pulling his gown about him, gathered himself for his big speech to the jury.

12

Russell was not a rhetorician; no purple patches ornamented his address. It was like the man himself; forceful, incisive, firmly based on fact.

He reminded the jury that there were two distinct questions for them to consider. Was it a death by arsenical poisoning? If they were not satisfied of that, there was an end to the case. If, however, they found that arsenic was indeed the cause of death, was such arsenic administered by the prisoner? If they were not satisfied of that, there was an end to the case also.

Russell then reviewed the medical evidence in detail. He recalled the opinions categorically expressed by the three eminent experts brought by the defence. He recalled the failure by the experts for the Crown to name a single symptom that was not shared in common by arsenical poisoning and gastro-enteritis. He recalled the long history of Maybrick's dyspepsia and the equally long history of his arsenic addiction. He recalled, in this context, the results of the analysis which disclosed only a small amount of arsenic in the corpse. He wound up this part of his speech, with a powerful plea deriving from long acquaintance with the psychology of juries.

"It would only be natural," Russell said, "that the thought should arise in your minds: if not arsenical poisoning, we should like to have some suggestion what it was. Now I am not called upon to advance any theory. Counsel representing the prisoner is entitled to stand upon a defence and to say 'You have not proved the case which you alleged.' But passing that by, is there no reasonable hypothesis? Is it improbable that a man who had been dosing himself, admittedly taking poisonous medicines—is it remarkable that this man's constitution had suffered so that he should always be complaining of derangement of the stomach? Is it or is it not reasonable to say that a man who had been pursuing such a course would have his constitution liable to attack from causes which in a healthy man would be of no effect?" And thus to the submission: "There is no safe resting-place on which you can justify to yourselves a finding that this was a death of arsenical poisoning."

This had become the strongest plank in the defence—so strong indeed that it would not have been surprising if the jury had acquitted without hearing any more. Russell himself seems to have half expected this. "I must ask you," he had said, "*even at the outset* whether it is possible for you to find the prisoner guilty." That was a broad hint that they could stop it if they wished.

But the jury did not stop it, and Russell, rightly declining any vestige of a gamble, went on to discuss the second question he had posed.

Had Mrs Maybrick administered arsenic (barring always the isolated instance of the meat-juice)? He summarized his previous points and added a few fresh ones. Mrs Maybrick, he emphasised, knew she was a suspect from 8 May. The searching of the house, with its abundant haul of arsenic, did not take place until the 11th or the 12th. Why, if she was guilty, did not Mrs Maybrick cover up the traces of her crime? "If a woman had the nerve and fibre to plan such a murder, cold and deliberate, would she have not also had the instinct of self-preservation?" Neatly, he made the large amount of arsenic found seem to operate in Mrs Maybrick's favour. "If, as is clear, there was in that house a quantity of poison capable of being fatally applied; if there was one packet of arsenic with which admittedly fly-papers had nothing to do; if there was a bottle in which grains of arsenic were found with which admittedly fly-papers had nothing to do; I ask why, with these means at her command, should she have resorted to the clumsy, the stupid contrivance of trying to steep fly-papers in water?"

There was no peroration in the accepted sense; no rolling periods, no high-flown similes. But who could fail to be impressed by the awful gravity with which he summoned the jurors to the climax of their task? "You are in number large enough to prevent the individual views and prejudices and prepossessions of one from affecting all, but in numbers small enough to preserve to each one of you the undivided sense of individual responsibility. The verdict is to be the verdict of each one of you and the verdict of you all. I make no appeal for mercy; let that be clearly understood. You are administering a law which is merciful; you are administering a law which forbids you to pronounce a verdict of guilty unless all reasonable hypotheses of innocence have been excluded. I end as I began by asking you, in the perplexities, in the doubts, in the difficulties which surround this case, can you with safe conscience say that this woman is guilty? If your duty compels you to do it you will do it, you must do it; but you will not, you must not, unless the whole burden and facts and weight of the case drive you irresistibly to that conclusion."

13

Addison's reply was vigorous and barbed. His assertions about Maybrick seemed to verge on the extravagant: he was not an arsenic-eater; he was a healthy, careful man; in April he was sick for the first time in his life. Addison bitterly criticised Mrs Maybrick's statement—"carefully thought out and ably delivered." He made a shrewd thrust at the suggestion that Maybrick took arsenic shortly before his death; "he, who knew medicines so well and was so fond of talking about them, never suggested to a soul that the symptoms might be due to that." Without mercy he dissected the famous note to Brierley: "I protest against the notion of any tenderness for a husband in a woman who wrote that letter." And finally: "If she be guilty, we have brought to light a very terrible deed of darkness, and proved a murder founded upon profligacy and adultery, and carried out with a hypocrisy and cunning which have been rarely equalled in the annals of crime."

It was the evening of the fifth day and the court rose. Next morning the judge began his long, painstaking, intermittently intelligible summing-up.

14

A word about the judge into whose hands the directing reins now passed.

Mr Justice Fitzjames Stephen was a man of high attainments. Littérateur of taste, essayist of note, close friend of Froude and of Carlyle, he embraced and enjoyed a wider range of interests than is customary among members of the legal profession. As a judge, he adhered to broad principles and disliked mere technicalities; his mind, hard and clear rather than subtle, was adept in the marshalling of facts. He was scrupulously fair, conscientiously humane, and a recognised authority on the rules of criminal evidence. Few men would have been better fitted to try the Maybrick case than Mr Justice Stephen in his prime.

But it is the undeniable and tragic fact that by the late summer of 1889 this able and distinguished mind was on the wane.

Four years earlier Stephen had had a stroke which caused him temporarily to give up work. Soon after he resumed a slow decline set in; gradually, over a period of years, his mental powers diminished: At last, prompted by reports of public uneasiness, the anxious judge consulted his physician. An insidious disease was diagnosed, and he instantly resigned.

How long this disease had flourished undetected cannot be asserted with precision, but everything suggests it was already stirring at the time of the Maybrick trial, twenty months before. The summing-up, so thorough in conception—it took the best part of two days to deliver—was in execution rambling and blurred. From first to last the judge seemed all at sea. He told the jury that the fly-papers had been purchased in March and was somewhat testy when corrected. He attributed the opinions of one doctor to another. He read out a letter which had not been put in evidence. He said things which were dangerously misleading ("If you can show a sufficient quantity of arsenic to cause death, why then, you need go no further"). He said things which were highly prejudicial in effect ("On that day began the symptoms of *what may be called the fatal dose*"). He said things which were free from any meaning whatsoever ("You are apt to assume a connection between the thing which is a proof in the result at which you are to arrive—because it is put before you—and in that way you may be led to do a greater or less degree of injustice according to the state of the case").

The complaint that lies against the judge is not one of undue bias. He did his best, no doubt, to hold the balance. His shortcoming was this: that he failed to clarify the issues, to state accurately the facts, and to group the evidence in appropriate perspective. Thus, at the end of a momentous and complicated case, the jury received no adequate direction.

Whether this particular jury would have profited by such is an entirely different matter.

15

At twenty past three on the seventh afternoon, the jury retired to deliberate in private.

If they had made up their minds in favour of acquittal, it might be assumed that they would not be absent long. If not, the field of discussion was so vast and the matters to be weighed so debatable and intricate, that an interval of hours could occasion no surprise.

They were back at five to four. Ten minutes later their verdict had been given and Mrs Maybrick had been sentenced to be hanged.

16

Whatever the immediate Liverpool reaction, the country as a whole was deeply shocked by this result. *The Times* condemned it editorially; leading lawyers and doctors set on record their disquiet; meetings were held to voice protest and dissent; petitions for reprieve were signed by tens of thousands. Nor were official circles lacking in activity. The Home Secretary, Henry Matthews, held a series of long conferences: with the judge, with the Lord Chancellor, with certain witnesses, with the judge again, with the judge and Mr Addison. These indications of misgiving in high places corresponded with the raging tide of public disapproval.

Meanwhile the days slipped by and the condemned woman lay in Walton Gaol, where the tedium of solitary confinement was relieved by the hammering of the workmen setting up her scaffold.

On 22 August, with only one more Sunday between her and the rope, Mrs Maybrick was reprieved. The death sentence was rescinded and replaced by one of penal servitude for life.

At that time reprieves were not come by two a penny, nor was there much squeamishness at the thought of hanging women. Mrs Maybrick's neck was saved for the most logical of reasons: because the case against her fell short of legal proof. "Although," said the Home Secretary, "the evidence leads clearly to the conclusion that the prisoner administered, and attempted to administer, arsenic to her husband with intent to murder, yet it does not wholly exclude a reasonable doubt whether his death was in fact caused by the administration of arsenic."

If there was "reasonable doubt", she was not guilty of murder. That was the only indictment upon which she had been tried. The life sentence was administratively imposed for an attempt to murder with which she had not been charged.

Russell, first as counsel, then as head of the judiciary, never ceased to press for Mrs Maybrick's release. He met with no success. He himself died in 1900; Mrs Maybrick was not freed till 1904. She had lost her youth, her spirit, and fifteen years out of her life.

17

Did Mrs Maybrick do it? That is not the problem. Was her guilt proved? Unquestionably no.

In later years a verdict so perverse would have been quashed by the Court of Criminal Appeal. In 1889 that Court did not exist. All that could be done was done, but this was not enough, and the verdict of that jury unhappily remains to mock at and discredit the fair name of British justice.

On her release in 1904, Mrs Maybrick returned to her native America and disappeared. In 1923 she was discovered living in a tiny shack in the Berkshire foothills of Connecticut, a small, bent woman calling herself Mrs Florence Chandler (her maiden name). Neighbours who accidentally discovered her identity were sworn to secrecy. She was said to have returned to Liverpool in 1927 and to have attended that year's Grand National steeplechase. In October 1941, she was found dead in her shack, amid several hungry cats nosing at empty milk saucers. Mrs Maybrick was seventy-nine years old.

THE MYSTERY OF THE POISONED PARTRIDGES

(Hubert Chevis, 1931)

C. J. S. Thompson

Who murdered young Lieutenant Hubert Chevis, and why? The case is as impenetrable now as it was in 1931. It is also one of the most sinister, since the murderer not only rejoiced at the agonizing death of Chevis but took equal delight in cruelly taunting his grieving family with exclamations of "Hooray!" The identity of the person behind the nom de meurtre J. Hartigan remains as bafflingly obscure as the motive for the murder. Charles J(ohn) S(amuel) Thompson was the author of two books of poisoning cases in the 1930s.

How did a brace of partridges which had been cooked and served for dinner become impregnated with strychnine was a problem that was presented to a coroner's jury during the inquiry into a remarkable poisoning case at Blackdown Camp near Aldershot?

In June 1931, Lieutenant Chevis, a young artillery officer, was occupying a bungalow at the camp where he was engaged on his military duties.

He was very popular in his regiment and was happily married;

his wife having a flat in London, she often joined him with their two children at the bungalow at Blackdown.

On Saturday, 21 June 1931, a brace of partridges was ordered from a poulterer at Aldershot and they were delivered at the bungalow in a van. They were placed by the cook in an open meat-safe kept outside the building, and there they remained until they were required for dinner in the evening.

Late in the afternoon some friends called to see Lieutenant Chevis and his wife, and after having cocktails they remained chatting for some time.

After they had left, Lieutenant and Mrs Chevis sat down to dine early, as they intended to go to the Military Tattoo which was taking place that night.

The dinner was brought in by the batman, who placed the roasted partridges before Mrs Chevis who was seated at the table, and she proceeded to serve them. Lieutenant Chevis took one mouthful and exclaimed: "It tastes horrible!" and he refused to eat any more. He asked his wife to taste the bird to see if she found anything wrong with it. She just touched it with her tongue and said it tasted "fusty" and could not get the taste out of her mouth for a long time afterwards.

Lieutenant Chevis then ordered the batman to take the birds away and have them destroyed. Fifteen minutes later he was taken violently ill. He lost the use of his legs and terrible convulsions followed. A doctor was sent for and the lieutenant was at once removed to hospital, where he died in great agony early on the following Sunday morning.

Mrs Chevis was also taken ill shortly after the meal and was seized with severe pains. She was medically treated and eventually recovered.

The Coroner was notified and inquiries were at once set on foot by the police.

A further element of mystery was introduced into the case when it was learnt that a telegram had been received by Sir William Chevis, the father of the deceased man, on the day of his son's funeral. It had been handed in at Dublin and contained the words: "Hooray. Hooray. Hooray." On inquiry it was found that the form was signed on the back with the name "Hartigan" and the address of a well-known Dublin hotel. It further transpired that no one of that name was known at the hotel, nor had any person called "Hartigan" been staying there.

Another strange fact connected with the telegram was, it had been sent off before any announcement of the tragedy at Blackdown Camp had appeared in the Press. The matter was taken up by the police of the Irish Free State who, it was stated, had found that a man answering the description of the person who had handed in the telegram in Dublin had purchased strychnine from a local chemist.

The inquest on the body of Lieutenant Chevis was opened on 23 June, but was adjourned until 21 July for the analyst's report. On 11 August it was resumed before a crowded Court by the deputy coroner for West Surrey.

In opening the proceedings he remarked that the evidence would clearly indicate the partridge as the means by which the poison had been conveyed. It was, however, a most unfortunate thing that both the partridges had been destroyed, especially the one served to Lieutenant Chevis, by his orders.

On the day of his funeral a telegram had been received at the house of his father, Sir William Chevis, who lived at Bournemouth, which contained the words: "Hooray. Hooray. Hooray." It was not signed, but on the original form being obtained for inspection there was found on the back a signature and address which read: "J. Hartigan. Hibernia." Although inquiries had been made by the Dublin police and every possible effort made, no trace could be found of the sender of the telegram, nor could his identity be established.

A photograph of the original telegram was published in the *Daily Sketch*, and on 2 August, a postcard was received addressed to "The Editor", purporting to have been written in London on 1 August. It read:

Dear Sir,
    Why do you publish the picture of the Hooray telegram.
                    J. HARTIGAN

This was followed by a further postcard addressed to Sir William Chevis and posted in Belfast on 4 August. It read:

It is a mystery they will never solve.
                    J. HARTIGAN   Hooray.

"To add to the mystery," the coroner continued, "the contents of the telegram were known to me before the last hearing, but it was deemed inadvisable to reproduce it at the last adjourned hearing. Although we thought this was assured, the telegram was published without consulting me or my officer.

"The great handicap in this case is that the bird was destroyed. Had that not been done the case was a simple one."

Captain Chevis, brother of the deceased officer, was then called, and said that the "Hooray" telegram arrived at five p.m. on 24 June, the day of his brother's funeral.

He did not know anyone in Dublin likely to send a telegram of the kind or anyone answering to the description which the telegraph clerk gave of the sender. His brother had never been in Ireland in his life.

Mrs Chevis in her evidence said she had given all possible information in connection with the inquiry. There were no telegrams belonging to her husband which might throw any light on the case.

Describing what took place at dinner on the evening of the tragedy, she said that her husband had two glasses of sherry after tasting the partridge, which he got for himself. Bulger, the batman, would have removed the dirty glasses and the cook would have washed them. She did not move them. The partridge she had on her plate tasted "fusty", but there was no bitter, sharp or offensive taste. Both the partridges were cooked together in a tin and they were basted in the same fat.

She only took one mouthful and it was vaguely unsavoury. She was absolutely sure that her husband told Bulger to burn the partridge. He was very anxious that the dog should not get it. She knew no one of the name of Hartigan and no one in the household knew anyone of that name. Lieutenant Chevis, as far as she knew, had no friends or relatives called Hartigan.

Dr J.H. Ryffel, analyst to the Home Office, was then called and described the results of his examination of the contents of the stomach of the deceased man and of other articles removed from the bungalow. The latter included sink-water from the drains of the bungalow, a basin containing dripping, a vegetable dish containing peas and potatoes, an empty tin, a packet of gravy mixture, some anchovy sauce, a bag of flour and a tin of carbolic. He also examined some material from Mrs Chevis after she had been taken ill. This and similar material from Lieutenant Chevis were mixed together and gave a yield of strychnine corresponding to a total in the amount received of .3 of a grain. The material from Lieutenant Chevis contained a large amount of strychnine. He also found a small amount of strychnine in the dripping and more in the gravy, which was very bitter. There was no strychnine in the water or other materials.

"I concluded," continued Dr Ryffel, "that the total quantity of strychnine associated with the partridges amounted to at least two grains. This is an extremely rough calculation and would depend on what other materials were employed. The total quantity would depend on the proportion of the bird eaten, which I understand was very small."

In his view if only a small proportion of the bird had been eaten the quantity in the bird was very considerable.

The minimum fatal dose of strychnine was half a grain.

Dr Ryffel added that he had received three partridges taken from the cold stores of the company who sold the partridges to Lieutenant Chevis, but none of them contained strychnine.

The coroner asked the witness: "Supposing this bird had picked up strychnine when alive, could it have been absorbed sufficient to show the amount eaten by Lieutenant and Mrs Chevis?"

"I do not think so," replied Dr Ryffel. "The only thing would seem to me that if a partridge had taken a large amount of strychnine material in its crop, after it was in cold storage the amount might have diffused into the bird." He understood, however, that the crop was cleaned at the shop before the birds were sent out and would not be included in the cooking. He did not think the bird could have absorbed the amount of strychnine into its own substance because it would be dead long before. On the other hand, if strychnine was injected into the substance of the bird it would stay there and stay during the cooking. But this is not strychnine taken by the bird in life. It is strychnine inserted into it afterwards.

"Strychnine itself is very insoluble, but it would be slightly soluble in fat, and two birds basted in the same fat would certainly give a proportion of strychnine on the second bird after cooking."

In answer to further questions, Dr Ryffel said: "Strychnine has to be absorbed from the intestines and when it is taken, as in this case, with a large amount of fat, the absorption is much slower than if taken by itself. The fact that Mrs Chevis's symptoms did not come on till later would point to her having less and to the fact that she did not pass her food on as rapidly as her husband. Strychnine could be fatal within two hours, but in the case of Lieutenant Chevis it was fourteen hours, because he was kept alive by artificial respiration and he ultimately died of failure of respiration."

A police-inspector of Camberley said he searched the bungalow and found nothing in writing connected with the case. He had searched the Poison Registers of chemists in Frimley, Farnborough, Bagshot and Camberley, but found no evidence of any sales of strychnine.

A brother-officer in the Royal Artillery stated that Lieutenant Chevis was very popular and as far as he knew he had no enemies. He saw Lieutenant and Mrs Chevis on the day of the fatal meal and they both appeared in perfect health and quite happy.

Nicholas Bulger, batman to Lieutenant Chevis, said he did not serve any drinks at dinner that night. Mrs Chevis served the partridges and he handed the vegetables. He came from the south of Ireland, but he did not know anyone of the name of Hartigan. He removed the bird and took it into the kitchen and gave it to the cook. Mrs Chevis told him to destroy it; not to burn it. When he took it to the cook, he said: "This is to be destroyed," but she put it on the fire.

Mrs Yeoman, the cook, said that the safe in which the partridges had been kept was outside the bungalow and had no lock. She noticed nothing unusual about the birds. She had no friends in Ireland and did not know anyone of the name of Hartigan.

The manager of the firm who sold the partridges said they came from Manchuria. They had sold Manchurian birds for years and never had any complaints. They were delivered to the bungalow in a covered van which was kept locked.

The Coroner then summed up and said there was no doubt that Lieutenant Chevis died from asphyxia following the poison cased by eating the partridge. There was no evidence to show how the strychnine came to be in the birds. He had sifted all the evidence and could find nothing to lead him to any conclusion as to whether this was a case of accidental death, a foul murder, or whether it was a case of negligent dealing with things served up to eat as amounted to manslaughter.

The proper verdict was asphyxia following strychnine poisoning caused by eating partridge, with insufficient evidence to show how the strychnine came to be in or on the partridge. The jury, after a consultation of five minutes, returned with an open verdict.

What is the solution of the mystery involved in this extraordinary case? Misadventure may be ruled out, as even if the partridges had picked up strychnine in Manchuria, it could not have been absorbed into the flesh of the birds. It is also most unlikely that a poison such as strychnine could have got into the partridges by accident. It must, therefore, be concluded that the strychnine must have been deliberately introduced into the birds by some person with the object of killing both Lieutenant Chevis and his wife.

The Home Office expert in his evidence said he concluded that a considerable quantity of strychnine must have been present in the birds, and as the flesh was so strongly impregnated with the poison it would appear as if a solution had been injected.

Strychnine hydrochloride occurs in small white crystals, the maximum dose being one eighth of a grain. It is only soluble in about forty parts of water, but it dissolves in about eighty parts of alcohol. Its taste is characteristic and extremely bitter. Sprinkled on the back of a bird, even in the form of a powder, it would not be absorbed into the flesh. It is a drug so readily recognizable from the taste that even an enemy would hesitate before using it to murder an unsuspecting person.

An obvious question arises; does a clue lurk in the cruel telegram sent from Dublin to the father of Lieutenant Chevis? How did the sender of that message know of the tragedy before it was published in the Press? There could have only been one object in sending it, and that was to express the sender's delight that the murderer had succeeded in his purpose.

No motive can be assigned for the perpetration of the crime, but the fact that the brutal telegram was addressed to the victim's father shows that the sender knew the anguish it would cause.

Taking all the circumstances known into consideration, one is led to the conclusion that the murder was the work of a homicidal maniac who had a fancied grievance against the family.

Armed with a hypodermic syringe charged with a solution of strychnine, which could be made from the tablets sold for that purpose, he would watch for his opportunity. The meat-safe was open to anyone outside the bungalow, and it would be but the work of a moment to inject the contents of the syringe into the birds and to slip away without being seen. The strychnine would thus be absorbed into the flesh of the birds and the cooking afterwards would assist it.

That murder was intended there can be no doubt. Whoever

the unknown miscreant may have been, he was never traced in spite of all the efforts of the police, and the mystery of the murder of the unfortunate young officer remains a mystery still.

THE OBSESSION WITH THE BLACK DAHLIA

(Elizabeth Short, 1947)

Russell Miller

In January 1947, the brutal murder of Elizabeth Short shocked America. Her naked body was found on a piece of waste land in Los Angeles. It had been cut completely in half, and was bruised and beaten. Elizabeth Short was an aspiring actress of twenty-two who'd drifted for several years, taking odd jobs and conducting brief affairs with a string of men. She'd also reportedly had liaisons with women, including (so it was said) Marilyn Monroe. The Black Dahlia tag derived from Elizabeth Short's black hair and clothing. When the story of the murder broke, several men and women confessed to the crime, but the police failed to validate anyone's story. The case, notoriously, attracted several false confessions. Although one woman has written a book naming her own father as the killer, the Los Angeles Police Department continue to list the case as unsolved. The mystery of the Black Dahlia seems still to weave a sort of magic for modern murder-fanciers, and the case has its own thriving website on the internet. This study of how the killing continues to fascinate was first posted there by American writer Russell Miller (b. 1969). In 1947, Miller's family owned the ranch where the alleged Roswell Incident UFO crash took place. His published work includes articles on racist cartoons, the JFK assassination and man-made UFOs.

"Another factor complicating the case was the obsession developed by men with the Black Dahlia in death—as many as had been obsessed with her in life."

—Finis Brown, LAPD.

On a typically mild winter evening right before New Year 1996, I stood at the corner of 39th and Norton near the Crenshaw area of Los Angeles. Clean-looking, middle-class houses stood shoulder to shoulder in a nondescript neighbourhood within eyeshot of the famous HOLLYWOOD sign to the north. Despite the fact that Watts and Compton weren't too far away to the south-east, it seemed pleasant enough. Not a bad neighbourhood if you *have* to live in L.A.

Standing at the corner of 39th and Norton is not unlike standing next to the ground zero monument at Trinity Site in my home state of New Mexico; the area looks so normal, you'd never guess what kind of insane goings-on went down on the same spot fifty years previously.

On 15 January 1947, in what was then a lot to the south-west of the intersection, the body of a young woman was discovered. Her nude, mutilated body was severed in half at the waist. Both halves of her body had been drained of blood.

By the following morning, the LAPD learned that she was twenty-two year-old Elizabeth Short, who had come to Hollywood from Massachusetts to be a star. As a joking nod to the Alan Ladd and Veronica Lake movie *The Blue Dahlia*, and because her hair and clothes were always jet black, she was known to some acquaintances in L.A. as "The Black Dahlia".

Despite the fact that the murder rocked the city like an 8.0 earthquake, and despite the fact that for months afterwards the police and Press battled bitterly to solve the crime, not a shred of evidence surfaced which pointed to anyone who might have been involved with the murder. It remains officially unsolved to this day.

I knew all of that. Years before, I read Kenneth Anger's *Hollywood Babylon II* and came away with the same story as everyone else: Elizabeth Short was a floozy prostitute who slept with every guy she met, finally angering one who butchered her in a fit of jealous rage. It was a case of unbelievable overkill, and all the more intriguing that the perpetrator of something so unspeakably horrible escaped so easily.

But then two years ago I picked up, by chance, a book by famed writer John Gilmore called *Severed—The True Story of the Black Dahlia Murder* (the book is being reissued by Amok Books in 1998). In it, Gilmore—who researched the Dahlia case on and off for some thirty years—dropped several bombs, probably the biggest being that the LAPD had, years after the murder, found the man responsible for killing the Black Dahlia.

For weeks after I finished the book, I was, for lack of a better word, haunted. The Black Dahlia wouldn't leave my head. And after a time it became a quest to figure out why.

I did my homework before I went back to L.A. in July of 1996 to do a Black Dahlia tour. From a Black Dahlia Website I found a bunch of articles, and discovered that there were thousands of others out there like me. More obsessed individuals making pilgrimages to 39th and Norton. Strange stuff—here we are, fifty years later, and the Black Dahlia refuses to fade away. In the summer of 1991 a crackpot, fifty-four-year-old woman in Southern California went to the police claiming it was her father who killed Elizabeth Short in 1947, and buried the evidence at her former home. A few years ago, James Ellroy's "Novel based upon Hollywood's most notorious murder case", *The Black Dahlia*, was published, even though it had barely anything to do with the case. Freaks with Black Dahlia tattoos walk the streets of America. Goatee-sporting, cappucino-sipping, wanna-be-arty gothic-types sit in coffee houses rambling on about Elizabeth Short, practically deifying the girl; in 1947, Elizabeth Short was just a confused chick who ran with a bad crowd. By 1997, she was a legend, an archetype of sorts—the most spectacular unsolved murder America has to offer.

My tour began where all Black Dahlia tours *must* begin—39th and Norton. Even though the intersection is ground zero for Black Dahlia buffs, there's nothing there in 1997 that recalls the Los Angeles of 1947. L.A. is the Rome of the western US; its layers deep in history. The excitement and glamour of Golden-Age Hollywood is now buried under tons of garbage and endless miles of clogged freeways. Likewise, the infamous lot where Elizabeth Short achieved worldwide fame is buried under dozens of houses.

I tried to picture the intersection on 15 January 1947. Vacant lot overgrown with weeds, punctuated by the nude body of a girl cut in half. The crime scene itself is impossible to ignore; for a single image which starkly and brutally sums up the state of affairs between men and women on this planet, look no further than any picture of Elizabeth Short at 39th and Norton. Her murder is a sobering reminder that no matter how far feminists think they've come, you can't fight tens of thousands of years of evolution. The brutal men of the world have always dominated the Elizabeth Shorts of the world.

I aimed my rental east down Martin Luther King and headed towards 31st and Trinity, where the house in which Elizabeth Short was murdered *used* to be.

Why do people who have even an accidental brush with the Black Dahlia's story wind up as fanatics? Different people offer different reasons. For some, the story is a link to an older, seedier, *noir*-like Los Angeles. To others, Elizabeth Short is the prime symbol for any number of social ills, ranging from the irresponsible Press to the irresponsible police.

Part of my homework was talking to John Gilmore, who, as it happened, also lived in New Mexico.

For Gilmore, who has written books about Manson (*The Garbage People*), Tucson's Charles Schmid (*Cold Blooded*), and James Dean (the newly released *Live Fast, Die Young—Remembering the Short Life of James Dean*), it's the body itself which laid the groundwork for endless generations of Black Dahlia zealots. "It's like this tremendous, bizarre magnet," he told me. "It gets to our unconsciousness, and it gets to us on a real subliminal level . . . So much hidden agenda went into that murder that it was inherent at the *scene* of the murder."

I wasn't going to argue with that—Gilmore is, after all, the world's number one Black Dahlia expert. As a child, he actually met Elizabeth Short—albeit briefly—at his grandmother's boarding house. In the early sixties, he hooked up with actor Tom Neal, who wanted to make a movie about the Black Dahlia. Neal assigned Gilmore the task of speaking with potential financiers, one of whom was a "weird, weird guy" in Barstow who wanted to touch Gilmore's hands, because they had touched the field where the body had lain. (A great bit on all of that appears in Gilmore's latest book, *Laid Bare*, which chronicles his relationships with, among many others, James Dean, Lenny Bruce, Janis Joplin, and Ed Wood, Jr).

A bit of a monkeywrench was thrown into the plan when Neal went to jail after murdering his wife in Palm Springs. Although it was no longer his intention to make it into a movie, Gilmore continued to research the Black Dahlia case for years after that ("I suppose

over the years I've had all the major Black Dahlia crackpots . . ."),
eventually hooking up with retired LAPD detective Finis Brown,
who, having personally worked on the Dahlia case, was a treasure
trove of information.

And Gilmore was right; that body does hit you—and *hard*—on
an unconscious level. But it wasn't the main reason I was having
difficulty ridding my brain of the Black Dahlia. There was more
to it than that.

Take the second biggest bomb dropped in his book. Gilmore
had access to the previously sealed Elizabeth Short autopsy report,
which revealed that because her genitals were not fully developed,
Elizabeth Short was incapable of having sex. (A startling release
generated for the *Severed* book focused exclusively on this point:
"STRANGE BLACK DAHLIA MURDER VICTIM WAS NOT A BEAUTIFUL
FEMME FATALE, BUT WAS A MAN". Well no, she wasn't *really* a
man, but she wasn't a whore either.)

Discovering that Elizabeth Short not only wasn't a prostitute, but
couldn't have been a prostitute, throws the story under an entirely
different light. So much for the countless Call-Girl-of-the-Night
stories. So much for James Ellroy's fantasy view to the facts.

If a beautiful girl who apparently bounced from guy to guy *wasn't*
sleeping with any of them, then what was going on? ". . . She knew
that she couldn't ever possibly become a full-blown woman in any
size, shape, or form," Gilmore told me between sips of coffee. "And
she decided she was going to do the role anyway. Because she did.
It was just a series of games, a series of encounters with people
that would lead to the romance-type situation, and then she would
disappear. I think she overlapped relationships, so she always had
a place to go, and a place to be transported to."

So the Black Dahlia herself had a secret so dark that she had to keep
it from the male acquaintances in her life. Probably the female ones,
too. Actually, plenty of folks think it's Short's past—not her murder—which is at the heart of the case. The autopsy certainly brought
an insane new twist to a story already replete with insane twists, but
there was still something else that I couldn't put my finger on.

I turned left onto San Pedro and then left again a couple of
blocks later onto 31st. It's amazing how quickly the landscape
changes in L.A. Only minutes away from the more-or-less cozy
atmosphere at 39th and Norton, the scenery becomes aesthetically
destitute at 31st and Trinity. A few badasses in tanktops glared at
me from a garage.

Unlike the Angelinos at 39th and Norton who are tired of countless morbid tourists snapping pictures of their houses, the blokes at 31st and Trinity are oblivious to their area's role in the Black Dahlia case. Although the house in question was torn down over thirty-five years ago, it was here, as Gilmore discovered through his research, that Elizabeth Short was actually murdered.

And so it's here that Jack Anderson Wilson, aka Arnold Smith, enters the picture.

The biggest question mark in the Black Dahlia murder has always been, obviously, the identity of the murderer himself. Many, like Sherry Mazingo (USC's associate professor of journalism), would argue that the case's endless momentum and *noir* mood was built around the fact that Elizabeth Short's murderer was never found. As Mazingo once wrongfully observed: ". . . Should the (Black Dahlia) murder have been solved, it would take some of the dramatic sheen off this beautifully dramatic story."

I couldn't disagree more. You do have to understand. Elizabeth Short's story to understand the Black Dahlia phenomenon, but it is Smith's place in the action which I find most engrossing. And, if anything, the drama only intensifies with Smith's arrival. Uncovering him gives the Black Dahlia story a beginning, a middle, and for the first time, an ending. It's a stunning ending, too. The kind that would be criticized by a Lit. professor as an easy way out.

Elizabeth Short is *Severed*'s dark woman of the night, but Smith—a thin alcoholic who stood around six foot four, walked with a limp, and had a five-page rap sheet and a dozen different aliases—is the mysterious shadow who lurks throughout the book, whom police could never quite pinpoint.

As the LAPD worked feverishly to solve the Black Dahlia murder, Smith's presence was felt here and there, fleetingly, but never long enough to come into focus. While Elizabeth Short was still alive, rich L.A. socialite Georgette Bauerdorf (an acquaintance of Short's) was murdered and left in her bathtub; police investigated all leads except one. A man who Bauerdorf had dated—a tall man who walked with a limp—couldn't be found.

Bauerdorf's murderer fled in her car, which was abandoned near 25th and San Pedro, right around the corner from 31st and Trinity. A week after the murder, *Herald Express* newspaper reporter Aggie Underwood received a tip that a tall, thin man walking with a limp was seen walking away from 25th and San Pedro.

Many, many years later (in late 1981), Arnold Smith emerged

as a suspect in the Black Dahlia case only because he related the story to an informant (that's how it reads in the book; incredibly, Gilmore himself is the one who brought Smith to the LAPD's attention), who in turn gave him money to stay loaded. However, Smith explained that *he* wasn't responsible for the murder. An acquaintance of his—one Al Morrison (extensive investigations by the LAPD didn't turn up any proof that Morrison ever existed)—murdered Short in a house on East 31st near Trinity, and later related the events to Smith.

After Gilmore took taped interviews of him to the LAPD, Smith—who until that point was always available for a drink—became "cagy" and impossible to track down. However, the LAPD and Detective Badge Number One, John St John, were hot to nail him. St John was sure that Al Morrison was just a "smoke screen" to keep the police off the trail of the real murderer—Smith himself. On the tapes Gilmore provided, Smith related details about the murder that only the murderer could have known; details that the hordes of confessed Black Dahlia murderers who had been turning themselves in over the years knew nothing about.

The LAPD felt sure they had their man. Now they had to catch him. With much difficulty, a meeting was finally arranged with Smith.

In the case's most astonishing twist, Smith nodded off while smoking only days before the meeting, and died in a fire in his tiny room in the Holland Hotel near downtown L.A. Carelessness, or suicide? Hard to say.

So the enigmatic spectre who was probably responsible for the enigmatic Black Dahlia's murder—and at least one other—reared his head years after the murder and then was suddenly gone. And it wasn't, as so many had assumed, a jealous doctor, a physician with the skill to cut Elizabeth Short surgically into two. It was just a drunken loser, one of countless zeros wandering around Los Angeles.

After his death, police learned that when he was younger, Smith had lived for a time with his mother near—surprise, surprise—31st and San Pedro. The whole area is Mr Smith's Neighbourhood.

Unanswered questions. Dark, impenetrenable shadows hiding crucial pieces of the puzzle. "I'm not going to say I solved the murder," Gilmore told me. "It's absurd. My research carried me to a certain point. *This* was the guy St John wanted to nail, so I handed everything over to the LAPD. But I'll never stand up and say, 'I solved the Black Dahlia murder!' No one can ever *solve* the Black Dahlia murder."

Despite Gilmore's disclaimer, the thin man who walked with a limp has become a permanent part of the Dahlia tapestry, and cannot be ignored. Arnold Smith is the biggest mystery in a story whose edges and borders are forever blurred by personal agendas (Smith's prints were lifted from Georgette Bauerdorf's apartment, but William Randolph Hearst—a friend to the Bauerdorfs—shut the investigation down, wanting to keep the Bauerdorfs and himself out of unflattering news) and shoddy police work (innocent suspect Leslie Dillon was grilled mercilessly by an incompetent LAPD "psychiatrist" and returned the favour by filing a $100,000 damage claim against the city), but there are many more myths and mysteries that distort the Black Dahlia case to this day. Most writers continue to report that the letters "BD" were carved into her thigh, that there were cigarette burns all over her body, and that her hair had been shampooed. Non-facts made up by hack writers through the years. Yet, they cause the haze that surrounds the case to grow thicker and more intriguing. It's as if the case's inertia attracts these myths like a magnet as it rolls on through time.

(The haze thickens considerably with a story Gilmore told me—that he's never written about—whereby he travelled to Indianapolis many years ago on a wild goose chase to find the apocryphal Al Morrison, actually found the man in a rough-nik bar, and then lost the nerve to talk to him. "This guy didn't look like a female impersonator to me," Gilmore explained after my jaw dropped open. "I asked the bartender, and he pointed to this guy—'That's Al Morrison'. I had a drink, but I didn't talk to him. I admit, it's one of the regrets of my life I didn't talk to this guy. It just wasn't right. I felt like I already knew all there was to know.")

Leaving 31st and Trinity, I wondered, as I had many times before, why on earth pretty Elizabeth Short had ever given Arnold Smith the time of day.

"With them, I think it was a very strange connection of the cripple," Gilmore told me. "She *was* crippled. She was a defective individual, and *he* was a defective individual. And you have a tense situation with people whose nerves are on the surface, where the antennas are very clear with one another. Very clear. I think he was a man who just overrode all boundaries. I don't think he even *recognized* boundaries in life . . . plus, he was stalking her, so it was simply a matter of *time.*"

I took San Pedro north to 8th, and navigated my way through downtown L.A, finally spilling onto 7th street east of MacArthur park. There stood the run-down, decrepit Holland Hotel, where Arnold Smith, the man who could have answered everybody's questions about the Black Dahlia murder, burned to death after eluding police for thirty-five years. *Thirty-five years.* Who would have thought that closure for the Black Dahlia story, such as it was, would be found in a dump like the Holland so long after her death?

How sad that Elizabeth Short's insecurities landed her, as they seem to do with so many women, in the wrong part of town with the wrong people, at precisely the wrong time. Gilmore had remarked that she was a driven girl, but afraid of running into herself.

". . . .She played these games out with men, and reached a point where . . . it was time to get up and do the act. And she *couldn't* do the act—I think it was a moment of great anxiety for her, which might have been all along leading up to a point where she fled. She left and ran. I think [Smith] was there at the right time, at the right place, as if to say, take my hand—the spider and the fly. And I think she was a willing fly. She was willing herself into the crime, as weird as that might sound.

"So you could look at him as an incidental thing, an appendage to her success or something, as a *noir* star, a dark star."

For a few minutes, I stood across the street from the rundown hotel where Arnold Smith bid adieu to planet Earth. A more perfect building couldn't have been dreamed up for the final chapter in the Black Dahlia saga; the Holland Hotel looked about as inviting as Norman Bates's house.

To my way of thinking, Smith was more than just an "incidental thing" in the Black Dahlia story. If it really had been a rich surgeon behind the murder, the story's ending would have been most un-*noir*-like, and boring at that. Throw Smith into the mix, and you have a paralysingly perfect tale—one that Hollywood's best writers *wish* they could've thought up. What were the odds that such a slippery, spooky guy was behind the whole damn mystery? How many things could Elizabeth Short have done differently after she arrived in L.A. to avoid her run-in with Arnold Smith on 14 January 1947? Standing there in the shadow of the Holland Hotel, I finally realized what it was about the Black Dahlia murder.

In its uniquely haunting way, Elizabeth Short's story is a play about randomness—the most profoundly disturbing and frightening play ever written about the consequences of Chance. By naïve, dumb chance, Elizabeth Short's path crossed that of a murderer. And from that point on, a shortly wound clock was ticking towards her macabre murder. It's a harrowing, *noir*-take on the worn-out Creation vs Evolution argument: was all this *created*, or did it happen by *chance*? The craziest things happen by chance, and Elizabeth Short—who may never have seen the end hurtling towards her like a freight train on 14/15 January 1947—is Chance personified.

TRUE LIES

(Hilda Murrell, 1984)

Judith Cook

When the body of Hilda Murrell was found in 1984, it seemed a straightforward, if particularly nasty, crime. She'd been attacked at her home in Shropshire, abducted in her own car and left to die in a copse several miles away. Police anticipated an early arrest. But then came the doubts, coincidences and conflicting stories. Evidence emerged linking Hilda Murrell's murder with British Intelligence and people connected with the nuclear industry. Investigative journalist Judith Cook (b 1933) published her first book on the case Who Killed Hilda Murrell? *in 1985. Five years later, private investigator Gary Murray produced two new witnesses, friends of Miss Murrell, whose "knowledge of deficiencies" in nuclear reactors at Sizewell was believed by some to have led to her death. Miss Murrell became known as Britain's Karen Silkwood, the American plutonium plant worker killed in a mysterious car crash in 1974. Judith Cook has written several books including a thriller novel and biographies of the writers Daphne du Maurier and J.B. Priestley. In 1994, Judith Cook published a second book on the Hilda Murrell case,* Unlawful Killing, *on which this account is based.*

On the morning of 24 March 1984 the body of an elderly woman was found in a copse six miles outside Shrewsbury. She was half-naked and there was superficial injuries. The probable cause of death was hypothermia. After a lengthy investigation, the police concluded that the woman's death was the result of a break-in by an opportunist thief which had gone "tragically wrong". They have never deviated from that conclusion.

The woman's name was Hilda Murrell and the murder has become a *cause célèbre*, passing into folklore as one of the great unsolved mysteries of its decade. It has been the stuff of legends, speculation, fantasy and fierce controversy. Theories abound. On the wild side it has been said she was the victim of some kind of satanic rite connected with the spring solstice. A strong body of opinion considers that she was a nuclear martyr as she was about to present a paper on nuclear waste to the Sizewell B inquiry and that somehow she had access to damning information which has never been revealed.

While the nuclear issue may certainly have played an indirect part in her death, it seems more likely—in spite of all the attempts to rubbish any but the official version—that her death was the result of a train of apparently disconnected events, a cock-up rather than a conspiracy. She died because she was the wrong person in the wrong place at the wrong time.

She was also a victim of the times. The first years of the Thatcher administration were marked by a climate of paranoia. "Political correctness" has now come to mean jokes about short people being described as "vertically challenged". Political correctness in 1984 was about being "one of us", fears of "the enemy within": a time when legitimate democratic dissent was regarded as little less than treasonable.

Many of the facts of the case are now widely known. At the time of her death, Hilda Murrell was seventy-nine and had long since retired from the family rose-growing business which she had run somewhat reluctantly, having hankered after an academic career—she read modern and medieval languages at Cambridge. She never married. In retirement she concentrated on conservation issues and felt passionate about nuclear energy.

We know that in the run-up to her death she suffered from anxiety, telling some of her friends she felt she was under some kind of surveillance. This culminated in an extraordinary phone call to Gerard Morgan Grenville of ECOROPA on 25 February 1984 which ended with her saying: "If they don't get me first I want the world to know that one old woman has seen through their lies."

On 21 March she had arranged to spend the day with friends in Wales. Returning from a shopping trip before setting off, she appears to have disturbed a thief or thieves. There was a struggle, after which the assailant drove her out of the town (sixty-nine witnesses saw the car) and dumped her in the copse. Her body was discovered three days later. The break-in was unusual. First the thief had disconnected the telephone. At first the police said it had been "expertly disconnected", then that the wires had merely been yanked out of the wall and, indeed, a policeman later appeared on television holding some broken wires. The thief then went on to search her files and papers thoroughly before leaving with a small amount of cash. A police statement that she had been sexually assaulted was later amended to there being signs of sexual activity: the thief had masturbated on some clothing.

Controversy over the investigation is also common knowledge: for instance, that her abandoned car was not checked out even though it was reported twice; that the owner of the land on which the body was found stated he had walked the area on the Thursday and there was no corpse there then; that a policeman had searched the house for two hours on the morning of 24 March without discovering she was not there.

After months of speculation, the inquest was held in December 1984, the coroner returning a verdict that she had been unlawfully killed. Detective Chief Superintendent David Cole confirmed the view that she had died at the hands of a random burglar, stating he had evidence in his incident room which led to that conclusion. That evidence has never been revealed. Following mounting criticism of the conduct of the police investigation, the West Mercia force called in their colleagues in Northumberland to undertake an inquiry. Six months later it was announced that, while there were minor criticisms of the way the investigation had been conducted, no real flaws could be found. The full report, like the information in the incident room, has also never been published.

So to the two main strands. First the nuclear issue. In January 1985, thanks to journalists assisted by Gary Murray, a private investigator, it was discovered that Sizewell B objectors had indeed been the object of surveillance. The operation on behalf of an anonymous client (consensus opinion being that it was MI5) was put out to Zeus Securities, a high-powered security firm with a clutch of Establishment names on its board. Presumably because it was considered a soft job, much of the work was, in turn, put out to the Sapphire Investigation Bureau of Acle in Norfolk run by Barry Peachman. He, in turn, contracted the work out still further to a man variously known as Vic Norris or Adrian Hampson.

Norris/Hampson, a convicted child sex-abuser, was known to have links with the extreme right. Indeed, he ran a Nazi memorabilia mail-order business from his office in Colchester. Zeus has always fiercely denied any knowledge of Hilda Murrell but agrees that it did assist in the surveillance: it could hardly do otherwise as there is copious documentary evidence of the three-way link.

After their activities came to light, everyone frantically back-pedalled. Everyone, that is, except Peachman who had admitted finding himself totally out of his depth over Sizewell. Three weeks after Hilda's murder, he blasted half his head off with a shotgun. The inquest heard that Peachman, a married man, had been under severe emotional strain due to his involvement with another woman. It was not quite like that. His relationship with his mistress had lasted many years, indeed she helped run his agency and they had a nine-year-old son, something that had long been accepted by his wife and family.

The world of private security firms is a murky one. It is also complicated. Some of those employed by one might well run another on their own account. All use freelancers. Much has been made of the fact that Hilda Murrell's name has not been found on any list of those under surveillance, but then it did not need to be. She belonged to a number of organizations which were listed and, for instance, telephone taps can be granted for an entire organization, covering any one in it. At its 1993 press conference on the Murrell murder, it was stated that "the Security Services" had assured West Mercia police that Hilda Murrell had never appeared on their files or been the object of scrutiny. In view of what has leaked out over the years with regard to other people considered mildly subversive, then it is hardly surprising this has been greeted with scepticism.

So to the *Belgrano* connection. Thatcher had been swept back to power in the 1983 election on a tidal wave of patriotic jingoism. The Falklands campaign had been a godsend; prior to it, her poll rating stood at the lowest for any prime minister since records began, an achievement now overtaken by John Major.

Just why she decided to tell the country, backed by her ministers, that the battleship had been sunk as it was sailing towards the British Task Force to attack it, rather than fleeing away back to Argentina, is unclear. As ex-defence minister Alan Clark said in his *Diaries*, most of the British people couldn't have cared less if it had been tied up in port. However, once having decided to prevaricate, her face had to be saved at all costs. The fly in the ointment was Labour MP Tam Dalyell, who worried at the issue like a terrier with a rat. By December 1983, his questions were getting so near the bone that a special committee, under Cabinet secretary Sir Robert Armstrong, was set up to look into the leaks.

By 19 March 1984, it was evident that Dalyell had material which was quite specific. That day there was, says an informed source, "a tremendous flap in Downing Street". Earlier attempts to discover the culprit or culprits had come to nothing. The order went out that they must be found at all costs, every avenue explored, however remote. This was before senior civil servant Clive Ponting, appalled at what he was being asked to do, sent documents to Dalyell. Could it be, it was suggested, that copies of "raw signals" concerning the sinking had come into Dalyell's hands? Rumours abounded. Had information come from a Lieutenant Sethia, a junior officer on the submarine *Conqueror* which had sunk the battleship? There was also deliberate misinformation. Newspapers were told the *Conqueror*'s log was missing, the inference being that it had been stolen. In actual fact, *Conqueror* had been acting as a spy for the USA, monitoring Soviet ships dropping sounding equipment and the Americans had demanded the log be sent to Washington after the Falklands campaign.

Back then to the signals traffic. Only one senior officer, Commander Robert Green, who had played a crucial role in naval intelligence at Northwood during the Falklands campaign, had since left the service. Green was Hilda's nephew. Again, when it was said recently that her name had never appeared on any list, civil or military, he pointed out that he himself had given it as next-of-kin when he had been positively vetted. It had to be on naval files.

No one who has looked into this affair has thought for one moment that Green was responsible for the leaks. If any further evidence is needed, then it can be found in his record at the time he left the Navy. He is especially praised for his liaison work with the security services. "He has been particularly good," it reads, "in strengthening the many contacts with outside intelligence agencies and has earned their respect to a greater degree than SOIs (Senior Officers, Intelligence) have done for many years."

It can now be said that Dalyell did receive material based on signals from *Conqueror*. Sethia was not the only officer who was sickened by the hypocrisy surrounding the whole affair. The material came into the hands of a London publisher (now dead) who, after taking advice from a colleague, had it passed on to Dalyell, who probably still does not know its origin.

The years passed and gradually interest in the Murrell affair diminished, although the mystery provoked a number of books, some fictional, and at least three plays. Then in 1993 a book appeared called *Enemies of the State*, by the private investigator Gary Murray. The Murrell murder was one of a number of examples instanced of state power having apparently got out of control. Murray is a maverick, has made powerful enemies and every effort has been made to dismiss him and what he has to say, but there is no doubt whatsoever that he does have access to a great deal of undercover information.

Murray's new information had come from a young woman, Triona Guthrie, who had been a friend of Hilda's in Shrewsbury. She had since taken up a conservation post in Lincolnshire and had also become a prison visitor. It was while visiting a prisoner in a north-country jail that she heard the story of a fellow-inmate, a story which she was recommended to pass on to Murray, the bare bones of which appeared in his book. Triona Guthrie swore her information on affidavit. No one who has spent time with her and questioned her closely can doubt her sincerity or balance and she cannot be described in any way as an obsessive.

As briefly as possible, the story is this. In March 1984, a group of freelancers, which had been used before by a shadowy north-of-England investigation agency which called itself "Ceres" and was the offshoot of a larger, unnamed organization, was brought together for a soft target operation. The liaison officer, whose name is known and who has openly bragged of his links with MI5 and MI6, called himself "Demeter". The team's task was to search Hilda's house, Ravenscroft, for papers. It was known (thanks to phone taps) that on 21 March she would be out all day. Four people actually went into the house, led by the man described in Murray's book as Team Member 3 and backed up by his girlfriend and two other men, one of whom was the source of the story.

Seeing her leave the house and assuming that she would not be back until the end of the afternoon, they had broken in, disconnected the telephone (a drawing of its state on the morning of 24 March

1984 has now been published) and begun their search. Team
Member 3 soon found the deeds to The Shack, Hilda's holiday
cottage on the Welsh border not many miles away, and he decided
to take his girlfriend and search there first, leaving the other two
men to continue going through Ravenscroft. Shortly after he left,
the two men were taken totally by surprise when Hilda returned.

There was a brief struggle, she was tied up and dumped on her
bed. One of the men, with a taste for violence, then tried to make
Hilda tell him if there were "stolen papers" in the house, roughing
her up in the process and becoming sufficiently sexually aroused to
masturbate. Team Member 3, returning soon after having found
no papers at all at The Shack, was appalled.

Here the story becomes somewhat confused, but basically it is
that it was decided to remove her, that she was taken first to a
deserted airfield known locally as Little America, before being
dumped in the copse on the Friday before she was found. After
which the professionals were called in to clean up the mess.

Needless to say, Murray's book met with a barrage of criticism
but, as a result, West Mercia police announced they were reopening
their inquiries.

Murray gave no names of those involved but it was known
that Team Member 3 had later died in Cleveland in 1987 after
a police chase. It did not therefore need the skills of Sherlock
Holmes to trace him. His name was David Gricewith and he had
been wanted in connection with the fatal shooting of a policeman
during an abortive robbery in Leeds in October 1984. He does not
seem to have been suspected locally of any criminal activity and,
indeed, lived in the village where he had grown up, ran a garage
business and seems to have been well liked, though neighbours
described him as a bit of a lad with the women. Interestingly,
he did look very much like the second artist's impression of a
man seen running away from Hilda's car shortly after it had been
abandoned.

In October 1984, two men had tried to hold up a sub-post office
in Leeds. Possibly there had been a tip-off, but in any events two
policemen saw what was happening and tackled them. One of the
robbers produced a gun, shot and wounded PC John Thorpe, then
fatally wounded Sergeant John Speed. During the hunt for the killer,
Gricewith was interviewed but his current girlfriend gave him an
alibi. Two different sources, both independent and unknown to
each other, have since claimed that Gricewith holed up for a while

afterwards in Hilda's house, The Shack, at Llanymynech shortly before it was severely damaged by fire. The culprits of the arson attack have never been found.

In fact, the police were convinced that the man they wanted was Anthony Kelly, an Irishman with a record of violent crime who had then got back to Dublin: indeed PC Thorpe was almost certain Kelly was his attacker and on the day of the murder a van stolen by the killer was seen parked outside the house of Kelly's former wife in Leeds. A 1,000 page dossier had been prepared, prior to asking for his extradition, but three years later Kelly was in prison in Dublin convicted of kidnapping.

On 12 February 1987, Gricewith drove his car into a supermarket car park in Norton, near Stockton-on-Tees. It is not clear why police were waiting there. One version says there had been a spate of supermarket thefts and all major supermarkets were under surveillance.

Another has Gricewith being specifically targeted and that it was a stakeout. Whatever the truth of the matter, Gricewith realized something was wrong and headed out of the car park, then dumped his car before fleeing on foot, taking with him a sawn-off shotgun and a pistol, and chased by a police Fiesta. He fired at the car, stopped it, dragged its driver out of the driving seat at gun point and drove off pursued by other police cars. He was chased to a nearby housing estate and up a dead-end where he ploughed into a brick wall. It was then, it is said, the fatal accident occurred. His shotgun had been across his knees and it went off, fatally wounding him.

Evidently he had not realized this and struggled violently with the police as he got out of the car, the fight being witnessed by a local resident. He still appeared to be relatively uninjured when taken to the police station but collapsed and died shortly afterwards. After his death just about every serious violent crime that had occurred in the area in the previous fourteen years was laid at his door. It must have done wonders for the local clear-up rate.

Shortly afterwards a number of arrests were made, including that of Gricewith's girlfriend who had given him his original alibi. One was of his partner in the abortive Leeds robbery, another a man said to have been a previous partner-in-crime. There is nothing to show that Gricewith had been such a Napoleon of crime, prior to his violent demise. Other information is, however, more interesting. Gricewith had known and long-standing links with the extreme right both in this country and in Europe. He had carried out undercover work for private security firms on previous occasions. He had been used as an *agent provocateur* during the miners' strike, being responsible for a particularly violent incident. He had an obsession with guns and had long been the object of interest to a number of investigators.

Eight months after the publication of Murray's book, the West Mercia police reported their findings. Their conclusions had already been trailed in *The Times*, under the heading "Police Clear MI5 over Death", where it was claimed there was no evidence to support Triona Guthrie's story or any link with the *Belgrano*. "Mrs [*sic*] Murrell's nephew, Commander Robert Green, was a member of the crew of *HMS Conqueror*, the Royal Navy submarine that sank the cruiser," averred the paper.

At a press conference held in Shrewsbury in February 1994, West Mercia police did indeed confirm that they could find no "shred of evidence" to support Triona Guthrie's informant's story. All the members of the anonymous team (except for "one now deceased") had been interviewed and eliminated from inquiries. It had been established that one of the alleged participants, currently serving a long prison sentence, had read an article about the Murrell murder in late 1989 and, in an attempt to focus media attention on himself and what he believed was his wrongful conviction, had made the whole story up, basing it on the article. Police had also visited "the Headquarters of the Security Services" (they did not specify which one) and "the Services" had cooperated fully. They had had no knowledge of Hilda Murrell prior to her death and were not involved in her murder. Had police had unrestricted access to intelligence files? No, but they had been given access to the parts of files which would have contained the relevant details had there been any to contain.

Criticism was levelled at all those who had sought, since the 1994 investigation, to suggest there was anything behind the murder other than the panic of an opportunist thief. Answers to questions from journalists were hampered by anything to do with "the Security Services" being disallowed on security grounds! The event was best summed up in a question asked by John Osborne of HTV, one of the first and most persistent journalists to have covered the Murrell affair: "Don't you realize," he said, "that the reason there has been so much speculation over the years is because people just don't believe the police theory of the random walk-in burglar? Because what you say simply isn't credible?" Assistant

Chief Constable Thursfield replied that he did not agree with this view but was prepared to defend Osborne's right to express it.

No one who has looked seriously into the Murrell affair believes MI5 was directly involved in the Ravenscroft break-in. All those denying any direct involvement are, therefore, speaking the truth. It cannot be proved, given known information, that the team described by Guthrie's informant as working for "Ceres" did exist. However, it is worth pointing out that if there had not been cast-iron evidence that an outfit called Zeus had organized the Sizewell surveillance and that a Nazi-sympathizing child-abuser had been one of the operatives, nobody would have believed it.

The newspaper feature on which the story was said to have been based appeared in *The Independent* in November 1989. The writer, Amanda Mitchison, was interested in the obsessive effect the murder has had on people. One section only deals with the murder itself. To base the "Ceres" scenario on it would take, one feels, the combined talents of P. D. James and Ruth Rendell. The instigator would also have had to weave in a host of previous associates and an employee of a security firm who does actually exist. And for what? How could it help him to focus media attention on his own conviction? If it was proved to be a pack of lies, then he would do his case no good at all and spend even more time in jail for wasting police time. If it proved to be true, then he could find himself tried as an accessory to one of the most notorious murders of the last decades. Finally, nowhere in *The Independent* was either The Shack or Little America mentioned, yet the informant knew of both. Indeed, regarding the latter, Mitchison quotes Green and Hilda's friend, Don Arnott, as saying they had found a disused stable where they thought her body might have been concealed.

Shortly after I delivered my book, a retired MI5 officer, often used as a consultant by the media, was casually asked about the Murrell murder. Freelance operatives had, he said, been sent in and they had panicked when the old lady returned unexpectedly. Their MI5 handler had been severely reprimanded.

WHO KILLED JOE ELWELL?

(Joseph Bowne Elwell, 1920)

Morris Markey

The Elwell murder, Alexander Woollcott observed, was marked by a set of extremely prominent teeth, but so conspicuous by their absence (upstairs in a glass of water) that they became important evidence in the case. Woollcott likened this strange absence with the fictional one in which Sherlock Holmes calls the attention of a Scotland Yard detective to the curious incident of the dog in the night-time. "But", the detective replied, "the dog did nothing in the night-time". "That", said Holmes, "was the curious incident". Here, in an essay for Esquire *magazine thirty years after Joe Elwell's mysterious death, journalist Morris Markey mentions the dentures only* en passant, *and even then the reference is clamped in someone else's quotation marks. But maybe Elwell's man Friday, Barnes, spoke no more than the truth when he pointed out that an undentured Elwell "would never have sat down with a lady, looking like that". Woollcott believed that Elwell was shot by a burglar or an enemy. But Markey (who, unlike Woollcott, used to shift himself out of his armchair to jam his foot in many a stricken door) thought suicide the most likely explanation. Morris Markey was the original Reporter At Large for the* New Yorker. *Many of his articles have become classics on American journalism courses.*

If you were looking for a boundary marker, as it were, between the Smart Set of the lobster-palace days and the Café Society of our own time, you could find its location easily enough, and indeed you could find the precise hour and minute when the old order passed, giving place to new.

The location is the four-story granite house at No. 244 West 70th Street in the City of New York. The time is thirty-five minutes past eight o'clock on the morning of Friday, 11 June 1920. For Mrs Marie Larsen went into that house at that moment and discovered her employer, Joseph Bowne Elwell, dying of a bullet wound in the exact center of his forehead.

Elwell was the very last of the men-about-town in the tradition of Van Bibber. The gentlemanly punctilio, the discreet elegance and gallantry that were essential to the role in those days were the very things that delivered a bullet into his brain. And, ironically enough, it was those identical qualities in the wellbred character of Edward Swann, the District Attorney, that made a solution of the puzzle almost impossible. The people involved in the affair were ladies and gentlemen of substance and refinement. Mr Swann could not bring himself to deal rudely or realistically with them. Indeed, he was so intent upon preventing a smirch on any name that he was deceptive in his dealings with the press to the point of downright dishonesty.

The dashing Elwell (who was forty-four years old when he died) was no Johnny-come-lately. He had put together a quite substantial fortune despite the fact that the only capital he possessed at the beginning was his nimble mind, plus instinctive good taste, plus the manners of a gentleman that he had learned at his mother's knee. On the morning that the bullet found him, he owned about $500,000 worth of real estate. He had about $100,000 worth of personal property. His stable of twenty thoroughbreds was racing at Latonia. He kept his yacht at Palm Beach for his annual winter sojourn there. He owned five automobiles and, of course, the house on 70th Street.

It is true that he laid the foundation of these riches at the card table, where he played bridge for ten dollars a point and, on one occasion at least, gained thirty thousand dollars. Yet, significantly enough, the very friends who lost to him insisted unanimously that he was by no means a professional gambler. "It was a pleasure to play with him," they said, "and it was worth it to have him beat you, because he had a cool passion for the science of bridge, the philosophy of a card game. He never seemed to give a thought for the money involved, whether he won it or paid it out."

Gambling at cards was not, in short, his weakness.

But he had a weakness. And it seems to have absorbed his time and his thoughts to an almost fantastic degree.

Among the countless distinguished men who were delighted to know him, he was a man of impeccable honor, of fastidious regard for the social conventions. He was generous and considerate, and his nod of assent was better than a signed contract. But among the countless beautiful women who were equally delighted to know him, he was an insatiable voluptuary, a heartless rake who, with neither compunction nor pity, took the full advantage of their frailty. He played upon a whole orchestra of women as a conductor upon the podium bends the fiddles and the woodwinds to his whim.

Elwell lived an odd sort of life in the 70th Street house. It was big, as city houses go, and superbly furnished. Yet he had neither butler nor cook nor maid to keep it for him. He employed a combination secretary and factotum, William Barnes, and a chauffeur, Rhodes, both of whom lived out. Mrs Larsen, the wife of a butcher, came every morning to prepare his breakfast (two breakfasts if a lady were present) and clean up the house.

It was this aura of secrecy, of a peculiar need for complete privacy which, in a time when expensive entertainment was expected of all prosperous gentlemen, first gave the citizens a hint that here was something rather special in the way of a mystery. "What does he do every night, when he goes home to that silent house and takes off his tail coat and white tie?"

Rhodes, Barnes, and a former chauffeur told the newspaper reporters all about it. If their comments were to be summed up in one statement, it would read like this: "During the four years I've worked for him he's had more than fifty women. Most of them were very high-class-looking dames, and I got the idea most of them were married to somebody else. But I don't know any of them by name, because that's where he was very careful. He'd tell me to go to some street intersection or some restaurant, and then he'd roll up the glass to cut me off from the back of the car. There would be a dame waiting for him, and she'd get in, and I couldn't hear a word they said even if I'd wanted to.

"When we got to the 70th Street house he would take the lady in, and wave me away, and I'd put the car in the garage and go on home.

"There were seven women to my knowledge, though, that had a key to the house. I think there were twelve, but seven to my knowledge. I don't know when they used the keys, because I never was around the place at night. When he drove out at night, he used taxicabs.

"But even all this blueblood didn't seem enough for him. Many a time we would be driving along the street and some woman on the sidewalk would catch his eye and he would signal me to pull up. He would always say to the dame, 'Why! I haven't seen you since Palm Beach!' or something like that. If the women looked insulted he would apologize for his mistake. But you'd be surprised how many of them didn't act insulted at all."

Now you should understand very clearly that amorous dalliance with the fair was a profoundly different game in the days of the Smart Set—particularly with the wedded fair. In our own time of Café Society, it is catch-as-catch-can, and few holds barred. But in the early Twenties, when an odd affair called the honor of a gentleman was an item in the moral currency, there were rules. Men simply did not take it kindly when their wives slept with other men, and so the most serious of all the rules was called the Unwritten Law. The cuckolded husband was assumed to have (unless some tedious jury failed to get the point) at least some small right to blow the brains out of the scoundrel who had seduced his wife.

The males of the city generally accepted this notion as an explanation of Elwell's sudden end. They made up a jingle which was a favorite at the cocktail hour:

> Who killed Joe Elwell?
> I, said the Banker,
> And now I will spank her.
> I killed Joe Elwell.

The ladies, quick to establish the honor of their sex, countered with their own explanation:

> Who killed Joe Elwell?
> I, said the lady.
> His conduct was shady.
> I killed Joe Elwell.

It was in this Cock Robin mood that an absurdly incompetent investigation of the affair got under way—an investigation that proved one thing: that a cop had better have a course in logic than a closet full of Old School Ties.

Elwell had been born into a respectable and moderately prosperous family in New Jersey. At twenty-five he was advancing steadily toward the top of a Brooklyn hardware firm. He had done well enough to join a club, small but socially correct, and it was there that he learned to play bridge whist. The game fascinated him utterly. He harnessed his mind to it, and before he was thirty he was the leading bridge expert in the country, with two published books on the subject behind him and eleven more to come. He was one of the most active members of the New York Whist Club, and a founder of the Studio Club—which was so exclusive that the membership was limited to twenty men of affairs.

He married and his wife bore him a son, but by 1916 Mrs Elwell had had enough of a man who drew women to him as a magnet draws needles. She obtained a legal separation, but not a divorce.

On New Year's Day of the year in which he died, Elwell was driven to Palm Beach by Rhodes, the chauffeur. Nothing seems to have transpired in his Florida sojourn that could have the least bearing upon his violent end. Late in May, he sent Rhodes back to New York with the car, and a few days later took the train for his own return journey. It was reported, after his death, that as soon as he returned from Palm Beach he called upon his wife and asked her to give him a divorce, saying that he would like to marry again, and that she refused. Mrs Elwell denied this and said that she had wanted a divorce at the time of their separation, but that Elwell preferred to remain married to shield himself from getting in too deep with other women.

On the night of 10 June, thirteen hours before the fatal shot, Elwell went to a dinner party at the Ritz-Carlton Hotel. The hosts of the occasion were Mr and Mrs Walter Lewisohn. Octavio Figueroa, a journalist from Buenos Aires, was a guest. And so was Viola Kraus, Mrs Lewisohn's sister. Indeed, Viola Kraus was the guest of honor. Three months before, she had won an interlocutory decree of divorce in the court at White Plains from her husband, Victor von Schlegell. On this night, the decree automatically became final, and the party was by way of celebrating the event.

Unhappily, something occurred to mar the gaiety of the occasion. As the Lewisohn party settled themselves in their chairs and the waiters scurried about them, a burst of hearty laughter came from a table only a few feet away. They turned their heads and saw von Schlegell, in merry humor, seated with a beautiful young woman dressed all in black.

When coffee and brandy were done, the Lewisohn party took the elevator to the roof to dance a little while, and von Schlegell and his young lady came to the same elevator. As far as can be determined, only one remark was made as the car swept upward: von Schlegell's companion said, "It seems we just can't keep away from each other." Nobody undertook to make reply. A little later, on the roof, Elwell and Viola Kraus were dancing a waltz when von Schlegell and his partner drifted close to them. Von Schlegell said, "Hello, Joe."

Viola Kraus and von Schlegell and the young woman in black all said afterward that Elwell smiled and returned the greeting. Walter Lewisohn disagreed with them. "I was seated at the table and watching everything closely," he said. "When Von spoke, Elwell's face did not change expression and he did not acknowledge the greeting."

At about ten o'clock, von Schlegell took his young lady away. Some half-hour later, Elwell went off in advance of the others to the New Amsterdam Theatre to get tickets for the Ziegfeld Midnight Frolics. When the rest of the party arrived he was waiting for them, tickets in hand. All of them danced, now, and sipped champagne, and enjoyed the floor show until about one-thirty in the morning. In the light of subsequent events, it seems almost certain that there was some misunderstanding within the little group at this period. When all hands decided to call it a night, and came down from the New Amsterdam roof, Elwell announced that he would walk home alone. He saw the others into a taxicab and then went away westward on 42nd Street toward Eighth Avenue.

Nobody knows how he spent the next hour. The telephone records of the Columbia Station showed that two calls were put through from the Elwell house—one at one forty-five and the other at two-four. Viola Kraus telephoned to him at two-thirty and found him at home, and attempted to patch up whatever unhappiness the evening had produced. He tried without success to get through to his sometime partner in the racing stable, W.H. Pendleton, at Cedarhurst, L.I. The operator later said she rang for some moments, but got no answer.

(It should be said here that Pendleton was at home. The telephone was beside his bed. He said that it never rang at all. The *New York*

Times reporter, desperate for news and being constantly misled by the District Attorney's office, made a great deal of this episode and, with elaborate innuendo, predicted the arrest of Pendleton within twenty-four hours. The idea was an absurd one. Pendleton was a staid, family sort of man. He had sold his share of the stable to Elwell, ". . . because I just couldn't keep up with Joe or go out with him. His pace was too fast for me. We had lost touch with each other, but I'll testify that he was a man of honor in all his dealings. I admired him and respected him.")

It was very hot that night. At three forty-five, John Isdale, chief engineer of a cargo steamer, got up from his bed in the house two doors away from Elwell's. He had been roused from uncomfortable half-sleep by the loud, popping exhaust of a racing automobile. He went to the window and saw the car drawn up in front of the Elwell house. "I didn't see anybody get out of it," he said, "and I didn't see anybody get in. I don't know the color or the make of the car. In about five minutes it went away, still popping that damned exhaust."

At six-thirty that morning of 11 June, Henry Otten, the driver of a dairy wagon, left a quart of milk in the vestibule of No. 244. He said that the glass-paneled entrance door was shut as usual, but the double-wing storm doors were wide open.

At seven-twenty, the postman entered the vestibule, saw the milk, and dropped four or five letters on the tiled flooring. He pushed the bell-button twice, as was his custom. He was never able to remember, afterward, whether he pulled shut the storm doors behind him as he went away.

At eight-thirty, Mrs Larsen arrived. The storm doors were shut and the latch had caught so that she had to use her key—the same key opening both storm doors and entrance doors beyond the vestibule. The milk was still where Otten had placed it. She saw no letters at all.

Mrs Larsen hurried back to the kitchen and threw open a couple of windows. She puttered around for a moment or two and went back toward the front of the house. In a small room, the "reception room," just to the right of the main-entrance hall, she saw something that stopped her in her tracks. Joseph Elwell was sitting upright in an upholstered chair, dressed in green silk pajamas and barefoot. His face was faintly streaked with blood. His breathing made a loud sound.

Mrs Larsen ran out the front door, and her cries brought Patrolman Henry Singer from his traffic post at the corner. When Singer got to the house, he ran back into the street, and found Otten the milkman on his way back through the street making collections.

The two of them had Elwell half out of his chair when Singer said, "Hey, wait a minute. This guy's been shot!" Otten looked again and saw that this was, indeed, the truth. They put Elwell back into the chair as they had found him, and Singer called headquarters. He looked about for a pistol, but found none.

The man-about-town was taken in an ambulance to Bellevue, where he died two hours later without recovering consciousness. By the time he drew his last breath, the house on 70th Street was half-filled with detectives under the field command of Captain Arthur Carey of the Homicide Squad. The next day John F. Joyce, an assistant District Attorney, entered the case.

The reception room itself was small. The furniture consisted of two upholstered chairs, a small table, and three pictures on the wall. Elwell's own chair stood with its back to the wall, in the usual place. There was no sign of disturbance whatever, except that the second chair had been moved a few feet from its ordinary position. It faced Elwell's chair, at a slight diagonal, some six feet away. Singer and Otten could not remember whether they had moved this chair when they undertook to put the dying man in a more comfortable position.

The bullet had passed directly through Elwell's head and imbedded itself in the plaster, some four inches above the back of the chair. During the first few minutes of his investigation, Singer had picked up an empty .45-caliber shell which had been ejected from an Army-type Colt automatic. The bullet, dug out of the plaster, matched the shell.

On the floor beside Elwell's chair were some of the letters that the postman had delivered that morning, all unopened. Another letter, a routine report from Lloyd Gentry, the trainer of Elwell's racing stable in Kentucky, was opened and lay stained with blood upon the floor at his left hand. None of the other letters, when opened by the police, proved to be of any significance.

Elwell had his cigarettes especially manufactured: cork tips for himself, gold tips and rose tips for the ladies. He had been smoking one of his own, which lay half burned out on the carpet beside his chair. On the marble mantel shelf there was a half-smoked cigarette of a common brand. It had been smoked from the wrong end and the brand name was burned away.

It was easy to decide that robbery was not the motive for the crime. There were two basement doors, both of them locked and neither tampered with. All of the downstairs windows were protected from intruders by ornamental iron grilles. In Elwell's bedroom on the third floor the clothes he had worn to the Lewisohn party were laid out where he had taken them off. On his bed also there was $400 in cash, and his diamond studs and cuff links, worth about $7000.

He had not slept in his bed (unless, perchance, it had been remade later), though indentations in the pillow indicated that he had lain there a little while on top of the counterpane. Beside the bed on the floor there was a copy of the *Morning Telegraph*, a racing paper, and an ash tray filled with his own cigarette ends.

In the closet of Elwell's bedroom the detectives found a pink silk negligee. A little square of the cloth, apparently bearing the embroidered name or initials of its owner, had been cut away with a knife. And that careful attention to the garment was the chief clue to Elwell's character, or at least to his code of behavior. It was a sample of his way of doing things. For, despite the scores of women who were so powerfully drawn to him, who pressed their favors upon him with discretion thrown to the winds, Elwell remained discreet. In his effects there was not found one letter from a woman. He kept no diaries. Rhodes and Barnes and Mrs Larsen all solemnly swore that they did not know the identity of any of these beautiful and breathless creatures.

The tale of door keys in the hands of special favorites was, unhappily, soon dispelled. The police found a locksmith who had changed the locks to the front doors more than six months earlier and had filed only two keys to fit them, one for Elwell himself and one for Mrs Larsen. And upon this point Mrs Elwell had an observation to make: "Joe wasn't a fool. He would never take a chance on two women using their keys the same evening. If he gave out keys at all, it was to people who would come and gamble with him."

Yet there was little evidence that Elwell had held gambling parties in his home. Only a single deck of cards was located—in a desk on the second floor. Part of a faro layout was found in a storeroom.

William Barnes had this to say: "It wasn't a woman who killed him, even if a woman could handle a gun that big. When they found him, he had left upstairs the toupee that covered his little bald spot, and his bridge of false teeth was upstairs too. He never would have sat down with a lady, looking like that. I figure how it happened was this: He brings some fellow home with him or maybe lets the fellow in when he rings the bell. He sits down and the fellow sits facing him, probably holding the gun in his hand and saying what he's going to do. I've seen Mr Elwell lose $50,000 in an evening at bridge, and never bat an eye about it. He didn't know what it was to be nervous or afraid. He wouldn't have begged or pleaded with this fellow or made any promises. He would have pretended the whole thing was a joke, even if he knew it wasn't a joke. I can see him now, reaching down to the pile of letters the postman delivered, and opening one and commencing to read it, and saying to this fellow, 'Very well, old chap. If you're determined to shoot me, go ahead. While you're waiting, I'd better go over my mail.' And so the fellow shot him. To my mind, he was some woman's husband or maybe brother."

Most of the investigation and the questioning of witnesses was carried on in the house at 70th Street, which for nearly ten days was the scene of feverish comings and goings, of lights that burned all night. Dr Charles Norris, the medical Examiner, published his report to the effect that:

"The medical evidence supports the factual evidence, in that Elwell was shot some time between the delivery of the mail and the arrival of Mrs Larsen. It seems apparent that the wound was received from ten to fifteen minutes before Mrs Larsen arrived at the house.

"The circle of powder marks about the bullet wound was three inches in diameter. Tests with a similar weapon show that the muzzle was held not more than three feet from his forehead and probably not more than one foot. Even assuming that the weapon was in the room, and that some misguided person secreted it before the arrival of detectives, it would be an awkward and unusual thing for a man to shoot himself directly through the center of the head. Suicide seems unlikely."

At this point District Attorney Swann, himself a gentleman of the old school, took personal charge of the inquiry. He permitted Joyce to stay with the case and he brought in another assistant named Dooling. Joyce and Dooling immediately began to bicker between themselves, but since the whole investigation turned into a masterpiece of incompetency, their bickerings seem inconsequential now.

A detective made a discovery in the cellar.

It was a hidden package containing a pink silk nightgown, a pink silk robe, and two pink silk slippers. Mrs Larsen was brought to the mat and finally confessed that she had taken them out of Elwell's bedroom closet (missing the negligee that was found) and tucked them away in the basement before the detectives arrived that fatal morning. "I thought," she explained, "that it wouldn't look nice for them to be found in his bedroom."

Mr Swann told the press that these articles belonged to a person whom they might call "Miss Wilson". And then, as Mrs Larsen's composure suffered another breach, it was revealed that "Miss Wilson" had appeared breathless at the Elwell house at almost the hour when he was breathing his last in Bellevue.

Mrs Larsen: "She wanted to run upstairs and get her things. But the upstairs was full of detectives by now, and anyway I told her I had hidden the things. She said, 'Isn't this an awful accident?' And I said yes, it was, and she went away."

At this hour of the day, no newspapers had appeared with reports of the Elwell shooting. There was, of course, no radio. The assumption was that Mrs Larsen, under the influence of her employer's gallantry, had telephoned the news to "Miss Wilson." She denied that she had been paid for her thoughtfulness or bribed to keep it silent.

More than a week passed before the insistent reporters drove Swann to the admission that "Miss Wilson" was, in reality, Viola Kraus. The District Attorney explained his subterfuge: "We are investigating a murder, not the frailties of womankind. I am loath to mention any lady's name. Was it not a Prince of Wales of whom his friends said, when he was called to testify upon a lady's honor, 'He lied like a gentleman'? "

With Viola Kraus now so intimately involved with Elwell's life, it was inevitable that her divorced husband, von Schlegell, should attract the attention of the authorities. He was questioned in the Elwell home for nearly five hours, and at the end Swann gave the reporters this account of the interview:

Von Schlegell, American-born, was an engineer. He had been educated at the University of Minnesota and was a partner in a New York firm. His meeting with Elwell and the Lewisohn party at the Ritz had been purely accidental. He did not remember the name of his companion of the evening. She was a Minneapolis girl who had got in touch with him when she came to New York.

He had, he said, delivered this young woman to her apartment at ten o'clock, following the Ritz dinner. Business required him to go to Atlantic City the next day, but his car had developed trouble. Late in the night he had taken it to his garage and insisted that it be repaired by morning. He had taken delivery of the car at about ten o'clock the morning of 11 June, and started for Atlantic City. At

Red Bank, the motor had quit again, and he had left the car there, going to Atlantic City by train. Having concluded his business, he had spent the night in a boardwalk hotel, taken the train to Red Bank, picked up his car, and driven to New York.

Under increasing attack from the press, Swann finally admitted that von Schlegell had not really denied knowing the name of the young woman in black. "I concealed her identity upon my own initiative," he said. "Enough names have been dragged through the mud in this case." He finally got around to saying that the girl was Elly Hope Anderson, the daughter of a prominent merchant in Minneapolis. She had been playing organ and studying voice in the East for some time. Swann accepted the statement she made to the press in Minneapolis:

"Von took me to my apartment at 10, directly from the Ritz. He didn't come in. I was leaving for home the next morning, but he asked me to come to his apartment for breakfast. I did go there, at about eight o'clock. I left him about nine, to go to the Grand Central for my train."

Swann's people never let Captain Arthur Carey do very much but run errands. The inference was that the Police Department, necessary but a trifle unpolished, might cause embarrassment among the important names involved if given too much rein.

It goes without saying that nobody has ever been arrested and accused of the murder of Joseph Bowne Elwell.

The lens of time, however, brings these affairs into a clean focus. And a theory clamors from the record: Joseph Elwell did, indeed, commit suicide.

So it is possible to pose a hypothetical question:

Did Mrs Larsen walk into the reception room that morning to discover that her godlike employer had killed himself? Did she see a pistol on the floor beside him? Did this spellbound woman think at that moment as she thought later, when she decided that pink silk things in Elwell's closet "would not look nice"? Did she think that it would be a shameful thing, no less, for the world to know that this paragon of mankind had taken his own life? And did she pick up the pistol and tuck it into her apron—whence it could be taken out again a little later and tucked into a pocketbook and carried away at the end of a dreadful day?

It is easy enough to reach the conclusion that the cigarette on the mantel was tossed there by Otten the milkman when he came into the room and was shaken by the sight of a bloody, dying man.

And it is easy to see how Joseph Elwell shot himself squarely in the middle of the forehead, as awkward and bizarre as that may seem at first thought. The next time you have an empty .45 automatic around the house, try holding it with both hands at arms length, and pointing it at your brow, and pressing the trigger with your thumb.

Be sure it is empty. Because it certainly would work.

DR JOHN BODKIN ADAMS

(Mrs Morrell and Mrs Hullett, 1957)

Eric Ambler

*In the mid-1950s, a rumour began in the genteel resort of Eastbourne,
on England's south coast, that a local general practitioner, Dr John
Bodkin Adams, was poisoning his patients and pocketing large legacies
from them. Suspicion took root in 1950 with the death of an elderly and
eccentric patient called Mrs Edith Morrell. Nurses observed Dr Adams
dosing Mrs Morrell with various medications including barbiturates,
doses that grew bigger as the stricken old woman sank deeper. After
her death, Adams received a chest of silver, an antique cupboard and
a Rolls-Royce motor car from Mrs Morrell's estate. Tongues wagged.
In July 1956, another elderly patient, Mrs Gertrude Hullett, died in
the care of Dr Adams, leaving him another Rolls-Royce car in her
will. Teacups in scandalized Eastbourne rattled louder than ever, and
the town's chief constable called in a team of detectives from Scotland
Yard's murder squad to investigate. Adams had treated hundreds of
old and wealthy patients, but the police drew up a dossier focusing on
nine suspicious deaths. Told that he was to be charged with murdering
old Mrs Morrell, Dr Adams blinked owlishly and replied: "Murder?
I do not think you could prove it was murder." He was right. They
could not.*

*Dr Adams, a church-going bachelor, had apparently lived a blameless
life, but the case against him was strong. At his sensational Old Bailey
trial in 1957, the doctor was said to have been a beneficiary in 132*

*wills, and to have amassed £45,000 in cash as well as silver, jewellery,
antiques, pictures and the two Rolls-Royce cars. When the trial began,
the assembled world's press, believing almost to a man that Adams was
guilty, reported the case recklessly. "Eastbourne's frenzied gossip pushed
Dr Adams's alleged victims as high as 400", trumpeted* Newsweek
*magazine, which was promptly fined for contempt and banned from
circulating for the remainder of the trial. Eric Ambler (b. 1909), the
best-selling writer of spy thrillers, was commissioned to cover the case.
When this account appeared in Eric Ambler's 1963 murder anthology*
The Ability To Kill, *Dr Adams made such a fuss that the book was
pulped. It was eventually published without the Adams chapter, which
appears here for the first time. Dr Adams himself died in 1984.*

Even during the summer holiday season, when the visitors are
down from London and the hotels and boarding houses become
filled, Eastbourne remains a quiet, dignified town. A great many
of its residents are well-to-do elderly persons who have gone there
to end their days in retirement. To succeed in Eastbourne a doctor
has to be more than a good physician. He also needs a good bedside
manner.

Dr Adams succeeded from the moment he arrived there in 1922.
And not merely because of his sweet smile and his Irish brogue. A
busily religious man, he was soon taking an active part in local
Salvation Army and welfare activities. Nor was his piety a spare-time
thing. He had the engaging habit of carrying a Bible and a selection
of religious tracts along with his stethoscope and manometer, and
of offering spiritual comfort with his medical advice.

Inevitably, he had his critics. Some members of the Salvation
Army discerned in their recruit an irritating tendency to regard
himself as the Almighty's personal representative in Eastbourne.
Relations cooled. Yet, those who dismissed him as a sanctimonious
humbug made no converts. Success did not spoil him. His older,
poorer patients were never neglected. He gave a weekly tea party
for the lonely ones among them so that they could meet and gossip.
And, of course, he helped them with prayer. If he had a vice—and
what man has not?—it was his passion for eating chocolates by the
boxful. Certainly, among his patients there was never any doubt
of his goodness or of the sincerity of his beliefs. He was fifty-seven
and a bachelor.

Early in 1956, the Chief Constable of Eastbourne became aware
of a strong undercurrent of rumour in the town. He also received
some related anonymous letters. Both the rumours and the letters
made the same allegation—that there was a connection between
the deaths of several of Dr Adams's wealthier patients and the fact
that the doctor had benefited under their wills.

The identity of those who started the rumours and wrote the
letters will probably never be known for certain. After the trial,
Dr Adams stated in a newspaper article that he himself had at
intervals been receiving anonymous letters accusing him of killing
"wealthy widows" since 1935. However, the rumours and letters
before the Chief Constable in 1956 were of too serious a nature
to be ignored. In the end, he decided to call on Scotland Yard
for help.

Scotland Yard sent Superintendent Hannam; and it was upon
the results of his work that much of the prosecution's case
subsequently relied.

The superintendent was forty-eight at that time, a self-educated,
ambitious and very able man. Some months earlier, he had been
responsible for investigating charges of police corruption in the
Metropolitan area and had done that disagreeable duty with
impressive thoroughness. At the Yard he had a nickname—"The
Count". When he gave evidence at the Old Bailey, the name did
not, in its urchin way, seem inappropriate. His tight-lipped manner
was a trifle imperious, and he used words like "quest" when he
meant "task" or "job" and "loquacious" when "talkative" would
have done. He also preferred phrases like "abuts on to" to a more
pertinent "is beside" and the medico's "cerebral vascular accident"
to the layman's "stroke".

Accounts of the number of deaths he investigated in Eastbourne
that summer have varied. At the height of the excitement some
newspapers put the figure as high as four hundred. About forty seems
a more likely estimate. But forty or four hundred, the investigation
gave the rumours something substantial to feed upon.

In August, the investigation began to come out into the open. At
a coroner's inquest on Mrs Gertrude Joyce Hullett, a wealthy widow
of fifty, Dr Adams appeared as a witness and said that he had been
treating her with sodium barbiturate. A government pathologist
said that he had found a fatal dose of it in Mrs Hullett's body. It
was revealed that in her will, she had bequeathed her Rolls-Royce
to Dr Adams. The jury returned a verdict of suicide. Depression

and ill health following her husband's recent death were thought to have been the cause. The coroner commented that there had been "an extraordinary element of careless treatment" on Dr Adams's part. He also asked Superintendent Hannam, significantly present in court, if Scotland Yard was investigating "certain deaths in this neighbourhood". Hannam agreed that it was.

Immediately after the inquest, Dr Adams was for the first time introduced to Hannam. The doctor told him that in view of the rumours that were going about he welcomed the investigation, and offered to help in any way he could. Apparently Hannam acknowledged the offer politely enough; but, with so much left unsaid (at this stage Hannam must at least have begun to believe that he was dealing with a murderer) it was a strained encounter.

Two days later, Hannam interviewed the doctor's solicitor and obtained from him a list of the wills under the terms of which Dr Adams had benefited in some way or other. The list was possibly quite extensive. Fifty or sixty years ago, when the social mores of most of the doctor's older patients were determined, it was quite customary to "remember" a friendly family physician in one's will.*

On 1 October, Hannam had what he later insisted was a chance meeting with the doctor outside the latter's garage. Yet, chance or not, within hours the newspapers were reporting that Dr Adams had again been interviewed by the Scotland Yard man. Eastbourne seethed with excitement. The world's press poured in to cover the story. The suspicion that there was a mass murderer in the town had by now become a conviction. On 24 November, Superintendent Hannam, accompanied by Inspector Pugh and Detective-Sergeant Hewitt of the Eastbourne police, went to the doctor's house. After questioning him about a list of drugs which he had prescribed for another wealthy widow, Edith Alice Morrell, who had died in 1950, Hannam took him to the police station. The doctor was there charged with thirteen offences under the Forgery and Cremation Acts.

The alleged forgeries were mainly concerned with prescriptions

---

* During the Eastbourne hearing Superintendent Hannam reported that he had mentioned his concern over the number of legacies received from patients to the doctor. The reply had been: "A lot of these were instead of fees. I don't want money. What use is it? I paid £1,100 super-tax last year."

for drugs. The four relating to cremation had a more sinister ring.

In England, before a person can be cremated, the doctor who attended must certify that he has no financial interest in the death. It was alleged that, in four such cases, the doctor had certified falsely. One of the cases was that of Mrs Hullett's husband. Another was that of Mrs Morrell.

The doctor was allowed bail. On 26 November, after an adjourned hearing on the charges, he asked to see Hannam. At that meeting, the doctor asked if Hannam intended to bring any more charges against him.

Hannam replied: "I am still inquiring into the deaths of some of your rich patients. I don't think they were all natural." He mentioned Mrs Morrell's name.

According to Hannam the doctor then said: "Easing the passing of a dying person is not all that wicked. She wanted to die. That can't be murder. It is impossible to accuse a doctor."

He was mistaken. At noon on 19 December Hannam, Pugh and Hewitt went again to the doctor's house, and arrested him for the murder of Mrs Morrell. Hannam delivered the usual caution.

The way in which Dr Adams responded and the intended meaning of his reply were later to be the subject of argument. The words he uttered were: "Murder? Murder? Can you prove it was murder?" A little later he added: "I did not think you could prove murder. She was dying in any event."

The following morning, he was taken before the Eastbourne magistrates, remanded in custody, and then sent to Brixton prison. On 14 January he was returned to the magistrates' court for the preliminary hearing. The Crown's case, conducted by Mr Melford Stevenson, QC, was in substance this:

Mrs Morrell had suffered from cerebral arterial sclerosis, a hardening of the vessels which supplied blood to the brain, and in June of 1948, when she was seventy-nine, had a stroke which had resulted in some loss of movement on one side of her body. Shortly after this she had come under Dr Adams's care. In spite of the fact that she had been in no serious pain, Dr Adams had begun prescribing morphine for her condition, and later heroin as well. It was contended that his purpose was to make her a drug addict and, therefore, dependent on him. In this way he hoped to induce her to provide for him generously in her will. During the next two years, the prosecution said, he had gradually stepped up the quantities of these drugs until, in November, 1950, he had administered fatal doses of both morphine and paraldehyde, one of which had killed her. He had then certified the cause of her death as cerebral thrombosis. On the cremation certificate, in answer to the question as to whether he had any financial interest in the death, he had written: "Not so far as I am aware." His explanation for this had been that he "always wanted cremations to go off smoothly for the dear relatives". Under her will he had received a valuable chest of Georgian silver cutlery and later received from her son a Rolls-Royce car which she had promised him. He had known that he would get these things, and that had been his motive for the crime.

If the case against Dr Adams had rested there (and, it must be pointed out, that is where it *did* rest when he was later tried at the Old Bailey) it would, I think, have been felt by most people, even those without any knowledge of the medical evidence available to the defence, that the Crown was on shaky ground.

The doctor was a well-to-do man with a substantial practice. The value of the Georgian silver which he had inherited from the dead woman was £276 (even her chauffeur had received more—£1,000 cash); the second-hand Rolls-Royce car had not been inherited, but given to him by the dead woman's son. Was it really feasible that the doctor would do murder for £276? If, in fact, he had been motivated simply by greed for money, would he not have tried to keep this wealthy, fee-paying patient alive as long as he could? As for the entry on the cremation form, the doctor's own explanation could perfectly well be true. Why create difficulties because of a chest of old cutlery? He did not seem to have valued it very much; six years later, when Hannam questioned him, it was still in his house—and he had not even troubled to unwrap it. Of course, it is very wrong to make false statements on legal documents; but most family doctors like things to go smoothly for the bereaved. There must be few who have not, at some time or other, signed a death certificate, knowing that the cause of death they have entered may not be precisely true, because they have seen no sense in insisting on a distressing and pointless autopsy. Of course, the wish for things to go smoothly can go too far. Dr Adams may well have done so.

At Eastbourne, however, there was no room for this sort of argument. After all the rumours, the prolonged and much publicized police investigation, the bringing of the thirteen lesser charges and the massive press coverage, it was virtually impossible to consider the case of Mrs Morrell on its isolated merits. Nor did the Crown attempt to do so. Having presented its case in respect of Mrs Morrell, the prosecution asked leave to introduce supporting evidence to show that Dr Adams's relationships with two of his other wealthy patients (Mr and Mrs Hullett) had followed a similar pattern—drugs, death, legacy—and that the pattern was one of wilful murder.

Mr Geoffrey Lawrence, QC, who defended the doctor both at Eastbourne and at the subsequent trial, argued strenuously against the hearing of the Hullett evidence in open court. His view was that the case had already received enormous publicity in the press; and that, if it were to go before a jury in another court, they would almost certainly have read about or been told about the Eastbourne proceedings. The trial judge might exclude the Hullett evidence as out of order, but it would be impossible for the jury to exclude it from their minds. If it had to be heard let it be heard *in camera*.

It is interesting to note that, in his summing up at the Old Bailey, Mr Justice Devlin expressed the same view.

However, the Eastbourne magistrates decided to follow the more usual practice, and allowed the Hullett evidence to be heard in open court. It amounted to this:

In December, 1955, Mr Hullett, a former Lloyd's underwriter of seventy-one, had been operated on for cancer. He was still convalescent in February when his general condition suddenly worsened. He had attacks of breathlessness and complained of pains in the chest and head. On 13 March, after one of these attacks, Doctor Adams had given Mr Hullett an injection of what the attending nurse had thought to be hyperduric morphia. Some eight hours later the patient had died. Dr Adams had told the nurse that the death had been due to a cerebral haemorrhage, but added words which suggested that the operation had not contained the cancer and that Mr Hullett had been doomed anyway. Under his will Dr Adams received £500. Again he had failed to declare his interest on the cremation certificate.

Four months later Mrs Hullett also died. At the inquest the coroner had said that Dr Adams had been "careless". The Crown said now that Dr Adams had followed the same procedure as in the case of Mrs Morrell, except that this time he had used his knowledge of the fact that she had suicidal tendencies. He had prescribed barbiturates for her and allowed her to possess enough of them for a fatal dose.

As Mr Lawrence pointed out, it was all a little far-fetched.*

Dr Adams pleaded not guilty, reserved his defence and was committed for trial.

Another man who had been tried for murder and then acquitted once wrote that the worst part of the trial was undoubtedly having to listen to counsel's opening speech for the prosecution, without being able to do or say anything about it. Moreover, everyone in court was watching you. If you controlled your feelings too well, that might be construed as callous indifference; if you responded visibly you might convey an impression of guilt and defeat. Whatever you did would be misinterpreted.

Dr Adams proved to be a stout, balding man of medium height with a round, florid face and a puckish nose. His manner was one neither of indifference nor defeat. He listened intently. When counsel drew conclusions with which he disagreed, he shook his head like an irritable schoolteacher trying to be patient with a backward child. Secure in the knowledge that, however imprudent he may have been, he was certainly not guilty of the crimes with which he was charged, his impatience was understandable. My impression was that the only person in court whom he really detested was Superintendent Hannam.

The Attorney-General, Sir Reginald Manningham-Buller, led for the prosecution, and he did so with an air of stolid confidence which he somehow managed to maintain to the end. Of the gaping holes in his case which the defence persistently exposed he seemed quite unaware. His look of surprise at the verdict could well have been genuine. It was as if the captain of a sinking ship had only just realised that the water was up to his neck.

Dramatically speaking, most criminal trials have a standard structure. The accused enters, the indictment is read, there is a plea of "not guilty", and the prosecution presents its case. One by one the damaging facts emerge. Then, come the witnesses for the prosecution, telling their individual stories. Counsel for the defence tries to shake them in cross-examination and usually gains a few minor points, but the general effect is unimpaired. Members of

---

* The Crown cannot have been entirely satisfied with its case. After the doctor's arrest, they exhumed two more of his former patients about whose deaths suspicions had been entertained. The deaths were found to have been entirely natural. Of course, this fact was never brought out in evidence.

the jury glance furtively at the prisoner in the dock, and you know what they are thinking. They are wondering why he should have thought for a moment that he could get away with it, and what lunatic advised him against pleading guilty. Then, later, when the defence presents its case, the whole thing swings the other way. Doubts enter. The battle is joined.

In the trial of Dr Adams everything happened quite differently.

The prosecution had decided to base its case against Dr Adams upon the indictment concerning Mrs Morrell; presumably because they felt that it was the strongest they had.*

The Crown's principal witnesses were the nurses who had attended Mrs Morrell during Dr Adams's treatment of her, and expert medical witnesses to give their opinions about the nature of his treatment. Since the Crown, to prove its case against Dr Adams, had first to prove that murder had in fact been done, the proceedings took on something of the character of an inquest.

The trained nurses were probably the most important figures in the case. These were the various day and night nurses who had been engaged by Dr Adams to attend Mrs Morrell at her house, from the time she left the nursing home in 1948 until her death two years later. The first of the three to give evidence was Nurse Stronach.

She was a small, faded woman with a short upper lip and a determined jaw. The jaw moved slightly but persistently as if she had sore gums or were chewing some kind of cud.

In reply to the Attorney-General's questions she drew for us a picture of Mrs Morrell's last days that looked bad for Dr Adams. We heard of his visits at night, of mysterious injections by him of unknown drugs, of poor Mrs Morrell lying doped and helpless, of further injections being pumped into her. Suggestions that Mrs Morrell might have been suffering pain were waved aside by Nurse Stronach. Mrs Morrell's complaints, she said firmly, were neurotic. She was the ideal prosecution witness.

Then, Geoffrey Lawrence rose to cross-examine.

His manner is quiet and gentle. He asks for the witness's help like a charity organizer wheedling a small subscription out of a

---

* There was a further indictment, for the murder of Mrs Hullett. However, no attempt was made (as there had been at the Eastbourne hearing) to introduce it. Evidently the Crown had no wish to burden itself with the obligation of proving "system".

millionaire. He is elaborately courteous. It is no part of his technique to undermine the witness's personal dignity or self-confidence. What he seems to propose is a friendly collaboration in his great task of getting the truth.

Unfortunately for Nurse Stronach, she chose to reject his proposal.

Lawrence began by reminding her that what she had described so confidently had taken place over six years ago and that she was relying upon her memory. At this not unreasonable suggestion Nurse Stronach took umbrage.

Her attitude was that she knew what she knew, and that nobody was going to trick her into changing her story. When asked about her numerous interviews with the police prior to Dr Adams's arrest, she became pert. The judge began to eye her coldly.

Lawrence, still very polite, began to question her about the record books kept by the nurses—the regulation nursing diary—and asked if such a diary had been kept for Mrs Morrell. Yes, of course. And it would be accurate? Oh, yes; everything pertaining to her medical history would be entered into it by every nurse concerned. Lawrence looked wistful. If only we had those records now we could see exactly what happened? Nurse Stronach agreed somewhat tolerantly that we could.

Then Lawrence pounced.

It so happened that we did have the books—he waved one aloft—and he would trouble Nurse Stronach to say if this entry, and that entry, and that, and that, and that, were in her handwriting. They were.

The prosecution's efforts to appear to remain calm under this assault were manful but forlorn. The Attorney-General recovered quickly enough to put up a counter-barrage of technical objections; but did not get very far. Nurse Stronach was too serious a casualty for technical first aid.

As Lawrence proceeded to demolish practically every statement she had previously made by making her read out what she had written at the time, Nurse Stronach got smaller and smaller.

Not that she gave in easily. She adopted an air of being importuned, while feverishly trying to clamber out of the trap by thumbing through the diary ahead of Lawrence's questions.

But he was not having that.

"Are you listening to me or are you reading that book?" he asked sharply at this point.

"Yes, I am listening," was the unhappy reply. She was chewing furiously now.

"Don't try to read them in advance," Lawrence persisted.

"I am not," said Nurse Stronach, bridling.

When the Attorney-General re-examined her in an effort to repair the damage, he found a witness almost as hostile to the prosecution as she had been to the defence. Nurse Stronach had had enough of lawyers for the day—all lawyers. The friendly pat on the shoulder she received from Superintendent Hannam when she left the witness box can have been small consolation to her.

The next prosecution witness, Nurse Mason-Ellis, suffered a different misfortune.

On the adjournment that day, the judge solemnly warned all three nurses not to discuss the case between themselves.

But the situation was too much for them. Together, that evening, they went back to Eastbourne by train. The following morning they returned to London, also by train. Their conversations on both journeys were overheard and reported to the defence. The ladies talked their heads off about the case.

Nurse Mason-Ellis, a nice-mannered little woman, was the one who had to admit publicly to the indiscretion. Lawrence made the most of it.

When she had been persuaded to admit that the conversations had indeed taken place, he asked: "Did one or other of you say, 'don't say that or you will get me into trouble'? "

Nurse Mason-Ellis after squirming a bit admitted that one of them had; but not her.

"Which one was it?"

"Must I answer?"

The judge intervened with a sharp, "yes".

The truth came out. It had been Nurse Randall, the nurse on duty when Mrs Morrell had died, and what she had been talking about was the important matter of how and where the dangerous drugs had been kept in the Morrell house. It also emerged that, on this same subject, one of the answers given by Nurse Stronach had been patently untrue.

Using the prosecution's own somewhat battered witness and the nursing diaries (the validity of which was not in dispute) Lawrence now proceeded to build up a picture of Mrs Morrell's last days totally different from that proffered by the Attorney-General in his opening address.

Sick she had certainly been; but she had also been senile and, at times, scarcely sane. She had been liable to sudden paranoid outbursts, during which, half-paralysed though she was, she would attempt to get out of bed, shout, scream and work herself into violent rages, abuse her nurses and accuse them of trying to kill her. In her condition this had been dangerous. She had needed heavy sedation, for only heavy sedation had had any effect. Her behaviour, as recorded in the diaries, even after massive injections of morphine and heroin, showed that clearly. She had died eventually because she was old and sick, and for no other reason.

By the time Lawrence had finished with the nursing diaries, Dr Adams was not the only person on trial there. What, it was being asked, would have happened if the diaries had not been found and produced? Presumably, the court would have accepted as true a lot of evidence it now knew to be false. Had those who had prepared the case for the Crown made any effort to find the diaries? Admittedly, after six years the chances of their still being available would be small; but had any effort at all been made?

Apparently not. After Mrs Morrell's death, it seems, the diaries had been delivered to the doctor's house in a bundle, put away with other records in a filing cabinet, and forgotten. It had not been until Superintendent Hannam had questioned him about some drug prescriptions which he had written for Mrs Morrell, that Dr Adams had remembered the diaries. This was when he was preparing to defend himself against the thirteen lesser charges, and some weeks before his arrest for the murder of Mrs Morrell. He and his solicitor had searched for and found the diaries. They had been handed over at once to the defence lawyers, who, of course, would have made them available if the Crown had inquired about them.

The Attorney-General's contention was that the diaries had been purposely kept by Dr Adams in case of any inquiry into Mrs Morrell's death; but this line of thought led him along a strange path. It ended at the dark suggestion that the doctor (driven, we had to assume, by an unholy passion for Georgian cutlery) had taken "the greatest care possible to secure that any entries put by the nurses in those books were not obviously incriminating to him and not obviously showing the design that he had formed".

How the doctor was supposed to have managed this, the Attorney-General did not explain. There had been no hint of a suggestion from any of the nurses that the doctor had told them what or what not to write. Indeed, they had all insisted

on the accuracy of the entries; and the books were all there; no
pages had been removed.

These were not the only nursing diaries to inconvenience the
prosecution.

The expert witnesses for the Crown were two Harley Street
specialists, Doctors Douthwaite and Ashby.

Dr Douthwaite, senior physician at Guy's Hospital, described
the causes of a stroke such as that suffered by Mrs Morrell in
Cheshire in 1948, and the treatment that, in his opinion, should
have followed such an incident.

The burden of his evidence was that there was no justification
for administering morphine to such a patient unless there was an
episode of acute mania. In that event a single injection only might
be given. Dr Adams's programme of morphine and heroin injections
had been quite wrong. It had led to Mrs Morrell's becoming an
addict of those drugs, and her tolerance of them had increased
to the point where she had been suffering withdrawal symptoms.
Finally, in Dr Douthwaite's opinion, Dr Adams had increased the
dosage drastically with the intention of murdering her.

These opinions were given simply, lucidly and temperately; but
also very positively. There was no doubt of the impression they
made upon the court.

When Lawrence rose to cross-examine, he was, we realised, faced
with the task of effacing that impression or, at least, of blurring
it pending the introduction of an expert witness or the defence
who would flatly contradict Dr Douthwaite's opinions. It had not
been expected that he would have as his unwitting collaborators
those who had prepared the case for the Crown. This is how the
cross-examination went.

Lawrence: "Are you saying that Dr Adams formed the intention
to terminate Mrs Morrell's life on 8 November and carried that
intention into effect over the next five days?"

Dr Douthwaite: "Yes."

Lawrence: "I think it follows from what you said to my Lord
yesterday that that murderous intent, in your view, was present in
his mind from and including 8 November onwards to the end?"

Dr Douthwaite: "Yes."

Lawrence: "A specialist's profession is a responsible one, but I
hardly suppose that you have often expressed a graver or more
fateful opinion on a matter than that, have you?"

Dr Douthwaite: "No."

Lawrence: "Before going into the witness box and expressing that view, have you satisfied yourself that you have every piece of relevant evidence before you on which to judge?"

Dr Douthwaite: "Yes."

Lawrence repeated this question in several different ways and received affirmative replies before going on: "Did you know that, when Mrs Morrell had the stroke over two years before she died, she was staying with her son in Cheshire?"

Dr Douthwaite: "Yes."

Lawrence: "Have you made any inquiries, before giving the evidence against Dr Adams that you gave yesterday, into· the symptoms of her stroke, the circumstances and the treatment she had in Cheshire before Dr Adams ever took her over in Eastbourne?"

Dr Douthwaite: "I have said in conferences it would be very interesting to know what treatment she had before she came under the care of Dr Adams."

Lawrence explored this answer a little and then continued: "If it was as relevant and as interesting as that, did you ask for that information to be found, or for attempts to be made to furnish you with it before you came to your final conclusion?"

Dr Douthwaite: "No."

Lawrence (sharply): "Why not, if it was relevant and material to the medical picture from the point of view of addiction, about which you told us so much yesterday?"

Dr Douthwaite must by now have suspected what was coming, but the hesitation before he replied was only momentary: "In the first place because I was told that the information was not available, and secondly because it would not have materially influenced the answers I have given in respect to the addiction."

Lawrence's face was quite expressionless as he produced the nursing record for the case of Mrs Morrell while she had been in the Cheshire cottage hospital. It contained all the information that Dr Douthwaite had been told was not available. The hospital physician had prescribed for her regular injections of morphine. The sedation treatment, which the Crown had postulated as an essential part of Dr Adams's wicked "design", had not been initiated by him.

The Attorney-General, while not going so far as to suggest that the cottage hospital in Cheshire had kept its nursing records for six long years solely in order to help Dr Adams defend himself against a charge of murder, dismissed the information in them as "irrelevant" Dr Douthwaite, however, was more interested. While still disapproving of the morphine injections, he conceded that the man on the spot was entitled to exercise his own best judgment. He also said that from six to twelve months would have been a reasonable prognosis in terms of expectation of life for Mrs Morrell after her stroke.

She had lived two years.

From this point on the trial became in effect a debate about the responsibilities of doctors towards their patients and of the ethical dilemmas involved.

Lawrence: "The reasonable object of a general practitioner's treatment for what he could reasonably expect to be the remaining months of that woman's life would be to make life as bearable as it could be to her and to those who had to look after her?"

Dr Douthwaite: "The first object would be to try to restore her health if possible."

Lawrence: "That is at the highest level the object of every doctor in every case, but human life being what it is there are some instances where every sensible doctor knows that, whatever he does, he cannot restore his patient to normal health. No doctor in his senses would think that, short of a miracle, he could restore a woman of seventy-nine or eighty to her pre-stroke health?"

Dr Douthwaite: "Oh, I agree."

He also agreed that when Dr Adams had been away and his partner had been confronted with a marked degree of cerebral irritation in Mrs Morrell's case, the partner had been right to increase the morphia administration.

Lawrence: "If a general practitioner decides that he has to make use of some sort of drug, he has to balance up the advantages and disadvantages of his choice?"

Dr Douthwaite: "Certainly."

Lawrence: "In the case of Mrs Morrell, one of the most prominent circumstances would be his reasonable prognosis at the time of her stroke that her expectation of life was about six to twelve months?"

Dr Douthwaite: "Yes."

Lawrence: "Therefore, with that short expectation reasonably entertained by the doctor, the disadvantages of addiction following from the selection of these opiates would be far less than if he was selecting them for a person whose prognosis was absolutely indefinite?"

Dr Douthwaite: "Yes."

In response to a further question on this point he went on: "The problem often confronts us, and my practice in teaching has been that if a patient is obviously dying it is ridiculous to worry about addiction. If the strong probability is that the patient will not live for more than a month or two, and if the drugs are indicated for the condition, you cannot worry about addiction."

Nevertheless, he persisted in his opinion that, in the last weeks of Mrs Morrell's life, Dr Adams had set about causing her death and had, in fact, done so. At the same time (it was all most confusing) he agreed that another physician with qualifications comparable to his own might well have a completely contrary opinion.

Dr Ashby put the ethical dilemma another way: "I think that once it can be established that a patient is dying, considerations of improving their health scarcely apply, and a doctor must give his first thought to the patient's comfort and well-being. If comfort and well-being are competing against the length of survival, he might properly give them precedence providing death is known for certain." In his opinion the test was this: if the doctor feels obliged to give priority to treatment of the patient's discomfort, then he must do so.

Or, in Dr Adams's words, he must "ease the patient's passing".

That concluded the case for the Crown.

Lawrence did not put Dr Adams in the witness box to give evidence on his own behalf. It would have been pointless to submit him to that ordeal. The evidence of what had been done in the case of Mrs Morrell was in the nursing records, and it was the best evidence because it depended on nobody's memory of things that had happened six years earlier.

He called only two witnesses for the defence. The first was Dr Harman, a consulting physician of St Thomas' Hospital.

Most laymen fall into two categories where their attitudes towards the medical profession are concerned: those who prefer to believe that most doctors are skilful and wise, and those who profoundly distrust the whole pack of them. For the former group, expert medical evidence is always disconcerting. What is an elderly invalid to think of a flat statement by Consultant X that the drug with which he is being regularly dosed should on no account be prescribed for elderly persons? Should he conclude that his own doctor is trying to murder him? Or should he wait for the reassuring news from

Consultant Y that what the doctor ordered is the very thing he needs? The patient has a dilemma, too.

In just under two hours Dr Harman contradicted, politely, good-humouredly, but quite firmly, practically every opinion about narcotic drugs and their use in treatment which had been given by the prosecution witnesses. Cross-examination did not shake him.

The one other defence witness was the matron of the Cheshire hospital to which Mrs Morrell had first been taken after her stroke. The patient, she said, had been "irritable and restless". As an illustration of what she meant by that phrase, the matron recalled that Mrs Morrell had thrown a reading lamp at one of the nurses.

In his summing up, Mr Justice Devlin said that not infrequently he had heard a case presented by the prosecution that seemed to him to be manifestly a strong one and sometimes he had felt it his duty to tell the jury so. He did not think he should hesitate in this case to tell them that here the case for the defence seemed to be manifestly strong.

He concluded: "It is the same question in the end, always the same. Is the case for the Crown strong enough to carry conviction in your minds? It is your question, you have to answer it. It will lie always with you, the jury, always with you."

The jury retired for forty-three minutes and then returned a verdict of Not Guilty.

The judge then mentioned the further indictment charging Dr Adams with the murder of Mrs Hullett.

The Attorney-General said that he had given the most anxious consideration to the course the Crown should pursue in that matter. He went on:

"One of the considerations I have felt it my duty to consider is that the publicity which has attended this trial would make it even more difficult to secure a fair trial on this further indictment. I have also taken into account the length of this trial, the ordeal which Dr Adams has already undergone, and the fact that the case for the prosecution on this further indictment is based on evidence given before the Eastbourne magistrates, and depends in parts on the evidence of Dr Ashby and very greatly on evidence not supported, as in Mrs Morrell's case, by the admission of the administration of drugs. Having given the matter the best consideration I can, I have reached the conclusion that in all the circumstances the public interest does not require that Dr Adams should undergo the ordeal of a further trial on a charge of murder . . ."

The trial had lasted over three weeks. For the last two, few of those present in court throughout the trial had considered a verdict of Guilty conceivable.

Of the few, I remember one in particular. He was an Old Hand with a knowing grin and, he assured us, access to inside information. Right up until the last day, this genial expert was firmly convinced that the Crown would win hands down; and he had a ten shilling bet on to back his judgment. Wasn't it obvious?

He was one of the policemen on the door of the courtroom.

Postscript

At Lewes Assizes in July of that year, Dr Adams pleaded guilty to certain of the offences under the Forgery and Cremation Acts with which he had originally been charged. The court considered that there had been mitigating circumstances, and a fine rather than a prison sentence was imposed. In view of the conviction, however, the General Medical Council considered it proper to strike his name from the medical register.

In November 1961, following an application by Dr Adams to the Disciplinary Committee of the Council, his name was restored to the register. At the hearing, it was stated that he intended to return to practice in Eastbourne, as an anaesthetist.

A SORT OF GENIUS

(Rev. Hall and Mrs Mills, 1922)

James Thurber

The Hall–Mills double murder of 1922 horrified and then mystified the American nation. But it was, as the Daily News *in New York remarked, "a nice, clean crime". It was also one of the first to be reported using modern transmission methods. The backstage star of the case was the world's biggest portable electric switchboard, property of the Western Union, which could handle 20,000 words an hour. Two hundred reporters covered the trial, including sixteen correspondents from the* Daily News, *plus fifty photographers. Ten of these were posted in the courtroom at Somerville, New Jersey; an eleventh fell through the skylight on the day the defence called Mrs Hall. At the end of eleven days, a total of 5 million words had been telegraphed from Somerville. At the end of eighteen days the total was 9 million. By the twenty-fourth day, it was 12 million, enough to fill a shelf of novels twenty-two feet long. The American humorist James Thurber (1894–1961) was a journalist in the 1920s when the Hall–Mills case broke. By the time he composed this account, in 1936, he was a full-time writer. This elegant essay from the creator of Walter Mitty reminds us of Thurber's extraordinary versatility, and his talents as (his widow's words) "the analyzer and the rememberer".*

On the morning of Saturday 16 September 1922, a boy named Raymond Schneider and a girl named Pearl Bahmer, walking down a lonely lane on the outskirts of New Brunswick, New Jersey, came upon something that made them rush to the nearest house in Easton Avenue, around the corner, shouting. In that house an excited woman named Grace Edwards listened to them wide-eyed and then telephoned the police. The police came on the run and examined the young people's discovery: the bodies of a man and a woman. They had been shot to death and the woman's throat was cut. Leaning against one of the man's shoes was his calling card, not as if it had fallen there but as if it had been placed there. It bore the name Rev. Edward W. Hall. He had been the rector of the Protestant Episcopal Church of St John the Evangelist in New Brunswick. The woman was identified as Mrs Eleanor R. Mills, wife of the sexton of that church. Raymond Schneider and Pearl Bahmer had stumbled upon what was to go down finally in the annals of our crime as perhaps the country's most remarkable mystery. Nobody was ever found guilty of the murders. Before the case was officially closed, a hundred and fifty persons had had their day in court and on the front pages of the newspapers. The names of two must already have sprung to your mind: Mrs Jane Gibson, called by the avid press "the pig woman", and William Carpender Stevens, once known to a hundred million people simply as "Willie". The pig woman died eleven years ago, but Willie Stevens is alive. He still lives in the house that he lived in fourteen years ago with Mr and Mrs Hall, at 23 Nichol Avenue, New Brunswick.

It was from that house that the Rev. Mr Hall walked at around seven-thirty o'clock on the night of Thursday 14 September 1922, to his peculiar doom. With the activities in that house after Mr Hall's departure the State of New Jersey was to be vitally concerned. No. 23 Nichol Avenue was to share with De Russey's Lane, in which the bodies were found, the morbid interest of a whole nation four years later, when the case was finally brought to trial. What actually happened in De Russey's Lane on the night of 14 September? What actually happened at 23 Nichol Avenue the same night? For the researcher, it is a matter of an involved and voluminous court record, colourful and exciting in places, confused and repetitious in others. Two things, however, stand out as sharply now as they did on the day of their telling: the pig woman's story of the people she saw in De Russey's Lane that night, and Willie Stevens's story of what went on in the house in Nichol Avenue. Willie's story, brought out in cross-examination by a prosecutor whose name you may have forgotten (it was Alexander Simpson), lacked all the gaudy melodrama of the pig woman's tale, but in it, and in the way he told it on the stand, was the real drama of the Hall–Mills trial. When the State failed miserably in its confident purpose of breaking Willie Stevens down, the verdict was already written on the wall. The rest of the trial was anticlimax. The jury that acquitted Willie, and his sister, Mrs Frances Stevens Hall, and his brother, Henry Stevens, was out only five hours.

A detailed recital of all the fantastic events and circumstances of the Hall–Mills case would fill a large volume. If the story is vague in your mind, it is partly because its edges, even under the harsh glare of investigation, remained curiously obscure and fuzzy. Everyone remembers, of course, that the minister was deeply involved with Mrs Mills, who sang in his choir; their affair had been for some time the gossip of their circle. He was forty-one, she was in her early thirties; Mrs Hall was nearing fifty. On 14 September, Mr Hall had dinner at home with his wife, Willie Stevens, and a little niece of Mrs Hall's. After dinner, he said, according to his wife and his brother-in-law, that he was going to call on Mrs Mills. There was something about a payment on a doctor's bill. Mrs Mills had had an operation and the Halls had paid for it (Mrs Hall had inherited considerable wealth from her parents). He left the house at about the same time, it came out later, that Mrs Mills left her house, and the two were found murdered, under a crab apple tree in De Russey's Lane, on the edge of town, some forty hours later. Around the bodies were scattered love letters which the choir singer had written to the minister. No weapons were found, but there were several cartridge shells from an automatic pistol.

The investigation that followed—marked, said one New Jersey lawyer, by "bungling stupidity"—resulted in the failure of the grand jury to indict anyone. Willie Stevens was questioned for hours, and so was Mrs Hall. The pig woman told her extraordinary story of what she saw and heard in the lane that night, but she failed to impress the grand jurors. Four years went by, and the Hall–Mills case was almost forgotten by people outside of New Brunswick when, in a New Jersey court, one Arthur Riehl brought suit against his wife, the former Louise Geist, for annulment of their marriage. Louise Geist had been, at the time of the murders, a maid in the Hall household. Riehl said in the course of his testimony that his wife had told him "she knew all about the case but had been given $5,000 to hold her tongue". This was all that Mr Philip Payne, managing editor of the *Daily Mirror*, nosing around for a big scandal of some sort, needed. His newspaper "played up" the story until finally, under its goading, Governor Moore of New Jersey appointed Alexander Simpson special prosecutor with orders to reopen the case. Mrs Hall and Willie Stevens were arrested and so was their brother, Henry Stevens, and a cousin, Henry de la Bruyere Carpender.

At a preliminary hearing in Somerville the pig woman, with eager stridency, told her story again. About 9 o'clock on the night of 14 September, she heard a wagon going along Hamilton Road near the farm on which she raised her pigs. Thieves had been stealing her corn and she thought maybe they were at it again. So she saddled her mule, Jenny (soon to become the most famous quadruped in the country), and set off in grotesque pursuit. In the glare of an automobile's headlights in De Russey's Lane, she saw a woman with white hair who was wearing a tan coat, and a man with a heavy moustache, who looked like a coloured man. These figures she identified as Mrs Hall and Willie Stevens. Tying her mule to a cedar tree, she started toward the scene on foot and heard voices raised in quarrel: "Somebody said something about letters." She now saw three persons (later on she increased this to four), and a flashlight held by one of them illuminated the face of a man she identified first as Henry Carpender, later as Henry Stevens, and it "glittered on something" in the man's hand. Suddenly there was a shot, and as she turned and ran for her mule, there were three more shots; a woman's voice screamed, "Oh, my! Oh, my! Oh, my!" and the voice of another woman moaned, "Oh, Henry!" The pig woman rode wildly home on her mule, without investigating further. But she had lost one of her moccasins in her flight, and some three hours later, at one o'clock, she rode her mule back again to see if she could find it. This time, by the light of the moon, she saw Mrs Hall, she said, kneeling in the lane, weeping. There was no one else there. The pig woman did not see any bodies.

Mrs Jane Gibson became, because of her remarkable story, the chief witness for the State, as Willie Stevens was to become the chief witness for the defence. If he and his sister were not in De Russey's Lane, as the pig woman had shrilly insisted, it remained for them to tell the detailed story of their whereabouts and their actions that night after Mr Hall left the house. The grand jury this time indicted all four persons implicated by the pig woman, and the trial began on 3 November 1926.

The first persons Alexander Simpson called to the stand were "surprise witnesses". They were a Mr and Mrs John S. Dixon, who lived in North Plainfield, New Jersey, about twelve miles from New Brunswick. It soon became apparent that they were to form part of a net that Simpson was preparing to draw around Willie Stevens. They testified that at about eight-thirty on the night of the murders Willie had appeared at their house, wearing a loose-fitting suit, a derby, a wing collar with bow tie, and, across his vest, a heavy gold chain to which was attached a gold watch. He had said that his sister had let him out there from her automobile and that he was trying to find the Parker Home for the Aged, which was at Bound Brook. He stuttered and he told them that he was an epileptic. They directed him to a trolley car and he went stumbling away. When Mrs Dixon identified Willie as her visitor, she walked over to him and took his right hand and shook it vigorously, as if to wring recognition out of him. Willie stared at her, said nothing. When she returned to the stand, he grinned widely. That was one of many bizarre incidents which marked the progress of the famous murder trial. It deepened the mystery that hung about the strange figure of Willie Stevens. People could hardly wait for him to take the stand.

William Carpender Stevens had sat in court for sixteen days before he was called to the witness chair, on 23 November 1926. On that day the trial of Albert B. Fall and Edward L. Doheny, defendants in the notorious Teapot Dome scandal, opened in Washington, but the nation had eyes only for a small, crowded courtroom in Somerville, New Jersey. Willie Stevens, after all these weeks, after all these years, was to speak out in public for the first time. As the *New York Times* said, "He had been pictured as 'Crazy Willie', as a town character, as an oddity, as a butt for all manner of jokes. He had been compared inferentially to an animal, and the hint of an alien racial strain in his parentage had been thrown at him." Moreover, it had been prophesied that Willie would "blow up" on the stand, that he would be trapped into contradictions by the "wily" and "crafty" Alexander Simpson, that he would be tricked finally into blurting out his guilt. No wonder there was no sound in the courtroom except the heavy tread of Willie Stevens's feet as he walked briskly to the witness stand.

Willie Stevens was an ungainly, rather lumpish man, about five feet ten inches tall. Although he looked flabby, this was only because of his loose-fitting clothes and the way he wore them; despite his fifty-four years, he was a man of great physical strength. He had a large head and a face that would be hard to forget. His head was covered with a thatch of thick, bushy hair, and his heavy black eyebrows seemed always to be arched, giving him an expression of perpetual surprise. This expression was strikingly accentuated by large, prominent eyes which, seen through the thick lenses of the spectacles he always wore, seemed to bulge unnaturally. He had a heavy, drooping, walrus moustache, and his complexion was dark. His glare was sudden and fierce; his smile, which came just as quickly, lighted up his whole face and gave him the wide, beaming look of an enormously pleased child. Born in Aiken, South Carolina, Willie Stevens had been brought to New Brunswick when he was two years old. When his wealthy parents died, a comfortable trust fund was left to Willie. The other children, Frances and Henry, had inherited their money directly. Once, when Mrs Hall was asked if it was not true that Willie was "regarded as essential to be taken care of in certain things," she replied, "In certain aspects." The quality of Willie's mentality, the extent of his eccentricity, were matters the prosecution strove to establish on several occasions. Dr Laurence Runyon, called by the defence to testify that Willie was not an epileptic and had never stuttered, was cross-examined by Simpson. Said the doctor, "He may not be absolutely normal mentally, but he is able to take care of himself perfectly well. He is brighter than the average person, although he has never advanced as far in school learning as some others. He reads books that are above the average and makes a good many people look like fools." "A sort of genius, in a way, I suppose?" said Simpson. To which the doctor quietly replied, "Yes, that is just what I mean."

There were all sorts of stories about Willie. One of them was that he had once started a fire in his back yard and then, putting on a fireman's helmet, had doused it gleefully with a pail of water. It was known that for years he had spent most of every day at the firehouse of Engine Company No. 3 in Dennis Street, New Brunswick. He played cards with the firemen, ran errands for them, argued and joked with them, and was a general favourite. Sometimes he went out and bought a steak, or a chicken, and it was prepared and eaten in the firehouse by the firemen and Willie. In the days when the engine company had been a volunteer organization, Willie was an honorary member and always carried, in the firemen's parades, a flag he had bought and presented to the firehouse, an elaborate banner costing sixty or seventy dollars. He had also bought the black-and-white bunting with which the front of the firehouse was draped whenever a member of the company died.

After his arrest, he had whiled away the time in his cell reading books on metallurgy. There was a story that when his sister-in-law, Mrs Henry Stevens, once twitted him on his heavy reading, he said, "Oh, that is merely the bread and butter of my literary repast." The night before the trial opened, Willie's chief concern was about a new blue suit that had been ordered for him and that did not fit him to his satisfaction. He had also lost a collar button, and that worried him; Mrs Henry Stevens hurried to the jail before the court convened and brought him another one, and he was happy. At the preliminary hearing weeks before, Simpson had declared with brutal directness that Willie Stevens did indeed look like a coloured man, as the pig woman had said. At this Willie had half risen from his chair and bared his teeth, as if about to leap on the prosecutor. But he had quickly subsided. Willie Stevens all through the trial had sat quietly, staring. He had been enormously interested when the pig woman, attended by a doctor and a nurse, was brought in on a stretcher to give her testimony. This was the man who now, on trial for his life, climbed into the witness chair in the courtroom at Somerville.

There was an immense stir. Justice Charles W. Parker rapped with his gavel. Mrs Hall's face was strained and white; this was an ordeal she and her family had been dreading for weeks. Willie's left hand gripped his chair tightly, his right hand held a yellow pencil with which he had fiddled all during the trial. He faced the roomful of eyes tensely. His own lawyer, Senator Clarence E. Case, took the witness first. Willie started badly by understating his age ten years. He said he was forty-four. "Isn't it fifty-four?" asked Case. Willie gave the room his great, beaming smile. "Yes," he chortled, boyishly, as if amused by his slip. The spectators smiled. It didn't take Willie long to dispose of the Dixons, the couple who had sworn he stumbled into their house the night of the murder. He answered half a dozen questions on this point with strong emphasis, speaking slowly and clearly: he had never worn a derby, he had never had epilepsy, he had never stuttered, he had never had a gold watch and chain. Mr Case held up Willie's old silver watch and chain for the jury to see. When he handed them back, Willie, with fine nonchalance, compared his watch with the clock on the courtroom wall, gave his sister a large, reassuring smile, and turned to his questioner with respectful attention. He described, with technical accuracy, an old revolver of his (the murders had been done with an automatic pistol, not a revolver, but a weapon of the same calibre as Willie's). He said he used to fire off the gun on the Fourth of July; remembering these old holidays, his eyes lighted up with childish glee. From this mood he veered suddenly into indignation and anger. "When was the last time you saw the revolver?" was what set him off. "The last time I saw it was in this courthouse!" Willie almost shouted. "I think it was in October 1922, when I was taken and put through a very severe grilling by—I cannot mention every person's name, but I remember Mr Toolan, Mr Lamb, and Detective David, and they did everything but strike me. They cursed me frightfully." The officers had got him into an automobile "by a subterfuge," he charged. "Mr David said he simply wanted me to go out in the country, to ask me a very few questions, that I would not be very long." It transpired later that on this trip Willie himself had had a question to ask Detective David: would the detective, if they passed De Russey's Lane, be kind enough to point it out to him? Willie had never seen the place, he told the detective, in his life. He said that Mr David showed him where it was.

When Willie got to the night of 14 September 1922, in his testimony his anger and indignation were gone; he was placid, attentive, and courteous. He explained quietly that he had come home for supper that night, had gone to his room afterward, and "remained in the house, leaving it at two-thirty in the morning with my sister". Before he went to bed, he said, he had closed his door to confine to his own room the odour of tobacco smoke from his pipe. "Who objected to that?" asked Mr Case. Willie gave his sudden, beaming grin. "Everybody," he said, and won the first of several general laughs from the courtroom. Then he told the story of what happened at two-thirty in the morning. It is necessary, for a well-rounded picture of Willie Stevens, to give it here at some length. "I was awakened by my sister knocking at my door," said Willie, "and I immediately rose and went to the door and she said, 'I want you to come down to the church as Edward has not come home; I am very much worried'—or words to that effect. I immediately got dressed and accompanied her down to the church. I went through the front door, followed a small path that led directly to the back of the house past the cellar door. We went directly down Redmond Street to Jones Avenue, from Jones Avenue we went to George Street; turning into George Street we went directly down to Commercial Avenue. There our movements were blocked by an immense big freight automobile. We had to wait there maybe half a minute until it went by, going toward New York.

"I am not at all sure whether we crossed right there at Commercial Avenue or went a little further down George Street and went diagonally across to the church. Then we stopped there and looked at the church to see whether there were any lights. There were no lights burning. Then Mrs Hall said, 'We might as well go down and see if it could not be possible that he was at the Mills's house.' We went down there, down George Street until we came to Carman Street, turned down Carman Street, and got in front of the Mills's house and stood there two or three minutes to see if there were any lights in the Mills's apartment. There were none." Willie then described, street by street, the return home, and ended with "I opened the front door with my latchkey. If you wish me, I will show it to you. My sister said, 'You might as well go to bed. You can do no more good.' With that I went upstairs to bed." This was the story that Alexander Simpson had to shake. But before Willie was turned over to him, the witness told how he heard that his brother-in-law had been killed. "I remember I was in the parlour," said Willie, "reading a copy of the *New York Times*. I heard someone coming up the steps and I glanced up and I heard my aunt, Mrs Charles J. Carpender, say, 'Well, you might as well know it—Edward has been shot.' " Willie's voice was thick with emotion. He was asked what happened then. "Well," he said, "I simply let the paper go—that way" (he let his left hand fall slowly and limply to his side) "and I put my head down, and I cried." Mr Case asked him if he was present at, or had anything to do with, the murder of Mr Hall and Mrs Mills. "Absolutely nothing at all!" boomed Willie, coming out of his posture of sorrow, belligerently erect. The attorney for the defence turned, with a confident little bow, to Alexander Simpson. The special prosecutor sauntered over and stood in front of the witness. Willie took in his breath sharply.

Alexander Simpson, a lawyer, a state senator, slight, perky, capable of harsh tongue-lashings, given to sarcasm and innuendo, had intimated that he would "tie Willie Stevens into knots". Word had gone around that he intended to "flay" the eccentric fellow. Hence his manner now came as a surprise. He spoke in a gentle, almost inaudible voice, and his attitude was one of solicitous friendliness. Willie, quite unexpectedly, drew first blood. Simpson asked him if he had ever earned his livelihood. "For about four or five

years," said Willie, "I was employed by Mr Siebold, a contractor."
Not having anticipated an affirmative reply, Simpson paused. Willie
leaned forward and said, politely, "Do you wish his address?" He
did this in good faith, but the spectators took it for what the *Times*
called a "sally", because Simpson had been in the habit of letting
loose a swarm of investigators on anyone whose name was brought
into the case. "No, thank you," muttered Simpson, above a roar
of laughter. The prosecutor now set about picking at Willie's story
of the night of 14 September: he tried to find out why the witness
and his sister had not knocked on the Mills's door to see if Mr Hall
were there. Unfortunately for the steady drumming of questions,
Willie soon broke the prosecutor up with another laugh. Simpson
had occasion to mention a New Brunswick boarding house called
The Bayard, and he pronounced "Bay" as it is spelled. With easy
politeness, Willie corrected him. "*Bi*yard," said Willie. "Biyard?"
repeated Simpson. Willie smiled, as at an apt pupil. Simpson bowed
slightly. The spectators laughed again.

Presently the witness made a slip, and Simpson pounced on it like
a stooping falcon. Asked if he had not, at the scene of the murder,
stood "in the light of an automobile while a woman on a mule went
by," Willie replied, "I never remember that occurrence." Let us
take up the court record from there. "Q.—You would remember
if it occurred, wouldn't you? A.—I certainly would, but I don't
remember of ever being in an automobile and the light from the
automobile shone on a woman on a mule. Q.—Do you say you
were not there, or you don't remember? A.—I say positively I was
not there. Q.—Why did you say you don't *remember*? A.—Does not
that cover the same thing? Q.—No, it don't, because you might
be there and not remember it. A.—Well, I will withdraw that, if
I may, and say I was not there positively." Willie assumed an air
of judicial authority as he "withdrew" his previous answer, and he
spoke his positive denial with sharp decision. Mr Simpson abruptly
tried a new tack. "You have had a great deal of experience in life,
Mr Stevens," he said, "and have read a great deal, they say, and
know a lot about human affairs. Don't you think it sounds rather
fishy when you say you got up in the middle of the night to go and
look for Dr Hall and went to the house and never even knocked on
the door—with your experience of human affairs and people that
you met and all that sort of thing—don't that seem rather fishy to
you?" There was a loud bickering of attorneys before Willie could
say anything to this. Finally Judge Parker turned to the witness and

said, "Can you answer that, Mr Stevens?" "The only way I can answer it, Your Honour," said Willie, scornfully, "is that I don't see that it is at all 'fishy'. " The prosecutor jumped to something else: "Dr Hall's church was not your church, was it?" he asked. "He was not a *Doctor*, sir," said Willie, once more the instructor. "He was the Reverend *Mister* Hall." Simpson paused, nettled. "I am glad you corrected me on that," he said. The courtroom laughed again.

The prosecutor now demanded that Willie repeat his story of what happened at two-thirty a.m. He hoped to establish, he intimated, that the witness had learned it "by rote." Willie calmly went over the whole thing again, in complete detail, but no one of his sentences was the same as it had been. The prosecutor asked him to tell it a third time. The defence objected vehemently. Simpson vehemently objected to the defence's objection. The Court: "We will let him tell it once more." At this point Willie said, "May I say a word?" "Certainly," said Simpson. "Say all you want." Weighing his words carefully, speaking with slow emphasis, Willie said, "All I have to say is I was never taught, as you insinuate, by any person whatsoever. That is my best recollection from the time I started out with my sister to this present minute." Simpson did not insist further on a third recital. He wanted to know now how Willie could establish the truth of his statement that he was in his room from eight or nine o'clock until his sister knocked on the door at two-thirty a.m. "Why," said Willie, "if a person sees me go upstairs and does not see me come downstairs, isn't that a conclusion that I was in my room?" The court record shows that Mr Simpson replied, "Absolutely." "Well," said Willie expansively, "that is all there was to it." Nobody but the pig woman had testified to seeing Willie after he went up to his room that night. Barbara Tough, a servant who had been off during the day, testified that she got back to the Hall home about ten o'clock and noticed that Willie's door was closed (Willie had testified that it wouldn't stay closed unless he locked it). Louise Geist, of the annulment suit, had testified that she had not seen Willie that night after dinner. It was Willie's story against the pig woman's. That day in court he overshadowed her. When he stepped down from the witness chair, his shoulders were back and he was smiling broadly. Headlines in the *Times* the next day said, "Willie Stevens Remains Calm Under Cross-Examination. Witness a Great Surprise". There was a touch of admiration, almost of partisanship, in most of the reporters'

stories. The final verdict could be read between the lines. The
trial dragged on for another ten days, but on 3 December, Willie
Stevens was a free man.

He was glad to get home. He stood on the porch of 23 Nichol
Avenue, beaming at the house. Reporters had followed him there.
He turned to them and said, solemnly, "It is 104 days since I've
been here. And I want to get in." They let him go. But two days
later, on a Sunday, they came back and Mrs Hall received them
in the drawing room. They could hear Willie in an adjoining room,
talking spiritedly. He was, it came out, discussing metallurgy with
the Rev. J. Mervin Pettit, who had succeeded Mr Hall as rector of
the Church of St John the Evangelist.

Willie Stevens, going on seventy, no longer visits the firehouse of
No.3 Engine Company. His old friends have caught only glimpses of
him in the past few years, for he has been in feeble health, and spends
most of his time in his room, going for a short ride now and then in
his chauffeur-driven car. The passer by, glancing casually into the
car, would not recognize the famous figure of the middle 1920s.
Willie has lost a great deal of weight, and the familiar beaming
light no longer comes easily to his eyes.

After Willie had been acquitted and sent home, he tried to pick
up the old routine of life where he had left it, but people turned
to stare after him in the street, and boys were forever at his heels,
shouting, "Look out, Willie, Simpson is after you!" The younger
children were fond of him and did not tease him, and once in
a while Willie could be seen playing with them, as boisterously
and whimsically as ever. The firemen say that if he encountered a
ragged child he would find out where it lived, and then give one
of his friends the money to buy new clothes for it. But Willie's
adventures in the streets of the town became fewer and farther
apart. Sometimes months would elapse between his visits to the
firehouse. When he did show up in his old haunts, he complained
of headaches, and while he was still in his fifties, he spent a month
in bed with a heart ailment. After that, he stayed close to home, and
the firemen rarely saw him. If you should drop by the firehouse, and
your interest in Willie seems friendly, they will tell you some fond
stories about him.

One winter Willie took a Cook's tour of Hawaii. When he came
back, he told the firemen he had joined an organization which,
for five dollars, gave its subscribers a closer view of the volcanoes
than the ordinary tourist could get. Willie was crazy about the

volcanoes. His trip, however, was spoiled, it came out, because someone recognized and pointed him out as the famous Willie Stevens of the Hall–Mills case. He had the Cook's agent cancel a month's reservation at a hotel and rearrange his schedule so that he could leave on the next ship. He is infuriated by any reference to the murders or to the trial. Some years ago a newspaper printed a paragraph about a man out West who was "a perfect double for Willie Stevens". Someone in the firehouse showed it to Willie and he tore the paper to shreds in a rage.

Willie still spends a great deal of time reading "heavy books"—on engineering, on entomology, on botany. Those who have seen his famous room at 23 Nichol Avenue—he has a friend in to visit him once in a while—say that it is filled with books. He has no use for detective stories or the Western and adventure magazines his friends the firemen read. When he is not reading scientific tomes, he dips into the classics or what he calls the "worth-while poets". He used to astound the firemen with his wide range of knowledge. There was the day a salesman of shaving materials dropped in at the engine-house. Finding that Willie had visited St Augustine, Florida, he mentioned an old Spanish chapel there. Willie described it and gave its history, replete with dates, and greatly impressed the caller. Another time someone mentioned a certain kind of insect which he said was found in this country. "You mean they used to be," said Willie. "That type of insect has been extinct in this country for forty years." It turned out that it had been, too. On still another occasion Willie fell to discussing flowers with some visitor at the firehouse and reeled off a Latin designation—*crassinae carduaceae*, or something of the sort. Then he turned, grinning, to the listening firemen. "Zinnias to you," he said.

Willie Stevens's income from the trust fund established for him is said to be around forty dollars a week. His expenditures are few, now that he is no longer able to go on long trips. The firemen like especially to tell about the time that Willie went to Wyoming, and attended a rodeo. He told the ticket-seller he wanted to sit in a box and the man gave him a single ticket. Willie explained that he wanted the whole box to himself, and he planked down a ten-dollar bill for it. Then he went in and sat in the box all alone. "I had a hell of a time!" he told the firemen gleefully when he came back home.

De Russey's Lane, which Detective David once pointed out to Willie Stevens, is now, you may have heard, entirely changed. Several years ago it was renamed Franklin Boulevard, and where

the Rev. Mr Edward W. Hall and Mrs Eleanor Mills lay murdered
there is now a row of neat brick and stucco houses. The famous
crab apple tree under which the bodies were found disappeared the
first weekend after the murders. It was hacked to pieces, roots and
all, by souvenir-hunters.

WHAT BECAME
OF MARTIN GUERRE

(Martin Guerre, 1560)

Elliott O'Donnell

No murder as such (at least, no murder that was ever proved) but two trials and a hanging. Quite whether any actual crime was committed is also a moot point. But there was certainly a mystery in the case of Martin Guerre's disappearance, and the mystery was never solved to anyone's satisfaction. The setting is sixteenth-century France, making this (historically) the oldest story in the present collection. Most modern readers will know the name of Martin Guerre as the eponymous hero of the hit musical by Alain Boublil and Claude-Michel Schonberg, the duo behind Les Miserables *and* Miss Saigon. *This version of the story appeared in 1927. Elliott O'Donnell (1872–1965) was a stage and film actor as well as a writer. He wrote mainly about unusual phenomena and the supernatural, his first book* For Satan's Sake *appearing in 1904. In all he wrote over sixty books, several radio plays, and hundreds of articles for newspapers and magazines.*

Sometime, during the sixteenth century, there lived in the little town of Artigues, in the district of Rieux, a young couple named Guerre,* about whom very queer stories were told. The reason was this.

Bertrande Rols, when little more than thirteen years of age, was married to her playmate, Martin Guerre, a youth of about sixteen; but, despite the fact that they were both strong and healthy, Bertrande possessing, in addition to a sound constitution, considerable physical attraction, they had no children.

Hence, the good citizens of Artigues, who like the majority of people at that time were very superstitious, came to the conclusion that the Guerres were bewitched; and consequently extraordinary rumours soon got into circulation concerning them. It was said, for instance, that they had gathered flowers in a certain woodland glade reputed to be fairy haunted, and that, as a result, they had come under a spell; and, again, that they had offended an old itinerant mendicant believed to possess the evil eye, and that he, in revenge, had cursed them.

Their friends and relatives, believing either one or other of these stories, and anxious to deliver the alleged sufferers from the charm or curse, as the case might be, recommended all sorts of supposed antidotes, such as consecrated cakes, the branch of an elder tree, a horseshoe (nailed over the entrance of their abode), and the red flowers of the hypericon or St John's wort (to be worn round their necks),† while the priests of the district composed special prayers for their benefit, and nearly drowned them in holy water. However, it was all of no avail; the enchantment continued: no children would come.

Now among the many admirers of Bertrande Guerre were several young men, who, being envious of Martin, combined with Bertrande's friends and relatives in trying to persuade Bertrande to divorce him and marry some one else, attributing her being childless

---

* See "All the Year Round", 29 June 1867, and "Celebrated Crimes," by Alexandre Dumas.

† Bassardus Visontius (ant Philos) commends to one troubled with heart-melancholy "Hypericon or St John's Wort" gathered on a Friday in the hour of Jupiter, "When it comes to his effectual operation (that is about the full moon in July); so gathered, and borne or hung about the neck, it mightily helps this affection and drives away all phantastical spirits." (Burton's *Anatomy of Melancholy*, Part II., sec. 5.)

to him, and declaring him to be a thoroughly worthless and abandoned character, capable of almost any wickedness. But Bertrande,
who was devotedly attached to her husband, indignantly repudiated
all these charges, and refused to be separated from him.

Then an event happened, which for the time being, at all events,
led to the total discomfiture of Martin's accusers. Bertrande gave
birth to a child, a boy, who was subsequently christened Sanxi*;
and this, of course, rendered any attempt at divorce extremely
difficult, if not impossible. However, not long after the birth of
this child, a robbery took place one night on the farm belonging to
Martin's father (who, though of Biscayan origin, lived in Artigues),
and owing to the discovery of certain tell-tale clues, suspicion at
once fell upon Martin; and, whether he could have exonerated
himself or not, no one could say, for while his wife and father, .
who believed him to be innocent, were waiting for him to take
that step he suddenly vanished.

He left his cottage one summer morning and set off down the
road, in the direction of his father's farm, and, after that, all trace
of him was lost. His enemies, naturally, spread the report that he
had absconded, remarking that if any sure proof of his guilt had
been needed, he himself had now furnished it. Fearing arrest and
the severe punishment meted out to thieves, they said (in those
days no matter how small the theft hanging was the penalty) he
had simply fled.

"You are well rid of him," they told Madame Guerre. "If he
hadn't robbed his father, you may depend upon it he would have
robbed some one else."

But again they were nonplussed; Bertrande stolidly refused
to be set against her husband. Moreover, she declared, in
public, her absolute belief in his innocence, and was cease-
less in her efforts to trace his whereabouts. In this she was
helped by Martin's father, who, although somewhat dubious
now as to his son's innocence (the circumstances, it must
be remembered, appeared to be dead against him), was still
fond of him, and only too willing to welcome him back to
Artigues.

However, despite the exhaustive inquiries made by these two,
no tidings of the missing man could be obtained. He had not
been seen in any of the neighbouring villages, nor apparently had

* Bertrande was now just twenty years old.

he been encountered by anyone in any of the roads or lanes round and about Artigues.

The years passed by. Martin's father died, and to prove that he bore Martin no ill will he left the bulk of his property to him. In the absence of any positive proof of Martin's death, the legal view of the matter was that he was still alive, a fact Martin's father, of course, would be well aware of when he drew up the will.

In Artigues, however, the opinion that Martin Guerre was dead prevailed, and great therefore was every one's astonishment, when, at the expiration of eight years from the time of his disappearance, the news was suddenly spread that he had returned. What actually happened was this.

One morning, a sunburned, weather-beaten man called at the house where Madame Guerre was living in solitary retirement, and asked to see her. Now the moment Madame Guerre caught sight of the stranger, perceiving at once that his features and stature were identical with those of her lost husband, with a wild cry of delight she threw herself into his arms. Later, the Guerres' friends and neighbours, becoming acquainted with the news, came crowding to the house, and as soon as they saw the stranger they also unanimously expressed the opinion that it really was Martin come back, and straightaway greeted him with the utmost cordiality.

The stranger, whom I will now call Martin, then chatted away with them, gossiping about old times, various escapades in which he had participated as a boy, and numerous adventures that had befallen him in more recent years, until finally, when they left him and returned to their respective houses, there was not one among them who was not fully convinced that he was and could be none other than Martin Guerre.

And it was the same with Martin Guerre's four sisters. They had no sooner set eyes on the stranger than they hailed him as their missing brother, while their uncle, Peter Guerre, following suit, acknowledged him to be his nephew, and subsequently made him his heir. So far, then, all was well. Martin Guerre had come back to life, and since, naturally perhaps, bygones were allowed to remain bygones, he was soon comfortably ensconced in the home he had left so abruptly, and under such a cloud.

And no one could have been happier than his faithful Bertrande, who, in course of time, presented him with two more children. One of them, it is true, died in its infancy, but this apparently was a mere detail, apart from which everything seemed to be going on quite swimmingly in the Guerre household. Nothing, in fact, of an unpleasant nature seemed in the least degree likely to happen, when one day a startling report concerning Martin was suddenly launched forth and spread throughout the village. It originated thus.

A soldier, arriving in the village from Rochefort, upon being told the story of Martin's disappearance and return, electrified his informers by declaring that the man whom they had welcomed, open armed, as the lost Martin Guerre was an impostor, and that the real Martin Guerre, whom he knew intimately, was still alive, although he had lost a leg in the recent war in Flanders.

The story was variously received. While some were inclined to believe it, others did not, arguing that, if it were true, the one-legged man would assuredly have come forward long ago and claimed his pretty wife and not inconsiderable property.

Now, it was while the citizens of Artigues were thus engaged in a somewhat heated controversy that the harmony in the Guerre household was threatened with a serious rupture.

Although Peter Guerre had handed over to his nephew the property he had inherited from his father, and of which he had been appointed trustee, he had not rendered an account of his trusteeship, and this omission gave rise to an incessant wrangling, which soon led to a violent quarrel. Martin brought an action against his uncle, and his uncle, losing his temper one day, knocked him down with an iron bar and would have killed him, had not the devoted Bertrande opportunely interfered and prevented him. Henceforth, however, Peter Guerre became Martin's inveterate enemy, and, with the intensity of feeling which was characteristic of him, gave himself up entirely to thoughts of revenge. Nor did he have to wait long for an opportunity to gratify such thoughts.

Martin, who seems either to have become suddenly aggressive or to have developed the unfortunate idiosyncrasy of arousing other people's animosity, quarreled with a man named Jean d'Escarboeuf, who, somehow, managed to get him put into prison. Here, then, was the opportunity Peter was looking for. Taking advantage of Martin's ignominy and absence, he did his level best to persuade Bertrande to desert her husband, declaring him—although he had up to that time unhesitatingly accepted him as his nephew—to be an impostor, and even going so far as to threaten to turn them out of their house if she refused. Bertrande, however, did refuse.

She said the story told by the soldier from Rochefort was untrue, merely another device on the part of Martin's old enemies, and that she was positively certain the man she had welcomed back as her husband was her husband.

"If it isn't Martin," she said, "then it is the devil in his skin."

This sentiment found an echo in the minds of many, including one Jean Loze, a highly influential person living near Artigues, who, upon Peter's applying to him for a loan to commence proceedings against Martin, indignantly refused to advance him a sou, at the same time remarking:

"If I part with any money, it will only be to defend Martin Guerre against those who are once again trying to deprive him of his good name."

The day after Peter Guerre's application had been thus summarily dismissed—it was said that he went out from the presence of Jean Loze raging—another sensation was caused in Artigues. Peter Guerre, accompanied by his four sons-in-law, all armed to the teeth, went to Martin's house, while he was at breakfast, and taking him by surprise, before he could lay his hand on any weapon with which to defend himself, marched him off between them to Rieux, where he was once again lodged in the jail which he had only quitted a few hours previously. Intensely surprised though they were upon hearing of this outrage, the inhabitants of Artigues were still more astonished when they learned that it had been approved of by Bertrande herself, and even perpetrated at her request. There seems, indeed, to be little doubt that such was the case, but it is extremely probable that Peter Guerre and his sons-in-law had "got at" her, and that she would not have acted as she did, had they not resorted to forcible persuasion, or what is termed in other words undue influence. There is, however, some uncertainty with regard to what were her real feelings and belief at this juncture. Some are of the opinion that she had long ago discovered that the man she was living with was not her husband, but that she had resolved to say nothing about it, since she had grown really fond of him, a state of affairs that would account for her not having yielded to the previous persuasion and threats of Peter Guerre; whereas others maintain that she still believed the arrested man to be her real husband and, having full confidence in his ability to prove himself such, she considered it advisable that he should have an opportunity of doing so in public. At any rate, as a sure indication, we may take it, that she still had some regard for him, about three weeks after the commencement of his incarceration, she sent him clothes, clean linen and money.

The trial before the Court of Justice took place at Rieux. He was put down on the indictment sheet as Arnold Tilh, commonly called Pansette, a native of Sagias,* and charged with having assumed the name, rank and person of Martin Guerre, claimed his wife, appropriated and spent her property, and contaminated her marriage. His chief accusers were Peter Guerre and the latter's sons-in-law.

The accused defended himself, and the story he told was apparently pronounced with so much candour and simplicity that, if he really were the impostor he afterwards declared himself to be, one can only say he should be classified among the very cleverest and most unscrupulous of criminals. He said that having seriously offended his father (although he was innocent of the robbery) he thought it best for financial reasons and his wife's sake to leave Artigues, and consequently he went off, without making known his intentions to a soul. Wandering about from place to place—he mentioned them by name and the various people he had come in contact with in each—he eventually enlisted, and served in the French army for eight years. Tiring at length of that, he deserted, and after being a soldier in the Spanish army for a short time, finding he could return to France without fear of punishment, he came back to Artigues, and being instantly recognized by his wife, his four sisters and all his relations and friends, he naturally resumed his old life. He described in detail the instant recognition of him by his wife and sisters, and the welcome they gave him, throwing themselves into his arms, and then said:

"If Bertrande, after thus receiving me back and living with me perfectly happily for three years, is now one of my accusers, it can only be because she has been intimidated and forced to turn against me by my enemies, of whom my uncle is the most bitter. I once had the misfortune to quarrel with him, and ever since then he has sought every opportunity to do me harm. I beg of you to have my wife released from his power and placed under the protection of some reliable and disinterested person."

The Court granted this appeal and deferred giving a verdict till inquiries concerning the truth of certain of his statements had been

* Arnold Tilh had mysteriously disappeared about the same time as Martin Guerre.

made, and more witnesses called. The trial was therefore adjourned
for a while. The result of the inquiries having tended to corroborate
the statements of the accused, regarding the towns he had visited
and the people he had encountered, the trial was resumed, and
the accused subjected to a rigorous cross-examination. He neither
wavered nor contradicted himself, but spoke easily and naturally
about his parents and wife, commenting on the dresses worn by
some of those present at his marriage, and recalling an amusing
incident that happened the night preceding that event, namely, a
serenade given him by a number of young men in the village, all
of whom he mentioned by name.

His accusers, however, noticing with satisfaction that he had
not made any allusion at all to the rumours that had, at one
time, been current in Artigues, with regard to the bewitchment
of Martin Guerre and his wife, commented upon this point to
the judges, who at once examined him on it, but his replies to
all the questions put to him were perfectly satisfactory, and tallied
in every detail with a statement in writing, relative to the same
subject, made by Bertrande Guerre.

A hundred and fifty witnesses were now called to say whether
they identified the accused as Martin Guerre or Arnold Tilh.
About sixty of them could not decide one way or the other.
Forty drew attention to certain marks on the accused, namely,
a scar on the forehead, a misshapen nail on the forefinger of his
right hand, several warts on various of the other fingers of the
same hand, and a conspicuous mole over one eye, declaring that
Martin Guerre, whom they remembered as a youth, had all these
marks, and therefore they were convinced that the man they now
saw before them in the person of the accused actually was Martin
Guerre; whilst, on the other hand, fifty witnesses pronounced the
accused to be Arnold Tilh of Sagias, whom they had known as a
boy, and who, they thought, might quite possibly have possessed
marks on his person similar to those said to have been seen on the
person of Martin Guerre.

As a further test, Sanxi, the acknowledged son of Martin Guerre,
was brought into Court. The majority of those present decided
that he bore no resemblance whatsoever to the accused; but, on
the other hand, they observed that Martin Guerre's four sisters,
who had preceded Sanxi in the witness box, bore a very close
resemblance to the accused.

Thus the pros and cons in the case seemed to be about equal, and considerable excitement ensued, when the judges, after conferring together for some time, returned to pronounce their verdict. It was to the effect that the accused, being found guilty of all the charges against him, was sentenced to be executed and quartered.

He made an appeal to a higher tribunal, and another trial was consequently arranged before the High Court of Justice, at Toulouse. In due course it took place.

One of the first witnesses called was Bertrande Guerre. Her past life, the fact that for eight years she had remained wholly loyal to her absent husband, resolutely refusing to divorce him or to marry again, had created a very strong impression in her favour, and this impression was enhanced by her extreme beauty, simple air and very modest bearing. It seemed impossible that she could descend to falsehood, or that she would have lived with a man, unless she had been thoroughly convinced he was her lawful husband. Yet, on being confronted by the accused and asked by him in his usual calm, steady voice to tell the Court whether he was or was not the real Martin Guerre, she dropped her eyes, looked confused and declined to give any definite reply. Fortunately for the accused, the judges were of the opinion that this hesitation on Bertrande's part was due to intimidation on the part of Peter Guerre and his sons-in-law. She was afraid to speak the truth because of them.

Thirty of the people who had figured as witnesses in the previous trial were re-examined, and, as before, they could not agree. While some of them declared the accused was Martin Guerre, others were equally positive he was Tilh. Those who remembered both Martin Guerre and Arnold Tilh as youths agreed that the likeness between Martin Guerre and Arnold Tilh had been remarkable, but that there were certain differences. Arnold Tilh, for instance, was more robust looking and upright than Martin Guerre. I have already referred to certain marks the boy Martin Guerre was declared to have possessed; some of the witnesses who had already affirmed that Arnold Tilh had several, if not all, of those marks, now differed as to the position of some of them, some declaring, for instance, that the scar had been over the right eye, and some over the left. Indeed, no two witnesses agreed *in toto*. And with regard to other testimony it was just as conflicting. An innkeeper of Rieux in the witness box swore that the accused had once told him in confidence that he was, in reality, Arnold Tilh; and two other witnesses said that, on a certain occasion, seeing the accused out of doors, in company with some of Martin Guerre's relatives, they were about to greet

him as their old friend Arnold Tilh, when he signalled to them to
be silent, and shortly afterwards one of them received a present
from him with a message to the effect that silence was golden.*
Also, an uncle of Arnold Tilh, on seeing the accused in Court
in chains, at once identified him as his nephew, and burst into
tears, which involuntary demonstration on the part of a witness
made a great impression on the judges, who regarded it as very
telling evidence for the prosecution.

Yet, as against all this and more testimony of a condemning
nature, certain witnesses, including the brothers of Martin Guerre,
were emphatic in their belief that the accused was the person
he purported to be, urging in support of their contention the
character of Arnold Tilh. Was it possible, they argued, that such
an incorrigibly lazy, mendacious and disreputable individual as
Arnold Tilh admittedly had been could have lived for three
years in perfect harmony with a woman of such an upright and
estimable a character as Bertrande? This was a poser. The judges
were perplexed; they did not know what to decide, and it is highly
probable they would have given a verdict in favour of the accused,
had not the prosecution, at this psychological moment, created a
big sensation in Court by producing a new witness in the person
of the man with the wooden leg, already referred to, who styled
himself the real Martin Guerre.

The accused, on being confronted with this new witness, did
not appear in any way startled or disconcerted. On the contrary,
he maintained the same calm demeanour which had characterized
him throughout. He declared the man with the wooden leg was
simply an impostor, bribed to appear against him by Peter Guerre,
and that it was all part of a conspiracy to deprive him of his lawful
wife and the property he lawfully inherited.

In giving his testimony, the man with the wooden leg, while
vehemently denying that he had been bribed, and protesting he was
the real Martin Guerre, appeared very flustered, and his evidence
struck many of those present as forced and unconvincing.

The next step, however, on the part of the prosecution, and
one which had probably been well rehearsed beforehand, was to

* In addition to this rather damning testimony, it was known that the
youthful Martin Guerre had been a good swordsman and could speak
Basque, his father's native tongue, whereas the accused had been proved
to be a poor swordsman and to be utterly ignorant of Basque.

confront the man with the wooden leg with the Guerres. This proved fatal to the accused. Directly the eldest of Martin Guerre's sisters saw the new witness, she threw herself into his arms, calling him her dear lost brother. Her three sisters followed suit. Then, amid the most tense silence, Bertrande was called. The moment she entered the Court and saw the man with the wooden leg, she became greatly agitated, and bursting into tears fell on her knees before him, crying out that he was her real husband and imploring his forgiveness.

That, in the opinion of the judges, settled the matter. They at once pronounced the accused to be guilty of all the charges brought against him, and sentenced him to be executed. Four days later, that is to say on 16 September 1560, the sentence was carried into effect.

The condemned man, bareheaded, clad only in his shirt, holding in one hand a burning taper, and with a rope round his neck, was, first of all, made to kneel before the door of the Church of Rieux and ask pardon of God, the King, the local authorities, the presumed real Martin Guerre, in other words the man with the wooden leg, and Bertrande. Then, with a cruelty characteristic of those times, he was taken to a scaffold, which had been erected just outside Martin Guerre's house, and in the presence of Bertrande and all the Guerre family, he was slowly strangled, his body being subsequently burned.

If Bertrande did feel any pity for him, she certainly did not manifest any, but seems to have remained perfectly indifferent to his sufferings. That he was an impostor should not, perhaps, be doubted, since it is said that he made a full and spontaneous confession of his guilt without any coercion whatever.

But, at the same time, it seems to me quite conceivable that this unfortunate man really may have been Martin Guerre, and that he made a false confession with regard to his identity, anticipating torture if he did not.

The question as to whether the man with the wooden leg was the real Martin Guerre may, I think, safely be answered in the negative. It must be remembered that the soldier from Rochefort had publicly declared, most probably at the instigation of Peter Guerre, that the real Martin Guerre, having lost a leg in the wars, was wearing a wooden one. What an inducement then for an adventurer, chancing to have lost a leg, to pretend to be Martin Guerre, the owner of no inconsiderable property and a pretty wife!

Learning, too, of Peter Guerre's fanatical hatred of the man who had for three years passed as Martin Guerre and was now accused of being Arnold Tilh, he would, of course, bank considerably on Peter Guerre's support, reckoning that with such an influential ally the risk of exposure would not be very great.

Or, again, and what, I think, is more likely, Peter Guerre may have engineered the whole thing and have bribed the man with the wooden leg to play the rôle of Martin Guerre.

As I have already stated, the man with the wooden leg appeared very confused in Court; his replies to questions put to him were evasive and shifty, and he gave not a few of those present in Court the impression that he was not genuine and merely acting a part he found extremely difficult to maintain. Were he the real Martin Guerre, many argued, he would surely have made known his presence in Rieux or Artigues before his appearance at the trial, and the fact of his not having done so suggested he was purposely kept out of the way, lest he should be asked too many questions.

The fact that Bertrande and Martin Guerre's sisters proclaimed the man with the wooden leg to be the genuine Martin Guerre the moment they set eyes on him proved nothing, since they had all been just as ready with their recognition in the case of "Arnold Tilh", so that, if they had been so easily deceived on one occasion, why should they not be on another?

But apart from the fact that their identification was thus proved to be futile, it is more probable than not that, in the case of the man with the wooden leg, they had all acted under the coercion of the vindictive Peter Guerre.

However, if neither the man with the wooden leg nor the man who had been executed was the real Martin Guerre, what had become of him? He was last seen, it will be remembered, that summer morning, some seven or eight years after his marriage, walking along the road leading from his home, through lonely lanes and fields, in the direction of his father's house. He was well known to have had several inveterate enemies, youths who bitterly resented his prosperity and coveted both his wife and fortune. What more likely, then, than that these envious youths had banded together and murdered him, burying his body in one of the many unfrequented spots all around Artigues?

I can find no definite statement that this explanation of his disappearance was seriously considered at the time, but so obvious is it that there was both motive and opportunity for murder, that were it not for Bertrande's having been so sure, to begin with, and apparently up to the commencement of his trial, that the man who claimed to be her husband, and with whom she subsequently lived for three years, was her husband, I should say that, without doubt, Martin Guerre was murdered. It is the inconsequent and unsatisfactory behaviour of Bertrande herself that, in my opinion, makes any certain solution to the mystery of her husband's disappearance impossible.

THE CASE OF THE
SALMON SANDWICHES

(Annie Hearn, 1930)

Daniel Farson

*Everything about Annie Hearn suggested a long, grey spinsterhood.
Plain, slightly dowdy and prematurely middle-aged, she had spent much
of her life nursing various ailing relatives in the north of England. In
1919, she claimed to have married a Dr Leonard Hearn in London, but
this appears to be unsubstantiated. So is her claim to have been widowed
within a week of the wedding. In the early twenties, Mrs Hearn moved
south to Cornwall, nursing an elderly aunt and a sister, both of whom
died under her care. A local farmer and his wife were in the habit of
taking Annie Hearn with them on various outings. For one of these trips,
she prepared tinned salmon sandwiches, dressed with her own homemade
salad cream. Two weeks later, the farmer's wife was dead from arsenical
poisoning. Annie Hearn disappeared, apparently into thin air. When
she was found, she was arrested and tried for murder, but the jury
acquitted her and Mrs Hearn walked free. The mystery of what really
happened to the poisoned neighbour was never solved. The case caught
the attention of the writer and broadcaster Daniel Farson (1927–97).
Farson was a rumbustious alcoholic who moved to the West Country
in the 1960s from London, where he was a familiar figure in louche
Soho circles. He wrote a book on Jack the Ripper, claiming the killer
was M.J. Druitt, a barrister who, on 8 September 1888, played cricket*

for Blackheath less than six hours after Annie Chapman was hacked to death in Spitalfields.

It became one of the most mysterious cases of murder this century, but it had a jaunty beginning. On the afternoon of Saturday 18 October 1930, three people set out by motor car from the small Cornish village of Lewannick, near Launceston, for a trip to the nearby seaside resort of Bude. William Thomas, a farmer, and his wife Alice were taking their neighbour Annie Hearn on an outing. Annie had been on her own since the death of her elder sister Minnie in July and the Thomases had decided that a trip might cheer her up.

Annie Hearn was something of a mystery in the neighbourhood. She lived at Trenhorne House, just outside Lewannick, a hundred yards or so up the road from the Thomases at Trenhorne Farm. She was a "foreigner" from the north of England who had come to Cornwall in 1921. She was apparently a widow, probably in her mid forties, though no one was certain of her age—not even Annie herself. She had known bad luck: her husband had left her only a week after their marriage; her aunt had died at Trenhorne House after a long illness, and then tragedy had struck again with the painful death of her sister Minnie. It was only natural that William and Alice should feel sorry for the lonely woman who lived nearby. Alice made her junkets and clotted cream, which her husband took to Trenhorne House. He had shown sufficient trust in her to lend her thirty-eight pounds two years earlier when she was short of money.

The three left for Bude in William Thomas's car at three p.m. One of the lesser resorts on the north Cornish coast, it was a drive of twenty miles (thirty kilometres). They went to Littlejohn's Café (no longer in existence), where they ordered tea. When they were seated, Annie produced a packet of sandwiches, carefully prepared by herself with tinned salmon and her own salad cream, as her contribution to the treat. By today's standards this seems an odd thing to do, but not then. "Remember," says a relative of Jack Littlejohn today, "you're in Cornwall now. That's the way they did things here, saving the pennies."

They ate most of the salmon sandwiches and afterwards the two women went for a stroll while William Thomas took a walk on his own. He stopped at the nearest inn, The Grove Hotel, for a couple of whiskies, with the excuse that he was feeling queasy. When he rejoined the ladies, his wife complained of "a sticky taste" in her mouth and asked if they could buy some fruit; her husband bought her some bananas.

They started the drive back to Trenhorne Farm at six forty-five p.m. but were forced to make a number of stops on the way because Mrs Thomas was suffering from vomiting and diarrhoea. On their return to the farm, they sent for Dr Graham Saunders, who arrived at nine thirty p.m. He found Mrs Thomas's symptoms consistent with food poisoning, but did not think she was seriously ill and recommended a diet of whitebait and water.

Now it was Annie's turn to play the good neighbour and she rallied nobly, staying at the farm to nurse Alice Thomas who improved steadily. Oddly, it was eleven days before Alice's mother, Mrs Parsons, heard of her daughter's illness, although she lived only five miles (eight kilometres) away—apparently Alice did not want her mother to be alarmed. Once she knew, she came over to nurse her daughter herself; Annie continued to run the house and do the household cooking. The doctor was sufficiently reassured to stop calling every day, and the following Sunday Alice Thomas was able to come down for lunch—a traditional meal of roast mutton, sprouts and potatoes, prepared by Annie. Alice ate hers in the dining room while the others stayed in the kitchen. At nine p.m. Thomas carried his wife upstairs, giving her an aspirin from a bottle that Annie had supplied.

During the night, Alice became ill again. In the morning Thomas sent for the doctor, who was so shocked by the change that had taken place in his patient that he called in a consultant. Alice was now delirious, partly paralysed and unable to use her legs—and the consultant agreed with Dr Saunders' suspicion that she had arsenical poisoning. They transferred the patient immediately to Plymouth City Hospital where she was admitted just before midnight on Monday 3 November. By nine thirty-five the next morning, she was dead.

Because of the doctor's report about possible poisoning, a post mortem was held. The organs sent to the Exeter city analyst were found to contain 0.85 grains (56 mg) of arsenic. This finding should have remained confidential, but William Thomas somehow got to hear of it. He warned Annie that there might be inquiries by the police and possibly an inquest. The rumours spread, and festered in the retelling, so that the funeral of Alice Thomas on Saturday 8

November took place in an atmosphere of high tension. Subjected to stares, whispers and innuendos, Annie Hearn braved it out until the accusations against her were finally voiced the following day in the Thomases' dining room at Trenhorne Farm. Percy Parsons, the dead woman's brother, said to Annie Hearn: "We haven't met, but I've heard about you and them tinned sandwiches you was responsible for. What d'you put in them? That's what I'd like to know. Something wrong from all accounts. This needs clearing up, 'tis not the end of it, no way."

Understandably distressed, Annie confided to her neighbour Mrs Spears, who lived in the other wing of Trenhorne House, "They seem to think I have poisoned Mrs Thomas with the sandwiches. They think down there all tinned food is poisoned!"

Meanwhile, the behaviour of William Thomas struck some people as peculiar, too. Far from accusing Annie, he asked her to stay on at the farm, but demanded some form of receipt for the thirty-eight pounds she had borrowed two years before. Distraught, she refused to sit down and eat with him, and burst out, "I'll never forget that horrid man Parsons and the things he said. I've lost my appetite . . . life isn't worth living." She ran off up the lane and, when she failed to return, Thomas called at her house. There was no answer.

On 11 November Thomas received a poignant letter from Annie, posted the previous afternoon from nearby Congdon's Corner, in which she insisted on her innocence but clearly threatened suicide. Or was the letter a bluff? The "awful man" was Percy Parsons, the dead woman's brother.

"Dear Mr Thomas,
    Goodbye. I am going out if I can. I cannot forget that awful man and the things he said. I am *innocent, innocent.* She is dead and it was my lunch she ate. I cannot bear it. When I am dead they will be sure I am guilty, and you at least will be clear. May your dear wife's presence guard and comfort you still. Yours, A.H. My life is not a great thing anyhow, now dear Minnie's gone. I should be glad if you send my love to Bessie and tell her not to worry about me. I will be all right. My conscience is clear, so I am not afraid of the afterwards. I am giving instructions to Webb about selling the things, and hope you will be paid in full. It is all I can do now.

Thomas immediately fetched a police officer and together they broke into Trenhorne House to find it empty. Annie Hearn had disappeared.

Was the letter an implicit admission of guilt despite her claim to innocence? Or was it the final testament of a woman weighed down by local gossip, attempting to do the honourable thing by saving the reputation of her friend William Thomas by destroying her own? Or could it have been a charade—a calculated deception by one guilty of murder? If that was the case, then Annie Hearn was a monster.

To start with, her movements were easy to trace. She had hired Hector Ollett, an ex-army man who ran the shop at Congdon's Corner where she had posted the letter, to drive her down to Looe about twenty miles (thirty kilometres) away on the south coast. She paid him eighteen shillings, and he dropped her off at the bridge. After that the scent went cold, until the police found her check coat several days later, near the edge of the cliff. The conclusion was obvious: Annie Hearn had killed herself by jumping from the clifftop.

On 24 November, little more than a month since that outing to Bude, the inquest into the death of Alice Thomas began in Plymouth. The coroner asked William Thomas these vital questions:

"Had you any rat poison?"—Thomas replied that he had, "locked in my desk".

"Did your wife ever object to Mrs Hearn coming to the house?"— "Never."

"You and Mrs Thomas were friendly with Mrs Hearn's sister?"—"Yes."

"Did you ever give your wife any cause to be jealous of Mrs Hearn?"—"Never."

A chemist from Launceston confirmed that he had supplied weedkiller for Mrs Hearn's garden four years earlier. The powder, he said, was practically "all arsenic". The verdict of the inquest was given on 26 November: "Murder by arsenical poisoning by some person or persons unknown."

The original assumption of the police that Annie Hearn had jumped to her death had changed dramatically after the local fishermen pointed out that, if she had fallen from the spot near where her coat was found, her body would have struck the rocks and remained on the beach. If she had been swept out, she would have been washed up almost at once because of the home winds that had been prevalent for the previous ten days. Two people had drowned in the area recently, and both were washed ashore within two days. Had she faked her suicide?

The police issued the following description, together with a photograph:

> Mrs Hearn is aged 45, 5ft 2ins or 3ins [1.57 or 1.60 metres] in height, with grey eyes, brown shingled hair, of sallow complexion, and medium build. There is a noticeable defect in one of the front teeth. She walks briskly, carries her head slightly to the left, and when in conversation she has the habit of looking away from the person she is addressing. She is well-spoken but has a north country accent. She is of rather reserved disposition.

The police now began to take an interest in the death of Annie's sister Minnie (Lydia) who had joined her at Trenhorne House in 1925. The sisters lived there with two other shadowy figures: an old Cornish woman called Mrs Aunger, who had since died; and Annie's aunt, Miss Mary Everard, who had fallen ill and died in September 1926 after being nursed devotedly by her niece. Now people remembered that the aunt had left everything she possessed "to my dear niece Sarah Ann Hearn, except my mother's picture." The deaths of her aunt, who was seventy-six, and her sister, who was only fifty-two but who had suffered from chronic gastric catarrh and colitis, had seemed natural at the time. Now, however, the Home Office announced a decision to exhume the bodies, because the symptoms of their illnesses were also consistent with arsenical poisoning.

In Lewannick they still remember that macabre exhumation, which took place on Tuesday 9 December 1930 in a storm of snow and sleet. Mrs White, who was a girl at the time and still lives in Lewannick today, recalled the two policemen who guarded the gates of the churchyard and the trouble they took in erecting a screen of tarpaulins to prevent the public looking on. But since they completely forgot the houses at the back that overlooked the churchyard, she had a good view: "We could see all their pots and a box on the grave. They had the coffins taken up and we could see them with their tongs dropping things into jars." These "things" were forwarded to Dr Roche Lynch, the Home

Office analyst. In the remains of both bodies he found "distinct quantities of arsenic".

And, on the same day that the exhumations took place, the *Daily Mail* brought the sensational case to a head with the spectacular offer of a reward of £500, a very great deal of money in those days, "for the discovery of Mrs Annie Hearn, the missing witness". WHERE IS MRS HEARN? asked the headline, IS SHE STILL ALIVE?

Now Annie Hearn had been revealed in a more sinister light as the possible murderer of *three* women. What had happened to her? The answer was that she had indeed faked her suicide. She had calculated her movements from the moment she arrived in Looe with a wicker basket as her only luggage. Half an hour later she bought an attaché case for three shillings and eleven pence. By ten p.m. she had arrived in Torquay by train, and signed the register at St Leonard's Hotel as Mrs Ferguson of Heavitree, Exeter. The next day she moved to simpler lodgings in Ellacombe Church Road, using yet another name, Mrs Faithful, with the explanation that her husband was ill in the local hospital.

She ordered some calling cards in the new name, and answered an advertisement for a cook-housekeeper. A week later she was employed by an architect, Cecil Powell. He was impressed by his new servant, who went to church on Sundays and seemed of above-average education, though he thought that at times she seemed preoccupied. This was hardly surprising—when she was alone in her room she was busy cutting out the pictures of herself in the national newspapers. One of these photographs, accompanying the *Daily Mail*'s reward announcement, had seemed familiar to Powell "in a vague sort of way". Though he saw a similarity, he was reluctant to act because of his wife's delicate health and his own aversion to publicity. It was Annie's own furtive behaviour that caught her out.

On 1 January 1931 she set out for the new year sales and chose a coat at Williams & Cox in the Strand, Torquay, presumably to replace the one she had abandoned at Looe. She needed to have it shortened, and left it in the shop with a deposit in the name of Mrs Dennis. When the errand boy delivered the coat a few days later, the door was opened by Powell's son, who said that there must be some mistake because no one of the name of Dennis lived there. Annie's subsequent attempt at explanation was so suspicious that the architect consulted his friend the mayor, who informed the police in Launceston.

In the fading light of the afternoon of 12 January Powell asked his housekeeper to go on an errand, knowing that she was to be watched and followed by a police sergeant. As she passed him under the lamplight, the constable stepped forward. "Mrs Hearn?" "Yes?" "I believe I know you. I think you know Lewannick." "Yes, I have been there." "Then I must ask you to come to the police station."

There she was charged "that between 18 October and 3 November 1930 at the parish of Lewannick, you did kill and murder one Alice Maud Thomas".

On 11 March Annie made her twelfth appearance before the Launceston magistrates, standing in an easy attitude with her hands clasped in front of her, wearing a long, claret-coloured coat with fur collar and cuffs. Percy Parsons told the court about the day of his sister's funeral: "Some lady met us at the door. I didn't know who she was." But he identified her now as "the lady sitting over there". He agreed that he had never visited the farm before in order to see his sister. "Was that on account of a family feud?" he was asked. "I can't say. I was never invited."

Superintendent Pill read the statement made to him by Annie shortly after midnight on the day of her arrest:

On the Sunday before Mrs Thomas was taken away, I prepared roast mutton for dinner. I have read in the newspapers that I might have carved Mrs Thomas's portion. I did not carve it, and I did not help with the gravy or anything. I remember Mrs Thomas complaining that a junket that Mrs Parsons [her mother] made was too sweet. She did not complain of the meals I prepared. Mr Thomas appeared to be very grateful to me for my help up to the time when he returned from Plymouth after Mrs Thomas's death. He then appeared more abrupt in his manner towards me. On one occasion he said to me, "They are going to send some organs to be analyzed. They will find out what it is. They will blame one of us. The blame will come heavier on you than on me . . ." It appeared as if somebody was going to be charged with murder . . . sooner than that I thought I would go my own way and take my life. I did go to Looe with that intention but later found that I could not do what I thought of doing.

Large crowds watched Annie Hearn's exit from Launceston Court, for this was market day and the farming families took a personal interest in the accused. Local opinion was completely against her, but at this low moment in a life that seems to have been dogged by misfortune, Annie's luck took a turn for the better. Her former employer, Cecil Powell, who had informed on his housekeeper and claimed his reward from the *Daily Mail*, behaved impeccably. He donated the £500 towards her defence, which is how she was able to afford the services of Norman Birkett, the most brilliant barrister of his time.

Birkett's first and shrewdest move was to send all the available evidence to the eminent forensic science expert Sydney Smith in Scotland. Smith told Annie Hearn's solicitor, Walter West of Grimsby, that there was no doubt about arsenical poisoning, though how and when it was administered was another matter. All the doctors agreed that genuine food poisoning could have accounted for Alice's illness after the tea in Bude, and that there was no evidence that she had taken arsenic then. But there was indisputable evidence that she *had* taken arsenic much nearer to the date of her death. Smith found the case of Minnie Everard, Annie's sister, much less conclusive and returned the documents with his opinion that Mrs Hearn was "probably innocent". He regretted, however, that his university classes prevented him from attending the trial.

But on 11 June he received this desperate telegram from West: "Birkett thinks it vital you should be at Bodmin on Sunday for consultation about six evening. I think so too and most earnestly beseech you to come. Wire reply at once." Smith felt that his students came first, but then he reconsidered: "I thought it would be the negation of all my teaching if it meant that an innocent woman might be convicted and hanged. So I went."

The trial of Annie Hearn opened on Monday 15 June 1931. From the outset, the prosecution made a mistake in including the death of her sister, because the medical evidence to support such a charge was shaky. Birkett extracted the admission from witnesses for the Crown that Minnie's death could have been due to natural causes. Sydney Smith had already fastened on a vulnerable point in the prosecution's case. He had no doubt that arsenic had been traced in the muscles, hair and nails of Minnie's corpse, but pointed out to West that, though this would have indicated poisoning if she had been buried in almost any other county in England, it did not lead to the same conclusion in Cornwall. Cornwall is famous for its tin—and and tin contains a high degree of arsenic. In other words, the soil in the graveyard where Minnie had been buried was impregnated with traces of arsenic.

Birkett exposed the ignorance of the Crown's chief witness, the Home Office analyst Dr Roche Lynch, with his very first question: "Have you ever examined a living patient suffering from arsenical poisoning?" Lynch had to admit he had not. Neither had he ever been involved in an exhumation in soil where the level of arsenic was as high as 125 parts in a million. Turning to another Crown witness, Birkett asked: "Am I right in saying that a piece of soil so small that you could hold it between your fingers dropped onto this body would make every single calculation wrong?" The expert had to answer yes to this question.

Birkett's next move was then inevitable: to prove how easily such a speck of soil, containing arsenic, could have inadvertently contaminated the organs during the exhumation, which had taken place under considerable difficulties on a windy, snowy day. "There was no expert to assist," he told the jury, "merely the police sergeant, the carpenter, and the sexton, the sergeant perhaps holding the corks of the jars with an ungloved hand." In other words, or so he implied, it was a botched-up analysis, which proved nothing except that a piece of arsenical dust on the instruments used in the exhumation might have accounted for all the arsenic found in Minnie Everard's body.

Norman Birkett had scored his first and vital point—he had discredited the claim that Annie had murdered her sister and therefore put doubt in the jury's mind regarding the other charge. Now the Crown turned to the alleged murder of Mrs Thomas, with Lynch's conclusion that "a dose of possibly ten grains [600 mg] of arsenic" had been administered to Mrs Thomas on the day of the outing to Bude. But Sydney Smith had conducted an interesting experiment. It was the obvious thing to do, but the police had failed to do it, and the result was devastating. He had prepared some salmon sandwiches, exactly as Annie Hearn had done, but mixing enough weed-killer to contain ten grains (600 mg) of arsenic with the tinned salmon. Half an hour later the sandwiches were stained heavily with the bluish-purple dye used in the weed-killer.

The conclusion was obvious—no one would have touched the sandwiches. Even if Annie had carefully poisoned one sandwich only, handing it directly to Mrs Thomas, the stain of Prussian blue would easily have been noticed; the risk would have been far too great. This dramatic deduction impressed the jury, who were able to imagine those alarming blue sandwiches. Furthermore, Lynch was forced to admit that he had not made the experiment himself. "You have not tried it!" Birkett exclaimed, outraged. "On the theory of the prosecution, surely that was the most terrible risk to run?"

Cleverly, Birkett did not call Sydney Smith for the defence; his invaluable guidance was conducted behind the scenes. Birkett called no witnesses other than the accused herself, a move that gave him the right to make the vital closing speech just before the judge's summing-up. Though by now he had scored two important victories, he knew that the case against his client remained serious and that a number of awkward points still had to be overcome.

There was the mystery over Annie's mysterious "husband"—who seemed never to have existed—which suggested that she was capable of lying. Then there were damaging remarks that had been made by her neighbour, Mrs Spears. She used to visit Minnie Everard during her illness, in order to pray and read the Bible to her. Minnie told Mrs Spears that Annie's medicine was too strong: it was "going into her hands and legs. When I called on Mrs Thomas, she complained that she had lost the use of her legs, and I thought it was very much the same as in the case of Miss Everard."

Birkett tried to soften this impression by suggesting that Minnie was "rather hysterical" at the time, but without success. She was "not hysterical," insisted Mrs Spears, "but frightened of being poisoned." The suspicion was left that Minnie believed she was being poisoned by her niece.

Then there was a diary kept by Minnie that Birkett succeeded in keeping out of court. The question remained and still remains: what was in it?

But perhaps most important of all, there was the crucial question of motive. Why should Annie Hearn have wished to kill Mrs Thomas, let alone her sister or her aunt? There seemed to be only one possibility as far as Mrs Thomas was concerned: Annie was in love with the farmer and wanted his wife out of the way. A whispered remark to Sergeant Trebilcock on the night of her arrest was an important factor in the evidence. It was alleged that Annie stated: "Mr Thomas used to come to our house every day with a paper. Of course, that was only a blind." Norman Birkett tried to call the policeman's bluff: "Listen to this. 'Mr Thomas used to bring a paper. He was very kind'. Don't you think you could have made a mistake?" "No," said the policeman emphatically, "I made no mistake."

What about the farmer himself? William Thomas was a key figure in the mystery, but had remained an enigma. He had not accused Annie, but neither had he sprung to her defence. In the circumstances this seems hard to explain, unless it was due to his awareness that his own position was becoming increasingly suspect. He admitted giving his wife medicine but denied he had ever given her arsenic. "I have never had arsenic in my possession," he told the court, adding, "except sheep dip and tablets which are things any farmer might have."

It was left to Annie to deny any sexual relationship between them when she finally stood in the dock to be questioned by Norman Birkett. "Was there at any time in your mind the thought that you might marry Mr Thomas?" he asked her. "Never." "Did you ever conceive a passion, guilty or otherwise, for Mr Thomas?" "No." "It is suggested that on 18 October you gave Mrs Thomas a poisoned sandwich in order to marry Mr Thomas. Is there a shadow of truth in that?" "Not a shadow of truth." "From first to last in this matter, have you administered or given in any shape or form arsenic, either to Mrs Thomas or your sister?" "I have not." "That", concluded Birkett, "is the case for the defence."

But there was still a sensation to come, though not one relevant to the evidence. The counsel for the prosecution, Herbert du Parcq, collapsed in the middle of his final address. Norman Birkett was at his side in a moment with a bottle of smelling salts. Clutching Birkett, who was supporting him, du Parcq managed to stumble from the court into the anteroom where he collapsed again.

When he finally returned to the courtroom, the judge insisted: "I don't think there ought to be any mystery about this. The fact is that after a meal one is apt to have a little pressure on the heart which causes faintness." When du Parcq wanted to continue standing "if I can", the judge ordered him to sit. "This has occurred to me once or twice since I began my professional career," he explained, "and here I am older than Mr du Parcq." His announcement was greeted by the usual outburst of laughter accorded to any attempt at levity by a judge, and the tension was broken. But the tension of the Crown's address had been broken, too. Du Parcq's collapse at such a critical moment was highly damaging for the prosecution, and the judge's comment that one often feels faint after a little food might well have reminded the jury of Mrs Thomas's illness after the sandwiches in Bude. If the members of the jury were at all superstitious, they might even have regarded the collapse of the prosecutor as a direct sign that the accused was innocent!

In fact the jury was not particularly prone to considering the role of divine providence, as Birkett discovered when he discussed his summing-up with Sydney Smith and Walter West as they strolled outside the court. "The Cornish are very religious people," he informed them, "and I intend in my speech to draw the attention of the jury to the difficulty of reconciling the loving care which the accused lavished on her sister with the fiendish project of slowly poisoning her with arsenic. I will read the fourteenth chapter of St John, her sister Minnie's favourite. Don't you think that will be effective, Mr West? You look doubtful?"

But West revealed that the jury had been asked the previous Sunday if they wanted to go to divine service or drive to the coast. They chose the seaside. "Oh lord!" exclaimed Birkett, "there go My Father's Mansions!"

Now it was up to the jury. The members had been chosen from outside the district, away from local prejudice. This was a relief for Birkett, who realized soon after his arrival that local people had already decided on their verdict—his client was as guilty as hell.

Norman Birkett's final address to the jury lasted four hours. He started by scorning the inexperience of the Crown's analyst: "Dr Lynch has never attended one person suffering from arsenical poisoning, yet he spoke of symptoms with exactly the same confidence as he spoke of other matters. Let the cobbler stick to his last. You are above all experts. The final word rests with you."

Having scrapped his proposed biblical text, he seized his opportunity when he reached the end of his speech and needed something dramatic for his closing sentence. He found it in the summer sunlight streaming through the windows of the Bodmin courtroom:

> For five months this woman has lived in Exeter jail during the darkness and dreariness of winter. She is now here before you in the sunshine of summer, but she is still walking in the valley of a great shadow. It is you, and you alone that can lead her back again to the road of sunshine, your voice alone that can speak the word of deliverance. I ask you to speak that word to her, to stretch forth that hand that will help her back into the sunlight away from the shadows which have haunted her so long. That is my last appeal to you all.

It was a stirring climax to a brilliant defence. The next day the jury returned after fifty-five minutes and gave their verdict—"Not guilty." Women sobbed and the young nurse who had been Annie Hearn's constant companion in prison seemed close to collapse.

The judge informed the jury: "You have another duty to perform, the case of Miss Everard." Then he revealed that the Crown was not intending to proceed with this—"You will therefore", he instructed, "return a second verdict of not guilty. Now, Sarah Ann Hearn, you are discharged and free." More than 2,000 people had assembled outside, but Annie exchanged hats and coats with her married sister Bessie Poskitt and managed to escape unnoticed by most of the crowd. Later she was seen having a meal at the King's Arms in Launceston. Then she went up to Yorkshire where she stayed with her sister.

Annie Hearn was acquitted, and it certainly looks as if she was innocent. Her brother-in-law told the *Yorkshire Post*: "She is so kind and good and faithful", and this is the impression conveyed by her fake suicide note and the letter of thanks she wrote to Sydney Smith, unless she was a woman of quite extraordinary guile.

But if Annie was innocent, who was guilty? Was William Thomas the murderer? The judge came straight to the point in his summing-up: "The issue is now down to two people—Mrs Hearn and Mr Thomas. It is no use beating about the bush."

But then the judge made a curious comment: "If you supposed that Mr Thomas were the guilty person, what could his motive be—passion, love, malice or hatred? There may have been some other women who moved him to passion; there is no evidence that Mrs Hearn moved him to passion." Some other women? This is a fascinating possibility—that farmer Thomas poisoned his wife and Annie Hearn bore the consequences, even at the risk of her life, so that he could further his relationship with another woman. But did such a woman exist? A lady in Lewannick today provides a possible clue—she remembers the postmistress gossiping after Alice Thomas's death, "He'll be able to have Mrs Tucker now."

There is one piece of evidence that looks incriminating against him. Copper was found in his wife's body as well as arsenic. The worm tablets in his possession contained copper, too. Had he given them to his wife as "medicine", pretending that they were aspirin tablets? Sydney Smith certainly implied so, pointing out that, apart from Annie, he was the only person who had access to his wife during the whole course of her illness.

But if Thomas was guilty of his wife's murder because of this other woman, then who killed Minnie Everard? Since he had no motive for that whatsoever, the theory is enhanced that in fact there was no other murder, and that Minnie died, as was thought by everyone at the time, of natural causes.

William Thomas died on 14 December 1949 on a remote farm at Broadoak, Cornwall, where he had lived a lonely existence as a recluse ever since the trial. The son of Annie Hearn's old solicitor, Walter West, who has taken over his practice in Grimsby, cannot divulge any information about his father's client, so that Annie Hearn's life after the trial can only be guessed at. It is possible—even likely—that she changed her name to escape unwelcome publicity, and lived in the north of England near her family. Whatever did become of her, there is no doubt that she was a woman of extreme courage, who may have shielded a man she was fond of, even to the extent of risking her own life for him on the gallows.

DEATH OF A MILLIONAIRE

(Sir Harry Oakes, 1943)

Julian Symons

At seven a.m. on the morning of 8 July 1943, the Duke of Windsor, former King of England and then governor of the Bahamas, took a telephone call. His friend and local businessman, Harold Christie, was on the line with the shocking news that Sir Harry Oakes had been brutally murdered in his bed. Oakes was one of the richest men in the British Empire. According to Christie, having spent an undisturbed night at the multi-millionaire's luxury Bahamian home after a dinner party there, he had discovered Oakes's battered and partly burned body not long after daybreak. The Duke took personal charge of the investigation and called in the police—but not the local police. Neither did he summon Scotland Yard from London, nor even the American FBI. Instead the Duke called the police department in Miami. Their investigation was a sham. They ignored the obvious suspect: Harold Christie himself, Oakes's business agent. Instead they arrested a twice-divorced French-Mauritian playboy, Alfred de Marigny, who had fallen foul of Bahamian society by marrying Oakes's eighteen-year-old daughter Nancy. The accused son-in-law was tried and acquitted, leaving the question of who killed Sir Harry Oakes unresolved. Julian Symons (1912–94) was one of Britain's leading crime novelists and critics, hailed as the heir to Dorothy L. Sayers or Agatha Christie. He was a highly versatile man of letters who believed strongly in the literary value of crime and detective novels. Symons was fascinated by real-life crime, and in Sweet Adelaide *(1980) proposed a solution to the Victorian case of Adelaide Bartlett (qv,* Murder Hath Charms *in this collection). In 1960 he published* A Reasonable Doubt, *a collection of true-life cases in which he questioned the verdicts in three British murder cases, and recapitulating others, such as the Oakes case, which remain unsolved.*

There was nothing unusual about the last day in the life of the Canadian millionaire, Sir Harry Oakes. He planted trees at Westbourne, his home near the Bahamas Country Club in Nassau. In the afternoon he played tennis at the Club with his friend Harold Christie, a local estate agent and a member of the Governor's Executive Council.

That evening there was a small dinner party at Westbourne, with Christie and two other friends of Oakes's as guests. The party broke up early but Christie stayed the night, as he often did. He told Sir Harry good night, went to his own room, which was separated from Sir Harry's by a bedroom and a bathroom, undressed, crawled under the mosquito net and went to sleep.

Christie woke after daybreak. He went to the screen door of Sir Harry's room on the northern porch and called "Hi, Harry", but got no reply. He then went into the bedroom, and there saw the millionaire's body. Oakes was lying on the bed, his body burned in several places. Fire was still smouldering in the mattress. The mosquito net was burned. There were burns on the carpet and on the wardrobe, and a fine soot was lying about the room. Christie did not notice all these things at once, but he saw enough to call a doctor and the police. Sir Harry Oakes was dead. At some time during the night he had been attacked, and his skull fractured by a hard, blunt instrument. Death was caused by this fracture, by a brain haemorrhage, and by shock.

Sir Harry's sudden and violent death shocked the whole island. The Duke of Windsor, who was governor-general, cancelled all his appointments so that he could take a hand in the inquiry. He telephoned to Miami, and the Florida police arranged to fly out two experts at once. Sir Harry Oakes died on the night of 7 July 1943, and on the following day Captain E. W. Melchen, homicide investigator, and Captain James O. Barker, fingerprint and identification expert, arrived. Sir Harry's body had been taken by plane to the United States for burial. Now the plane was recalled for an autopsy. Melchen and Barker moved swiftly. Three days after the death Sir Harry's son-in-law, Marie Alfred Fouqueraux de Marigny, was charged with murder.

So opened one of the most curious crime puzzles of this century, a puzzle still unsolved. It is remarkable partly for the characters of the participants, and partly because "expert evidence" of identification through fingerprints has seldom, if ever, been so utterly destroyed in cross-examination.

Let us look at the people and their backgrounds. Sir Harry Oakes was a remarkable man by the standards of any period. He had tramped Canada in youth as a poor prospector. Kicked out by a railway guard when he hitched a lift in a car travelling north to Northern Ontario, he found the second richest goldfield in the world on Lake Shore, one reputed to bring him an income of a million pounds a year.

Oakes looked for the railway guard and had him pensioned. His generosity was multifold, his influence international. He gave £90,000 towards the rebuilding of St George's Hospital. He had homes in Florida and Maine, a house in Kensington Palace Gardens with separate flats for each of his five children by the Australian girl he had married, an estate of 850 acres in Sussex. When he decided to settle in the Bahamas, he financed Bahamas Airways for inter-island communication, built Oakes Airfield, and stocked a 1,000 acre sheep farm with sheep specially imported from Cuba. In the early days of the war he had made a gift of £5,000 to the Ministry of Aircraft Production for a fighter plane, and more recently had given £10,000 to provide two Spitfires, named Sir Harry and Lady Oakes.

The multi-millionaire, now in his late sixties, was a man of simple and unpretentious tastes. In the Bahamas he wore often the slouch hat, khaki shirt, corduroy breeches and top boots of a prospector. Generous in the ordinary affairs of life, and indulgent to his children, he was not a man who took kindly to having his wishes thwarted. He made no secret of his disapproval when, in 1942, his daughter Nancy secretly married Alfred de Marigny, two days after her eighteenth birthday. The marriage took place in New York, just after Nancy had left school. Sir Harry and his wife learned of it on the evening after the wedding. It is hardly surprising that they were displeased, and what they knew of the man generally called Count Alfred de Marigny cannot have reassured them.

He was not, as his name implied, a French nobleman, nor was

his name Marigny. He had been born in Mauritius, and although his mother's name was de Marigny, his father's was merely Alfred Fouqueraux. The Count had blended the names and added the title, although his friends called him Freddie. He had come to the Bahamas in 1937 with his first wife, was active in yachting circles, bought and sold estates. He was a fast, fluent talker, a playboy devoted to all kinds of sport, lavishly hospitable. Where his money came from—whether, indeed, he had any money—was not known. In fact, he was in receipt of £100 a month from his first wife.

From the beginning Sir Harry disliked his son-in-law, and an incident a few months after the marriage widened the estrangement. Nancy became very ill with typhoid while travelling with her husband in Mexico, and her state of health on recovering from this was so bad that an operation was necessary to terminate her pregnancy. Marigny came into hospital at the same time for a tonsil operation, and occupied the room next to his wife's. Sir Harry told him to get out of this room, or he would kick him out. Marigny left the hospital. His feelings were not openly expressed at the time, but may be imagined.

On 10 February, Marigny went to see a lawyer named Foskett, who acted for the Oakes family, and asked Foskett to do his best to establish good relations with Sir Harry. He was a gentleman, Marigny said, and he was not treated as one. Foskett said that he disapproved of the way in which Marigny had pursued Nancy in New York, and had married her without the knowledge of her parents. He refused to give any help. Five days later Foskett prepared a new will for Sir Harry by which, although the body of the estate was to be divided among the five children, none of them obtained a share until they reached the age of thirty.

In the following month there was a furious scene. Sir Harry went to Marigny's house in Nassau where his eldest son, sixteen-year-old Sydney Oakes, was staying the night. He made Sydney get up, dress and leave. He was like a madman, said the foreman of Sir Harry's Nassau estate, as he called Marigny a sex maniac, said that he had better not write any more letters to Lady Oakes, and threatened to horsewhip him if he did not leave the Oakes family alone. After this Nancy wrote a letter in which she said that the Marignys were cutting themselves off from the Oakes family until they had confidence in Alfred.

So much for the background. How had Marigny spent the evening of 7 July? With his wife Nancy away in the United States, Marigny, in the company of his friend and fellow Mauritian the Marquis Georges de Visdelou Guimbeau, had entertained the wives of two RAF officers to dinner. Mrs Dorothy Clark and Mrs Jean Ainslie testified that Marigny drove them home at one-thirty in the morning. This, however, did not provide him with an alibi, since the time of death was placed between half past two and five o'clock. Marigny said that he had gone straight home, and his friend the Marquis de Visdelou was prepared to support that statement.

A neighbour had seen a light on in Marigny's room between twelve-thirty and four a.m. on the vital night. On the following morning, very early, he had come in to the local police station, with bulging mouth and wild eyes, to make some routine inquiry about a car.

Slowly the prosecution accumulated evidence. Fingerprint expert Barker found the print of Marigny's little finger on a screen drawn across Oakes's bed. He also carried out a heat test and found that Marigny's beard, and the hair on his hand, forearm and head all showed signs of scorching under a microscope.

Homicide investigator Melchen found smudge marks in the hall. He reconstructed the case to show that Sir Harry had staggered into the hall, pyjamas aflame, had gripped the stair railing and tottered against the wall. Then he had been dragged back to his room, and the bed set on fire.

Melchen said Marigny had told him: "Oakes hated me for marrying his daughter, Nancy. I hated him because he was a stupid old fool who could not be reasoned with."

The prosecution suggested that Marigny, tired of attempting to reason with Sir Harry, had planned and executed his murder, and then attempted to burn the body. The strong points of their case were the expert evidence relating to fingerprints and scorched hair. It was essential to the prosecution to prove these beyond question in court.

Into the small court room at Nassau people crowded every day to watch the case, bringing sandwiches and ice cream sodas, often sitting two to a seat. The preliminary investigation in the Magistrates' Court had opened a week after Marigny's arrest. It was adjourned more than once, dragged on through August. The trial

itself finally opened on 18 October in the Supreme Court, before Sir
Oscar Daly, Chief Justice of the Bahamas. The Attorney-General,
the Honourable Eric Hallinan, led for the Crown, with one of the
colony's leading lawyers, the Honourable A. F. Adderley, to assist
him. The Honourable Godfrey Higgs led for the defence.

The trial lasted more than three weeks, with preliminary chal-
lenging of many jurors by both sides, and several others providing
medical certificates to say that they were unfit to serve. During
those three weeks the prosecution saw the case steadily slipping
away from them, because of the inefficiency of many of the police
officials who worked on it.

Consider that vivid reconstruction of the case made by Captain
Melchen, when he said that Sir Harry had staggered into the hall,
tottered against the wall and been dragged back to his room. In
face of positive medical evidence that Sir Harry never got out of
the bed in which he was found, Melchen retracted this evidence.
He admitted that no analysis had been made of the material used
to light the fire in the bedroom. Certain hand marks on the wall
of Sir Harry's room had not been measured.

There followed the curious story of the bloodstained towels.
Major Herbert Pemberton, head of the CID in the colony, had
removed a bloodstained towel from Sir Harry's bed. He had
also found a towel with what appeared to be bloodstains on it
in Christie's bedroom.

While giving evidence in the Magistrates' Court Pemberton had
forgotten all about these towels, and indeed denied seeing them.
He was tired, he explained, and didn't recollect the matter. As
a matter of fact the towel in Sir Harry's room had been in his
possession for some weeks, and he had forgotten all about it. As
for the towel in Christie's bedroom, why, it had just been left there.
He had not made a note of finding the towels, Pemberton told an
astonished court room, and did not think they were important.

How had bloodstains got on to Christie's towel? The estate
agent explained that when he found Sir Harry's body he poured
water in his mouth, wet a towel and wiped his face with it. He
believed that the towel came from his own bathroom. There were
certain bloodstains on the glass door and screen door of Christie's
bedroom, and he said that these were probably from his own hands,
after he had found Sir Harry.

A strange story was told by Captain Sears, the Assistant
Superintendent of Police. Driving in Nassau on the fatal night

Captain Sears had seen a station wagon with Christie sitting in the front seat, and somebody else driving. Sears, however, must have been mistaken, for Christie said positively that he did not leave Westbourne on that night.

The severest blow struck at the prosecution came with the evidence of Captain James Barker. It was evidence which at times turned the tragedy into something like a farce. It was also evidence of historical importance about the methods of obtaining fingerprints.

The first step in taking fingerprint evidence is usually to photograph the prints. This fingerprint expert, however, had left his fingerprint camera behind. Perhaps Pemberton might have one? Well, yes, he had, but it was out of commission.

Without bothering to make any further inquiries about cameras or to send for his own camera, Barker proceeded to take prints by "lifting" them on to Scotch tape. This is a recognized method. When he ran out of tape he "lifted" them on to rubber, a procedure which has the effect of destroying the original print. Having done this, he forgot all about the print on the screen for ten days when, he said, he examined it and found that it was Marigny's.

Judge Daly called Barker's conduct "quite incomprehensible", and his forgetfulness was really extraordinary. In court he identified the place on the screen where the print had been found—and it turned out to be the wrong place. He said that certain lines on the screen were not made by him—and they turned out to be marked with his initials. Looking at the lifted print, this expert was unable even to say which way the finger was pointing.

There was worse to come. It was obvious that, for the fingerprint evidence to be effective, Marigny must have had no possible access to the screen before it was fingerprinted. Now, Marigny had been taken upstairs at Westbourne to be interviewed on the day Barker took the prints. Had he gone before or after the work was done? In the Magistrates' Court all the police officers agreed that it was after.

Pemberton said the screen was under constant police guard. Two other police witnesses said that Marigny, on strict instructions, had not gone upstairs in the morning, while the screen was being fingerprinted. Melchen confirmed that he had taken Marigny upstairs between three and four in the afternoon.

At the trial, however, Mrs Clark and Mrs Ainslie said that they had been summoned to Westbourne that morning, and that Marigny had been taken upstairs between eleven o'clock and noon. Now, quite suddenly, the prosecution evidence on this point collapsed. The police guards admitted that they had been mistaken about the time, and so did Melchen. It was just a mistake, he said.

"What a mistake," defence counsel commented ironically. "What a coincidence that you and the constables should make the same mistake."

In his final speech for the defence Higgs plainly accused these winesses of perjury. While Melchen was examining Marigny upstairs Barker had come to the door and asked if everything was OK. The defence suggested that Marigny had been taken upstairs deliberately, to get his print on to the screen.

By the time that Marigny went into the witness box, the incompetence or corruption of the police had made his acquittal almost inevitable. He explained that the burnt hair on his beard and forearms had been caused when he lit a cigar over a candle in a hurricane shade. He was a confident witness, laughing, joking occasionally, winking at his wife.

The jury voted nine to three for acquittal. They unanimously recommended Marigny's deportation.

Talking to reporters afterwards Marigny told them to keep out of prison. "It's a hard life," he said. "I could see that I had a good foreman to guide the jury. By the way, did you notice that he was the only one who was awake all the time?" Asked if he would try to solve the mystery he said, "I'll leave that to Erle Stanley Gardner."

Echoes of the case can be heard occasionally through the years. In 1950 a Finnish seaman said he had been told the name of the Oakes murderer by an American landscape artist, and a search was made for a blonde model named Betty Roberts, who gave evidence in the case. When found, Miss Roberts, now happily married, proved to have nothing to say. In this same year Betty Ellen Renner, who came to the Bahamas to investigate the case, was murdered and put into a well. At this time, also, Marigny was heard of, working as a part-time French translator in New York. His marriage to Nancy Oakes had been annulled. In 1953 Barker was shot dead by his son, after a quarrel. But these are mere sidelights on some of the characters. Neither Erle Stanley Gardner (who was there as a reporter) nor anyone else has ever solved the problem: who killed Sir Harry Oakes?

Any investigation of the Oakes case is bound to leave one with the feeling that much less than the whole truth has been told. But in the welter of contradictory evidence, and the evasions of police officials (the jury expressed their regret that no evidence had been obtained from Lieutenant-Colonel Erskine-Lindop, Commissioner of Bahamas Police, who left to take up another appointment between the Magistrates' hearing and the trial), some questions stand out. They are questions that seem, strangely enough, never to have been asked:

(1) Oakes was killed in his bedroom, as the result of a blow with a heavy instrument. The night of the murder was stormy, but still, there must have been considerable noise. Why was it not heard?

(2) Where did the inflammable material come from that was used to set the fire?

(3) And why, having decided to burn the body, did the murderer make such a bad job of it, when he had apparently all night at his disposal? Was he disturbed? Or was the body-burning an elaborate pretence to lead suspicion away from the real murderer?

There are other questions too, which it is not possible to ask publicly, even fifteen years after Marigny's trial. But the Oakes case is one on which the file is not completely closed. It is possible, at least, that one day an answer will be provided to one of the most remarkable murder mysteries of the twentieth century.

THE MYSTERY OF THE HANSOM CAB

(Nan Patterson, 1904)

Alexander Woollcott

On 4 June 1904 an wealthy gambler called Francis Thomas Young (known as Caesar) was riding along Broadway in a New York City hansom cab. Sitting alongside him was his mistress, a twenty-two-year-old showgirl called Nan Patterson. A shot rang out, and bystanders heard Miss Patterson exclaim: "Look at me Frank. Why did you do it?" She directed the cab to a nearby drugstore and then on to a hospital, where Young was pronounced dead on arrival. The couple had been quarrelling over a proposed elopement; Young had agreed to go to Europe, but with his wife. The unhappy Miss Patterson had told him (falsely or mistakenly) that she was pregnant. She claimed Young had committed suicide when she upbraided him for agreeing to his wife's request for a connubial holiday. This was at odds with the ballistics evidence over the position of the bullet entry wound in Young's head, which suggested that he could not have shot himself. However the comely Miss Patterson managed to convince not one but two juries of her innocence. In fact, to the delight of thousands of excited New Yorkers, there were three trials. The first was aborted when a juror suddenly died. The second ended in deadlock when the jury failed to agree on a verdict. When the jury in the third trial also became confused and finally confounded, the judge ordered Nan Patterson's release. It was a hugely popular outcome,

and Miss Patterson (who'd been a member of the chorus in the musical
Florodora) *went on to scale new heights in her musical and theatrical
career. The case is included not for its forensic complexities but for its
treatment by one of America's most original writers on murderous matters,
the journalist and critic Alexander Woollcott (1887–1943). Fat, owlish,
lazy, acid-tongued, Woollcott was, in the words of one contemporary,
"first, last and always a reporter . . . distinctly a one-man show". He
was fascinated by murder, and often included a note on a current or
historical case in his Shouts And Murmurs column in the* New Yorker.
*Woollcott's homosexual inclinations were thwarted by the singular fact
that he was to all intents and purposes a eunuch, born with a hormonal
imbalance, a shortage of testosterone. There was a certain wistfulness
about the way in which Woollcott related a story about Lord Reading's
marriage to a woman some forty years younger than himself. Woollcott
quoted the London* Times *account which ended with the unfortunate
tidings: "The bridegroom's gift to the bride was an antique pendant."
Alexander Woollcott recalled the case of Nan Patterson ("the handsome
alumna of the* Florodora *sextette") in a 1934 anthology of his journalism
that became his first bestseller,* While Rome Burns.

It was in 1905 on 3 May, my dears, that, for the second and last
time, the case of the People of the State of New York (ever a
naïve litigant) against Nan Randolph Patterson was entrusted to
the deliberations of an infatuated jury. After being locked up all
night, they tottered from the jury room to report that they, like the
susceptible twelve who had meditated on the same case six months
before, were unable to decide whether or not this handsome wench
was guilty of having murdered Cæsar Young. At that report the
exhausted People of the State of New York threw up their hands
and, to the cheers of a multitude which choked the streets for
blocks, Nan Patterson walked out of the Criminal Courts Building
into American legend.

It was in the preceding June that the killing had been done.
Cæsar Young—that was a *nom de guerre*, his real name was Frank
Thomas Young—was a gay blade of the race tracks, a bookmaker,
gambler, and horseman, personable, rich, generous, jovial, English.
For some two years he was enchained by the loveliness of this Nan
Patterson, a brunette, pompadoured, well-rounded show-girl from
the sextette of a *Florodora* road company. He had picked her up on

a train bound for California where, according to testimony, which later put all manner of ideas into Eastern heads, they spent several days together in what must have been a singularly liberal-minded Turkish Bath. But by the spring of 1904 he had returned penitent to the bosom of his wife and, for a healing voyage of reconciliation, the Youngs booked passage on the *Germanic*, due to sail from her pier at the foot of West Fulton Street at nine-thirty on the morning of 4 June.

On the night before, they had come in from Sheepshead Bay after the fifth race and taken lodgings for the night with Mrs Young's sister in West 140th Street. Indeed that last evening, Young's life was fairly swarming with in-laws, all bent, I suspect, on seeing that this, their Cæsar, should not change his mind at the last moment and run back to that dreadful Patterson woman. At seven next morning Young jumped out of bed, dressed, and sallied forth, explaining to his wife that he needed a shave and a new hat and would meet her on the pier not later than nine o'clock. He never kept that appointment and, too late to get her heavy luggage off the boat, poor Mrs Young decided to let it go on without her.

Young never reached the pier because, at ten minutes before nine, just as the hansom he had picked up in Columbus Circle was rattling along West Broadway near Franklin Street, he was shot through the chest. The cabman, although subsequently disinclined to recall having noticed anything at all that morning, was at the time sufficiently alert to draw up in front of a drug store. Passers-by who hurried forward found within the cab a dying man. Oddly enough the pistol which had killed him lay hot in the pocket of his own coat and he had fallen forward across the knees of the fair creature who was sharing the cab with him. Nan, for it was she, was extremely emotional and clasping her hands in supplication to the Deity, exclaimed (with admirable presence of mind, the State afterwards contended), "Cæsar, Cæsar, why did you do this?"

In the following November, the American people settled back to enjoy a real good murder trial, with Nan's face pale in the shade of a vast black picture hat, with her aged father, a patriarch superbly caparisoned with white mutton-chop whiskers, sitting beside her and kissing her in benediction at the end of every session. For the State appeared the late William Rand, who looked rather like Richard Harding Davis in those days. He was a brilliant advocate, although in talking to a jury, the tobacco-chewing members of the bar would tell you, he did rather suggest an English squire addressing the tenantry. For the defence the humbler Abraham Levy had been retained – the mighty Abe Levy who looked like a happy blend of cherub and pawnbroker and who, as the most adroit and zestful practitioner of the criminal law in this country, was called for the defence in more than three hundred homicide cases. The foreman of the first jury was the late Elwood Hendrick, eventually Professor Hendrick of Columbia, if you please, but—marvellous in this restless city—still living in 1930 in the East Fortieth Street house which he gave as his address on that day when Nan, after looking him sternly in the eye, nodded to her counsel as a sign that he would do as a juror for her.

The aforesaid American people, fairly pop-eyed with excitement, were at first defrauded. On the tenth day of the proceedings, one of the jurors succumbed to apoplexy and the whole verbose, complicated trial had to be started all over again. This form of mishap occurs so often in our courts that there is considerable backing now for a proposed law to provide a thirteenth juror who should hear all the testimony but be called on for a vote only in such an emergency. Roughly the idea is that every jury ought to carry a spare.

In the testimony it was brought out that Nan, aided by her sister and her sister's husband, had in that last spring worked desperately to regain a hold over her once lavish lover, trying every trick from hysterics to a quite fictitious pregnancy. On the night before the murder they had spent some clandestine time together in what was supposed to be a farewell colloquy. It was begun late in the evening at Flannery's saloon in West 125th Street, with one of Mrs Young's plethora of watchful brothers-in-law sitting carefully within earshot. Nan had reached the morbid stage of predicting darkly that Cæsar would never, never sail next day. Profanely, he taunted her with not even knowing on what boat his passage was booked. Indeed he tossed a hundred-dollar bill on the beer-stained table and offered to lay it against fifty cents that she could not name the ship.

"Cæsar Young, Cæsar Young," she made answer, while abstractedly pocketing the stakes, "Cæsar Young, there isn't a boat that sails the seas with a hold big enough or dark enough for you to hide in it from me to-morrow morning."

Between two and three on the morning of the fourth, they parted—unamicably. Indeed there was testimony to the effect that at the end he called her by an accurate but nasty name, slapped her in the mouth, and threatened to knock her damned block off. It was the more difficult for the State to surmise how a few hours later they ever came together in that hurrying and fatal hansom. It was seven-twenty when he left his wife in West 140th Street. It was not yet nine when he was shot at the other end of the city. Nor was all of that brief time at Nan's disposal. For the new hat was on his head when he was killed. And somewhere, somehow he had also paused for that shave.

There were sundry such *lacunæ* in the State's case. The pistol had been sold the day before in a pawnshop on Sixth Avenue but the proof that it had been bought by Nan's sister and her husband was far from water-tight. Anyway the jury must have been left wondering why, if these people had all been battening on Cæsar Young, they should have wished so golden a goose slain. Another weakness was Young's general rakishness. But the State's chief weakness, of course, was Nan herself. She was such a pretty thing.

The strength of the State's case lay in the fact that it seemed physically impossible for anyone else to have fired the pistol. The direction of the bullet, the powder marks, the very variety of the trigger-action all pointed only to her. To the ill-concealed rapture of the reporters, a skeleton was trundled into court as a model whereby to convince the jury that Cæsar Young would have had to be a contortionist to have pulled the trigger himself, as Nan implied he did. Of course she was not sure of it. It seems she was looking dreamily out of the window at the time and was inexpressibly shocked at his having been driven so desperate by the thought of a parting from her.

It is needless to say that Mr Levy, who managed to suggest that he was just a shabby neighbour of the jurors, seeking to rescue a fluttering butterfly from the juggernaut of the State, made the most of that "Cæsar, Cæsar, why did you do this?" At such a time, could this cry from the heart have been studied.

"Is there a possibility," Mr Levy argued, "that within two seconds after the shot she could have been so consummate an actress as to have been able deliberately to pretend the horror which showed itself in her face at that moment? Do you believe that this empty—frivolous, if you like—pleasure-loving girl could conceive the plot that would permit her at one second to kill, and in the next second to cover the act by a subtle invention? Why, it passes your understanding as it does mine. My learned and rhetorical and oratorical and brilliant friend will tell you that this was assumed. My God, you are all men of the world. You are men of experience. Why, you would have to pretend that this girl possessed ability such as has never been possessed by any artist that ever trod the boards, not even by the emotional Clara Morris, not even by the great Rachel, not even by Ristori, not even by Mrs Leslie Carter!"

Reader, if you are faintly surprised to find the name of Mrs Carter in that climactic spot, consider that it may have been a delicate tribute to her manager, Mr Belasco, who was attending the trial as a gentleman (*pro tem*) of the Press. Then, as always, the Wizard's interest in the human heart and his warm compassion for people in distress took him often to murder trials, especially those likely to be attended by a good many reporters.

Mr Levy's "learned and rhetorical friend" was not impressed. Indeed, he could not resist pointing out that Levy himself, while no Edwin Booth precisely, nor any Salvini either, had just read that very line with considerable emotional conviction.

"It does not require the greatness of histrionic talent," Mr Rand said dryly, "to pretend that something has happened which has not."

Mr Levy referred a good deal to Nan's dear old dad sitting there in court and, to play perfectly safe, he also read aloud from Holy Writ the episode of the woman taken in adultery. The jury disagreed.

The State tried again in the following April, moving the case for trial this time before Justice Goff, perhaps in the knowledge that, despite his saintly aspect, that robed terror to evil-doers could be counted on to suggest to the jury, by the very tone of his voice, that hanging was too good for Nan. In his final argument, Colonel Rand was magnificent. In after years at the civil bar he argued in many cases of far greater importance and it was always one of the minor irritations of his distinguished life that laymen everywhere always tagged him as the man who prosecuted Nan Patterson. This gaudy prestige even followed him overseas when he was a high-ranking member of the Judge Advocate's staff stationed at Chaumont for the prosecution of those of us in the A.E.F. who were charged with cowardice, rape, insubordination, and other infractions of the military code.

"Oh, gentlemen, gentlemen," cried Mr Rand in his peroration, reaching at last his guess at the scene in the hansom cab. "We are near the end, we are near the end now. Going back to revisit his early home and his old friends, a richer, stronger, heartier man than Cæsar Young that morning you shall not find. But the harvest of the seed he had sown was still to be reaped and the name of the reaper was Nan Patterson. And his companion, what were her thoughts? What were her reflections as she sat there by his side? One call, you may be sure, was insistent in her thoughts. One call she heard again and again. 'You have lost, Nan, you have lost. The end has come, your rival has triumphed, the wife has won. The mistress has lost, lost her handsome, generous lover. No more riots, no more love with him. He is going back, he is going back. Cæsar is going back, Nan. Back, back, to his first love. Back to his true love. Cæsar is going back, Nan. Back, back to the woman who had shared his poverty, who had saved his money, who has adorned his wealth. Back. Cæsar is going back to the wife he had sworn before God to love, honour and cherish.' Oh, if she had doubts, they vanished then; then she saw red; then the murder in her heart flamed into action, and she shot and killed. A little crack, a puff of smoke, a dead man prostrate on a woman's knee, the wages of sin were paid!"

Thus the District Attorney. But again the jury disagreed and after a few days he moved for a quashing of the indictment. It was immediately announced that Nan would be starred in a musical show called *The Lulu Girls*. It opened a fortnight later in Scranton, Pennsylvania, and got as far as Altoona, where, although billed by that time as *A Romance of Panama*, it quietly expired. Shortly thereafter Nan was remarried, after a lively vacation, to an early husband from whom she had been obscurely divorced. She then vanished from the newspapers, although there occasionally finds its way into print a legend that she is living in Seattle a life given over to good deeds and horticulture.

Ten years ago an elderly and indignant washerwoman living in a shanty in White Plains found herself surrounded one morning by a cordon of reporters and photographers all conjured up by a fanciful and self-sprung rumour that she was Nan Patterson. The White Plains *blanchisseuse* was furious, as it seems she was not Nan Patterson at all. Why, she had never been in a hansom cab or a Turkish Bath in all her life. She had never even been in *Florodora*.

A COINCIDENCE OF CORPSES

(Brighton Trunk Murder, 1934)

Jonathan Goodman

Between the wars, the golden age of rail travel produced a sanguinary slew of trunk crimes. In Brighton, a raffish seaside town on the English south coast, there were two in the same summer, that of 1934; only one was ever solved, leaving the other (so to speak) still to be called for. The unsolved case became known as the Brighton Trunk Crime No. 1. The victim—a woman—was never identified, and her killer never caught. By the most extraordinary of coincidences, barely a month later, a second corpse was found in a second trunk in the same town. This time, the remains were identified; they were those of Violette Kaye, a one-time dancer turned prostitute, whose lover, a petty crook calling himself Tony Mancini, was tried for her murder in a case known as the Brighton Trunk Crime No. 2. Thanks to an Olympian defence by his lawyer, the great Norman Birkett KC, Mancini was acquitted. Sensation (eventually) followed sensation: forty years on, in 1976, in an interview with the News of the World headed "I've Got Away with Murder", Tony Mancini confessed his guilt. Trunk Crime No. 1, meanwhile, remains unsolved. This account is by Jonathan Goodman (b. 1931), unquestionably Britain's leading historian of crime. A former theatre and television director, his dissection of the Wallace case in Liverpool in 1931 (see F. Tennyson Jesse's Checkmate *pp. 81-93), published in 1969 as* The Killing of Julia Wallace *remains an unrivalled achievement of original research and forensic insight.*

If they say that it rains
Or gives rheumatic pains,
  'Tis a Libel. (I'd like to indict one.)
All the world's in surprise
When any one *dies*
  (Unless he prefers it)—at Brighton.

—"Arion", *Blackwood's Magazine*, 1841

Dear Brighton, in our hours of ease,
A certain joy and sure to please,
Why have they spread such tales as these
  About thy smells?

—Anon., *Society*, 1882

By midsummer of 1934, that year had the stench of decay about
it. It was the sort of year that is remembered for what most people
who lived through it would prefer to forget.

   In Callander, Ontario, an accident of fertility called the Dionne
quins was perverted into a multimillion-dollar industry. Only a day
or so after the births on 28 May, while it was still touch-and-go
whether any of the babies would survive, the father received an offer
for them to appear, a constellation of stars outshining singular freaks
of nature, at the Chicago World's Fair; he signed the agreement
after consulting the local priest, who gave his advice in return for
a commission on the deal. But before long other offers, and more
lucrative ones, poured in, giving ample reasons to welsh on the
bargain with the Chicago promoters, ample funds to contest their
claim. The Dionne Quins (yes, with a capital Q by now) went
on to become an advertising symbol, a public relations exercise,
a product to boost sales of other products. It never occurred to
anyone that they might need protection against anything other
than breach of contract.

   On the sweltering-hot Sabbath-day of 22 July, John Dillinger—
"Public Enemy No. 1" and the first gangster to have a fan-club—was
shot to death by an impromptu firing-squad of FBI agents as he left
the Biograph Cinema, Chicago, after seeing *Manhattan Melody*, in
which a prosecutor (played by William Powell) convicted his friend
(Clark Gable) of murder. Following the shooting, the most human
gesture was that of a policeman, so delighted to see Dillinger dead

that he shook hands with the corpse. Spectators dipped hankies in the blood; some lady onlookers went so far as to kneel and soak the selvedges of their skirts in it. As soon as the inquest was over, a queue-shaped mob surged past the body as it lay in state in a mortuary. A crowd even more dense—5,000 strong, it was reckoned, many carrying picnic-hampers—was locked outside the cemetery (and was drenched but not depleted by a thunderstorm—"God's tears," according to someone who was prevented from attending) while Dillinger's remains were interred. Those remains, for which Dillinger's father had turned down an offer of $10,000, weren't quite complete: during the autopsy—a select, all-ticket affair—a light-fingered person with a quaint taste in mementoes had pocketed the brain.

June 30 ended as the Night of the Long Knives: Adolf Hitler, self-styled as "the supreme court of the German nation", organized the massacre of ninety or so people whose political views and morals did not coincide with his own. And on 25 July, over the border in Austria, the Heimwehr Fascists attempted a *coup d'état*. The timing was awry, though: the Nazis turned up at the Chancellery just after the Cabinet had gone to lunch. Still, Dr Dollfuss was shot as he tried to escape. The Nazis refused to allow anyone out of the building to summon medical help, and the "little Chancellor" bled to death on a red leather couch.

Few people in Great Britain seem to have been specially concerned about the atrocities in Germany and Austria—least of all, Oswald Mosley's black-shirted biff-boys, who were far too busy carrying out atrocities of their own, all in the name of King and Country. On 8 June, members of parliament expressed disquiet at the scenes of well-drilled thuggery they had witnessed at a Nuremburg-style rally at Olympia, the night before, and the Home Secretary recited an assurance that "the situation is under most careful scrutiny". Maybe it was some consolation to victims of blackshirt brutality to know that the Home Office was watching what was happening.

A casual scanning of newspapers of 1934 gives an impression of a year that had more than its fair share of death; but this is probably an optical illusion induced by a large tally of banner-headlined accounts of bizarre deaths and post-mortem occurrences. On a blustery day at the recently-opened Whipsnade Zoo, a man seeking to retrieve his bowler from the lions' den fell on the fatal side of the barrier . . . the first man to be hanged in Austria for fifteen years was a half-witted hobo who had set fire to a hayrick . . . the wife of the

Nepalese Minister to Great Britain having died, she was cremated
at an alfresco, coffin-less ceremony at Carshalton, South London
. . . in America, a resident of the buckeye state of Ohio suffered
a slapstick-comedy death by slipping on a banana-skin. And in
Brighton—addendum to attractions that were part and parcel of
the holiday season—bodies were treated as baggage.

> BRIGHTON. County borough, Sussex, 51 miles south of
> London (3rd-class return rail-fare, 12/10d.); on English
> Channel; magnificent promenade (3 miles) with two piers;
> fisheries. Pop. (1933 census) 146,700.

Its fortune founded in the middle of the eighteenth century by Dr
Richard Russell of Lewes, who enticed rich sufferers from scrofula
(otherwise known as the King's Evil) to bathe in—and even to
quaff—the sea-water at Brighthelmstone, a fishing village whose
sole claim to fame was as the place where Charles II embarked
for France following his defeat at Worcester, Brighton owed much
of its subsequent prosperity and growth, and all of its architectural
splendour, to the morally insane but aesthetically inclined George,
Prince Regent, who was a regular visitor in summers from that
of 1783 till that of 1820, shortly before he was crowned King,
and in half a dozen summers afterwards. The First Gentleman's
influence was at least two-fold: his presence acted as a magnet to
others, and aspects of his taste were mimicked in the design of
houses and hostelries that were erected to cope with the rush.

In 1934, Brighton was still the most resplendent seaside resort
in England, perhaps in Europe. Pebbledashed and Tudorbethan
residential nonentities were already blemishing the hem of the town,
and office blocks, posing as architecture, degrading the skyline, but
these were just first symptoms of a disfiguring rash. The general
impression was of the Regency: of bowfronts and balconies, of
faded stucco, of snooty squares, terraces and crescents (some of
which in propinquitous Hove had conveniences for dogs, few of
which took advantage of them).

In this setting—and, by a perverse visual alchemy, seeming to
be apt to it—there were all the gaudy trappings of a trippers'
town: red-blue-and-predominantly-white seafood stalls, assailing
the nostrils with the intermingled scents of vinegar and brine . . .
fortune-tellers' booths, their velveteen-curtained windows patched
with pictures of customers as celebrated as Tallulah Bankhead,

Isaac Leslie Hore-Belisha (whose lollipop-like beacons appeared on the streets that year) and Amy Johnson . . . arcades crammed with penny-in-the-slot peepshows and pin-tables . . . a display of waxwork dummies . . . hundreds of greasy-spoon cafés ("Thermos Flasks Filled with Pleasure") and near as many pubs . . . dance-halls . . . an aquarium . . . souvenir emporiums that did a roaring trade in miniature-po ashtrays, sticks of rock-candy, boaters with ribbons that extended invitations such as "KISS ME QUICK", and naughty postcards painted by Donald McGill. There was even, on the prom, a store that offered not only Rhinestone jewellery and strings of paste beads but also—unsurprisingly, come to think of it—"Ear Piercing While-U-Wait".

Since the days of the Prince Regent and his *corps-d'amour*, Brighton had enjoyed a reputation as a place where sexual illicitness was allowed, expected, invited even; when the town was mentioned in conversation, a knowing wink was very nearly implicit. "A dirty weekend at Brighton" was a catch-phrase so familiar as to suggest that the town had cornered the market as a venue for sexcapades—that weekends were never at all grubby at resorts like Frinton, Lytham St Anne's and Bognor Regis. As is often the case, with people as well as with places, the reality was less exciting than the reputation.

Brighton had acquired more nicknames over the years than anywhere else in the land. In the decade or so following the Great War, when the race-course and the town were infested by villains, "Doctor Brighton", "London-by-the-Sea", "Old Ocean's Bauble" and other chamber-of-commerce-nurtured sobriquets were joined by "Soho-on-Sea" and "The Queen of the Slaughtering Places". But the preposterous coincidence of the town's being the scene of three of the five known trunk-crimes in Great Britain made "Torso City" perhaps the most deserved nickname of all.

The first trunk-murder was committed in 1831 by John Holloway, a twenty-six-year-old labourer on the Brighton Chain Pier, who was assisted in his post-executional chores by the fact that his victim, his wife Celia, had stood only four feet three inches tall. His crime was brought home to him at Lewes Assizes on 14 December, and he was hanged two days later.

The next two trunk-murders were London sensations.

In 1905, Arthur Devereux, a chemist's assistant, poisoned his wife and two-year-old twin sons with salts of morphine, and crammed the bodies into a tin trunk fitted with a home-made air-tight cover, which he deposited in a warehouse at Kensal Rise. Three months later, in April, his mother-in-law got permission to have the trunk opened. Arrested in Coventry, Devereux was tried at the Old Bailey in July; the jury rejected his plea of insanity (which was supported by a clergyman who asserted that Devereux was "a little bit off the top"), and he was hanged in August.

The third trunk-employing murderer was John Robinson, an estate agent who in May 1927 did away with an aspiring prostitute called Minnie Bonati in his office facing Rochester Row Police Station, and afterwards dismembered the body, packed the portions in a trunk and deposited the trunk in the left-luggage office at Charing Cross Station. Robinson, who had scattered incriminating evidence as if it were confetti, was, like Devereux, hanged in the month of August and at Pentonville Gaol.

As far as is known, there was a lull of nigh on seven years before Brighton, home of the inaugural trunk-crime, became the main setting for more than one.

17 June 1934, the day when a large amount of the first-discovered body came to light, was a Sunday: a bright, tranquil day, one of many that summer, with the temperature on the south coast rising into the seventies by early afternoon. In Brighton's railway station, on the brow of Queen's Road, the sunlight, softened by its struggle through the grimy glass of the vaulted canopy, descended in dust-dotted, steam-flecked columns that emphasized the shadows.

Four o'clock; the median of a busy day at the station; a hiatus of calm between the arrival of the last of the special trains that had brought thousands of trippers to the town and the departure of the first of the trains that would take most of them—moist, pink-faced, salty-lipped—away after a Nice Day by the Sea.

It was stuffy in the left-luggage office. Occasionally, the movement of a bus, cab or car in the forecourt of the station would send a breeze scuttling across the linoleum-surfaced counter; but this merely rearranged the stale air. And it certainly had no deodorizing effect on an item of luggage that, at that moment, was being discussed in unflattering terms—and not for the first time—by William Vinnicombe and James Lelliot, the attendants on the two-till-ten shift.

The plywood trunk was brand-new. Its covering of light-brown canvas was clean, unscratched—marred only by the counterfoil of the threepenny ticket, number G. 1945, that had been dabbed on the lid when the trunk had been left for safe-keeping eleven days before, on 6 June.

The trunk stood solitary on the stone floor, as if shunned by the pieces of luggage on the tiers of wide, slatted shelves. Actually, it had been left on the floor because of its weight. Harry Rout, the attendant on the other shift who had accepted the trunk, had told Vinnicombe that he remembered saying how heavy it was to the man who had handed it in. The only other thing that Rout had recalled of the transaction was that it had taken place some time between six and seven on the Wednesday evening. In his memory, the depositor of the trunk was faceless, formless; he might, just might, recognize the man if he saw him again—doubtful, though. After all, 6 June was Derby Day, and crowds of racegoers returning from Epsom Downs had combined with the usual early-evening commuter-rush to overcrowd the station.

Now, standing as distant from the trunk as the confines of the left-luggage office would allow, Vinnicombe and Lelliot agreed that the smell from it—which they had first noticed a couple of days before and wrongly attributed to a shoulder of lamb insufficiently wrapped in sheets of the *Brighton Argus*—was growing stronger, more pungent, with every minute that passed. Before long—and in no time at all if the fine weather persisted—the odour would be unbearable.

Something was rotting within the trunk; there was no doubt about that. But what? The smell, as well as being noxious, was unique in their experience. In all probability, both men surmised what was causing the smell. Neither of them, however, was prepared to put the thought into words.

"Whatever is is," William Vinnicombe prevaricated, "it's definitely not lilies of the valley."

The conversation about the trunk drifted on; aimlessly, repetitively, uncertainly. At last—spurred, perhaps, by a specially rich whiff—Vinnicombe decided that enough was enough. Leaving Lelliot to hold the fort and to endure the smell alone, he went in search of a railway policeman.

As it happened, the officer he found was hidden from public gaze, having a chat with the constable of the Brighton police force assigned to uphold law and order in the environs of the terminus. Neither officer was pleased at having his unofficial tea-break interrupted, but when Vinnicombe explained the reason for his own absence from his post, both of them accompanied him back to it. Having sampled what troubled the attendant, they agreed with him—and with the more talkative Lelliot—that the trunk gave cause for suspicion; they only nodded their agreement, then hastened from the left-luggage office and began breathing again. Talking to each other, they concluded that the trunk had to be opened and its contents examined, but that the adding together of their respective years of service did not equal the authority to take on the task. The Brighton policeman "got on the blower" to his station, which was a section of the town hall, and within a few minutes (the town hall being just over a quarter of a mile away, close to the sea) they were joined by Detective-Constable Edward Taylor. The latter, a man of action, borrowed his uniformed colleague's truncheon and used it to prise open the two catch-locks on the side of the trunk. Then he flung back the lid. And then, his need for resuscitation easily over-coming his curiosity, he staggered out on to the concourse. Perhaps it was his imagination, but he was sure that the fumes from the trunk had seeped into his clothing. (Perhaps not imagination at all: even a year later, the trunk, sans contents and having had dozens of drenchings with disinfectant, gave off such a disgusting odour that the spare room at the police station where it was kept was dubbed the "stink-hole".)

Taylor was joined by another detective-constable, Arthur Stacey (whose slight delay is explained by the fact that, having been ordered to proceed to the terminus, he had decided to wait for a tram rather than make himself intolerably sweaty by walking). The two of them dashed into the left-luggage office, stared into the trunk, observed a large brown-paper parcel tied with cord of the type that was used in venetian blinds, scrabbled some of the paper away, sufficient to reveal a female torso, and dashed out again. Having recovered, Stacey telephoned the police station to request—no, to insist upon—the despatch of the head of the CID (never mind if it was his Sunday off) and other senior detectives and an undertaker's shell and canvas screens and the police surgeon and a posse of uniformed constables to what he described as "the scene of the worst crime we've had in donkey's years".

By the time the rush of homeward-bound day-trippers got under way, the left-luggage office was obscured by decorators' sheets; a scribbled notice apologized for the inconvenience of temporary closure. The offensive trunk, contents and all, had been removed to the mortuary. Its floor-space had been scrubbed with boiling water and lysol soap, and half a dozen detectives (known in Brighton as "splits") were perusing the remaining left-luggage for indications of the presence of the limbs and head that had been detached from the torso. No such parts were discovered. (But the search did reveal other human remains. A battered Moses-basket, on the lid of which the initials VP had been partly scratched away, was found to contain the body of a baby—a girl who, if she had lived at all, had survived no longer than a few days. As the basket had been deposited as far back as 23 February, Detective-Inspector Arthur Pelling, the officer in charge of the investigation, felt confident in saying that there was "no possible connection between this discovery and the trunk case".) The search was still going on when Captain W.J. Hutchinson, the ex-soldier who was chief-constable of Brighton, got in touch with the duty officer at both Scotland Yard and the London headquarters of the railway police, to ask for all left-luggage offices in the south of England—in coach depots as well as railway stations—to be scoured for suspicious baggage.

At the mortuary, the trunk was unpacked by the police surgeon. Not all at once, but over the next couple of days, the following facts were established apropos of the contents:

Excepting the wounds of decapitation and dismemberment, the torso appeared to be uninjured; a small pimple below the left breast was the sole distinguishing mark.

As well as the brown paper and the venetian-blind cord (19 feet of it; disappointingly unpeculiar, available from thousands of hardware stores at a halfpenny a yard), there were some hanks of cotton wool (used to soak up the blood?) and a once-white face-flannel with a red border. Written in blue pencil on one of the sheets of wrapping paper were letters that looked like f-o-r-d; there seemed to be a preceding letter—d, perhaps, or a hasty l—but this was only just visible, on the right-hand edge of a patch of congealed blood. Was "ford" the end of a surname? Or of a place name?—Dartford, Guildford, Stafford, for instance. Or was "ford" a misreading? Were the letters actually h-o-v-e?—and, if so, was there a connection with the so-named western continuation of Brighton? (None of those questions would be answered. Towards the end of the week, the sheet of paper would be sent to the government laboratories in Chancery Lane, London, but none of the new-fangled tests, using chemicals and ultra-violet rays, would bring to light the letter or letters that lay beneath the blood; and

later, any number of people practising as graphologists would
come up with any number of different readings of the visible
letters.)

On Monday morning, Inspector Pelling enlisted the help of the
press. "What I should like," he said, "is that members of the public,
particularly those residing in the Southern Counties, including
London, should contact the Chief Constable of Brighton if a
female relative or friend disappeared without explanation on or
prior to the 6th of this month." (The response to the appeal was
over-gratifying: by the beginning of September, twelve thousand
letters, cards and telegrams—not to mention many telephone
calls—had been received; more flowed in during the autumn and
winter, but no one at the police station bothered to count these.)

While Arthur Pelling was talking to reporters—guardedly concerning the crime itself—some of the policemen assigned to the
investigation were scanning the Brighton and Hove missing-persons
files, others were trying to establish whether those files required
deletions or additions, others were at the railway station, working
in the left-luggage office or quizzing staff and travellers in the hope
of finding people who had been there between six and seven on
Derby Day and noticed a man who, perhaps with assistance,
was carrying, pushing, pulling or in some less conventional way
transporting a trunk.

And at other stations, policemen of other forces were sniffing
unclaimed baggage or, more fastidious, standing by or back while
left-luggage attendants sniffed on their behalf. One of these stations
was, of course, King's Cross, a primary metropolitan terminus of
the LNER. There it was, on Monday afternoon, that William
Cope, a porter deputizing for an attendant who was on holiday,
sniffed and then unhesitatingly opened a cheap brown suitcase.
Crammed inside the case were four objects wrapped in brown
paper and copies of national newspapers, those wrappings soaked
from within by blood and from without by olive oil. Cope looked
no further before hailing a constable, who, having taken a fleeting
glance at the discovery, blew his whistle to summon other, more
senior officers, one of whom felt obliged to pay greater heed to
the parcels. Finding that two contained a human leg apiece and
that the other two each contained a human foot, he assumed
that the feet had been cut from the legs, and that this had been
done because, whereas the four parcels fitted snugly inside the

case, two larger ones, roughly L-shaped, could not have been accommodated.

The first of those assumptions was confirmed by Sir Bernard Spilsbury, the honorary Home Office pathologist, who, once the legs and feet, still in the case, had been removed to the St Pancras mortuary, went there to examine them. As well as noting that the legs and feet were, so to say, a matching set, he concluded that they had been chopped from the body of a woman—a natural blonde, he believed, basing that opinion on a microscopic examination of the faint down on the legs. The state of the feet—free of corns or other blemishes, the nails expertly trimmed—led Sir Bernard to believe that the woman had worn decent shoes (size $4\frac{1}{2}$, he reckoned) and that she had paid regular visits to a chiropodist, the final visit being shortly before her death.

By the time the police received the pathologist's report, officers at King's Cross had learned that the suitcase had been deposited round about half-past one on the afternoon of 7 June, the day after the trunk was left at Brighton station; they had interviewed Cyril Escott, the attendant who had issued the ticket, but had been unable to jog from him the slightest recollection of the person to whom he had issued it. However, the newspapers that had been used as wrappings—one dated Thursday, 31 May, the other Saturday, 2 June—seemed to provide a small and very general clue: after looking at the blood-and-oil-sodden sheets, a newspaper printer said that the "make-up", and "compositor's dots" on a front page, showed that the papers were copies of editions distributed within about fifty miles of Fleet Street.

Sir Bernard Spilsbury travelled to Brighton to examine the torso. He was occupied for three hours (during which time a crowd gathered outside the mortuary—a few locals, several reporters, and many holidaymakers, including "jazz girls", some conspicuous in beach-pyjamas, some of these and others rendering the hit-song, "It's the cutest little thing, got the cutest little swing—hitchy-koo, hitchy-koo, hitchy-koo", over and over again) and then informed Inspector Pelling that:

> internal examination of the torso had not revealed the cause of death;
>
> the legs and feet found at King's Cross belonged to the torso;
>
> the victim had been well-nourished (which, put with the

chiropody, suggested to Spilsbury "a middle-class background"); she had been not younger than twenty-one
and not older than twenty-eight, had stood about five
feet two inches, and had weighed roughly eight and a
half stone;
    she was pregnant at the time of her death.

On the Monday afternoon, Brighton's seaward newsboys, standing
at corners on the promenade or crunching through the pebbles on
the front, had a cry in common:
    "Horrible murder in Brighton! Dead body in trunk!"
    The cry gave a man known as Toni Mancini the worst shock of
his twenty-six years of life. Since the start of the holiday season, he
had been employed as a waiter and washer-up at the Skylark Café,
which took up one of the man-made caves beneath the promenade,
entered from the beach. On this particular day, his attention had
been almost wholly directed at the kitchen-sink. Therefore, he had
heard nothing of the discovery at the railway station.
    "Toni Mancini" was not his real name but just the current
favourite among an accumulation of aliases that included Jack
Notyre, Luigi Pirelli and Antoni Luigi. He had committed a
few petty crimes, but the Italianate aliases, rather than being
inventions aimed at misleading the police, were symptoms of his
Valentinoesque dream-world; so was the way he smarmed his dark
hair diagonally back from a central parting, and so was his attitude
towards a string-thin moustache, which was there one week, gone
the next. Actually, he was a native of the South London borough
of Deptford, where he had been born on 8 January 1908 to an
eminently respectable couple—the father a shipping clerk—with a
determinedly unforeign surname; the parents had borrowed from
the nobility for his Christian name and made the mother's middle
name his, thus arriving at Cecil Lois England.
    Still, to save confusion, we may as well refer to him as Toni
Mancini. He was already calling himself that when, in 1932 or
thereabouts, in London, he met up with and soon moved in
with a woman sixteen years older than himself. Though her first
name was Violet, and despite the fact that she was still married
to a man named Saunders, she insisted on being called Violette
Kaye, which was the name she had used during an ill-fated career
as a dancer in chorus-lines—first, "Miss Watson's Rosebuds";
finally, "The Parisian Pinkies"—at tatty provincial music-halls.

Subsequent to terpischory, she had turned to prostitution, and she was well versed in that trade when Mancini joined forces with her, soon to add business to pleasure by appointing himself her pimp. The partners moved from London to Brighton in the spring of 1933. Occasionally, slumps in the never great demand for the forty-one-year-old Violette's services forced Mancini to work; but more often than not he spent afternoons and evenings in dance-halls, usually either Sherry's or Aladdin's Cave, for he was as much a master of the tango and the fox-trot as Violette had ever been mistress of tap and clog-dancing routines. They shared a succession of small flats, the last being in the basement of 44 Park Crescent, almost opposite the Race Hill Inn on the main Lewes Road.

That was their residence on Wednesday, 10 May 1934, when (according to the account given by Mancini a long time afterwards) he finished a stint at the Skylark Café, went home for tea, had a flaming row with Violette, who was the worse for drink or drugs, and, in the heat of the moment, threw a coal-hammer at her—with such unintended accuracy as to kill her. Flummoxed, he left the body lying on the floor, close to the fireplace. When he eventually thought that he must put it out of sight, rigor mortis was complete, which meant that he had the devil's own job fitting it, standing in an upright pose, into a wardrobe (within which, as the rigor wore off, it dropped in fits and starts, making rather alarming noises while Mancini was trying to sleep). To forestall the arrival of Violette's sister, who was looking forward to spending a week in Brighton, sleeping on the Put-U-Up, in the basement flat, he sent her a telegram:

GOING ABROAD GOOD JOB SAIL SUNDAY WILL WRITE VI

A week or so later, he decided for some reason to move from Park Crescent to the diminutive basement flat at 52 Kemp Street, the southern bit of a dingy thoroughfare that, after being crossed by a main road, became Station Street—so named because its western aspect was the blind side-wall of Brighton's railway terminus.

In preparation for the move, he purchased a black fibre trunk from a dealer in secondhand goods, not haggling at the asking-price of ten shillings. Having stowed his and most of Violette's belongings in cardboard boxes and suitcases, he transferred the corpse from the wardrobe to the trunk, packed the crevices with female garments that remained, scattered a bag of moth-balls over the contorted body, closed and locked the trunk, and threw away the key. As, on his own, he could hardly shove the trunk, let alone lift it, he borrowed a wheelbarrow, then persuaded two acquaintances, a blind piano-accordionist named Johnnie Beaumont and a kitchen porter named Tom Capelem, to help him lug the trunk to the barrow and trundle the barrow to Kemp Street. When Capelem enquired, "What yer got in 'ere—a body?", Mancini replied, with every appearance of nonchalance, "Silver and crockery do weigh surprising heavy, don't they?"

He involved himself in additional expense in the basement flat, for he decided that as he intended to use the trunk as a makeshift seat when he had more than one tea-time guest, he needed to cover it with something: he bought a square of pretty, primrose-patterned American cloth from Woolworth's. Though, as the weeks went by, the trunk became increasingly malodorous and began to leak body fluids, Mancini continued to have visitors. He was fortunate in one respect: the landlady had no sense of smell—and when she commented on the fluids seeping into the floorboards, he told her that they were a unique blend of French polishes, so were enhancing the boards rather than disfiguring them, a reply that pleased her so much that she asked for a quote for spreading the stuff wall-to-wall. On one occasion, a lady guest broke off from munching a muffin to say, "Do excuse my curiosity, but I'm wondering if by any chance you breed rabbits or . . . um . . . skunks." "That funny smell, you mean?" Mancini asked. "I must apologize for it. And when I have a minute to spare, I'll remove the cause—which (I hesitate to admit this) is an old pair of football boots, reminders of my lost youth: QPR were keen to sign me on, you know. Won't you partake of the raspberry junket? I made it with my own fair hands, and it would be such a shame to let it go off."

When, on the afternoon of Monday, 17 June, Mancini was allowed a five-minute break from his chores in the kitchen of the Skylark Café, he sauntered between the white-painted cast-iron tables and out on to the beach. There he heard the newsboys' cry. Assuming, reasonably enough, that he was the only person in or anywhere near Brighton who had lately put a body in a trunk, he furthermore assumed that Kemp Street was at that moment a hive of police activity; and, once he was able to hear his thoughts above the beating of his heart, he registered surprise, astonishment even, that the only uniformed person within arresting distance of him was a deck-chair attendant. Extending his five-minute break, he staggered across the pebbles to where the occupant of a deck-chair was reading a copy of a special edition of the *Brighton Argus*. Forcing himself to look over the man's shoulder, he read the headlines above, and stared at the picture illustrating, the report of the trunk-crime. Of a trunk-crime that was quite independent of his own. At last believing the unbelievable, he strode back to the café. And he whistled a happy tune.

You will recall that when Toni Mancini first heard of what came to be called "Brighton Trunk-Crime No. 1"—differentiating it from the death and subsequent bundling of Violette Kaye, which was billed as "Brighton Trunk-Crime No. 2"—Sir Bernard Spilsbury was toiling over the torso in the mortuary. Also, policemen were traipsing the town, some checking on whether women reported missing were still astray, others looking in empty premises and even burrowing in rubbish dumps on the offchance of happening on the head and arms to augment the portions found fifty-one miles apart; and, at police headquarters, a trio of detectives was considering the first suggestions from the public regarding the identity of the victim (who, by the way, had already been dubbed "The Girl with the Pretty Feet" by a London crime-reporter—the same man, perhaps, who would call Violette Kaye "The Woman with Dancer's Legs" and her terminal souteneur "The Dancing Waiter"). And, some time during the same period, Captain Hutchinson, the chief constable, had a word with Inspector Pelling and then telephoned the Commissioner of the Metropolitan Police to request that Scotland Yard detectives be sent to Brighton to take control of the investigation; by making the request promptly, Captain Hutchinson ensured that the cost of the secondment would not have to be met by local rate-payers.

The "murder squad" detective chosen for the assignment was Chief Inspector Robert Donaldson, who was, in comparison with most other policemen, quite short. His relative diminutiveness and neat apparel might have led people to believe that he was a "desk-top detective"; also that he lacked endurance. Both notions would have been far from the truth. Not only had he taken part in a number of murder investigations, but on several occasions he had "gone in mob-handed" to arrest violent criminals, some carrying firearms. Any doubts about his stamina would be dispelled by his sojourn in Brighton, during which he worked eighteen hours a day, seven days a week, for months on end.

The detective-sergeant who accompanied Donaldson to Brighton was Edward Sorrell, who at twenty-six had only recently joined Scotland Yard. Donaldson had not worked with him before, but chose him as his assistant after talking to him and getting "an impression (proved accurate) of intelligence and alertness". (That and subsequent otherwise unattributed quotations are from letters that Robert Donaldson wrote to me from his home in New Zealand in the early 1970s.)

Donaldson knew that it was vital to get the support of Arthur Pelling, who might feel put out at having had control of the investigation taken away from him. This he succeeded in doing; indeed, the two men became friends. Donaldson considered Pelling "a very competent detective. A Sussex man whose father had been in the force, he was serious-minded and conscientious. He showed no resentment that Scotland Yard were summoned to the inquiry, and it was largely through his efforts that the Brighton Constabulary, as a whole, were most co-operative."

Captain Hutchinson arranged for Donaldson to have a team of a dozen detectives and uniformed officers, and promised that additional manpower would be provided if and when it was required. As no large offices were available to be turned into "trunk-crime headquarters" at the police station, Captain Hutchinson asked the town clerk if there was space to spare in any council-owned premises, ideally in the centre of Brighton. Thus it was that the investigators took over three apartments adjoining the music salon in the Royal Pavilion, and there, amidst the chinoiserie bequeathed by George IV, and sometimes to the muffled accompaniment of string quartets and of choirs eager with hosannas, got on with the task of trying to identify the Girl with the Pretty Feet, of trying to establish who had gone to such lengths to make that task difficult.

The police did all the things one would suppose they would have done; and many that were out of the ordinary. The investigation, uniquely thorough, comprised a myriad of activities, some of long duration, others of a day or so or a matter of hours. For instance:

As a result of what the press called "the great round-up", 732 missing women were traced. A questionnaire was sent to every hospital and nursing home in the country. Hundreds of general practitioners and midwives were interviewed. At Queen Charlotte's Hospital, London, five thousand women, some from abroad, had received pre-natal advice or treatment between the beginning of February and the end of May; all but fifteen were accounted for.

Statements were made by several residents of Worthing, just along the coast, to the effect that a man who had until recently owned a sea-going vessel had offered them the opportunity of seeing a rather unusual double-bill: first, the murder of a woman, then her dismemberment. The would-be exponent of *grand-guignol* was tracked down, interviewed, and dismissed as being "all mouth and no achievement". Much the same description was applied to the several men and two women who insisted, despite clear evidence to the contrary, that they were the "trunk criminals". Donaldson's men took notes but little notice of what clairvoyants, water-diviners, teacup-readers, numerologists, vivid dreamers, and people who had been given ouija-boards for Christmas had to say. (One of the clairvoyants, known to his many fans as Grand Wizard of the Past and Future, told a Brighton detective—and, after being shown out of the Royal Pavilion, a reporter for the *Sunday Dispatch*—that "the trunk criminal is probably called George; he has busy hair, works in a wholesale seed-store, and originally used the brown paper found in the trunk for wrapping up tyres".)

Police throughout the country asked register-office clerks whether in the past few months couples had given notice of marriage but not turned up to complete the transaction. The thought behind this question was that whoever had made the trunk-victim pregnant may have bolstered the conning of the girl with indications of legitimizing intentions.

Of the many people who responded to repeated appeals that anyone who was at Brighton railway station between six and seven on the evening of Derby Day should come forward, two women and a man, the latter a retired warrant officer of the Royal Engineers, claimed to have seen the—or *a*—trunk being transported towards the left-luggage office. The trouble was that, whereas the women—fellow-Tory-travellers from a garden party at North Lancing—were convinced that they had seen just one man coping with a trunk, the ex-soldier was sure that he had seen two men sharing a similar load. Still, his description of one of the men—"about forty-five, tall, slim, dark, clean-shaven, and quite respectably attired"—came close to the description arrived at (perhaps after much "No, you're wrong, Mabel"—"I'm certain I'm right, Edna" discussion) by the women; and as all three witnesses had been at the station within a period of a few minutes, it was reasonable to hazard a guess—based on the station-master's notes of the actual times that trains had reached Brighton—that if the trunk was brought to the station by rail, its journey was short, probably from the west and no further away than Worthing. An artist was called in to make a portrait from the witnesses' specifications, and copies of this were shown to staff at local stations; but though one or two railwaymen raised hopes by saying that the drawing slightly resembled someone or other who at some time or other had entrained to somewhere or other, the eye-witness evidence led nowhere.

An imperfection was observed in the serration of a piece of brown sticky tape affixed to part of the wrapping that had been round the torso. Therefore, policemen called on every single stationery supplier in London and the Southern Counties, trying—but without success—to find a saw-blade cutter with one tooth blunted in a peculiar way.

So as to check a London suspect's alibi, particles of sand found in his car were compared with samples of sand from near Brighton and from sandy-beached resorts east of Bournemouth and south of Yarmouth. The sand turned out to be unique to Clacton, in Essex—a fact that lent support to his story.

Upon completion of one of the early-begun tasks—the interviewing of residents of Brighton who might help to establish the where-abouts of women who had suddenly become conspicuous by their absence—Donaldson ordered that the interviews be repeated. A roster was prepared, its aim being to ensure that everyone already interviewed was revisited—and by a different officer.

Right at the end of the first sweep, one of Violette Kaye's customers had called at 44 Park Crescent and, having been told by the landlady that "Mr and Mrs Mancini" had gone, she knew not where, reported the prostitute's departure to the police. On Saturday, 14 July, a constable had traced Toni Mancini to the Skylark Café and, not liking the look of him, decided to take him to the Royal Pavilion rather than question him at his place of employment. But after Mancini, ostensibly quite at ease, had said that his "old friend Vi" was trying her luck in France, Germany, or somewhere like that—and that she was forty-two, at least fourteen years senior to the trunk-victim—he was allowed to leave.

But Mancini did not return to the Skylark Café; nor did he go to the house in Kemp Street—the front of which had since the day before been latticed with scaffolding, put there on behalf of a firm of decorators who were to start repointing the brickwork on Sunday. No; he sought out a girl-friend and treated her to a plate of cod and chips at the Aqua Café, which was at Old Steine, near the Palace Pier. He was not his usual cheery self. Ever the perfect gentleman, though, he commented that the girl looked rather nice in her new dress (which was not new at all: once the possession of Violette Kaye, Mancini had presented it to the girl a week or so after Vi's demise, suggesting that it could do with dry-cleaning). The girl was still eating when Mancini abruptly asked for the bill, paid it, left an over-generous tip, and, muttering something that the girl didn't catch, walked out of the café. The waitress scurried across to bag the tip. Lifting the cup of tea that Mancini had barely touched, she pointed out to the girl that he had left her a message, scribbled in blue crayon on the tablecloth: SEE YOU LATER, DUCK.

Mancini was already on his way to the northern outskirts of the town, where he would hitch a ride to London.

On Sunday morning, just as one of Donaldson's team was about to leave the Royal Pavilion to start a round of repeat-interviews, including a second chat with Toni Mancini, at his home this time, a telephone call was received from a foreman-decorator, who insisted that the police come to 52 Kemp Street at once. Why? Well, for the simple reason that he and his mates, repointers all, needed gas-masks against the dreadful smell coursing into the street from the nether regions of the dilapidated house.

The detective with 52 Kemp Street on his list of addresses was told to delay his departure. When he left the Royal Pavilion, he was accompanied by colleagues, one of whom was Detective-Constable Edward Taylor—who, you may recall, was the officer who had opened the stinking trunk at the railway station exactly four weeks before. Arriving outside the house, the detectives at once followed the example of the waiting decorators and turned up their noses; Taylor afterwards expressed mystification that the smell, which must have been polluting the outside air for days, had not offended any of No. 52's neighbours, nor the scaffolders, into complaining about it to a health officer. As there was no reply when the detectives banged on the front door (it turned out that the landlady and her husband—he as senseless of smell as she was—had arranged to be away on holiday while the external decorations were being done), they broke it down.

Having descended the uncarpeted steps to the basement, the

detectives first of all flung open the windows, front and back. Then the highest-ranking of them pointed an accusing finger at the black trunk and twitched another finger in Taylor's direction, indicating that he had been selected to open it. The detectives, every one of them, were sure that the trunk contained the missing head and arms. Taylor grabbed a sharpening iron from among the stuff on the draining-board and, his head reeling from a blend of stink and *déjà vu*, prised open the locks and pulled back the lid.

You will be aware—basically at least—of what was revealed. Though predictable, mention must be made of the fact that the contents were lavish with maggots, the most gluttonous of which were more than an inch long.

In the afternoon, Sir Bernard Spilsbury visited Brighton for the second time within a month. Following his examination of the body of Violette Kaye, he noted on a case-card that

> she had been five feet two inches in height and well-nourished;
> she had used peroxide to turn her brunette hair blonde;
> her head was badly bruised, and she had been killed "by a violent blow or blows with a blunt object, e.g. head of hammer, causing a depressed fracture extending down to the base, with a short fissured fracture extending up from its upper edge".

Even before Spilsbury's arrival, Robert Donaldson—depressed that he now had two trunk-crimes to deal with, though "Brighton Trunk-Crime No. 2" seemed to be virtually solved—broadcast a message to all police forces, giving a description of Toni Mancini and asking that he be apprehended.

At about eleven o'clock on the night of Thursday, 18 July, Police Constables William Triplow and Leonard Gourd were sitting in a patrol-car near the Yorkshire Grey pub in Lewisham, South London, close to Mancini's birthplace. All at once, Triplow nudged his partner and pointed through the windshield in the direction of a well-lighted roundabout. A man was walking towards an all-night café. "So what?" Gourd muttered. "Look at his walk," Triplow said. Gourd looked. Yes, there was something odd about it: it was more of a prance than a walk; the feet merely dabbed the ground, making one think of a liberty-horse—a tired liberty-horse. "I reckon it's the Brighton-trunk bloke, the 'dancing waiter',", Triplow said. With that, he left the car and ran towards the man.

"Excuse me, sir," he said, "but do you happen to be Mr Marconi?"

"Mancini," he was corrected. "I couldn't half go a cup of tea and a sandwich or something."

Triplow and Gourd took Mancini to the local police station. A phone call was made to Scotland Yard, and from there a message was sent to Brighton police headquarters, saying that Mancini would be arriving under escort in the town in the early hours of the morning.

The arrest was front-page news on papers that reached Brighton at about the same time as did Mancini. The reports heaped praise on William Triplow, one going so far as to call him "the sharpest-eyed policeman in the Metropolis". (When I met him at his home in Lewisham in 1970, he had been blind for several years.)

Presently, a queue began to form outside the magistrates' court. Most of the queuers were young women, some of whom bragged of having partnered Toni on the dance-floor, others of whom went farther in boasting of their knowledge of him. Soon there were more than fifty people in the queue. As there were only fifty seats in the gallery of the court, the thousand or so latecomers disorganized themselves into a cheering, singing, waving-to-press-photographers mob. Mounted policemen were needed to bisect it when Mancini, flanked by detectives, made his first public appearance as a celebrity. He looked as if he had been allowed to shave, but his clothes—dark blue jacket, grey shirt, white tie, flannel trousers—were crumpled. He smiled in response to the shouts and screams of "Hello, Toni," "Keep your pecker up," "Don't worry, love, all will be well," and frowned concernedly when a woman in beach-pyjamas fainted, either from sheer emotion or from absence of underwear on a rather chilly morning. The girl he had treated to fish and chips at the Aqua Café stood apart from the mob; she was again wearing the dress he had given her.

Similar scenes were enacted when he left the court, having been remanded in custody, and when, over the next few weeks, he was brought from Lewes Goal, first for further remands, then for the committal proceedings, at the end of which he was ordered to stand trial at the forthcoming Lewes Assizes.

The trial lasted four days. Beforehand—perhaps on his own

initiative, perhaps at the suggestion of his counsel, Norman Birkett—he had done some preparation:

"I had carefully rehearsed my lines like an actor. I had practised how I should hold my hands and when I should let the tears run down my cheeks. It might sound cold and calculating, but you have to remember that my life was at stake."

His story—in its essentials, entirely false, as he admitted when the rule against double-jeopardy protected him—was that he had found Violette Kaye lying dead when he returned to the basement flat in Park Crescent on 10 May. As he had a record of convictions for petty crimes (none involving violence—an important point in his favour, Birkett contended), it would not have occurred to him in a month of Sundays to report the matter to the police: "I considered that a man who has been convicted never gets a fair and square deal from the police." So—very silly of him, he now understood—he had bought the trunk, wedged the body in it, and moved, trunk and all, to a different basement.

Birkett brilliantly abetted the lies, saliently by patching together disparate answers from prosecution witnesses so that they seemed to support the theory that Violette Kaye had either taken a mite too much morphine and fallen down the area steps or been pushed down them by a dissatisfied, over-eager or jealous client—and that, whatever had caused the fall, she had struck her head on a projecting rail or a pilaster of masonry.

Holes gaped in both Mancini's story and Birkett's theory: but the jury, having stayed out for some two hours, returned to the bijou court with a verdict of "Not guilty".

Was Mancini surprised? One cannot tell. When he entered the dock to hear the verdict, he was wearing an overcoat—indicating that he expected to walk out into the high street a free man—but when the foreman of the jury spoke two words rather than the fatal one, he staggered and stared, and when he was at last able to speak to his counsel, muttered, "Not guilty, Mr Birkett—not guilty?", as if he were a character in someone else's dream.

(The following summer, Mancini toured fairgrounds with a sideshow featuring a variation on the trick of sawing a woman in half. Instead of a box, he used a large black trunk; his "victim" was his wife, whom he had met at Aladdin's Cave shortly before his flight from Brighton and married a week after his acquittal. He did not draw the crowds for long, and was almost forgotten by 1941, when he was serving in the navy. In that year, a man who really was named Toni Mancini was hanged for a gang-murder in Soho, and people recalled the earlier case, the self-styled Toni Mancini, and said, "Now there's a coincidence.")

While Brighton Trunk-Crime No. 2 had been delighting the populace, Robert Donaldson and his eventually reduced team of helpers had been working hard to solve Trunk-Crime No. 1. Donaldson had reason to believe, but was never able to prove, that one or both of the missing arms had been burned on the Sussex Downs, close to a place where, after the Great War, the bodies of Hindu soldiers who had died in hospitals in or around Brighton were cremated. As to the whereabouts of the head—well, perhaps Donaldson obtained a general indication of its resting place when, early in September, he was put in touch with a young man of the town. The latter stated that "shortly before the discovery at the railway station, he and his girl had been walking along Black Rock, to the east of Brighton. In a rock pool they found a head. It was the head of a young woman. The man explained to his sweetheart that they should leave it alone as it was probably the remains of a suicide and that the police had removed all they needed of the body".

As soon as Donaldson received this information, he caused a search to be made of the whole beach: "Nothing relevant was found, so I consulted various marine authorities on the question of where the head might be; the sweep of the tides indicated that it could have been taken out to sea and then swept ashore at Beachy Head, but nothing was found there either."

The courting couple's silliness was just one thing among many that Donaldson had to hide his anger about. His greatest reason for anger was the action of a high-ranking policeman stationed at Hove.

By early July, Donaldson had garnered indications that the person directly or indirectly responsible for Trunk-Crime No. I was Edward Seys Massiah, a man in his mid-fifties who hailed from the West Indian island of Trinidad. One of Massiah's parents had been white, the other black, thus making him a mulatto, his skin dark but not ebony, his hair more wavy than crinkled, his lips quite thin. He had an impressive collection of medical qualifications: MD, MB, B.Ch, DTM. All but the last of those designatory letters, which stood for Doctor of Tropical Medicine, were scratched larger than his name on his brass shingle, which in 1934 gleamed beside the imposing entrance to a slightly less imposing house within sight of the sea at Hove: 8 Brunswick Square.

The fact that he lived as well as practised there was something he stressed in conversation with prospective patients and with gentlemen whose lady-friends were pregnant or at risk of becoming so; he was, so to speak, open all hours, and that convenience was allied with a guarantee of confidentiality. No doubt you will have guessed that he was an abortionist; and it will have occurred to you that abortion was a criminal offence.

Now, a likely cause of the death of the Girl with the Pretty Feet was a mishap during an attempt to abort her embryonic child; if that *was* the cause, then a person who had been involved in the arrangements for the abortion or the person who had tried to perform the operation, or both, would have been most anxious that the transaction and, more important, their roles in it remained secret.

When Robert Donaldson had put together diverse reasons for being suspicious of Edward Massiah (whose qualification of B.Ch was, by the way, a shortened form of the Latin *Baccalaureus Chirurgiae*, meaning Bachelor of Surgery), he found a sum greater than its parts. But as that sum did not equal justification for making an arrest, he came to the obvious conclusion that efforts were needed to ascertain whether there were additional reasons for suspicion—or whether there was a single exculpatory fact. Towards that end, he gathered a number of people together in one of the apartments at the Royal Pavilion; among those present at the meeting were Captain Hutchinson, Inspector Pelling, key-members of the trunk-crime team, and a senior officer from Hove. Donaldson enumerated the points that seemed to tell against Edward Massiah, invited discussion of them, and then—speaking specially to the man from Hove—requested covert collection of information regarding the doctor's background, his present activities and acquaintances, and his movements on Derby Day. He emphasized the word *covert*.

However, that emphasis was overlooked or ignored by the Hove policeman. Having come upon—and kept to himself—a further unflattering fact about Edward Massiah, he went, uninvited and unexpected, to 8 Brunswick Square and laid Donaldson's cards on the consulting-room table. Massiah paid attention, smiling the while, never interrupting. The sun shining through the tall windows glistened on the ranks of surgical instruments, on the green and crystal-clear pots of medication, on the framed diplomas, tinctured the red-plush couch, nestled in the careful creases of the doctor's pearl-grey cravat, black jacket and striped trousers, flashed from the unspatted parts of his patent-leather shoes. Towards the end of the policeman's speech, the doctor took a silver pencil and began jotting on a pad. Notes of what he had said and was saying, the policeman guessed.

But no, he was wrong. When he had quite finished and, pleased with himself, was feeling in a pocket for his own pad—he would need that to record the doctor's exact response—he was nonplussed by what the doctor was doing: carefully tearing the sheets from the pad on the ormolu table, turning them round, and using one manicured finger to prod them towards him. He looked at the writing. Names. Addresses, too. Telephone numbers following some of the addresses. Many of the names he recognized: they belonged to important personages of Sussex, or to national celebrities, members of noble families, or extravagantly wealthy commoners who gave financial support to worthy causes. The doctor explained. These were people who, if he were ever threatened with court proceedings and, in turn, threatened them with publicity relating to services he had rendered them, would do all in their power to protect him and ruin his accuser or accusers. The list of names was only a small sample—come to think of it, he had omitted the name of Lord So-and-So, of the member of parliament for the Such-and-Such constituency, of the owner of the Thingummyjig group of newspapers . . .

It seemed to the policeman that the sun had gone in: all of a sudden, the consulting room was a place of sombre shadows. The doctor was speaking again—quoting the forewarned-is-forearmed adage, thanking the policeman for revealing each and every fact known to Donaldson, adding that he was much obliged since he could now set about sanitizing most of those facts. And, needless to say, he would make blessed sure that Donaldson—whom he would be delighted to meet some time—made no further headway towards his objective of foisting responsibility for Trunk-Crime No. 1 on a quite innocent person: himself, he meant. Could the officer find his own way out . . . ?

The officer could. And did.

Of course, he didn't volunteer an account of the interview to Robert Donaldson. The latter learnt of the visit from one of the people named by Edward Massiah. The doctor had just happened to mention it—casually, with all the humour of a hyena—to that person, whose consequent fear was manifested as a quietly-spoken threat to Donaldson. The threat didn't worry Donaldson; but the disclosure of the Hove policeman's action made him very angry indeed. Even so, though he got the full story of the interview from the policeman himself, and berated him for "putting ambition before professionalism", he did not instigate disciplinary action.

(Shortly afterwards, Edward Massiah left Hove and started practising in London. There, a woman died following an illegal operation that he had performed. It would be wrong to say that there was a "cover-up", but somehow or other he managed to escape retribution; his name was not erased from the Medical Register. By 1938, he had left England and was living in a fine house, "Montrose", near Port of Spain, Trinidad. Not until December 1952 did the General Medical Council strike his name from the Register, and then only because he had failed to respond to letters.)

At about the time of the Massiah incident, Robert Donaldson brought his family to Brighton: "Not wanting this to be found out by a gossip-columnist, we lived in a private hotel under the name of Williams. I was supposed to be an engineer. My wife and I briefed the children as to their new surname and we thought all would be well. However, my six-year-old younger son, not realizing what was at stake, would solemnly ignore the injunctions of 'Andrew Williams, come here,' etc., and would tell all and sundry that he was a Donaldson. My cover was quickly blown."

Months later, the strain of the inquiry took its toll on Donaldson: "I found that I was having trouble with my eyes. I went to an oculist in London, and after extensive testing he said there was nothing organically wrong with my eyes. He recommended that I see a nerve specialist. His diagnosis was that I had been overworking. Under the circumstances, that was somewhat self-evident. However, I was then given a Detective-Inspector—Taffy Rees—to help me. But Taffy too became a casualty with a stomach ulcer."

There is a final—one could say unforgivable—coincidence to be mentioned. In September 1935, Robert Donaldson took a well-earned holiday. He went motoring in Scotland. On the way home, he parked his car near the border-town of Moffatt and sat on the bridge at Gardenholme Linn for a quiet smoke. Beneath the bridge, tucked well out of sight, were some of the neatly-parcelled remains of Dr Buck Ruxton's common-law wife and of his children's nursemaid, Mary Rogerson. By the time Donaldson reported back to Scotland Yard, those parcels and others had been discovered, and it goes without saying that it was he who took charge of the London end of the inquiry into the north-country variant on bodies-as-baggage. Though not a superstitious man, he must have been at least slightly worried when he learnt that Dr Ruxton, guilty beyond doubt, was to be defended by Norman Birkett, the barrister who had been so helpful to Toni Mancini. But no: this time Birkett's client was found guilty and was duly hanged.

THE SECRET
OF IRELAND'S EYE

(William Burke Kirwan, 1852)

William Roughead

Here is a case in which the outcome was almost certainly a miscarriage of justice. William Kirwan, an artist, was convicted of murdering his wife and sentenced to death. In the event he was reprieved and served nearly thirty years of penal servitude. But subsequent medical opinion suggests that the woman died of natural causes. Kirwan appears to have been a victim of some intangible intuition on the part of the Dublin Court that he was guilty, although the evidence strikes the modern reader as flimsy in the extreme. Journalist Richard Lambert believed the case to have been beset by "a sort of nightmarish atmosphere, a murk in which judges, witnesses, lawyers and jurymen seem to stray as if bewitched . . . If the law at that time had allowed the accused to go into the witness box and undergo cross-examination, the mystery would probably have been dispelled." This unravelling of the mystery is by the Scottish lawyer and writer William Roughead (1870–1952). Roughead rejected the label of "criminologist", preferring to be described as a teller of "plain tales from jails" but he agreed that his study of criminology had encouraged his admiration for the ingenuity of the human race. Dorothy Sayers hailed Roughead as "the best showman that ever stood before the door of a chamber of horrors" and he is especially celebrated in America. President Roosevelt collected Roughead's works, and his relaxed, but acute, style has earned him a cult status that has eluded him in Britain.

> *O, that it were possible we might*
> *But hold some two dayes conference with the dead!*
> *From them I should learne somewhat, I am sure,*
> *I never shall know here.*
> *—The Dutchesse of Malfy*

"People who like legal mysteries and the arts of the literary detective"—the phrase is Andrew Lang's—can hardly fail to appreciate the Kirwan case. It presents a puzzle sufficiently perplexing to intrigue even a blasé taste, and to stimulate the Sherlockian spirit that sleeps in the bosom of the most blameless of Watsons. It is, in the first place, a trial for murder quite out of the common run. The circumstances of the crime, if crime in fact there was, were at the time unprecedented: the drowning of a wife by her husband; and they remained unparalleled in our annals until the revelations made upon a trial in 1915, when one Mr Smith was found to have eclipsed the achievement of his forerunner of the fifties by drowning no less than three wives in succession. But the quantitative element apart, the earlier case is much the more interesting and instructive. Smith was a mere mechanic, ingenious if you will, and clever at his job; a capable craftsman enough, but lacking imagination and the sense of style. Instead of making his first success a stepping stone to higher things, he was so stupid as to stereotype his method. Further, none but his counsel, *ex officio*, was ever known to doubt his guilt, whereas many have maintained the innocence of his predecessor. The staging, too, of the respective tragedies differed markedly in scenic effectiveness. Smith's theatre was the domestic bathroom of drab lodgings in mean streets; Kirwan's, a desolate island of the sea. As to motive, Smith was but a footpad, murdering for money; Kirwan's act, if he indeed committed it, was of the passionate cast so tenderly regarded by the law-courts of France.

The astute reader will notice that I have safeguarded myself from pronouncing upon Mr Kirwan's guilt. It was an Irish case, vehemently discussed; and although the passage of some seventy years ought to have cooled the ashes of that old controversy, I am not going to take any risks. Convicted by a Dublin jury, with the approval of two eminent judges of the Irish bench, the prisoner after a three days' trial was duly sentenced to death. The tide of public opinion, which had set strongly against the accused man from the start, then turned in his favour, and as the result of much popular agitation the question was begged in the usual British fashion—how we love a compromise!—the extreme penalty was remitted, and the convict was sent to Spike Island for life. All of which pleased nobody and left the subject in dispute precisely where it was before.

Personally, in the matter of alleged judicial errors I am rather sceptical. Miscarriages of justice have, of course, from time to time occurred, owing to the fallibility of the human agents, but this danger is now discounted by the opportunity provided for review by a competent tribunal. It may be that a Court of Criminal Appeal, had such been available, might on the merits have reversed the jury's finding. Certainly, it was a narrow case; the evidence was purely circumstantial and called for very nice and cautious estimation; had the trial happened to be held in Scotland, our national *via media* of Not Proven would probably have been followed. In hearing, reading, or writing about these cases I always feel how much there is behind the scenes that one ought to know in order to arrive at a fully informed judgment; how much that, by reason of sundry rules of the game played by counsel with the prisoner's life for stake, is never allowed to come out in court. Thus in the present instance we know next to nothing of the personality of the man, upon which the solution of the problem so largely depends, or apart from the evidence of a single quarrel are we told anything of his usual relations with his wife. The second "Mrs Kirwan" is not produced, and on the important question as to the lawful wife's knowledge of her rival's claims, or even of her existence, we have no information beyond the opposed statements of the contending counsel. Relatives and family friends could have dispelled these doubts and also have settled the vital matter of the dead lady's general health and habits: the Crown representing her as a perfectly sound, healthy woman; the defence, as an epileptic. Again, she is alleged at once to have been a strong and daring swimmer, and not to have been able to swim a stroke! Upon these and many other points the state of the proof is disappointingly nebulous. The medical evidence, too, is unsatisfactory and inconclusive. The conditions were plainly unfavourable, but surely nowadays science should be equal to giving a more decisive answer. What weighs most with me is the conduct of Mr Kirwan himself, in the brief glimpses we get of him on the island and after his return to Howth. And those dreadful screams, heard over the water by the five witnesses, re-echo across the years today in a very ugly and suggestive manner for such as have ears to hear.

A mile off the harbour of Howth, in County Dublin, lies the little island with the picturesque name: Ireland's Eye. Visitors to that agreeable watering place are in the habit of taking a boat to the romantic and rocky isle, lying so invitingly in view out in the sea, for purposes "not unconnected", as the newspapers say, with picnics. A ruined chapel of St Nessan, a Martello tower, a fine stretch of beach, a beautiful and extensive prospect: these form the chief attractions. Upon the seaward side a narrow creek or gully, called the Long Hole, will claim our special attention later. Altogether it is a pleasant spot in which to while away the hours of a summer day, and the last place one would associate with a treacherous and cruel crime.

At ten a.m. on Monday, 6th September, 1852, two persons embarked at the harbour in the boat of a local fisherman named Patrick Nangle. They had with them a bag and a hand-basket, their object being to spend the day upon the island, as they had already done on two or three former occasions. The stout, dark man of about five-and-thirty was Mr William Burke Kirwan, an artist; the handsome, well-made woman of thirty was his wife, Maria Louisa Kirwan; the bag contained the materials of his art, together with the bathing costume, cap, and bath sheet of his spouse, a constant and enthusiastic bather; the basket held provision for an exiguous al fresco meal. Married for twelve years and without a family, the Kirwans lived at No. 11 Upper Merrion Street, Dublin. They were then staying in summer lodging at Howth, where they had been for some six weeks; and as they were to return to Dublin on the morrow, this was their last excursion.

A commonplace couple enough, one would say; and yet Mr Kirwan's domestic habits present on closer acquaintance certain singular features. Though then on holiday, it was his custom, in his landlady's phrase, to "sleep out" three times a week, going on these occasions to Dublin and returning to Howth next day. Such periodic abstentions from the family bosom were not, as one might suppose, due to the exigencies of his profession as an anatomical

draughtsman and furnisher of coloured maps in the city. No; during
the whole period of his married life Mr Kirwan had been leading
what is figuratively termed a double life. He kept a mistress, one
Teresa Kenny, by whom he had no fewer than seven children, and
he maintained his Hagar and her brood in a house in Sandymount, a
suburb of Dublin, provided her with a servant, and endowed her with
the style and title of "Mrs Kirwan". To what extent his legitimate
lady was aware of this redundant *ménage*, and if she knew of it, how
she viewed the pluralistic peculiarities of her lord, there is no proof.
Upon this point the prosecuting counsel thus addressed the jury:

"It so happened, or was so managed, that neither Maria Kirwan
nor Teresa Kenny had either of them the least notion or idea of
each other's existence until a comparatively recent period . . .
These facts, gentlemen, will appear in the evidence; nay, more,
with such consummate art was this system of double deception
carried on, that it was only within the last six months that either
of these two women became aware of the fact that each had a rival
in the prisoner's affections."

Not only did these facts *not* appear in the evidence, but counsel
for the defence in his speech declared:

"The connection alluded to was not a new one; his wife knew
of it and forgave it, and she and her husband were reconciled."

Here, again, no evidence is produced in support of this statement,
and we must choose between the *ipse dixit* of learned counsel on
each side of the bar. Whether or not an attractive young wife would
be likely to acquiesce in such an arrangement is for the reader to
judge, according to his experience of human nature.

Despite the famous dictum of Mr Justice Stephen in the Maybrick
case, adultery of itself is not necessarily an incitement to murder.
If it were so, I am afraid our criminal courts would be sadly
congested and the hangman would be worked to death. The
domestic atmosphere of the Kirwan home, however, is unusually
dense, and does need more light than the trial affords. As we shall
find, the husband had been heard of late to beat and abuse his
wife, and even to threaten her life, acts which exceed the customary
amenities of the married state. But more of this later: we are keeping
our pleasure-seekers waiting.

They landed below the Martello tower at the north-west corner
of the isle, and the boatman was instructed to return for them at
eight o'clock—a long day, and a late hour for the autumn season;
the sun set that evening at six thirty-six. At noon Nangle's boat

came again to the island, bringing over another family party, who remained there till four o'clock. During the day these people saw the Kirwans, singly and together, at various times and places, but did not speak to them. When leaving in the afternoon for Howth one of the party, observing that the lady looked intently after the boat, called to her did she wish to go ashore; but she answered no, the men were to come back for her at eight. So for the next four hours this man and woman remained alone together upon the isle. What passed between them can never be known; no human eye could see how they employed their time, nor watch the act which certainly brought about the violent death of one of them. But human ears, by a strange chance, heard something of that unwitnessed tragedy. The shadows lengthened, the daylight waned, there was a heavy shower about six o'clock, and still silence brooded over the island, wrapped in the gathering dusk. At seven o'clock a fishing boat, making for Howth harbour, passed Ireland's Eye to the west of the isle, within ten perches of the Martello tower. She was a hooker of thirty-eight tons, with a crew of nine men, of whom one only was then on deck: the steersman, Thomas Larkin. It was "between day and dark". As the boat glided by before a light north-west breeze—the night was quiet and there was no sea—Larkin was startled by a loud scream, "a great screech", from the direction of the Eye. No one was visible on the shore, though there was light enough in the sky for him to have seen anyone there. In five or six minutes, during which the boat increased her distance, he heard a second scream, but lower; and two minutes afterwards, more faintly, a third. The boat was by then half way to the harbour. The cries were like those of a person in distress; he mentioned the matter at the time to his mates, who being below heard nothing. Night had fallen when they reached Howth.

Other four people on the mainland severally heard these cries. Alicia Abernethy lived at Howth, near the harbour. Her house was directly opposite the Long Hole, a mile off across the water. That evening she called upon her next-door neighbour to ask the time, and was told it was five minutes past seven. She returned, and while leaning over her garden wall, looking towards the Long Hole on the Eye—"it was between the two lights" and she could just see the island—she heard "a dreadful screech, as of a person in agony and pain". She then heard another, not so loud, and next a weaker one. The cries, she thought, were those of a woman. She told her family about them that night. Catherine Flood, employed in a house on the quay of Howth, was standing at the hall door at five or six minutes past seven, when she heard "great screams" from Ireland's Eye. The first was the loudest—"a very wild scream"; the last was cut off in the middle. There was a minute or two between them. John Barrett, from the door of his house at the east pier, heard about seven o'clock "screeches abreast the harbour". Going over to the pier, he heard two or three more; they declined in loudness and seemed to come from Ireland's Eye. Hugh Campbell, "between day and dark", was leaning over the quay wall, when he heard from the direction of the island three cries, "resembling the calling of a person for assistance"; some three minutes elapsed between the cries, which became successively weaker. *Half an hour later he saw Nangle's boat leave the harbour and go over to the island.** He had often before heard voices from the Eye.

These five persons were all reputable folk of the place, credible witnesses, whose testimony cross-examination failed to shake. So we have the fact clearly proved that about seven o'clock that night there rang out upon that little isle three lamentable screams of terror and distress, so piercing as to be audible a mile off upon the mainland. Yet Mr Kirwan, rendered deaf by anxiety for, or indifference to the fate of his vanished wife, or wholly engrossed with his sketch-book in making the most of the failing light, as appears, heard nothing.

At twenty minutes to eight o'clock Patrick Nangle, and his cousin Michael, accompanied by other two men, left Howth harbour as arranged to bring back the pleasure-seekers. The boat reached the island about eight o'clock, and landed close to the tower. It was then getting very dark and they saw nothing of their party; but on their calling out, the voice of Mr Kirwan replied: "Nangle, come up for the bag." Patrick went ashore; he found Mr Kirwan standing by himself on the bank and received from him his bag and sketch-book. Patrick, taking these down to the boat, met Michael going up, who, seeing Mr Kirwan coming towards the boat and finding he was alone, at once exclaimed, "Where is the mistress?"

"I have not seen her for the last hour and a half," was the reply.

"Sir," said Michael, "you should have had the mistress here,

---

* This statement is important as disposing of one of the defence theories as to the cries, namely, that they were those of the boatman and Mr Kirwan, calling for his wife during their search for the missing lady.

and not have to be looking for her at this hour of the night; what way did she go?"

"She went that way," said Mr Kirwan, pointing in the direction of the Long Hole. "I was sketching at the time. She left me after the last shower. She did not like to bathe where I told her to bathe, because there was a bad smell there." Michael and Mr Kirwan then went to look for her along the strand, Patrick going back to the boat. "Maria, why don't you answer?" called her husband. "The boat is waiting." Michael too kept calling "Mrs Kirwan!" but there was no response. Their search included the Long Hole, so far as the state of the tide permitted, and *while there Michael could hear Patrick hailing from beside the tower.** Returning, they found he had been equally unsuccessful. "This is a fine job," said Michael, "to be here at this hour of the night! Where are we to find this woman? Let us leave the other two men in the boat and we will go round again; if Mrs Kirwan comes in the meantime, they can go on the top of the bank and hail us." The three then started to retrace their steps. Descending the rocks into the Long Hole Mr Kirwan stumbled and fell. At that instant Patrick Nangle cried out that he saw "something white" below.

The Long Hole is an inlet, some 360 feet in length, narrow at the entrance and wider towards the head, enclosed by steep banks and frowned upon by cliffs. From low to high-water mark the distance is 163 feet. This area is divided into two channels by a large rock in the middle, 22 feet high, on which the tide rises on the landward side about a foot at high water. The surrounding strand is of coarse gravel, interspersed with lesser rocks, and 12 feet above low-water mark a low barrier of these stretches across the channel, here 28 feet in breadth. Just within this barrier, at the base of the south-eastern side of the gully, is a small rock, 3 feet long and 12 inches high, upon which was found the body of the dead lady.

The tide was out. She lay upon her back, the head hanging down over the edge against the barrier rock, the arms extended, the knees bent, and the feet in a shallow pool. Her wet bathing dress was gathered up about her armpits, leaving the whole body exposed, and beneath her was a wet bathing sheet, upon which she partly lay. Her bathing cap was missing—it was found a fortnight later at high-water mark, the strings tied in a tight knot—but she

---

* So cries from one end of the island were audible at the other.

wore bathing boots; seaweed and gravel were entangled in her hair. The body was still quite warm and flexible. The mouth was frothing; there was blood upon the face, blood upon the breasts, and blood was flowing from the ears and from other parts. Patrick, for decency, adjusted the bathing dress, straightened the arms and legs, and tied the sheet twice about her at the neck and knees, all before Michael and Mr Kirwan, who had been searching the other side of the cove, came up. "Mr Kirwan said 'Oh, Maria, Maria!' " and told the men to look for her clothes: "we would get them there on the rock"—pointing to the high centre rock before mentioned. Patrick went up and searched as directed, but could find nothing. Mr Kirwan then went up himself, and coming back in a few minutes with a shawl and "something white" in his hand, bade Patrick go up again, which the latter did. This time he at once found the clothes in a place where he had already looked without result: "I had searched the very same place before and did not find them." The shawl was then wrapped about the head; what the "something white" was we shall see in the sequel. Patrick next proposed that the boat be brought round for the body, so he and Michael left accordingly. Mr Kirwan refused to go, and threw himself upon the corpse. It was now about nine o'clock and it took them an hour to fetch the boat; when they reached the Long Hole they found Mr Kirwan just as they had left him, "lying with his face on the breast of the body". The remains, wrapped in a sail, were carried to the boat by one of the men, who got wet up to the knees during the operation, but none of the others got wet, nor according to them did Mr Kirwan, who took no part.

Arrived at Howth the body of Mrs Kirwan was taken on a dray to her lodgings and laid on the floor of her room. Mrs Campbell, the landlady, was short-sighted and much upset: she did not examine it closely; but she saw that Mr Kirwan's legs were wet, and she helped him to change his stockings. Other three women in the house that night proved that his boots, stockings, drawers and trousers were wet, and that as he sat on a chair by the kitchen fire drying them, water dripped from him on to the door. These dames—one, Mrs Lacy, was a sick-nurse of forty years' standing—were ordered by him to wash the body. When they pointed out to him that the police would not allow it to be touched until an inquest was held, the bereaved husband made this remarkable retort: "I don't care a damn for the police; the body must be washed!" So washed it accordingly was, and laid out as for burial before it was seen by a medical man. Whatever the propriety and whatever the motive of Mr Kirwan's action there is no doubt that it resulted in the loss of very valuable evidence. The washing was done by Anne Lacy and Catherine M'Garr, one taking the right, the other the left side, while Mary Robinson held a candle. The account given by these women of the appearances noted by them is of the last importance. There was a large quantity of blood on the sail where the lower part of the body had lain. The body was quite limber.

> "The face was covered with blood; the blood came from a cut about the eyes, and on the cheek and forehead; the ears were also loaded with blood, which was still running from the inside of them; I sponged and washed the ears, but the blood continued flowing afterwards for nearly half an hour; I had to put a flannel petticoat to prevent it flowing down."

There was a cut on the right breast, which bled freely, and a discharge of blood, which was not natural, from another part. The right side of the body was black from shoulders to feet. The lips were much swollen, the eyes "as red as blood", the neck was slightly twisted. The body was healthy looking and finely formed: "she was a beautiful creature". Thus Mrs Lacy, whose long experience gives weight to her testimony. Mrs M'Garr noticed wounds about the eyes, "as if torn". The nose was "crooked", the lips swelled and covered with slime, blood flowed from the ears, the left breast, and from another part. Mary Robinson observed that the eyes were bloodshot and the ears bleeding. These details, though repellent, are essential to a determination of how this lady came by her death.

Between one and two o'clock on the following day, Tuesday, 7 September, by order of the Coroner the body was professionally examined. Of distinguished members of the faculty there was then, as now, no lack in County Dublin, and it seems unfortunate that the duty was entrusted to a medical student named Hamilton, who stated his qualifications as "having been attending lectures during the last six years". He made what he himself describes as "a superficial examination", the result of which will presently appear, and having no reason to suspect foul play, he assumed it to be a case of simple drowning and reported accordingly. The inquiry opened later in the afternoon before Mr Coroner Davis, the authorities having apparently no suspicion that the death was other than fortuitous. The Nangle cousins were examined. "Mr

Kirwan took an active part in the investigation," said the Coroner at the subsequent trial; "I remember his interrupting one of the witnesses who was giving his testimony; I do not remember what he said to him; I believe the witness in question was one of the Nangles." Now, as appears from the evidence of Patrick Nangle at the trial, just as he was beginning to tell the Coroner about the sheet and the finding of the clothes, he was interrupted by Mr Kirwan and was "put back", another witness being called. Thus as to these most material facts he "was not allowed to speak". The evidence of Mr Kirwan was as follows:

"I am an artist, residing at No. 11 Upper Merrion Street, Dublin. The deceased lady, Maria Kirwan, was my wife; I was married to her about nine or ten years. I have been living with Mrs Kirwan in Howth for five or six weeks. I was in the habit of going over to Ireland's Eye as an artist. Mrs Kirwan used to accompany me; she was very fond of bathing, and while I would be sketching she would amuse herself roaming about or bathing. Yesterday we went over as usual. She bathed at the Martello tower on going over, but could not stay long in the water as the boatmen were to bring another party to the island. She left me in the latter part of the day, about six o'clock, to bathe again. She told me she would walk round the hill after bathing and meet me at the boat. I did not see her alive afterwards, and only found the body as described by the sailors."

It will be observed that no mention was made by Mr Kirwan of the three screams, and that he did not allege, as was later done in his behalf, that his wife was subject to epilepsy. The five witnesses who heard the cries had not then come forward. Neither the landlady nor the women who washed the corpse were examined. Upon these insufficient premises the jury founded a verdict of accidental death. Unfortunately for the ends of justice, a grave was chosen in the wettest part of the cemetery at Glasnevin, the remains of Mrs Kirwan were buried there, and the affair seemed in a fair way to be forgotten.

If Mr Kirwan was innocent of his wife's death he was curiously unlucky in his reputation. The fact that he had a mistress with seven children became generally known and raised a strong prejudice against him in the public mind. He was even said to have committed bigamy with her, but the woman, as appears, was merely a chronic concubine. One Mrs Byrne, his next-door neighbour in Dublin, did not scruple to promulgate his guilt. Indeed, this lady had foretold the event: "Kirwan had taken his wife to some strange place to destroy her"; and being but human, she was naturally gratified by the fulfilment of her prophecy. She further alleged that "Bloody Billy", as she impolitely termed him, had murdered her own husband. Two other charges of murder were also brought against Mr Kirwan in the Dublin Press. It was there stated:

1. That in 1837, he, Kirwan, burglariously entered Bowyer's house in Mountjoy Street, and carried away Bowyer's property, which he converted to his own use; and that for this offence he was tried before the Recorder, and only escaped upon a point of law.
2. That having thus obtained possession of Bowyer's property he murdered him.
3. That in order to keep Mrs Bowyer quiet, he paid her an annuity of forty pounds a year, blood money.

Whatever be the truth as to these allegations, it is plain that Mrs Bowyer, like Father Paul of the *Bab Ballads*, did such things "singularly cheap". The other charge of murder related to his brother-in-law, Mr Crowe. "That Kirwan murdered him, according to the statement of the parties preferring the charges, was beyond all doubt, because he accompanied him to Liverpool, and Crowe was not heard of since."

The Nangles and the nurses talked of the amount of blood they had seen about the body, and the report spread that the deceased had been done to death with a sword cane. Then Mrs Kirwan had been a Catholic and her husband was a Protestant, facts which in Ireland are still of more than spiritual import, and belief in Mr Kirwan's guilt or innocence became largely a matter of faith. Finally, the authorities realized that the case was one which called for further investigation, so the body was ordered to be exhumed. On 6 October—thirty-one days after death—Dr George Hatchell, assisted by Dr Tighe, made a post-mortem examination, the results of which will presently appear. The coffin was found to be lying in two and a half feet of water, due to the dampness of the soil. Following upon the doctors' report Mr Kirwan was apprehended on a charge of murder. The warrant was executed at his own house in Dublin, where the police found Miss Kenny and her young brood installed in the dead wife's room.

The trial, originally fixed for November, was at the instance of the accused postponed, and did not open till Wednesday, 8 December 1852, when it took place before a Commission of Oyer and Terminer held at Green Street, Dublin, the presiding Judges being the Hon. Philip C. Crampton and the Right Hon. Richard W. Greene. John George Smyly, QC, Edmund Hayes, QC, and John Pennefather conducted the prosecution; Isaac Butt, QC, Walter Burke, QC, William W. Brereton, QC, and John A. Curran appeared for the defence. The charge against the accused was that on 6 September, at Ireland's Eye in the county of Dublin, he "did wilfully, feloniously, and of his malice prepense kill and murder one Maria Louisa Kirwan", to which he pleaded "Not Guilty". Mr Smyly, in the absence of the Attorney-General, having opened the case for the Crown, proceeded to call witnesses in support of the indictment.

The first was Alfred Jones, surveyor, who had prepared plans of the *locus* and made certain calculations and measurements at the Long Hole. The place where the clothes were found was about the middle of the central rock, 5 ft 6 in. above the strand, and at high tide 1 ft 6 in. out of the water. On 6 September it was high water at three-thirty p.m., and at that hour there would be 7 ft of water over the "body" rock; at six-thirty 2 ft 6 in.; at seven, 1 ft 9 in.; at seven-fifteen, 1 ft 4½ in.; at seven-thirty, 1 ft; at eight, 3 in.; and at nine-thirty the tide would be 2 ft below the "body" rock. The distance from the Martello Tower to the Long Hole was 835 yds; from where Mr Kirwan was standing when the boat arrived, 792 yds. Cross-examined by Mr Butt, a person about to bathe might step down to the strand from the rock where the clothes were found.

Mrs Margaret Campbell told how the Kirwans came to her as lodgers in June, and of Mr Kirwan's habit of absenting himself three nights a week. During the first month of their stay she noticed quarreling between them more than once.

"I heard angry words from Mr Kirwan to his wife. I heard him say he would make her stop there; I heard him miscall her; I heard him call her a strumpet. I heard him say 'I'll finish you!' I do not think they had been a month with me at that time. On the same evening I heard her say to him, 'Let me alone, let me alone!' Next morning I heard her say to him she was black from the usage she had got the preceeding night—across her thighs."

Witness heard a rush in their room, and "thought he beat her". There was no one else in the house at the time except Anne Hanna, who was with witness in the kitchen. Mrs Kirwan used to bathe every day at the ladies' bathing place. She was in good health all the time she was at Howth. On the Thursday and Friday before her death she and her husband spent the day on Ireland's Eye, returning home about nine o'clock. Mrs Campbell then described the bringing back of the body, and the condition of Mr Kirwan's nether garments, as before narrated. Cross-examined by Mr Butt, she had heard them quarrelling at different times; it was on the first occasion that she heard the threatening language; subsequently "they had an odd word now and again"; he never used violence but the once. She had heard Mrs Kirwan's mother, Mrs Crowe, caution her not to be too venturesome in bathing.

Anne Hanna, who washed for Mrs Kirwan, corroborated as regards the first quarrel. She heard the furniture being knocked about, and a man's voice say: "I'll end you, I'll end you!"

Patrick Nangle described the happenings on the island, with which we are already acquainted. When he recovered the sail in which the body had been wrapped, he found a great deal of blood on it: "I had to scrub it with a broom." Cross-examined by Mr Brereton, he was sure the body was not stiff when found; none of the limbs was stiff. There were several scratches about the eyes. The mouth was frothing. Blood flowed from the lower part of the body. The scratches could not have been caused by crabs; there were no crabs where the body lay. Mr Kirwan did not say, when he (witness) saw him on the bank, that his wife must be in the boat. There was no swell that night to bruise the body. The injuries could not have occurred by scraping on the gravel. The sheet was under the body when he found it; he saw no shawl until he came back with the boat. He did not care how dark it was: he had searched the rock and found nothing, where, after Mr Kirwan had gone up, he found the clothes. He demanded and got two pounds for his trouble that night. No one could have been on the island after four o'clock without his knowledge. Mr Kirwan could not have got wet in the pool where the feet lay: there was not enough water in it.

Michael Nangle gave his version of the facts, which, with one exception, tallied with that given by Patrick. He had never before heard of ladies bathing at the Long Hole; the rocks were sharp and dangerous. He looked for the clothes along the strand; Patrick searched the rock. Mr Kirwan came down "bringing down something white in his hand like a sheet, ·and also a shawl". Witness did not see the body closely till the next day; he only saw the face, on which were cuts or scratches. Mr Kirwan did not get wet while in their company. The water in the Long Hole was as smooth as in a well. During their search Mr Kirwan seemed "uneasy"—which, in any view, is not surprising.

Michael differed from Patrick only in that he thought the sheet was brought down from the rock by Mr Kirwan, whereas Patrick was positive that the sheet was beneath the body when discovered, *that it was wet*, and that he tied it twice about the body before Michael and Mr Kirwan came up. It was dark at the time; Patrick, who examined and handled the body, is more likely to be right than Michael, who did neither. The significance of the wetness of the sheet, as sworn to by Patrick, appears to have been overlooked: however dark it was, that is a matter on which he could not well be mistaken, and had Mrs Kirwan left the sheet with her clothes upon the rock, it would like them have been dry, for they were found above high-water mark. What, then, was the "something white" selected by Mr Kirwan from his wife's clothes? Most probably, her chemise; for though we have an inventory of all the garments removed from the rock, there is no word of a chemise, which, as we shall find, was missing, while that she wore one will hardly be disputed.

Thomas Giles, one of the boatmen, corroborated the Nangles to the extent of his knowledge, and Arthur Brew, of the picnic party, told what he had seen of the Kirwans when on the island. Then followed the five witnesses who heard the cries. Mr Butt worked hard to bring out minor discrepancies in their statements, such as, for instance, the number of minutes that elapsed between the several screams, and so forth; but upon the cardinal points that each *did* hear about seven o'clock three distinct screams, decreasing in volume, coming from Ireland's Eye, their testimony was unscathed.

The next group of witnesses was the women who had washed and laid out the corpse, and who now deposed to the condition in which they found it as before described. They stuck gallantly to their guns, and Mr Butt failed to impair the value of their evidence. Mrs Lacy, the dame of forty years' practical experience, maintained in cross-examination: "There was nothing like the bite of a crab on the body." The hearing was then adjourned.

Next day, 9 December, began with the evidence of Joseph Sherwood, Sergeant of Constabulary, stationed at Howth. He had seen the face of the body on the night of Mrs Kirwan's death; it was scratched, there was a cut on the right temple, the mouth was swollen, and the eyes were bloodshot. He noticed that Mr Kirwan's clothes were wet from the knees downward. Upon arrest of that gentleman at his house in Upper Merrion Street, on 7 October, witness there saw the woman Kenny and her children. He was present when the bathing cap was found at high-water mark in the Long Hole on 11 September; the string was tied in a hard knot. Shouts at Ireland's Eye were audible at Howth; he himself had heard such on the mainland. Cross-examined by Mr Butt, the bundle of Mrs Kirwan's clothes did not include a chemise. The clothes were clean and free from bloodstains.

Ann Molloy, the Kirwans' servant, said she had been with them for twelve months. They had no family. Miss Theresa Kenny was then called, but failed to appear. It would have been interesting to have heard her evidence. William Bridgeford stated that he was the owner of the house in Sandymount occupied by Mr Kirwan who became his tenant in 1848. Witness saw there occasionally a woman whom he understood to be Mr Kirwan's wife. There were children in the house. He had received notes, presumably on business, from the woman, signed "Teresa". Catherine Byrne, Mr Kirwan's servant at his "home from home", said that a woman lived with him there who was known as "Mrs Kirwan". They had seven children. A strange lady called once to make some inquiries.

Thomas Alexander Hamilton, the medical student who had seen the body, was next examined. It was, he said, then prepared for burial. He made a superficial examination of the head, but found no fracture. There was a scratch on the right temple, and scratches around the eyes, which were closed; he did not open them; the eyelids were livid. The lobe of one of the ears was cut. There was froth, thin, light, and stationary, upon the mouth. The abdomen was full and firm. He did not examine the body very closely, and saw no blood, or anything else that attracted his attention. Cross-examined, he noticed no marks of violence. He had never before examined the body of a drowned person. He knew nothing at the time to excite suspicion.

Dr George Hatchell, who made the post-mortem examination thirty-one days after death, was next called. He was present at the exhumation. The coffin lay in two and a half feet of water, which had entered it, and the body was to a certain extent macerated. The scalp showed no marks of violence. He found abrasions or scratches about the right eye. The eyes were injected with blood. The lobe of the right ear was wanting. There were no other injuries about the ears that he could observe, decomposition being too far advanced. The lips were swollen and very vascular; the tongue was marked above and below by the teeth. On opening the head, the brain was found to be in a semi–fluid state and of a light pinkish colour. The base of the skull was not fractured. There was nothing remarkable about the trachea or the larynx, and the vertebrae of the neck were not dislocated. On the right breast was a superficial cut or scratch. There was extensive lividity on the right side, due probably to gravitation of the blood. The lower orifices of the body were swollen and their interior very vascular, much more than was usual. The lungs were congested by engorgement of blood; the heart was empty on both sides. He had visited and inspected the *locus*.

"From the appearances you observe on the body, are you able as a medical man, to form an opinion as to the cause of death and what is that opinion?—I am of opinion that death was caused by asphyxia, or a sudden stopping of respiration. From the congestion in the—, from the engorgement of the lungs, and other circumstances, I should say that in all probability the simple stoppage of respiration must have been combined with pressure of some kind, or constriction, which caused the sudden stoppage. I do not think that simple drowning would produce to the same extent the appearances I saw."

Cross-examined by Mr Butt, the extreme congestion which he had found could not be produced by drowning alone. He had never seen such engorgement caused by simple drowning. There must have been a struggle for life, whether by herself or with another. There was no internal injury to the ears nor any sign of a sharp instrument having been thrust into the body. Bathing on a full stomach might bring on a fit; but he had never heard of a person who fell in a fit of epilepsy giving more than one scream.

Henry Davis, the Coroner, who held the inquest on Mrs Kirwan, stated what took place at that investigation. Cross-examined, he said that in his opinion the scratches on the body were due to the bites of green crabs. In re-examination, he described Mr Kirwan's behaviour at the inquiry, as already mentioned. The case for the Crown closed with the reading of Mr Kirwan's deposition before the Coroner, and Mr Butt addressed the jury for the defence. He

began by begging them to dismiss from their minds anything they
might have heard out of doors to the prejudice of the accused. The
evidence upon which the Crown asked them to conclude that his
wife had died by his hands was (1) the appearances of the body,
(2) the suspicion against him and the cries from the island, and
(3) the stain upon his character as a husband. It was impossible
for the prisoner to bring any evidence as to what had happened. He
was not a competent witness, and he and his wife were alone upon
the island when she met her death. That the cries heard were hers
was merely a conjecture; even if they were so, that was consistent
with her death in a fit. He asked the jury to disbelieve the evidence
of the witnesses who said they heard the cries on the mainland;
Larkin's was the only evidence on which they could rely, but the
guilt of the prisoner could not be deduced from it. The cries he
heard might have been those of Mr Kirwan, calling for his wife
before the boat arrived. If this was a murder, how did he do it?
Did he strangle her? Did he go into the water and drown her? If
her death was the result of violence and Larkin heard her death
cries, how was it that eight minutes elapsed during the first and
second? What was a strong woman doing in the meantime? It was
a natural supposition that she had been attacked by epilepsy on
going into the water with a full stomach after her dinner, and that
she shrieked first, revived afterwards, and shrieked again. With
regard to the prisoner's unfortunate connection, that could supply
no motive for the crime. It was an old affair; his wife knew of it and
forgave him, and it would be monstrous to suppose that because he
had been unfaithful to her he was capable of imbruing his hands
in her blood. As to the appearances presented by the body, no
marks of violence were found; there was no internal injury to the
ears or other parts, and drowning in a fit would account for the
bleedings and congestion. Dr Hatchell in his report mentioned
"strangulation", but the neck and throat were uninjured. Did he
mean by "compression" that she was seized and crushed to death?
No force was possible without injury to some vital organ. The
cuts and scratches, the Coroner told them, were due to the bites
of crabs; or they might have been caused by struggling among the
rocks: her hair was full of sand and seaweed. A murderer would
not begin by scratching her face, and there were no scratches on
his face, such as might have been expected. If he had followed her
into the sea and drowned her, his arms and coat would have been
wet. He might have got his feet wet in the very pool in which her

feet lay. "If he loved his wife, as it seemed evident that he did," he who flung himself upon the body, and remained so long alone with it, could not be the murderer.* As to the position of the sheet and the finding of the clothes, these rested solely on the evidence of Patrick Nangle, to which no weight should be attached; that of Michael Nangle was upon these points to be preferred. This accusation would never have been brought but for the prisoner's previous character; if they dismissed from their minds that consideration, they should acquit him, and he would leave the court a wiser and a better man.

Two witnesses only were called for the defence, Drs Rynd and Adams, who were present in court and had heard the evidence. Dr Rynd said the appearances described pointed to death by asphyxia, or stoppage of the breath and circulation. If caused by external violence there should be manifest marks thereof; there were no such injuries here. All the appearances could be produced by a fit of epilepsy, without any concurring cause. An epileptic might give several screams. Bathing with a full stomach would be apt to cause a fit. Congestion of the brain would account for the bleeding from the ears; general congestion for that from the other organs. Cross-examined by Mr Smyly, witness admitted he never knew of such bleeding in a case of simple drowning. The blood continued fluid in drowned bodies for a considerable time after death. The amount of congestion would depend on the efforts made by the drowning person to save himself. Counsel referred witness to the notorious case of Burke and Hare, where, although no external marks of violence were visible, suffocation was effected; and asked whether a wet sheet held over the mouth would produce the appearances described, without leaving any marks of violence. Dr Rynd admitted that it would do so. He had seen Mrs Kirwan professionally six years before; she appeared to him a fine strong young woman. He had heard, from a person deeply interested in the trial, that her father had died of epilepsy.

Dr Adams concurred generally in the evidence of Dr Rynd, but admitted that it was unusual for an epileptic to scream more than

---

* The case of Dr Pritchard in 1865 affords a sufficient answer to this argument. During the four months in which he was torturing his wife to death the doctor habitually slept with her, and she died in his arms. At the funeral he caused the coffin to be opened that he might kiss her for the last time.

once—"the first scream is the rule". Cross-examined, a wet cloth over the mouth and nose would produce all the effects of drowning. If a person was held under water it would cause congestion. It all depended upon the mouth and nose being under water. He had never known a case of accidental drowning where similar bleeding from the organs occurred, nor had he ever heard of a case of epilepsy accompanied by such bleedings. Re-examined, pressure applied to the chest would leave some external marks of violence.

> "*Mr Justice Crampton*—Supposing death to have taken place by forcible submersion, or from accidental drowning, would you be able, from the appearances described, to state to which species of death they were attributable?—My Lord, in my opinion, no man living could do so."

The case for the defence being here closed, Mr Hayes replied on the part of the Crown. He told the jury to disregard the rumours which had been circulated to the prisoner's prejudice, and defended the prosecution from the animadversions of Mr Butt. Having reviewed the accused's connection with the woman Kenny, whom he had represented as "Mrs Kirwan", counsel dealt with the quarrel and the threats against his wife's life.

> "Is it reasonable to suppose that a man had been living with a concubine for ten years, and during all that time gave her his name, while he was beating his legitimate wife at Howth, could entertain connubial affection for the woman he treated so grossly?"

He then described the fatal excursion to the island on 6 September. As to the fact of the three screams, sworn to by five witnesses, there could be no possibility of doubt; that they were the shrieks of epilepsy was an ingenious suggestion, unsupported by proof.

> "If there was any evidence that this lady had been previously affected by epilepsy or anything of that kind, there might have been a shadow of ground upon which to found the assertion. As the prisoner has forborne to produce such testimony, it is not too much to infer that there was none to produce; we must take it as proved that the deceased was a perfectly healthy woman."

Why did Mr Kirwan say nothing about the screams? He must have heard them; he hadn't seen his wife for an hour; "and yet this affectionate husband is deaf to these dreadful shrieks". If he knew she were subject to fits he would have run to her assistance but he is found calmly waiting for the boat, and all he says is "Nangle, come up for the bag!" The first mention of the missing lady comes from the boatman, not from the distracted, agonized husband. Two hours after this lady set out to bathe, the search for her is begun in the dark. At first it is fruitless. They would note that Patrick, calling out near the boat, is heard by Michael at the Long Hole. Was it too much to suppose that if the prisoner had been at that part of the island he would hear screams from the Long Hole? The search was renewed, the body was found, and the question now arose, whether, upon all the facts and circumstances of the case, death was caused by accident or by Mr Kirwan. No direct evidence was possible; and it was from circumstantial evidence alone that the jury could arrive at a conclusion. How came that sheet beneath the body? It should have been left high and dry for her use when she came out. The position of the bathing dress, too, was inexplicable. At seven o'clock, if this lady was then bathing, the tide was going out, and there was 1 ft 9 in. of water over the "body" rock, which was 1 ft high. She was an expert swimmer: was it likely that she should be accidentally drowned there?

"Let us suppose her in this water, 2 ft 9 in. deep; let us suppose the prisoner coming into the Hole with the sheet in his hand, after taking it from the place in which it was left, ready to put it over her head; let us suppose she saw his dreadful purpose: can you not then conceive and account for the dreadful shrieks that were heard, when the horrid reality burst upon her mind that on that desolate, lonely island, without a living soul but themselves upon it, he was coming into that Long Hole to perpetrate his dreadful offence? Would not the consequence have been the dreadful shrieks that were heard and sworn to? If he succeeded in putting her under the water, notwithstanding her vain efforts to rise, struggling with all her energy against his greater strength, can you not imagine the fearful, agonizing, and fainter shrieks that men and women from the mainland depose to having heard? That is not a mere imagination; it is a rational deduction from the evidence; and it is for you to say whether, upon all the facts of the case, that might not have occurred, or whether the prisoner lost his wife without any fault of his own."

As to what happened when the body was found, Patrick Nangle was a better witness than Michael, who on his own showing saw but little of it. If the deceased left her husband about six o'clock, and if he did not see her thereafter, it was very strange that he should be able at once to know where her clothes lay, in a spot to which he pointed and in which Patrick, who was familiar with the place, had failed to find them. The discrepancy between the Nangles with respect to the sheet is reconciled if what Kirwan brought down from the rock in his hand with the shawl was the chemise. That chemise was not forthcoming: it was for the jury to say whether it was not the "something white" to which Michael referred. With regard to the prisoner's insistence on the washing of the body, he, a gentleman of position and education, was sworn to have said: "I don't care a damn for the police; the body must be washed," although he knew his wife had met her death suddenly on a lonely island, and that every circumstance as to the state of the body was most important to the ends of justice. Moreover, he was actually warned of the coming investigation. The women who washed the body were positive that the scratches were not caused by crabs.

> "You will ask yourselves, gentlemen, whether or not these scratches have any reference to the time when the horrible sheet was being put over the face of the deceased; whether at that awful moment she might not have put up her hands to try and remove the sheet, and in endeavouring to do so, tore herself in the manner described."

The bathing cap, found at high-water mark, with the strings tied tight, was also against the supposition of death by epilepsy or accident. Might it not have been torn off in the struggle that took place before the sheet was thrown over her head? Dr Adams, with all his great experience, never knew a case of death from simple drowning or epilepsy in which such bleeding occurred, and yet in the face of that testimony they were asked to say that Mrs Kirwan's death was accidental! If, apart from the medical evidence, the conduct and demeanour of the prisoner together with the whole facts and circumstances of the case, left no rational doubt of his guilt, it was their duty to find him guilty.

In charging the jury, Mr Justice Crampton referred to the mantle of mystery spread over the case, and explained the nature and effect of circumstantial evidence. Having reviewed the undisputed facts, his lordship went through the proof at large. That the parties were not living on good terms as husband and wife was proved by the character and conduct of the prisoner. The testimony of all the medical men was, substantially, that the external injuries could not have been the cause of death. While they found no marks of violence, that did not exclude the mode of destruction suggested by the Crown—the forcible application of the sheet—which the doctors admitted would leave no signs distinguishable from those of drowning. All were agreed that the appearances, external and internal, were consistent with either simple drowning or forcible immersion. Dr Hatchell went further: he thought the congestion greater than could be accounted for by drowning alone. Thus the jury were left by the doctors in a state of much uncertainty. His Lordship then commented on the demeanour of the prisoner on 6 September. The jury would consider whether that was due to genuine grief or was merely affected to avert suspicion. As to the sheet, it was for them to decide which of the Nangles was in error. Both seemed anxious to tell the truth; but it was very dark at the time, a fact which should also be kept in view with reference to the finding of the clothes. Patrick Nangle's account of his being interrupted by Mr Kirwan at the inquest was corroborated by the Coroner. It was admitted that three cries from Ireland's Eye were heard that evening about seven o'clock. If the screams heard by Larkin came from the Long Hole they must have come across the island, and consequently must have been heard by the prisoner. The credit of the five witnesses who heard these cries was unimpeached. If they were uttered by the deceased lady, what caused them? Undoubtedly, pressing and imminent danger of some kind. Were they the screams of a person seized by epilepsy, or were they due to pain or fear caused by another? The jury would consider whether the character of the cries was consistent with an attack of epilepsy to a person bathing. They would also consider whether this lady, an experienced bather and an expert swimmer, was swimming in two feet nine inches of water when she was seized with epilepsy and gave the screams described. It was impossible that she herself placed the sheet where it was found, as the rock was then covered by water.

How came she upon that rock? Was it probable that the tide threw her on it and left her there? Again, did she ever in her life have an epileptic fit? Suspicion must not be confounded with evidence. But if they could not reconcile these facts with the prisoner's innocence, they must not pass them over; if, on the other hand, they were not satisfied that Mrs Kirwan's death was the result of violence, they would acquit him.

At seven o'clock the jury retired to consider their verdict. Returning in forty minutes, they intimated that they could not agree, and the Court adjourned till eleven o'clock. On its reassembling, however, the jury were no further forward, and it was proposed to lock them up all night and to take their verdict in the morning. They asked for a little more time, and wished to hear Dr Adams repeat his testimony, but the judge supposed that gentleman was then fast asleep; he gave them his own recollection of the doctor's evidence: that death might have been caused by either simple or forcible drowning. The jury then said they were likely to agree, and in fifteen minutes arrived at a verdict of guilty. The Court adjourned.

When the Court met next day to pronounce sentence, Mr Butt moved that certain questions of law be reserved for the decision of the Court of Criminal Appeal,* namely, whether the evidence of the prisoner having lived at Sandymount with a woman who called herself "Mrs Kirwan" was admissible: whether the verdict was founded on the testimony of Dr Adams, a witness for the defence; and whether the deposition of the prisoner at the inquest ought to have been admitted? The Court refused the application. Asked what he had to say why sentence of death should not be passed against him, the prisoner, "in a firm and perfectly calm voice", made no fresh statement and merely repeated the facts known to everyone in court. Mr Justice Crampton said:

> "I am sorry to interrupt you at this painful moment, but you must be well aware that your counsel entered into all these subjects. It is impossible for me now to go into the evidence."

* In fact the Court was the Court of Crown Cases Reserved which had jurisdiction under the provisions of the Statute 11 & 12 Victoria, c. 78.

His Lordship then pronounced sentence of death, intimating his own concurrence and that of his learned brother in the rightness of the verdict, and pointing out that there was no hope of pardon on this side of the grave. The prisoner, again protesting his innocence, was removed under escort to Kilmainham Jail, and the Court rose.

The Official Report of the trial concludes: "By order of the Executive Government the sentence was commuted to transportation for life." The result was achieved by the joint endeavours of the Rev. J. A. Malet, who produced a brochure entitled *The Kirwan Case*, and of J. Knight Boswell, a Dublin solicitor, who published a pamphlet on similar lines. Both tracts give an *ex parte* review of the evidence and contain a series of declarations by divers persons, more or less relevant to the issue, as to which it may be generally observed that such irresponsible pronouncements, not upon oath, are plainly of less value than statements sworn to in court. I have space but to glance at this new "evidence".

The Kirwan Case crop includes Mrs Crowe, the mother of Mrs Kirwan, who said she was in constant touch with her daughter and that Mr Kirwan was always a most kind, affectionate husband. She makes no reference to the Sandymount establishment, and as regards her daughter's health, condescends only upon sleeplessness; she does not mention fits. Her daughter was "very venturesome in the water, going into the deep parts of the sea, and continuing therein for a much longer period than other ladies". Mrs Bentley said that she knew the deceased intimately. Mrs Kirwan became aware of the Kenny connection within a month of her marriage, and "exhibited no emotion on the subject". Two years before, she told the declarant that she had a fit in presence of her husband. Two other ladies severally averred that Patrick Nangle had equivocated about the sheet, and had expressed an intention to "pinch" Mr Kirwan at the trial. There follows a certificate by ten Dublin physicians and surgeons, proceeding upon the "sworn testimony annexed", that the appearances were "quite compatible with death caused by simple drowning or by seizure of a fit in the water"; and that they were "given to understand that Mrs Kirwan's father died of a fit eight years ago".* The great Dr

---

* These gentlemen had not the advantage of inspecting the body or of hearing the evidence. The "testimony" on which they rely was, as we shall see, *not* "sworn". It is also to be noted that Mrs Crowe says nothing about the manner of her husband's death.

Taylor wrote on 20 December, 1852, denouncing the verdict: we shall hear his opinion presently. Anne Maher, Kirwan's servant, said that two years before Mrs Kirwan had a fit in presence of her husband and one Kelly. Arthur Kelly said that he had been Kirwan's "assistant" for twelve years; he assisted at two fits, one two years ago and another in June last, just before Mrs Kirwan left for Howth. *Neither of these declarations were upon oath*—Anne Maher could not write.* An uncle and a cousin of the deceased said that she often complained of blood to the head and "confusion of ideas"; adding with delightful, if unconscious humour that she spoke in the highest praise of her husband's conduct and "always appeared in the full and affluent enjoyment of comfort and respectability". Mr Butt wrote to say that the epileptic theory was not thought of till the second day of the trial, when it was suggested by a medical witness, too late to call evidence in its support—as though he had not had an opportunity of consulting his own client! The remaining volunteers allege that Kirwan had nothing to do with choosing the wet grave, that the Crown expert's measurements at the Long Hole were defective, that the acoustics of the island were other than as represented, and that Mrs Kirwan once told a servant, with reference to a little boy who came to the house enquiring for "dada", "that it was Mr Kirwan's son, and he had two or three more of them". Here endeth *The Kirwan Case*.

Islands would seem to have exercised a baleful influence upon Mr Kirwan's fortunes. Fatal, in any view of his behaviour, were the hours spent by him upon Ireland's Eye; and now his Excellency the Earl of Eglinton, the Lord Lieutenant, whether dissenting from the verdict, or impressed by these declarations, or yielding merely to popular clamour, commuted the sentence to penal servitude for life, and the convict was immured accordingly on Spike Island in Queenstown harbour.

In the other pamphlet, Mr Boswell discusses the controversial points of the case, and publishes among certain statements a declaration by Teresa Kenny. But the second "Mrs Kirwan" is disappointing: she was plainly in no mood for revelations. She very handsomely accepts sole responsibility for the liaison,

---

* This is the "sworn testimony" which weighed with the ten physicians. It is remarkable that Mr Kirwan omitted at the inquest to mention these seizures, and that he did not instruct his counsel to adduce at the trial evidence of such importance.

of which she alleges the wife was all along aware, and says
that in 1847 Mr Kirwan urged her to go to her brother in
America, a proposition declined by her in the spirit of Ruth's
refusal to forsake Naomi. She was unable to bear witness at the
trial, having cut her thumb. Since her protector's arrest she and
her children had suffered much persecution at the hands of the
righteous. But what the testimony of Teresa lacks in sensation
is amply atoned for by the statement that on 6th September
there was upon the island another man, one John Gorman, who
avouched "that Kirwan was as innocent of the murder as the child
unborn"! Unfortunately, this person, having unbosomed himself
to Mr Malet, absconded, alleging, with some show of reason, that
"he was afraid of being implicated himself", and no trace of him
could be found. So the pamphlet is not enriched by his declaration
which, like "an affidavit from a thunderstorm or a few words on
oath from a heavy shower", desiderated by a certain chancellor,
was not forthcoming. Mr Boswell has a stronger hand to play in
Dr Taylor. That forensic autocrat had contributed to the medical
press an article, reprinted at length in the pamphlet. As this is not
a medical journal and not all my readers are medical jurists, I do
not propose to accompany Dr Taylor in his pathological excursus.
Those professionally interested may read him for themselves. His
conclusions are as follows:

> "I assert as my opinion, from a full and unbiased examination of
> the medical evidence in this case, that so far as the appearances
> of the body are concerned, there is an entire absence of proof
> that death was the result of violence at the hands of another.
> Persons while bathing, or exposed to the chance of drowning,
> are often seized with fits which may prove suddenly fatal,
> although they may allow of a short struggle; the fit may
> arise from syncope, apoplexy, or epilepsy. Either of the last
> conditions would, in my opinion, reconcile all the medical
> circumstances of this remarkable case."

While admitting the force of the moral and circumstantial evidence
against the accused, Dr Taylor holds that, "looking at the unsatisfactory nature of the medical evidence of violent death, it would
certainly have justified a verdict of Not Proven".

The doctor, however, was not to have it all his own way. There
was published by Professor Geoghegan the result of his examination

of the same facts, which led him to a very different conclusion. The copy of this pamphlet now before me is interesting as having been presented by the author to Mr Smyly, QC, who conducted the prosecution. Why that learned counsel did not put the Professor in the box is an additional mystery. To me, a layman in such matters, Dr Geoghegan's arguments upon the medical evidence seem much more cogent and convincing than those of Dr Taylor. His summing up is as follows:

"The preceding considerations, I think, suffice to indicate that the entire series of medical facts leads to the following conclusions:

1. That the death of Mrs Kirwan was not the result of apoplexy, or of epilepsy, nor yet of epileptic or of suicidal drowning.
2. That the combined conditions of the body (both external and internal) were incompatible with drowning, unattended by other violence.
3. That the appearances observed may have been produced by strangulation alone, or combined with compression of the chest, or with partial smothering.
4. That they are also consistent with a combination of the preceding mixed or simple process of strangulation, with drowning; the submersion not having been continuous from its commencement."

That Dr Geoghegan was in the better position to form a judgement would appear in the following circumstances: he had been consulted by the Crown at an early stage of the case, had personally inspected the *locus*, and heard the whole trial, none of which advantages was enjoyed by Dr Taylor. Further, he ascertained from witnesses who had seen the body certain conditions not elicited in evidence. From observations made by him at the Long Hole, Dr Geoghegan believed that the deed was done at the landward side of the "body" rock, in shallow water; the presence of seaweed and gravel in the hair favoured that view, and there would be less chance of detection from wetting of the perpetrator's clothes. "The arrangement of the deceased's bathing-dress, and of the sheet beneath her, with the orderly position of the body, seem clearly to show that wherever death may have occurred, the corpse was placed subsequently on the rock."

Actuated as I always am by a laudable desire to give the reader full value for his money, and believing that the opinion of a modern authority on forensic medicine might prove helpful, I consulted, unprofessionally, my friend Dr Devon, who was so good as to make a careful study of the whole phenomena, and to favour me with his conclusions. Of the competency of Dr Devon to pronounce upon the question, it would be impertinent to speak. His report is too long for quotation here, and I must be content to quote one pregnant paragraph:

"In this case it was suggested that deceased had an apoplectic stroke; but there was no evidence in the brain of any haem-orrhage. Syncope was also put forward as a cause of death; but the appearances found pointed to death from asphyxia. Epilepsy was also advanced as a cause, with as little evidence to support it. Granting, however, that deceased fell into the water either from an epileptic or a fainting fit, and there was drowned, how could she have sustained the injuries she had received and be found lying on her back? Had she fallen forward against projecting rocks or stones, might she not have cut her face and breast and bruised her right side? Possibly; but if she fell *forward* and got injured and drowned, how did she fall *backward* on a sheet, with her clothes up under her armpits? I am unable to imagine any accidental or suicidal drowning in which the deceased would be found in the position and with the injuries of Mrs Kirwan. And how might it have occurred? If the sheet on which she was found lying had been put round her when she was alive, in some such way as it was put round her dead body before it was removed, she could easily have been submerged in shallow water. If she had been shoved in from behind, the injuries might have been received from the rocks or stones in the bed of the water. There was no evidence of throttling and there were no injuries on her back. The body seems to have been taken to the place in which it was found, and in the process the clothes might have been drawn up to the armpits. It was a simple murder, clumsily carried out. If the body had been left in the water there would have been less room for suspicion, but it is a common thing for people under emotional stress to get exhausted mentally and to behave with a degree of stupidity that is amazing."

Who shall decide when the doctors disagree? Dr Taylor asks "Whether any amount of moral evidence can compensate for a deficiency of proof of the cause of death?" But though medical opinion be thus divided, some weight must surely attach to other facts and circumstances indicating foul play, hardly to be reconciled with death from natural causes. If so, the secret of the island would seem to be rather an open one after all, and like the song the Syrens sang, not beyond all conjecture.

A quarter of a century after the trial the following paragraph appeared in the *Freeman's Journal* (3 February 1879):

AN OLD TRAGEDY REVIVED

More than twenty-five years ago, a man named Kirwan, who lived in Upper Merrion Street, and had official employment as a draughtsman, was convicted in the Courthouse, Green Street, of the murder of his wife at Ireland's Eye, under circumstances of peculiar atrocity and horror. Sentence of death was pronounced; the gallows was prepared, the hangman retained, and the rope ready for its work; but at the last moment powerful influence of a very special character was successfully exerted, to rescue the culprit from the grasp of the executioner. Kirwan's death sentence was commuted to penal servitude for life, and after a short stay at Mountjoy Prison he was sent to Spike Island, where he spent nearly twenty-four years as a convict. Last week he was liberated, on condition that he should leave the country, and he has sailed, *via* Queenstown, for America. One who saw him just before his departure describes him as an aged and very respectable-looking gentleman, white-haired, bent, and feeble, and with nothing in his aspect or manner to suggest that he was guilty of the awful tragedy on Ireland's Eye.

Some further particulars are furnished by Mr M'Donnell Bodkin, K C, in his recent account of the case, on the authority of the late Dr O'Keeffe, formerly prison doctor at Spike Island, who "accompanied Kirwan when, on his release, as the last prisoner on Spike Island (before it was turned to its present use), he proceeded to Liverpool, whence he sailed to America, with the intention of joining and marrying the mother of his children, whose name figured so prominently at his trial". A reunion sufficiently remarkable, whatever view you take of the mystery. The local tradition that a venerable and flowing-bearded stranger, who some years afterwards visited Ireland's Eye and remained wrapped in contemplation of the Long Hole, was Mr Kirwan, surveying the scene of his adventure, may be dismissed as legendary.

THE MYSTERY OF MERSTHAM TUNNEL

(Robert Money, 1905)

Sir Edward Parry

One of the more puzzling of a rash of railway murders from the days of steam, the death of Mary Money has never been properly explained. As Sir Edward Parry notes, "the last act of the drama will never be written," in spite of the bizarre death, seven years later, of the dead woman's brother. His Honour Sir Edward Parry (1863–1943) was a barrister and county court judge who pursued various literary endeavours, producing a number of books and plays over a period of some forty years. These included books of criminology, poetry and historical biography, along with works so startlingly diverse as the play What the Butler Saw *(produced at Wyndham's Theatre in 1905) and a book with surely the most narcoleptic title of 1918,* Pensions Past and Present.*

Readers of Edgar Allan Poe will remember his masterpiece, *The Mystery of Marie Roget*, whose sudden disappearance produced such intense excitement in Paris, and whose atrocious murder was a problem too difficult for the Parisian police to solve. Had Edgar Allan read the story of Mary Money he might have solved the mystery of her death, but the police made nothing of it. There were various theories put forward at the time. Seven years afterwards these were reconsidered and revised. But the solution, whatever it is, will always remain a mystery. The last act of the drama will never be written. The scenes that were played out are peculiarly horrible and extraordinary. They are of the kind that lovers of the Grand Guignol revel in. There is a certain fascination in mere horror which finds its place in drama. But it would be impossible to invent stranger tales of terror and mystery than the stories of Mary Money and her brother Robert.

Mary Sophia Money was a pleasant girl of twenty-two, who was in September, 1905, working as a book-keeper for a dairyman at 245 Lavender Hill, Clapham Junction. She had been in her situation for over a year. She was in good favour with her neighbours, who one and all spoke well of her as a kindly girl of good reputation. There was a very honest young fellow near by who wrote letters to her and walked out with her, and she had other friends and acquaintances suitable to her class. No one suspected her of any social intrigue, nor had she, as far as appeared, ever absented herself from her work or been away from the household where she lived for any length of time.

On Sunday evening, about seven o'clock, she left the house, telling her fellow assistant that she would not be long and was going for a walk. Her dress contained no pocket. Round her neck was a flimsy silk scarf like a motor veil. She carried in her hand a handkerchief and a small black knitted purse with money in it. At No. 2 Station Approach, Clapham Junction, she entered a sweet shop a few minutes after seven, and bought six pennyworth of chocolates. At that time she was alone. The lady who served her knew her well and was sure no one was waiting for her outside the shop. She mentioned that she was going to Victoria. From that moment no one, as far as the world knew, ever spoke to the poor girl again.

About five minutes to eleven o'clock on the same Sunday night a sub-inspector of the South Eastern Company was patrolling the Merstham Tunnel. There were men at work relining the brickwork. He entered the tunnel at the Coulsdon end, and before he came to the outlet he found what appeared to be a bundle of clothing lying between the down line and the tunnel side. He turned his lantern upon it and was horrified to find it was the corpse of a woman terribly mangled by the wheels of a train. The body was still warm. He ran for help to Merstham Station, and the body was removed to Merstham, and a doctor sent for, but the poor woman was beyond human aid.

The injuries were very terrible. Both thighs were fractured, the left leg only hung by a shred, a wheel had eviscerated the lower part of the body, and a portion of the fluffy scarf was pushed into the brain. The police constable reported, too, that he found about a foot of this scarf wedged into the woman's mouth, apparently gathered up from the knot under the chin and thrust down the throat. Unfortunately he pulled it out before any experts could examine it. The doctor who first saw her and examined the remains with the police constable came to the conclusion that the woman had been gagged by someone who was travelling in the carriage with her, and thrown out into the tunnel through an open door by a person of considerable strength. No money, purse or railway ticket was found.

A police description was issued on the Monday, which included the laundry mark 245, which was the number of the shop at which Mary Money was employed. It appeared that she had a brother living at Kingston Hill. He, too, was in the dairy business. By Tuesday he seems to have heard that his sister was missing. He went down to Merstham and recognized the remains.

The Press representatives who saw him describe him as a young and prosperous-looking dairy farmer. He has a sad task before him, and they are naturally sympathetic and respect his sorrow. The police take him to identify the remains, which are locked in a dark shed. They illuminate the grim scene with a flickering stable lantern. The young man bears himself bravely. There is no doubt it is his sister.

The inquest threw little light on the affair. The young fellow who had walked out with her had clearly never been in her company during that day. The evidence of railway men and others, who thought they had seen her in company with someone, was of little or no value and very vague and contradictory. There was no trustworthy evidence that anyone ever saw her after she left the sweet shop. Robert Money, her brother, was merely called as a witness to identify the body. Afterwards, it was alleged that friends noticed a strangeness in his manner, and it was asserted that he complained to some of them that the police suspected him. As a matter of fact he was not suspected, and no questions were asked of him as to his movements. Other witnesses were examined as to their movements and accounted for them satisfactorily.

There were experts who favoured the theory of suicide, but Dr Wilcox was satisfied that the bruises on the right arm and wrist were not due to contact with the train but were inflicted. He considered there was evidence to show that she was attacked and then jumped or was thrown out of the train whilst she was alive. If the police officer is to be believed—and there is no reason to doubt his accuracy—the poor girl was choked with the scarf, which was stuffed down her throat, and then thrown from the train into the tunnel.

Who did it and why? That is the mystery which probably will never be solved. There seemed to be no clues to follow up, and the affair was forgotten or only remembered as an unanswered problem in the history of crime. No one seems at the time to have taken any note of the demeanour of brother Robert. It is not likely that he betrayed any peculiar emotion over his sister's death, since students of criminology tell us that moral insensibility is a characteristic of the instinctive and habitual murderer.

It seems harsh to use such a phrase in relation to a blameless milkman, but we cannot but wish some eager detective had paid more intimate attention to the movements of brother Robert. After his sister's death we hear nothing of him for about a year. Then he appears to have sold his share of the milk business for £1,000, which he invested in house property in Kingston, the rents from which seem to have been his sole legitimate income.

We must now occupy ourselves with a different history. About 1907, two sisters, Florence and Edith, were living with their parents at Clapham. Florence became acquainted with a fascinating young fellow named Robert Hicks Murray. He had plenty of money and had been a captain in the Gordon Highlanders. He spoke of his people as being in Scotland and on the continent. His father was a barrister at Watford. He persuaded Florence to live with him at a house in Clapham, which he furnished for her.

He, too, had property in Kingston, so he said, and also drew money for Army work. He had a bank account, and his affairs, whatever they were, flourished. There were two children of this union, and for a year or two Captain Murray was very kind to Florence and her children. He had no regular business. He rose early, helped in the domestic duties of the house, then strolled on the Common until dinner time, after which he went to a cricket match or a boxing match, so he said, and returned to tea. He was very fond of the theatre and the music hall. He used to take

Florence to the play or the halls. At first they went to the stalls and dress circle, but latterly they had been content with the upper circle or pit. Sometimes he was away on Army or other business.

During these years, although he was kind and generous, Florence was somewhat afraid of him. He was a strong muscular man and very passionate at times. She had doubts about his identity, and once he caught her searching his pockets to look at his letters and threatened to kill her. She seems to have surmised that he was not all he pretended to be; but, though she lived with him for several years, she had no knowledge of the channels from which he obtained money except what he told her about his rents from Kingston and the alleged Army business, on account of which he said he drew pay.

In the summer of 1910, Florence's sister, Edith, came to see them. The fickle Murray fell in love with her at first sight. Edith, on her part, seems to have been only too ready to meet his advances. They were married at once, but the Captain did not wholly desert his first love. He lived at various places with his real wife, and would return to spend a few days from time to time with Florence and her children.

Towards the end of 1911, the cost of two establishments seemed to be exhausting his resources, and he told Florence that he had sold his Kingston house property. In July, 1912, he took her with her children down to Eastbourne, where they went to some rather poor lodgings and passed under the name of Stirling. Here he left her very much to herself. For at the same time he was living, unknown to Florence, in a better part of Eastbourne with his real wife, Edith, and her child, for whom he had taken a villa in the name of Charles Richard Mackie, posing as an American.

On the morning of Saturday, 18 August, the housekeeper at the villa was told that Mr and Mrs Mackie would not require her services for a time, as they were going away, and would send her a wire when they returned. The tradesmen were told not to call until Tuesday. Edith was last seen alive at about six-forty, when she was out shopping. There is no doubt that the husband shot his wife and child on Saturday night and locked the bodies in a room on the first floor.

On Sunday afternoon he went to fetch Florence and the children and their luggage. He told her that a brother officer named Mackie had lent him a villa and they would go there. He took their luggage to the railway station and put it in the left-luggage office, and on his way to the villa purchased two cans of petrol. He then took Florence and her children to the empty villa, explaining to her that the owner had locked the door of the first-floor room, as he had left his silver there, and she was not to open it.

That night he shot Florence whilst she was in bed, and, believing he had killed her, went into the room where his children were lying and shot them dead. Then he poured the petrol over their bodies and set fire to the bed, and as the flames arose turned his revolver upon himself and ended his life.

Florence struggled out into the street and saved her life. The flames were put out, and the remains of Murray, Edith and the three children were taken possession of by the police. In the house was found a note signed C. K. Mackie, stating that he was absolutely ruined and had killed everyone dependent upon him.

It was the facsimile of this letter published in the Press that disclosed the identity of Murray or Mackie. A relative who saw it said at once, "That is Bob's writing," and the murderer was clearly identified as Robert Henry Money.

That this man was a typical homicide there can be no question. This does not, of course, prove that he was the murderer of his sister, but it is unfortunate that his movements on the night of her murder were never traced. What induced this dairyman to pose as an Army man with connections in Scotland and elsewhere? What were the sources of his wealth? What was the business which called him away from home? These are riddles which must always remain unanswered.

THE DUMB BLONDE WHO KNEW TOO MUCH

(Marilyn Monroe, 1962)

Kirk Wilson

In August 1962, the world's most glamorous film star Marilyn Monroe was found dead in bed at her home in Los Angeles. At first her death was said to have been caused by a drugs overdose; later, however, several people claimed that Monroe was given a lethal injection or otherwise murdered, claims that have been bitterly disputed over the years. The favourite conspiracy theory surrounding her death is that she had affairs with both President John F. Kennedy and his brother, US Attorney General Robert Kennedy, and that Monroe was murdered because she knew too many state secrets. In 1973 the American writer Norman Mailer published a biography Marilyn *in which he argued that, although Monroe had been deeply depressed at the time of her death, she had not committed suicide. Mailer attacked Marilyn's last husband, playwright Arthur Miller, and reported that while making her last film* The Misfits *she had resumed an affair with Clark Gable. "Who is the first to be certain that it was of no interest to the CIA, or to the FBI, or to the Mafia, and half of the secret police of the world, that the brother of the President was reputed to be having an affair with a movie star who had once been married to a playwright denied a passport for supporting Communist movements", Mailer wrote.*

> *"Being a sex symbol is a heavy load to carry,*
> *especially when one is tired, hurt, and bewildered."*
>
> —Clara Bow

> *"It's all make believe, isn't it?"*
>
> —Marilyn Monroe

In the world she moved through, nobody who mattered used their real names. The names they used were made up for them, like magical incantations. But she was never sure of her real name, so even by the standards of this world of make-believe, she was an insubstantial creature. The actress the world knows as Marilyn Monroe created herself anew each day. What she created was a dream, a myth, the closest thing our times have summoned to a love goddess in the flesh. The death that came to her had all the scope of emotive possibilities she had brought to every day in life. From one perspective, it was squalid, pointless, and pitiable. From another, it was of itself a myth, an epic role in a drama involving the most potent names and players of her age.

Sometime in the night of 4 August 1962, Marilyn Monroe slipped away into the ultimate unreality, riding a massive dose of Nembutal and chloral hydrate. The Chief Medical Examiner of Los Angeles County made a hedging call on the cause of death—*"probable suicide"*. Other investigators, with considerable evidence but no hard proof, are still calling it murder.

Murder, accident, or suicide, Marilyn's death is a mystery today not because of differing interpretations of the facts, but because this mistress of make-believe had been playing in a real and dangerous world, and the monarchs of that world were powerful enough to rewrite the script of her last hours.

In life and death, Marilyn embodied a supremely surreal and ambiguous version of the all-American success story. Raised in orphanages and foster homes, she became the Queen of Hollywood, using her talent and her body in equal measure to ascend from one imagined tier to the next. By the end she had achieved everything any starry-eyed bit player could dream of, and along the way she had bedded a president, married a sports legend and a literary giant, and captured the adulation of the world more completely than any actress of any time. She could be in turns a bitch and a baby, cunning and helpless, the goddess of sexual promise and the ghost of oblivion. She was a woman who could move, in the same afternoon, from a trembling mess of insecurity and self-doubt into an absolute master of her art. No one before or since has put more electricity and magic onto a piece of film.

The baby girl born at Los Angeles General Hospital at nine-thirty a.m. on 1 June 1926, was named Norma Jean Baker. The first name was inspired by the actress Norma Talmadge. The last was a convenience, borrowed from her mother's departed second husband. Though the matter has been endlessly researched, the identity of Marilyn's real father has never been firmly established. There are several candidates, the leading one a man named Gifford, who worked with her mother. The search for a father would become one of the themes of Norma Jean's strange life. A number of surrogates—in fantasy, Clark Gable was a favorite—would fill and abandon the role.

The child who would be Marilyn had little more in the way of a mother. At the time of her daughter's birth, Gladys Pearl Baker Mortenson was a delicately beautiful woman in her mid-twenties, working as a negative cutter at Consolidated Film Industries. She had two other children—a boy and a girl—who were living in the custody of her first husband's family.

Norma Jean spent her first eight years with foster families while her mother worked, visiting the child on weekends. In 1934, mother and daughter lived in the same household for a few months—the longest period they would spend together during Norma Jean's childhood—until Gladys suffered the first of many mental collapses and entered the same state hospital in which her own mother had died. The mother of Marilyn Monroe would spend most of the rest of her days in institutions, diagnosed—like her parents and brother before her—as a paranoid schizophrenic.

At nine, Norma Jean entered an orphanage and slept by a window overlooking the RKO studies. Beginning at eleven, she migrated from foster homes to guardians. Biographers have charted a total of twelve different households, not including the orphanage, inhabited by young Norma Jean before her marriage at sixteen. This upbringing did little to build a stable personality. After her transformation into movie stardom, Marilyn would milk the poor-orphan story for all it was worth with writers and studio publicists. Her accounts included an attempted smothering by her grandmother and no fewer than ten episodes of rape or molestation, beginning at age six. Even allowing for her exaggerations and self-contradictions, there is no doubt that Marilyn's childhood was a perfect breeding ground for insecurity and loneliness.

Norma Jean's first marriage, to a twenty-one-year-old former high school hero named Jim Dougherty, was more or less arranged by her guardian of the moment, who was moving out of state and preferred not to take the teenage girl along. In later years, Jim would remember the marriage more fondly than Marilyn. However happily it may have begun, the marriage was doomed when Jim shipped out with the merchant marine and the head of his luscious young bride was turned toward a career in modeling. With every stunning photograph, with every line of agent's hype and every leer from ad executives and movie producers, Norma Jean moved closer to rebirth as Marilyn.

The official incarnation happened while Norma Jean was working as a contract player for 20th Century-Fox in 1946. Ben Lyon, the Fox casting director, borrowed the name Marilyn from an actress he admired named Marilyn Miller, Marilyn herself contributed Monroe—it was the maiden name of her grandmother.

Her first screen appearance came the following year, at the age of twenty-one. Marilyn briefly rowed a canoe in an insipid movie starring a team of mules and titled *Scudda Hoo! Scudda Hay!* The infamously jiggling-Monroe walk had its debut in a bit part in a Marx Brothers movie called *Love Happy* (1949), causing Groucho to evaluate the young starlet as "Mae West, Theda Bara, and Bo Peep all rolled into one." The importance of these early cameos was that Marilyn's uncanny ability to make love to a camera lens was being noticed by the men who owned the cameras. She was not, by Hollywood standards, an exceptionally beautiful woman. She was an exceptionally photogenic woman, and that was all that mattered. Remembering his first session with Marilyn in an early screen test, veteran cinematographer Leon Shamroy says, "I got a cold chill. This girl had something I hadn't seen since silent pictures. She had a kind of fantastic beauty . . . she got sex on a piece of film."

She also knew how to use sex on a casting couch, and her talents in this line contributed as much to her early successes as her undeniable screen presence. One advantageous relationship was with the seventy-year-old Joseph Schenck, the head of production at Fox and one of the founders of the company. Another was with a powerful agent named Johnny Hyde. Marilyn minced no words in describing her attitude at this stage of her career. "I spent a lot of time on my knees." There were genuine love affairs to go with the affairs of business, and a good deal of near-pathological abandon. By the end of her life, Marilyn may have undergone as many as fourteen abortions.

Hampered by the studios' unfortunate choices of vehicles to showcase her talents, the on-screen Marilyn remained more a sexpot than a major star until her twentieth picture, *Gentlemen Prefer Blondes* (1953). A succession of movie classics followed, among them *The Seven Year Itch* (1955), *Bus Stop* (1956), and *Some Like It Hot* (1959).

She was the movie star she had dreamed of being, lived to be. More than that, she had become a marvelous, if difficult, actress who worked long and seriously at her craft. She built these powers by a force of will, but the one thing she could never build was a complete and secure human being to occupy Marilyn's—or Norma Jean's—celebrated body. Take the time to sift through the recollections of those who knew her, and one word of description will occur more frequently than any other. The word is not "sex"—though the person described packaged and sold sex more powerfully than anyone. The word is "child". Marilyn Monroe was a child, sometimes petulant and obnoxious, sometimes spontaneous and effervescent and living to charm and please, but more times than anything, afraid. Afraid of being unloved and alone.

Though lacking in formal education, this child-woman was not the dumb blonde she played in the movies. The saber wit and the insights into character were not created by the scriptwriters. One example. An attempt is made to blackmail the studio because Marilyn's nude image has been discovered on a cheesecake calendar, which will make millions for its publishers but which was shot years before when Norma Jean needed the fifty bucks she was paid for the session. The time is the prudish early 1950s, but Marilyn skates through the thin ice to an enormous publicity advantage with a crowded press conference.

Reporter: Is it true you didn't have *anything* on when these pictures were taken?

Marilyn: We had the radio on.

In January of 1954, just as she ascended to the heights of stardom, Marilyn married another star who had been longer and even more widely adored. He was Joltin' Joe DiMaggio, the Yankee Clipper, one of the greatest baseball players ever to swing a bat and the man who had held America in his grip during the entire summer of 1941, hitting in fifty-six straight games. The courtship had made good copy for a year and a half. The marriage lasted nine months. Joltin' Joe, it seemed, wanted a wife more than a movie star. Still, Joe could "hit homes runs" in bed; but more than that, he was something Marilyn couldn't find in Hollywood. He was "genuine" and he loved her as a woman. He would reemerge as a friend and protector in the last year of her life, and he would be the guardian of her violated body at the end.

In the summer of 1956, a second star from an entirely different constellation joined the goddess of love in marriage. Arthur Miller was—with Tennessee Williams—one of the two great living playwrights in America. For Marilyn, who desperately wanted to be taken seriously as an actress, the oh so serious playwright held all the fascination of the one who supplies the deathless words for the one who speaks them. In the media, it was the wedding of the Beauty and the Brain, the Egghead and the Hourglass. It proved to be a storybook romance that could not survive a prolonged reading by the eyes of the real world. After many difficulties, the divorce came at the beginning of 1961.

There was, or at least there may have been, another "marriage". This marriage—if real—would have been the second, before DiMaggio and after Jim Dougherty. Though undocumented, this marriage is of great interest to those who believe Marilyn Monroe was murdered, for it was to the man who has maintained a single-minded crusade to expose the murder to the world, a man named Robert Slatzer. Slatzer is a writer and producer who met Marilyn in the summer of 1946, when he was a young fan-magazine reporter and she was the struggling model and would-be starlet Norma Jean Mortenson. Slatzer has subsequently claimed that he and Marilyn fell in love and were married in an alcoholic haze in Tijuana, on 4 October 1952. According to his account, the young couple lived together as man and wife "about three days", until they were strong-armed by Darryl F. Zanuck—the head of 20th Century-Fox and Marilyn's boss at the time—into annulling the marriage and having all records of it destroyed.

Monroe's biographers are divided on the marriage story. It is well established that Robert Slatzer and Marilyn were certainly good friends, and that their friendship extended from the late 1940s until her death in 1962. In any case, Slatzer's credibility is a crucial issue in the murder story, as much of the first-hand evidence in the case comes either directly from him or from his long and determined legwork.

To accompany the confirmed and could-be husbands there is a Homeric list of confirmed and could-be lovers. Marilyn could be ambivalent about how much she personally enjoyed the sex act, but there is no doubt she enjoyed attracting men. "If fifteen men were in the room with her," said one Hollywood publicist, "each would be convinced he was the one she'd be waiting for after the others left." Through personal magnetism, compulsion, or both, she raised the art of seduction to a new level. Not too surprisingly, a vast number of the men who had speaking acquaintances with her have claimed at one time or another to have shared her bed. But for our purposes the most interesting of the lovers are those who could not afford to brag. Of these there are two more interesting than all: the President of the United States and his brother, the Attorney General.

Some accounts trace the origin of Marilyn's affair with John F. Kennedy to the early 1950s, when Kennedy was a rising star in the US Senate and Marilyn was an established sex symbol in Hollywood. Other sources say the romance began just before Kennedy received his party's nomination for president in 1960. Whenever it may have started, the affair—judging by the independent testimony of several who witnessed it first-hand—seems to have reached its peak in the early, heady days of the Kennedy presidency, through the offices—and in the beachfront Santa Monica home—of the President's brother-in-law, actor Peter Lawford. The timing of the coupling is significant. Marilyn was at the end of a marriage and in a downward spiral both professionally and personally, due to heavy drug abuse and the endless drain of her own insecurities. John Kennedy was very much married and the most powerful man in the world. As a security risk, the unstable Marilyn was as risky as they come.

Not that John Kennedy was above taking risks where sexual adventure was concerned. The list of *his* confirmed and could-be liaisons rivals Marilyn's in its proportions. For Kennedy—and his brother Robert—the indiscretions may have seemed a sort of family tradition. "Dad", JFK revealed to Clare Boothe Luce, "told all the boys to get laid as often as possible." Joe Kennedy had taken his own advice. He himself had reportedly enjoyed Hollywood girlfriends in his heyday, the most famous being Gloria Swanson.

Robert Kennedy's fling with Marilyn is less well documented than his brother's, and its beginnings are no less difficult to trace. There are those who claim Robert was the first Kennedy to date Monroe. At least one first-hand account, however, suggests that Robert's affair began as the President's was ending—in the summer and fall of 1961. The inference has been drawn that the younger Kennedy was enlisted to soften the blow of the end of the President's dalliance, and that he, like so many others, found Marilyn's temptations impossible to resist. However and whenever it started, this affair appears to have continued until just prior to Marilyn's death in August of 1962. At least from Marilyn's viewpoint, there was an important difference between the ways the two brothers conducted their affairs. From what she reportedly told others, it seems the love goddess took Robert Kennedy's attentions more seriously than John's. Speaking of the President, she could be lighthearted: "I think I made his back feel better" and "I made it with the Prez." Of the Attorney General: "Bobby Kennedy promised to marry me."

Again, the timing relative to Marilyn's state of mind is important. Her life, never securely anchored, was becoming increasingly unraveled as the decade of the 1950s wore into the 1960s. Her attempted "suicides"—some or all of which were accidental overdoses—had recurred perhaps a dozen times, with increasing frequency in later years. Her tendency to keep whole, and enormously expensive, film production ensembles awaiting her appearance for hours and even days had increased to the point that she had been fired from her last film, *Something's Got to Give*, on 8 June 1962, after showing up on the set only twelve times during thirty-three scheduled shooting days. Marilyn's last day before the cameras had been 1 June, her thirty-sixth birthday. Her psychiatrist had noted an alarming disintegration beginning in the summer of 1961, including "severe depressive" reactions, suicidal tendencies, increased drug use, and random promiscuity. She may have been a goddess, but she was not a goddess to be trusted with anybody's secrets. And the Attorney General of the United States may have trusted her with the most important secrets that he knew.

The source for this intriguing possibility is Robert Slatzer. Slatzer was one of a number of friends in whom Marilyn confided about her affairs with the Kennedy brothers, but he appears to be the only one she told about Robert Kennedy's weakness for dangerously indiscreet pillow talk. Slatzer says Marilyn told him Bobby had become annoyed when she forgot things he had told her during previous visits, and that she had resorted—unbeknownst to the

Attorney General—to making notes of their conversations in a red diary. Ten days before she died, Marilyn showed Slatzer the diary, as they sat on a beach at Point Dume, north of Malibu on the Pacific Coast Highway. Most of the entries, Slatzer says, began with "Bobby told me." He remembers entries about Kennedy's war with Jimmy Hoffa and the Mafia, with Kennedy swearing to "put that SOB behind bars". But most chillingly, he remembers an entry that read, "Bobby told me he was going to have . . . Castro murdered."

The Kennedy administration's bungling attempts to kill Fidel Castro—through the strangely combined efforts of the CIA, anti-Castro Cubans, and the American Mafia—first came to light during U.S. Senate hearings in the mid 1970s, and have since become common knowledge. But in 1962, a revelation of this kind would have been the most dangerous political fiasco imaginable. It could certainly have done critical damage to the administration; it could feasibly have started a nuclear confrontation; it could even cause the assassination of the President of the United States—which, as matter of fact, it may well have.

According to Slatzer, Marilyn not only knew these state secrets, she was prepared to tell the world about them. He says she talked of plans to call a press conference and "blow the lid off this whole damn thing," revealing her affairs with the two Kennedys and the broken "promises that had been made to her". The date allegedly mentioned for the press conference was Monday, 6 August 1962—the day after she was pronounced dead. Slatzer says he asked if Marilyn had told anyone else of her plans for the press conference and she replied that she had told "a few people". He claims to have warned her that what she knew was "like having a walking time bomb," but that she said she "didn't care at this point . . . these people had used her . . . and she was going to . . . tell the real story."

Some confirmation of Slatzer's story comes from Peter Lawford's ex-wife Deborah Gould. Gould has said that—years after the fact—Lawford broke down and offered a tearful account of the end of Marilyn's life. Taken as a whole, Lawford's "confession" raises as many questions as it answers. But in this case Lawford's alleged account echoes Slatzer's: Marilyn tells Lawford, "I've been used . . . thrown from one man to another . . . and I'm going public with everything." If Marilyn wanted word of this threat to get back to the Kennedys, she could have chosen no better vehicle than Peter Lawford.

There is no record that Marilyn notified anyone in the media about plans for a press conference. The fact remains that the mere suggestion of such an ultimatum could have been an extremely dangerous gambit. It appears Marilyn was desperate enough to play this card in hopes that it would force Robert Kennedy to contact her. She had told several friends that Robert had abruptly ended the affair, and no longer called her or returned her phone calls. He had gone so far, she said, as to disconnect the private number he had given her, and the Justice Department operators refused to put her calls to the main switchboard through. Marilyn's frequent calls to Justice during July of 1962 are documented on her phone records. The last call for which records are available was placed 30 July, the Monday before her death.

Marilyn's reasons for calling Robert Kennedy may have gone beyond the sting of the spurned lover. In late June, she told an interviewer, "A woman must have to love a man with all her heart to have his child . . . especially when she's not married to him. And when a man leaves a woman when she tells him she's going to have his baby, when he doesn't marry her, that must hurt a woman very much, deep down inside." Between late June and early July, she told several friends that she had lost a baby, without specifying abortion or miscarriage. To some friends she confided that the father had been John Kennedy, to others, Robert. At least two sources have reported that there was an abortion, performed in Tijuana by an American doctor. Depending on which authority you trust, this may have been the fourteenth abortion of Marilyn's life, an especially sad count for a child-woman who spent her final interviews talking about how much she wanted a child of her own. During the same period, Marilyn told several friends—to universal disbelief—that she and the Attorney General would someday be married.

In the available accounts of these last scenes of her life, there is another word that crops up frequently in descriptions of Marilyn. The word is scared. One long-time friend, Arthur James, recalls that Marilyn was "frightened stiff". Slatzer says she told him that "because of circumstances that led all the way to Washington", she was "scared for her life". James and others say she became convinced that she was being watched, that her phones were bugged, and that she resorted to making personal calls from a phone booth in a park near her home, lugging pocketfuls of change for this purpose.

Marilyn may have had paranoid tendencies, but in this instance she was very much in tune with the real world. She was right about the phones. She was right about being watched. In fact her whole home was bugged, and so was Peter Lawford's home, where she had rendezvoused with her two most powerful lovers. The bugging was not being done by the government.

Though she almost surely did not know it, the recording devices and the sinister people behind them may have been precisely the reason Robert Kennedy had become incommunicado. Kennedy was in the fifth year of a personal war against organized crime in general and Teamsters Union President Jimmy Hoffa in particular. The struggle had been joined when Kennedy was Chief Counsel to the McClellan Committee in the US Senate, and carried on, with unprecedented force, when he became Attorney General. Hoffa was convinced Robert Kennedy had used the attack on his union as a stepping stone to national power for himself and his brother, and in a sense he was right. The union boss and his mob friends hated both of the elder Kennedy brothers enough to want them dead—and were reportedly not above saying so, among themselves—but they especially hated Bobby.

In the course of the struggle, Robert Kennedy had created a special "Get Hoffa" strike force in the Justice Department, with the FBI, the IRS, and the government itself aligned on his side. But Jimmy Hoffa and his Mafia allies were not without their own resources and their own considerable army of foot soldiers. Hoffa knew the Kennedys were vulnerable because of their womanizing. When he learned of the amorous dance of John and Robert and Marilyn Monroe—by one account the information came to him as early as 1957—he must have rubbed his hands in glee.

The ideal weapon for this phase of the war on Kennedy happened to be a human being who happened to already be on Hoffa's payroll—the man acknowledged by his peers to be the best wiretapper in the world, one Bernard Bates Spindel. Spindel had learned the basics of his trade in the US Army Signal Corps and in army intelligence during the Second World War. One of the ironies of his remarkable career is that he could easily have served on the Kennedy side in the bugging wars: as a young man he applied for a job with the CIA but was rejected. Though he is said to have worked both sides of the fence thereafter, Bernie Spindel spent the bulk of the rest of his days beating the government spooks at their own game. Spindel had been taping Robert Kennedy for his client Jimmy Hoffa since at least the late 1950s. According to

Hollywood-based private eye Fred Otash, Spindel got the Marilyn Monroe assignment in the summer of 1961.

Otash has said Hoffa summoned him and Spindel to a meeting in Florida that summer. Hoffa wanted "to develop a derogatory profile of Jack and Bobby Kennedy and their relationships with Marilyn Monroe and with any other woman. The strategy . . . was to use electronic devices." The first target was Peter Lawford's home, where bugs were placed not only on the phone lines but "in the carpets . . . under chandeliers and in ceiling fixtures." Otash says the tapes from the Lawford bugging contained conversations between both Kennedys and Marilyn, and phone conversation to arrange rendezvous between both Kennedys and Marilyn, and both Kennedys and other women.

Another private detective who worked on the assignment, John Danoff, has been more graphic in his description of the tapes from the Lawford house: it "was cuddly talk and taking off their clothes and the sex act in the bed—you could hear the springs squeaking and so on."

If this was good stuff, maybe better stuff could be had at Marilyn's home, the modest Spanish-style house in Brentwood in which she spent the last months of her life. Marilyn's friend Arthur James says he was asked in the spring of 1962 to get Marilyn out of the house so that "people could come in there and bug . . . for the purpose of getting evidence on Bobby Kennedy." James says he turned the request down, and never told Marilyn about it. The house was bugged anyway. Examination in later years turned up indications of eavesdropping devices both on the phones and on the premises.

Despite all these frightening developments, there are indications Marilyn had rebounded to some extent from her depressions during her last few days. The studio, with reluctance but with little choice in the matter, had rehired her on *Something's Got to Give*, and shooting was set to resume before the end of 1962. She was negotiating on other film projects, giving interviews, enjoying setting up and landscaping the Brentwood house, the first home she had bought and lived in on her own. She had set several appointments for the week that would follow her death. Though never a model of stability, she did not appear to be a person who was contemplating suicide.

The Brentwood household included a housekeeper-companion, a sixty-year-old woman named Eunice Murray, who had been installed by Marilyn's psychiatrist, Dr Ralph Greenson. Mrs Murray, who seems to have had some experience dealing with psychiatric patients, came on the scene after Marilyn had alienated a succession of nurses. It was Mrs Murray who had found the Brentwood house for Marilyn to buy, and Mrs Murray who brought her own son-in-law into the household as a salaried handyman. The housekeeper and the handyman were two of many links between the film star and the psychiatrist. During her final summer, Marilyn saw Dr Greenson in his professional capacity as often as twice a day. She also relied on him increasingly for advice and moral support, spent a great deal of time in his home, and became close to his children. Marilyn came to depend on Greenson so heavily that some of her friends observed that the doctor was, in effect, running her life. It was a pattern she had lived through before with her acting coaches, and if it troubled her there is only one indication that she may have been trying to change it: a report that she made inquiries about replacing Mrs Murray with a housekeeper of her own choosing at the end of July, just before she died.

As it happens, Mrs Murray has become the enigma within the riddle of the Marilyn Monroe case. Her evidence is critical, because, according to the officially accepted version of events, she was the only other person in the house when Marilyn died. But beginning with her first statements to police that night, and stretching almost to the present day, her accounts have been so abstruse, ever-changing, and self-contradictory that they may be interpreted in any number of vastly different ways. In the impossible event that any party or parties were ever put on trial for the murder of Marilyn Monroe, one can imagine Mrs Murray in the role of witness for either the defense or the prosecution, depending on the story she chooses to tell on that particular day. It is hard to escape the conclusion that this kindly and soft-spoken old lady is either impossibly befuddled or is doggedly hiding a dangerous truth.

Mrs Murray is not alone in her capacity for confusion about the last hours of Marilyn's life. In fact, virtually all of the small number of people who spent extended periods of time with Marilyn that weekend have shown an alarming tendency to forget or to offer contradictory stories, so much so that their testimony would seem highly suspicious even if there were no other reason to doubt the official suicide verdict. And there are plenty of other reasons.

Given all the fuzzy recollections, it is impossible to reconstruct with any certainty the last two days Marilyn Monroe spent on

this earth. There are a few documented facts. One is that Robert
Kennedy was in California that weekend. With his wife and four
children in tow, he was to address the American Bar Association
meeting in San Francisco, staying at the ranch of a lawyer named
John Bates, about sixty miles south of the city. Marilyn knew
Kennedy was coming, and was still desperately trying to contact
him. Her phone records for the four days she lived in August were
mysteriously confiscated, but an enterprising reporter established
that she made several calls to the San Francisco hotel where the Bar
Association had reserved rooms for Kennedy, and that the calls were
not returned. Bit by bit, evidence has emerged that Kennedy left the
San Francisco area to visit Marilyn that weekend. His host John
Bates has steadfastly insisted that this could not have happened.
A number of other witnesses, including Los Angeles police, claim
otherwise.

For her part, Marilyn spent the early hours of Friday shopping
for plants to landscape her yard. She visited her doctor and her
psychiatrist. No one has clearly established what she did that
night. One of the questionable sources for Marilyn's activities that
weekend, her press aide Pat Newcomb—who later worked for and
was close to the Kennedys—has said she and Marilyn dined at
one of their favorite Santa Monica restaurants that evening, but
that she could not recall the name or location of the restaurant.

At dawn on Saturday, 4 August, Marilyn's friend and self-
described "sleeping-pill buddy" Jeanne Carmen received a phone
call from Marilyn, speaking in "a frightened voice . . . and very
tired—she said she had not slept the entire night" and complaining
about " 'phone call after phone call after phone call' with some
woman . . . saying, 'you tramp . . . leave Bobby alone or you're
going to be in deep trouble.' " During this call and twice later in
the day, Marilyn asked Carmen to come over and "bring a bag of
pills" but Carmen was busy and couldn't comply.

Marilyn made a number of other phone calls during the
morning—one to her friend and masseur Ralph Roberts, making
a tentative plan for dinner at her home that evening. At one point
Mrs Murray's son-in-law Norman Jeffries, Jr encountered Marilyn
while working on the kitchen floor. She was wrapped in a bath
towel, looking "desperately sick" as though "she must have taken
a lot of dope . . . or was scared out of her mind. I had never seen her
look that way before." Late in the morning, Marilyn's hairdresser
Agnes Flanagan visited and observed that Marilyn was "terribly,

terribly depressed" at the delivery, via messenger, of a stuffed toy tiger. The significance of the tiger has never been explained.

The afternoon is a mystery about which very little clear information is available. The only reported event with several sources to support it is a visit by Robert Kennedy to Marilyn's home. If Kennedy did visit, it would not have been the first time. Jeanne Carmen says she was once at Marilyn's when Kennedy arrived, and Marilyn, fresh out of a bath and dressed in a bathrobe "jumped into his arms" and "kissed him openly, which was out of character for her".

A private investigator working for Robert Slatzer reports that a neighbor of Marilyn's was hosting a bridge game on the afternoon of 4 August, and that the ladies at the game—understandably interested in the comings and goings at the home of their famous neighbor—observed Robert Kennedy arrive in the company of another man "carrying what resembled a doctor's bag". A daughter of one of the women at the game (the woman is deceased) has repeated the story, adding that the hostess was harassed for weeks by men warning her "to keep her mouth shut". Robert Kennedy himself allegedly testified in a deposition—no record of which is available—that he did visit Marilyn's home that afternoon escorted by a doctor, who injected the distraught actress with a tranquilizer to calm her down. Mrs Murray, having denied over the course of twenty-three years that Kennedy had been in Marilyn's home that Saturday, finally admitted on camera in a 1985 BBC documentary that the Attorney General had been there during the afternoon, though she offered no details. Peter Lawford's ex-wife Deborah Gould says Lawford told her Kennedy went to Marilyn's that Saturday to tell her once and for all that the affair was over, and the confrontation left her "very very distraught and depressed". A neighbor of Lawford's says he saw Robert Kennedy arrive by car at Lawford's home during the afternoon.

Marilyn's psychiatrist, Ralph Greenson, fills in the story as of about four-thirty or five p.m. Dr Greenson has said Marilyn called him in an anxious state, seeming "depressed and somewhat drugged". He went to her house, spending "about two and half hours" there. According to his carefully worded account, she told him she had been having affairs with "extremely important men in government. . . at the highest level", and that she had expected to be with one of these men that evening, but had been disappointed. At around six-thirty p.m., the masseur Ralph Roberts called to confirm the dinner plans. Roberts recognized Dr Greenson's voice, as it told him Marilyn was not home. Joe DiMaggio's son Joe Jr tried to call twice, reaching Mrs Murray, who said Marilyn was out. The press aide Pat Newcomb had spent the night in the house and had been on the scene all day. According to Greenson, Marilyn now became angry with Newcomb, and he asked Newcomb to leave.

There is an interesting sidelight to this seemingly minor incident. One source—a friend of Newcomb's who also knew Marilyn—has said that Pat Newcomb, a bright and attractive young woman, was herself "deeply in love with Bobby Kennedy". Marilyn considered the younger Newcomb a rival as well as a friend, and had been jealous of her in the past. Newcomb, who was sequestered in the Kennedy compound at Hyannis Port immediately after Marilyn's death and who subsequently became a Kennedy employee, has long refused comment on the Kennedys' relationships with Marilyn.

Though Marilyn "seemed somewhat depressed", Greenson had seen her "many, many times in a much worse condition". He had a dinner engagement, and, according to his account, he judged that Marilyn was sufficiently recovered that he could return to his home around seven-fifteen, asking Mrs Murray to stay the night as a precaution. At about seven-forty p.m., Greenson says, Marilyn called him to report that she had talked to young DiMaggio. She sounded in better spirits.

The Kennedys' brother-in-law, Peter Lawford, gave a number of differing accounts of the night Marilyn died to a number of different people. In all of them, he claims to have had a phone conversation with Marilyn at about this time, in which she turned down his invitation to come to dinner at his home. The dinner party may have been the gathering Marilyn had hoped to attend with Robert Kennedy that night. By this time, she was in no shape to go.

As far as anyone knows for certain, the only person on the scene with Marilyn at this point was Mrs Murray. Of the many stories she has told of the fatal night, this is essentially the original—the one repeated in the first police reports:

At around eight p.m., Marilyn says good night and, taking one of her two phones with its long cord in with her, closes her bedroom door.

Mrs Murray tidies up about the house and goes to her own room. At about three-thirty a.m., for some reason—perhaps alerted by a "sixth sense," as Dr Greenson somewhat mystically referred to it—Mrs Murray arises and notices that Marilyn's light is still on and that the phone cord is still under her door. The phone is normally disconnected at night. Mrs Murray is too timid to knock and risk awakening Marilyn, but alarmed enough to call Dr Greenson. He tells her to knock on the locked door, and she does. There is no response. He tells her he is on the way and instructs her to call Dr Hyman Engleberg, Marilyn's personal physician. As she awaits the doctors' arrival, Mrs Murray goes to the front of the house and uses a fireplace poker to pull back the curtains and peek in. She sees Marilyn lying nude on the bed. At about three thirty-five a.m., Greenson— who lives nearby—arrives, breaks the bedroom window, and enters the room. Marilyn is lying face down with the phone clutched "fiercely" in her right hand. Greenson realizes immediately that she is dead. Dr Engleberg arrives about five minutes later. The police are finally called at four twenty-five a.m.

On the face of it, the story almost makes sense, though it certainly has its queer touches. For one, it has Mrs Murray awakening a psychiatrist in the middle of the night before she makes any effort on her own to find out if anything is really wrong. Odder still, it shows us two doctors –who knew their obligations in what was clearly a coroner's case—waiting, inexplicably, almost an hour to report the death of their most famous patient. There are other serious discrepancies that are not so immediately apparent. One is that Mrs Murray could not, as she claimed, have first been alarmed by the light under Marilyn's bedroom door. The house had newly installed white wool carpeting that brushed firmly enough against the bottom of the door to make it difficult to close. No light showed through.

This early account of Marilyn's death is not, as it may seem, stranger than fiction. It *is* fiction.

The first cop on the scene had immediate misgivings about the story he was told. The belated call to the police had been placed by Dr Engleberg. It had been taken by the Watch Commander on the West Los Angeles desk, a Sergeant named Jack Clemmons. Given that the death of Marilyn Monroe had been reported, Clemmons was curious enough to make the run to the scene himself. Clemmons was a tough-minded and experienced cop. Ironically, he was also a friend of Marilyn's ex-husband Jim Dougherty, who became a policeman years after his divorce from his famous first wife.

The doctors showed Clemmons a Nembutal bottle among the fifteen bottles of medication cluttering Marilyn's bedside table.

The bottle was empty and had its top in place. Its label came from the San Vicente Pharmacy in Brentwood, and indicated a prescription from Dr Engleberg, filled on Friday, 3 August. Engleberg told Clemmons the bottle had contained fifty capsules when full. No suicide note was in evidence.

Perhaps more significantly, no water glass was in evidence either, and the water in the adjoining bathroom was turned off because of work on the plumbing system. People who knew Marilyn well have said she could not bear to swallow even one pill without water. Swallowing fifty pills without water was out of the question. It has been noted that photographs of the room show what appears to be a Mexican-style ceramic jug on the floor that could have held water. Apparently no one thought to see if it did, or ask if it was used for that purpose.

Clemmons had an "uneasy feeling" about the behavior of the doctors and of Mrs Murray. There was something about the death scene itself he couldn't buy. It was too pretty, too arranged, to jibe with the death throes by overdose in his experience: "It looked like the whole thing had been staged." Marilyn's body was in rigor mortis. By Clemmons's experienced guess, she had not died during the early hours of that morning, but may have been dead as long as eight hours. He did not like the fact that Mrs Murray was busying herself by doing laundry and packing boxes when he arrived, or that her son-in-law had already been called to repair the broken bedroom window. Most of all, he did not like the time sequences he was given.

Though his concerns did not find their way into the final version of his written report, Clemmons has insisted that Mrs Murray told him she first became alarmed about Marilyn "immediately after midnight". He says the two doctors were present when she made this statement, and *did not disagree.* Clemmons's impression was that Drs Greenson and Engleberg had been on the scene themselves since around midnight, and he remembers questioning the doctors "very pointedly" about why they had waited not one hour but four to call the police. He got no satisfactory reply. When Sergeant Clemmons went off duty that Sunday morning and turned the case over to other officers, he was highly suspicious. By the time the official suicide verdict was returned, he was convinced that Marilyn Monroe had been murdered. He remains adamantly convinced today, though his refusal to accept the official line in the case cost him his job with the Los Angeles police.

Twenty-three years after the fact, Mrs Murray told the BBC interviewer that it had indeed been "around midnight" when she first became concerned about Marilyn. In this version of her story, she says she did wait until three-thirty a.m., to call Dr Greenson. Why did she wait so long? She can't remember.

In fact there were hours of frantic activity—beginning well before midnight—in Marilyn's house that night that Mrs Murray can't remember. It was about eleven p.m.—perhaps even slightly earlier—when Marilyn's press agent Arthur Jacobs's enjoyment of a Henry Mancini concert was interrupted by an urgent message. Jacobs's widow Natalie, who accompanied him to the Hollywood Bowl that night, remembers: "About three-quarters of the way through the concert someone came to our box and he said, 'Arthur, come quickly . . . Marilyn is dead, or she's on the point of death.' " Mrs Jacobs believes the message came from Pat Newcomb, an employee in her husband's firm. She says Jacobs dropped her off at their home, and she saw nothing of him for two days thereafter. In her phrase, "he had to fudge the Press".

Presumably one of the things Jacobs had to fudge was the possibility that Marilyn did not die at home after all. In the early hours of the morning she left the premises for an ambulance ride. The ambulance story first surfaced during a District Attorney's review of the case in 1982, and has since been confirmed by writers and reporters. The ambulance driver has been identified as one Ken Hunter, and the attendant as Murray Liebowitz. The ambulance belonged to Schaefer Ambulance, the largest private company of its kind in LA at the time. Hunter and Liebowitz, who has since changed his name, have confirmed the call at Marilyn's house, but have been mysteriously reluctant to talk about it. The owner of Schaefer Ambulance, Walter Schaefer, has not. Schaefer insisted Marilyn was alive, but in a coma—apparently suffering from a drug overdose—when she was picked up and taken to Santa Monica Hospital. The time has been reported as two a.m. Schaefer believes Marilyn died at the hospital. An obvious problem with this opinion is that, if the time report is correct, Marilyn was found in rigor mortis just two and one half hours later. Rigor mortis takes from four to six hours to set in.

Records of the ambulance company are only kept for five years, and have been destroyed. Hospital records for the period are likewise not available, and no one has been located who worked at the hospital in 1962 and who remembers treating Marilyn Monroe that night. It is of course possible that she was treated but, lacking makeup, not recognized, and possible that she died en route to the hospital. The autopsy records no evidence of medical attempts to resuscitate her from an overdose. Still, it seems incredible that Schaefer and his two employees could be mistaken about so memorable an emergency call. And the case for an attempt to save a dying Marilyn was reinforced by Mrs Murray, whose on-again, off-again memory recollected during a 1985 version of her story of a late night visit by an unidentified doctor while Marilyn was still alive.

What was happening at Marilyn's house between the time someone—Pat Newcomb?—sent Arthur Jacobs the message that Marilyn was dead or dying around eleven p.m. and someone called for an ambulance, perhaps about two a.m.? And if she did ride to the hospital, who took her body home? It wasn't Schaefer: Marilyn's trip in the ambulance was one-way. It would have been no mean feat to make a corpse vanish from an emergency room. Standard procedure in such a case would be for the Medical Examiner to be called and to officially release the body only after an autopsy. A clever manipulation—or the wave of some powerful hands—would have been required to bypass the system.

With each new revelation in the case, the scene at Marilyn's house grows more crowded. One of her lawyers, Milton "Mickey" Rudin, reportedly appears at around four a.m., calling Peter Lawford's agent on the phone and telling him Marilyn is dead.

Peter Lawford himself appears. According to his ex-wife Deborah Gould, he shows up to purge the house of any evidence of contact with the Kennedys. He even finds and destroys, in the story as Gould reports it, a suicide note. Several of Lawford's later accounts of the evening feature a distress call from a slurry-voiced Marilyn telling him to "say goodbye to Jack, and say goodbye to yourself, because you're a nice guy". Two of his dinner guests have confirmed that there was some discussion about whether Lawford should go to Marilyn's and check on her. Judging by the statements of the guests, his trip to the house happened sometime after eleven p.m.

Private detectives and their operatives troop in and out. Fred Otash recalls that Lawford—unaware that he is hiring one of the men who have been bugging his home—bursts into his office around three a.m., "completely disoriented and in a state of shock . . . saying that Marilyn Monroe was dead, that Bobby Kennedy was there, and that he was spirited out of town by some airplane, that they [Marilyn and Robert Kennedy] had got in a big fight that evening, that he'd like to have . . . someone go out to the house and pick up any and all information . . . regarding any involvement between Marilyn Monroe and the Kennedys."

And all of the actors on this crowded stage play out their parts for at least five hours—and probably more—before anyone feels safe enough to call the police and tell them Marilyn Monroe is dead. No wonder Marilyn's body was already in rigor mortis—indicating she had died at least four to six hours earlier—when Sergeant Clemmons arrived and found only the two doctors and Mrs Murray on the scene.

Where is the leading man? There is no proof that Robert Kennedy was back at Marilyn's house the night she died, but there are several reports that place him at Peter Lawford's house, only minutes away. Police sources have said Kennedy was seen at the Beverly Hilton during the afternoon, was at Lawford's house that night, and broke a dinner date with Marilyn. An enterprising photographer named Billy Woodfield ran down a lead to the owner of an air charter company often used by Lawford and his guests. Woodfield says the charter man showed him logs indicating that Kennedy had been picked up by helicopter at Lawford's house around two a.m. Sunday morning, and flown to Los Angeles International. Neighbors were awakened by the sound of the helicopter. Another report, from Deborah Gould, confirms Woodfield's story. She says Lawford told her Kennedy left by helicopter during the night, going back to his accommodations near San Francisco. According to Gould, the stall in calling the police served two purposes: allowing time for incriminating evidence of the affair to be removed, and for Kennedy to make his escape from the area.

If such an elaborate—and swiftly arranged—cover-up seems unlikely, consider that what we have seen thus far are only the more visible suggestions of a remarkably thorough scheme of damage control that seems to have reached federal law enforcement agencies, the phone company, the coroner's office, and the Los Angeles Police Department.

Not long after daybreak on Sunday, two men "with Eastern accents", identified by two knowledgeable sources as FBI agents, appeared at the offices of General Telephone and purged Marilyn's phone records for the four days she lived in August. The agents obviously acted with the quickly secured cooperation of high-ranking phone company officials. Like many of the actions in the Monroe cover-up, the seizure of the records was illegal. They have never been recovered, and the FBI has denied any involvement. A Santa Monica newspaper publisher who was a close friend of a telephone company division manager has said he was told the missing records showed "a call to Washington on the night Monroe died." A police leak during the highly secret Monroe investigation indicated that a wadded piece of paper with a White House telephone number had been found among the sheets on Marilyn's bed.

At nine-thirty a.m. on Sunday morning, Marilyn's body went under the knife of the world's most famous coroner, Dr Thomas Noguchi. The results of the autopsy are as controversial as anything in the controversial case. Noguchi, then working as a medical examiner under Chief Medical Examiner of Los Angeles Dr Theodore Curphey, noted the somewhat unusual presence of the D.A.'s liaison to the coroner's office, Deputy District Attorney John Miner, at the autopsy. Though Dr Englebert had reportedly given Marilyn an injection as recently as Friday, and despite the alleged injection by Robert Kennedy's "doctor" companion on Saturday afternoon, Noguchi—after "searching painstakingly"—"found no needle marks". Miner has confirmed the thoroughness of the search. A fresh bruise was found on the lower left back and hip, which Noguchi notes "might have indicated violence".

Despite the fact that Marilyn supposedly swallowed as many as fifty Nembutal capsules and chased them with a handful of chloral hydrate, Noguchi found "absolutely no evidence of pills in the stomach or the small intestine". There was some diffuse, pinpoint hemorrhaging evident in the stomach lining, but there were no partially digested capsules, with the yellow color that gives Nembutal its street name "yellow jackets". No residue. No refractile crystals in a smear of gastric contents. Nothing.

Marilyn was a pill popper. She did not do drugs with needles. Much has been made of her surprisingly empty stomach, and some have insisted that this fact alone proves she was murdered.

If the fatal dose was not taken orally, murder by injection is one obvious possibility, and despite the absence of needle marks the door to this theory remains at least partially open. Noguchi himself has said that it is possible that "punctures made by fine surgical needles" could "heal within hours and become invisible". Other coroners concur: depending on the type of injection and the needle used, a needle mark can be extremely difficult to find.

There is another possibility, supported by more evidence: Marilyn was given the fatal dose in an enema.

Noguchi's autopsy report notes the presence of "purplish discoloration" of the colon, or large intestine. This discoloration, as John Miner—who has seen five thousand autopsies in the course of his career—puts it, "is not characteristic of a barbiturate OD death". To Miner, the discolored colon is "the most puzzling" aspect of the autopsy, as it "does indicate the possibility that the drugs, or some portion of the drugs, were introduced into the large intestine rather than being swallowed".

If the task at hand was the murder of a known pill addict, enema would certainly be a clever choice of method. Empty a few pill bottles, and a high concentration of drugs in the body would be expected. There would be no incriminating needle marks. And there would be no obvious residue remaining in the colon because the drug would have been administered in liquid form.

Aside from the forensic evidence, the death-by-enema theory is supported by a thoroughly odd remark attributed to Peter Lawford. Asked by ex-wife Deborah Gould exactly how Marilyn had died, he allegedly replied, "Marilyn took her last big enema."

Noguchi has written that the absence of pill residue in the stomach did not surprise him in the least. In the belly of a pill addict like Marilyn, he says, pills would be familiar visitors and would be rapidly "dumped" into the intestinal tract, just as familiar food is easily digested, while exotic food causes indigestion. Other reputable coroners—including those interviewed for this book—have disagreed, saying that such a massive dose of pills should leave some telltale residue behind.

The high level of barbiturates found in Marilyn's liver does suggest that drugs were taken over a period of hours, rather than in one dose, and could offer some explanation for the lack of residue in her stomach. At the same time, the liver concentration does not negate the fatal-dose-by-enema theory. No doubt Marilyn had been taking pills over a period of hours, as was her habit. A fatal dose administered into the colon on top of her self-administered oral dosages would reach the liver through "portal circulation"—entering the blood vessels directly from the large intestine—rather than through the usual digestive process.

The enema explanation and other forensic theories in the case remain theories not because of anything Dr Noguchi said or did, but because of an incredible slip-up in another part of the coroner's office.

Noguchi made the following notation at the bottom of his autopsy report:

"Unembalmed blood is taken for alcohol and barbiturate examination. Liver, kidney, *stomach and contents*, urine and *intestine* are saved for further toxicological study." [My emphasis].

Standard procedure, then and now. But in Marilyn Monroe's case, standard procedure went out the window. The blood and the liver were tested, revealing a blood level of 8.0 mg% chloral hydrate and a liver containing 13.0 mg% pentobarbital (Nembutal), "both well above fatal dosages". But the stomach and its contents, the intestine, the other organs, and tissue samples taken for microscopic analysis *somehow disappeared* and were never tested. Noguchi, who has nothing to do with this aspect of the examination, has speculated that the toxicology department may have *assumed* suicide because of the blood analysis and the empty pill bottles. If so, the assumption has fed the flames of conspiracy theories, and with good reason. A thorough analysis of the stomach, its contents, and the intestine could have shed more light on the crucial question of whether the fatal drugs entered Marilyn's body through her mouth or through some other avenue.

Elsewhere in the coroner's office toiled a deputy coroner named Lionel Grandison, who happened to be the man who signed Marilyn's death certificate, and who surfaced years later to provide one of the more bizarre sideshows in the case. Robert Slatzer stumbled across Grandison—by this time a radio engineer—while appearing on a program at a Los Angeles radio station in 1978. Slatzer was eager to talk with Grandison, and in the course of the recorded interview, Grandison made a number of startling allegations. He claimed to have seen, among Marilyn's personal possessions, the red diary Marilyn had told Slatzer about. Grandison said he skimmed the diary and saw references to the President, the Attorney General, and Fidel Castro. The diary subsequently disappeared, as did other things of Marilyn's, particularly a scribbled note Grandison assumed was a suicide note. He claimed there were numerous bruises on Marilyn's body that were not mentioned in the autopsy report. He said he had to be forced to sign the death certificate, for he did not agree with the suicide ruling. And he topped his story off with the revelation that there were necrophiliacs in and about the coroner's office who had taken liberties with Marilyn's corpse.

The necrophilia tale, together with the discovery that he had done six months on a forgery rap, damaged Grandison's credibility on more salient points. His allegations remain unproved.

If Grandison's story was manufactured, what did happen to the red diary? One of the private detectives hired by Peter Lawford to destroy evidence at Marilyn's house may have just missed it. He reported entering the house, with the help of a police contact, at around nine a.m. Sunday morning, just four and a half hours after the police were first called to the scene. His brief search revealed a filing cabinet in the garden room that had been jimmied. Marilyn apparently used the filing cabinet to hold valuable papers. She had recently had the lock on it changed. A friend of Joe DiMaggio's has said that when Joe went to the house later Sunday, he was looking for "what he referred to as a book". He didn't find it. The book and other personal papers were long gone. The implication is intriguing: Lawford's clean-up team *was not the only one at work*. Whoever rifled the filing cabinet must have done it either before the police were called, or while there were still police officers in the house.

At the coroner's office, the fine line between bad judgment and deliberate cover-up is difficult to distinguish. At the police department, the line appears to have been blatantly crossed. The Police Chief at the time was William Parker. The head of the Intelligence Division was Captain James Hamilton. Both men were friends and admirers of Robert Kennedy. Parker reportedly made the amazing statement during the investigation that he expected to be named FBI Director when Robert Kennedy became President. Robert Kennedy had alluded to Hamilton as "my friend" in the foreward to his book *The Enemy Within*, and later recommended him for the job of Chief of Security with the National Football League.

Very early on in the investigation, Chief Parker took the unprecedented step of yanking the Monroe case from Homicide and making it the exclusive domain of the Intelligence Division. Thereafter, in the words of Parker's successor Tom Riddin, nobody outside Intelligence "knew a bloody thing about what was going on". A file that ran to hundreds of pages was reportedly developed on the case, but only a few innocuous fragments from the file exist—so far as is known—today. When former Los Angeles mayor Sam Yorty asked to see the Monroe file, he was told it could not be found.

Reddin has said that the only justification possible for making the Monroe case a secret Intelligence Division operation would be "a national security problem".

No doubt the police file contained much information that could make the Marilyn Monroe case less a mystery than it is today. Like so much of the material on the John F. Kennedy assassination, it has been withheld from public view by a few individuals who have decided for the rest of us that ignorance is preferable to unpalatable truths. Again like the Kennedy assassination, the difficult business of learning the truth has been left to private citizens—to writers, researchers, and investigators—whose collective efforts have pieced together much of what is known about the case today.

One of the most visible of these citizens is a private detective with the colorful name of Milo Speriglio. Speriglio is Director and Chief of Nick Harris Detectives in Los Angeles and a public figure in his own right who has, among other things, run unsuccessfully for mayor of the city. In 1972, Speriglio accepted Robert Slatzer as a client. In so doing, he joined Slatzer's crusade to prove to the world that Marilyn was murdered, a crusade that continues to the present day.

Speriglio has written two books on the case himself, is at work on a film and a third book, and is periodically featured in splashy tabloid articles with headlines like "Marilyn Was Murdered by the Kennedys". Despite all their efforts, Speriglio and his client Slatzer have produced no conclusive proof that Marilyn was killed. They have, however, filled in a great deal of the story that would otherwise be unknown, and have provided some chilling suggestions in the process.

Perhaps the most chilling is the possibility that Marilyn's murder may have been recorded on audio tape. It is well established that clandestine recording devices were in place at her home at the time. Speriglio claims to have been contacted, in August of 1982, by an informant who, twenty years previous, had been in the employ of ace wiretapper Bernie Spindel, the man who bugged Marilyn and the Kennedys for Jimmy Hoffa. The informant provided Speriglio with technical tidbits about the bugging of Marilyn's home, including the band frequency used and the pioneering hardware Spindel brought to his assignment—bugs smaller than matchbooks with VOX, or voice-activated, capabilities that turned on the recorders only when audible sounds were present.

The informant had not actually heard the tapes himself, but

heard them described by an associate Speriglio calls Mr M, who supposedly still had, as of 1982, a copy of the tapes in his possession. According to the informant, Mr M had described what he took to be the tape of the murder, with Marilyn being "slapped around". Speriglio, who at first accepted this account and repeated it in his first book, now believes that the slapping was not the murder but an earlier event. He remains convinced that the murder tape once existed—and may still exist.

In checking out the story, Speriglio says he made contact with a newspaper reporter who in turn located Mr M. M—identified as a "well-respected" Washington attorney with offices in the Watergate complex and a former associate of Bernie Spindel's—denied having the tapes and would not admit having heard them.

Speriglio also claims to know of a phone call—likewise recorded by a bug—to Marilyn's house the night she died. The call came from San Francisco (the operator's voice is heard) and the caller asks an unknown party, "Is she dead yet?" Since the Kennedy party was in San Francisco at the time, Speriglio speculates that the caller may have been a Kennedy aide, and the call may have occurred sometime after Marilyn was put in the ambulance en route to the hospital.

These reports are hearsay, and, pending the discovery of the tapes themselves, they should be weighed accordingly. Still, there were bugs in Marilyn's house—and on her phones—the night she died. If the bugs were active, they presumably produced tapes. Where are those tapes? And if we could play them back today, what would we hear?

In addition to the copy supposedly possessed by Mr M, Speriglio believes other copies of the tapes were once held by Bernie Spindel's widow, by Jimmy Hoffa, and by the New York County District Attorney, who carried off a collection of bugging tapes during a raid of Bernie Spindel's home in 1966. Hoffa's "foster son" and associate Chuck O'Brien has confirmed that Hoffa had tapes of the Kennedys and Marilyn.

There may have been still another copy. Researchers for a 1985 BBC documentary discovered that the tapes were a potential time bomb placed dead center in Robert Kennedy's career path. In 1968, when Kennedy was the most promising Democratic candidate for President, a right-wing Republican group hired a journalist named Ralph De Toledano to find the rumored Marilyn–Kennedy tapes. According to De Toledano, an investigator was hired, who reported back that the tapes could be had—through an unnamed ex-policeman—for $50,000. The Republican group agreed to the deal on 4 June 1968, but requested "a couple of days" to raise the money. That night, as he celebrated his California primary victory at the Hotel Ambassador in Los Angeles, Robert Kennedy was fatally shot. (As a final irony, the autopsy on Robert Kennedy—which would also become a matter of controversy—was performed by Dr Thomas Noguchi.) The plan to buy the tapes was dropped. De Toledano says he is certain the tapes would have been used against Kennedy if he had lived to be nominated for the presidency.

Interviewed for this book, Speriglio says he is still "positive" Marilyn was murdered, but less sure anything will ever be done about it. The authorities are "not planning to do a damn thing . . . One of the best things they could have gotten was the tapes, if they wanted to prove what really happened, and they never made an effort." The detective claims to have given an LA District Attorney specific information on where a copy of the tapes could be found, and "he never went after it".

Speriglio's latest theory is that two men—he says he knows who they were—murdered Marilyn on orders from Chicago mob boss Sam Giancana. Giancana's private army was involved in the CIA–Mafia plots to kill Fidel Castro—the same plots we are told Marilyn had documented in her red diary and threatened to reveal in a press conference. The gangster shared with John Kennedy a sexual involvement with starlet Judith Campbell. And his organization had reportedly done Kennedy a favor—either by request or gratuitously—by suppressing information on the President's alleged involvement with another starlet, Judy Meredith, as recently as the spring of 1961. He had even bragged that his machine delivered Illinois to Kennedy in the 1960 election. Marilyn spent the last full weekend of her life, stoned and disorderly, at the Cal-Neva Lodge, a mob hangout on the Nevada border in which Giancana once had an interest. Could she have said or done something that made her a target? Could Giancana have wanted her dead because of her threat to talk about the top-secret Cuban plots?

Giancana and his henchmen were active players in the Hollywood power game. For that matter, their successors still are. If they killed Marilyn, it would not have been the first time real blood has been spilled in the land of make-believe to serve the purposes of their secret society.

The mob was a partner with the Kennedy administration in Cuba, but a bitter enemy at home, due to Robert Kennedy's unrelenting attacks on organized crime. Because of this two-edged relationship, Speriglio finds it difficult to choose between two motives in his mob-killed-Marilyn theory: "to embarrass the Kennedys . . . or as a favor to them, we've never been able to put that together".

Speriglio's theory echoes that of one of the case's original investigators. The late Frank Hronek was a Los Angeles DA's investigator in 1962. According to his family, he suspected that Sam Giancana and his associate Johnny Roselli—another link in the CIA-Cuba connection—were involved in Marilyn's death. Hronek also mentioned his suspicions of the CIA's involvement in either the death or the cover-up. Hronek's report file, like the police file, has mysteriously disappeared.

In 1982, due largely to the efforts of Slatzer, Speriglio, and others who had joined the cause, the Monroe case was reopened by the Los Angeles District Attorney's office. A great deal of new information came to light—the ambulance ride, details of the cover-up, etc.—but despite these intriguing developments the case was dropped with the conclusion that "no further criminal investigation appears required".

Many disagree. John Miner, the Deputy District Attorney who stood beside Dr Noguchi during the autopsy, has never been comfortable with the suicide ruling. This may be particularly significant, because Miner appears to have information on Marilyn that is possessed by no one else. During the original investigation, Miner conducted a four-hour interview with Dr Greenson, Marilyn's psychiatrist. Speaking with a guarantee of confidentiality, Greenson opened up to Miner, told him the reasons he did not believe Marilyn was a suicide, and played a forty-minute tape of Marilyn talking, presumably to prove his point. The tape was not a recording of a psychiatric session, but a statement Marilyn had specially recorded on her own for her psychiatrist to hear and to keep. According to Miner, Greenson (who died in 1979) later destroyed the recording.

Miner has steadfastly refused to tell anyone what the psychiatrist told him, and continued to honor his twenty-seven-year-old promise when interviewed for this book. A crucial question, of course, is whether Greenson offered any reason to believe Marilyn was murdered. Refusing direct comment, Miner points out that any information he had from Greenson was "a product of either single or . . . double hearsay . . . it's not admissible in court, it's not valid for any purpose legally". He did, he says, write a memo about the Greenson interview to the coroner and the Chief Deputy District Attorney that included a phrase he remembers as, "I believe I can say definitely that it was not suicide." After writing the memo, Miner worried that he would be called before a grand jury, and might be cited for contempt for refusing to answer questions on ethical grounds. There was no grand jury. Not surprisingly, the memo has disappeared.

Caught off guard by a phone call from a reporter, Greenson himself may have suggested some of what he revealed to Miner. The reporter had his recorder running. The resulting tape exposes an exasperated Dr Greenson saying, "I can't explain myself or defend myself without revealing things that I don't want to reveal . . . It's a terrible position to be in . . . because I can't tell the whole story." Greenson ends the conversation with a few cryptic words of advice: "Listen . . . talk to Bobby Kennedy."

No one can talk to Bobby Kennedy now. Or to Dr Greenson, Peter Lawford, Sam Giancana, Police Chief Parker, and others of the major players in the drama. All are dead. It is still a safe bet that there are people who live today with secrets that could reveal the truth in the case. And there still remains the macabre possibility that the last few moments of Marilyn's life may be recorded on a tape that may someday be played for the world to hear. The red diary—if it still exists—would be a fascinating find, but would likely prove nothing as far as the cause of death is concerned. The key to the question of whether Marilyn was murdered is in the bungled autopsy: if she swallowed a fatal dose of pills, she was probably a suicide or the victim of an accidental overdose; if she didn't swallow the fatal dose—and the evidence suggests that she did not—her death was caused by someone else. The key to the questions of how and why she was killed is on the hidden tapes and in the hidden thoughts of her killers and their silent accomplices.

In her last interview with *Life* magazine, published days before her death, Marilyn Monroe unknowingly delivered an epitaph for herself as fitting as any other: "I now live in my work." She was a brilliant performer, and she is best remembered in the images of that vast and all-forgiving screen of unreality that were her gift to the world. The story of the real Marilyn, the abandoned and vulnerable child who played with a powerful fire and was burned, is perhaps too painful and too full of disillusion to live in our memories for long.

TEMPTATION AND THE ELDER

(William Gardiner, 1902)

Jack Smith-Hughes

A genuine mystery, and a real period piece, from Edwardian rural England, with religious rectitude challenged by the fleshly temptations of a lusty country girl. The victim, Rose Harsent, was by all accounts a nymphomaniac who had set her cap at an older, married man called William Gardiner. He was a stalwart of the local Primitive Methodists whose wife was expecting their eighth child, but whether he killed Rose Harsent when he discovered that she, too, was pregnant is a moot point. The question divided and defeated not one jury but two, with the result that Gardiner was freed to spend the rest of his days in obscurity. But the writer here, Jack Smith-Hughes (1918–94), is unequivocal and makes out a strong case against the accused man. Smith-Hughes played a key role in the resistance movement on the island of Crete during the Second World War. After the war, he qualified as a barrister and worked in the Army Legal Service for much of the 1950s. During this time he also wrote several true crime collections. In 1958 he joined the Northern Circuit, but after the death of his wife in 1972, Smith-Hughes emigrated to the British Virgin Islands and eventually established his own legal firm there. He also served as chief magistrate and acting attorney-general in the town of Tortola.

'Tis here, but yet confus'd:
Knavery's plain face is never seen till us'd.

Shakespeare, *Othello*, Act ii, sc. i

The year of grace 1902 was one of those vintage years of crime. It witnessed such memorable events as the arrest of the poisonous Polish publican, George Chapman (by some regarded as the original Jack the Ripper): the trial of Kitty Byron for the murder of her stockbroking lover: the liquidation of the Darby family by Edgar Edwards: the murders on the barque *Veronica*; and the mysterious death of Rose Harsent at Peasenhall. This last case has long been a favourite of criminologists but, at least until recently, the line taken by those who have written about it—Sir Max Pemberton, H. L. Adam, Guy Logan, and Elizabeth Villiers to name only four—has been that the suspect was a monstrously wronged man, and many have followed Sir Max's lead in suggesting that the village belle died by misadventure and that there was never a murder at all. In 1934, however, William Henderson edited, in the *Notable British Trials* series, a comprehensive account of the mystery and refused to be bamboozled by the fact that the suspect was outwardly a deeply religious man of a puritanical disposition.

As a race, we English instinctively distrust Puritans: we doubt if Cromwell's army was all that model, and we know that the Puritans suppressed bear-baiting not because it was cruel to the bear but because some people enjoyed it. The attitude of their Victorian descendants was admirably satirized for our fathers in the song, "Of course you can never be like us, but be as like us as you're able to be." We jealously guard our right to smoke, drink, dance, and be merry when we want and not when the godly want. And although we do not, if we are honest with ourselves, suspect them all of hypocrisy, we derive a modicum of pleasure from the spectacle of one of them being found out: nor are we surprised that they should be so found out from time to time.

Only very recently we have witnessed the downfall of an Australian teetotal politician who had earned the style of "Lemonade" Ley from his devotion, even at public banquets, to that worthy if unsatisfying beverage: we know now that he kept a mistress, that he promoted shady companies, that he was a brazen liar, and that he organized at least one murder. An earlier generation recalls Norman Thorne, that refulgent member of the Alliance of Honour (which eschewed the anticipation of connubial bliss by the affianced) who not only maintained two mistresses at the same time, but actually buried the dismembered remains of one of them under his chicken-run. Again, at least three of our medical poisoners were outwardly good churchmen: Palmer of Rugeley was a regular communicant: Pritchard of Glasgow and Cross of Shandy Hall both kept diaries in the most sanctimonious terms: yet all three expedited the demise of their wives. The type however reaches its apogee in Scotland and my readers who wish to study the Caledonian hypocrite are referred to the sparkling pages of William Roughead. For me, the most fascinating of his collection is "Holy Willie" Bennison, poisoner, bigamist, and a lay preacher on behalf of the Primitive Methodists in the city of Edinburgh.*

And now to meet another Primitive Methodist elder, Mr William Gardiner of Peasenhall, a charming Suffolk village. The place of his birth does not seem to be recorded, but the event took place in about 1867: he married a girl from Yoxford, Georgina Cady, in October 1888 and settled in Peasenhall (which is some three miles from his wife's village) about a year or two later. The union was blessed with no less than eight children, of whom six were living at the time of their father's tribulations. For many years he had worked for a local firm of agricultural implement makers, with whom he had risen to the position of foreman carpenter: he was held in high esteem by his employers but, even though he was sufficiently well thought of to represent them at the Paris exhibition, he was paid no more than twenty-seven shillings a week. There is no doubt that he was industrious but, in his little community, he is said to have been respected rather than liked. However, since he was, after all, a foreman, this is not exactly surprising. He is described as "a dark, swarthy-complexioned man of heavy build" by Mr Henderson, and by Sir Max Pemberton as of almost Spanish appearance. He also affected a jet-black beard. Nature had clearly equipped him suitably for a Calvinistic role and this he played superbly in the Primitive Methodist community at Sibton, an adjoining hamlet, where he fulfilled the functions of superintendent, treasurer, and trustee of the Sunday school, assistant society steward, and choirmaster. It was his association with the choir which proved his ultimate downfall, for amongst the choristers was a girl named Rose Anne Harsent whom he had seen grow from an attractive child to a desirable woman.

* See his *Rogues Walk Here*, pp. 259–85 (Cassell, 1934).

Rose was on friendly terms with his wife and, had he desired an amorous dalliance, there were none of the usual difficulties in his path. Nor was the girl likely to demur.

In the year that Queen Victoria died, Rose was twenty-two, and Gardiner was twelve years her senior. She was the daughter of a carter employed at the Drill Works of which Gardiner was the foreman. She was herself employed as a domestic servant by the local Baptist elder, Deacon Crisp, in whose establishment she had replaced a girl who had been dismissed some three years previously in a condition alike embarrassing to herself and interesting to everyone else. The Crisp residence, known as Providence House, was unfortunately suited to the immoral desires of its handmaidens, whose room was immediately over the kitchen and access to it was by a separate stairway: the Crisps were old, and the Deacon somewhat deaf. Mr Henderson makes no attempt to court East Anglican susceptibilities and says of Rose, "living as she did in a part of England not notably celebrated for a particularly high standard of moral purity, she was probably a fair specimen of the girlhood of her district". As he had, only a sentence or so earlier, put on record that the attentions of this girl's admirers "had not been altogether free from certain gross accompaniments" and that "the cruder side of her amorous adventures was not entirely distasteful to her", the Suffolk grandmother of today may well feel aggrieved. It would have been more courteous to have compared her with Alexandrine Vernet, that dangerous schoolmistress of Nohèdes who was, H. B. Irving tells us, "twenty-two years of age and comely after a bold and alluring fashion, perpetrated atrocious efforts at poetry, and had a pronounced taste for dirty literature".

Rose did not, in fact, write poetry, but she made up for this deficiency by preferring her dirty literature to be rhymed. She had been sufficiently intrigued by the pornographic ditties sung by the younger villagers of an evening to request the youth who lived next door to supply her with written copies of these edifying verses; for a maiden of half a century ago, she was singularly advanced, and her contemporaries must have shuddered at her depravity. She was also not unacquainted with certain of the franker passages of holy writ to be found in *Genesis* and *Proverbs*. In short, Rose Harsent enjoyed her role of village belle and was a most unsuitable companion for a susceptible young elder whose wife's frequent confinements entailed for him the occasional period of sexual abstinence. For William Gardiner was clearly a full-blooded male and it may be that his visit to Paris had not been without resulting effect on his character.

On 1 May 1901, Mrs Gardiner was once again in the last stages of pregnancy and on that evening Rose was seen to enter a little thatched building known as the Doctor's Chapel:* this was the place of worship of old Crisp, and one of her domestic duties was to sweep it out: it stands a little way back from the main road, is immediately opposite the Drill Works (where Gardiner was employed), and is only a minute's walk from Providence House. Rose was observed by two inseparable young men who were also employed at the works. One of them, George Wright (known in the village as "Bill"), was twenty years of age and came directly under Gardiner: the other, Alphonso Skinner (known as "Fonzo"), was somewhat older and worked under another foreman. They were intrigued to see Gardiner follow the girl in and both subsequently admitted that they crept up outside the chapel in the hope of hearing something indecent, from which one can only infer that rumour had already linked the names of the choirmaster and the chorister. Certainly, if they were to be believed, their eavesdropping was amply rewarded: nor can their tale have been wholly fabricated since, though he strenuously denied the dialogue, Gardiner admitted being in the chapel with the girl.

The conversation they overheard was significant: Rose was heard to exclaim "Oh! Oh!" and her exclamations were followed by a rustling sound and by merry feminine laughter. Wright then lost his nerve and slunk away but the more mature Skinner was determined to hear more. Rose, so he said, then asked Gardiner if he had noticed her reading her Bible on the previous Sunday: the elder asked her what she was reading about and she replied, "I was reading about like what we have been doing here to-night. I'll tell you where it is. Thirty-eighth chapter of Genesis", with which she mentioned the particular verse to which she referred. Now this chapter is devoted to the remarkable adventures of the widow Tamar at the hands of Onan her brother-in-law and Judah her father-in-law. Even in the verbatim account of the trial the actual verse is not specified, but whichever one it was we cannot

---

* So called because it was built on the land of Dr Lay: his son succeeded him as village doctor and gave evidence at the trial. The chapel was subsequently disused for religious purposes and was used as a schoolroom for the doctor's children.

but agree with Sir Max that the passage was so compromising to her virtue that, assuming the incident to be true, the nature of their relations was left in no doubt.

Bill and Fonzo were not pleasant young men: not content with spying, they proceeded to spread the scandal around Peasenhall. Some, no doubt, rejoiced that the sanctimonious foreman was not, after all, above the selfish lusts of the flesh: others were horrified that a young woman could quote scripture to such purpose. At the risk of irrelevance, I note that times have changed and that Alexander Woollcott has placed on record that a well-known American critic has named a favourite canary after Tamar's brother-in-law. Within a short while, the rumour reached the ears of Gardiner himself and, on 8 May, he sent for both youths at the works and demanded a written apology. They refused and insisted that they had only told the truth: Gardiner was later to say that they gave as the reason for their refusal that if they withdrew their allegations they would have been hooted in the village, but even if this was said it is not an admission of lying.

The reason why an abject written confession of lying was required was because Gardiner wanted something to lay before his brother elders at the forthcoming investigation at Sibton into his conduct. It is not clear who was responsible for initiating this inquiry: Gardiner claimed that it was held at his request but it appears that the person who in fact wrote to the circuit superintendent, the Rev. John Guy, was a septuagenarian lay preacher named Rouse. As Rouse claimed to have supported Gardiner on this occasion (although he certainly did not do so later) it may be that he wrote his letter at the instigation of his traduced colleague. Accordingly on 11 May, a score of senior Primitive Methodists forgathered at Sibton under the presidency of Mr Guy. They heard the evidence of Skinner. They heard the evidence of Wright. They heard the denials of Gardiner. They did not bother to hear Rose at all, presumably because they did not feel it right to put that sort of question to a young girl. Guy decided that the case had not been made out: he may have told some members of the sect that Skinner's tale was a fabrication from beginning to end but his considered judgment seems to have been that, in such a case, it was safer to rely on the word of one member of the sect than on that of two strangers who worshipped in the Church of England. It is obvious that the main purpose of the investigation was to smother the scandal, if it were possible, and if the facts did not prove too blatant to ignore.

Gardiner resigned all his offices but was solemnly re-elected to them all. Guy had a word in private with Rose who assured him that she had never been guilty of any impropriety with the choirmaster: he also warned Gardiner against being too friendly with the female choristers, while Gardiner conceded that in the past he had been indiscreet. In short, the case was, in Scots usage, not proven which, we are told, means "not guilty, but don't do it again".

The acquittal was certainly not as honourable as Gardiner himself would have liked and we must now consider three letters that he either wrote or had written. The first two, from internal evidence, seem to have been written between 8 May and 11 May, and were sent to Rose: they were later found among her possessions—the little minx proving too sly to destroy them—and it was then suggested that they were carefully composed epistles whose purpose was to warn the recipient what policy to adopt. One ran:

Dear Rose,
 I was very much surprised this morning to hear that there's some scandal going the round about you and me going into the Doctor's Chapel for immoral Purposes so that I shall put it into other hands at once as I have found out who it was that started it. Bill Wright and Skinner say they saw us there but I shall summons them for defamation of character unless they withdraw what they have said and give me a written apology. I shall see Bob* tonight and we will come and see you together if possible. I shall at the same time see your father and tell him.
Yours &c. WILLIAM GARDINER

Presumably it was not practicable, or deemed impolitic, to arrange the meeting, since a second letter followed in which Gardiner as good as said that, while he had no doubt of his own ability to bluff and brazen his way out of the predicament, he did not entertain such sanguine hopes about her capacities in such a direction, indeed he had reluctantly come to the conclusion that she would give the show away. To quote him:

* It does not appear who Bob was and no witness at the trial possessed this Christian name. It appears from my own inquiries, half a century later, that he was *not* one of Rose's five brothers.

Dear Rose,

   I have broke the news to Mrs Gardiner this morning, she is awfully upset but she say she know it is wrong for I was at home from ½ past 9 o'clock *so I could not possibly be with you an hour* so she wont believe anything about it. I have asked Mr Burgess to ask those too [*sic*] Chaps to come to Chapel to-night and have it out there however they stand by such a tale I don't know but I dont think God will forsake me now and if we put our trust in Him it will end right but its awfully hard work to have to face people when they are all suspicious of you but by God's help whether they believe me or not I shall try to live it down and prove by my future conduct that its all false, I only wish I could take it to Court but I dont see a shadow of a chance to get the case as *I dont think you would be strong enough to face a trial.* Trusting that God will direct us and make the way clear, I remains

Yours in trouble, W. Gardiner

This strikes a much less confident note than the earlier letter. It is curious that Gardiner's wife should be ready to supply him with some sort of alibi, but he was able to point out to her that Wright had been caught spying on her own brother some years earlier when her brother was courting in Wright's mother's orchard: perhaps it was a telling debating point. The meeting in the Doctor's Chapel was to be admitted, but its duration was to be cut down, in order that an innocent explanation might be more readily accepted.

   But whatever he may have felt of Rose's shortcomings as a witness, it is known that Gardiner did consult a solicitor. The man of law certainly told him that, against penniless youths, he would not recover his costs and may have told him that to allege unchastity *against a man* was actionable as slander only in rare cases, e.g., against a beneficed clergyman, and that Gardiner's unpaid offices hardly brought him within the exceptions. However, the solicitor did write to Wright and Skinner on 15 May to threaten legal proceedings unless they apologized in writing within seven days: the bluff failed. There was no apology from either, nor was a writ ever issued. The matter was officially dropped and might, in time have been completely forgotten. What is uncertain is whether the association between Gardiner and Rose now ceased.

   It cannot have ended completely, as they must have met at choir practices during the week and at the Sunday services. It is, however, worthy of record that only one person subsequently alleged anything untoward between them, and that person was that bumbling busybody Henry Rouse who had been so largely responsible for the solemn *Vehmgericht* of the Sibton elders. Nine months after the original scandal, Rouse said he saw Gardiner and Rose walking down a lane at nine o'clock at night: he bade them good night but neither vouchsafed a reply. Nine days after that, he called Gardiner aside after a Wednesday prayer meeting and berated him for continuing an association which could only "do the chapel a great deal of harm". If Rouse is to be believed (and Gardiner denied the conversation in its entirety) Gardiner expressed the hope that his wife would not be informed and, upon receipt of this assurance, undertook to refrain thenceforth from such nocturnal peripatetics.

A second incident, also denied by Gardiner, is said to have occurred a month or so later. Though improbable and seemingly senseless, there is contemporaneous evidence that, whether or not it was true, there was certainly a complaint about it. The redoubtable Rouse chanced to glance behind himself while ranting from the pulpit and was horrified to see Gardiner with his feet up on Rose's lap. "You gentlemen," said Rouse in the witness-box, "know what I mean by the lap of a person. I ceased to speak, with the intention of telling one of them to walk out of the chapel but something seemed to speak to me not to expose them there." In the end Rouse did not speak to his colleague at all: instead, on April 14th, he dictated to his wife what was to be an anonymous letter to Gardiner, correctly assuming that her writing would not be recognized. Gardiner kept this letter and it was read at the trial:

Mr Gardiner,
    I write to warn you of your conduct with that girl Rose, as I find when she come into the chapel she must place herself next to you, which keep the people's minds still in the belief that you are a guilty man, and in that case you will drive many from the chapel, and those that will join the cause are kept away through it. We are told to shun the least appearance of evil. I do not wish you to leave God's house, but there must be a difference before God's cause can prosper, which I hope you will see to be right as people cannot hear when the enemy of souls bring this before them. I write to you as one that love your soul, and I hope you will *have her sit in*

some other place and remove such feeling which for sake she will do [*sic*].

It is thus clear enough that Gardiner, in spite of the scandal, was not averse to sitting beside the girl in the choir. Such conduct was incautious, to say the least, and the more unfortunate when it is realized that, at about the end of the previous November, Rose had had intercourse with some man that had resulted in pregnancy. She seems to have kept her condition secret as long as she could, but her situation was not one that permitted indefinite concealment. She borrowed a book on abortion from the obliging youth next door who had previously supplied her literary desiderata, but her pregnancy continued uninterrupted. About the middle of May, she was taxed with her condition by her mistress, Mrs Crisp: she denied it, but obviously the time was coming when she would have to follow her domestic predecessor into retirement. In such circumstances, she could do only one thing, to seek assistance from the man, whoever he was, who was responsible for her impending motherhood. In view of her secrecy in the matter, one assumes that this man was unable to marry her because he already had a wife: an unmarried man would have been jostled to the altar by the mere weight of local opinion. And so, at the end of May, there was a married man in Peasenhall, on the verge of exposure and, if he held any position of respect, of shattering disgrace.

At twenty past eight on the morning of 1 June, Rose's father called at Providence House to bring his daughter her laundry. It was a Sunday and the previous night had been marked by a heavy thunderstorm. Old Harsent was surprised to find the back door open: he went into the kitchen, to find his daughter dead on the floor. Her body was in a pitiful condition, turned towards the wall of a room only ten feet six by eight feet six inch with its head towards the staircase. Rose had been wearing stockings and a nightdress but some paraffin had been spilt and an attempt made to burn the body which had consumed most of the nightdress while merely charring her arms and lower part of the body. The fire was not the cause of death, as there was a wound in the chest which a medical expert later said had been made with an upward thrust: her throat had been cut twice, practically from ear to ear and with such force as to sever the windpipe. Some blood had spurted towards the staircase, and there was a large pool of blood between her head and the wall. There were no footmarks in the blood, and therefore no reason to assume that the murderer had been stained. Although it should have been obvious that the unhappy girl had been suddenly struck down by the blow to the chest, turned over to the wall so that the blood would spurt away, and then despatched with no more ceremony than a sheep or goat, such was not the original police theory.

Harsent covered his daughter's body with a rug but otherwise moved nothing except the metal top portion of a broken lamp that was lying beside her. As he was doing so, Crisp's brother came to the door followed by other villagers, for bad news never takes long to circulate. Someone sent for the village constable and this worthy, Eli Nunn, arrived at twenty minutes to nine. The briefest of conversations with the Crisps, the most cursory examination of the almost naked body, must have told him that Rose was well advanced in pregnancy. But, in the absence of bloody footprints, Nunn decided that this was a case of suicide. The local police have been rightly ridiculed for holding such an opinion, even momentarily, but it is quite wrong to suggest, as has been so often done, that the delay enabled the murderer to destroy incriminating evidence. Nunn did not know of the crime until just before nine o'clock and we shall see what Gardiner had been doing as early as eight o'clock that morning.

In any event, it is doubtful if the suicide theory was held for long. By the body was another source of paraffin in addition to the broken lamp, a smashed bottle that had recently held paraffin but which had once held medicine: nor was there any doubt as to its ownership as it still bore the label *For Mrs Gardiner's chdn*. There was also a charred piece of newspaper, with which the fire had been started: it came from a 30 May copy of the *East Anglian Daily Times*, a paper not taken by the Crisps although delivered daily to Gardiner at the works, curiously enough by Rose's fourteen-year-old brother. A search of her bedroom proved more interesting still, revealing as it did not only Gardiner's two letters about the torrid interchange in the Doctor's Chapel but also a third note in what looked remarkably like the same handwriting. With it was an envelope, postmarked 31 May: the letter was an assignation for midnight on the night of the murder and was couched in the following terms:

D R,
    I will try to see you tonight at 12 oclock at your Place if you Put a light in your window at 10 oclock for about 10

minutes then you can take it out again. dont have a light in
your Room at 12 as I will come round to the back.

It was not signed, so it is evident that the writer knew that his
hand would be recognized. It was equally clear that the writer
lived in Peasenhall if he was able to see the warning signal. It
was unfortunate for Gardiner that the similarity of writing was
immediately detected and also that his home should be only 208
yards away from Providence House with a clear view of Rose's
bedroom from his front doorstep: he also not infrequently returned
home at about ten o'clock and his route from the works passed
Providence House. From the outset he was the obvious suspect,
and such he has remained.

Since Gardiner had left his home at nine o'clock to take his
children to Sunday school, it was some time before he was told
of the violent death of his favourite chorister. He was told at eleven
o'clock and evinced no surprise whatsoever: as he had known her
since childhood and had been meeting her twice a week at least
for choral reasons at Sibton chapel, it was felt that he should have
been more shocked than he appeared to be. And it is hard to believe
that a bearded elder would fail to expatiate on such a death unless
he was singularly preoccupied.

The case was handed over to Superintendent Staunton who, on
the Monday morning,* called on Gardiner at the Drill Works and
taxed him with writing the letter of assignation: Gardiner denied it,
but conceded that the writing was remarkably like his own. During
the lunch interval, Gardiner left the works and did not thereafter
return: in modern parlance, he was assisting the police with their
inquiries. Meanwhile a significant additional piece of information
had come to light: Burgess, a bricklayer, remembered chatting with
Gardiner outside his house for a quarter of an hour at about ten
o'clock on the night of the murder, and also recalled noticing a
light at the top of Providence House when he walked away. The
inference that Gardiner was watching for the signal was almost
irresistible. On the Tuesday evening, after the coroner had opened
his investigation, William George Gardiner found himself taken
into custody and formally charged with murder: for the purposes of
completeness, it should be recorded that he denied the charge.

---

* Evidence of James Rickards: this clearly refutes any suggestion of serious
delay on the part of the police.

Subsequent to his arrest, further evidence came to light to suggest that no mistake had been made. A gamekeeper named James Morriss, whose detective instincts were acutely developed, said that he had been walking along Peasenhall's main street at five o'clock in the morning and had seen a single set of footprints in the mud left by the rain leading from Gardiner's house to Providence House and back again. Being aware of the Harsent scandal—his superior gamekeeper's brother was Wright's landlord—he was interested and mentioned the matter to his superior when he met him, about two and a half hours *before* the murder was even discovered: at half-past eleven, he heard of the murder and realized its importance. Before the coroner he stated that he would be able to describe the sole marks and, since he was a gamekeeper, his evidence should have been reliable: a juror drew a blank sole on a piece of paper and passed it to Morriss, who proceeded to draw two parallel bars across it. The evidence was not particularly helpful to the police at this stage: they had collected all of Gardiner's known clothing from his wife in the hope of finding something incriminating but they had found no such shoes. But, on June 6th, a policeman called on Mrs Gardiner to ask if she had any india-rubber-soled shoes: she then produced a pair that she said had been given her by her brother when up in London during the week previous to the murder. *The markings coincided with Morriss's drawing.*

But what the police proved incapable of discovering was the time at which Rose had been killed. The doctor judged, from the state of *rigor mortis*, that she had died between half-past twelve and half-past six, with the probabilities in favour of half-past four. The police preferred to link the crime with the time given in the assignation, i.e., midnight. The Crisps admitted to having been awakened by the storm, whereupon Mrs Crisp had come downstairs to make sure the rain was not coming in: they were later re-awakened by a scream and a thud which the Deacon refused to permit his consort to investigate, pointing out that Rose had been told that, if ever she was nervous, she could come to their bedroom. Mrs Crisp told the coroner on 3 June, and again on 16 June, that the scream had occurred between one and two o'clock, but it later transpired that she had not looked at a clock in making this guess. All that can be said for certain about the time factor is this: the girl expected a caller at midnight, by which time a storm was raging and continued to rage for at least an hour and a half longer. The rain had ceased by four o'clock. We know that Rose expected him to come, as her bed had not been slept in: presumably she did not wish to fall asleep as she had to let him in when he arrived. She would not have expected him until the storm had died down: the nature of the visit was presumably intended, at least by her, to discuss her future, now that her mistress's suspicions were aroused, rather than for further trysting.

On other aspects of the case, the police had some tenuous technical evidence available. A handwriting expert's conclusions were damning to Gardiner. And, although no blood-stains were to be found on any of his clothes, a penknife of his which, in the view of a medical expert, could have inflicted the fatal injuries, proved to have been newly sharpened and had been scraped inside, but even so there was some blood inside the hinge. Gardiner explained this by saying that he had been hulking (vernacular for disembowelling) a rabbit and since the expert was able to say no more than that the blood was not more than a month old and mammalian, his explanation was not wholly unsatisfactory.* There was also a small piece of woollen material found by Rose's body which, it was assumed, might have been torn off in the fatal scuffle, but hopes of matching it with the arrested man's clothing had failed. On the other hand, the envelope containing the assignation note proved to be identical with those used at Gardiner's place of employment. Though not an especially strong chain of circumstantial evidence, it was thought sufficient to justify sending him for trial. It is worth noting that, at this stage of the case, that over-observant elder, Henry Rouse, had not given evidence, either before the coroner or before the bench, and that there was no evidence of any association between the accused and his alleged victim during the year that followed the episode in the Doctor's Chapel.

Since the strength of the prosecution's case would lie in Gardiner's motive, it had become essential to show that Wright and Skinner were witnesses of truth. And so, on 28 July, Constable Nunn went to the chapel with Burgess and the two youths and re-enacted the amatory vignette that they claimed to have overheard: acoustically speaking, it was not impossible. And shortly before the opening

---

* But I am told that it is not the practice in Peasenhall to eat rabbit except between the months of October and February since their meat, when they are "struck", produces intestinal disorders. At the trials Gardiner agreed that the rabbit was inedible and had to be buried.

of the Ipswich Assizes, the police became aware of an important witness who had not so far seen fit to reveal himself. This person was Herbert Stammers and his house overlooked the yard at the back of Gardiner's home: he claimed that, at half-past seven on the Sunday morning, over an hour before the murder had been discovered, Gardiner had gone to the wash-house and lit a large fire. The inference was that he had been burning incriminating clothing, since it was not the practice to light fires of that size on a Sunday morning: I should add that, oddly enough, Gardiner claimed to be in possession of only two shirts at the time of the crime.

Gardiner's trial took place on 6, 7, 9 and 10 November 1902: the intervening day was a Sunday and the jury protested at the proposal to keep them cooped up in Ipswich, pointing out that it would be more pleasant to spend the weekend at Felixstowe, even though out of the season; the judge arranged for them to spend the day at the seaside under supervision, but they had to return to Ipswich for the night. The judge was Mr Justice Grantham, a popular foxhunting squire but an indifferent lawyer and all too liable to make up his mind at an early stage of the proceedings that he was called upon to try: as he was not particularly adept in concealing his prejudices, he was not the most suitable judge for a case where the balance of evidence was so evenly poised. The prosecution was in the hands of Mr H. F. (later Sir Henry) Dickens, a son of the novelist and a conspicuously fair man: the defence was led by Mr E. E. (later Sir Ernest) Wild who established his reputation by his conduct of the case. Both were to end their days as contemporary Old Bailey judges, the one as Common Serjeant and the other as Recorder. That Wild's efforts on behalf of his client were magnificent cannot be gainsaid, but he showed unwarranted irascibility with witnesses, with Dickens (even descending to personalities), and, in the subsequent trial, with the judge: he drew inferences against witnesses that lacked justification: with greater justification he muddled the jury with several choice red herrings.

As the first trial proved abortive, we need not be much concerned with it, save to note certain differences between it and the repeat performance some ten or eleven weeks later. Rouse was not subjected to much cross-examination and Mrs Gardiner suggested that he was lying because he was jealous of her husband's superior position in the chapel hierarchy. There was an unfortunate misunderstanding with the judge when Skinner was telling of his interview with Gardiner: it appears that the accused man told Skinner that the tale was "made up out of old stuff" which Grantham took to mean that there had been previous talk of the association, although Dickens conceded that the phrase, in the vernacular, meant no more than rubbish, without reference to its age. Wild also elicited from the police superintendent that a newspaper reporter had been present at the post-mortem: as this produced an indignant outburst from the judge, Wild took the opportunity to comment on the prejudice shown against Gardiner in the local press, although it elsewhere appears that the *East Anglian Daily Times* had largely contributed to the defence funds.

The first suggestion made by the defence was that Rose's neighbour and purveyor of pornography was at least as good a suspect as Gardiner himself: a certain amount of prejudice had already been imported into this side of the case by having this meretricious literature read to the jurors in private rather than have it recited in open court. The writer, Frederick James Davis, admitted to knowing Rose, though he denied ever having intercourse with her or even going out with her. As a grocer's assistant, it was his duty to call at her kitchen several times a week and it was at her request that he had supplied her with sundry salacious ballads and selected excerpts of Holy Writ. He had also written her a torrid love-letter, but he again denied being her lover. He had begun this course of conduct in September 1901 and on a date not later than December of that year (at which time she will have been one month pregnant) he had supplied her with a book which discussed abortion: she had asked him for it and he had supplied her with it in the hope, vainly, that she would yield to his amatory overtures. The book also mentioned a remedy for sore feet, from which he suffered: after Davis had agreed that he owned a pair of indiarubber-soled shoes, Dickens interrupted to say that he would call Davis's father to give the unhappy youth an alibi for the whole of the evening. Wild explained that this was not necessary, as all that the defence alleged against Davis was that he was responsible for her condition. After the judge had told him that his "abominable conduct" was a disgrace to humanity, the witness withdrew.

Opening for the defence, Wild once more complained of local prejudice and said that Gardiner had been portrayed in a waxwork exhibition in the very act of killing the girl. The allegations of immorality against the accused remained unproved and Gardiner had therefore no motive to kill her. Nor did the time factor help the prosecution as it had been suggested that the murder had taken place at about half-past one, although at that time Gardiner and his wife were with a friend who was terrified of thunder: Mrs Gardiner could say that she had gone to bed with her husband at two o'clock and that he had not left their bedroom until eight o'clock the next morning. He would also call evidence that the footprints seen by Morriss, if indeed they had ever existed, were certainly not in evidence at four o'clock that morning and, in those circumstances, can hardly have been made by Gardiner. The label on the bottle had led the police astray: the real assassin possessed a suit of clothes like the fragment of cloth that had been found, but Gardiner possessed no such suit.*

Although prisoners had been allowed to give evidence on their own behalf for only three or so years, there had already grown up a practice that such evidence should be given *before* the other defence witnesses, if only, as far as possible, to make fabrication of evidence more difficult. But Wild seems to have been allowed, without objection, to call Gardiner last. His first witness was Mrs Gardiner, who claimed to have been unable to sleep that night until five o'clock owing to aches and pains that she attributed to the thunder: she remembered remarking to her husband, at about twenty past two, that it was beginning to get light: in cross-examination she conceded that her husband had not told her of the scandal until the morning of the Sibton inquiry.†

Amelia Pepper said that she lived next door to the Gardiners and, owing to the thinness of the partition, was able to hear everything that went on in their house. She had herself gone to bed at one o'clock and had heard her neighbours retire at two o'clock: at twenty past two she had come downstairs and had remained there until a quarter past four, apparently because she was worried by the storm. She had stayed in the front room and had from time to time opened the front door to see if the storm had stopped: at no time did she notice any footsteps or hear anyone leave the Gardiners' home, although

---

* But, according to local tradition, Gardiner had a "pepper-and-salt" suit that was committed to the flames, together with his third shirt. Unfortunately Mr Stammers, who rejoiced in the local style of "Old Hardeye", could not see what was burned that morning.

† This seems to be corroborated by Gardiner's second letter to Rose.

she did hear somebody moving about and understood it to have been Mrs Gardiner (who admitted getting up to look at one of the children). Amelia Pepper's tale was an odd one but, if believed, it provided an alibi for Gardiner after two o'clock: the lady must be distinguished from Rosanna Dickenson, the brontophobe with whom the Gardiners claimed to be until two o'clock.

Martha Walker was called to corroborate Mrs Gardiner's explanation of the broken bottle, which was that she had filled it with camphorated oil and given it to Rose about Eastertime for a cold. Mrs Walker was a regular attendant at the Sibton chapel and had known the Gardiners for some twelve years: her daughter was a member of the Sibton choir. She was able to remember Rose telling her that she had cured a cold with camphorated oil given her by Mrs Gardiner: this conversation was not strictly admissible in evidence, but the prosecution generously did not object to it.

Gardiner then gave his evidence. It was mostly a string of denials of each separate incriminating fact. To account for the blood on his knife, he told the rabbit story and swore that he had not cleaned the knife since 31 May. To account for being seen outside his house at ten o'clock, he said that he was watching the storm coming up. In view of the nature of his evidence, it is not surprising that he was unshaken by cross-examination.

Wild then sought to show that the Rev. Mr Guy had described the evidence of Wright and Skinner as a fabrication and for this purpose proposed to call an elder named Abraham Goddard. The judge doubted if this was admissible, Wild referred to Lord Denman's Act, and the judge then said that it might be wiser to admit the evidence even if, strictly, it was inadmissible. Goddard then quoted Guy as having called the youths' tale a fabrication, but it emerged in cross-examination that the superintendent had also said that it was a case of two for and two against and that he preferred those within the chapel to those without.

Of the other witnesses who contradicted Nunn's audition tests and Gurrin's handwriting evidence, little need be said: they made a poor showing and Wild, in his final address, obviously realized their shortcomings. He explained that Gurrin was a professional witness: the defence witnesses were not and were therefore at the mercy of a skilled cross-examiner like Mr Dickens. On the other hand, both Gardiner and his wife had stood up to this last test and emerged unscathed. He also made the amazing suggestion that the footprints seen by Morriss may have been a blind to draw suspicion in the direction of Gardiner, which hardly seems a fruitful line of argument. Dickens replied, expressing the hope that he had discharged with consideration his distasteful duty of cross-examining the prisoner and his wife: in the prosecution view, the murderer had to fulfil certain conditions and Gardiner was alone in fulfilling them all. I deal so cavalierly with counsels' arguments as we shall be meeting them on a second occasion.

On the other hand, Mr Justice Grantham was to have only one occasion to address his mind to the Peasenhall problem. His summing up was strongly adverse to the prisoner, but not unwarrantably so: it certainly did not justify all the bitter strictures that have been passed upon it by posterity. He began, as seems to have been his custom,* by saying that the case was a remarkable one and that he could not remember one in which the issues were so difficult. The jury did not have to decide the truth of the scandal in the chapel, nor could they place any reliance on the verdict of the Sibton elders in view of their obvious preference for the version given by their colleague: the important fact was that, as a result of the affair, Guy had felt it incumbent on himself to caution Gardiner about his attitude to the charming chorister. There was no evidence that Davis was aware of the girl's pregnancy and no reason to suspect him of the murder. Crimes of this class were as a rule committed by the last person one would suspect, and therefore the prisoner's good character did not affect the matter much. The murder was deliberately planned, and Gardiner's conduct, both in the six months preceding the crime and upon hearing of it, struck his lordship as suspicious: it was odd that he should have displayed no emotion on hearing of her death. The evidence of Morriss was most important: no bloodstains were found, but then the jury was well aware of the ease with which indiarubber soles could be washed: the judge did not appear to realize that it was never suggested that

* I find that his lordship told the jury that tried Chapman in March 1903, "This case is unique, not only from a medical point of view or a chemical point of view, but also unique from a legal and criminal point of view." When trying Robert Wood of Camden Town in December 1907 he told the jury "You have been engaged in one of the most remarkable trials that is to be found in the annals of the Criminal Courts of England for many years—certainly the most remarkable in my time, which has not been a short one." Such words certainly flattered the vanity of the jury and, it may be, the vanity of the man who uttered them.

the murderer stepped in the blood at all. It did not matter that Mrs
Crisp had originally timed the scream between one and two o'clock
but could no longer be sure: in such circumstances, it was hard
for anyone to be sure. The presence of the charred paper was not
important, since the newspaper concerned had a wide circulation: of
far greater importance was the little bottle with Gardiner's name on
it, and the jury might think it improbable that the girl would herself
have filled it with paraffin. The similarity of the envelopes was not
important since they were of a common type. The evidence as to
the similarity of handwriting given by Gurrin was highly significant
and the contradiction of his evidence by the defence witnesses was
"lamentably deficient". In short, Mr Justice Grantham ran true
to form.

The jury retired at a quarter past four and returned at half-past
six to ask the judge what was the inference to be drawn from the
absence of blood on the accused's clothing. Grantham properly
advised them that it was a point in his favour, although it was not
and could not of itself be conclusive of his guiltlessness. The jury
again retired until twenty minutes to nine when they announced
their inability to reach a verdict. It was soon evident that eleven
were for conviction when the dissentient was asked by the judge if
further time might make him change his opinion. "I have not made
up my mind not to agree," was the reply, "if I was convinced that
the prisoner was guilty, but I have heard nothing to convince me
that he is guilty." There was a swiftly suppressed burst of applause,
and the jury was discharged. It was subsequently suggested that
the juror was not a believer in capital punishment, but a careful
analysis of his remark suggests rather that he was not a believer
in circumstantial evidence.

And so Gardiner had to be tried again. Both prosecution and
defence had shown their hand and both were aware of what they
had to meet. The English practice, in the ordinary way, results in
the prosecution putting all its cards on the table, while the defence
need disclose nothing until there is no time to refute its story.
Gardiner's advisers were therefore somewhat at a disadvantage,
but they used the opportunity to bring forward some fresh evidence
and in particular to unearth certain derogatory incidents from the
past of that hoary old pry Henry Rouse. For a while there was a
suggestion of entrusting the defence to Sir Charles Gill but this
was felt to be unfair to Wild and most amply did he justify the
trust reposed in him. The same counsel accordingly crossed swords

again at Ipswich on 21 January 1903, for another four-day trial of
the old issue.

The judge, on this second occasion, was Mr Justice Lawrance. His
Chancery background had not fully prepared him for the hurlyburly
of the criminal courts but he had by now experienced twelve years in
the King's Bench Division and his was a more judicial personality
than that of Mr Justice Grantham. He was strong enough to
rebuke Wild when necessary and it will not be anticipating the
story too much to say that he was not too favourably impressed
with Gardiner's version of his relations with Rose.

Dickens was never a brutal prosecutor: he had just come from
the Old Bailey where he had put up a valiant though vain effort
on behalf of Kitty Byron. He opened his case temperately and was
far too good a tactician to overcall his hand: counsel can never be
sure that a witness will come up to his proof. His survey of the
facts was accurate, apart from his adding a decade to the prisoner's
age. In his view, the interchange in the Doctor's Chapel and in
particular the details of it given by Skinner were beyond invention
and this incident was the keystone to the case. He indulged in a
little theorizing in respect of the oil lamp and the broken bottle,
but his theory was sound and met all the facts: the murderer had
brought the bottle of paraffin to start a fire, but he had corked it so
well that he was unable to open it: he had then dismantled the oil
lamp, but had been unable to extract the combustible fluid from it
and had then smashed the bottle, forgetting that it bore his name.
This evidence, and all the other evidence, pointed at Gardiner as
the culprit.*

After plans and photographs had been proved, George Wright
told his story. Wild tried to discredit him by suggesting that he
had been reprimanded at the works by Gardiner but, since the

---

* The theory is open to the objection that no person in his senses would
seek to burn a body with one newspaper and a tiny bottle of paraffin, but
presumably the intention was to incinerate the girl in her bed, for which
purpose there was sufficient to *start* a fire. It is doubtful if Gardiner ever
realized that his name was on the bottle, but in any case he may have
lost his head when Rose screamed, for fear the Crisps should come down
to investigate. In 1946, one Arthur Clegg threw a baby in the Thames
after carefully removing all clothing to avoid identification: he forgot the
existence of a tape round its wrist which had been attached in hospital
to prevent confusion: the tape bore the words "Baby Clegg" and its
grandfather paid for his negligence on the scaffold.

first trial, Wright had ascertained the exact date of the rebuke and it had been *after* the chapel incident: witness said that, if anything, he was grateful to the accused, who had been responsible for his promotion to wheelwright. He agreed that five or seven years earlier he and his friends had observed one Cady* and his young woman from a tree: pressed by Wild as to why he had talked about it, he made the reasonable reply, "They were in my mother's orchard and they had no business there." He could have added that he cannot have been more than fifteen at the time.

Alphonso Skinner, the older observer, was more firmly handled by Wild who was so domineering that first Dickens and then the judge had to intervene. To the suggestion that he had learnt his story by heart came the reasonable retort that he had by now told it many times, to the elders, to the magistrates, to the coroner, and at the previous trial. When pressed too hard to concede that Gardiner had always denied the indecency and always admitted being in the chapel with Rose, Fonzo remarked that, at the works, Gardiner had originally denied ever going to the chapel at all. Wild sat down hurriedly.

The Rev. John Guy, superintendent of the Wangford circuit, told of the inconclusive investigation at Sibton: he agreed that he had, at one time, mistakenly said that Rose Harsent was questioned by the elders. He became angry when counsel suggested that his memory was defective, and denied ever describing the chapel incident as a trumped-up affair. It was quite clear that the minister was never satisfied of Gardiner's innocence but he pointed out that one of the difficulties of pursuing the matter was that the next investigatory body was comprised of himself, Gardiner, and one other elder. In his view Rouse was senior to Gardiner in Primitive Methodist hierarchy since he was a lay preacher and Gardiner was not. Rather surprisingly, Wild elicited from Guy that he had himself been taxed on one occasion with comparable indiscretions: as counsel took the same line with Rouse, the jury can hardly have formed a favourable impression of the Sibton elders, of whom of course the accused was one.

Henry Rouse gave his age as seventy-three and claimed to have been a Primitive Methodist for thirty-five years. He had come to

---

* Presumably a brother-in-law of the accused, whose wife's maiden name was Cady, a point that has previously been missed and which was not taken at the trial.

Sibton some two years prior to the chapel incident, in which, so he claimed, he had taken Gardiner's part. He told his tale of the subsequent association between the accused and the dead girl but, however much Wild might seek to discredit him, there was no gainsaying that in the April, *when Rose was pregnant but before Mrs Crisp had taxed her*, Rouse had had that letter written to the choirmaster taxing *him* with excessive familiarity. Rouse had to admit bringing a charge of arson against a thirteen-year-old boy which was dismissed by the magistrates. This was the second murder trial at which he had given evidence but it was not his fault he had not given evidence in the police court. It was true that he had himself once been accused of misconducting himself with the wife of a farmer whom he had persuaded to look after a sow for him, and it was said that, under the joint pretence of visiting the sow and spreading the gospel, he had called on the lady for other than religious purposes. This was quite false, as was an accusation of misconduct with another woman, although it was true that he had left the district shortly after these accusations. He was not much more fortunate in his new abode, where he quarrelled with a villager over money and pursued his quarrel by telling the vicar that his enemy's daughters were a couple of whores. It was not an impressive performance, and Wild had once had to interrupt him by saying, "I don't want any preaching." This amazing man had been a lay preacher for a quarter of a century: in private life he described himself as a labourer.

Harry Harsent, Rose's fourteen-year-old brother, said that he had often taken letters between Gardiner and his sister in both 1901 and 1902: he agreed that at the previous trial he said that he had taken no such letters in 1902 and supposed that was the truth: Constable Nunn had not tried to make him remember since. On the other hand, Wild did not cross-examine the postman who had delivered the assignation note at a quarter past three on the afternoon before the murder, although he claimed to have delivered similar envelopes to Rose on three or four other occasions. It should be made clear that Gardiner admitted writing twice to Rose, and that she had written once to him, about the choice of hymns for choir practice. Rose was a girl who kept her letters and, if there had been others, it is curious that they too had not been preserved, if not for romantic reflection at least with an eye on subsequent proceedings in bastardy.

With Mrs Georgina Crisp, Wild showed himself at his worst.

The lady, it will be recalled, was no longer definite about hearing the scream between one and two o'clock and it suited Wild that she should revert to her original timing, because of the footprint evidence. Instead of approaching her tactfully, Wild practically called her a liar and lost his temper when she kept calling him "Mr Wild": for this she is hardly to be blamed as Wild had called on her three weeks before the trial to inspect the scene of the crime. His attacks on her failed to produce the result he desired, although they did impel the Deacon (who had been given a seat on the bench beside the judge) to intervene: Mr Justice Lawrance silenced the Deacon, and Wild sneered "Is this the *deaf* gentleman?": counsel then produced the red herring that Crisp had behaved badly in not investigating the scream at the time. In the end, Mrs Crisp became so muddled that she was unable to say whether or not the storm was continuing at the time of the scream: had she been handled more gently, she would probably have accepted Wild's contentions as not impossible.

Wild did not bother much with Burgess: there was no doubt that he was on his doorstep at ten o'clock, but so were many other villagers. Mrs Rosanna Dickenson was almost a defence witness. She said that Mrs Gardiner had come to her home at about half-past eleven and that Gardiner had followed about half an hour later: they had both left together at about half-past one, just as the storm was passing over. The Crown left it to the jury to infer, if they so wished, that the crime was committed *before* Gardiner called on this witness: it certainly appears that Gardiner had originally suggested that he had gone to the witness together with his wife.

This was somewhat sloppy, since Morriss, who was the next witness, made it clear that the footprints that he saw between Providence House and Gardiner's house had been made after the storm was over, as otherwise all trace of them would have been washed away. He agreed with Wild that if the police had not come to him, he would probably never have mentioned the matter at all. Stammers told of the fire lit by Gardiner on the Sunday morning: he denied that he had been coaxed by the judge at the first trial into saying that it was a *large* fire and that he had originally described the conflagration without the adjective: on being pressed, Stammers added that, in the twelve months that he had lived opposite the Gardiners, he had not known them light a fire there on a Sunday morning.

John Samuel Rickards produced samples of Gardiner's handwriting: the reprimanding of Wright had been subsequent to the chapel incident: envelopes similar to that which had contained the assignation note were used at the Drill Works: they were very ordinary and cost about three shillings per thousand.

After Rose's father had told of finding her body, Constable Nunn described the appearance of the corpse: the constable had collected all Gardiner's clothing and found him to possess only two shirts.* Wild's cross-examination of him was directed largely to show the inadequacy of his acoustic tests at the Doctor's Chapel and brought a rebuke from the judge: "You put it offensively to him and then blow him up if he makes an observation; it is not fair to any witness." Wild's next gambit was that the indiarubber shoes were visible to Morriss when he made his sketch, but this suggestion was clearly groundless. He then tried to persuade Nunn that he had been improper in interviewing Mrs Gardiner while her husband was more or less under arrest: Nunn retorted that he felt it his duty to stop the pair getting together, even if no admission from the wife would have been admissible against her husband. Nunn did agree that he had altered his record of his conversation with the wife in his notebook, but otherwise his evidence was practically unshaken.

Superintendent Staunton said that the only difference between Gardiner's and his wife's version of their movements was whether or not they had gone to Mrs Dickenson together: he said they had, she said they had not. Wild used the opportunity of having him in the box to put in three separate confessions to the murder by palpable lunatics. Dickens protested mildly, but the judge said that he would not be too strict. Wild suggested that one of the letters might have come from a brewer called Goodchild but Dickens elicited the fact that this man was never in the right place to post the assignation letter. It was just another of Wild's red herrings: the merit of the letters may be summed up by one quotation from one of them: "Must I give myself up to the law? I cannot. My beard is grown like Brother Gardiner's. I must wander on the sea."

The medical evidence is already known to the reader, and was

---

* In fairness to Gardiner, it must be conceded that his other shirt was dirty and ostensibly of the previous week. In his summing up, the judge said cryptically, "The accused had had a clean shirt on that morning, and how, after a fortnight's wear, that could be managed, I do not know." Mrs Gardiner washed fortnightly.

not particularly helpful. Dr Stevenson, the senior Home Office
analyst, told of his unsuccessful search for blood-stains and paraffin
on Gardiner's clothing, and of the minor discovery on the penknife:
the condition of this knife was certainly curious:

> It was a little oily and had evidently been freshly cleaned and
> sharpened. *It had been scraped inside the haft.* On examining
> the interior of the handle and between the metal and bone of
> the handle I found a minute quantity of mammalian blood.
> I should say the blood inside had not been more than a
> month there.

Dr Stevenson's evidence about the little bottle hardly fitted the
prosecution theory, as he thought that some, if not all, of the
broken bits had been fractured by heat. He agreed that the cork
had been so forced into the neck that it could not be prised out by
the fingers: this fitted Dickens's theory. Wild did not cross-examine
him at length, contenting himself with the fact that the expert had
found a minute piece of cloth which did not match with any of
Gardiner's known clothing: on being asked where he found it, the
doctor gave the curious reply:

> It had dropped out of the paper containing the glass, which was
> in a small box. I did not find it during my first examination,
> but a day or two after when it turned out amongst the debris
> of the bottle.

So, although Wild relied largely on this fragment, it may well be
that it had nothing whatever to do with the case.

It is unnecessary to follow the luckless Davis through his admissions and denials: asked if he was not surprised that Rose should
have asked him for the dirty ditties, he said that there were worse
girls than Rose "at the present day". Wild again conceded that he
did not suggest that Davis was the murderer. Still less, as this is
not a text-book, need we follow the evidence of Thomas Gurrin,
the handwriting expert: it seems an almost irresistible conclusion
that it was Gardiner who wrote the letter making the midnight
appointment.

Wild opened the defence by pointing out that Gardiner had spent
234 days in custody, besides making the conventional attack on
circumstantial evidence. Gardiner was "perhaps not too popular

owing to the fact that he is a teetotaller, and that he is a man professing religion" but he was certainly no scoundrel. In any case, would a man commit misconduct with a girl less than two hundred yards from her home "with the louts loitering about"? Gardiner was cleared of the scandal at the time and, if Guy said that he was in a dilemma, Guy was mistaken and there was no dilemma at all: as for Rouse, he was nothing but a prurient old scoundrel unworthy of credence. Even if the jury believed that Gardiner wrote the letter of assignation, that did not show him to be guilty of the murder, however grave the suspicion might be. Certainly he did not keep the appointment for midnight, and the prosecution seemed to suggest that he had visited the girl at about half-past one. In any event, it was dangerous to convict any man on the evidence of handwriting experts. The accused would explain the blood on the knife, and his wife would explain how the bottle came to be in Providence House. Morriss's evidence was probably mistaken. Stammers had exaggerated the size of the fire: if anything had been burnt, Stammers would have smelt it and the police would have found the remains. Gardiner could not have done the murder without getting scratched or getting his clothing stained, and there was no suggestion that this had happened. The evidence pointed just as strongly at Davis as it did at Gardiner, and one of the confession letters suggested that the real murderer was trying to blame Goodchild. Not only was the case against Gardiner not proven: he was entitled to a verdict of not guilty on this unjust charge brought against him.

Mrs Gardiner was examined at length: she had always believed her husband innocent of the Harsent scandal and said that, apart for a brief period about eleven o'clock when she went over to Mrs Dickenson and he followed after assuring himself that their children were safely tucked up in bed, they had been together all the evening. She fainted before she could be cross-examined and was evidently in a high state of nervous tension. "There had been much cruel suspense connected with the case," comments Mr Henderson, "but a belief in her husband's innocence might have been expected to inspire her with greater fortitude, unless of course she was in weak health or abnormally temperamental." She admitted that a fire had been lit in the yard on the Sunday morning, although only for the purpose of boiling a kettle. And she agreed that her husband had not seemed much shocked at the violence of Rose's end.

Her cross-examination had to be postponed, and Gardiner himself

then gave evidence. His explanation of the chapel incident was that
Rose had asked him to help her with the door which was somewhat
stiff. His story generally was an out-and-out denial: Wright, Skinner,
Rouse, and Stammers were all liars: Morriss was in all probability
mistaken. His writing was similar to that in the letter of assignation,
but he had not written that letter. He could not remember cleaning
his knife about the time of the murder, nor did he ever recall scraping
it inside: he had hulked the rabbit in May, which he conceded was
rather late for so doing, indeed the rabbit was breeding and had had
to be buried. He possessed only two shirts and knew nothing about
them as his wife bought them and supplied him with clean ones as
he required them: he agreed that his laundry was washed fortnightly
and that he changed his shirt every Sunday, which makes the feat
somewhat difficult to accomplish.

Mrs Pepper had to agree that the person she heard moving in
Gardiner's house at twenty past two in the morning might have
been Gardiner himself and that it was only Mrs Gardiner's own
statement that made her think it was not. Her story of waiting
downstairs for a couple of hours hardly strikes one as credible.
After her performance, Mrs Walker recounted the history of the
medicine bottle and an accountant and a bank clerk said that they
did not believe Gardiner had written the letter in question. A fowl
dealer said that he had passed by Providence House at four o'clock
in the morning and had not noticed the footprints observed by
Morriss. An architect and a quantity surveyor said that they had
made tests at the Doctor's Chapel and that, in their view, it was
not possible to hear from outside what was going on inside. The
defence solicitor was also called, ostensibly to support them but,
one suspects, rather for Wild to import some more prejudice into
the case: he received short shrift from the judge.

> MR WILD: I believe it is a fact that the notice of the character
> of Rouse and Stammers's evidence was served upon you at
> the last moment, just before the last Assizes?
> LAWRANCE, J.: There is nothing to complain of in that.
> MR WILD: No, my lord.
> LAWRANCE, J.: Then why bring it up?

A host of elders were called to contradict the memory of the Rev.
Mr Guy, which they did reluctantly, and to declare their faith in
the accused, which they did more enthusiastically. Brother Abraham

Goddard said that Guy had called it a fabrication and a trumped-up affair: in cross-examination, he agreed that Guy had used the word dilemma and had said that he preferred to believe his own church. Brother Cripp, who had known Gardiner for twenty-eight years, said that he was first asked to give evidence less than a week before the second trial began. Guy had certainly called the affair a fabrication but had not mentioned the word dilemma in the discussion with Brother Goddard. Brother Noah Etheridge agreed with Brother Cripp: he too had not given evidence at the first trial. Brother Samuel Goddard said that Guy had expressed the view that Gardiner was "in the clear" and had never used the word dilemma, although he believed that the minister had stated his preference for believing two in the church rather than two out. Similar evidence was given by Brother Fiddler. The trial seemed to be more concerned with what Guy had said in 1901 than with what Gardiner had done in 1902: Dickens commented on the skill with which the brethren remembered a conversation that had taken place twenty months before.

Wild said that, apart from the cross-examination of Mrs Gardiner, that concluded the defence. The judge said that he had caused the man Goodchild to be brought to the court and that if the defence made any suggestion that he had anything to do with the murder, he would be given the fullest opportunity to defend himself. The court adjourned with Wild expressing the hope that he had said nothing improper. On the next day, Mrs Gardiner threw a fit of hysterics on the way to the court. Wild called Brother Etheridge to say that she was in no state to give evidence and that, on the previous day, she had lain on the table in the waiting-room for four hours in a state of collapse. A doctor was sent to her and she was recalled. She was not seriously shaken by Dickens: she had slept on the night of the murder only from five till eight o'clock and her husband had certainly not lit the fire in the yard at seven o'clock as suggested by Stammers. She made her husband's shirts and he had only two: if he got wet, "he had to get dry again".

Wild's final speech does not lend itself to condensation. It began with an appeal to the jurors' sympathy: "Shall it go forth to the world that this poor country girl"—she had been married thirteen years and borne eight children*—"who has staggered from her illness in order

---

* Speaking of Davis, Wild had earlier observed, "If ever you wish to minimize the importance of a man, you call him a lad: he is twenty."

to face the ordeal of cross-examination is the wife of a murderer?" It underlined the main points of the defence, admitting that if they did not believe Mrs Gardiner and thought her husband was guilty that she must then be an accomplice in the murder of his paramour. It conceded that Gurrin's evidence was good enough for a civil action, but was not to be acted on in a criminal case. And ended up in an impassioned plea to say that the case was not proven and that the accused was, in England, therefore entitled to be acquitted.

Dickens replied that this was not a case where the jury should be misled by sympathy for the accused's relatives. Murder had been done and, although he had refrained from taking technical objections, everything pointed at the accused as the guilty man. Why should they, as the defence suggested, look for an unknown man—for neither Davis nor Goodchild were guilty—when they had the letter, the footmarks, the signal, the knife, the association, the shoes, and the bottle all pointing to Gardiner. People did not swear a man's life away recklessly and there was no reason whatever for thinking that Skinner, a man of twenty-seven, or Rouse, or Stammers, would swear to seeing what they had not seen.

Mr Justice Lawrance pointed out the difference between direct and circumstantial evidence and went on to analyse certain aspects of the evidence. The most improbable part of Skinner's story was the language attributed to the dead girl but, after considering the literary compositions found in her possession, the improbability immediately disappeared. As far as the Sibton investigation went, it did not matter what Guy thought of the facts: what did matter was what the jury thought. It had been suggested that Rouse was an evil-liver, but had this been the case, would he have been allowed to remain in a position of trust in his church? Judging the similarity of handwriting was a matter for the jury, but experts were useful in pointing out similarities and Gurrin was the best in his class. Someone made an appointment with the girl, someone kept it and the girl had died. Very strong suspicion must be cast on the writer of such a letter. The defence had not contradicted the fact that, from in front of Gardiner's doorstep Rose's window was clearly visible, and where was Gardiner seen at the time that the signal was to be given? Stammers had seen a fire early that morning. Morriss had seen footprints and, had the police not wasted time speculating on suicide, somebody else might have remembered these prints. The evidence about the condition of the knife was not important taken by itself, but it was certainly significant in the light of the other evidence. The label on the bottle was significant. The absence of bloodstains on Gardiner was a point in his favour, but there was no suggestion that the blood had been stepped in: the evidence about his possessing only two shirts was perplexing. The murderer might not have been the father of the girl's unborn child, but he probably had good reason to suppose that he would be given the credit for her condition. If they had a reasonable doubt, the accused was entitled to the benefit of it but such doubt must be fair and reasonable and not trivial "such as the speculative ingenuity of counsel might suggest". The only certainty they could have would be what they had seen with their own eyes but they had to act on the sort of evidence that they would act on in their ordinary lives. It depended so much on what people meant by a moral certainty. If the facts led them to the conclusion that the accused, although no human eye saw him, was the man who did the murder they would be justified in giving effect to such opinion. Otherwise, Gardiner was entitled to their verdict.

The jury retired at five o'clock and were out for nearly two and a quarter hours before returning to announce that, like their predecessor, they were unable to agree. The judge had correctly assumed that standards of what was a moral certainty varied, and it was later understood that once again it had been eleven votes to one, though on this occasion eleven were for acquittal. Although double disagreements are not unknown, it is as far as I know unique for there to be one in a murder case. The practice is to put the accused on trial a third time and offer no evidence, thus giving him the advantage of a full acquittal: there is much to be said for this course as it is hard to say that a case has been proved beyond reasonable doubt when two juries have already disagreed.

On this occasion the procedure was varied. Five days after the second disagreement, the Attorney-General lodged a *nolle prosequi*, thereby intimating that it was not intended to proceed with a third trial. Gardiner was accordingly released from Ipswich Gaol and, after removing his distinctive beard, departed for London and was not thereafter heard of again with any certainty. Legend in Peasenhall has it that he once visited Yoxford, his wife's village, and his children are said to have visited Peasenhall itself. He is variously supposed to have found employment in London as a wheelwright and to have taken over a tobacconist's. If he was innocent, then his tribulations were those of Job, but I fear that my sympathies are with the majority of the first jury.

The reader need not agree. He may even find solace in the accident theory. According to this school of thought, Rose slipped on the stairs as she came to the door to let in her lover. She fell on the little bottle which was in her hand, thereby cutting her throat in two places and wounding herself in the chest: the lamp dropped from her hand and broke on the floor, setting fire to the paraffin. The lover entered and fled in horror, presumably leaving behind his old copy of the *East Anglian Daily Times*.

There is also the detective story solution. I have always assumed that it was in reference to the Peasenhall case that ex-Detective Sergeant Leeson wrote:

> A sequel . . . may be found in the evidence given at a murder trial some years ago. The victim had been done to death in her own house by someone who had visited her, and the evidence on which the prosecution relied to prove the case consisted of footprints which they endeavoured to prove were made by the accused man. There was no doubt that the boots produced belonged to the prisoner, and fitted the prints, but he was acquitted for want of substantiating evidence.
>
> It is true that the footprints were made by someone passing to and from the prisoner's home, but to my mind the evidence, had it been weaved differently, would have proved the prisoner's wife to have been the guilty person.*

It is true that it was theoretically possible for Georgina Gardiner to have carried out the murder, but her demeanour in the witness-box hardly fits her for the role of Lady Macbeth. She may have had the will to destroy the viper that threatened to destroy her home, but she would hardly have borrowed her husband's knife for the purpose: nor, in the broadest sense of the word, was the murder of Rose Harsent a ladylike operation.

---

* B. Leeson: *Lost London* (Stanley Paul). Mr Leeson left Scotland Yard after being wounded in the Battle of Sidney Street.

THE HOOP-LA MURDER TRIAL

(Jessie Costello, 1933)

Sydney Horler

To everyone's surprise, Jessie Costello was cleared of murdering her fireman husband by dosing him with a poisonous compound used to burnish her kitchen boiler. The American Edmund Pearson, who was at the trial in 1933, put the comely Mrs Costello's acquittal down to twelve male jurors "as helpless as twelve rabbits under the influence of those glittering ophidian eyes". This account is by a British author, Sydney Horler (1888–1954), a former Daily Mail *reporter who wrote dozens of thrillers in the 1920s and 1930s in the style of Edgar Wallace. Never one to mince his words, Horler described Mrs Costello's acquittal and subsequent Broadway career, as "the most astonishing crime-farce within living memory".*

In these days of highly-publicized crime, murderers often get newspaper space which might well be devoted to more worthy individuals. At least, that is the plaint of the moralists, the high thinkers and the what-nots generally. Well, they have this consolation: if things are bad enough in this country, they are very much worse in America. Every now and then in that continent of fierce turbulence of one kind and another, there springs up a crime possessing so many bizarre features that something like 120 million people are held enthralled, fascinated, or repelled according to the nature of their mentality.

Having delivered ourselves of this brief homily, let us now examine in some detail the truly astonishing case of Jessie Costello. This woman may be said to have run the whole gamut of human emotions, not through her own merits but through the stark fact that she was accused of murdering her husband by means of cyanide of potassium poisoning. During her trial she became the most important figure in all the Americas: immediately after the trial she was besieged by film and music-hall agents with dazzling offers—and, final and most bewildering phase of all, two months after her acquittal from an ordeal which a spirited writer in the *New Yorker* called "as luscious a trial as any in the gaudy annals of American jurisprudence," she stood beside Mrs Aimée Semple Macpherson, the hot-gospeller revivalist, and sang "The Old Rugged Cross", maybe with fervour, but certainly with an eye to the main chance.

If ever a woman can be said to have determined to capitalize the notoriety due to having stood in the dock on a charge of murder, it was Mrs Jessie Costello. She had believed—and hoped—that she would find her inevitable way to the Bright Lights of Broadway as a result of having been placed in the pen; but when the wheel of Fate turned about and landed her instead by the side of that other truly remarkable character, Aimée Semple Macpherson, she felt not only bewildered but reproachful. As the writer in the *New Yorker* so ably put it, "as she faced 8,000 devout people in Boston's Arena, even the ecstatic amens and hallelujahs that greeted her throaty blues-singer's voice did not completely banish her resentment. Her trial had brought her to God instead of to Broadway, and if she was a bit rebellious who can blame her?"

All things considered, I am of the opinion that the Costello trial—practically unknown in this country, let it be added—and what followed it constitutes the most amazing piece of criminal jurisprudence within the last fifty years. If any should doubt this assertion, and it is very possible, all I ask is for that sceptic to read on.

The remarkable Jessie was a Maid of Salem. Before her great advancement she strutted on the meagre stage of Peabody, Massachusetts. Peabody is a small, drab, entirely undistinguished factory town of 20,000 inhabitants, distant some thirty miles from Boston. Born in 1902, Jessie had always disliked school, and at the age of fourteen had refused ever to return. She is said to have resembled her father, a breezy, blunt, go-to-hell type of a fellow, with a temper to match his ham-like hands. From an early age—but here I must borrow again the inimitable prose of the *New Yorker* writer:

> Jessie was destined for higher things. The success she achieved at the Salem Court-house was perhaps no surprise to those connoisseurs of seductiveness who, lolling against corner lamp-posts, had watched Mrs Costello's provocative and rather hefty sensuosity wriggle off into the distance. Frequently, in the past, they had given her dark, intense figure, whose ample torso bent a little forward from burgeoning hips, that accolade of approval expressed by the phrase "get a load of that!" In their way, they were pioneers. Perhaps, too, those of Mrs Costello's neighbours who had engaged with her in certain fierce debates were not surprised by the fire and dash she later revealed. She had a certain masculinity of expression, rich, varied and yet precise, which she occasionally employed in the heat of combat.

From the above, a very good impression will be gathered of the type of woman this was.

She could not settle down to any ordinary employment; perhaps the visions of her future greatness prevented it. In any case, she tripped, in a single year, from a bakery shoppe, to the operation of an adding machine, and from this on to a Peabody Corset Emporium, where she was the chief sales-girl. (With her impressive bust she made a good model, no doubt.)

Well, there Jessie was—an opulent-breasted, big-hipped wench, full of zing, craving for life, never able to stay put for very long in one place, attracting the attention of all the males in the neighbourhood, seeing all the movies, attending all the dances, reading all the highly-spiced sex magazines in which American journalism abounds. It was, we are told, "a rich, full life"—and it was to be infinitely richer and infinitely fuller.

When she was seventeen—that was in November 1919—Jessie, looking at least ten years older in spite of the short skirts which were the fashion in those times, attracted the attention, whilst standing on a street corner selling poppies for the disabled veterans of the world war, of a tall, bleak-faced young fireman of Celtic cast, who was walking swiftly by. In the ordinary way, William J. Costello, himself a veteran of the war, and now an employee in the Fire Department of the Peabody Corporation, did not pay any attention to females; he was not that type. Sex meant nothing in his austere life. But this girl was different: when Jessie, reaching out, nabbed him by the arm, passers-by smiled; it was such a characteristic gesture of this go-getting wench. To those who were not beset with arid puritanism, the picture might have been a pleasant one—these onlookers could not have seen the shadow of death hovering in the distance.

Shortly after Jessie pinned a poppy on the coat lapel of William J. Costello, they began courting. Four years later they were married.

Now it does not require a skilled psychologist to opine that a girl of Jessie's characteristics and mentality was a piece of human dynamite to which to be hitched—unless the husband could manage her with a firm hand.

Bill Costello, we are informed, was a bit on the staid side. Compared with his exuberant bride, he looked like one of the Pilgrim Fathers. He had not told the life-loving Jessie beforehand that he spent several hours every day on his knees; that he was given to brooding not only on his God but on his stomach: for Bill, the fireman, was both religious and suffered from chronic indigestion. Furthermore, Bill was not much of a one for talking. In this he clearly resembled the late President Calvin Coolidge who, when asked by his wife what the Sunday sermon was about, briefly answered: "Sin", and when further asked what views the preacher had expounded, coughed up the laconic rejoinder: "He didn't approve of it."

To be fair, as every historian should be, I must say that Bill Costello could not have been by any manner of means a lovable character—he was too grim, too rugged, too introspective for that. Apart, altogether, from his unfashionable habit (in these days) of praying for hours on end, his indigestion, and his introspection, he had a somewhat nauseating habit of taking his boots off when he got home from duty and propping his socked feet on the radiator. It does not require much imagination to agree with the *New Yorker* writer already quoted, Mr Richard O. Boyer, that "Bill had little of the tender sparkle of the heroes Jessie read about in *True Stories*."

But whatever failings the Peabody fireman possessed, he must

have satisfied—at least, for the time being—his wife's requirements as a husband. He did his duty—perhaps grimly, perhaps
introspectively, but he did it: after the marriage, we are told, "there
were four children in a sequence almost as swift as biology would
allow".

But children bring diapers—and diapers weren't much in Jessie's
line. She regarded them as an unpleasant adjunct of modern
civilization. What was more, four young children, all requiring a
mother's loving care, cramped her style; she was now no longer
the admired girl on the sidewalks; marriage had caught her fast
in its toils, and she was buried and lost amidst the multitude
of other young housewives of Peabody. It was a melancholy
reflection—especially as she had gained forty pounds in weight
and had now passed her thirtieth year. Oh, dear!

In a word, Jessie was ripe for mischief when Fate sent across her
path the man who was destined to become nationally known as
the "kiss-and-tell-cop".

This shortly-to-be-blazoned-abroad personage was a pouty-
mouthed and tow-haired patrolman (constable, in this country)
called Edward J. McMahon. This ornament to the Peabody Police
Force moved through life in the typically lethargic manner peculiar
to his kind; he could aptly, we are told, be described as both mawkish
and moon-calfish; nevertheless, he was a great favourite with the
ladies. There was, no doubt, a reason.

Almost immediately after our heroine made the acquaintance
of McMahon, she was seen to undergo a renaissance. Questioned
on the matter, she said—only in plainer, blunter terms—that the
relationship between her and the patrolman ("Big Boy") was entirely
spiritual, and that she admired McMahon only in a platonic way.
When this statement is compared with the astonishing confessions
of lecherous intimacy, which McMahon, surely one of the strangest
self-accusers who ever stepped into a witness-box, made at the
trial, Jessie's love of the truth was, with some degree of fairness,
questioned.

But the main thing is that "Big Boy's" admiration and adoring
tactics provided a much-needed tonic for Jessie. She might have
posed at this stage of her life, as a "before" and "after" witness:
if the patrolman had had some rejuvenating pills named after
him, his testimony would have sold a wagon-load at every street
corner.

Yes, Jessie bloomed again. Once again she came to the forefront,

glorying in the limelight. Leaving her dishrags and diapers, she set
out to "go places and do things". She sold tickets for Policemen's
Balls; she participated in Penny Bazaars; she collected funds for the
Unemployed, and was a member of several committees. Altogether,
a remarkable recrudescence was hers.

"Love had planted roses in her heart," the newspapers later said.
The newspapers *would* . . .

And then came that fatal February. Up to this time, any thought
of a hand of the Law—that same Law with which she was at
this time so intimately connected—reaching out to grab her, was
unthinkable, but—

The actual date of Jessie's arrest was 17 March 1933. This
was exactly a month after the death of her husband, who—poor
man!—a long, lank, lugubrious corpse, as in life he had been a
long, lank, lugubrious fireman—was found sprawled outside the
bathroom of his home on Fay Avenue, a rosary lying near it.

In her dim, fumbling way, Jessie had always dreamed of
Greatness—and now the newspapers thrust this dubious quality
upon her with unstinting hands.

Disregarding the fact that she had passed the age of physical
perfection (remember the extra forty pounds motherhood had
thrust upon her) it pleased the US journalistic world to portray
her as "Beauty in Distress". We are informed that "reporters unable
to talk to the widow because of gaol rules, were forced to create their
own version of her." Thus, they thrust upon her all the seductiveness
of Helen of Troy, one paper going demented and declaring that "all
the modest sex appeal of Lady Godiva plus clothing but minus horse
was hers". For a few hectic weeks, Jessie thrust all the fashionable
film stars away from the front page; she became the shopgirls'
ideal. Photographs in abundance were published: "Male members
of lonely hearts' clubs all over the country went to bed thinking of
Jessie!"

The Boston Press, usually reflecting the real New England
modern puritanism, cast aside all its former restraint and went
stark, raving mad. Here was a chance to cash in on their own
special sensation, and they did so with such wild abandon, that
their *confrères* all over the American Continent followed suit. To
quote the spirited Mr Boyer once again: "The Boston Press beat the
tomtoms so wildly that their echoes were heard by the journalistic
brethren from coast to coast and brought them on the run. Perhaps

some genuine *aficionados* of the murder trial ran a bit reluctantly. One might not have expected to find the perfect American trial, with all the hoop-la and idiocies the genre require, in austere New England. Salem, where the House of the Seven Gables* still casts its bleak Puritan shadow, seemed to lack the lavishness of temperament that was needed."

When the alleged murderess (for the charge against Jessie was the specific one of poisoning her husband by means of cyanide of potassium) made her appearance in the dock, she was seen wearing a black dress, ornamented simply with white collar and cuffs. This dress soon became as well known as her smile. (She smiled throughout the trial, let it be added.) The jury, we are told, did not at first display that goggling undisguised admiration that they were to evidence later. They were coy to respond; the Costello magic took time to cast its spell. The bailiff who shortly was to send a bouquet of roses to the prisoner each day, on the opening morning behaved as official decorum dictated; in other words, he looked straight ahead of him and concentrated purely on his duty. Nor did the crowd, who were to cheer Jessie wildly each day as she made her triumphant progress from gaol to court-house, develop these maniacal tendencies until later. In short, the opening morning of the trial gave small indication of the tempest of excitement which was to follow.

Indeed, had it not been for the striking personality of the accused, this might have been just another murder trial. But, and here again I have resource to Mr Boyer,

> facing a possible death sentence, Jessie bloomed like a rose. Her personality dominated the proceedings. Even dull moments seemed to contain a certain breathlessness, a certain lilt, derived, perhaps, from the cadenced hop, skip, jump, wave and smile with which Jessie, four times a day, streaked to and from her limousine through the cheering crowd on her way in and out of the court-house. Then she would pant up the stairway, the fortunates in the building racing in the wake of her broad and straining buttocks. Gaining the second floor, she would stand at the window and wave to the crowd in the street beneath. One day a retinue of vaudeville midgets stood below and received Jessie's wave as if it were a benediction.

* A reference to Hawthorne's grim story, *The Scarlet Letter*.

Their manager henceforth advertised them as The Troupe
That Had Been Waved At By Jessie!

Word of the wonderful things that were to be witnessed at the Salem
court-house soon got abroad; with his finger characteristically on the
American reading-public's pulse, that overlord of the printed word,
W.R. Hearst, began to press buttons. He sent such notable United
States writers as Will Irwin, Katharine Brush and Adela Rogers St
John thither to write their flowing cadences. The Hearst papers,
we read, "were full of typographical aphrodisiacs. Every phrase
describing Jessie as a glamorous siren, irresistible to men, seemed
to increase the irrelevancy of her guilt or innocence."

Stimulated by reading such purple prose, was it any wonder
that the crowd panting to get into the court-house increased every
day—indeed every minute? Once the populace, led by the Press, had
firmly come to the opinion that Jessie was the most lovely feminine
creature that had been reared in New England for a decade, was it
any wonder that the jurors caught the general infection? After all
(as Mr Boyer so sapiently points out), they were only men, and
Jessie was merely a woman.

Sentiment—mawkish, heavily-scented, sex-pulsating, dreamy-
eyed—ruled the camp. Justice went overboard—and who can
wonder at it amidst such an atmosphere? It is recorded that one
of the jurymen actually inquired if he could send the prisoner a box
of candies as a slight gesture of his esteem! So crazy had become the
atmosphere of the court-house that, during the recesses, the jurors
formed a male voice quartette, and the hot summer air vibrated
to their renderings of such songs as "Sweet Adelaide", "My Wild
Irish Rose", and "Let Me Call You Sweetheart".

If Jessie became the heroine, her "Big Boy", the "kiss-and-tell-
cop", became the villain—after all, you can't have two heroes
in a murder trial: that's asking too much! Even the Hearst
papers jibbed at printing all of McMahon's testimony; this was
so sizzling in character that strong men were seen to blush, and
haughty matrons to (pretend to) swoon. A particularly daring
publisher put the moving words into a little red booklet, and
this sold in cart-loads. Meanwhile, "Jessie, heady with adulation
and resembling some buxom *prima donna* entering the opera-house
amid the cheers of her admirers, cantered through the crowd from
limousine to court-house and back again."

The American male is a chivalrous if simple creature—and

seeing Jessie as the heroine of this sordid piece, he commenced to write letters to the prisoner at the rate of five hundred a day. Here are two which were read in Court—both of them in verse, it will be seen.

The first:

> Tear-drops on a velvet rose,
> Tear-drops—in your eyes,
> Make me wonder if there'll be
> Tear-drops—in Paradise.
> Freedom-home.
> —Robert E. Lee.

The second:

> May your life be long and happy,
> May your trouble be but few,
> May you find a home in Heaven,
> When your earthly life is through.

A Mr J. E. Hazeltine was responsible for this much more mature effort.

Mr Hazeltine, whilst pouring out his admiration for Jessie, poured out also a liberal dose of verbal prussic-acid for the man who had confessed that he went to bed with Jessie on innumerable occasions—especially when Bill the fireman was out looking after his fires. He wrote of McMahon in the following blistering words: "I would not give him a job cleaning out a pig-pen. I would have more respect for the pigs."

Mr Hazeltine was evidently a deep and profound thinker.

This astoundingly egregious criminal farce wound its way slowly to a close. Every day the radiant happiness of Jessie could be seen depicted more clearly on her dimpled face. For by now there had entered another element: inspired by what they had read in the newspapers, and getting all hot under their vests at the photographs they had seen printed, agents for the burlesque theatre (where "art" is confined to shapely women provocatively taking off their clothes, piece by piece) arrived on the scene. They all carried contracts in their hands.

Before the Defence had closed its case, there were men in the crowd who talked knowingly of screen tests. Newspapers were said to be prepared to bid fortunes for the rights of Jessie's life story. The Bright Lights of Broadway seemed as inevitable as acquittal when she faced the jury and said simply, but with dignity: "Gentlemen, send me back to my children".

How could they—being men with hearts beating—do anything else? Yes, although the most was made of the evidence, Jessie was acquitted.

She came back to the world, her head dizzy with prospective further triumphs: amongst other tangible proofs of her popularity, she had a contract for eleven hundred dollars, representing two appearances daily for four days in a New York theatre. Besides the contract, she had also been provided with a maid, a theatrical agent, two thousand four hundred dollars for the exclusive newspaper rights of her life-story, and two reporters who were to act as her Boswells.

Jessie sped like a meteor—rather a weighty one, with too much flesh round her hips and sagging breasts—towards the Bright Lights of Broadway. In doing so, she disappointed at least one of her admirers—that same Mr Hazeltine, who has been mentioned earlier in this chronicle. Mr Hazeltine was a knight who would not have disgraced himself sitting at King Arthur's table; he had believed that his heroine might struggle for vindication, but never for profit. To commercialize her great ordeal in the way she had done, was something that threatened to break Mr Hazeltine's heart. As for Mr Robert E. Lee, it is said that he talked darkly of taking his life . . .

America never does anything by halves; this truism was rarely better demonstrated than in the case of Jessie Costello. Contracts were thrust upon Jessie by the handful; they descended upon her like the autumn leaves. And, being so much sought after, Jessie became capricious; amidst the frantic hullaballo in which she now lived, amidst the never-ceasing, hard, unwinking Bright Lights of Broadway, she turned down scornfully a $20,000 contract for a ten-week burlesque appearance. Her lady-like excuse was that "she didn't think that taking off her clothes in public was refined," and so she hurried back to her main occupation—which nowadays was shopping. Feeling that she was a great person in her own right, she conducted it on a lavish scale. "A dozen pairs of shoes in one place, half a dozen hats in another, silk underwear by the bundle, hosiery, dresses by the score—everything," was the description one of her reportorial Boswells wrote, swimmy-eyed, in his paper.

Arrayed in all this finery, Jessie did not lead a retired life: on the contrary, she was frequently seen in the fashionable places. In these resorts of the élite she could be seen, "the cynosure of all eyes, as she sits down in a beautiful gown and ermine wrap, a smart, self-possessed, well-groomed widow".

When such famous Broadway columnists as Walter Winchell of the New York *Daily Mirror* and Ed Sullivan of the New York *Daily News* came up to be introduced, she was graciousness itself "as they offered sympathy for the trouble and torture she had been forced to endure." The picture of Walter Winchell, that hard-boiled commentator on mankind's frailties, offering sympathy for the troubles and tortures which Jessie had endured, should have been photographed—as, no doubt, it was.

Meanwhile Hollywood itself had got busy. Those modern magi, who know what the public wants even before the public has given any indication of it, were gathering in the offing like so many pot-bellied vultures. Presently they descended in shoals, demanding the radiant widow's appearance on the screen.

So here she was, sitting pretty as the saying goes, being besieged by all kinds of *entrepreneurs*. It must have been a gorgeous sight for the observing gods.

Even more gorgeous was the spectacle which almost immediately followed. There was a certain, but as yet inarticulate, portion of the American public, that saw not the trailing clouds of glory, but national disgrace in the acquitted widow's wholesale grabbing of newspaper-space. They resented the fact that a woman who had been accused of murder, and who, according to the man who said he had been her lover, had displayed lascivious tendencies too shocking even to be printed in the newspapers, should be thrust upon the public's consciousness in this manner. They were old-fashioned enough to think that, hidden away somewhere or other, was the merest hint of bad taste. Just a *soupçon*, perhaps, but still there.

So they went to Mr Will Hays, who, as the world knows, is the judge of what shall and shall not be seen in American motion pictures.

Mr Hays, who has been described as "that great Presbyterian moralist," saw eye to eye with them. The result was swift, devastating and astonishing; told in plain language that this was one of the things that *must* not be done, the screen magnates lost all interest in the fascinating widow overnight, and the next morning Jessie was left high and dry. All washed up, in fact.

Difficulties now descended upon Mrs Costello, even more quickly than her former successes. It was not to be wondered at, perhaps, that Jessie did not quite understand the difficulties that now lay in her path. She was still artistically obstreperous. She began her second day in the Metropolis, we are told, by

> actually rejecting an $18,000 contract in burlesque, before hurrying out to do some more shopping. She had been about to sign the document, which stipulated 1,600 dollars a week payment for twelve weeks, when her duties were explained—these duties consisted of acting a little scene, "clean but affectionate" between herself and an actor impersonating the unspeakable McMahon. For an instant Jessie was her old trenchant, eloquent self as she ejected the agent. Then she rushed out and bought a refrigerator, furniture for her six-roomed country cottage, gifts and clothing for her children, and purchases for her friends.

But the thunderclouds were rapidly gathering; the bad news was broken to Jessie by one of her Boswells that she was no longer saleable. Instantly she changed her front; from being the pursued, she was now the pursuer. No story-book detective could have been more assiduous in tracking down the murderer than she was in tracking down the agents who, warned by Mr Hays, were determined now to have nothing more to do with this bad risk. (As Mr Boyer put it: "It wasn't fair; it was almost un-American.")

Despairing of the films, she thought twice about the burlesque theatres. Perhaps, after all, what she had been asked to do was not too bad; she went to the manager who had offered her the $18,000 contract referred to above. To her indignant surprise, she was now told that the offer no longer held good. The Bright Lights of Broadway were dimming with a vengeance.

Jessie stood alone.

There was nothing else for it but to return to her Boston home.

She returned with no contracts, little money, and a magnificent wardrobe. She returned to find a city of angry critics—and no real friends.

Reaction, you see, had set in; the public had switched their views within an hour. Whereas before there were none so cruel as to impugn her motives, now she found none so brave as to support her. The general comments were summed up in a pregnant phrase by a leader in the campaign for decency. He said: "Public morals forbid commercializing such a tragic event."

Determined to snatch what little might remain of her previous astonishing glory, Jessie descended the scale with a sickening thud. No longer able to show herself on stage or dance-hall, she took to the sawdust floor of a Boston public-house. This was owned by Jack Sharkey, the highly temperamental Lithuanian, who had once been heavy-weight champion of the world. In the month of September she entered Sharkey's employ as a "hostess".

Then came the most amazing turn-about of this whole epic of hoop-la. Jessie had been working among the sawdust, the spittoons, the drunks and the photographs of other great prize fighters for a fortnight, when she sent word to the local newspapers that she had something to tell them.

The result was this: On October 3rd the local Press carried a statement signed by her to this effect: "I am about to be associated with the noted Los Angeles Evangelist, Mrs Aimée Semple MacPherson."

To quote the fuller details about this staggering prospect, she explained that "she had gained Sister Aimée's consent and would begin work for the Lord on 15 October, when Sister Aimée would open a revival in Boston."

In order to dress befittingly for the part, Jessie, we are told, "bought a becoming nun-like costume of black and went immediately into training". Her trainer was the Rev. Mr William McLam, Boston's Representative of Aimée's nation-wide organization. After a long training session, the Rev. Mr McLam emerged into the open and reported progress.

"I'm always glad," he said to the reporters, "to co-operate with anyone seeking to enter the Harvest Field. The Master is calling for labourers. We hope Mrs Jessie will come into the great blessing of God's love. I get down on my knees and pray with her."

Well, what could be fairer than that?

Clemenceau, when he had been a newspaper-man, would have found the opening night of the Revival (Jessie's) a fitting subject for his pen. But even then the withering cynic could not have done justice, perhaps, to this mighty theme.

In the absence of Clemenceau, let us be content with recording the heart-searing words of Mr Boyer:

> When the great night arrived, Sister Aimée's heart must have dropped a beat when she saw her glowing protégée. No one knew better than this aged prima donna of the sawdust trail, that the allure which had called so many to God, was beginning to fade. Yet she had retained her coquettish technique. The years that had lined her face had given her such skill that she could sometimes still create the illusion of youth, providing that no younger person stood near.
>
> But now, in the glare of the Boston Arena's lights, she stood before 8,000 people, and, beside the electric Jessie. It was a cruel contrast. The young widow radiated triumph. After many vicissitudes, she had gained an audience. There was something tense, positive, and compelling about her figure. In contrast, Aimée's ageing muscles seemed to sag.

But the old warrior did not go down without a fight.

"I have in mind to-night," Aimée said, "a woman who has been separated from her children, and is now finding her way back to God."

It was unfortunate, no doubt, that her voice sounded thin and reedy; or that her white nurse's uniform, her straw-coloured hair and her pasty face blended with the yellow lights and made her difficult to see: on the other hand, it was even more unfortunate, from her point of view, that Jessie's solid figure was in black.

Aimée continued:

"You must, you know, be broken at the feet of Jesus before you can do anything worth while. Mrs Costello told me, 'Oh, sister, I have been broken at the feet of Jesus and think I can help the poor.' She told me she'd like to do something for Jesus and that she 'didn't want to die empty-handed.' "

Called upon to do her stuff, Jessie began her Evangelist work by lifting up her voice and singing that old favourite, "The Old Rugged Cross". She gave it all she had—which was plenty—and, it is recorded by the faithful Press present on the occasion, "the more orthodox 'Amen!' was drowned in secular cheers."

The sound must have been wine to Jessie—it recalled, no doubt, the resounding huzzas of the Salem court-house—and she warmed to the 8,000 of the faithful.

She spoke in a husky voice, tremulous with emotion.

This is what she said:

"I want to say to-night that I thank God I am saved and that He has brought me back again."

With that, according to the strict instructions she had received beforehand, she made about to retire. But the crowd would not have it. Again to quote the sprightly Mr Boyer,

> surely it was not the redeemed who rudely shouted the widow's name as her rival fought onwards with the service. There was a miniature sailboat on the stage. The pale-faced Evangelist gestured towards it and one could see her mouth open and shut as she recited her parable. Now and again she tortured her face into a smile, and sometimes phrases sounded through the confusion—"sinking in the sea of sin, sinking to rise no more"—and then at last it was over. Sister Aimée had fought the good fight and it had not been pleasant. Sister Jessie received an ovation as she distributed paper-bound copies of the New Testament; when similar scenes happened on succeeding nights, it was unbearable. Mrs Aimée expelled Sister Jessie from her organization, declaring that she had not been sufficiently trained to preach or to make public appearances for the Lord.

The hard-boiled reporters panted for revelations.

"Are you jealous of her?" they asked pertinently.

The reply was as good as could be expected in the difficult circumstances.

"In the Lord's work," said Aimée Semple MacPherson, "one is not afraid of a pretty face." Her own was twisted as she spoke; she might have been eating a sour plum.

That was the end. Released from the Lord's service, Jessie had no further cards to play; she bumped down-hill as though she were descending to Avernus on a rickety toboggan. "Expelled" by Sister Aimée, it was just as though she was the victim of a curse.

She fought back. She even wrote to President Roosevelt about it, but it was no good; her cup became filled to overflowing; bitterness seeped into her soul.

One must have a certain sympathy with this extraordinary woman. She had been granted a vision of glamour and wealth, and this died hard. She had been told to expect illimitable riches—whereas, all she had actually gained was a sum equivalent to £700, plus clothing, furniture, presents and living expenses.

No heroine of maudlin fiction suffered more or so intensely. She became the heroine of Victorian melodrama; she was ejected from her old home—exactly twelve months after her triumphant acquittal. It snowed that day . . .

In May of the following year, she was forced to ask for relief. She was entitled to do this because her husband had been in the world war, and she was thereby enabled to claim protection under the State Soldiers' Aid Fund. The authorities gave her the exact sum of sixty-five dollars a month, to keep her and her four children.

The end?

My friends, it is a sad one. According to the latest information to hand, our heroine is still alive. But, alas, oblivion has descended upon her in a blue-black cloud. On the afternoon that she received the first instalment of the Soldiers' Aid Grant, she moved with her four children to a five-roomed apartment on the second floor of a two-family house on Ethel Avenue, Peabody. Her rent there was twenty-five dollars a month, and she paid it from her welfare allowance. Is it any wonder that one of her friends recently declared "that the children might do with a little more clothing, and that food is not too plentiful"?

Jessie is now said to be thin, although there are no grey hairs on that once thickly thatched black head. Her skin, we are told, is still very white. She can look out of her kitchen window and see her old home just one street away. Perhaps sometimes she thinks of the fireman on his knees—and lying starkly still outside the bathroom.

One might have thought that her spirit would have been broken. Not at all; the same courage that enabled her to face the applauding audiences at her trial now enables her to plan for the future. She has an eye, we are told, on another residence, which could be bought for just over one thousand pounds. She has not the money, but she is hoping that this will turn up.

Perhaps a New Hampshire farmer who knocked at her door

one night, his face flushed like a crimson moon, and who said apologetically that "he hated to bother her, but he wanted to marry her. His wife had died and he was pretty well off," could have been prevailed upon to provide it—but Jessie said "No!" For, you see, there was a tag tied to the offer: the New Hampshire farmer naturally wanted a wife who would live with him down on his farm.

Jessie did not see her way to grant such a request. Living in the backwoods was not for her. After all, she had once been a great figure—her name had been in every paper, crowds had cheered wildly every appearance she made. How could she hide herself away in the bleak Middle-West? She turned this farmer down—cold.

The last recorded words of our heroine may or may not be pathetic. When a reporter called upon her concerning the last offer of marriage, she swept a hand round her present shabby abode and said contemptuously: "This is only temporary, I shall climb again."

Time alone will provide the answer to this statement.

Time—and that ever-crazy country, America.

JACK THE RIPPER

(The Whitechapel Murders, 1888)

Philip Sugden

The identity of Jack the Ripper, who slaughtered six prostitutes in the East End of London in the autumn of 1888, remains the greatest unsolved crime mystery of the Victorian age. The case is thick with theories. Candidates for the killer have ranged from known criminals to luminaries of Court and Social; he (the assumption has to be that the Ripper was male) is said to have moved in several unlinked (and, one is tempted to add, ever-decreasing) circles: medicine, midwifery, butchery, sorcery, Freemasonry, to name but a few. The late twentieth century has thrown up some likely and unlikely suggestions, including Queen Victoria's physician, Sir William Gull, an American quack called Tumblety, and even James Maybrick, the unlikely author of the disputed "Ripper diary", who stumbles into the frame from another Victorian puzzle, that of his own lingering death in Liverpool six months after the last Ripper murder (qv, Florence Maybrick elsewhere in this volume). This review of the case and the clues comes from the historian Philip Sugden (b. 1947), who published his authoritative full-length survey of the facts in his book The Complete History of Jack the Ripper *(Robinson, London 1994).*

"Hunt the Ripper" is almost as old a game as the murders themselves.

In 1888, at the height of the Ripper scare, Sir Charles Warren, Commissioner of the Metropolitan Police, told Sir James Fraser, his counterpart in the City of London: "We are inundated with suggestions and names of suspects." And four years later Chief Inspector Abberline, the man who had co-ordinated the police investigation on the ground, remembered it as a time of despair. "Theories!" he snorted in an interview for *Cassell's Saturday Journal*, "we were lost almost in theories, there were so many of them."

Today, more than a century on, little has changed. The identity of Jack the Ripper is almost a British obsession and the production of new and improbable theories a cottage industry for amateur sleuths. The term "Ripperologist" is now widely used to describe these theorists and may one day find a place in the *Oxford English Dictionary*. Some genuine researchers and an entirely respectable periodical devoted to the murders acknowledge the term, but in common parlance it has come to denote the Ripper charlatan or crank. Unfortunately, too many of the contributors to the steadily growing stack of Ripper books have been written by authors of this stamp and they have taken us away from, not towards, the truth. For there is an important distinction between the methods of the historian and the archetypal Ripperologist. The historian sets out to recover the facts by patient research and the rigorous evaluation of primary sources, and his conclusions follow upon the evidence he has uncovered and studied. The Ripperologist works in the reverse order. First he decides who he wants Jack the Ripper to be. And then he plunders the sources for anything that will invest his candidate with a veneer of credibility. In doing so, inevitably, he perverts, if not suppresses, evidence that conflicts with his theory, and in the worst instances he has not scrupled to buttress his case with "evidence" that has been completely invented. The historian seeks truth. The Ripperologist is too often only intent upon selling a theory and his business is confidence trickery.

In 1910 Dr L. Forbes Winslow was falsifying evidence on the Ripper and he was not the first of his kind. However, since the early 1970s, when alleged royal connections with the case stimulated fresh public interest, the potential rewards for marketable theories—and consequently the temptations to fake evidence—have grown. Stephen Knight's *Jack the Ripper: The Final Solution*, published in 1976, was a worldwide bestseller. In Knight's tale the victims were murdered to prevent them revealing that Prince Albert Victor, Queen Victoria's grandson, had married a Catholic, and the principal killer was none other than Sir William Gull, Physician-in-Ordinary to the Queen herself! It was based upon "revelations" made by the artist and picture restorer Joseph Sickert, but only two years after Knight's book came out Sickert pulled the rug out from under his feet by admitting that the story had been "a hoax . . . a whopping fib". In 1991 extracts from fake Abberline diaries were published and in 1993 another fraudulent diary, this one purporting to be that of the Ripper himself, was marketed amidst huge publicity. Few readers appear to have been deceived. But in all this welter of speculation and falsehood there is a real danger that the few facts we know about Jack the Ripper will be lost and it is important that we keep them before us.

Let's recall them now.

Because the Ripper was never caught we cannot be certain how many murders he perpetrated. Detectives and surgeons involved in the case themselves disagreed on the true total of his victims, estimates ranging from four to nine. Both Robert Anderson, Head of CID, and Abberline, the senior Yard man on the spot, opted for a tally of six. This was, and is, a common view, and it is the one adopted here, but it is important to understand that the existing evidence permits lower or higher figures to be plausibly argued. All six victims were prostitutes and all were slain within a single square mile of the East End of London in the late summer and autumn of 1888.

The first murder now widely attributed to the Ripper was that of Martha Tabram, found dead on the first floor landing of George Yard Buildings, a tenement block in George Yard, off Whitechapel High Street, on the morning of Tuesday, 7 August 1888. Martha had been stabbed frenziedly to death. Dr Timothy Killeen, who conducted the post-mortem examination, found thirty-nine stab wounds on her body. Two different weapons appeared to have been used. Most of the wounds could have been inflicted with a penknife but there was a deep wound in the breast which Dr Killeen felt could only have been made by a strong, long-bladed weapon like a dagger or bayonet.

The number of wounds and the use of more than one weapon suggest the possibility that more than one attacker was involved but the mysteries surrounding Martha's death were never dispelled. Just over three weeks later, on the last day of August, another woman was killed.

The second victim was Mary Nichols, known to her friends as

Polly, a hard-drinking forty-three-year-old Londoner. Like Martha Tabram before her she was living apart from her husband and, also like her, was supporting herself by soliciting on the streets. At about one-twenty on the morning of her death, 31 August, Polly was turned out of a common lodging house in Thrawl Street because she couldn't afford fourpence to pay for a bed. She was wearing a new black straw bonnet trimmed with black velvet and, as she left the house, told the deputy to keep her bed for her until she raised the money. "I'll soon get my 'doss' money," she said laughing, "see what a jolly bonnet I've got now!" About an hour later she was seen, very drunk, on the corner of Osborn Street and Whitechapel Road. And not much more than an hour after that she was dead. Her body was discovered at about three-forty by a carman walking to work along Buck's Row (present Durward Street), Whitechapel.

Charles Cross, the carman, may have disturbed and scared away the killer because medical opinion placed the time of death only minutes before he arrived on the scene. Even so Polly had sustained horrific injuries. Her throat had been cut down to the spinal column and her abdomen ripped open, exposing her intestines. A post-mortem examination was made by Dr Rees Llewellyn. He concluded that the wounds had been inflicted with a strong-bladed knife and that the murderer had exhibited "rough anatomical knowledge". No further clues came to light. Police made numerous inquiries in the neighbourhood but the killer seemed to have vanished without leaving, as Chief Inspector Swanson reported, "the slightest shadow of a trace".

A week later he struck again. On this occasion the victim was a forty-seven-year-old widow named Annie Chapman. Annie supplemented meagre earnings from crochet work, antimacassars and flower selling with casual prostitution. Her fate was strikingly similar to that of Polly Nichols. Expelled from a common lodging house in Dorset Street because she lacked the money for a bed, Annie was on the streets in the early hours of Saturday, 8 September, and just before six her dead and mutilated body was found in the backyard of No. 29 Hanbury Street, Spitalfields. The throat had been ferociously severed, the abdomen laid open and the womb, together with parts of the vagina and bladder, extracted and carried away by the murderer. The pitiful contents of Annie's pocket—two combs and a piece of coarse muslin—were found carefully arrayed by her feet.

It was the Hanbury Street murder that yielded what appeared

to be the first important clues to the identity of the killer. Dr Phillips, the police surgeon who carried out the post-mortem, told the inquest that in his view the culprit had displayed both anatomical knowledge and surgical skill. And this time there was a witness. At five-thirty, shortly before Annie was killed, Mrs Elizabeth Long saw her talking to a man outside No. 29. Unfortunately, she only saw the man's back. But she remembered that he was only slightly taller than Annie (Annie was about five feet tall), that he was wearing a dark coat and brown deerstalker hat and that he was of "shabby genteel" appearancc. She thought he was a foreigner over forty years old.

The macabre slaying in Hanbury Street plunged Whitechapel and Spitalfields into panic.

For some days afterwards excited crowds gathered about the murder sites in Buck's Row and Hanbury Street, turning furiously upon anyone they fancied to blame. Several times police had to rescue innocent eccentrics from the hands of lynch mobs. After dark the streets were deserted except for patrolling constables and homeless vagabonds. And in Mile End a vigilance committee was established to raise a reward for the capture of the murderer.

The CID investigated numerous suspects. The most famous at this stage of the murder hunt was John Pizer, known throughout the neighbourhood as "Leather Apron". Pizer was an unemployed shoemaker. He fell under suspicion because of his reputation for bullying local prostitutes and after the Nichols murder newspapers linked him with the crime in a series of lurid articles. Terrified of mob vengeance, Pizer took refuge at his brother's house in Mulberry Street. The police arrested him there on 10 September but subsequent questioning soon established that he had sound alibis for the dates of the murders. Indeed, when Annie Chapman was killed Pizer was hiding at his brother's house, afraid to venture out. "I will tell you why," he informed the inquest, "I should have been torn to pieces!"

By the end of the month the East End had recovered its nerve. But then, on the morning of Sunday, 30 September, two women were slain, only one hour and some three-quarters of a mile apart.

The first was Elizabeth Stride, a widow and well-known prostitute, whose last place of residence was a common lodging house in Flower and Dean Street. At about twelve-thirty on the fatal morning PC William Smith, on patrol in Berner Street, off Commercial Road, saw her talking with a man. Her companion looked about twenty-eight years old, stood five foot seven or eight inches tall, and sported a small dark moustache. He was respectably dressed in a black diagonal cutaway coat and dark deerstalker and he was carrying a parcel wrapped up in newspaper. Fifteen minutes later another passer-by, Israel Schwartz, actually saw a man throwing Elizabeth down on the pavement outside Dutfield's yard in Berner Street. Schwartz, too frightened to intervene, cowardly scurried away. But he later furnished the police with a good description of the assailant: "Age about thirty, height five foot five inches, complexion fair, hair dark, small brown moustache, full face, broad shouldered; dress, dark jacket and trousers, black cap with peak." Elizabeth's body was found in the passage communicating between Berner Street and Dutfield's Yard at about one. Her throat had been cut from left to right, as in the cases of Polly Nichols and Annie Chapman, but there were no other mutilations.

Just forty-five minutes after the discovery in Berner Street an even more gruesome one was made in Mitre Square, within the eastern boundary of the City of London. City PC Edward Watkins patrolled the square at one-thirty and found it deserted. Entering it again at one forty-four, however, he discovered the dead body of a woman in the darkest and southernmost corner. The throat had been ferociously severed from left to right, the head and face cruelly slashed, there were severe abdominal injuries and the left kidney and part of the womb had been cut out and taken away. "She was ripped up like a pig in the market," said PC Watkins later, "I have been in the force a long while but I never before saw such a sight."

The Mitre Square victim was a forty-six-year-old charwoman and prostitute named Kate Eddowes. What is thought to have been the last known sighting of her alive occurred at one thirty-five. Joseph Lawende, a commercial traveller, was leaving the Imperial Club in Duke Street when he noticed a couple standing at the entrance of a passage which led from Duke Street into Mitre Square. The man looked "rather rough and shabby". He was five foot seven or eight inches in height, of medium build and appeared to be about thirty years old. The clothes included a pepper-and-salt coloured jacket, a reddish neckerchief and a grey cloth cap with a peak. Lawende thought he looked like a sailor. Ten minutes after this sighting Kate's body was found in the square.

A piece of Kate's apron, still wet with blood, was found discarded a few streets away in the entry to Nos. 108–119 Wentworth Model

Dwellings, Goulston Street. Just above it, written in white chalk on
the right-hand side of the doorway, were the words:

> The Juwes are
> The men That
>   Will not
> be Blamed
>   for nothing.

If this message was written by the murderer—and it probably
was—it was the only tangible clue he ever left behind. Its correct
interpretation, however, is problematical. On the face of it it
suggested that the killer was a vengeful Jew and for this reason
Sir Charles Warren, afraid that it might provoke retaliatory attacks
upon the Jewish community, ordered it to be erased before daybreak.
Nevertheless, the prevailing police view at the time was that the
message was a deliberate red herring, intended to throw them off
the scent of the real culprit.

The great disparity in the injuries inflicted upon Elizabeth Stride
and Kate Eddowes has led some writers to contend that they were
slain by different men. This is not impossible. But Elizabeth may
have escaped mutilation only because her killer was disturbed by
Louis Diemschutz, the man who found the body, and it is now generally believed that the Ripper walked into the City to find a second
victim when his desire to mutilate the first had been thwarted. If so
his return to Whitechapel, where he discarded the piece of Kate's
apron, undoubtedly suggests that he lived in the East End.

After the double murder the police unwittingly increased apprehension in the East End by giving publicity to a letter received by
the Central News Agency. This letter, purportedly sent by the
murderer, was written in red ink and promised further killings. "I
am down on whores," it ran, "and I shan't quit ripping them till
I do get buckled." The letter was dated 25 September, five days
before the double killing, and was signed "Jack the Ripper". The
police posted facsimiles of the letter—and a postcard written in the
same hand—outside police stations in the hope that someone might
recognize the handwriting but the scribe was never traced. There is
nothing in the content of the documents, however, to suggest that
they were really written by the murderer. The police themselves
came to regard them as hoaxes and many years later a suspicion
existed at the Yard that Tom Bulling and Charles Moore, two

journalists at the Central News, had been responsible. Whatever the identity of the hoaxer, the only significance of the letter now is that it gave the murderer the gruesome nickname by which he seems destined to be remembered: Jack the Ripper.

The horrific murder of Mary Kelly in her room at No. 13 Miller's Court, Dorset Street, on Friday, 9 November 1888, was the last generally attributed to the Ripper.

Mary was a young Irish prostitute. At the time of her death she was more than six weeks in arrears with her rent and when last seen, at about two on the fatal morning, was soliciting in Commercial Street. A casual labourer named George Hutchinson saw her meet a well-dressed client there and take him to Miller's Court. The man had a large moustache curled up at the ends. He was of Jewish appearance, dark, about thirty-four or thirty-five years old and five foot six inches in height. His attire was impressive. Hutchinson remembered a dark felt hat, a long coat with the collar and cuffs trimmed in astrakhan, a large gold watch chain displayed from the waistcoat and a horseshoe pin affixed in the tie. He was carrying a small parcel in his left hand.

At about four two residents in Miller's Court thought they heard a scream of "Murder!" Some seven hours later the landlord's assistant, calling at No. 13 for rent, discovered Mary's body. It lay on the bed, naked except for the remains of a linen undergarment. She had been appallingly mutilated. The throat had been severed, the face hacked beyond recognition, the breasts cut off and the abdomen laid open. The viscera had been extracted and deposited in various places around the body. The flesh from the abdomen and thighs had been stripped away and placed on a bedside table. The heart had been cut out through the abdominal cavity. It was never recovered.

There were similar murders in the East End after 1888 but these are now generally regarded as copy crimes. After Miller's Court, seemingly, the Ripper vanished, as "if through a trapdoor in the earth", as one contemporary quaintly termed it.

Some serial killers have claimed far more victims than the Ripper but few have terrorized a community so completely as he did the East End of 1888. Partly this was because his crimes were grotesque, partly because they were so concentrated in time and place. "No one who was living in London that autumn will forget the terror created by these murders," wrote Sir Melville Macnaghten, ex-Head of CID, many years later. "Even now I can recall the foggy evenings, and hear again the raucous cries of the newspaper boys: 'Another horrible murder, murder, mutilation, Whitechapel.' Such was the burden of their ghastly song; and, when the double murder of 30 September took place . . . no servant-maid deemed her life safe if she ventured out to post a letter after ten o'clock at night."

So who was Jack the Ripper?

Well, the historical record does suggest a few clues. The witnesses tended to describe a white male, relatively young, in his twenties or thirties, of medium height or less and respectably dressed. Dr Gordon Brown, who carried out the post-mortem examination of Kate Eddowes, was convinced that the murderer had demonstrated surgical skill as well as anatomical knowledge in his extraction of the left kidney. Certainly most of the doctors who saw the Ripper's handiwork felt that *some* degree of anatomical knowledge had been involved. And the close geographical grouping of the crimes, together with the killer's return to Whitechapel from Mitre Square, suggest a local man.

Can we go further? Can we put a name to the Ripper? The answer to that one, despite the blandishments of the Ripperologists, is an emphatic no.

The police investigated hundreds of suspects. It is sometimes said that there was a principal suspect but this implies a consensus of view that simply did not exist within the detective force. Some suspects were more interesting than others but different officers held different theories. Many police records from the period have been lost but enough survives for us to identify some of the main suspects. Indeed, as a result of intensive research over the last thirty years we probably know more about these men than the police did at the time.

One of the most interesting police suspects was Aaron Kosminski, a poor Jewish barber committed to Colney Hatch Lunatic Asylum in 1891. Interesting because his appears to have been the only case in which the police procured evidence to link a suspect with any of the crimes. Sir Robert Anderson certainly came to believe that Kosminski was the Ripper and refers to him in his memoirs, published in 1910. By Anderson's account Kosminski was identified by a witness, the "only person who had ever had a good view of the murderer", but the police were unable to charge him because the witness, also Jewish, refused to give evidence against a fellow-Jew.

Unfortunately, the more we learn about Kosminski the less likely a suspect he seems. Most of the documentation is lost but the clues we have suggest that the witness was Joseph Lawende, the man believed to have fleetingly seen the Ripper on the night of the double murder, and that he did not identify Kosminski until 1890–91, about two years after the event. A great deal of research has been conducted into identification evidence of this kind since Anderson's time and it has taught us that at periods of a year or more after the original sighting it is worthless. There are other doubts about whether Kosminski can have been the Ripper. We have no clear evidence that he possessed anatomical knowledge. And although he spent more than twenty-five years in asylums (he died in Leavesden Asylum, near Watford, in 1919) the doctors who monitored his progress there explicitly and repeatedly described him as a harmless patient.

Melville Macnaghten, who joined the Metropolitan Police in 1889 and became Head of CID in 1903, held to a different theory. In his view the Ripper was Montague John Druitt, a man who committed suicide by throwing himself into the Thames shortly after the Miller's Court tragedy. However, Macnaghten's data on Druitt is now known to have been seriously flawed. He thought, for example, that he was a doctor. In reality Druitt was a schoolteacher and barrister. No one has ever proved a connection between Druitt and the crimes, or even the East End. On the other hand there is evidence to suggest that he spent his summer vacation on the south coast in 1888 and hence may not have been in London when Martha Tabram and Polly Nichols died. Thus, on 1 September, the day after Polly was murdered, Druitt was in Canford, Dorset, playing for the local cricket team against Wimborne.

George Chapman (real name Severin Klosowski), executed in 1903 for the murder of Maud Marsh, fits what we know about the Ripper better than either Kosminski or Druitt. Ex-Chief Inspector Abberline undoubtedly believed that Chapman and the Ripper were the same man and after the trial he congratulated Inspector Godley, who had apprehended Chapman, with the words: "You've got Jack the Ripper at last!"

Before coming to London in 1887 Chapman was trained as a surgeon in his native Poland. In 1888 he lived in Cable Street, within walking distance of the murder sites. His appearance matches descriptions of the Ripper well. And he was violent and cruel. Chapman was fascinated with weaponry and adorned his walls with swords and firearms and he terrorized a succession of female consorts, threatening one with a knife, another with a revolver and physically abusing several. Maud Marsh was the third "wife" he poisoned to death between 1897 and 1902.

If Chapman was the Ripper he must have abandoned the knife

in favour of poison and some writers have not found a change of *modus operandi* as dramatic as this credible. The fatal flaw in the case against Chapman, however, is the simple fact that not a scrap of tangible evidence was ever adduced to connect him with a single one of the Ripper crimes.

Perhaps the most important document to come to light in recent years is the Littlechild letter. Discovered in 1993, it is a letter written by Ex-Chief Inspector John Littlechild, one-time Head of the Special Branch, to the journalist George R. Sims in 1913, and it introduced us to a police suspect hitherto unknown to researchers: an American quack doctor named Francis Tumblety.

Tumblety was in London at the time of the murders. On 16 November 1888 he was charged at Marlborough Street Police Court with homosexual offences and bailed to appear at the Central Criminal Court, but he violated bail and fled, first to France, and then back to America.

Littlechild considered Tumblety a "very likely" Ripper suspect and an interesting circumstantial case can indeed be alleged against him. He had pretensions to medical knowledge, he was a known misogynist and he collected anatomical specimens. His collection included, according to one who saw it, jars containing wombs from "every class of women", and it will be remembered that in two of the Ripper murders the womb had been extracted and taken away.

Yet Tumblety, no less than Kosminski, Druitt and Chapman, must be exonerated. It is clear that the police had no hard evidence implicating him in the killings for had they possessed such information they would have charged him with the murders or, after his flight, sought his extradition. In important respects, furthermore, Tumblety does not fit the Ripper evidence. In 1888 he was fifty-six years of age, far older than any of the men seen with victims. And the murderer would appear to have been a much smaller man. Annie Chapman and Kate Eddowes are known to have both been about five foot tall. Mrs Long, who saw Annie with a man, almost certainly her murderer, thought that Annie's companion was only a "little taller" than she was, and Joseph Levy, Lawende's companion on the night of the double murder, estimated the man they saw talking with Kate Eddowes to have been only "about three inches" taller than Kate. Tumblety, however, was tall, perhaps six foot in height. Someone who knew him said that he "looked like a giant".

The only sensible conclusion one can draw from the existing evidence is that the police investigation failed and its failure left detectives grasping at straws. It is impossible to find a credible case against a single one of their suspects.

We should not judge the police too harshly. In most murder cases victim and killer are known to each other and careful inquiry into the past and circumstances of the victim will usually suggest suspects and motives. This was not so in the Ripper's case. He was an example of that still fortunately rare phenomenon, the murderer of strangers, and such killers are exceedingly difficult to detect. Even today their crimes often go unsolved and modern aids to detection like fingerprinting, the biochemical analysis of blood, DNA fingerprinting and psychological profiling were unknown or undeveloped in 1888. The Ripper's crimes were facilitated, moreover, by the character of the area in which he worked and the kind of victim he targeted. The Victorian East End was an intricate warren of tiny courts, alleys and backyards, impossible for the police to patrol effectively, and the Ripper's victims readily played into his hands. Most of them were poor middle-aged women, deprived of male support by bereavement or separation, and for such women casual prostitution was often an instrument of survival. At the height of the Ripper scare prostitutes fled the district or took refuge in workhouse casual wards, but on any normal night in Whitechapel and Spitalfields large numbers of them could be found soliciting on the streets, eager to sell their bodies and conduct clients to secluded alleys and backyards for the price of a drink or a doss.

Given the failure of the police investigation in 1888 it is extremely unlikely that the Ripper can be unmasked now. Speculative theories will continue to assail us but any proposed solution to the mystery will only carry conviction if it presents a suspect who matches what we know about the Ripper and, crucially, is backed by authentic evidence linking him to the crimes. So far very few of the reckless accusations cast about by Ripperologists have satisfied the first criteria, none the second. As Jonathan Goodman has amusingly observed, the search for Jack the Ripper has come to resemble a horse race in which Chapman is the dubious favourite against a "current line-up of no-hopers, none of appropriate pedigree and most of them zebras in horses' clothing."

More than anything else, however, it is the riddle of the killer's identity that lies at the root of our perennial fascination with the case, it is the very facelessness of Jack the Ripper that keeps his legend alive. If the mystery were to be solved, if some diligent and lucky scholar could prove, for argument's sake, that the Ripper

was John Smith, an obscure Whitechapel slaughterman, the rest
of us would probably lose interest in him altogether. As it is, our
inability to unmask him enables writers and film makers to make
of him what they will. And because of that the mystery of Jack the
Ripper looks set to remain, after more than a century, the classic
whodunnit.

THE MURDER OF MARGERY WREN

(Margery Wren, 1930)

Douglas G. Browne and E. V. Tullett

This unsolved case from 1930 is taken from the casebook of the British pathologist Sir Bernard Spilsbury (1877–1947) hailed as the "greatest medical detective of the century". Spilsbury's professional links with the Home Office began in 1910, when he was called in to examine the mutilated remains of Cora Crippen, wife of the infamous doctor who had since fled London with his mistress, Ethel le Neve. It was the first of a long series of cases in which Spilsbury was retained by the Home Office over a period of nearly forty years. The rather forlorn case of Miss Wren, robbed in her seaside shop and left for dead, is included in the best-selling biography of Spilsbury published by Browne and Tullett in 1951. Douglas G. Browne was a kinsman of Hablot Knight Browne, better known as Phiz, who illustrated the works of Charles Dickens. Tom Tullett was chief of the Daily Mirror's *crime bureau, who claimed to be the only journalist to have been a detective in the CID.*

If there are degrees of wickedness in murder, only a shade less atrocious than the killing of children is the deliberate battering to death of elderly women living alone. These crimes are almost always committed for gain. In the majority of cases the murderer picks out some one known to him—a woman keeping a small shop, or with a reputation for hoarding money—but the evidence shows that there is also a type of monster who sets to work, by a system of trial and error, to find a suitable victim. Though murder may not always be intended, whether it results or not seems to be a matter of indifference to this class of criminal. From his point of view the victim is usually better dead; and only too often, the hammer or poker having silenced her, the bloody task is completed.

Such brutes are always with us, as the newspapers show, and their crimes recur with terrible frequency in Spilsbury's records. Some of these cases have been mentioned. Among those occurring in this middle period of his career two stand out—the murders of Miss Wren at Ramsgate and of Mrs Kempson at Oxford.

The Wren case, which in its shocking details differs little from a score of others, is remarkable for the character and behaviour of Miss Wren herself. She was eighty-two, and she had a small sweet-shop in Ramsgate. She possessed some house property, and had money in the bank. Like so many people of her age and class, she kept cash in tin boxes and other receptacles stowed away in various hiding-places. This dangerous habit got known, as it usually does, and her hoards, no doubt, were much exaggerated, the more so because she lived like the traditional miser, in squalor and discomfort.

About six o'clock on 20 September 1930, a girl of twelve who lived opposite the shop was sent across the street to buy a blancmange powder. The shop door was locked; peering through the window, the girl saw Miss Wren sitting in her back room. When eventually the old woman came to the door blood was streaming down her face, and she could only whisper; but though, in fact, she was suffering from injuries that might have killed her on the spot, she went behind the counter and fetched a number of packets for the child to choose from. The girl ran back to her parents, and to their horrified inquiries Miss Wren gave the unlikely explanation that she had fallen over the fire-tongs.

She was taken to hospital, where she lingered for five days. She had been savagely attacked, and on the third day Scotland Yard was called in. As her mind wandered she made rambling and contradictory statements, from which glimpses of the truth emerged, to the nurses and the police, and to the magistrate who, later, waited beside her bed. It was an accident; a man had attacked her with the fire-tongs; he had a white bag; it was another man with a red face; it was two men; then, again, it was an accident with the tongs. Once she admitted that she knew her assailant, but she would not name him. "I don't wish him to suffer. He must bear his sins . . ." Just before the end she said, "He tried to borrow ten pounds." More than this they could not get from her, and to Superintendent Hambrook, who was in charge of the case, she was the most determined, inflexible woman he ever met. On the afternoon of the 25th she died, still keeping her secret.

Performing the post-mortem on the following day, Spilsbury enumerated eight wounds and bruises on the face, and seven more, lacerated or punctured, on the top of the head. In addition, there had been an attempt at strangulation. The injuries were undoubtedly inflicted with the tongs which figured in the poor woman's stories, and on which hairs were found.

The circumstances of this murder suggest that it may not have been premeditated, as it so often seems to be in similar cases. Miss Wren was seen alive and well at five-thirty, and she usually kept her shop open after six. At that hour, in September, with Summer Time in force, it was not dark. There were people going up and down the street, and children playing. If violence was intended it was an extremely rash project. On the other hand, there can be no doubt that the murderer came for money, and, like all his type, was prepared to go to great lengths to get it. It was probably he who locked the shop door. Perhaps disturbed by another caller—for no money seems to have been taken—he escaped by the backyard. Apart from the evidence of Miss Wren's admissions, it is clear that he knew of her habits, and was familiar with the premises.

At the inquest certain persons were referred to by letters of the alphabet. Superintendent Hambrook says that there were six suspects, of whom *A*, *B*, and *C* were able to clear themselves. One of the remaining three *D*, *E*, or *F*, was the murderer. Miss Wren knew which, and the police may know too. But it has never been possible to pin the crime on him.

THE ZODIAC KILLER

(Zodiac Killings, 1968)

Colin Wilson

One evening just before Christmas 1968, a teenaged courting couple parked their car by a reservoir in the hills above San Francisco Bay, California. Minutes later, they were murdered in cold blood by a gun-wielding maniac. The killer was to become notorious throughout the United States as "Zodiac". Six months later he struck again, but this time one of his victims survived and described the killer. Impatient at the inability of the police to catch him, the killer sent letters and a coded message to three different newspapers. Once deciphered, the cryptogram made chilling reading, but it took the police no nearer to the killer's identity. After five murders, the killing stopped, but the mocking letters continued. The British author Colin Wilson (b. 1931) writes prolifically on crime, the occult and the paranormal.

It was the perfect night for young lovers: calm, moonlit and cold enough outside for the inside of the estate car to seem the most delightful place in the world. David Farraday and Bettilou Jensen were out on their first date on the night of 20 December 1968. They had spent most of the evening at the high school Christmas concert in nearby Vallejo, a small town about twenty miles (thirty kilometres) north-east of San Francisco, California.

Now, at eleven-fifteen p.m., they had just parked near a concrete pump-house above Lake Herman reservoir. The heater blew warm air, the radio played pop music, and the seventeen-year-old boy and sixteen-year-old girl began to get better acquainted.

Suddenly, a man appeared at the window, and David Farraday found himself looking straight down the barrel of a gun. As the youth opened the door and started to climb out, the gun exploded. David Farraday fell dead instantly with a bullet wound behind his left ear. Bettilou flung open her own door and began to run. In the moonlight, it was impossible for the gunman to miss her; five shots ploughed into her back and she collapsed seventy-five yards (sixty-eight metres) from the car.

Only a few minutes later, another car drove past the pump-house. The woman driver saw the two bodies clearly in the headlights, but she did not stop; on the contrary, she put her foot down on the accelerator and drove fast towards the next town, Benicia, about six miles (nine kilometres) away, where she was going to meet her children from the Saturday evening cinema. A few miles further along the road she saw, with relief, the red, flashing light of an oncoming police car. Within minutes, two deputy sheriffs and a detective sergeant were on their way to the pump-house on the Vallejo–Benicia road.

The young couple were both dead, and the warmth of their bodies told Detective Sergeant Leslie Lundblad that they had died recently. But beyond that there seemed to be no clues. David Farraday's wallet was intact in his pocket. Bettilou Jensen lay exactly as she had fallen, and her clothing was undisturbed. This, however, did not entirely rule out sex as a motive—it was conceivable that the killer had been disturbed by the passing car and taken refuge temporarily behind his victims' car until it had gone. The woman driver had, it turned out, shown very good sense in not stopping to investigate.

There were two more possible explanations. The most obvious was jealousy. David Farraday was a good-looking young man; Bettilou was a pretty girl. Perhaps some rejected lover had followed them as they drove towards the lovers' lane. The other possibility was rather more disturbing: that the killer was not a rejected lover, merely a reject—and a man who hated *all* lovers.

Lundblad's investigations soon disposed of the jealousy theory. David and Bettilou were ordinary high-school students. Both had good scholastic records and David was a scout and a fine athlete. Neither had any "secret life" to investigate. It became clear to

Lundblad that the two victims must have been chosen at random. Their killer had probably been hiding near the pump-house—a well-known resort for young lovers—waiting, like a hunter, for someone to arrive. It seemed probable that he had parked his car out of sight and sat in it until David's estate car had arrived. Even that was only a guess; the ground was frozen too hard to show tyre tracks. Only one thing seemed clear: sooner or later, this hunter of human beings would probably experience the urge to kill again.

Six months passed and David Farraday and Bettilou Jensen became just two more statistics in California's huge file of unsolved crimes. It looked as though their murders were an isolated incident until, shortly before midnight on 4 July 1969, another young couple parked their car in Blue Rock Springs Park, Vallejo, only two miles (three kilometres) from the place where David and Bettilou had died. The car, a brown Ford Corvair, belonged to the girl, twenty-two-year-old Darlene Elizabeth Ferrin, a Vallejo waitress and mother of a young child. With her was nineteen-year-old Michael Renault Mageau, who worked for his father, a Vallejo businessman.

Soon after the couple drove into the car park, another car came and parked beside them. They were not particularly disturbed at this: there were various other cars in the park, the nearest of which contained several people. In any case, this second car soon went away, leaving them in peace. Ten minutes passed, and suddenly the same car returned, this time parking on the other side of the Corvair. A blinding beam of light, like a searchlight, shone through the window on the passenger side, which made the couple think that it was a police patrol car. A man opened the door and came over towards them. Suddenly there was an explosion of gunfire. Two shots struck Darlene Ferrin as she sat at the wheel; another ploughed into Michael Mageau's neck and went up into his mouth, causing him to scream with agony. Then the man turned and walked back to his own car. He paused and fired another four shots, then drove away, backing out so fast that he left a smell of burning rubber behind him.

Michael Mageau, still conscious, saw him drive away. By this time he was lying on the ground beside the car, trying to reach the nearest other car in the park. But before he succeeded, this car also drove away: the occupants were obviously anxious not to get involved. Michael Mageau lost consciousness.

At four minutes past midnight, the switchboard operator at the

Vallejo Police Headquarters received a call. A man's voice told her, "I want to report a double murder. If you go one mile east on Columbus Parkway to a public park, you will find the kids in a brown car. They are shot with a 9 mm Luger. I also killed those kids last year. Goodbye." Then the line went dead.

When the police patrol car arrived at Blue Rock Springs Park, the officers discovered that the caller had been mistaken about one detail: it was not a double murder. Michael Mageau was still alive, although the bullet that had passed through his tongue prevented him from speaking. Darlene Ferrin was dead.

Michael Mageau slowly recovered. When he could speak, he was able to describe his assailant as a stocky, round-faced man, about five foot eight inches (1.72 metres) tall, with light brown wavy or curly hair. His age was around thirty. The gun he had used was not the same one as in the previous case; this one was a 9 mm whereas the other was a .22. But the Solano County Sheriff's Department had little doubt that the caller was telling the truth when he admitted to killing David Farraday and Bettilou Jensen. And Lundblad now knew that his worst apprehensions were confirmed. The killer's motive was not robbery, rape, or jealousy. This was simply a "nut", a homicidal maniac who killed at random.

Again, there were no clues. Even the discovery that the killer had used a public telephone booth in a garage two miles from the murder scene failed to provide a lead. The garage had been closed at the time, so no one had seen the caller. The likeliest inference was that the killer was an inhabitant of Vallejo, or was at least familiar with the town, and knew where the garage was and that it would be closed. And since Vallejo was a small town, that seemed a promising lead. Surely somebody would recognize Michael Mageau's description of the stocky, wavy-haired man who drove a brown car, probably a Ford?

But it seemed that no one did. And four weeks after the 4 July murder, the killer himself apparently became impatient with the police's lack of progress and decided to liven up the investigation. On the morning of 1 August 1969 the editor of the *Vallejo Times-Herald* received a crudely scrawled letter, signed with a circle containing a cross, which looked ominously like the telescopic sight of a rifle. The letter-writer described himself as the man who had shot both couples, giving details that made it clear that he knew more about the murders than had been made public. For example, he gave precise details of the type of bullets that had killed Darlene Ferrin. He also mentioned the clothing worn by Bettilou Jensen, evidence that he had taken a close look at her body before fleeing from the scene.

The letter contained an enclosure—a third of a sheet of paper, covered with a strange cipher. What had happened to the other two thirds? The answer soon came. They were enclosed in two more letters, sent simultaneously to the *San Francisco Chronicle* and the *San Francisco Examiner*. The letters to all three newspapers were identical; the code was not. But the letter-writer explained that if the three fragments of the ciphered message were decoded and joined together, they would reveal his identity.

It was the signature on the letters—the circle with a cross inside it—that provided the killer with his nickname. The sign is the astrological symbol for the zodiac, the circle of twelve heavenly constellations. From then on, the newspapers called the killer "Zodiac". All three letters contained the same threat: that if they were not published that same day, 1 August, the writer would "go on a rampage": "This will last the whole weekend and I will cruise around killing people who are alone until Sun night or until I kill a dozen people."

The letters were published—but not in their entirety. Certain details were withheld, including the murder threats. Most major murder cases provoke false confessions from the mentally ill; by withholding part of the letters, the police had a useful method of distinguishing between a harmless crank (who would not be able to say what was missing) and the real killer, if they were to make an arrest.

All three newspapers published the complete text of the cryptogram, together with a request that the letter-writer should provide more proof of his identity. Zodiac responded promptly, sending the *San Francisco Examiner* a letter beginning: "This is Zodiac speaking", in which he gave more details of the crimes. But he provided no further clue to his identity.

Public attention now centred on the cryptogram. It was sent to naval code experts at the nearby Mare Island Naval Yard, but they failed to crack it. Amateur cryptanalysts all over the state experienced the same lack of success. But one man—a schoolteacher named Donald Harden, who lived in Salinas, California—had the inspired idea of looking for groups of signs that might fit the word "kill", on the grounds that this word would be used more than once. When he had found the suspected group of signs, he began the long, slow business of working out other letters that might be associated with it—for example, endings like "-ing" or "-ed". It took Harden and his wife ten hours to decode most of the letter. It read:

> I like killing people because it is so much fun it is more fun than killing wild game in the forest because man is the most dangerous animal of all to kill something gives me the most thrilling experience it is even better than getting your rock off with a girl the best part of it is when I die I will be reborn in paradise and all I have killed will become my slaves I will not give you my name because you will try to slow down or stop my collecting slaves for my afterlife . . .

The decoding was made more complicated by the fact that the cryptogram was full of spelling errors (such as "forrest" for forest and "sloi" for slow), and it ended in an incomprehensible jumble: "ebeori st me thh piti."

But the threatened massacre (the "rampage") did not materialize. Perhaps Zodiac was satisfied with the partial publication of his letter, or perhaps he never had any intention of going on a murder rampage on a weekend when every police officer in California would be looking for him. The threat was simply to cause the maximum amount of panic.

The public offered more than a thousand tips, and every one was checked by the police. Yet ten weeks after the murder of Darlene Ferrin, they were still apparently no closer to solving the crimes. The long, blazing hot summer drew to a close. On the afternoon of Saturday 27 September, two students from Pacific Union College, a Seventh Day Adventist institution above Napa Valley, went out for a picnic on the shores of Lake Berryessa, about thirteen miles (twenty kilometres) north of Vallejo. Bryan Hartnell was twenty years old, and Cecilia Shepard was 22. They had just finished eating at about four-thirty p.m. when they heard a noise behind them. From the shadow of a tree, a hooded figure stepped out. On the part of the hood covering the figure's chest was a zodiac sign, drawn in white. The short, pudgy figure advanced towards them, a gun in one hand and a knife in the other.

In a gruff voice, the man asked Hartnell for money, and the young man said he was welcome to the small amount he had on him. The hooded man then declared that he was an escapee from Deer Lodge State Prison in Montana, where he had killed a guard, and said that he needed to take their white sports car so that he could get to Mexico. Then he produced a length of plastic clothes-line and proceeded to tie them both up. As he tied Hartnell's hands, the young man was able to see through the eye-slits in the hood that their assailant wore glasses and had brown hair. When he had tied both victims by the wrists and ankles, the man announced: "I'm going to have to stab you people." Hartnell replied, "I'm chicken. Please stab me first—I couldn't bear to see her stabbed." "I'll do just that," said the man, and plunged the knife again and again into Hartnell's back. Sick and dizzy with pain, Hartnell then watched the man attack Cecilia. This, obviously, was what the killer had been looking forward to. After the first stab he went into a frenzy, driving the knife again and again into her back. Then he turned her over and stabbed her repeatedly in the stomach. When he had finished, he went over to their car, took out a black felt-tipped pen and wrote on the passenger door. Then he left.

Fighting off unconsciousness, Bryan Hartnell managed to struggle over to Cecilia and undo her wrist bonds with his teeth. It made no difference; she was too weak to move. But fortunately help was already on the way. A fisherman on the lake had heard their screams and had seen the two bodies lying on the shore. He rowed straight to the headquarters of the park ranger and within half an hour Ranger William White was kneeling by the two victims, who both looked close to death. They had just been rushed off to hospital when the Napa police arrived. They, however, had not been summoned by the fisherman or the ranger. They had been alerted by an anonymous telephone call, a man with a gruff voice telling them: "I want to report a murder. No, a double murder. They are two miles north of park headquarters. They were in a white Volkswagen Karmann Ghia. I'm the one that did it." There was no click to end the call; the man had apparently left the telephone to dangle off the hook.

Bryan Hartnell and Cecilia Shepard arrived at hospital in Napa; neither was able to speak. Cecilia died two days later without recovering from her coma; Bryan Hartnell recovered slowly, and was later able to describe their attacker. But by then the police already knew they were dealing with Zodiac. They found his sign on the passenger door of the sports car. He had also written two dates, 20 December and 4 July, the dates of the first two attacks; and a time, four-thirty, the time of the third attack.

Only six blocks from the police headquarters in Napa, the police found the public telephone from which Zodiac had made the call; the telephone receiver was still hanging off the hook. Technicians found three fingerprints on it, but this clue also led nowhere. The killer's prints were not on police records in California; apparently he had no criminal record in the state. A check with Montana's Deer Lodge State Prison revealed what the police already took for granted: the killer's talk about escaping and killing a guard there was pure fantasy.

Two weeks later, on the evening of 11 October 1969, a student and part-time taxi-driver named Paul Stine picked up a passenger near the Fairmont Hotel on Nob Hill in San Francisco; he was a stocky man with brown hair and horn-rimmed glasses. A quarter of an hour later, two youths standing at the intersection of Washington Street and Cherry Street heard the sound of a gunshot. It came from a yellow cab that had pulled in to the kerb. As they watched, a man got out of the back seat, and leaned through the window into the front of the cab. There was a tearing noise, then the man began wiping the cab with a piece of cloth. Suddenly aware that he was being watched, he left the cab and began to walk rapidly along the street towards the great open space called the Presidio.

The youths alerted the police, who were at the spot within minutes. Paul Stine was slumped forward over the wheel of the cab. The twenty-nine-year-old student of San Francisco State College was dead, shot in the back of the head. The motive was robbery—his wallet was missing and so was the cash from previous fares. The tearing noise the witnesses had heard had been Stine's shirt, which the killer had used to wipe the cab, presumably to eliminate fingerprints.

It looked like a typical armed robbery, the kind that often occurs in San Francisco on a Saturday night. The only unusual feature about this particular crime was its sheer ruthlessness—the driver had been killed when he could just as easily have been left alive. It was not until the following Tuesday that the police realized that they had come close to catching Zodiac. The *San Francisco Chronicle* received a letter that began: "This is Zodiac speaking. I am the murderer of the taxi driver over by Washington and Maple Street last night. To prove this here is a bloodstained piece of his shirt. I am the same man who did in the people in the south bay area. The S.F. [San Francisco] police could have caught me last night if they had tried . . ."

The letter went on to jeer at the police for not making a thorough search of the Presidio, and commented on how much the killer detested the sound of the police motor cycles. It continued:

"Schoolchildren make nice targets. I think I shall wipe out a school bus some morning. Just shoot out the tyres and then pick off all the kiddies as they come bouncing out."

The letter was signed with the mark of the Zodiac. By that time, a check on the bullet that had killed Stine showed that it came from the same .22 that had killed the first two victims ten months before. There could be no doubt that the letter was genuine. The bloodstained piece of cloth was from the tail of a shirt, and it fitted the torn shirt left on Paul Stine.

Was the killer serious about shooting children from a school bus? Probably not—he had never, so far, taken any real risk; he liked to kill stealthily, then run away. But the threat could certainly not be ignored. Armed deputies started to ride on all school buses, not only in San Francisco but in all the surrounding towns. Drivers were instructed not, on any account, to stop even if shots were fired; they were to drive on at top speed, sounding the horn and flashing the lights.

But all these precautions proved unnecessary. The murder of Paul Stine was the last officially recorded crime of the Zodiac killer. The murderer may well have felt that the hunt was getting too close; the police by now had good descriptions of him, and had issued "Wanted" notices showing a man with a crew-cut and horn-rimmed glasses. Police from Napa to San Francisco were permanently on the alert; and there was a noticeable drop in the number of courting couples using lovers' lanes at night. The team hunting Zodiac now believed they were getting close, and that it would only be a matter of time before their net snared the man whose fingerprints matched those found on the telephone. But this optimism proved to be unfounded.

Zodiac had decided to stop killing, but his craving for publicity was unsated. In the early hours of 21 October, ten days after the murder of Paul Stine, the switchboard operator of the Oakland Police Department heard a gruff voice saying, "This is Zodiac". He went on to make a number of remarks that later convinced police that he was the man who had so far killed five people. What he really wanted, said the caller, was to give himself up. He would do that on condition that he was represented by a famous lawyer—preferably F. Lee Bailey or Melvin Belli, both well known lawyers at the time. He would also, he said, like to speak on a famous television talk-show that went out on breakfast television.

The requests sounded absurd, but the Zodiac squad decided that it was worth a try. They immediately contacted Melvin Belli, who had an office in San Francisco, and asked if he would be willing to try to help them trap Zodiac. He agreed without hesitation. Then they asked the chat-show host, Jim Dunbar, if he would reserve space for a telephone call on his show at six forty-five that morning. The police then got in touch with the only three people who had heard Zodiac's voice: victim Bryan Hartnell and the two switchboard operators who had taken Zodiac's calls.

When the show went on the air at six forty-five a.m., silver-haired Melvin Belli was sitting beside the presenter Jim Dunbar. Dunbar told his audience that they were hoping for a call from the Zodiac killer, and asked them to keep the telephone lines clear. The audience cooperated. Those who saw the opening moments of the show rang their friends to tell them what was happening and, as a result, the show reached a record audience for that time of day in the San Francisco Bay area.

Almost an hour went by, while Belli and Dunbar discussed the murders. Then, at seven forty-one a.m., a soft, boyish voice came on the line. He rang off immediately, but rang back five minutes later. This time he identified himself as Zodiac, but said he preferred to be called Sam. In the studio, Bryan Hartnell and the two switchboard operators shook their heads. Unless Zodiac had been deliberately lowering his voice when they heard him, this call was a hoax.

Sam rang off and rang back fifteen separate times. He stated that he had been suffering from headaches "since I killed that kid last December", and he frequently groaned with pain, explaining, "it is the headache speaking". Belli tried twice to persuade Sam to give himself up, without success. But finally, with the broadcast sound cut off so that the television audience could not hear, Belli persuaded the caller to meet him in front of a shop in Daly City, south of San Francisco.

Predictably perhaps, the mysterious caller failed to arrive. Members of the Zodiac squad hidden at various points near the shop told themselves in consolation that they did not believe the caller was Zodiac anyway. Yet that conclusion is by no means as obvious as it looks. If the caller was a hoaxer, then it would seem logical to expect that the real Zodiac would lose no time in denouncing him. Nothing of the sort happened. And when, that Christmas, the lawyer Melvin Belli received a letter from a man who called himself Zodiac, it began "Dear Melvin", as if he and Belli were old acquaintances. To confirm his identity, the writer enclosed another piece of Paul Stine's bloodstained shirt. Handwriting experts confirmed that this letter bore strong resemblances to the earlier ones. The letter seemed to indicate that the writer's mental state was deteriorating. The spelling was worse than usual, and there was a note of desperation that sounded genuine: "The one thing I ask of you is this, please help me. I cannot reach out for help because of this thing in me won't let me. I am finding it extremely difficult to hold it in check and I am afraid I will lose control and take my ninth and possibly tenth victim. Please help me I am drowning . . ."

The claim that he had killed eight people, not five, led to frenzied activity in the San Francisco Police Department, where records were checked and re-checked for other possible Zodiac murders that had gone unrecognized. The only unsolved case that seemed to fit Zodiac's pattern was the murder of an eighteen-year-old student, Cheri Jo Bates, who had been found dead in her car in the college car park with her throat slashed. If she was a Zodiac victim, then she pre-dated all the others, and it seemed odd that Zodiac had not taken the opportunity to boast about this crime at some time, as the had done about the others. If Cheri Jo Bates was the first victim and Zodiac was counting the two men who had recovered, that would explain the "eight" mentioned in his letter.

One big problem for the police was that hoaxers and mentally disturbed people were jumping on the Zodiac bandwagon; some of these showed a disturbing note of sadism. In one letter, the writer threatened to torture his victims before he killed them by tying them over anthills to watch them squirm or driving splinters under their nails. In some cases, the writers snipped out letters or words from newspapers and glued them to postcards. One read: "The pace isn't any slower! In fact it's just one big thirteenth. Some of them fought. It was horrible." But police were able to dismiss most of these; the real Zodiac usually went to some trouble to prove his identity. On 16 March 1971 the *Los Angeles Times* received a Zodiac letter, postmarked from Pleasanton, near Los Angeles, in which the murderer taunted the police for being unable to catch him. This letter included the figure "17+"—an attempt to imply that the death toll was rising.

Three years passed. In January 1974 Zodiac was still hungering for attention; a letter postmarked San Francisco hinted that the number of his victims had now reached thirty-seven; it added that he would "do something nasty" if the letter was not publicized. Internal evidence suggested that this time the letter was genuine—and there were others, too, which appeared to be authentic communications from the killer.

The 1974 letter is, in its way, as significant as any of the crimes themselves. What it reveals is a man whose deepest craving is for attention; he clamours for it like a badly behaved child. This point was noted by one of the USA's top psychiatrists, Dr Laurence Freedman, who commented, "He kills senselessly because he is deeply frustrated. And he hates himself because he is an anonymous nonentity. When he is caught he will turn out to be a mouse, a murderous mouse." He added that he was convinced that Zodiac was insane.

Freedman's psychological portrait of Zodiac is based on the crimes themselves which, studied closely, reveal a certain pattern. The first element is a complete lack of courage. It appears that Zodiac ordered David Farraday out of the car, then started to shoot almost immediately, as if afraid he himself might be attacked. He approached the car containing Michael Mageau and Darlene Ferrin and began to shoot immediately; then he jumped into his own car and drove off so fast that he burnt the rubber of his tyres.

It is also significant that two of his male victims survived. In the case of Bryan Hartnell, it is obvious that the killer's real interest was in his friend Cecilia Shepard, who was a beautiful girl. He stabbed Hartnell only in the back. But when he began to stab Cecilia he lost control, stabbing her repeatedly in the back then turning her over and stabbing her another twenty-three times in the stomach. In all probability, this violence brought him some kind of sexual satisfaction, but there was no evidence of rape or attempted rape in the case of any of his three female victims. This seemed to suggest a man who was repressed and inhibited in his relations with women.

The case of the taxi-driver Paul Stine again illustrates the same combination of nervousness and extreme caution. It took place at a late hour on a foggy night, and he ordered the driver to pull up in a deserted street. The motive was robbery, but he was not willing to risk simply holding him up and taking his money; he preferred to guard against being identified by shooting his victim in the back of the head. When he realised he was being watched, he fled instantly. The next day, his courage restored, he wrote the police a jeering note and enclosed a fragment of his victim's bloodstained shirt.

As significant as the killer's cowardice is his craving for attention. After the first double murder, he drove off hastily, perhaps alarmed by the headlights of the oncoming car whose driver noticed the bodies only minutes after they had been shot. He made no attempt to contact the police or to publicise the murders. Yet immediately after shooting Michael Mageau and Darlene Ferrin, he rushed to the nearest telephone to inform the police of what he had done. And it was after this shooting that he wrote the letters to three newspapers, including one in code, and threatened to go on a murder rampage and kill twelve people. By then he was convinced he had got away with it and wanted to boast, to defy authority, to make people cringe. He was no longer an "anonymous nonentity". He would force the world to pay attention.

If, in fact, the telephone caller to the Jim Dunbar show was Zodiac—and the later letter to Melvin Belli makes this highly probable—then this episode is rather ironic. The "anonymous nonentity" had caused shock waves all over California; he had had the satisfaction of knowing that hundreds of people were trying to puzzle out his cryptogram—it must have felt rather like being a bestselling author. He had certainly achieved a kind of fame. The murder of the taxi-driver brought him yet more publicity, and after the threat of an attack on a school bus, he was the most talked-about man in the USA. When he rang the San Francisco Police Department on 21 October, he undoubtedly wanted to appear on Jim Dunbar's show. The fact that the caller to the show had a "boyish voice" is no proof that he was not Zodiac. Various other people described Zodiac as having a gruff voice, but any man can lower his voice to make it sound gruff—in fact, this is the easiest way of disguising the voice. And if "Sam" was not Zodiac, then who was he? One thing that seems fairly certain is that if Zodiac had changed his mind about ringing through to the programme and a hoaxer had taken his place, Zodiac would have lost no time in denouncing the phoney; his sense of publicity would have guaranteed that.

Yet all this fame was ultimately self-defeating since, though he could walk along a street and think, "I am famous", nobody knew him—he was still an anonymous nonentity. He could address the famous lawyer as "Dear Melvin"—but he did not dare to sign his own name. He tried to keep the excitement alive with more letters, hinting at more killings, but he was crying wolf too often and the newspapers eventually relegated him to the back page. The only way of keeping the excitement alive would be to commit more murders, but next time he might be caught. Besides, being a temporary "celebrity" had released some of the frustration that had turned him into a killer. As it was, the police had come dangerously close, with an accurate description of him and three fingerprints. So the "murderous mouse"—unless he has since been arrested and jailed for another crime, perhaps in another state where he was not recognized—has presumably lapsed back into obscurity, telling himself that at least he had made the world sit up and take notice of him. Other police theories are that he is in hospital or has died. The Zodiac killings could be used to illustrate one of Freud's most disturbing assertions: that if a child only had the power, it would destroy the world.

There is one more speculation. In his first letter, Zodiac asserted that the decoding of the cipher message would reveal his identity. It did not do so. The logical assumption is that the killer never meant to reveal his identity, but intended the claim to act as bait and cause widespread effort to crack the code. Yet one thing that may strike anyone who looks at the first few lines of the cipher message is that Zodiac sometimes used the letter "Z" to signify an "E". Might the killer have, in fact, hidden his own name in the message, and could the solution to the case now lie in the hands of another cryptanalyst?

AND TO HELL WITH BURGUNDY

(Florence Bravo, 1876)

Dorothy Dunbar

One of the earliest puzzles of the Victorian age to earn the description of "mystery" was the death of Charles Bravo at Balham, south-west London. Bravo, possessed not only of a dashing name but also of an enviable position in polite society, was a bored barrister of thirty whose ambitions to stand for Parliament were abruptly dashed when he died of poison in the spring of 1876. The two main suspects were his beautiful wife Florence and her paid companion, the unprepossessing Mrs Jane Cox. A third candidate presented himself in the shape of Dr James Gully, a celebrated but elderly hydropathic doctor at Malvern, with whom Florence had conducted an affair between her brief first marriage and this, her second. The American writer Dorothy Dunbar (1923–76), whose mother was one of the first women crime reporters in the US, offered this unique perspective on the Bravo case in her 1964 survey of domestic murders Blood in the Parlor.

Some women attract men; some women attract trouble. Florence Bravo was a double-barreled magnet; she attracted both. Her small voluptuous figure, which no corset or bustle could distort, her coquettish chestnut hair, which no curling iron or crimpers could restrain, and an irresistible siren song of helplessness made up a small but potent package of sex appeal. It was just her luck to fatally fascinate an alcoholic, a married man, and a spoiled boy.

As for trouble, Florence was a feather, caught in every emotional downdraft that came along, and she got trapped in some cross-ventilation when she overstepped the unalterable code of Victorian womanhood. In an age when the sanctity of woman was as jealously institutionalized as chivalry had been in the days when knighthood was in flower, the pattern of Victorian dualism fell into inflexible categories. A woman was either "pure" or "fallen". She had to be one or the other, and there was no room for a twilight zone, such as our current popular myth of the "prostitute with the heart of gold". A pure woman was a virgin with chaste thoughts and sexual *rigor mortis*, a woman who granted her husband bleak conjugal submission and periodic heirs, or a spinster who lightened the heavy load of her days with the subliminal sop of John Ruskin's Italian-art criticism or pure-thinking literature like *Sesame and Lilies*.

A fallen woman encompassed everything from the dashing, feather-boa-ed belles, who toyed with champagne and men in private dining rooms, to gin-logged slatterns. But Florence Bravo didn't realize that never the twain shall meet. If she had followed the rigidly mapped course of either a good or bad woman, there would have been no nineteenth-century shocker known as the "Balham Mystery", but because she wanted to have her cake and eat it, too—Florence Bravo was just plain murder!

Florence Campbell was the daughter of Robert Campbell, a wealthy London merchant. Everything points to a spoiled, petted childhood and to a familiar twentieth-century spectacle—well-meaning parents who are unable to cope with the teenaged Frankensteins they have created.

In 1863, when she was eighteen, Florence visited Montreal, and, to her, one of the greatest attractions of the brave new world was Captain Ricardo of Her Majesty's Army. Captain Ricardo listed as assets a dashing uniform reminiscent of a Strauss operetta, a name with an evocative Latin ending, and a comfortable fortune. In 1864, two doom-ridden events took place: Maximilian, that harassed Hapsburg, became Emperor of Mexico; and Florence Campbell married her colorful captain. Some men accept marriage with stoicism, while others luxuriate in the matrimonial state. There are men who fight it—wifebeaters, etc., and there are men who avoid it, e.g., bachelors. Captain Ricardo by nature and inclination, belonged to the latter group. He had an inordinate liking for women, and he was an avid companion of the grape. Florence, at a dewy, well-developed eighteen certainly must have appealed to him, but marriage was the price for capitulation. So Captain Ricardo bartered bachelorhood for maidenhood.

Like most young brides, Florence embarked upon matrimony with high hopes. Perhaps she even subscribed to the age-old delusion that marriage changes a man. In any event, the honeymoon came to an abrupt end when it became apparent that "hearth and home" were just two rather unfamiliar words in the English language to Captain Ricardo. He was keeping mistresses and making a cult out of the empty bottle. To Florence, spoiled and petted, six years of violent scenes, pitying smiles from friends and relations, and a husband's total lack of concern over her happiness were devastating blows to her ego. Captain Ricardo alternated between sessions with pink elephants and fits of black remorse, and in the middle of this emotional maelstrom, was Florence, her self-confidence shaken, her ego badly fractured. To help soften the ugly edges, she started drinking herself. If you can't beat 'em, join 'em, seemed to be her attitude. Let there be no mistake that Florence's drinking fell under the proscribed limits of social drinking for Victorian females. The sip of sherry or blackberry wine, the gulp of stronger spirits for medicinal reasons were not for Florence. She drank as she did everything else—whole heartedly, on the spur of the moment, and all the way. Any self-respecting AA would unabashedly tip his hat to the capacity of this frail Victorian belle.

By 1870, Florence was on the verge of what would now be called a nervous breakdown. Six years of marriage to Captain Ricardo plus the solace of the vine was just about all an emotionally weak woman could stand. Mr and Mrs Campbell suggested that Florence and her captain go to Malvern, a famous spa, to take the cure, but it was useless. Captain Ricardo had retired from the army and was now devoting his full time and energy to drinking, so Florence's parents insisted upon a deed of separation. In the following April, Captain Ricardo died in Cologne as he had lived—with a transient mistress in his bed and the eternal bottle at his elbow. His will was unaltered, and Florence was now set to become a very merry widow with an income of £4,000 a year to be merry on and Dr Gully to be merry with.

In 1842, Dr William Gully had developed a water cure and offered it to an ailing public. Dr Gully was no quack. He was a thoroughly trained medical man, and his water cure put the town of Malvern on the map, so to speak. Applications of water were used in every form—packing in wet sheets, compresses, spinal washes, friction with dripping towels—and his patients included Tennyson, Carlyle, Charles Reade, Bulwer-Lytton, an all-star cast from the social register, and many other water-sodden Victorian greats and near greats. Dr Gully himself had literary aspirations. He wrote articles on medical subjects and wrote a play adapted from Dumas's *Mademoiselle de Belle-Isle*, which was produced at Drury Lane in 1839. Dr Gully himself was sixty-two at the time Florence came to Malvern with her problem husband. He is described as handsome, if not tall, with clean-cut features and an erect bearing. He was also the possessor of a disastrous amount of personal magnetism, and a wife in her eighties whom his water cure could not help; she had been in an insane asylum for thirty years.

It was this man that Florence met when she came to Malvern. At the time she was emotionally ill, and Dr Gully's warmth and sympathetic understanding must have been every bit as effective as his water treatments. Florence was headstrong but not self-reliant, and Captain Ricardo had proved a broken reed upon which to lean. Dr Gully, a pillar of strength by comparison, was a welcome change from Captain Ricardo's highhanded, drunken treatment and groveling sober remorse. Florence recovered under his care. Today, when everyone nonchalantly tosses off the argot of psychoanalysis, transference is an every day word, and Gully's age was no detriment after Florence's experience with a young husband. Picture Dr Gully, well-to-do, attractive, respected, confronted with a rampant Florence seething with devotion and flattery.

Just when Dr Gully's bedside manner began to assume personal overtones is not clear. Florence steadfastly maintained nothing improper had occurred during her marriage to Captain Ricardo. However, early during her widowhood her parents refused to see her because of her relations with Dr Gully and because of her continued drinking. For four years, Florence was cut off from her family and was beyond the possibility of a social circle, but she had Dr Gully, emotional security, and her wine.

It was during this isolated, if not celibate, widowhood that Mrs Cox entered the scene. Florence was visiting her solicitor, Mr Brooks, and there she met Mrs Jane Cannon Cox. Mrs Cox was the down-at-the-heel widow of a Jamaican engineer with three sons, and through the kind offices and advice of a Mr Joseph

Bravo, who had interests in Jamaica, she had bought a small house in Lancaster Road, Notting Hill, as an investment, had placed her sons in a school for destitute gentlefolk, and obtained the post of governess to Mr Brooks's children. Mrs Cox, with her solid figure inclined to dumpiness, heavy-featured face, glittering spectacles, and skintight hairdo was no beauty, but she made up for it by relentless efficiency, an air of unassailable respectability, and a grim desire to please.

It wasn't long before the pretty but lonesome widow appropriated Mrs Cox as her companion. And it was, at the time, an ideal arrangement for sheltered, beautiful Florence and plain, unsheltered Mrs Cox. Mrs Cox ran Florence's house, controlled the servants, and understood perfectly the comfort and elegance that Florence wished to enjoy, without exerting any effort. And Mrs Cox had it made. She had exchanged the life of uncertainty, drudgery, and poor pay of a governess for the role of "friend of the bosom" to Florence Ricardo. They were on the footing of social equals; it was "Florence" and "Janie". She received a salary of £100 a year, clothes, and incidental expenses, and her three boys could spend all their school holidays with her.

In 1872, Dr Gully sold his practice amid testimonials and demonstrations from the citizens of Malvern, and, wherever Mrs Ricardo lived, Dr Gully's home was sure to be within spitting distance, and their friendship continued. In 1873, the pair made a trip to Kissingen, and the tangible result was a miscarriage. During this illness, Mrs Cox attended Florence, but claimed she did not know the real nature of the trouble.

In 1874, Mrs Ricardo moved into what was to be her permanent home, the Priory. It was a pale-tinted structure with arched windows and doorways, winding walks, flower beds, melon pits, a greenhouse, and the house was luxurious with a sparkling Venetian glass collection, a lush conservatory with ferns that cost twenty guineas each, and every expensive horror of Victorian decoration. Here Florence Ricardo settled down, with the perpetual Mrs Cox, to enjoy life's three greatest pleasures—gardening, horses, and drinking. And Dr Gully, whom one is tempted to nickname Johnny-on-the-spot, bought a house just a few minutes from the Priory. There were lunches, dinners, drives, and several nights of illicit bliss when Mrs Cox was away. Dr Gully had a key to the Priory. Then, one day in 1875, Mrs Cox wished to call on her benefactor, Mrs Joseph Bravo, and Mrs Ricardo went with her. There she met Charles Bravo, the spoiled son of the house. The meeting itself was without incident, but its repercussions are now called the Balham Mystery.

In October 1875, Mrs Ricardo and Mrs Cox went to Brighton and there again met Charles Bravo, a sulky handsome young man with a weak chin. He was a young man her own age and of her social position, and when Florence returned to the Priory she told Dr Gully that she was going to break off their "friendship" and reconcile with her family because of her mother's health. Actually, Florence was, in all probability, weary of her "back street" existence. She had snapped her garter at the world, and, instead of being told she was cute, was knuckle-rapped by social ostracism. What she did not tell Dr Gully was that she was also going to marry Charles Bravo. Dr Gully was hurt when he found out about the engagement, but later wished Florence happiness. Perhaps the demands of a young capricious mistress had begun to tell on the sixty-seven-year-old doctor, and the prospect of placid days and monastic nights had an attraction.

But in spite of Florence's injunction that they must never see each other again, they did. According to British law at that time, every possession and all property of a woman marrying automatically became the property of her husband, unless specifically secured to her by settlement. Florence wanted the Priory and its furnishings secured to her, but Charles sulked and muttered he wanted to sit in his own chairs or he'd call the marriage off. Florence arranged a meeting with Dr Gully to discuss the impasse, and they met at one of the Priory lodges. Dr Gully advised her to give in on the matter and wished her luck. As usual, Florence backed down, and "Charlie" won the moral victory of "sitting in his own chairs".

Charles Bravo was not a wealthy man in his own right and was mostly dependent on his father's spasmodic handouts, since his law practice only netted him £200 in the last year of his life. However, his future was bright. He was his stepfather's heir, and his prospects for becoming a member of Parliament were good, and here was a young, infatuated, wealthy widow, with a belated yearning for respectability and security, palpitating on his door-step.

Charles and Florence told each other "all". He had had a purple passage with a young and willing woman in Maidenhead but had made a final settlement with her before breaking off. Florence told him about her idyll with the autumnal Dr Gully, and Charles seems to have accepted it with equanimity. Charles was what might be called "rotten spoiled". He was charming when things went his way, extremely conscious of money, probably because he had been around it so much, yet had so little of his own. And the prospect of marrying a wealthy widow—even one with a sexual slip-up in her past—was attractive. Certainly he was not consumed with jealousy. When he went to see Florence's attorney about the settlement, he received the lawyer's congratulations with the remark, "to hell with the congratulations, it's the money I'm interested in!"

Mr Bravo, Sr, settled £20,000 on Charles as a wedding present, but Mrs Bravo refused to attend the wedding. She didn't like Florence. For that matter, she probably wouldn't have liked any girl her son married. And so Florence and Charles Bravo were married and settled down at the Priory, and they might have lived happily ever after if Charles Bravo hadn't been so stingy.

They seemed like an average, happy couple. Charles brought his business associates to dinner and heartily endorsed the institution of marriage. The servants all thought the Bravos a happy, devoted couple, but Mrs Cox was worried. Charles was cutting down on the overhead. He wanted Florence to give up her horses and her personal maid which she did, and he wanted her to dispense with Mrs Cox. He had put together a pound here and a pound there and figured out that the genteel companionship of the widow was costing £400 a year—enough to keep a pair of horses. And Florence, who operated on an anything-for-the-sake-of-peace basis and who was charmed by her young attractive husband, decided to give up her horses and maid, and Mrs Cox could see the handwriting on the wall. Her relatives in Jamaica had been pressing her to return, and now Mr Joseph Bravo and his son were urging the same thing.

During this period of surface serenity, several curious events occurred. Mrs Cox had several meetings with Dr Gully; whether they were planned or accidental, they have all the aspects of Mrs Cox trying to stir something up. Mrs Bravo had had a miscarriage, and Mrs Cox, at one encounter, asked Dr Gully, who knew Florence couldn't take regular opiates, to send something to her house on Lancaster Road. The doctor sent some laurel water and thus laid himself open to later insinuations that he was supplying Mrs Bravo with abortive medicines, a rather empty charge in view of the fact that a child would have been just what Florence Bravo needed to cement her newly established respectability and reconcile Charles's mother to the marriage. And then, just after Charles Bravo figured out the cost of Mrs Cox's companionship, he was taken suddenly and mysteriously ill one morning on his way to his chambers in Essex Court. So ill, in fact, that he reported to his father he was afraid people might think he was drunk from the night before, and Charles Bravo had the digestion of an ox.

That was the situation at the Priory Easter weekend, 1876. Charles Bravo had his attractive wife and her equally attractive fortune. Florence was recovering from her miscarriage and appeared devoted to her husband, and Mrs Cox was brooding about the imminence of a trip to Jamaica. Charles Bravo laid out a tennis court, played with Mrs Cox's boys, who were down for the Easter vacation, and wrote to his mother that he had "loafed vigorously and thoroughly enjoyed the weekend".

Tuesday, 18 April, Mrs Cox set out to look at houses in Worthing where the Bravos were planning to go for Florence to recuperate from her miscarriage and with her she took a flask of sherry to fortify herself. Mr and Mrs Bravo drove into town, and he went to his club at St James Hall for lunch, while Florence returned to the Priory, after doing some shopping, for lunch, which she polished off with a bottle of champagne. Mrs Bravo understandably spent the afternoon resting. Late in the afternoon Mr Bravo returned home and went riding. The horse threw him, and he returned home with his dignity and himself rather badly bruised. Mrs Bravo suggested a warm bath before dinner, and then went upstairs herself to change. Mrs Cox returned from her house hunting with a photograph of the house, and, it is presumed, an empty sherry flask. She did not have time to change for dinner, she did go upstairs to clean up a bit.

Dinner, consisting of whiting, roast lamb, a dish of eggs, and anchovy bloater was not a sparkling meal. Mr Bravo was still smarting, both literally and figuratively, from his fall. Mrs Bravo had dry pipes from the champagne and was trying to put out the fire with sherry, and Mrs Cox had things to think about. Mr Bravo drank his three customary glasses of burgundy, but the ladies put him to shame. Between them, Mrs Bravo and Mrs Cox polished off two bottles of sherry, and the butler later testified that he had decanted the usual amount of wine that evening.

After dinner, they retired to the morning room where again conversations languished. In about a half hour, Florence announced she was going to bed and asked Mrs Cox to bring her a glass of wine. Since her miscarriage Mrs Cox had been sleeping with her, and Mr Bravo had been relegated to a guest room. Mrs Bravo went upstairs and was followed by the obliging Mrs Cox with a glass of wine. Mary Anne Keeber, a maid, came in to help Mrs Bravo undress and was asked by Mrs Bravo to bring her some wine. Mary

Anne brought a tumbler of marsala and was still in Mrs Bravo's
room when Mr Bravo entered to make the understatement of the
Balham Mystery. He accused his wife of drinking too much wine
and stormed off to bed. Mary Anne withdrew and saw as she left
the room that three-bottle Florence had taken the count and was
asleep, while Mrs Cox sat by her bed fully dressed. As Mary Anne
started downstairs, the door to Mr Bravo's room flew open and he
cried, "Florence, Florence. Water!"

And Mrs Cox, who sat fully dressed and wide awake by Mrs
Bravo's bedside, heard nothing until Mary Anne called her. From
the time of Mr Bravo's cries for water, there began a procession of
doctors and a progression of statements by Mrs Cox. Mary Anne
and Mrs Cox rushed into Mr Bravo's bedroom, where they found
him standing by the window vomiting. Mrs Cox ordered Mary
Anne to rush for an emetic and Dr Harrison. When Dr Harrison
arrived Mrs Cox told him Mr Bravo had taken chloroform to ease a
toothache, but the doctor said there was no smell of chloroform.

Mrs Bravo was by this time aroused and sent for Dr Moore
and Royes Bell, a Harley Street surgeon and friend of the Bravo
family. Mrs Bravo threw herself down by her husband, spoke to
him fondly, and promptly fell asleep and finally had to be carried
to her own room. Obviously, she hadn't had time to sleep it off.

Dr George Johnson arrived with Royes Bell, and they are told
by Mr Bravo that he has rubbed his gums with laudanum for his
toothache.

"But laudanum," Dr Johnson tells him "will not account for
your symptoms." But Mr Bravo stubbornly insisted that he had
taken nothing else, no other drug.

At this point, Mrs Cox takes Mr Bell aside and confides to him
that, while "Charlie" was vomiting at the window, he told her, "I
have taken poison. Don't tell Florence."

Mr Bravo's reply to this is "I don't remember having spoken of
taking poison," and again insisted he had only rubbed his gums
with laudanum. Dr Harrison was annoyed with Mrs Cox for not
telling him about the poison. "You told me," he said petulantly,
"that he had taken chloroform."

Mr Bravo by now was in a bad way. He was frequently sick and
had intense stomach pains, but he kept his wife by him, drew up
a will leaving everything to her, and sent word to his mother to
"be kind to Florence". Again he swears to the growing assembly
of doctors that he had taken nothing but laudanum and with a

trace of his old money consciousness says: "Why the devil should I send for you, if I knew what was the matter with me?"

Mr and Mrs Joseph Bravo arrived, and the elder Mrs Bravo took charge of the sick room. However, when the doctors had declared the case hopeless, Florence roused herself from her despair and her hangover to take action. "They have had their way, and I as his wife will have mine." And proceeded to try water treatments and small doses of arsenicum, both approved of by the doctors, as harmless.

Then Florence calls in Sir William Gull, a physician who wore as a crown the credit for having cured the Prince of Wales of typhoid fever.

"This is not a disease," Sir William tells Bravo. "You have been poisoned. Pray tell me how you came by it."

But Bravo persists that he has taken nothing but laudanum and on Friday morning, April twenty-first, the much harassed, much questioned Charles Bravo mercifully died.

The inquest had more of the air of a family tea than anything else. Mr Carter, the coroner for East Surrey was informed in a note written for Mrs Bravo by Mrs Cox that "refreshments will be prepared for the jury", and the inquest was held in the dining room of the Priory. Mr Carter, an experienced official, had the idea that there was something amiss and out of deference to two respectable families did not even send notices of the inquest to the papers. Test of specimens and organs revealed that Mr Bravo had died from a large, economy-sized dose of antimony administered in the form of tartar emetic, which is easily soluble in water and tasteless. Mr Joseph Bravo went to Scotland Yard and Inspector Clark, an expert on poisoning cases, was instructed to make inquiries to see if antimony could be traced to the Priory, because the senior Bravo suspected the story of death by accident. Both Mrs Bravo and Mrs Cox had medicine chests and the house contained innumerable bottles of medicine, but nothing lethal. But Mr Joseph Bravo refused to believe Mrs Cox's story that his son had committed suicide.

The coroner felt it was an embarrasing case of suicide, however, and closed the hearing without allowing Drs Johnson or Moore to testify and without calling Mrs Bravo, who was suffering from shock. Mr Bravo even admitted to the coroner's direct question, he did not suspect foul play, but there were a lot of drugs in the house. The verdict was "that the deceased died from the effects of the poison antimony, but there was no evidence as to the circumstances in which it had come into his body."

Mr Bravo was buried on April twenty-ninth, and Mrs Bravo and Mrs Cox, probably fortified by several flasks of sherry, departed for Brighton. But the end was not in sight. Charles Bravo had been popular in his circle of friends and colleagues, and they were dissatisfied with the summary verdict from the coroner's inquest. A week later, *The World* ran a provocative paragraph titled "A Tragedy?" It was done in the gossip-column style of today with no names mentioned but easily identifiable. Charles Bravo was referred to as "a rising young barrister recently married".

The following day, 11 May, the gathering storm continued, in which the *Daily Telegraph* became more explicit, naming names and premiering the sobriquet, "The Balham Mystery". The *Telegraph* also commented on the secret and unsatisfactory inquest and called for a reopening of the investigation. The case aroused great interest, and journals and newspapers were deluged with suggestions as to how Mr Bravo clashed head on with the antimony. Two schools of thought emerged. Either the fatal dose had been administered in his burgundy at dinner or in the water bottle which sat on his night stand and from which he was in the habit of drinking before he went to bed. Because of the time element the water jug was a 2-to-1 favorite. The doctors in the case were bitten by the literary bug. Drs Moore and Harrison wrote for the *Daily Telegraph*, and Dr Johnson gave a medical history in *Lancet*.

Mrs Bravo was aware of the drift of public sentiment. She was receiving anonymous letters, and, on the advice of her father, offered a reward of £500 to anyone who could prove the sale of antimony or tartar emetic "in such a matter as would throw a satisfactory light on the mode by which Mr Bravo came to his death".

The Home Secretary (afterwards Lord Cross) issued a statement that his office was "entirely dissatisfied with the way the inquiry had been conducted". Mrs Bravo's consent was obtained for a thorough search of the Priory. The investigation lasted two days and every medicine in the house was tested. Nothing was discovered that Charles Bravo could have taken, but five weeks between Bravo's death and the investigation were ample time to get anything incriminating out of the way.

On 27 May a private inquiry was called, and, although Mrs Bravo and Mrs Cox were not asked to give evidence, they both asked to make statements. Mrs Cox's statement, made after consultation with Mr Brooks, her former employer and Mrs Bravo's solicitor, dropped a bombshell. She deposed that through a misguided effort to shield Mrs Bravo's character, she had not given full particulars at the inquest. What Mr Bravo had actually said was, "I have taken poison for Gully—don't tell Florence." However, Mrs Cox had to admit that Mrs Bravo had had no contact with Dr Gully since her marriage and characterized Dr Gully's relations as "very imprudent" but of an innocent character. Mr Bravo had a hasty and violent temper and four days before his death had had a violent quarrel with his wife in which he called her a selfish pig, wished he were dead, and said "let her go back to Gully". He constantly stated he hated Gully.

Mrs Bravo's statement said that Bravo had pressed her constantly to cut down on expenses and turn away Mrs Cox. That he was short tempered and had once struck her, that his mother was always interfering, and that he read all her mail. She had told him about her attachment to Gully, and he had told her of his kept woman at Maidenhead, and they agreed never to mention these names. Florence, in this statement, described her relationship with Gully as innocent. "Nothing improper had ever passed between us." Mrs Bravo said that her husband had constantly harped on Gully after their marriage. The day he had taken ill they had had a fight about Gully on the way to town. Florence refused to make up. "You will see what I do when I get home." He thought she drank too much sherry, but she had given it up to please him. (Certainly one glaring untruth in Mrs Bravo's statement.)

On the strength of this private inquiry, Mr Clark was ordered to hold a new inquiry with a fresh jury. It opened on 11 July 1876, in the billiard room of the Bedford Hotel next to Balham Station. And if the first inquiry had been a furtive affair, the second was a field day for the public. The room was crowded with newspaper reporters and the curious, of which there were many. After the jury had viewed the exhumed body through a small piece of glass in the coffin, a grim legal formality, Mr Joseph Bravo testified that Charles was full of life, that he was interested in forensic medicine, and that they were on intimate terms. He had never heard Charles mention Gully's name. The last three letters Charles had written to his family, just before his illness, were in the best of spirits.

Mr Bravo said that Charles had discussed Mrs Cox with him, that he had nothing against her, but that she cost too much. Mr Joseph Bravo had agreed and advised Mrs Cox himself to return to Jamaica. She said she would not return. Mr Bravo also commented that while her husband was dying Mrs Bravo did not "appear much grieved" in any way at the state of affairs. He did admit that his son was quick tempered.

The doctors presented a solid antisuicide wall. They said they had never heard of a case of suicide by antimony, that the time of action was variable, and they positively stated that antimony could be administered without any taste in either water or burgundy. Several of the doctors testified to drinking out of the water bottle; but admitted that in the confusion it would have been easy to either switch or clean out the water jug. Dr Johnson testified that Mrs Bravo overheard him mention poison to Mrs Cox. Mrs Bravo asked: "Did he say he had taken poison?" "Yes, he did," replied Mrs Cox. And that was the end of the conversation.

Rowe, the Butler, testified that Mr Bravo drank three glasses of burgundy at his last meal and that the half-full decanter was put away. On 19 April he opened another bottle of burgundy. He did not remember who drank it, but the other half bottle must have been gone. With Florence around it's not surprising. He had never heard quarreling and called Charles Bravo "one of the kindest gentlemen I ever knew".

Mary Anne Keeber, the maid, said she thought Mr and Mrs Bravo were very fond of each other and saw no signs of jealousy or ever heard Dr Gully's name mentioned. She had emptied and cleaned the basin Mr Bravo had been vomiting in at Mrs Cox's request.

Amelia Bushnell, Mrs Joseph Bravo's maid, had heard Mr Bravo say he had taken nothing but laudanum and testified that Mrs Charles Bravo had been blaming his illness on something he ate at the club, cooked in a coppery pan.

John Pritchard, Dr Gully's butler said there had been a great attachment between Dr Gully and Mrs Ricardo, but that, in November of the previous year, Dr Gully had given him instructions not to admit Mrs Ricardo or Mrs Cox. Dr Gully had returned pictures, presents, and key to the Priory, and Mrs Ricardo had done the same.

Colleagues testified that Charles Bravo had no worries or cares, that he had made a special study of forensic medicine, and would never knowingly take such a painful or uncertain medicine.

Mrs Campbell testified she was met by Mrs Cox when she arrived during Mr Bravo's illness and was told it was poison, while Florence was still chattering about coppery pans at Charlie's club.

Mrs Cox, spectacles glinting, looking middle aged and dumpy

in her black, said Charles Bravo had said she was welcome at
the Priory, that he received an anonymous letter accusing him of
marrying Gully's mistress for her money. She had seen Dr Gully
several times since Mrs Bravo's marriage, had asked him for his
remedy for ague and Jamaica fever, also something to make Mrs
Bravo sleep after her miscarriage. Bravo had asked her, "Why did
you tell them? Does Florence know I poisoned myself?"
"I was obliged to tell them. I could not let you die."

Asked why she had not mentioned this conversation, Mrs Cox
replied imperturbably, "He did not wish me to." She had not
mentioned Dr Gully's name at the first inquest because it might have
injured Mrs Bravo's reputation. When she mentioned chloroform to
Harrison, she was confused and meant poison. "Dr Gully was a very
fascinating man—one who would be likely to interest women very
much." She said she had done everything she could to restrain Mrs
Bravo from her habit of drinking, but without much success.

Mrs Bravo, immersed in grief and a voluminous mourning veil,
testified that it was 26 April before she knew her husband was
dying of poison. Bravo harped about Gully in spite of her 16 April
letter to Mrs Bravo that Charles was happy as a king. At Brighton,
after the first inquest, Mrs Cox told her Charles had poisoned
himself on the account of Gully. She made a full admission of her
"criminal relations" with Dr Gully, but even under a heavy barrage
of insinuation, she maintained, under oath, that she was innocent of
any extra-marital activities during her marriage to Captain Ricardo.
But her protests of innocence were badly shaken when she was
handed a letter, written by her to a woman named Laundon,
who had been her maid. It was dated 17 November 1870, a date
that preceded Captain Ricardo's death by six months. In part the
letter said: "I hope you will never allude in any way to anyone of
what passed at Malvern." Asked what she referred to, Mrs Bravo
answered: "It was my attachment to Dr Gully, but not a criminal
attachment then." She burst into tears and appealed to the coroner
to protect her. So much for semantics.

Then Griffiths, a former coachman to Dr Gully and Mrs Bravo,
took the stand. He had worked for Mrs Bravo but had been
fired by Mr Bravo for carelessness. He seems to have been a
nineteenth-century hotrod and was accident prone. His testimony,
however, established the presence of antimony in the form of tartar
emetic at the Priory. He had bought a large amount to treat the
horses. He had kept it locked in a cupboard in the stable and

poured it all down the drain when he left. However, no inquiry was made as to what kind of lock was on the cupboard, and there is only Griffiths's word that after being fired, he conscientiously poured a large âmount of medicine down the drain. It would seem more natural for him to go off in a huff, leaving the tartar emetic for the next coachman. But although Griffiths was called an "unreliable witness", he did establish, for the first time in the case, the presence of the poison which killed Charles Bravo.

Dr Gully was the last witness to be called during the twenty-three-day inquest, which rivaled the Tichborne trial in public interest, if not length, when a 350-pound pretender consumed eight years and a total of 290 days trying to prove he was the long-lost Sir Roger Arthur Orton. Dr Gully's testimony backed up Florence Bravo's contention that there had been nothing improper pass between them during Captain Ricardo's lifetime, but when asked about his relations with Captain Ricardo's widow his rueful reply was "too true, sir; too true". He swore he had nothing to do either directly or indirectly with Charles Bravo's death and told of his chance meetings with Mrs Cox who told him repeatedly that Mr and Mrs Bravo were "getting along well".

The verdict turned out to be the most damaging aspect of the inquest. It concluded that "Charles Bravo was willfully murdered by the administration of tartar emetic, but there is not sufficient evidence to fix the guilt upon any person or persons." The jury significantly declined to use the standard, more familiar wording, "administered by some person or persons unknown".

And by the verdict of the jury, the Balham Mystery remains an official cipher. The suicide theory, with a nod of admiration in the direction of a lurking Mrs Cox, does not hold up. Against the unsupported word of Mrs Cox, there is a parade of friends, colleagues, and family who picture Charles Bravo as a happy man, contented with his career and marriage. His letters both to Florence and his family reflect Bravo's unsuicidal, rather complacent state of mind. As for Mrs Cox's statement that "he took poison for Gully", he had known of Dr Gully's relationship to Florence before he married her, and, according to every witness, Mrs Bravo never saw Dr Gully after her marriage. The only other possibility for suicide would be delayed-action remorse and jealousy, and Charles Bravo just wasn't the brooding type. His repeated denials to the doctors that he had not taken poison and his affectionate attitude toward his wife at his sick bed also lower the boom on the suicide theory.

The accident theory can quickly be eliminated. The only place that antimony in the form of tartar emetic was kept at Priory was in the stables, and it is hardly conceivable that Mr Bravo would ever dose himself in the stable on horse physic, while all medicines found in the house tested out as harmless.

Sir John Hall, considered the leading authority on the Bravo case, claims that it had to be both Mrs Bravo and Mrs Cox because they supported each other consistently in their statements, so at variance with all the other witnesses. But consider, Florence Bravo's actions after her husband is taken ill. Still befuddled by wine, she sends for the nearest doctor and later for specialists. She talks of food poisoning from the coppery pans at his club. The conversation between the doctor and Mrs Cox, which she claims not to have heard, could also be the result of combined hysteria and hangover.

Mrs Bravo said she first heard of poison and suicide when Mrs Cox broke the news to her after they were settled at Brighton. Since Mrs Bravo was in a state of shock and did not appear at the first inquest, she begins backing up Mrs Cox only after the Brighton sojourn. So, Mrs Bravo emerges as an upset, concerned wife, extremely fond, talking of food poisoning, and then after the trip to Brighton with Mrs Cox she accepts and, by testimony, backs up the suicide theory and fortifies Mrs Cox's position.

Something happened at Brighton, and everything points to a little genteel blackmail. Mrs Cox knew her relationship with Dr Gully was more than a harmless infatuation. She knew of her heavy drinking. She knew of the post-Kissengen illness—not hard for a woman with three sons and sickroom experience to diagnose as a miscarriage. And Florence Bravo, must above all, be considered within a specific frame of reference, that of nineteenth-century morals and manners. Within this frame, you have a woman who has made a slip and bounced from the category of "pure" to "fallen" woman. She had made an attempt at being respectable again, and Mrs Cox knew intimately the details of the transition. Her knowledge could bounce Florence right back into the latter category. In an age when women blushingly asked for a "slice of bosom" when being served chicken and female legs were as unmentionable as four letter Anglo-Saxon words, public disgrace could assume more importance than suspected murder; and, in Florence Bravo's case, it did.

At Brighton, Mrs Cox probably told Florence that her husband said, "I have taken poison for Gully." She told the young widow that if she would follow her lead, Mrs Cox would protect her reputation. In view of all the public agitation, they would have to make statements. The arrangement was that Mrs Cox would tell of Bravo's "Gully statement" but would testify that relations between Florence and Dr Gully were imprudent but innocent and Charles Bravo was jealous of his wife's past. Florence, in turn, would tell her story of her husband's baseless jealousy of Dr Gully. This way Florence's character would stay comparatively blameless, while Mrs Cox's suicide theory would be reinforced. And how could Florence say no to perpetrating this half-truth, when the entire truth would mean ruin. Besides, she probably believed Mrs Cox's story of Charlie's suicide.

So, Florence Bravo became an ex post facto accessory. By the time Mrs Cox threw her to the wolves at the second inquest in the interest of self-preservation, Mrs Bravo had gone so far in her statements that she was irrevocably implicated. During the second inquest, Mrs Cox had begun to panic. She could bolster the suicide theory by admitting that Mrs Bravo had told her of her intimate relations with Dr Gully and that Charles Bravo knew and brooded over his wife's past sins, or she could protect Mrs Bravo's reputation. Mrs Cox couldn't afford to let the suicide theory languish, or she would be in a most suspicious position. So Florence's reputation had to go by the boards, and, too late to do anything, Florence realized with growing horror, that Mrs Cox was not the friend she pretended to be, but a blackmailer consumed with some dark purpose of her own. Florence was left with no alternative but to admit her "criminal relationship" with Dr Gully, which gave the illusion that she was still "backing up" Mrs Cox, while in actuality these two sherry-sipping ladies had come to a parting of the ways.

Mrs Bravo moved to Buscot to live with her mother. Mrs Cox stopped in Manchester Street and planned to leave for Jamaica at the close of the inquiry. Florence was no intellectual giant, but she knew when she had been had.

It is the only theory that could account for Florence Bravo's opposite actions before and after Brighton. Mrs Bravo, by herself, had neither sufficient character or motive to do the dirty deed. Nor did she have a strong enough reason to act in conjunction with Mrs Cox. She certainly wouldn't condone the murder of her husband to keep Mrs Cox from returning to Jamaica. The weakness of Florence Bravo's character forms the strength of her innocence. To complain, to pout, to shed a few tears was her course of action, not poison. There have been suggestions that the relationship between Mrs Bravo and Mrs Cox was of an unhealthy hue. But with Florence's affinity for men, about the only unhealthy thing about their relationship was the amount of sherry they consumed.

Mrs Cox, too, falls with rigid delineation into this frame of reference. In our own era of the freewheeling career girl, it is difficult to remember that in Mrs Cox's day a working woman was an unhappy exception, just a cut above serfdom. In most cases, a governess, a companion, or a poor relation who "earned her keep" was a step above the servants and a step below the lord and lady of the house, isolated on a lonely plateau without social contacts or standing.

When Charles Bravo showed unmistakable symptoms of snapping the purse shut and shipping her back to her Jamaican home and family, it was not simply a matter of a new job or surroundings. It was social and financial annihilation, and it was a motive. By removing Charles Bravo, she could relieve the pressure being exerted for her to return to Jamaica. She would be once again the dear friend of Florence, whom she could completely dominate, and return to the good old days when Dr Gully's courtly charm caused a flutter under her formidable black bombazine exterior and Florence's home and funds were at her disposal.

Mrs Cox, however, did not know her poisons as well as she knew the gentle art of conniving. By administering a large, economy-sized dose of poison, Mrs Cox was under the impression that Charles Bravo would die immediately. She did not realize that antimony was a variable and unpredictable poison. When it became apparent that Mr Bravo was going to linger awhile, Mrs Cox had to come up with some quick answers off the top of her chignon, and she was in a good position. Bravo was in an incoherent state, and Mrs Bravo, during those first chaotic hours, had a case of the hot-and-cold shakes and dry pipes, while the servants were trained to take orders unquestioningly from Mrs Cox. It is only after the doctors agreed that it was a case of irritant poisoning that Mrs Cox came up with the "I took poison—Don't tell Florence" statement. Only after there is a strong suspicion of murder and a second inquest is looming does Mrs Cox add Dr Gully's name to the statement to give the suicide theory a strong motive. And only at the second inquest, when the jury and public were taking an increasingly dimmer view of the suicide theory, did she tell of the conversation when Bravo asks, "Why did you tell them?" Only Mrs Cox heard these three conversations with Charles Bravo. There were no witnesses except the necessarily mute Charles, and these words are the only indications of suicide. All the other testimony, all the other facts pointed to murder. Mrs Cox may not have been telling the truth, but she was a fast girl with a cue.

But in spite of Florence's sex appeal and money, in spite of Mrs Cox's strong, decisive character, things just didn't work out as they did in Florence's favorite romantic novels. Florence Bravo died within the year from a combination of emotional collapse, guilty knowledge, and hitting the bottle, never a healthy combination in her case. In Mrs Bravo's will, the only mention of Jane Cannon Cox is a reference to her as the mother of three boys to whom Florence Bravo left bequests of £1,000 each. Dr Gully, his name removed from the rosters of all medical societies, dies seven years later, full of age, if not honor. And Mrs Cox was last heard of beside a sick bed in Jamaica, a bad place for her.

Of course, no one actually saw Mrs Cox sneak antimony from the stable. No one saw her toying with Mr Bravo's burgundy decanter or water bottle, but she was the only person involved in the Balham Mystery who had the character, the opportunity, the motive, and an abiding faith that the Lord helps them that help themselves.

The jury at the inquest voiced their opinion in the damning phraseology of the verdict. The man in the street borrowed some meter from Oliver Goldsmith and circulated their own, less carefully phrased verdict.

> When lovely woman stoops to folly
> And finds her husband in the way,
> What charm can soothe her melancholy?
> What art can turn him into clay?
> The only means her aims to cover,
> And save herself from prison locks,
> And repossess her ancient lover
> Are burgundy and Mrs Cox.

It's a little hard on Dr Gully and Florence Bravo but gratifying to see Mrs Cox getting public recognition for all her work and effort.

FOOLS AND HORSES

(Shergar, 1983)

John Edwards

In 1983, Shergar, winner of the Derby and the world's most famous racehorse, was kidnapped from a stud farm in Ireland. It was an extraordinary crime, somehow peculiarly Irish, and it was never solved. John Edwards, who covered the story for the Daily Mail *in London, recalls the events of that bitterly cold February in Kildare.*

Much boredom and routine had now settled around the new life of the great Shergar since they retired him from racing to make a fortune as a sire. One day was the same as another.

If it changed, it was only when he smelled the air and got the scent of another mare in season being brought for him to "cover". Even then he had to get used to the briefest of affairs—fifteen minutes of passion for £80,000. The mare paid. Or at least the people who owned her did.

Everything had to be right if he was to create a new foal. The weather was part of it. A cold day was not so promising as a warm one.

And 8 February 1983 began with hailstones and an ice-cold wind coming over the empty roll of The Curragh, County Kildare, which is heartland country in the Irish horse business. Sometimes the hail joined up to form a solid block driving through the air. The infra-red lamp above Shergar in his stable at the Ballymany Stud was turned up to throw more heat onto his handsome back. Horse races on television are watched in the distance. There is no indication of size. But a champ like Shergar is huge and stands like a giant with his fine head still almost out of reach when anyone put up a hand to try and smooth his silky cheek.

They let Shergar alone that Wednesday because it froze from dawn to dusk. Even when they took him to the five-acre paddock for a run he galloped over and sheltered under leafless trees watching the hail with those big, dark eyes. "We'll have him back now," Liam Foley said to the stable boy, Jim Fitzgerald, who watched him all the time because he was a jewel worth £10 million. The title "stable boy" sticks for life. Jim was a stable boy when he was fourteen. He had just had his fifty-eighth birthday. It was the simplest of jobs and he made just enough to keep himself and his wife Madge and some of his seven children.

Liam was called the Stallion Man, which made him many stripes above a stable boy. He was the boss of Shergar any time business wasn't involved. The horse was part of his family. He treated him almost as if he was human.

Jim led Shergar clip-clopping back to his very special loose box with his name in brass letters over the door. It was routine for both horse and man. Jim first bolted the door over which Shergar had stuck his head with the shiny white blaze.

Then he locked the main door, which shut the horse off completely. Shergar could only look across the centre aisle into the face of another fine stallion called Nishapour. But they never became friends. They would have fought to the death if they could have got at each other.

Jim Fitzgerald turned and said something to Shergar which he doesn't remember now. It was probably "settle down now, fellow," he said later. He tried to dodge the weather when he went to his house in the stud which came with the job. It became dark so early he had everything locked up by four p.m.

No good for going anywhere, Jim said to his wife, so they settled in for what turned out to be the most incredible night ever dreamed of in the history of horse racing.

In twenty-four hours Jim's name would be in every newspaper in the world. He would be famous for bad reasons, afraid to go out, so shaken he couldn't talk. It was twenty-four hours in which he would look straight into the barrel of a gun and wait for death.

One of the great stories ever was about to explode around the Ballymany Stud. Shergar, beginning to lower himself into the straw to sleep, was about to become a legend which struck his name into history many more times effectively than sailing home in The Derby with Walter Swinburn aboard.

Ghislain Drion, the stud manager who spoke better French than English, peered through the windscreen wipers of his Nissan Patrol 4WD and was dazzled by his headlights reflecting off the flurries of snow. He parked next to his mansion outside the stud complex and checked the telex for messages from any of the thirty-four people in the Shergar syndicate.

Chief Superintendent James "Jazzer" Murphy of the Kildare County Garda Force went to his house, which was towards Dublin, and was quite relaxed because there was nothing much in his tray.

It had also been an easy day for the chambermaids at the Keadeen Hotel in Newbridge, a mile from the stud, because only nine of the thirty-two rooms were occupied.

A nasty mid-winter night in Kildare couldn't even get people out to the pubs. The one call made to the local police station was to report a car going off the road. Fog had joined the hail and snow. It was about eight-thirty p.m.

Security cameras couldn't hunt through the wall of weather. They were faulty anyway. No guards stood at the gate. Only a five-bar gate protected the stud. A kid could open it.

The gate was up the drive off the main road to Dublin. Nobody heard the gate open or saw the black shape of an unlit Granada pulling a horsebox as it turned down the drive into the stud. A van and another car pulled off the road and parked by the gate. The Granada turned inside the stud and the driver stopped the engine when it pointed back to the main road, the classic get away position. The slow turn made a noise when the wheels spread gravel. Jim Fitzgerald thought he heard the sound of a car but he wasn't in charge of security so didn't have to react to noises. Not even a knock on the door bothered him. His son Bernard was nearest. When Bernard opened it the silhouette reminded him of a man in police uniform. There was something different, though. He had never seen a policeman in a mask before.

He thought the man said something like: "Is the boss in?" Bernard turned to shout to his father. The blow in the small of his back sent him face down on the floor.

Jim pushed his way towards the door. His first memory was of Bernard on the floor. And then it was the glint of poor light on a pistol barrel pointed at his heart.

Who could these people be? The IRA? Hardly. The IRA didn't operate much in southern Ireland. They weren't harried a lot by the authorities. As long as they behaved they were tolerated. Even a murderer was pretty safe when he crossed from the North. That was the way the Dublin Government had quietly decided to play it.

Jim thinks he said: "What do you want us for because we haven't done anything?" Bernard got up slowly. Madge stood in the kitchen where a peat fire smoked in the grate and terror ran all the way through her.

Other masked men came into the kitchen, maybe as many as eight. Everything seemed to have been spoken by the gunman. "We've come for Shergar and we want £2 million for him. Call the police and he's dead."

One of the other men took a gun from his pocket. Jim had an escort to Shergar's stable. He lifted the bolt and heard Shergar move and snort. The smell of warm straw and horses flew out into the night.

The gunman prodded Jim along to Shergar's loose box which was the furthest from the door. There was some light from the infra-red lamps. Somebody behind him, a different voice this time, told Jim to get some tack and put it on Shergar. So he put a head collar on him and a bridle and bit. He heard straw being picked up and saw it scattered in the back of the horsebox. Jim's old coat, the one he always left hanging on a hook, was lifted down and he remembers one of the gang putting it on. The coat smelled of Jim. Shergar got a whiff and walked without stress. It was the smell he knew well. The man who put a gun on Jim, first took Ghislain Drion's private number and told Jim to pass a message that he would be contacted next day.

What Jim saw flashing through his brain now were the words "Kidnap and Ransom". Jim was frightened into a shiver. He gave Shergar a last pat on his neck. The back of the horsebox banged closed and the bolts went down. If Jim called the police or anybody, the gunman said, he had signed his death warrant. The horsebox went into the night. Jim caught a view of Shergar's hind-quarters. And a wonderful, blue-blood animal, innocent of everything, his fine aristocratic head strapped to a slat of a cheap horsebox, was taken away to begin his final journey.

In days gone by he had gone to Epsom and Ascot in his special box painted in grand colours like a royal coach. A band played for him once.

On that Wednesday night, 8 February 1983 the fog closed in around a miserable-looking shed on wheels and Shergar would have begun to feel the despair, a vet said afterwards.

Three terrorists nudged Jim back to his house and trained a handgun on him as he sat with his family. None of the words spoken for the next three hours were recalled by Jim.

He was full of fear and shook visibly. Exactly after three hours, the kidnappers made to leave Ballymany Stud. They whispered: "Call the police and you all die."

Jim thought it was all over until one of the men pushed him outside. He was marched to the gate and pressed to the floorboards of the van which had been parked unnoticed for hours.

A knee was in his back holding him down. Jim could never be sure how far they drove but he was completely lost when they kicked him out on a empty piece of road. At least he was still alive, he kept telling himself.

Madge called a friend and stuttered out the story at around midnight. The friend called the police.

Ghislain Drion was an aloof man and mixed little in company which didn't include titles or the gilded circles of international racehorse owners and breeders. Shergar was going to produce so much money for the syndicate, figures such as £100 million were being mentioned.

Syndicate members like the Aga Khan and Robert Sangster, Sheik Al Maktoum and Stavros Niarchos took special interest in the Ballymany Stud.

When the local cops called on him in the sleepiest hours of the night he said: "What do you mean stolen?" Since he was best in French, the cops had difficulty making their point. Which was when "Jazzer" Murphy was awakened. The name Shergar registered in the brain of "Jazzer" just as if he had been told that somebody had snatched a king or a queen.

The Det. Chief Supt warmed up his car, adjusted his famous trilby hat and toed it to the police station. No case he had handled was so short of clues. Crime: Kidnapping Shergar. Leads: Nil. That was a hell of a way to start the investigation.

Jim Fitzgerald's head was still so wobbly that what Murphy got out of him was hardly revealing. What stuck there was something Jim remembered about the gang mentioning a ransom of £2 million.

Drion had told the Aga Khan and Robert Sangster, but nobody connected with the syndicate was very open with Murphy. When he drove down to the stud for the second time he noticed a queue of hire cars full of reporters pulling into the Keadeen Hotel.

Murphy was pressed to hold a news conference on the steps of Newbridge garda station. "I really don't have any news," he said. "Look, I can't say it was the IRA or anybody. Nobody's seen the horse for sixteen hours. He could be anywhere."

In his mind he suspected somebody had already contacted Drion or another member of the syndicate and discussed a ransom. But he had not been told. Next time he saw Drion he told him it would be the worst thing possible to even think about paying the money.

After four days Murphy was still without a lead. And the trail was stone-cold. The detective couldn't even pin down positively that a £2 million demand had already been made to the syndicate.

A week went by. Then another week. The investigation was going backwards. The old cop couldn't entertain the Press with new lines. The story slipped from the front pages and the lead item of TV news shows. Clairvoyants kept troubling him with visons and he followed up one or two. It was that bad. Where WAS Shergar? WHO was holding him?

The incident room had logged reported sightings in Libya, The Channel Islands and almost every county in Ireland.

More and more Murphy figured it must have been the IRA. He worked out that every day they kept the horse away from the stud it would cost the syndicate thousands. They would pay up for sure. In fact they never entertained paying. The Shergar case faded away. It went down as "unsolved".

Almost a decade afterwards in 1992, the story stirred again. Sean O'Callaghan, an IRA top-gun turned informer, who ran the IRA's Southern Command, began saying things inside Maghaberry prison, Belfast. He said his duties in 1983 involved high-profile kidnaps to raise funds for arms and expenses. Shergar was the first big one. O'Callaghan said another IRA terrorist, Kevin Mallon, a racing expert, was picked to handle it.

This is how his information became reported: "The horse quickly became distressed. It threw itself into a frenzy. It couldn't be pacified. It was killed within hours."

The IRA gang panicked. They dug a huge pit in the wild mountains near Ballinamore, Co. Leitrim, 100 miles from Ballymany. Shergar, his coat still glistening with the sweat of fright, was thrown in the hole and covered. The gorgeous animal, innocent of everything, was dumped like rubbish. His kidnapping and killing were a complete waste. Horses were like children in the policy of the IRA—expendable in pursuit of the cause.

Ballymany had been turned into a kind of Alcatraz. The new security systems were immense. But nobody ever went there without having Shergar's stall pointed out. And those who worked there said his ghost was still around and they saw him in the paddock almost every day.

CALIFORNIA'S WORST CRIME

(Mabel Mayer, 1927)

Guy B. H. Logan

Unrecorded in the standard chronicles of crime, the ugly murder of a defenceless teenager, Mabel Mayer, nevertheless panicked the citizens of Oakland for several weeks in the high Californian summer of 1927. Witnesses spoke of a mysterious woman seen with the dead girl hours before the killing, and her last journey by street-car after a family card party places the crime firmly in different, distant days. Guy B.H. Logan, a prolific British writer on crime in the 1920s and 1930s, couldn't resist a parting homily, but the killer of Sunshine Mabel was never caught.

There was no prettier or more popular girl in the town of Oakland, California, than fifteen-year-old Mabel Mayer, who lived with her parents at 2008 Eighty-Sixth Avenue, and who, on the night of Saturday, 2 July 1927, was brutally seized and murdered within a stone's throw of her own house.

The crime was of a nature, at once atrocious and mysterious, to strike terror and consternation in any community. For weeks after the event parents were afraid to let their children, especially their daughters, go out alone, and the failure of the police to trace the stealthy criminal, though all the forces of detection were brought to bear, only served to spread and increase the public alarm and dismay. Clues, of a kind, there were in plenty, but they, unfortunately, led nowhere, and the tireless endeavours of the authorities, backed whole-heartedly by those in neighbouring states, failed to track down the merciless slayer. The murder itself was of the sort most difficult to solve. It closely resembled, in many of its features, the comparatively recent murder of Miss Learoyd, at Ilkley, Yorkshire, and the same type of miscreant was probably involved. In each case the man got clear away from the scene of butchery, leaving his mangled victim to be discovered by the first passer by, and in each case he has yet to be punished for his frightful crime.

On the fatal Saturday morning, Mabel Mayer, a happy and contented girl, living in comfortable and well-to-do surroundings, of unsullied reputation, and with no secrets, one imagines, from her parents, left her home at ten o'clock to visit her dentist. It was known that she was to stay in Oakland during the morning for her music lesson, and she would then proceed to Berkeley, a neighbouring town, where she would have her dinner and spend the remainder of the day with her uncle, Mr Christian Mayer, who lived at 2417 Sacremento Street, The girl expected to stay the night at her uncle's house, and it had been arranged that her father, John Mayer, and her brother, William, three years her senior, should go to Berkeley the next morning to escort her home.

At six o'clock on the Saturday evening Mabel reached her uncle's house. She had gone to the dentist, where she was treated for an aching tooth, had turned up at 456 Lee Street, Oakland, where her music teacher, Miss Doris Olsen, had a studio, just before noon, and after a light lunch at a tea rooms, had gone to a cinema, which she left at four o'clock. At four-thirty she was seen and spoken to in one of Oakland's principal streets by two boy friends, Les Partington and Earl Stanley, who said that with her was an older woman, a stranger to them. Mabel did not tell them who this person was and the woman herself did not speak. It was never discovered who this stranger was—she did not come forward—and where Mabel went or what she did between four-thirty and six the police were never able to discover. It is improbable, however, that this hiatus in the time of her movements had any bearing on the crime, and it is just possible that the two lads were mistaken in supposing that the "older woman" was in her company.

At any rate, Mabel Mayer reached her uncle's house at six o'clock, and at six-thirty was seated at dinner with him and his friends. Her manner was, as usual, bright and cheery, and she seemed to have nothing on her mind. "She was full of fun and banter," said Mr Christian Mayer afterwards, "and I am convinced that she had no appointment with anyone. She was a very sensible girl, with all her vivacity, and quite able to take care of herself."

At eight o'clock Mabel received a telephone call from her brother William. Her father also phoned a few minutes later. He told the girl that he and William were going to a card party at the house of friends, Mr and Mrs George Farley, 2025 Eighty-Sixth Avenue, and suggested that she should join them. Mabel, after conferring with her uncle, agreed to this, and said that she would come on the next Southern Pacific electric train. Would they meet her at the Blanche Street station at ten o'clock?

At nine-fifty William Mayer went to meet the train, but, a little to his surprise, his sister had not come by it. He waited till all the passengers had left the station, and then returned to the Farleys' house, and reported to his father that Mabel was not on the train.

"Oh, she'll come by the next one," said Mr John Mayer. "I'll meet the ten-twenty and bring her home."

William then went on to his father's house, and Mr Mayer soon afterwards walked to the station. Mabel, however, was not on the ten-twenty train either, and her father, after one or two attempts to phone his brother's house at Berkeley—most of the public call offices had closed—went home. He was not unduly alarmed. Mabel had stayed the night at her uncle's on several previous occasions, and he supposed that she had done so now. He thought that she had changed her mind about coming home.

At eight fifty-five, Mabel said good-bye to her uncle's friends, and left for the station in his car. When they got there they learned that the train had already departed, and, instead of waiting for the next one to Oakland, due to depart in twenty minutes, Mabel asked to be driven to the street-car terminus. She left her uncle's automobile at that point, and boarded a street-car for Oakland at nine-six.

A man named Garrison was the conductor of that car, and he was able to remember the girl by the green bag she carried. He stated that she left the car in the downtown section of Oakland at nine twenty-five, after asking for a transfer to another car that would take her close to her own home. Arnold J. Porter, the conductor of that car, said that she alighted at nine forty-five near her home. He recalled the fact that she tried to get off the car backwards and that he had assisted her to alight. On leaving the vehicle, the girl was seen to walk up Eighty-Sixth Street, which led to her home.

Early on the following morning, a Sunday, two men, L. C. Hall and C. M. Wilcox, both living at 9229 Olive Street, set out to walk to Eighty-Sixth Avenue, where, at the back of a vacant house, No. 1738, they were engaged in constructing a garage. It was a beautiful morning, a little after seven o'clock, and they were laughing and chatting gaily together in the best of good spirits, but the fine day was completely spoiled for them by what they came upon after turning the rear corner of the vacant house.

They almost fell over the body of a young girl. She was lying on her back, with legs spread apart, and her clothing rolled up under her waist. Her face was most frightfully lacerated and battered, so much so as to look scarcely human, and blood had poured from her wounds. Lying near her was a green bag, and, not far off, the hat she had been wearing. She herself was lying, twisted and crumpled, in a flower-bed, and one arm, which was broken, was still raised as though to ward off the merciless blows that had been rained upon her face with a wooden mallet or club. The wrist-watch she had been wearing had stopped at ten-six.

Wilcox and his friend had not stayed to observe all this. They had been too shocked and horrified to take more than one glance at the blood-bespattered form, and had then, sick and shaken, hurried off to telephone the police, who, led by Captain B. A. Wallman, were quickly on the scene.

The medical examination seemed to strengthen the belief, already entertained, that the crime was the purposeless act of a homicidal maniac. In spite of the disarranged clothing, pointing to a motive for the attack, the poor child had not been ravished, her skirts having collected round her waist when she was dragged to the spot where she lay. The murder took place in the backyard at the rear of the vacant house, where considerable blood marked the culminating point of the struggle. The weapons used were found near the body. They consisted of two pieces of timber, one 34 inches long, with a nail at one end, and the other a piece of flooring, about three feet, sharpened at one end, and both bore stains of blood. The girl had been carried or dragged from the side-walk up a driveway which lay between the empty house and a vacant lot. Smears of blood, the imprint of a hand, were found on the side of the house, but owing to the roughness of the pieces of board used to commit the murder, no finger-prints could be made out on these. The Chief of Police, Donald A. Marshall, stated that part of a finger-print was found on the small green hand-bag. This was not the victim's, but a whorl of composite pattern, elliptical in form, with fine, clear ridges. The pieces of timber used were taken from the unfinished garage, showing that the murderer had not brought a weapon with him, but had picked up the first implement to hand.

No injury was done to the skull, which was very thin, and there was no wound found on the body below the throat. The murderer had struck at the face only, grasping the thirty-four-inch board with both hands, and had destroyed the nose and had lacerated the mouth and chin, fractured both upper and lower jaws in a number of places, and knocked out nearly all the teeth. Death had been caused by concussion, shock, and hemorrhage. There were, in addition, several fractures of the left forearm, with which the poor little victim had attempted to shield her face from the pitiless blows. The body had been dragged about four and a half feet from the spot where she had been first struck down, near a fence between the two lots, over which she may have been attempting to make her escape, to where she lay when found.

There having been no apparent attempt at molestation, and robbery being ruled out, what was the motive for this atrocious crime?

Before endeavouring to answer that question in the light of the known facts, let us try to reconstruct the crime, bearing in mind that the night was somewhat dark, the moon obscured, and the thoroughfare at that hour a lonely and deserted one.

We have already traced Mabel Mayer to the place where, at nine forty-five, she alighted from the street-car. In proceeding up Eighty-Sixth Street on her way home the girl would pass the vacant house, in the shadows of which the murderer crouched, waiting either for this particular victim or any other young girl or woman to come along. Mabel Mayer, suspecting nothing, fearing no one, passes swiftly up the street, unconscious of her impending doom, and nears the vacant house. The man springs from the side of it as she passes, seizes her in a grip of iron, and, in spite of her cries and struggles, carries, pulls, or drags her to the rear of the house. Already he has pounded her in the face with his fists, for blood is flowing, and it marks the woodwork of the house's side. Her hat falls off and she is dragged up the narrow driveway from the street, but when they reach the yard, the girl, in her frenzy of fear, wins free from her assailant, and dashes to the door of the empty house. She bangs on it with her fists in a vain belief that there may be someone within to open, to shelter her—there are the bloody smears on the door itself. When no help comes, and the fiend, momentarily uncertain, is about to attack her again, she races to the 3-foot fence which separates the weed-grown yard from the adjoining one. The man seizes a piece of board, darts to the girl, and strikes her a blow with it that fells her to the ground. Then, in his blood lust, he drags her body clear of the fence, and, standing over her prostrate form, rains blows upon the upturned face. She is still at last, and, alarmed at some sound, foiled in his original purpose, fearful for his safety, he throws his bloody clubs down by his victim, darts through the driveway, and by ten-fifteen or ten-twenty is gone.

I do not think there can be any doubt as to what his original purpose was. Crimes of the kind indicated here are, in nine cases out of ten, the hideous work of sex-mad degenerates. This man dragged his victim to the rear of the empty house with one object only, and he killed her when he found that not even threats of violence could bend her to his will. That he would have slain her anyhow, after the act, is only too likely, but the primary object of the attack was clear enough. Whether he had followed Mabel Mayer after she had left the street-car, and, knowing that she must come that way, had contrived to slip past her in the darkness and hide himself at the side of the vacant house, we have no means of knowing. It may be that he was there to pounce on the first unprotected female that might chance to pass that way.

Although there must always be a first attempt of this nature, the sadist never stops at one. For a time his blood and sex lust may be satisfied, but, sooner or later, as in the case of Peter Kuerten, the urge comes upon him again, and other victims are added to the first. The Ilkley monster, who is still a menace, if he is not dead, will, at some other time, strike again. Theodore Durrant, though well aware that he was under some suspicion, had to lure a second girl to the church his first murder had already defiled. The terrible Vacher's sex crimes, like those of Joseph Phillippe before him, were spread over a number of years. Neil Cream, that top-hatted, be-spectacled, frock-coated horror, haunting the sordid streets round Waterloo and Westminster, offering liquid refreshment—and pills of strychnine—to the South London prostitutes, found himself totally unable to resist his sadistic tendencies, once started on his nightmare career. And a young Welsh boy, Harold Jones, emulating, on a small scale, the atrocities of the American youth, Jesse Pomeroy, was compelled to find a second victim, even though he had only just recently escaped conviction for the murder of his first.

The discovery of the body in the Oakland case was made at seven-fifteen on the Sunday morning, and by seven-fifty the police were on the scene. Letters in the green purse bag disclosed the identity of the girl victim, and her father and brother were located at Berkeley, where they had gone on learning over the telephone that Mabel had not, as supposed, slept the night at her uncle's house. Mr Mayer and William were terribly distressed, the poor father in particular, but neither, of course, could throw any light on the crime. Nor could Mr Christian Mayer, who could merely describe the circumstances in which his niece had left the house the previous evening. Every member of the family was convinced that Mabel had no particular man friend, and all expressed themselves satisfied that the crime had been committed by a stranger. The girl was the last one in the world to indulge in secret "petting" parties or in any other of the "orgies" which modern American youth, even girls of a tender age, is said to favour.

A Mrs Howell, who lived at 1745 Eighty-Sixth Avenue, Oakland, volunteered what appeared to be important information, but it was discounted in advance by the time factors in the case.

She said that she was sitting in her parlour between eight-thirty and ten on the Saturday night, reading a book. At about nine-thirty she heard a scream in what she took to be a feminine voice, and it seemed to come from the vacant house. She could not express an opinion as to whether it was a cry of pain or distress. At nine-thirty, however, be it remembered, Mabel Mayer was certainly on the street-car which took her to Eighty-Sixth Avenue and East Fourteenth Street.

Mrs Margaret Paterson stated that she happened to be passing the empty house and unfinished garage at about nine-forty on the Saturday night. There was a small touring car drawn up in the roadway near the house, and beside it were two men who seemed to be labouring under some excitement. They spoke in broken English and a language that she could not understand. All very well this, but Mabel Mayer did not leave the second street-car until nine forty-five, and could not have reached the scene of the murder until five minutes to ten.

People named Brown, residing at 1742 Eighty-Sixth Avenue, next door to the yard in which the girl was killed, returned from a motoring expedition at as nearly as possible ten o'clock on the fatal night. They neither saw nor heard anything to cause the least alarm, an amazing fact considering that the murderous attack had then begun.

Reports that a mysterious light had been seen in the empty house on the night before the murder suggested that someone of the tramping class might have taken up his unlawful abode therein, and the police obtained entry. There was nothing to show that any person had recently been in, and the dust was undisturbed.

There was one circumstance that gave the police much anxious thought. The dead girl had been seen in the centre of the town at four-thirty on the Saturday afternoon. She had been recognized by her two boy acquaintances, who said "Hulloa, Mabel" as they passed her. With her, they said, was a woman of about twenty-eight or thirty, of whom, a stranger to them, they could only give a vague description.

Mabel, however, did not reach her uncle's residence until about six o'clock, and the police were much exercised to know where she had been in the interval. That was the only period of time on the Saturday that could not be accounted for.

It was thought to be absolutely certain that the escaping murderer must have had blood upon his person. The blows with the bludgeon had been struck at close quarters, and there were smears of blood wherever the man and the victim had been. Surely, it was asked, someone must have noticed his condition. Though the hour was late, there were still people in the streets on a Saturday night, and the street-cars were still running. The site of the murder was in a quiet, residential neighbourhood, but busy thoroughfares were close at hand. The guilty man, with tell-tale stains upon his clothing, must have gone to some place for the night—unless he walked the streets—and yet the cordon the police had drawn round the town and the many arrests of suspected-persons, mostly tramps, had yielded nothing.

The Chief's idea was that it was not the miscreant's first murder. He checked up on recent cases of the kind, criminal assaults committed by morons and insane persons, and invited information on that unsavoury topic from near and far.

Information on that line came from a place called Salinas. A pretty schoolgirl, thirteen years of age, belonging to Valla Vista, had gone on a visit to friends at Salinas. A man driving a car that carried either the Washington or Montana licence had invited her to "have a ride round," and the child, suspecting no harm, had consented. Seven miles from the town, in open country, he criminally assaulted her, and turned her adrift on the turnpike road.

The man's description was sent to the Oakland police. He was said to have been from thirty-five to forty years of age, of medium height, with a spotted face and reddish hair. Whoever this blackguard was, his description did not help the Oakland and Berkeley police, and, as a matter of fact, he was never apprehended. No doubt he, too, having escaped capture and punishment, will repeat his dastardly attack when opportunity presents itself.

On the Wednesday following the murder, however, an event occurred which seemed to justify the supposition that the wretch had been caged.

The police received information to the effect that a very suspicious looking man was in hiding under a warehouse on the water front. They proceeded to the spot indicated at express speed, and, under an abandoned warehouse near Third and Webster Streets, came upon a man with bloodstains on his garments and in an insensible condition. There was a gash across his throat and wounds in his chest, and he was rushed to the hospital. The doctors declared that the injuries were self-inflicted, and that they were probably three or four days old.

For two days police officers took it in turns to watch at the bedside of this man, and when, after many hours, he recovered consciousness, he was at once questioned about the murder which Oakland and Berkeley were still talking of with bated breath.

The stranger, in a weak voice and with tears, protested his innocence. He had, he said, never heard of Mabel Mayer, and was unaware that a murder had been committed.

"Good heavens, man," exclaimed one of the detectives present. "Don't you ever see a newspaper? Don't you know that the folks here have talked of nothing else since last Sunday?"

"I have been in no state of mind to read the papers," said the wounded man, "and I've too many troubles of my own to concern myself with other people's calamities, though I'm sorry for this girl's people, whoever they are."

"How did you come by those wounds?" he was asked.

"I wanted to kill myself," the man replied. "I tried to, and I crept under the warehouse to die. When did this killing happen?"

"At ten o'clock on Saturday night, 2 July," he was told.

"I was at the Avalon Hotel at that time," said the man, "and if you ask the people there, they will prove it. My name is Selenker. I left the hotel on the Sunday, having paid my bill. I had no money left and nothing to live for, and on Monday I wounded myself in the way you see."

His story was true, his alibi complete. At ten p.m. on the Saturday he was in bed at the small hotel named, and this was sworn to by Mrs Neases—what odd names you get in America !—the landlady of the house.

So that little flame ended in smoke, and Mr Selenker being held blameless for anything worse than cutting and maiming himself, with a view to "putting a period to his existence," as the old style reporter was fond of describing a suicide, the police had to begin all over again.

An uneasy feeling prevailed that the murderer was still lurking in the neighbourhood. After all, it was said, and not without reason, there was no evidence to show that he was a tramp, a maniac, or a stranger to the district. It was at least possible that the unknown miscreant was a native of the town, outwardly sedate and respectable, living, perhaps, close to the scene of the crime, and even, maybe, known to the victim, by sight at any rate.

With the idea that the murderer might return to the scene of the crime—though why it was expected that he should do anything so unwise it is not easy to see—a careful watch on the empty premises was kept at night for two or three weeks after the event, the Oakland and Berkeley reporters being especially zealous in this way. Two of them, W. Pale and F. Loughrin, reported a strange incident.

At midnight on 16 July these two men were in the yard at the back of the empty house, moodily smoking their pipes while they gazed at the bloodstains, still visible in the moonlight, on the white sides of the building and the low fence.

Suddenly, there came into the yard from the drive-way the dark figure of a man, taking, probably, the same path by which the killer had fled on the night of the crime. Stealthily he approached the house, and, silent and spellbound, the two newspaper men watched him, the same thought in the mind of each—was this the slayer of "Sunshine Mabel", as the girl had been endearingly called, come back to gloat over the place where he had destroyed that innocent life?

The stranger appeared to be unkempt and dishevelled, his garments old and dirty. He wore a cap, and from it protruded long, entangled hair.

When he started to shuffle up to the fence the two watchers, with one accord, moved towards him, and, in an instant, with a wild look round, he was gone. Hurrying round the house to the roadway, Loughrin sped along until he almost ran into two uniformed policemen patrolling the district in a car. To these he imparted his news, and they, bidding him enter the car, raced towards Olive Street, two blocks north of the murder yard, in the belief that the shaggy stranger would emerge into that thoroughfare. The alarm was spread, and a cordon of police and citizens formed about the district, which was diligently searched from end to end, but the prowler had contrived to slip through it in the darkness, and was no more seen.

The following description was issued and the public warned to stop any person answering to it until the police could be fetched and his arrest effected.

"About five foot eleven inches, from thirty-five to forty years of age. Well built and active. Dark complexion, unshaven for some days, hair long and matted. Dressed in shaggy, dark blue coat, baggy and crumpled trousers. Of sinister aspect generally."

One decidedly significant fact about this mystery man was that some strands of blue cloth had been found snagged under a splinter on the rear door of the empty house. The man had moved so quickly and so silently that it was thought that he must have been wearing canvas shoes.

A fourteen-year-old girl, Rosalie Morgan, living at 2205 Eighty-Fourth Avenue, had reported to the police on the previous Monday morning a very curious story.

She was returning home from evening church service at about eight-thirty on the previous night, alone. Tall grass and weeds ran along the side walk of Nineteenth Avenue, and from these sprang out a wild-looking man, dressed in an old and tattered blue coat, who caught her by the arm and muttered something. She snatched her arm away and ran for her life, never looking back until she reached a frequented part of the town. The most minute search was made for this sinister stranger, but he, too,—or it may have been the same man—got clear away.

The murderer of pretty Mabel Mayer has not been caught. Luck, as it sometimes does, favoured the culprit, but the police do not forget, and some day or other, when, as he inevitably will, he tries to waylay and slay again, he will be found. If, as some think, he is a native of Oakland, an apparently respectable and harmless citizen, who knew Mabel, by sight at least, and who is still hugging his guilty secret to his breast, let him beware. The mills of God grind slowly.

THE CAMDEN TOWN MURDER

(Robert Wood, 1907)

Nina Warner Hooke and Gil Thomas

Sir Edward Marshall Hall rejoiced in the title The Great Defender. His full-blooded style was at its best in a case that touched his sympathies and emotions. The Camden Town murder case was one of these, but when he took it on, Marshall Hall's career was in low water. The year before, in 1906, he'd been overwhelmed by a run of misfortune: his hopes of a political career had been dashed when he lost his seat in Parliament, and a series of clashes with various judges had temporarily shattered and almost destroyed his practice. He needed a big, high-profile case to restore his position at the Bar. In November 1907 it came. "This", he exclaimed, hurrying into a colleague's room and throwing a huge pile of documents on to his desk, "is the greatest case I've ever had in my life. If you have an idea, however remote or far-fetched, come in and tell me. The man's innocent, and a chance idea may mean life or death to him." The papers flung on to the desk were the depositions in the Camden Town murder case. The accused man was Robert Wood. "When the case was over," reported one of Marshall Hall's biographers, "the newspapers took the view that the result was a foregone conclusion, but this was far from being true. It was a great triumph for Marshall

Hall and English justice. " *Its low-life setting in the dingy hinterland of Euston station, a transient world of four-ale bars and seedy sex, offers a lurid, if slightly dog-eared, snapshot of Edwardian London.*

Prostitution is a dangerous trade in most western countries and will continue to be so until man throws off the shackles forged by centuries of religious discipline. Christian dogma teaches him to equate sex with sin and eternal punishment. He is taught to be ashamed of his body, not to glory in its beauty and potency; to despise it as the gross expendable husk of a spirit body which will survive it on another plane of existence. His sacred literature makes it clear that human reproductive processes are repugnant to his God who spurned them when He came to earth Himself in man's shape. It is further impressed on him that, partly by virtue of this attitude, Christian and civilized nations are superior to unenlightened and less fortunate peoples. It is only the heathen who may regard sexual desire as an appetite like hunger and thirst, the satisfaction of which is natural, simple and enjoyable. It is only heathens who may recognize the fact that a man's virility outlasts a woman's and make due allowance for it. By a curious and unfair coincidence it is only in such heathen countries that sex crimes are uncommon.

Civilized man's distrust of the rational is only excelled by his fear of the pleasurable. He still lives in dread of hell fire. The flames have abated slightly but the embers are hot and the pit still yawns. Since he cannot eradicate the erotic impulses of his body and cannot gratify them extra-maritally without incurring moral censure, he drives them deep into hiding. Here, like healthy plants deprived of light, they wilt, become diseased and may mutate into monstrous forms.

The woman who caters for these secret lusts is the easy prey of the pervert, the sadist and the obsessionist who sees in her an amalgam of Eve, the original temptress and the serpent, the devil's emissary. Driven by remorse and terror he destroys her and is revenged for his banishment from Eden.

The murder of Emily Dimmock, a Camden Town prostitute, in the autumn of 1907 is regarded by criminologists as a classic example of this type of sex crime. It had all the ingredients necessary to titillate a sensation-loving public—a woman killed in her sleep, the discovery of her dead body with its throat cut, the long search for a murderer who had slipped away through the garden, the grief of the woman's lover who discovered the crime and the eventual arrest of a young artist named Robert Wood who was charged with the murder.

It is a curious feature of the case that widespread sympathy was extended to the accused young man and very little was felt for the victim of the crime. It could be argued that a girl who deliberately leads an immoral life, according to the tenets of our moral code, has abandoned any claim to sympathetic consideration. It is not generally accepted, at any rate in this country, that the prostitute fulfils a useful function without which the incidence of rape and violence towards women would be even worse than it is. Whatever view one takes of this trade no one but a fool would argue that its practitioners are all good or all bad. There are among them harpies in the true classical sense, both vicious and dishonest, who prey on the weakness of men and will cheat them if they can. Emily Dimmock was not one of these. In her own way she did at least give value for money.

Though her Christian names were Emily Elizabeth she was known in the area where she lived and worked as Phyllis. The dreary tenements of Walworth where she was born have produced a genius in the form of Charles Chaplin; but for one Chaplin there are ten thousand Emilys.

She was the youngest of a family of fifteen. When she was still a girl her father removed his brood to Northamptonshire where most of them, including Emily, went to work in a factory. This phase did not last long in her case. Returning to London she went into domestic service at East Finchley, but found the hours too long and the work too hard and before long had taken to the streets. Her new occupation had probably been described to her as offering an easy living. In fact it was not only strenuous but carried with it an occupational hazard which was to cost her her life at the age of twenty-three.

Readers of Patrick Hamilton's trilogy of novels about the London underworld will recognize in the second volume an almost exact description of Emily and her feckless way of life.* It is more than likely that her story formed the inspiration for the character of Jenny Maple. Emily, like Jenny,

---

* *Twenty Thousand Streets Under the Sky* by Patrick Hamilton (Constable, 1936).

was neat, slim and attractive, dressed well and had pleasant manners.

She lived in two rooms in St Paul's Road, Camden Town, an area which had passed through many vicissitudes. Even in the street guides of twenty-five years ago there was no mention either of St Paul's Road or of near-by Liverpool Street. St Paul's Road was a thoroughfare running parallel to the main railway line from St Pancras to the north. Within a short walking distance was the Caledonian Road and the old Caledonian Market. Emily was thus well situated for the transaction of her business. She could take a bus from Camden Road to the West End or she could find her clients in the numerous local public houses.

In 1907 the area around St Paul's Road was a shabby-genteel backwater where rooms were cheap and no questions were asked as long as the rent was promptly paid. The lusty life of the Caledonian Market engulfed it on Tuesdays and Fridays but for most of the week only the clip-clop of horses' hooves, the cries of children and street traders and the sound of passing trains disturbed the quiet. Prostitutes are not early risers and they prefer quiet neighbourhoods.

Emily shared her home with a man named Bertram Shaw and passed as his wife. Shortly after eleven o'clock on the morning of 12 September an elderly lady called at the house in St Paul's Road. This was Mrs Shaw. She had travelled from the Midlands to visit her son who, she understood, had recently married. Mrs Stocks, the landlady, told her that her son's wife was still in bed. They talked together in the hallway for about fifteen minutes until Bertram Shaw returned from work. He was employed as a dining-car attendant on the Midland Railway whose main lines ran to Leicester, Nottingham and Sheffield. His hours of work enabled him to catch the seven-twenty a.m. train from Sheffield to St Pancras and to reach his home shortly before eleven-thirty.

After exchanging a few words with his mother and the landlady Shaw went to call Emily. Receiving no answer when he knocked at the door he tried to open it and found that it was locked. He went to the kitchen and borrowed a duplicate key from Mrs Stocks who followed him into the parlour. Evidence of an intruder was all over the room. Drawers had been ransacked and their contents strewn over the floor. The folding doors leading to the bedroom were also locked and the key was missing. Again Shaw knocked and, receiving no answer, broke into the room. The blankets were in a heap on the floor. The sheets covered something on the bed from which a pool of blood had trickled down on to the floor. The room was dimly lighted through half-opened shutters.

Shaw, thoroughly alarmed, rushed to the bed and dragged aside the sheets. To his horror he discovered the nude body of Emily Dimmock lying face downwards. Her throat had been cut from ear to ear.

A search of the room disclosed that some of her personal belongings were missing. A gold watch had gone together with a silver cigarette case bearing Shaw's initials, a silver chain and a purse. On top of the sewing-machine lay a postcard album from which some of the contents had been torn out and scattered around.

Shaw had taken Emily from the streets to live with him. She had promised to abandon her way of life on the understanding that he would marry her. Why he had not done so was never explained. He had told his mother a lie. Mrs Stocks also was under the impression that the couple were married. It is possible that he never had any intention of keeping his word but had merely acquired cheaply an attractive bed-companion and housekeeper.

Unluckily for Shaw he had provided an excellent cover for Emily to have the best of both worlds. By day she was Mrs Shaw, the respectable married woman. At night she reverted to the life of the streets. There is a supposition that Shaw knew she had returned to her former ways and that he was turning a blind eye while taking advantage of the additional comforts she provided. Shaw, of course, denied any knowledge of Emily's duplicity and in the absence of evidence to the contrary this must be accepted. His position was both awkward and dangerous. Whatever happened he now had to disclose his real relationship with the murdered girl and could not escape suspicion.

Events moved slower in those days than they do now. There were no police cars with two-way radios. The divisional police surgeon did not arrive at the house until after one o'clock. After examining the body he gave his opinion that the murder had been committed between four and six o'clock that morning. There were signs that the killer had washed himself before escaping through the french windows and across the garden.

Once arrived on the scene the police lost no time in starting their inquiries. During the rest of the day they collected all available information about Emily's movements on the day before her death.

This was Wednesday, 11 September. She had spent much of it on household tasks such as washing and ironing. Presumably Shaw was with her since he left in the afternoon soon after four o'clock to catch his train to Sheffield as usual. Between then and eight-fifteen Emily was seen about the house, dressing herself and curling her hair. One of the garments she put on was a light-brown skirt. Nothing out of the ordinary was heard that night, either by Mrs Stocks or anyone else in the house.

Mrs Stocks got up about five-thirty next morning, knocked on Emily's door at nine o'clock and, getting no answer, concluded that her tenant was having what she called a "lie in". Nothing further happened until the arrival of Shaw. Shaw's movements were checked. His employers confirmed that he had been to Sheffield and could not possibly have got back to London until after Emily was dead.

By the following day, Thursday, the police had an almost complete dossier on the dead woman. She had plenty of men friends apart from her clients, some of whom were regular and some casual. She was young enough and attractive enough to be sure of making a good living; but like so many of her type she was open-handed with her money and was more concerned to have a good time in the present than to save for the future. She was an amusing companion and could play the piano well which added to her popularity in public-house circles. She had once been an inmate of a brothel kept by a man named Crabtree and had lived at many addresses in the Oxford Street and Tottenham Court Road area. She had a collection of postcards which had come from many parts of the world, most of them from clients who remembered her and no doubt intended to seek her out again when they returned to England.

Under the name of Phyllis she was well-known at the Rising Sun public house in Camden Town. It was here that the police located their first important witness, a ship's cook named Roberts. Having been paid off in the previous month he was now spending the last of his money before going back to sea. He had met Phyllis in the Rising Sun, taken a fancy to her and gone home with her on the Sunday night and on the next two nights preceding the one on which she was murdered—at a cost to himself of two pounds and a bottle of whisky. On Wednesday night he slept at a lodging-house since Phyllis said she had another engagement. Roberts's story was suspicious but his alibi was confirmed by the proprietress of the lodging-house and a fellow boarder. Roberts was thus eliminated from the murder hunt. He was however able to give the police a

piece of valuable information. On the Wednesday morning, while
he was dressing, he said, two letters were pushed under the door
which he picked up and handed to Phyllis. One was a circular, the
other a private letter. After reading the letter she passed it to him. He
remembered some of the contents, including the opening words:

Dear Phillis [*sic*],
    Will you meet me at the Eagle, Camden Town, 8.30
tonight, Wednesday?

The letter was signed "Bert". There was a postscript but Roberts
had not been allowed to read this. The girl then handed him a
postcard which she had taken from a chest of drawers. On one
side of it was a picture of a woman embracing a child. On the
reverse side was a message:

Phillis darling,
    If it please you meet me 8.15 p.m. at the—(here followed
a sketch of a rising sun).

Yours to a cinder,
Alice.

Roberts noticed similarities between the letter and the postcard.
Both were written in indelible pencil by the same hand and both
contained the same mis-spelling of Phyllis. The letter was burnt,
presumably because it was signed by a man and would be a
dangerous item to leave lying around. The postcard was returned
to the chest of drawers, presumably to add to the collection. The
signature of Alice made it harmless.

The charred remains of the letter were found in the grate but
the postcard did not come to light until Shaw, on packing up to
leave the apartment, found it under a sheet of newspaper lining
one of the drawers. Roberts identified it as the one he had seen
on the Wednesday morning.

Owing to the nature of the crime and the mysterious circumstances in which it was committed the case received wide publicity
while the investigation was going on. A leading article in the *Daily
Chronicle* reflects one aspect of public opinion:

To the moralist and every serious-minded citizen who considers the state of society, how terrible are the sidelights which

the case throws on life in London. Of scandals in high life we often hear much, and the publicity which they attract is perhaps out of proportion to their proper dimensions. Here we have the limelight thrown on scandals in low life and it is a saddening and sickening spectacle that is revealed. How awful is the picture of the murdered woman—"the lowest of the low" as she is called—passing at the end of the week as the wife of one man and for the rest of it consorting promiscuously, ending with her throat cut by some stray companion. Englishmen are proud of their civilizing mission in the dark countries of the world. We are not among those who would ridicule or discourage such work, but is there not some civilizing to be done nearer home? There are savages, as we call them, who would be ashamed to live the life that is led by some in Camden Town.

Despite this editorial exhortation it would seem that things have changed little in this neighbourhood in the last sixty years. It is not long since the murder of a newspaper reporter by a gang of louts on the fringe of Camden Town.

The most important clue so far was the postcard with the sketch of the rising sun, but it did not go far towards solving the mystery, since there was no means of identifying the writer. The Commissioner of Police enlisted the co-operation of the Press in this matter. In the album found in Dimmock's bedroom were other postcards written in the same handwriting and it was obvious that the writer had been a regular associate of the dead girl. The postcards, four in all, were circulated to the Press. The *News of the World* was quick to take advantage of this circulation booster. This newspaper used a facsimile of the Rising Sun card over the bold caption: "Do you recognize this handwriting?" A reward of one hundred pounds was offered for information.

Among the readers of this popular Sunday paper was a young woman named Ruby Young. She called herself an artist's model but in fact followed the same profession as Emily Dimmock, though possibly in a somewhat higher class. She recognized the handwriting on the postcard and wrote a letter to the newspaper attaching the cutting. But she never posted it. That same evening she had a visitor, a young artist and an ex-lover of hers whose name was Robert Wood.

Wood was in a responsible position as an artist-engraver in the

glass works of Messrs J. R. Carson of Holborn. His father was a
Scot who had worked for a quarter of a century as a compositor on
the *Scotsman*. Wood's boyhood was normal and unremarkable save
for the marked artistic talent that he showed at an early age and which
was encouraged at the church school he attended. When he grew up
he took a job as an assistant steward at the Medical Students Club
in Chancery Lane where he was frequently asked to draw medical
diagrams and copy illustrations from technical papers. When the
club was disbanded owing to financial losses Robert Wood went to
Carson's and rose steadily in the firm. His character was excellent.
He was good-natured and kind-hearted and everybody liked him.
His work attracted the attention of the great William Morris who
gave him personal encouragement and advice.

But Wood had a weakness for low company. His friendship with
Ruby Young had developed into a love affair. He apparently had
no objection to the girl's mode of life which was continued after
they became lovers. Ruby at one time lived quite near his home at
King's Cross but moved with her mother to Earl's Court. Wood
found the journey somewhat tiresome and began to meet her less
frequently. The break in their relations came when Ruby heard
that he was associating with other women. In July they had a
serious quarrel. Their next meeting was a chance one in the street
in August after Wood had returned from a holiday in Belgium.
After this casual encounter they made no further arrangements to
meet. But on Friday, 20 September, a week after the murder of
Emily Dimmock, Ruby received a telegram from Wood asking her
to meet him at the Phit-Eesie shop in Southampton Row. This had
been their former rendezvous. Ruby kept the appointment. Directly
they met, and almost before they had exchanged greetings, Wood
said, "Ruby, I want you to help me. If any questions are ever asked
you by anyone, will you say that you always saw me on Monday
and Wednesday nights?"

This was an odd request to make from a girl who had been
treated somewhat shabbily. Ruby was justifiably curious and a little
annoyed, particularly since he refused to give her any explanation.
However after a good deal of argument she consented to the request
and they parted. Wood next called on a friend of his who was
employed by a bookseller in Charing Cross Road. This man, whose
name was Lambert, had been in the Eagle public house opposite
Camden Town Station on the Wednesday before the murder. He
had seen Wood there accompanied by a young woman with her

hair in curling pins who apologized for her untidiness, saying she had "just run out". When Lambert inquired what had brought him to a public house he did not normally visit Wood replied that he had business to attend to. When Lambert left Wood had remained behind with the girl.

Lambert now guessed that the girl must have been Emily Dimmock and this was confirmed when the purpose of Wood's visit to the bookshop emerged. Wood had come to ask him to say, if questioned, that they had had a drink together but not to mention the girl. "I can clear myself," he said, "but I don't want it to come to my father's ears."

During the following week Wood took Ruby to a theatre and on the way home reminded her of the promise she had given him: "Don't forget now. Mondays and Wednesdays."

There were further meetings and a lot of discussion before they finally concocted a plan. Ruby Young said: "The best thing for me to do is to say that I met you at six-thirty at Phit-Eesie's and we had tea at Lyons' Café, and after tea we went down Kingsway to the Strand and on to Hyde Park Corner. Then we'd better say we walked along the Park out to Brompton Oratory and got there at half past ten. We'll say that we parted there and that you went back by tube to King's Cross and got home before midnight." Wood agreed to this whole-heartedly.

They met several times during the ensuing week and each time Wood reminded Ruby of her promise. She was by now getting thoroughly irritated as well as worried and she repeated that she would keep her word. "But don't keep bothering me. It's getting on my nerves."

Ruby Young was a most unsuitable ally in a cloak and dagger plan of this sort, for she could not keep a secret. She confided her worries to a girl friend. The friend repeated the story in confidence to a reporter on the *Weekly Dispatch*. The newspaper informed Scotland Yard and Inspector Neill, who was in charge of the case, was sent to interview Ruby Young. The outcome was that she went to meet Robert Wood with the Inspector in attendance and as she shook hands with her former lover he was taken into custody. After an identification parade on 5 October, when he was identified by a number of people as having been seen in the Eagle on the night of the murder in Emily Dimmock's company, he was formally charged with her murder.

From the time of his first talk with Arthur Newton after delivery of the brief, Marshall Hall was convinced of Robert Wood's innocence. But the task of formulating a defence in the face of Wood's tissue of lies about his whereabouts on the night of the crime needed all his ingenuity and the painstaking assistance of his colleague Wellesley Orr.

Marshall was well aware that a great deal hung upon the outcome of this case not only for his client but for himself. It was the most important criminal trial that had come his way since his fortunes began to mend. He needed to test his newly restored confidence in an arena lit by the full glare of publicity and he was determined to make the utmost of this opportunity.

Not least among the many difficulties with which he had to contend was Wood's peculiar behaviour. Marshall formed the opinion that he had a dual personality. He was certainly abnormal in one respect for he seemed unable to comprehend the appalling situation he was in. Wellesley Orr considered that the evidence of the ship's cook was of great importance. He also felt that Wood must be called in his own defence. Marshall Hall opposed this, believing that because of his obvious abnormality he would make an unreliable witness. But Orr insisted that if Wood were not called he would certainly hang. Marshall had still some lingering doubt as to whether he could, or should, trust his own judgment and allowed himself to be overruled. Accordingly the form of declaration he customarily used in such eventualities was sent to Wood who signed it, thereby giving his consent to be called.

The trial opened at the rebuilt Central Criminal Court on Thursday, 12 December, before Mr Justice Grantham. Sir Charles Mathews, K.C. appeared for the prosecution assisted by Archibald Bodkin and L. A. Symmons. Marshall Hall led for the defence with Herman Cohen, Huntly Jenkins and J. R. Lort-Williams.

Marshall had had few cases which looked more hopeless at the start. He had also had few which offered more scope for his particular brand of shrewd, lucid and hard-hitting advocacy. He did not make the mistake which a lesser man might have done. He did not say, "Wood must be innocent because X is guilty." He maintained throughout the trial that there was insufficient evidence to convict *anyone*. He was thus absolved from defending one man by accusing another and in consequence had a freer hand.

Mathews opened quietly and reasonably, making the most of Wood's futile efforts to cover up his association with the dead woman. The main point he brought out was the similarity of the handwriting on the Rising Sun postcard and the charred letter found in Dimmock's room. If the evidence of Roberts was to be believed Wood had arranged to meet Emily at the Eagle on the night she was murdered. The curling pins seen in her hair on the Wednesday night were still there when her body was found. The inference was that Wood intended to kill her either on Wednesday evening or Thursday morning and arranged to meet her at a place where he was unlikely to be recognized. The hair curlers indicated that she was going to meet someone she knew very well. The Crown also relied on the evidence of another witness, McCowan, who said he had seen Wood in the area of St Paul's Road at the time when, according to the medical evidence, the crime had been committed. Mathews stressed the importance of this evidence. At the identity parade the witness had unhesitatingly picked out Wood by his walk. Corroboration of the fact that Wood walked with a nervous jerk or twitch of the shoulder came from Ruby Young.

Mathews gradually built up his case into a formidable indictment against Robert Wood. The state of the apartment, he said, when the murder was discovered showed that Wood had gone to considerable lengths to find and destroy the Rising Sun postcard. The shutters had been half opened to admit light. Why had the murderer wasted valuable time looking through the postcard album unless it contained something of an incriminating nature? The articles which were missing had obviously been taken to provide a robbery motive for the crime; but if robbery was indeed the motive why had more valuable articles been left behind?

The case against Wood, although circumstantial, was strong. Great care in the handling of the defence was needed. Marshall Hall scored his first point when dealing with the street plan prepared by Sergeant Grosse. The inference to be drawn from this plan was that St Paul's Road was in a brilliantly lit area. Under cross-examination the sergeant admitted that the street lights were extinguished at four thirty-seven a.m. Marshall saw the opportunity he needed and asked:

"If that is so, they would be useless for lighting purposes at five minutes to five?"

"Yes."

"Do you think this is a fair plan?"

"I do."

"I put it to you, have you ever seen a more misleading plan in your life?" No answer.

"Would not anybody, looking at this plan, come to the conclusion that the light was reflected upon the front of 29 St Paul's Road?"

"Not on the front of the house, but in the neighbourhood."

"You *know* the electric standard lights were extinguished at four thirty-seven on the morning of 12 September?"

"Yes."

"You know it was a dark, muggy morning. If the electric standards were extinguished at that time they would be useless for any purpose of light at five to five?"

"Yes."

"Is it not the case that, this being so, you have been specially asked to prepare a map that would show, as your evidence suggests, a sufficiency of light coming from the railway cutting forty feet below the road?" No reply.

"If it was a drizzly, thick, muggy morning, the refracting and reflecting power of the arc lights would be at a minimum, would they not?"

"Yes."

"Is there, at the railway bridge, a wall nine feet high? High enough to prevent me, for instance, from seeing over?"

"Yes."

"Is that wall shown on the map?"

"No, it was not necessary."

By this forceful questioning Marshall Hall was able to cast doubt on the veracity of the police in relation to the street lighting at the time Wood was said to have been seen in St Paul's Road. His purpose was to challenge the identification of Wood by other witnesses, and it was a move both shrewd and subtle.

Much has been written about Marshall's talent as an orator. But less attention has been paid to his ability to elicit by clever questioning the priorities in a line of reasoning. He was faced with the fact that no other suspect in the case had both the means and the opportunity to commit the crime. He had to break one by one the links in the chain of evidence against his client.

Roberts, the ship's cook, was the next witness. In his cross-examination it is fascinating to see how the man is manoeuvred into a difficult position and forced to admit that he might have invented his story.

"Do you know a woman named May Campbell?"

"By sight, yes."

"Have you ever spoken to her?"

"Yes."

"Did you talk about the case?"

"It was talked of all over the place."

"Did May Campbell give you a description of someone who, she said, was known as a friend of Dimmock?"

"Yes."

"And did that description correspond very much with the description of the accused?"

"It tallied very much."

"So you could have picked him out from May Campbell's description?"

"Not unless I knew him."

"Was the description, published in the newspapers on 22 September of the man who was wanted, and which was described as official, very like the description Campbell gave you?"

"Yes."

"Was the description: 'Age twenty-eight to thirty. Height five feet seven inches. Sallow complexion. Dark hair. Clean shaven. Peculiar difference about eyes'?"

"Something like it."

"Almost word for word, was it not?"

"Yes."

"Did she add: 'Pimples on lower part of face and neck'?"

"She said something about pimples. Pimples do not always stay there."

"Do not argue. Were you not in a great fright when you heard of the murder?"

"No, I was not in any fright."

"When you heard of the murder did you realize that except for the murderer—"

"That I was next to him."

"Yes."

"Yes, I realized that. That is why I stopped at the Rising Sun when I heard of the murder. I said I would stop all night until the police came."

Having strengthened his attack on the question of identification by suggesting that Roberts and May Campbell had acted in collusion Marshall turned to the charred letter Roberts claimed to have read.

"How could anybody writing that on the Tuesday write 'tonight' for Wednesday?"

"You generally write that way to let a person know."

"Do you usually, when writing on a Tuesday to make an appointment for a Wednesday, write 'Meet me tonight'?"

"I do not."

"I put it to you that that piece of burned paper is a fragment which might have come from anywhere and which never came through the post."

"It did."

"Where did the name 'Bert' come from?"

"I tell you it was written."

"If the object had been to put suspicion on Shaw, the suggestion would have been very useful?" No answer.

At this point Sir Charles Mathews interrupted to ask if Marshall Hall were accusing Roberts of the murder.

"Most certainly I am not," said Marshall.

The second day of the trial produced further proof that Marshall had fully regained his skill in cross-examination. Confidently and ruthlessly he discredited three of the Crown's witnesses by making them so confused that the evidence they gave was worthless. One of these was the man McCowan, on whose statement that he had seen Wood coming out of 29 St Paul's Road on the morning of the murder the prosecution placed great reliance.

With Ruby Young Marshall dealt more gently. She had incurred general resentment by her betrayal of Wood for, it was alleged, the reward offered by the *News of the World*.

"Have you ever thought that, having regard to the evidence of Doctor Thompson who places the time of the murder at three or four in the morning, the alibi arranged with you from six-thirty to ten-thirty on the evening previous to the murder would be a useless alibi for the murder but a perfect one for the meeting of the girl?"

"It did not strike me then that it was a useless alibi."

"But it does now, does it not?"

"Yes, it does now."

Some accounts of the trial pinpoint this question as the foundation of Marshall Hall's defence, on the grounds that the ineffectual alibi proved Wood's ignorance of the time the girl had been murdered. But it proved nothing of the kind. Medical evidence as to the time of death is not completely reliable even today with all the advances in forensic science. In 1907 methods were far more haphazard and less account was paid to the factors governing the onset of rigor mortis and blood coagulation. It should be borne in mind that the crime was committed during one of the hottest weeks of the year. The heat in Dimmock's bedroom was attested by the fact that all the bedclothes save the sheets had been pushed on to the floor. It is by no means impossible that she had been killed much earlier than the time estimated.

It seems to us that the real foundation of the case for the defence was Marshall's destruction of the evidence of identification. Without positive identification of Wood as the man seen leaving the house in St Paul's Road early in the morning after the crime was committed, the Crown's case was purely circumstantial. He had gone to enormous trouble to challenge Sergeant Grosse in the matter of street lighting, had walked the whole area himself and had studied the properties of light in relation to atmospheric conditions.

The intention of the Crown was to prove, if possible, that Wood and Dimmock were acquainted before 6 September when Wood claimed they had first met. To this end a number of witnesses were called to show that the two had been on close terms for some eighteen months before this date. They were respectively a man named Crabtree, a brothel keeper, who said that Wood visited the girl when she lived at his house; another man, named Lyneham, who had seen them regularly in the Rising Sun; a woman, Mrs Lawrence, who had seen them together in another public house, The Pindar of Wakefield; and a second woman, Gladys Warren, who had not only seen them together on many occasions but could give specific dates. Marshall Hall weakened the value of their evidence by exposing their bad characters. But the character of these witnesses was not important. Their statements were; and since they were unknown to each other they could not have acted in collusion.

Towards the end of the fourth day Marshall Hall submitted to the judge that there was no case to answer. But he was overruled. The main points of his opening speech for the defence were: the absence of positive identification, the absence of motive and the absence of a weapon. He dismissed the false alibi concocted with Ruby Young as the misguided act of a young man wishing to conceal his double life from his family. He drew attention to the fact that Wood's father and brother confirmed that he had spent the night of the murder at home. He called the charred letter an invention of Roberts's to divert suspicion from Roberts to Shaw. He agreed that McCowan had seen a man leaving the house in

St Paul's Road but this man was not Wood. He would call several
witnesses to prove that Wood had no peculiarities of gait.

Wood, called in his own defence, was a thoroughly bad witness.
He seemed incapable of giving a straight answer to a question.
When asked by Marshall Hall, "Robert Wood, did you kill Emily
Dimmock?" he smiled and said nothing at all. The question was
repeated.

"You must answer."

"I mean, it is ridiculous," was Wood's reply.

"You must answer straight."

"No, I did not."

Throughout the examination he was the despair of his counsel and
even Sir Charles Mathews, then at the height of his powers, could do
little to break through his apparent indifference. He seemed to be
regarding the proceedings as an observer rather than a participant,
making sketches of the personages involved in the trial—including
the judge, Mathews, Ruby Young and himself. The salient point
of Mr Justice Grantham's summing up was the statement: "In my
judgment, strong as the suspicion in this case undoubtedly is, I do
not think the prosecution has brought the case near enough home
to the accused."

In the face of this clear direction the jury could do nothing else
but bring in a verdict of "Not Guilty".

There was no doubt that Marshall Hall had scored a great
triumph. In the words of Basil Hogarth:

> It was a splendid defence, the production of a marvellous
> forensic technique, and in architectonic structure Marshall
> Hall himself never improved on it. There was not a question
> that had not its appropriate answer, not a doubt but had its
> resolution.*

There were cheers in court on Wood's acquittal and the streets
around the Old Bailey were packed with excited people. Mrs
Beerbohm Tree rushed on to the stage of a West End theatre to
announce the verdict. In contrast, there was universal vilification
of Ruby Young who had to be smuggled out of the Court disguised
as a charwoman to save her from a mob who would have lynched

* *The Trial of Robert Wood*, edited by Basil Hogarth (Notable Trials Series.
William Hodge and Co. Ltd, Edinburgh).

her. Seldom in the annals of our legal history has the hysterical sentimentality of an English crowd gone to such lengths.

Looking back from a distance of almost sixty years it would seem probable that this public demonstration, ostensibly of sympathy for Robert Wood, was in point of fact adulation of Marshal Hall, his saviour and deliverer. After this there could be no doubt in anyone's mind that Marshall was restored to his old eminence and popularity.

It is significant that when he first accepted the brief he was absolutely convinced of Wood's innocence. But many years afterwards, on one of the rare occasions when he discussed his work with his daughter Elna, he told her that he had since reversed his opinion.

It certainly seems odd to the student of this baffling case that Wood should have been at pains to conceal his association with Dimmock from his family when they must have known about his friendship with Ruby Young—whose mode of life was much the same. Again, it cannot be ignored that the murderer, whoever he was, searched through the postcard album looking for something he suspected to be there, something which might incriminate him, and which could not have been anything else but the Rising Sun postcard. Marshall Hall's theory that the charred letter found in the bedroom grate existed only in Roberts's imagination was generally unsupported. Wood's own explanation of it was totally unbelievable. He said that the fragments were of some sketches and writings of his which Emily had appropriated. In that case, what was her reason for burning them—especially in the presence of Roberts? They were quite innocuous, according to Wood.

Out of this jumble of admission and denial, charge and counter-charge, only one thing emerges plainly, that Robert Wood was the only possible suspect once Roberts and Shaw had been eliminated. He had the opportunity, but what was the motive? Poor little Emily Dimmock represented no danger to him. Her few belongings were hardly worth stealing, even had he been so short of money as to contemplate robbing her. It is most unlikely that he was in love with her and swayed by jealousy. One is thrown back on the suggestions of a schizoid personality and a long association with Dimmock as a regular client. Given these factors, it is not difficult for anyone familiar with the elements of psychopathology to visualize a possible sequence of events—the young man of unblemished reputation in his own circle, with his church school education and repressive

Scottish upbringing, waking in the small hours in a sleazy bed beside a woman who meant nothing to him and to whom he was merely a customer for the night, the uprush of shame and disgust and the uncontrollable impulse to destroy the partner of his guilt. But here again one is faced with an insoluble problem. If the crime was the result of a sudden impulse to violence he would not have had with him the means to commit it. It takes a very sharp blade to cut a woman's throat so savagely that her head is almost severed. Shaw's two razors were in the bedroom, but it was established through microscopic examination that neither of these had been used.

From that day to this the Camden Town murder has fascinated criminologists, both amateur and professional, but they are no nearer a solution than the clientele of the Rising Sun who discussed it so avidly during that sultry autumn of 1907.

Ernest Raymond used it as the theme of a novel, *inventing for his murderer the character of an elderly lover of Dimmock's who met her by appointment after she left the Eagle on 12 September, and went home with her.

Someone else has advanced an ingenious theory whereby Shaw, by catching an earlier train and jumping from it while it was halted outside St Pancras Station, could have walked into the house, guessed what Emily had been up to and killed her in a wave of jealous fury. This of course presupposes that Shaw had previously been ignorant of Emily's activities, which is not very probable. Returning as he did each morning to a disordered room, to a bed in which the girl often lay sleeping off the weariness of the night's business in soiled and rumpled sheets, he must have been blind if he did not know what had been going on. Undoubtedly he knew about and condoned Emily's trade for the sake of the benefits it brought him; in which case to kill her would be killing the goose which laid the golden eggs.

Was there anyone who had the means, the opportunity and a possible motive? If so, it must have been someone who had access to the house or lived in it. It is worth considering the other inmates of 29 St Paul's Road. There was another lodger, a Mrs Lancaster who rented the upper floor. Mrs Stocks, the landlady, lived in the basement, and Mrs Stocks had a husband, a railway carriage cleaner. Stocks said in evidence that he heard nothing unusual on

* For Them That Trespass by Ernest Raymond.

the night of the murder. He had wakened at five o'clock when the alarm went off but had fallen asleep again.

This is interesting because it argues a break in pattern. He had to report for duty at the railway yard at five-thirty and had done so for many years. If he had been liable to oversleep, in those days he would have got the sack for unpunctuality. Why did it happen on that particular morning? Had he perhaps had a disturbed night? Both he and his wife deposed at the trial that they knew nothing of Dimmock's nocturnal activities. She was out every evening and seldom returned before they had gone to bed. Whether they slept in the back or the front room of the basement it seems impossible that they could have been ignorant of what was taking place in their house. Emily Dimmock had lived there some eight or nine weeks.

If in fact Stocks did know the truth about her, who knows what thoughts may have passed through his head? He might have made advances himself and been repulsed. Did he lie abed listening to the comings and goings overhead and brooding on forbidden joys, the resentment burning and boiling in him till it erupted into action? Possibly. But although McCowan's identification of Wood had been discounted by Marshall Hall under cross-examination, the man could not be shaken on the point that he had seen *someone* leave the house early on the morning of the murder—someone who presumably lived elsewhere. But again, this could have been some chance caller, a client of Emily's returned from abroad, who entered the house in the usual way, knocked on her door and, obtaining no answer, went out again. In any event the front door was not the only means of access. Emily's room had a french window that opened on to the garden and formed a convenient entrance for those of her clients who preferred to visit her surreptitiously. In hot weather the french window was sometimes left ajar. The murderer could have come and gone unseen by McCowan or anyone else.

When all the possibilities have been eliminated, only the impossible remains. One theory that has not so far been advanced is that Emily Dimmock was killed not by a man but by a woman. It does not require any great strength to sever a throat with a sharp instrument. The fact that no murder weapon was found on the scene argues that the crime was premeditated. Jealousy is the motive that therefore springs to mind. The trouble between Robert Wood and Ruby Young had begun when she found out that he had been associating with other women. There were presumably others besides Emily Dimmock, and Ruby may not have been the only jealous one. One can theorise indefinitely but in the end one is thrown back on the fact that, circumstantial though it was, the Crown's case against Wood was defeated only by the exceptional brilliance of the defence put up by Marshall Hall.

Up to a few years ago Robert Wood was alive and living in Australia. Many of the sketches that he made in court and in prison remain in this country. They are proof of exceptional talent, but what do they tell us of the enigmatic personality of the artist? Preoccupation with the symbol of the rising sun is obvious in one. But in the other the sun is not rising. It is setting. Of what state of mind is this brilliantly executed and imaginative picture indicative? The old man, moribund, lying in the snow, the desolate scene, the forlorn and shivering dog and the stark caption *Silence*—what would a psychologist have made of this? There were no psychiatric experts in 1907. Perhaps this was as well for Robert Wood.

ARNOLD ROTHSTEIN'S FINAL PAYOFF

(Arnold Rothstein, 1929)

Damon Runyon

Arnold Rothstein was the most prominent underworld figure in 1920s New York. A suave and urbane gambler, Rothstein (b. 1882) was known variously as New York City's "Big Bankroll", "The Brain" or simply "AR". In 1919, he achieved notoriety as the man who bribed the Chicago White Sox baseball team to throw the World Series. During the Roaring Twenties he accumulated a fortune by financing most of the East Coast rackets, but on 4 November 1928, during a poker game at the Park Central Hotel, someone shot Arnold Rothstein. "I won't talk about it", he told police from his hospital bed, "I'll take care of it myself." He died two days later without naming his killer. Police believed that Rothstein welshed on $300,000-worth of gambling debts to a group of men including George "Hump" McManus. McManus was duly indicted for murder, at a series of hearings attended by the writer and journalist (Alfred) Damon Runyon (1884–1946). Runyon's reports, filed to the New York American, *read like an electric charge, with their characteristically racy language, laced with jargon and slang from the street. Material from this and similar cases involving organized crime informed Runyon's best-known collection* Guys and Dolls *(1932), later the basis of a hit musical (1950) and film (1955).*

New York City, 19 November 1929

If the ghost of Arnold Rothstein was hanging around the weather-beaten old Criminal Courts Building yesterday—and Arnold always did say he'd come back after he was dead and haunt a lot of people—it took by proxy what would have been a violent shock to the enormous vanity of the dead gambler.

Many citizens, members of the so-called "blue ribbon panel", appeared before Judge Charles C. Nott, Jr, in the trial of George C. McManus, charged with murdering Rothstein and said they didn't know Rothstein in life and didn't know anybody that did know him.

Arnold would have scarcely believed his ears. He lived in the belief he was widely known. He had spent many years establishing himself as a landmark on old Broadway. It would have hurt his pride like sixty to hear men who lived in the very neighborhood he frequented shake their heads and say they didn't know him.

A couple said they hadn't even read about him being plugged in the stomach with a bullet that early evening of 4 November a year ago, in the Park Central Hotel.

Well, such is fame in the Roaring Forties!

They had accepted two men to sit on the jury that is to hear the evidence against McManus, the first man to pass unchallenged by both sides being Mark H. Simon, a stockbroker, of No. 500 West 111th Street, and the second being Eugene A. Riker, of No. 211 West 21st Street, a traveling salesman.

It seemed to be a pretty fair start anyway, but just as Judge Nott was about to adjourn court at four o'clock, Mark H. Simon presented a complication. He is a dark complexioned, neatly dressed chap, in his early thirties, with black hair slicked back on his head. He hadn't read anything about the case, and seemed to be an ideal juror.

But it appears he is suffering from ulcers of the stomach, and this handicap was presented to Judge Nott late in the day. James D. C. Murray, attorney for McManus, George M. Brothers, Assistant prosecuting attorney, in charge of the case for the State, and three other assistants from District Attorney Banton's office, gathered in front of the bench while Mark H. Simon was put back in the witness chair and examined.

The upshot of the examination was his dismissal from service by Judge Nott, which left Riker, a youngish, slightly bald man, with big horn specs riding his nose, as the only occupant of the jury box. Judge Nott let the lonesome looking Riker go home for the night after instructing him not to do any gabbing about the case.

The great American pastime of jury picking took up all the time from ten-thirty yesterday morning until four o'clock in the afternoon, with an hour off for chow at one o'clock. Thirty "blue ribboners", well-dressed, solid looking chaps for the most part, were examined and of this number Murray challenged a total of fourteen. Each side had thirty peremptory challenges. Attorney Brothers knocked off nine and four were excused.

George McManus, the defendant, sat behind his attorney eyeing each talesman with interest but apparently offering no suggestions. McManus was wearing a well-tailored brown suit, and was neatly groomed, as usual. His big, dark-toned face never lost its smile.

Two of his brothers, Jim and Frank, were in the court room. Frank is a big, fine-looking fellow who has a nifty tenor voice that is the boast of the Roaring Forties, though he can be induced to sing only on special occasions.

Only a very few spectators were permitted in the court, because there wasn't room in the antique hall of justice for spare chairs after the "blue ribboners" were all assembled. A squad of the Hon. Grover Whalen's best and most neatly uniformed cops are spread all around the premises, inside and out, to preserve decorum.

Edgar Wallace, the English novelist and playwright, who is said to bat out a novel or play immediately after his daily marmalade, was given the special privilege of the chair inside the railing and sat there listening to the examination of the talesmen, and doubtless marveling at the paucity of local knowledge of the citizens about a case that he heard of over in England. Mr Wallace proved to be a fattish, baldish man, and by no means as young as he used to be.

A reflection of the average big towner's mental attitude toward gambling and gamblers was found in the answers to Attorney Murray's inevitable question as to whether the fact the defendant is a gambler and gambled on cards and the horses, would prejudice the talesmen against him. Did they consider a gambler a low character?

Well, not one did. Some admitted playing the races themselves. One mumbled something about there being a lot of gamblers in Wall Street who didn't excite his prejudice.

Attorney Murray was also concerned in ascertaining if the talesmen had read anything that District Attorney Banton had said about the defendant, and if so, had it made any impression on the talesman? It seemed not. One chap said he had read Banton's assertions all right, but figured them in the nature of a bluff.

Do you know anybody who knew Rothstein—pronounced "stine" by Mr Brothers, and "steen" by Mr Murray—or George McManus? Do you know anybody who knew either of them?

Do you know anybody who knows anybody connected with (*a*) the District Attorney's office? (*b*) the Police Department? Were you interested in the late political campaign? Ever live in the Park Central? Ever dine there? Know anybody connected with the management? Did you ever go to a race track?

Did you ever read anything about the case? (This in a city of over 4,000,000 newspaper readers, me hearties, and every paper carrying column after column of the Rothstein murder for months!) Did you ever hear any discussion of it? Can you? Suppose? Will you? State of mind. Reasonable doubt—

Well, by the time old John Citizen, "blue ribboner" or not, has had about twenty minutes of this he is mighty glad to get out of that place and slink home, wondering if after all it is worth while trying to do one's duty by one's city, county and state.

20 November 1929

A client—or shall we say a patient—of the late Arnold Rothstein popped up on us in the old Criminal Courts Building in the shank o' the evening yesterday. He came within a couple of aces of being made juror No. 8, in the trial of George C. McManus, charged with the murder of the said Rothstein.

Robert G. McKay, a powerfully built, black-haired broker of No. 244 East 67th Street, a rather swanky neighborhood, was answering the do-yous and the can-yous of James D. C. Murray as amiably as you please, and as he had already passed the State's legal lights apparently in a satisfactory manner, the gents at the press tables were muttering, "Well, we gotta another at least."

Then suddenly Robert G. McKay, who looks as if he might have been a Yale or Princeton lineman of say, ten years back, and who was sitting with his big legs crossed and hugging one knee, remarked in a mild tone to Murray, "I suppose I might say I knew Arnold Rothstein—though none of you have asked me."

"Ah," said Attorney Murray with interest, just as it appeared he was through with his questioning.

"Did you ever have any business transactions with Rothstein?"

"Well, it was business on his part, and folly on mine."

"Might I have the impertinence to ask if you bet with him?"

McKay grinned wryly, and nodded. Apparently he found no relish in his recollection of the transaction with "the master mind," who lies a-mouldering in his grave while the State of New York is trying to prove that George McManus is the man who tossed a slug into his stomach in the Park Central Hotel the night of 4 November, a year ago.

Attorney Murray now commenced to delve somewhat into McKay's state of mind concerning the late Rothstein. He wanted to know if it would cause the broker any feeling of embarrassment to sit on a jury that was trying a man for the killing of Rothstein, when Judge Charles C. Nott, Jr, who is presiding in the trial, remarked, "I don't think it necessary to spend any more time on this man."

The late Rothstein's customer hoisted his big frame out of the chair, and departed, a meditative expression on his face, as if he might still be considering whether he would feel any embarrassment under the circumstances.

They wangled out six jurors at the morning session of the McManus trial, which was enlivened to some extent by the appearance of quite a number of witnesses for the State in the hallways of the rusty old red brick Criminal Courts Building.

These witnesses had been instructed to show up yesterday morning with the idea that they might be called, and one of the first to arrive was "Titanic Slim", otherwise Alvin C. Thomas, the golf-playing gambling man, whose illness in Milwaukee caused a postponement of the trial a week ago.

"Titanic Slim" was attended by Sidney Stajer, a rotund young man who was one of Rothstein's closest friends, and who is beneficiary to the tune of $75,000 under the terms of the dead gambler's will. At first the cops didn't want to admit "Titanic Slim" to the portals of justice, as he didn't look like a witness, but he finally got into the building only to learn he was excused.

The photographers took great interest in the drawling-voiced, soft-mannered, high roller from the South, and Sidney Stajer scowled at them fiercely, but Sidney really means no harm by his scowls. Sidney is not a hard man and ordinarily would smile very pleasantly for the photographers, but it makes him cross to get up before noon.

The State's famous material witness, Bridget Farry, chambermaid at the Park Central, put in an appearance with Beatrice Jackson, a telephone operator at the same hotel. Bridget was positively gorgeous in an emerald-green dress and gold-heeled slippers. Also she had silver stockings and a silver band around her blond hair. She wore no hat. A hat would have concealed the band.

Bridget, who was held by the State in durance vile for quite a spell, is just a bit stoutish, but she was certainly all dressed up like Mrs Astor's horse. She sat with Miss Jackson on a bench just outside the portals of justice and exchanged repartee with the cops, the reporters and the photographers.

Bridget is nobody's sap when it comes to talking back to folks. Finally she left the building, and was galloping lightly along to escape the photographers, when her gold-heeled slippers played her false, and she stumbled and fell.

An ambulance was summoned posthaste, as the lady seemed to be injured, but an enterprising gal reporter from a tab scooped her up into a taxicab, and departed with the witness to unknown parts. It is said Bridget's shinbone was scuffed up by the fall.

Some of the State's witnesses were quite busy at the telephone booths while in the building getting bets down on the Bowie races. It is a severe handicap to summon a man to such a remote quarter as the Criminal Courts Building along toward post time.

21 November 1929

Twelve good men, and glum, are now hunched up in the jury box, in Judge Nott's court, and they are all ready to start in trying to find out about the murder of Arnold Rothstein.

But the hours are really tough on a lot of folks who will figure more or less prominently in the trial. Some of the boys were wondering if Judge Nott would entertain a motion to switch his hours around and start in at four p.m., the usual hour of adjournment, and run to ten-thirty a.m., which is a gentleman's bedtime. The consensus is he wouldn't.

George Brothers, one of District Attorney Banton's assistants, who is in charge of the prosecution, will probably open the forensic fury for the State of New York this morning, explaining to the dozen morose inmates of the jury box just what the State expects to prove against the defendant, to wit, that George McManus is the party who shot Arnold Rothstein in the stomach in the Park Central Hotel the night of 4 November, a year ago.

You may not recall the circumstances, but McManus is one of four persons indicted for the crime. Another is Hyman Biller, an obscure denizen of the brightlights region of Manhattan Island, who probably wouldn't be recognized by more than two persons if he walked into any joint in town, such is his obscurity.

Then there is good old John Doe and good old Richard Roe, possibly the same Doe and Roe who have been wanted in forty-nine different spots for crimes ranging from bigamy to disorderly conduct for a hundred years past. Tough guys, old John and Richard, and always getting in jams. McManus is the only one on trial for the killing of Rothstein, probably for the reason he is the only one handy.

22 November 1929

"Give me a deck of cards," said "Red" Martin Bowe plaintively, peering anxiously around Judge Nott's court room in the dim light of yesterday afternoon, as if silently beseeching a friendly volunteer in an emergency.

"Get me a deck of cards, and I'll show you."

You see Red Martin Bowe had suddenly come upon a dilemma in his forty-odd years of traveling up and down the earth. He had come upon a fellow citizen who didn't seem to savvy the elemental pastime of stud poker, and high spading, which Martin probably thought, if he ever gave the matter any consideration, is taught in the grammar schools of this great nation—or should be.

So he called for a deck of cards. He probably felt the question was fatuous but he was willing to do his best to enlighten this apparently very benighted fellow, Ferdinand Pecora, the chief representative of Old John Law on the premises, and to show the twelve good men, and glum, in the jury box just how that celebrated card game was conducted which the State of New York is trying to show cost Arnold Rothstein his life at the hands of George McManus.

But no deck of cards was immediately forthcoming. So Martin

Bowe didn't get to give his ocular demonstration to the assembled citizens, though a man came dashing in a little later with a nice red deck, while even Judge Nott was still snorting over Martin Bowe's request.

Possibly if Mr Pecora can show a night off later some of the boys who sat in the back room yesterday might be induced to give him a lesson or two in stud poker. Also high spading.

Martin Bowe is a big, picturesque looking chap, who is getting bald above the ears, and who speaks with slow drawl and very low. In fact all the witnesses displayed a remarkable tendency to pitch their voices low in marked contrast with their natural vocal bent under ordinary circumstances and the attorneys had to keep admonishing them to talk louder.

"Gambler," said Bowe, quietly, and without embarrassment, when asked his business. Then he went on to tell about the card game that will probably be remarked for many years as Broadway's most famous joust. It began on a Saturday night and lasted into the Sunday night following. Martin said he previously played five or six hours at a stretch, and then would lie down and take a rest. He stated:

"It started with bridge, then we got to playing stud. The game got slow, and then some wanted to sport a little so they started betting on the high spade."

"I lose," remarked Bowe calmly, when Pecora asked how he came out. McManus was in the game. Also Rothstein, "Titanic", Meyer Boston, Nate Raymond, "Sol—somebody". A chap named Joe Bernstein was present, and several others he didn't remember, though Sam Boston later testified Bernstein was "doing something and he wasn't playing". It is this Bernstein, a California young man, who "beat" Rothstein for $69,000 though Bernstein was never actually in the play. He bet from the outside.

As near as Bowe could recollect, Raymond, Rothstein, McManus and Bernstein were bettors on the high card. He heard McManus lost about $50,000. Rothstein was keeping a score on the winnings and losings. McManus paid off partly in cash and partly by check, while Rothstein was putting cash in his pocket, and would give out IOUs. Bowe said he heard Rothstein lost over $200,000. The redoubtable "Titanic" won between $20,000 and $25,000 from McManus. Pecora asked: "What about Meyer Boston?"

"He wins."

Under cross-examination by James D. C. Murray, Bowe said he

had often known McManus to bet as much as $50,000 on one horse race and never complain if he lost. He said:

"It's an everyday occurrence with him. He always paid with a smile."

After the game, he said, Rothstein and McManus were very friendly; they often ate together at Lindy's. Rothstein won something from McManus in the game, but Bowe didn't know how much.

It was a rather big day for the defense. In his opening address to the jury, George Brothers, assistant district attorney, didn't seem to offer much motive for the possible killing of Rothstein by McManus other than the ill feeling that might have been engendered over the game in which they both lost.

That, and the fact that McManus fled after the killing, seemed his strongest points, while Attorney Murray quickly made it clear that part of the defense will be that Rothstein wasn't shot in room No. 349 at all, and that he certainly wasn't shot by George McManus.

Murray worked at length on Dr Charles D. Norris, the city Medical Examiner, trying to bring out from the witness that the nature of the wound sustained by Rothstein and the resultant shock would have prevented Rothstein from walking down three flights of stairs, and pushing open two or three heavy doors to reach the spot in the service entrance of the hotel where he was found, especially without leaving some trace of blood.

During the examination of the doctor, the expensive clothes that Arnold Rothstein used to wear so jauntily were displayed, now crumpled and soiled. The white silk shirt was among the ghastly exhibits, but the forty-five-dollar custom-made shoes that were his hobby, and the sox were missing. Dr Norris didn't know what had become of them.

The jurors, most of them business men on their own hook, or identified in salaried capacities with business, were a study while Martin Bowe and Sam Boston were testifying, especially Bowe, for he spoke as calmly of winning and losing $50,000 as if he were discussing the price of his morning paper.

You could see the jurors bending forward, some of them cupping their hands to their ears, and eyeing the witness with amazement. That stud and high spade game had been mentioned so often in the papers that it had come to be accepted as a Broadway fable. Probably no member of the jury, for none of them indicated in their examination that they are familiar with sporting life, took any stock in the tales of high rolling of the Broadway gamblers.

But here was a man who was in the game, who had lost $5,700 of his own money, and who knew what he was talking about. It was apparent the jurors were astounded by the blasé manner of Bowe as he spoke of McManus dropping $50,000 as "an everyday occurrence," and even the voluble Sam Boston's glib mention of handling hundreds of thousands of dollars yearly in bets on sporting events impresses them.

28 November 1929

Nothing new having developed in the life and battles of Juror No. 9, or the Man with the Little Moustache, the trial of George McManus for the murder of Arnold Rothstein proceeded with reasonable tranquility yesterday.

Just before adjournment over Thanksgiving, to permit the jurors to restore their waning vitality with turkey and stuffin', the State let it out rather quietly that it hasn't been able to trace very far the pistol which is supposed to have ended the tumultuous life of "the master mind" a year ago.

On a pleasant day in last June—the 15th, to be exact—it seems that one Mr Joe Novotny was standing behind the counter in his place of business at No. 51 West Fourth Street, in the thriving settlement of St Paul, Minnesota, when in popped a party who was to Mr Joe Novotny quite unknown, shopping for a rod, as the boys term a smoke-pole.

Mr Novotny sold the stranger a .38-calibre Colt, which Mr Novotny himself had but recently acquired from the firm of Janney, Sempler & Hill, of Minneapolis, for twenty-two dollars eighty-five. The factory number of the Colt was 359,946. Mr Novotny did not inquire the shopper's name, because it seems there is no law requiring such inquisitiveness in Minnesota, and Mr Novotny perhaps didn't wish to appear nosey.

No doubt Mr Novotny figures the stranger was a new settler in St Paul and desired the Colt to protect himself against the wild Indians and wolves that are said to roam the streets of the city. Anyway, that's the last Mr Novotny saw of pistol No. 359,946, and all he knows about it, according to a stipulation presented by the State of New York to Judge Nott late yesterday afternoon, and agreed to by James D. C. Murray, attorney for George McManus, as Mr Novotny's testimony.

It may be that some miscreant subsequently stole the gun from the settler's cabin in St Paul or that he lent it to a pal who was going to New York, and wished to be well dressed, for the next we hear of No. 359,946 is its appearance in the vicinity of Fifty-sixth Street and Seventh Avenue, Manhattan Island, where it was picked up by one Bender, a taxi jockey, after the shooting of Arnold Rothstein. A stipulation with reference to said Bender also was submitted to Judge Nott.

The State of New York would have the jury in the trial of George McManus believe it was with this gun that Rothstein was shot in the stomach in room 349 in the Park Central Hotel, and that the gun was hurled through a window into the street after the shooting. It remains to be seen what the jury thinks about this proposition.

It is not thought it will take any stock in any theory that the gun walked from St. Paul to the corner of Fifty-sixth Street and Seventh Avenue.

If the settler who bought the gun from Mr Novotny would step forward at this moment, he would be as welcome as the flowers in May. But those Northwestern settlers always are reticent.

It was around three o'clock in the afternoon when Mr James McDonald, one of the assistant district attorneys, finished reading the 300 pages of testimony taken in the case to date to Mr Edmund C. Shotwell, juror No. 2, who replaced Eugene Riker when Mr Riker's nerves bogged down on him.

It was the consensus that Mr Shotwell was in better physical condition than Mr McDonald at the conclusion of the reading, although at the start it looked as if Mr McDonald would wear his man down with ease before page No. 204.

Juror No. 9, who is Norris Smith, the man with the little moustache, whose adventures have kept this trial from sinking far down into the inside of the public prints long ere this, sat in a chair in the row behind the staunch juror No. 2, which row is slightly elevated above the first row. Juror No. 9, who is slightly built and dapperly dressed, tweaked at his little moustache with his fingers and eyed the press section with baleful orbs.

What juror No. 9 thinks of the inmates of the press section would probably be suppressed by the censors. And yet, without juror No. 9, where would this case be? It would be back next to pure reading matter—that's where.

Juror No. 9 was alleged to have been discovered by newspaper

men bouncing around a Greenwich Village shushery and talking
about the McManus trial, though he convinced Judge Nott that
he hadn't done or said anything that might impair his status as
a juror in the case. Finally it was learned juror No. 9 was shot
up a bit in his apartment at No. 420 West Twentieth Street on
February 29, 1928, by a young man who was first defended by
James D. C. Murray, now McManus's counsel.

30 November 1929

Draw near, friend reader, for a touch of ooh-my-goodness has
finally crept into the Roaring Forties' most famous murder trial.
Sc-an-dal, no less. Sh-h-h!

And where do you think we had to go to get it?

To Walnut Street, in the pleasant mountain city of Asheville,
North Carolina. Folks, thar's sin in them hills!

Here we'd been going along quietly for days and days on end
with the matter of George McManus, charged with plugging
Arnold Rothstein with a .38, and the testimony had been pure
and clean and nothing calculated to give Broadway a bad name,
when in come a woman from the ol' Tarheel State speaking of the
strangest didoes.

A Mrs Marian A. Putnam, she was, who runs the Putnam grill
in Asheville, a lady of maybe forty-odd, a headliner for the State,
who testified she had heard loud voices of men, and a crash coming
from the vicinity of room 349 in the Park Central Hotel the night
"the master mind," was "settled". And that later she had seen a
man wandering along the hallway on the third floor, with his hands
pressed to his abdomen and "a terrible look on his face".

Well, there seemed nothing in this narration to mar the peaceful
trend of events, or to bring the blush of embarrassment for this
city to the cheek of the most loyal Broadwayer. Then James D. C.
Murray took charge of the witness and began addressing the lady
on the most tender subjects, and developing the weirdest things.
Really, you'd be surprised.

Handing the lady a registration card from the Park Central
Hotel and assuming a gruff tone of voice several octaves over the
perfunctory purr that has been the keynote of the trial to date,
Murray asked, "Who are the Mr and Mrs Putnam indicated by
that card as registered at the Park Central on 28 October 1928?"

"I am Mrs Putnam."

"Who is Mr Putnam?"

Mrs Putnam hesitated briefly, and then replied, "A friend of mine to whom I am engaged."

There were subdued snorts back in the court room as the spectators suddenly came up out of their dozes and turned off their snores to contemplate the lady on the witness stand.

Mrs Putnam wore a rather smart-looking velvet dress, with a gray caracul coat with a dark squirrel collar, and a few diamonds here and there about her, indicating business is okay at the Putnam grill.

But she didn't have the appearance of one who might insert a hotsy-totsy strain into the staid proceedings. She looked more like somebody's mother, or aunt. She described herself as a widow, and here she was admitting something that savored of social error, especially as the lady subsequently remarked that "Mr Putnam" had occupied the same boudoir with her.

The spectators sat up to listen and mumbled we were finally getting down to business in this trial.

Murray now produced a death certificate attesting to the demise of one Putnam, who died in 1913, the attorney asking, "The Mr Putnam who occupied the room with you wasn't the Mr Putnam who died in 1913, was he?"

At this point Mrs Putnam seemed deeply affected, possibly by the memory of the late Mr P. She gulped and applied her handkerchief to her eyes, and the spectators eyed her intently, because they felt it would be a thrill if it transpired that the deceased Putnam had indeed returned to life the very night that "the master mind" was shot.

But it seems it wasn't that Mr Putnam, and Mr Murray awoke some very antique echoes in the old court room as he shouted, "Who was it?"

Well, Mrs Putnam doubtless restrained by a feeling of delicacy, didn't want to tell, and Judge Nott helpfully remarked that as long as she didn't deny she was registered at the hotel, the name didn't seem important. Murray argued Mrs Putnam's fiancé might be a material witness for the defense, so Judge Nott let him try to show it.

Finally Mrs Putnam said the man's name was Perry. He is said to be a citizen of Asheville, and what will be said of Mr Perry in Asheville when the news reaches the sewing circles down yonder will probably be plenty. Not content with touching on Mr Perry

to Mrs Putnam, the attorney for the defense asked her about a Mr
Elias, and then about a Mr Bruce, becoming right personal about
Mr Bruce.

He wanted to know if Mr Bruce had remained with Mrs Putnam
one night in her room at another New York Hotel, but she said
no. Then Murray brought in the name of a Mr Otis B. Carr,
of Hendersonville, N C, and when Mrs Putnam said she didn't
recall the gentleman, the attorney asked, "Did you steal anything
out of a store in Hendersonville?"

Mrs Putnam said no. Moreover, in reply to questions, she said
she didn't steal two dresses from a department store in Asheville
and that she hadn't been arrested for disorderly conduct and fined
five dollars. Before Murray got through with her some of the listeners
half expected to hear him ask the lady if she had ever personally
killed A. Rothstein.

Mrs Putnam couldn't have made the State very happy, because
she admitted under Murray's cross-examination that she had once
denied in Asheville, in the presence of Mr Mara, one of the district
attorney's assistants, and County Judge McCrae, of Asheville,
that she ever left her room in the Park Central the night of the
murder.

She said her current story is the truth. Mr Murray asked her if
she hadn't said thus and so to newspapermen in Asheville. She
replied, "I did".

A young man described as Douglas Eller, a reporter of an Asheville
paper, was summoned from among the spectators in the court room
and brought up to the railing, where Mrs Putnam could see him.
The lady was asked if she knew him, and she eyed him at length
before admitting she may have seen him before. Mr Eller retired,
blushing slightly, as if not to be known by Mrs Putnam argues
one unknown in Asheville.

Murray became very curious about the Putnam grill in Asheville.
Didn't she have curtained-off booths? She did, but her waitresses
could walk in and out of them at any time, a reply that Mrs Putnam
tossed at Murray as if scorning utterly the base insinuation of his
question.

Did she sell liquor? She did not. She had been shown pictures
of Rothstein and McManus and Biller, but she couldn't recognize
any of them. She was mighty reluctant about telling the name of a
lady friend with whom she dined in her room the night of the killing,
but finally admitted it was a Mrs Herman Popper. She explained

her reluctance by saying, "I don't want to get other people mixed up in this".

3 December 1929

The most important point to the State in the trial of George McManus yesterday seemed to be the key to room 349 in the Park Central Hotel, which, according to testimony, was found in a pocket of an overcoat hanging in the room.

This overcoat bore the name of McManus on the tailor's label in the pocket.

The prosecution will, perhaps, make much of this as tending to show the occupant of the room left in a very great hurry and didn't lock the door, besides abandoning the overcoat, though Detective "Paddy" Flood said the door was locked when he went there with a house detective to investigate things.

It was Detective Flood who told of finding the key. He was relating how he entered the room and found, among other things, an overcoat with the name of George McManus on the label. He was asked, "What other objects did you find?"

"A handkerchief in the pocket of the overcoat with the initials 'G. Mc'. There were other handkerchiefs in the drawer in the bedroom and a white shirt."

"Did you find anything else in the coat?"

"A key, in the right-hand pocket, for room 349."

"A door key."

"Yes."

Aside from that, the testimony brought out that "the master mind," as the underworld sometimes called Arnold Rothstein, died "game."

Game as a pebble.

In the haunts of that strange pallid man during his life, you could have had ten to one, and plenty of it, that he would "holler copper", did occasion arise, with his dying gasp.

Indeed he was often heard to remark in times when he knew that sinister shadows hovered near—and these were not infrequent times in his troubled career, living as he chose to live, "If anyone gets me, they'll burn for it".

And cold, hard men, thinking they read his character, believed they knew his meaning. They felt he was just the kind when cornered by an untoward circumstance, that would squeal like a pig. It shows you how little you really know of a man.

For when the hour came, as the jury in Judge Nott's court room heard yesterday, with the dismal snow slanting past the windows of the grimy old Criminal Courts Building—when Arnold Rothstein lay crumpled up with a bullet through his intestines, knowing he was mortally hurt, and officers of the law bent over him and whispered, "Who did it?" the pale lips tightened, and Rothstein mumbled, "I won't tell and please don't ask me any more questions".

Then another "sure thing" went wrong on Broadway, where "sure things" are always going wrong—the "sure thing" that Rothstein would tell.

But as the millionaire gambler lay in the Fifty-sixth Street service entrance of the Park Central Hotel that night of 4 November 1928, with the pain of his wound biting at his vitals, and the peering eyes of the cops close to his white countenance, he reverted to type.

He was no longer the money king, with property scattered all over the Greater City, a big apartment house on fashionable Park Avenue, a Rolls-Royce and a Minerva at his beck and call, and secretaries and servants bowing to him. He was a man of the underworld. And as one of the "dice hustlers" of the dingy garage lofts, and the "mobsters" high and low he muttered, "I won't tell".

A sigh of relief escaped many a chest at those words, you can bet on that.

Detective Flood, who knew Rothstein well, was one of those who bent over the stricken man.

Patrolman William Davis, first to respond to the call of the hotel attendants, also asked Rothstein who shot him, but got no more information than Flood.

The head of the millionaire gambler was pillowed on a wadded-up burlap sack when Davis reached the scene, which was important to the State in trying to show that Rothstein was shot in the hotel, in that it had been said that Rothstein's overcoat was put under his head.

Before the session was completed, the tables in the court room were covered with exhibits of one kind and another taken by Flood and other officers from room 349 in the Park Central.

There was a layout of glasses and a liquor bottle, and ginger ale bottles on a tray. But, alas, the liquor bottle was very empty. Also the State had the dark blue overcoat with the velvet collar that was found in a closet of room 349, said overcoat bearing a tailor's label, with George McManus's name on the label.

Likewise, handkerchiefs found in the room were produced and these handkerchiefs were elegantly monogrammed. One was inscribed "g Mc M.," another like "G. M. A." with the "G" and "A" in small letters, and the "M" big. A third was monogrammed "J. M. W." with the "J" and "W" in small letters on either side of the large "M" while the fourth bore the marking "J. M."

A white shirt with collar attached, some race tracks slips, and a window screen with a hole in it, were spread out for the jurors to see. Also the .38-calibre pistol, which one Al Bender, a taxi driver, picked up in Seventh Avenue.

This is supposed to be the pistol with which Rothstein was shot, and the screen is supposed to be the screen through which the pistol was hurled out into the street after the shooting, though the point where the pistol was picked up is quite a hurling distance from room 349.

While Flood and some other officers were in the room Hyman Biller, a cashier at the race track for McManus, and under indictment with McManus for the murder of Rothstein, came in with Frank and Tom McManus, brothers of George, and remained about twenty minutes.

It was the failure to hold Biller on this occasion that brought down much criticism on the heads of the Police Department, for Hymie was never seen in these parts again.

The lights were burning in room 349 when Flood got there. Four glasses stood on the table which is the basis of the indictment returned against McManus, and Biller, and the celebrated John Doe and Richard Roe. The State claims four men were in the room when Rothstein was summoned there by a message sent by McManus to Lindy's restaurant.*

Vincent J. Kelly, elevator operator at the Park Central, testified he was working on the service elevator the night Rothstein was shot, and saw Rothstein in the corridor, holding his hands across his stomach, and didn't see him come through the service doorway, through which he must have passed to make good the State's contention he came from upstairs.

He heard Rothstein say, "I'm shot".

---

* The State inferred Rothstein was summoned to pay the overdue IOUs given in the high spade game described by Martin Bowe.

Thomas Calhoun, of Corona, Long Island, thirty-two, a watchman on the Fifty-sixth Street side of the hotel at the time of the murder, saw Rothstein at ten forty-seven standing in front of the time office at the service entrance. Calhoun ran and got Officer Davis.

He heard Rothstein say something to the policeman about taking his money, and it was his impression that Rothstein had his overcoat over his arm and that it was put under his head as he lay on the floor, which impression was not corroborated by other testimony.

Through Calhoun, Attorney Murray tried to develop that Rothstein might have come through the swimming pool by way of Seventh Avenue. While cross-examining Calhoun, Murray suddenly remarked, testily, "I object to the mumbling to the District Attorney".

He apparently had reference to Mr Brothers, of the State's legal display. Everybody seemed to be a bit testy yesterday, except the ever-smiling defendant, McManus, who just kept on smiling.

Calhoun heard Rothstein say, "Call my lawyer, 9410 Academy".

Thomas W. McGivney, of No. 401 West 47th Street, who was also near the service entrance, testified he had taken Rothstein's overcoat off his arm and placed it under his head. Rothstein's overcoat hasn't been seen since the shooting.

McGivney, a stout looking young man with a wide smile, and a rich brogue, gave the spectators a few snickers, but by and large it wasn't an exciting day one way or the other.

Although George McManus was indicted for murder, Judge Nott eventually ruled there was insufficient evidence against him and ordered the jury to return a verdict of not guilty. Arnold Rothstein's murder was never solved. One theory holds that he was killed by members of a new crime cartel because Rothstein controlled so many rackets. The whereabouts of his fortune remained undiscovered, but AR's criminal empire was quickly carved up by his minions, including Jack "Legs" Diamond.

THE DEATH OF
BELLA WRIGHT

(Bella Wright, 1919)

Edmund Pearson

If ever a man worked hard to put a rope around his own neck, declared one seasoned crime reporter, it was Ronald Light. But in spite of himself and his foolish behaviour, Light was cleared of murdering Bella Wright and her death has remained a total mystery ever since. She was last seen alive on a summer's evening in 1919 accompanied by an unknown stranger on a green bicycle. The couple rode off into the dusk gathering over the remote Leicestershire countryside. Less than an hour later, twenty-one-year-old Bella was found dead in the road, shot in the head. Some six months later, a green bicycle dredged from a canal at Leicester was traced to Ronald Light. With it was a revolver holster containing live cartridges. Light admitted encountering Bella Wright on his bicycle, but said their ways later parted and he left her alive, albeit with a wobbly wheel. Spooked by the publicity over the girl's death, Light said he panicked and ditched his green bicycle and holster in the canal. "I didn't make up my mind deliberately not to come forward," he later explained. "I was astounded and frightened at this unexpected thing. I kept on hesitating and, in the end, I drifted into doing nothing at all." Edmund Pearson (1880–1937) wrote on the case in a collection of pieces on murder published the year before he died. Pearson was a trained librarian, and worked at the New York public library from 1914 until

1927, when he resigned to take up a full-time writing career. In 1923, following in the tradition of de Quincey, he wrote an essay on murder considered as one of the fine arts. "The study of murder", he wrote, "is the study of the human heart in its darkest, strangest moments. Nothing surpasses it in interest". The following year Pearson published Studies in Murder, *his best-known work which established his international reputation as the leading American writer on famous crimes.*

There was a murder case in England which not only needed a Sherlock Holmes but seemed as if it had been devised in solemn conclave by Conan Doyle, Holmes, and Watson themselves. It could be entitled The Mystery of the Green Bicycle; or, The Curious Incident of the Dead Raven.

Unfortunately, there was no great hawk-faced detective from Baker Street in it. Only, at the beginning, a local constable named Hall. Perhaps that is why one of the men best informed on this case says that it has "considerable claims to be regarded as the most fascinating murder mystery of the century".

Bella Wright was twenty-one and lived with her father and mother in a tiny place called Stoughton. This is within a mile or two of the city of Leicester, and in that city she was employed in a rubber factory.

She was a girl with good looks and good character, and was engaged to be married to a stoker in the navy.

The country round about Leicester is full of little villages connected by old Roman roads or by lanes with high hedges. To the north is the famous hunting center of Melton Mowbray.

The lanes are charmingly picturesque and lonely, but were made for a less motorized age. They are sometimes full of surprises and excitement for the pedestrian or the cyclist. At a curve he may suddenly be confronted by a flock of sheep just as an enormous motor bus, brushing the hedge on either side, comes up behind him.

Miss Wright was accustomed to go to and from her work on a bicycle, and sometimes, in the long daylight hours of the English summer evenings, to cycle from one hamlet to another to do errands or to call on her friends. Her uncle, a man named Measures, lived in the village of Gaulby, three miles from her home.

She was on the late shift at the factory, and one Friday evening in July rode home from her work at eleven o'clock, going to bed soon after. Next day seems to have been a holiday, so she thoroughly made up her sleep, not getting up again till four o'clock Saturday afternoon. Then, after writing a few letters, she rode with them to the post office at Evington. Again she came home, but finally, at six-thirty p.m., set out on her cycle in the opposite direction, away from Leicester. Her mother had seen her start for Evington, and never after that saw her alive.

At nine twenty that evening (still daylight) a farmer named Cowell was driving cattle along the old Roman road called the Gartree Road or *Via Devana*. At a point about two miles from Gaulby, where the way is very lonely and the hedges, at that season, more than eight feet high, Cowell found Bella Wright lying dead in the road. Her head was covered with blood, and her cycle lay askew, with its front wheel pointed toward Stoughton—that is, toward home.

The farmer supposed that she had been killed by a fall or similar mischance. He placed her on the grass at the side of the road. Her body was still warm. Close to the spot where it was found—and this may be important—there was an opening in the hedge: a field gate which led into the grassy meadow beyond.

Constable Hall and a doctor came later, after it was dark. The doctor's hasty examination led to nothing more than a general impression that Miss Wright, being thrown from her bicycle, had fractured her skull on a stone. Cowell's statement as to his discovery of the body seems to have been accepted as quite satisfactory. This was due, I suppose, to his good reputation, since the only witnesses he could call to prove his story were his cows.

Miss Wright's body rested that night in a cottage nearby. Early next morning Constable Hall decided to make further investigation. He carefully examined the road; and seventeen feet from the bloodstain which marked the spot where the girl's head had lain in the dust he found a bullet, caliber .45, partly embedded in the road as if it had been stepped on or run over.

He made another exceedingly curious discovery: the gate which led into the field was painted white, and on the top bar were marks of claws—marks in blood. There were tracks of these claws, also in blood—twelve such sets of tracks, six going and six returning—leading from the body to the gate. In the field the constable came across a large bird with black plumage—dead. This bird was found to be gorged with blood. Indeed, that surfeit of blood was supposed to have killed it.

In England everybody is keen about birds and their habits. As soon as the Leicester police said that this bird was a raven, other folk flew to the defense of ravens. They said that (*a*) there were no ravens around Leicester; and (*b*) if there were, they had never been known to drink blood.

(The bird of which the Book of Job says "Her young ones also suck up blood" is not the raven but the eagle.)

This creature, said the bird experts, must be a rook or a carrion crow.

Whatever bird it was, there are two schools of thought about it, and all the authorities, Messrs H. R. Wakefield, Edward Marjoribanks, and others, have discussed it. There are the severely practical ones, who think that the raven (or rook) had no connection with the death of Bella Wright; and there are the romantics, who believe there was a very close connection.

At all events, how did the bird obtain so much blood from the poor dead or dying girl as to cause its own death? Was that really the cause of its death? How did it chance to be in that vicinity at the moment? Since the body is supposed to have been found within a few minutes of death, how was there time for all this gruesome feasting and tracking back and forth from road to gate?

Let's return now to Constable Hall and the bullet. He and the doctor made another examination of the body. After the blood had been washed from the girl's face, they found a small bullet wound one inch below the left eye, and another slightly larger, the mark of the exit of the bullet, in her hair. Thus it seemed that this heavy bullet had passed through the girl's head, yet had gone no farther than seventeen feet from her!

At all events, this was murder; and it was the duty of the police to inquire where she had been, and with whom, between six thirty and nine twenty of that summer evening—daylight all the time.

At seven thirty she had ridden up to the cottage of her uncle, Mr Measures, in Gaulby. Calling on Measures at the time was his son-in-law, a man named Evans. So both of them were important witnesses to her arrival and departure. With her, when she came, was another cyclist, a young man. Bella Wright went in, leaving the young man outside. She remarked that he was "a perfect stranger", and added:

"Perhaps if I wait a while he will be gone."

Yet she did not ask her uncle to drive him away, as if he were objectionable. And when, an hour or more later, they came out again, the young man was still there—having either returned or waited. This time, he greeted her, so said Measures and Evans, with the remark:

"Bella, you *have* been a long time. I thought you had gone the other way."

Evans had some friendly conversation with the stranger about his bicycle. And finally, the girl and the young man pedalled away together—at, say, eight-forty. Forty minutes later, or thereabouts, Cowell, the farmer, was finding Bella's dead body in the Gartree Road.

Now, as the reader has noticed, there are some contradictions in this. If the man was "a perfect stranger", how had he progressed so far as to call her Bella? This has been answered by the statement that what he really said was "Hello!" And that certainly goes more reasonably with the rest of his remark.

How is this for an explanation of the incident? That he was a stranger, as she said, who had joined her as she rode along; and that, while his company was perfectly tolerable to her, she had offered a little tribute to strict propriety when she said to her uncle that if she waited around a bit he would go away. Girls do not, today—if they ever did—scream and say, "Sir, I have never met you!" when a presentable stranger starts conversation, while riding along a country road. They may welcome it, or they may simply bear it, not wishing to make a fuss, and knowing that, in most cases, the man will soon go away without becoming an annoyance.

Measures and Evans had had a good look at this man and his cycle, and so in a few days the police were offering a reward for a man of thirty-five, about five feet seven to nine inches in height, hair turning grey, and with rather a high-pitched voice. They gave a description of his clothes and various other particulars.

The notable thing was that he rode *a green bicycle*.

And for the next few months each man in Leicestershire unfortunate enough to own a green bicycle wished to heaven that he had never bought it. After he had satisfied the police as to where he had been on that July evening, he had to encounter the jeering remarks of his friends as to his diversions and his murderous disposition.

But the man really sought—the last man alive with Miss

Wright—was not so easily discovered. Scotland Yard had a try at it, but could do nothing with the murder, the missing green bicycle, or the dead raven.

Half a year went by, and Bella Wright had long been lying in the churchyard, past which she rode that evening. Then, one day in February, something happened: a most peculiar chance, which, for a time, probably revived faith in the ancient falsehood, "Murder will out."

A canal boat was passing through Leicester, carrying a load of coal to the rubber works where the dead girl had been employed. A boatman named Whitehouse was idly watching his towrope when he saw it slacken down into the water and then tighten. As it became taut it brought up part of a bicycle, which hung in plain sight for a moment—long enough to change the whole current of a man's life—then slipped back into the water. Whitehouse had not forgotten all those police advertisements and the reward: he came back next day and dragged the canal. He hauled up the bicycle frame again, and, as he hoped, it was green.

The police were soon busy—dragging the canal for other interesting objects and examining the one the boatman had found. From the canal they fished other parts of the machine; also a revolver holster with twelve ball and seven blank cartridges in it.

The green bicycle was of a special model, made in Birmingham, and from it the name and number plate and other identifying marks had carefully been removed. But, in an obscure place, was found the number 103,648—and this was the number of a bicycle sold years before to a Mr Ronald Vivian Light.

This gentleman was found teaching mathematics at a school in Cheltenham. He was a good-looking, rather earnest man; a little prematurely old in appearance, possibly as a result of his experiences in the war. He was a Rugby School boy; a civil engineer, who had served four years in France, part of the time with an officer's commission. Shell-shocked and slightly deaf since the great German attack in 1918, he had been discharged in 1919. For about a year thereafter (the year 1919, in the summer of which Miss Wright was killed) he had been out of work and living in Leicester with his mother. His present position dated only from January, 1920, the month before the discovery of the green bicycle.

Invited by a police inspector to explain how the fragments of his bicycle happened to be at the bottom of the canal, Mr Light proceeded to tell a pack of lies. He said he had never owned a green bicycle; he had never seen Bella Wright; he had never been in the village of Gaulby—certainly not on that crucial evening last July.

Naturally, there was nothing to do but arrest him—especially as Bella's uncle, Mr Measures, and Evans also, positively identified him as the mysterious man who rode away with her so shortly before the murder. And two little girls, Muriel Nunney, aged fourteen, and Valeria Caven, twelve, believed they recognized him as a man who had followed and frightened them, about five thirty on the day of the murder, and in the same vicinity. They remembered this many months after the event. Some of the cartridges, by the way, found in the holster suspiciously near the sunken bicycle, had bullets like the one found in the road. But of course Mr Light denied the holster as firmly as he did all the other relics.

Now, here was a beautiful case of circumstantial evidence. The net was drawn tight around the poor young man, who would, of course, be convicted—as in the detective novels.

About three months after his arrest, Ronald Light was placed on trial. The Attorney General stated the case against the prisoner in all its deadly detail. He began to prove by his witnesses that the bicycle belonged to Light; that he was with the girl shortly before her death; that he had concealed evidence, and lied about it, over and over again.

In the middle of this testimony, the prisoner's counsel quietly interrupted. This was Sir Edward Marshall Hall—the famous defender of accused persons, for whom everybody sent in time of great trouble. Sir Edward courteously intimated that the learned Attorney General was going to unnecessary pains. He need not prove that the bicycle belonged to the prisoner; they admitted it. He need not prove that his client rode up to Mr Measures's house that evening, with Bella Wright; they admitted that. Most of the Crown witnesses would not be cross-examined by the defense; only one or two points did they deny.

The Attorney General and the police were probably somewhat disgusted. Here was the defense conceding three quarters of the case at the outset. What about the other quarter?

Sir Edward denied, and his client would deny, that his client had used the name "Bella". He had said "Hello". And Sir Edward took in hand, very kindly and gently, the two little girls, who said they had met Ronald Light near the scene of the murder, and who described him going about the lanes seeking to molest unprotected damsels.

When he got through with Miss Muriel and Miss Valieria, they no longer looked like two little angels of justice, but rather more like two busy little brats who, feeding for months on sensational newspapers and pictures, had suddenly begun to remember something which *might* have happened to them on some day or other—but which they obligingly fixed for a *certain* day, after the police had suggested the date.

At the end of the trial the judge advised the jury not to trouble themselves at all with the testimony of Miss Muriel and Miss Valeria.

When he began to present his case, Sir Edward played his ace. He called the prisoner to the witness stand. Ronald Light was serious, calm, and dignified. He was what we call "a shell-shocked veteran", who had, moreover, become partially deaf as the result of an exploding shell. There was no attempt to emphasize Light's wartime services, except in so far as his shattered nerves might explain some of his conduct.

Light now testified that he had never had a revolver or pistol since he had been sent home from France on a stretcher. On the evening of the murder he left home at about five forty-five for a bicycle ride, expecting to return at eight o'clock. He rode through Gaulby, a district he did not know very well, and at six forty-five he was near a place called Little Stretton. He did not see the two small girls anywhere. As it was still early, he turned about to go home by the long route, and this led him again toward Gaulby.

He met a girl, who was a stranger to him, standing at the roadside examining her bicycle. She asked if he had a wrench. He had not, but he looked at the front wheel, which seemed merely to wobble a little. There was nothing he could do for it. They rode on together, chattering as they went. She said that she was going to see some friends in Gaulby, and added:

"I shall only be ten minutes or a quarter of an hour."

Light then testified:

"I took that as a sort of suggestion that I should wait and we should ride back together. I waited for ten minutes or more, then walked my machine up the hill to the church. Here I got on the bicycle to ride back to Leicester, when I found the rear tyre flat. I pumped it up, and sat down on a gate; but the tyre went down again and I had to mend the puncture. By this time it was eight fifteen, and I knew I was late anyhow. I thought I would ride back and see if this girl had come out. She came out the gate as I rode along, and I said, 'Hello, you've been a long time. I thought you'd gone the other way.' I talked with Evans, and all that he says is correct, except that I did not say 'Bella'."

He further testified that they rode together for only about ten minutes; that he had still more trouble with his tyre; and that the girl left him at a crossroads. He kept on the upper or more direct road; she took the lower, the Gartree Road. He had to walk nearly all the way home and did not arrive till nearly ten. On the following Tuesday he heard of the death. He read the description of Bella Wright and of his own bicycle and came to the conclusion that he was the man wanted.

He was utterly terrified. Both for his own sake and for his mother's, who was an invalid, he wanted to escape the horror of an investigation, perhaps a trial. Foolishly, as he now admitted, he refrained from going to the police at once, and drifted into a policy of silence, then of concealment, and finally of falsehood. He never went out on the green bicycle again, but hid it and at last broke it up and threw it (together with the holster) into the canal. He now frankly admitted all the lies told when the police came to him.

"I see now, of course," he said to the judge, "that I did the wrong thing".

He must have been astounded again when the evidence rose against him from the canal. It is recorded that he had looked at this water from his cell, while he was awaiting trial, and exclaimed:

"Damn and blast that canal!"

Ronald Light's story, as he now told it, could not be contradicted or disproved in any detail. Five hours of cross-examination failed to trip him once.

His lawyer, who was himself an expert on firearms, sharply questioned the Crown witnesses who testified on technical points: about the wound, and about the bullet. Sir Edward maintained that such a heavy bullet, fired, as they thought, from a distance of seven feet, would have blown out the back of the skull. It was absurd that it should not have travelled farther. The only explanation would be that she was shot as she lay on the ground, and even this was not wholly satisfactory.

That it was the same caliber as bullets found in Light's holster meant nothing: bullets like this one had recently been made in

England by the thousand million. Sir Edward suggested that the bullet found in the road might not be the fatal one at all, and that she might have been killed by an accidental shot fired from the neighbouring field. It could be a rifle bullet.

No one had appeared who could testify that Light and the girl were together on the Gartree Road; he was never placed at or even very near the scene of the crime.

The Crown had shown no motive. It was not a lovers' quarrel; the two were strangers. There had been no sexual assault. Why should Light have shot her?

The defense, of course, slid over the fact that certain kinds of murders, particularly of women and children, are committed for no apparent motive whatever.

The judge, in his charge, seemed rather to lean to the side of the defense. The jury argued the case for three hours, standing nine to three in favour of the prisoner. Then the three were won over, and they reported Ronald Light "Not guilty". The verdict was cheered.

But who did kill Bella Wright? Probably we shall never know. Probably, also, we shall never know whether we ourselves, if innocent, but in a predicament like that of the rider of the green bicycle, would behave any better.

Now to come back to our raven. A gentleman named Trueman Humphries went down to the Gartree Road, took pictures, and looked about. At the end he wrote, for the *Strand*, an entertaining bit of fiction. He imagines a scientific detective challenged to solve the mystery of the green bicycle. This detective organizes, in the neighbourhood of Gaulby and Little Stretton, a shooting match. A prize is offered and all the boys and men in the region are drawn in.

There are various targets: disappearing images of deer, running rabbits, or the like. All of them are sprung upon the contestants suddenly and as a complete surprise. Before one of these sportsmen—a young lad—as he lies on the ground, firing, there rises what seems to be a dark hedge cut in the middle by a white gate. And on this gate sits a raven!

The boy tumbles over in a faint. When he comes to, he is ready to make his confession. He was in the field near the Gartree Road that July evening. He had sighted a bird of some kind on the white gate. He lay behind a sheep trough two or three hundred yards away (there is really such a trough) and fired. He killed the raven—but the bullet also killed the girl who rode by the gate at that moment.

Far-fetched? Very likely. But it's not unworthy of the great Sherlock!

MURDER HATH CHARMS

(Edwin Bartlett, 1875)

Christianna Brand

The case of Adelaide Bartlett is one of a clutch of Victorian poisoning dramas that galvanized the British murder-reading public during the closing years of the nineteenth century. There were several crowd-pleasing features: the accused woman, at thirty, was still young and presentable, born in France, and the widow of a prosperous grocer ten years older than she was. Adelaide was accused of murdering him with liquid chloroform. The fact that she had slept with her husband's brother within a year of her marriage furnished a further frisson. Although acquitted, most observers of the case believe that Mrs Bartlett was a very lucky woman. Her case has prompted a number of full-length books, including a novelised interpretation by the crime writer Julian Symons, Sweet Adelaide. *This miniature treatment first appeared in 1974, in a collection of (mostly fictional) short crime stories by the detective writer Christianna Brand (1909–88). Her mystery novels (including* Green for Danger, *which was filmed starring Alistair Sim) appeared over a period of some forty years. She also wrote books for children, most notably* Nurse Matilda *(1963), illustrated by her cousin Edward Ardizzone.*

Murder hath charms, we must confess, for those of us not too closely brushed against it; and how much more so "when a lady's in the case"—those delicious pouter-pigeon ladies who so closely followed each other into the dock in the latter half of the last century: with their bosoms and their bustles and their tight little waists, all starry-eyed. And when, furthermore, the truth of their innocence or guilt must now be for ever in doubt—they are surely irresistible? Mrs Bravo so plump and pretty, lacing the wine or the water with antimony—*did she or didn't she?* Poor Florence Maybrick, adding to her elderly husband's already sufficient consumption of aphrodisiac arsenic—*did she or didn't she?* And Adelaide, sweet Adelaide, with her great big brown eyes and her great big brown bottle of chloroform—*did she or didn't she . . . ?* We shall never know now.

It was in the year 1875 that the friends of Miss Adelaide Blanche de la Tremoille purchased for her a husband—in the shape of a Wicked Grocer named Edwin Bartlett, who thenceforward kept her in a cage most cruelly all day—and in a separate bed most cruelly all night. Or so said Adelaide, on trial for his murder eleven years later. For he believed that a man should have two wives, one for use and one for companionship; and Adelaide, he explained to her, was to be the one for companionship.

To add to the improbability of her name, Adelaide Blanche de la Tremoille was, as Miss Austen would say, the natural daughter of Somebody—rich enough to have provided for her adequately, "decent enough to have wished for concealment". She was nineteen when the marriage was arranged but Edwin, having "a reverential regard for advanced learning" of which he himself had very little, packed her off to boarding school for the next three years and only then received her permanently into his home. He had invested his own purchase price in the family grocery business and now had a chain of flourishing shops. They set up house in rooms over one of these establishments in Herne Hill.

There she remained, poor young creature, very friendless, occupying herself with her needlework, music and the care of some Newfoundland dogs which her husband bred "for showing"—one gets the impression that there was not very much that Edwin did just for fun—and which were kept in kennels close by. Her sole companion was her aged father-in-law who, devoted to his son, with whom he incessantly talked business, had disapproved of the marriage and henceforward disliked and distrusted her.

After two years of this she petitioned for a baby of her own; and at last, evidently feeling that the better the day the better the deed, Edwin relented and on a Sunday afternoon "a single act" took place. Adelaide became triumphantly pregnant and, attended only by a midwife named Annie Walker, in due course she was delivered of a child. But the baby was stillborn. She went through a bad time, declared herself unwilling to have any more children; platonic relations were resumed and that was that.

Or so said Adelaide.

After several changes of residence, in the course of which they got rid of the company of Bartlett senior, the couple finally came to rest in Claverton Street, Pimlico a typical London house of that period, of which so many still exist—one of a long, stuccoed terrace, with steps up to the front door and two pillars and a balcony forming a porch. But it was not much of a life for an active and alertly minded young woman: two first-floor rooms, divided only by partitioning doors, and all the housework and cooking done by a landlady . . .

Or it wouldn't have been; but by now a new and exciting element had been introduced. The Reverend George Dyson had arrived upon the Bartletts' scene.

The Rev. George was attached to a Wesleyan chapel, where his duties appear to have been light for soon he was spending a great deal of time with the Bartletts, both of whom quite doted upon him (a young man with a large, plummy face, soft, dark eyes and a plentiful, black drooping moustache, it is nowadays hard to find much charm in him)—and soon he had undertaken to promote even further the advanced learning for which Edwin had so much regard. Latin, history, mathematics and geography—the last perhaps somewhat in the general direction of Oh, my America, my new-found-land!—a poem by a fellow cleric considerably more literate, if a great deal naughtier, in verse than the Rev. George. For while Donne addressed himself strictly to his bird, with George it was all his birdie—

> Who is it that hath burst the door
> Unclosed the heart that shut before,
> And set her queen-like on its throne
> And made its homage all her own?—
> My birdie!

This effusion went on for many stanzas, all with the same refrain. After Edwin Bartlett died, the author was at great pains to get it back from Adelaide: and who can blame him?

The lessons took place in the front room at Claverton Street and often lasted all day; not surprising that sometimes Adelaide was so exhausted as to have to take them sitting on the floor, her head resting against George's knee, the curtains drawn across and even pinned together, to take the strain from her eyes. These were very dark and large in an oval face, crowned by close-cropped, curly dark hair. The mouth is full-lipped and rather sensuous. No wonder that at last it was all too much for George who went to Edwin and confessed that he was becoming "too interested" in Adelaide.

Edwin was unperturbed. He begged George to continue as before and soon a somewhat astonishing situation emerged, which certainly was understood and accepted by all three—in which it was agreed that Edwin had some obscure condition which gave him not much longer to live and that Adelaide was more or less made over to George in advance, as his prospective wife.

October. November. On 8 December—in 1885, this is, the eleventh year of the marriage—Adelaide sent round the corner for the nearest available doctor. He found Edwin very low, weak and deeply depressed, suffering from sickness, diarrhoea, and haemorrhage of the bowels. On looking into the mouth, he observed also a blue line round the edge of the gums which suggested that at some time the patient had taken mercury. This in turn suggested what counsel later referred to euphemistically as "a pestilent disease" which, however, Edwin to the last refused to admit to; (one wonders a little, all the same, about that baby, stillborn to a perfectly strong and healthy young woman; and it does seem that Edwin was ever a prey to undefined, perhaps secret, fears). It later emerged that as a young man he had decided that dentures would be better than the real thing and had accordingly submitted to the awful agony of having all his own perfectly good teeth sawn off at the gums. The stumps had now decayed and his entire mouth was in an appalling condition. Within the next twelve days he had sixteen of these stumps removed; they revealed an underlying fungoid growth with resultant sloughing, eroding and sponginess which we may feel it more agreeable to pass over.

By the 19th however, things were much improved and the doctor wanted the patient to go away for a change—preferably without his wife who, said the doctor, "petted him too much".

But though brighter, Edwin was now terrified about his health and refused, and on the 23rd his fears seemed—to himself at any rate—justified. Whatever a lumbricoid worm may be, he passed a lumbricoid worm.

By this time it really seems fair to describe the wretched man as half out of his mind with fear, distress and a very understandable self pity. He felt worms constantly wriggling up and down his throat and one night, he told the doctor, he arose and stood before Adelaide as she slept, "extracting the vital force from her to himself". And each time he grew a little brighter, fresh disaster struck. Now necrosis of the jaw was suggested and it had a frightening ring to it. On 31 December, New Year's Eve, yet another stump of tooth must come out.

In preparation for this event, he ate for his breakfast half a dozen oysters and a large helping of jugged hare. On return from the dentist, "this remarkable invalid" had another half dozen oysters, a quantity of mango chutney—all by itself?—cake and tea; and ordered a large haddock for the next morning's breakfast, saying that he would wake up early in anticipation of this treat.

Alas, he was destined never to wake up again.

Adelaide, meanwhile, had been looking after her husband with a truly devoted assiduity, sitting up with him all night and every night, holding his toe which seems to have afforded him some obscure satisfaction. On 27 December, however, four days before he died, a most curious event had taken place. She had—apparently accidentally—run into the Rev. George Dyson in the street, and had sent him off upon an errand. He was to obtain for her quite a large quantity of chloroform. Edwin had long suffered from an internal complaint, she explained, about which he was too sensitive to speak to anybody, and nothing but chloroform had ever been able to soothe him and send him to sleep. She had previously got it from her friend, the midwife, Annie Walker—this was untrue—but Annie Walker was now abroad. She could not ask the doctor for it as he would never understand how skilled she was in its use.

She said nothing about keeping the matter secret and George could not, later, say why he should have gone such an odd way about obtaining it—going round to three different chemists—collecting the amount in three small bottles—telling lies as to its intended purpose—transferring it all to one bottle and handing it to Adelaide surreptitiously; though that, he explained, was only because Edwin was present.

The bottle was never seen again; and four days later Edwin Bartlett lay dead with a large quantity of chloroform in his stomach.

Adelaide had awoken, she said, at four o'clock in the morning; had turned him on his back, tried to pour brandy down his throat—there was a smell of spilt brandy on his chest and half a glass of it on the mantelpiece within reach of his bed. She had sent the maid for the doctor and called up the landlord. He testified that the room had smelt "of paregoric or ether" and especially the brandy glass.

Edwin's father arrived. He had long been making not very thickly veiled suggestions that his daughter-in-law was trying to poison her husband and he now kissed his dead son and at the same time sniffed at his lips: and announced that there must be a post mortem. The Rev. George, on the other hand, was concerned only and immediately with Number One. He began to panic about that chloroform and—on his way to chapel to take a service—disposed of the original three small bottles under separate bushes on Wandsworth Common. He then rushed to Adelaide and demanded the return of My Birdie; and receiving no satisfaction from her, proceeded to unburden his heart to friends.

Adelaide, betrayed, sought out the doctor and unburdened hers. She had really wanted the chloroform, she now declared, because Edwin, in his brief moments of returning spirits showed signs of wishing to claim rights which he had never demanded before. Feeling herself to have been almost officially handed over to the Rev. Dyson, she had felt this to be not quite decent. She could hardly explain it to a clergyman, so she had told him a tarradiddle to persuade him to get her the chloroform, privately proposing to sprinkle it on a handkerchief, wave it in her husband's face and so subdue his unwelcome passions. She had had no occasion to use it, but on that night, the evening of his death, she had felt so bad about keeping a secret from him that she had broken down and confessed it all and handed over the bottle. They had had a talk, "serious but amicable" and he had put the bottle on the mantel-piece by the bedside, turned over and gone to sleep—or to sulk, she rather unexpectedly amended. Next morning she had taken the bottle, not observing whether or not any of the contents was missing, and put it in a drawer of her dressing-table. There the police had—somewhat unaccountably, it must be confessed—overlooked it in their search and when she left the house for ever she had taken it with her and thrown it from the window of the train into a pond. It must be added in Adelaide's disfavour that at this time the pond in question is said to have been frozen over.

A simple little story—allowing for Adelaide's undoubted tendency to embroider the truth. It had only one drawback: nobody believed it.

On the other hand . . .

On the other hand, thundered the medical witnesses at her subsequent trial, it was impossible to administer chloroform to a conscious person without an agonised struggle and outcry: and in this case there had been demonstrably been none. And it was equally impossible for anyone unskilled to administer chloroform to an unconscious person, without leaving signs of burning in the throat; and in this case there were none. No attempt at murder by this means had ever been recorded.

So with all the bad will in the world—how could Adelaide have got the chloroform down her husband's throat?

Suicide and accident were of course canvassed. She had left him for some little time while she went into the next room to prepare herself for the night's vigil—which for some reason she appears to have spent fully dressed. But if he had then accidentally—or for that matter, purposely—drunk from the bottle, he must have cried out in pain and she must have heard him through the partitioning doors which were all that divided the two rooms. At any rate, she would not have found him when she came back, apparently peacefully at rest. There seemed no alternative to murder. Only—how?

By first rendering him partially insensible by inhalation of the chloroform, suggested the Crown, either while he was asleep (extremely difficult, protested the medical witnesses) or by some sort of persuasion; and then pouring the fatal dose down his throat. But, declared a specialist in such matters, though in a person losing consciousness there might be a moment between the time they were still able to swallow and the failure of that reflex—"the most careful doctor could not measure or predict its existence".

Very well, said the Crown (in essence) *you* know that: but Adelaide didn't, did she? Suppose she just had a bash and struck the lucky moment?

Or, it has since been suggested, might she not easily have persuaded him to take a dose?—trusting her implicitly as he did and with his deep respect for her "learning". He had been suffering from sleeplessness and nothing else so far had done him any good. (It is put forward in a recent book on the case that Adelaide was in fact a thoroughly wicked woman who all along had been poisoning her husband; that she had borrowed the lumbricoid worm from one of the Newfoundland dogs—not a very charming idea—and introduced it deliberately, further to cast gloom and despondency; and that finally *under hypnotism* she induced him, to take the dose.)

But the question always seems to come back to this—why should she? They all three believed that Edwin had not long to live—or why the arrangement, which undoubtedly existed, about handing her over to the Rev. Dyson? Dyson, by the rules of his church, could not marry for some little time to come, and meanwhile she was free, indeed encouraged, by her husband to spend most of her time with him—curtains drawn, head on knee, My Birdie and all the rest of it. Moreover, no one was ever found to say that to the end she had been anything but an affectionate, tenderly careful and much loved wife. So why take so appalling a risk?—why with so little care or concealment court a death-sentence for murder? Adelaide was a clever creature, the very readiness and glibness of her innumerable fibs proves that: would she for a moment have trusted George Dyson—a man of God, after all—to keep silent when his purchase of the chloroform became known?—nor had she ever asked him to keep the matter secret. Then—just to tip the stuff down her husband's throat, leaving no possible alternative to her own guilt when, as must inevitably happen, the cause of his death was proved. No attempt to set the stage for accident or suicide: why the removal of the chloroform bottle which made either impossible? And she was already aware that the embittered old father-in-law was accusing her of causing his son's illness.

The consensus of opinion is probably that Adelaide Barlett murdered her husband. This is to some extent on account of her lies—but we are nowadays sufficiently familiar with the phenomenon of the self-dramatist, the compulsive liar?—and the monotony and uselessness of her life would have conduced to both. Mostly, however, it is for lack of any alternative. And yet . . .

That Adelaide really cared two hoots for the Rev. Dyson, it is impossible to believe—except as a diversion from the tedium of her friendless life. But here was Edwin, however much she may have been devoted to him—with his toothless gums, sloughing and sponging and all the rest of it, with worms imaginary or otherwise crawling up and down his throat, with his crumbling jaw and that ominously suggestive blue line . . . Not exactly a proposition for a fastidious young woman, already sentimentally inclined elsewhere. And yet how to avoid wounding his feelings in his present extremely manic-depressive condition? She has been used, perhaps, to employing chloroform in her work with the dogs? At any rate, she sets about obtaining some. And sure enough, on New Year's Eve, after his supper of aphrodisiac oysters, the mango chutney and cake—Edwin shows signs of rising uxorious desires.

Who can say what was done or spoken that night? She genuinely believed, perhaps, that she could quieten him down?—and he detected something and so she confessed it all? Or she had thought of a better plan: she would simply explain to him that her spiritual betrothal to George Dyson—which Edwin himself had promoted—forbade marital relations between them. Either way, she handed over the bottle, left it standing there unused on the mantel-shelf—they had a good talk and Edwin turned over and went to sleep.

Or to sulk, Adelaide had said.

Of course it was all nonsense about Edwin and his platonic relations with his wife: another of those tarradiddles so pointless as to suggest a guiltless, pathological cause for all Adelaide's untruths. The famous "single act" on a Sunday afternoon which had resulted in the stillborn baby, was reduced to commonplace by the testimony of the midwife: "On all other occasions a preventative was used." Edwin, in his fitful feelings of well-being, was simply asking for his customary cuddle. And for the first time, Adelaide was saying no.

Poor man! He is hateful to himself with his upset stomach and his gums and his necrosis and his lumbricoid worm; and now it seems he is hateful to Adelaide also. She has withdrawn her favours from him; she and George, the admired and beloved friend, appear to be calmly anticipating a near future when he, the obstructive husband, shall be out of the way . . .

A bottle of chloroform within reach. A glass of brandy to hand. He tips a large dose of the one into the other. The chloroform hangs in the brandy*, suspended at its centre like a yolk in the white of an egg. Wrapped within its cocoon, the dose passes without pain or burning, all at one gulp—down the throat of the suicide.

Adelaide comes back from the other room. Edwin lies doggo. She settles herself for the night.

In the early hours of the morning she awakes; and he is dead.

As we have seen, Adelaide Bartlett was no fool. All along, the horrid old father-in-law has been making overt accusations and now his son is indeed dead, and it is she who has—apparently secretly, and giving false reasons—introduced the fatal dose. What to do? Get rid of the bottle of chloroform, at any rate, just get rid of it and trust to luck; nothing can be worse than leaving it here beside Edwin. Rinse out the glass, spill a bit of brandy around: but get rid of that bottle.

That she put it in her dressing-table drawer, we may take leave to doubt: laced into her corsets, more likely—no one went so far as to search her person. Then to send for the doctor (may he not, considering the patient's long sickness, issue a death certificate without more ado?)—summon up the landlord, give way to a doubtless quite genuine grief. And when the Rev. George comes rushing round in a state about the chloroform, stamp your foot and cry out, "Oh, damn the chloroform!"—that none of it has been used and he had better just forget all about it and pipe down . . .

George on the contrary piped up and to such effect that he shortly afterwards found himself standing in the dock beside her, both of them charged with murder.

They let him go almost immediately—to testify against her with all the vehemence of his shocked and terrified heart. But then, after all, he believed her guilty.

The jury believed it too; but they couldn't get round the doctors' evidence in her defence and they brought in a verdict accordingly. "Although we think that grave suspicion attaches to the prisoner . . ." The court waited to hear no more: a huge burst of cheering rang out and for the only time in his long and brilliant career, her counsel, Sir Edward Clarke, put his head in his hands and wept.

---

* I discovered this myself by experiment.

"Now that Mrs Bartlett has been found not guilty of murdering her husband," said the wits afterwards, "it seems only fair that in the interests of science, she should tell us how she did it."

THE MAN WHO CONTRACTED OUT OF HUMANITY

(Stanley Setty, 1949)

Rebecca West

In 1949, Donald Hume, misfit and psychopath, stabbed Stanley Setty to death, sliced up the body and ditched it (rolled up in a carpet) from the air over the Essex marshes. That, at least, is the official version: indeed Hume himself eventually made a confession, paid for by a newspaper. But some observers remained sceptical, among them the writer and historian Rebecca West, who attended Hume's trial and wrote an extensive study of the case. Perhaps the real story of how Stanley Setty met his death has never been told.

During the Second World War, Brian Donald Hume, a failed RAF trainee, posed as a Battle of Britain hero; while not yet twenty-one he became, on his own admission, "an undesirable and unreliable character". Discharged as unfit for service, Hume opened an electrical shop in Golders Green, north London. He prospered, to the extent that, by 1947, he'd expanded the business, hired extra staff and acquired a luxury car. In 1949, by chance, he ran into an unscrupulous second-hand car dealer called Stanley Setty. It was their second encounter; Hume had met Setty a year or so earlier in Warren Street, doing dubious deals on the pavement, recalling that he had "a voice like broken bottles, and pockets stuffed with cash". When Setty was last seen alive in October 1949, he was carrying about £1,000 in five pound notes. Not long afterwards,

Setty's dismembered and headless body was found rolled in carpet on the Thames marshes near Southend, where it had been dumped from the sky. Staff at Elstree aerodrome remembered Hume hiring a plane, and tipped off the police.

Hume was arrested at his cramped maisonette near Golders Green station. Rebecca West, who covered Hume's trial for murder, followed the police trail, toiling up the "dark, steep and narrow staircase with a murderous turn to it" in search of atmospheric detail. In January 1950, Hume entered the dock at the Old Bailey clad in checked sports jacket, pullover and flannels, "all chosen", Rebecca West reported, "to look raffish, which was then the uniform of the spiv . . ." Hume pleaded not guilty, blaming the murder on three of Setty's shady associates, Mac (or Maxie), Greenie and a man known as "The Boy". There were, in the event, two trials; the first, aborted when the judge was taken ill, lasted only one day. The second began straight away with a new judge, but at the end of a seven day hearing, the jury failed to agree a verdict. A fresh jury was sworn. But when the Crown offered no evidence against Hume on a charge of murder, the new jury was directed by the judge to return a not guilty verdict. Hume did, however, plead guilty to a second charge, of being an accessory after the fact to murder. On this count, he was jailed for twelve years.

When Rebecca West wrote about the case in 1950, Stanley Setty's killer remained (technically, at least) unconvicted, unknown and unnamed. Rebecca West filed her impression of Donald Hume's trial for the London Evening Standard.

Every murder trial, like every murderer, has unique fingerprints. It has its own personality. The trial of Brian Donald Hume, who was accused of murdering Stanley Setty, had a personality stronger and stranger than most.

It was great relief when it was over, when the jury disagreed, the prosecuting counsel announced that he was not going to demand a retrial, and brought forward a second indictment on the charge of being an accessory after the fact of murder, to which Hume pleaded guilty.

Much was mentioned at the trial which seemed to me irrelevant. All the expert witnesses, it seemed to me, might just as well have stayed at home. They discussed at length, and with spectacular evidence of conscientious deliberation, whether Mr Setty could have been killed by one assailant or if one or more men must have held him while another assailant stabbed him.

But all this was the purest speculation, as they had not got Mr Setty's head. It might well have been that a single assailant could first have hit Mr Setty on the head and rendered him unconscious and then stabbed him.

They never mentioned this possibility, which today, when the cosh is more of a feature of urban life than it has been since Victorian times, is more than a possibility—it is a probability.

But it would have been supremely relevant if any clotted blood had been found in Hume's flat, for blood flowing from the corpse of a man who had just been murdered clots. There was plenty of blood in Hume's flat, but the impression left was that it was all liquid, as blood is when it flows from a corpse which has been murdered for an hour or two.

I do not remember the prosecution explaining that if there were clotted blood in Hume's flat there was a strong presumption that he had been murdered there; and as a spectator I was left with the impression that, as the blood in the flat was liquid, it would have been feasible for Mr Setty to be murdered elsewhere and brought to Hume's flat.

On this, and on several other scores, it could be pronounced improbable that Hume murdered Mr Setty, and the jury could not agree to find him guilty of it.

But if Hume were convicted of a crime less than murder, it was still abominable enough. That was what contributed to the strangeness and horror of the pattern described by this murder, which consisted of patches of crude colour set against a quiet and lovely background. That pleasant background was made up of people who were very nice indeed; the crude colour was laid on by people who were not so nice.

It happened again and again during the trial that one listened to a witness and remembered that the real wealth of Great Britain lies in the number of decent men and women it produces, and that we are not bankrupt yet.

There was the enchanting manageress of the dyeing and cleaning establishment at Golders Green, with her shining yet reserved smile, her comfortable, fussed-over good looks, her perfect manners.

It would have been worthwhile attending the trial if only to see the tender and amused and generous gaze she directed on the learned counsel who did not know that a carpet cannot be dyed without being cleaned.

"Poor dear," she was evidently saying to herself, "surely common sense ought to have told him that. But, there, he probably knows a great many things I don't."

There was the domestic worker, Mrs Stride, who used to turn out Mrs Hume's flat one afternoon a week, and was not told what to do by Mrs Hume when she arrived. Oh, no. When the learned counsel suggested that might have been the routine, Mrs Stride's face, which had been round and pleasant under the little plain hat, became stern and marmoreal, as if she were one of the more respectable Roman Empresses among the statues in the British Museum.

She gave learned counsel to understand that she knew her work, and that when she got to the flat she started on that work and went on till she had finished it, and she doubted if Mrs Hume or anyone else could help her in that achievement.

Here was a woman who was obviously on top of her environment, who had made the resources within her reach serve her need to be self-respecting and independent and creative.

There was also Mr Sidney Tiffen, who found Mr Setty's torso on the Essex marshes and who did not let it go, as you or I might have been tempted to do, but dug a stake in the mud and struggled with the horrid parcel until he had fixed it to that stake.

We saw Hume's uninhibited quality, for it unfortunately happened that his cross-examination by the prosecuting counsel at times turned into a slanging match.

Bad temper was let loose, so it came about that Hume shouted: "Now it's you that's romancing," and "That's all boloney."

Now, Hume did not murder Mr Setty: but when he talked of his dealings with Mr Setty's corpse, of how he had propped up one parcel when it had fallen askew in his car, of how he had lost his footing when he was carrying another and slithered downstairs with it, he seemed as atrocious as if he had committed the greater crime.

Indeed, many murderers have shown more respect to their victims than he showed to this corpse which he had agreed to dispose of for money.

It was as if he had contracted out of humanity.

Humane instinct withered in him. He had become as full of death as Mrs Stride, Mr Tiffen, the manageress of the dyeing and cleaning establishment, are full of life.

So far as one could see, it is work that makes the difference. Mrs Stride had dedicated herself to the technique of making things clean; you should have seen the light of expertise burning in her eye when she discussed different sorts of noise made by two different types of vacuum-cleaner.

But Hume had been a "wide boy" since the war ended. He described himself as "semi-honest" and it is plain that he spent his life hanging round the neighbourhood of any control to see who would pay him for procuring a breach of it.

There was a time when dishonesty involved a certain degree of craftsmanship: a pickpocket had to pick pockets well if he could hope to make a living: and he will not even have to look for his clients. He can advertise himself as a dishonest dealer by prodigious tailoring and his station on certain notorious sites.

The currency racket is as simple. In both these rackets Hume had been involved.

He was following a way of living which did nothing to develop his own nature, and therefore isolated him from the knowledge and respect of others; so that in the end he could cart about a body that had been a man as if it were a piece of meat, and put his own body in the danger of death, and escaped it only to spend the years of his maturity in prison.

This is the specific criminal problem of our age. We live in a time of shortages, and shortages evoke controls, and the illegal breach of controls leads to quick and easy profits.

This is not merely a political problem. The rule by which a new car cannot be sold till twelve months after its owner has acquired it is not a Government regulation but a condition of sale legally imposed by the British Motor Traders' Association; and it was instituted with the object of checking wild profiteering and speculation which would have thrown the motor-dealing business into complete and disreputable disorder.

Nevertheless, it has created crime. It is necessary; but some of its effects are pernicious.

The community has never had a much more difficult problem to solve. It can be met only by the coldest scrutiny of all controls and the abolition of all that are unnecessary; by a national determination to end the days of shortages; and by a lively recognition that crime is not funny, but filthy.

That was what gave the Hume case its memorable quality. It showed a poor wretch who, human to start with, had gone past his humanity, not to animalism, for that has its saving instincts, but to callousness; and it showed other people who had kept their humanity and bettered it.

Brian Donald Hume was released from prison in February 1958, ҭaving earned full remission. In June of that year, the Sunday Pictorial *splashed his confession to the murder of Stanley Setty, Hume having first taken the precaution of fleeing to Switzerland. By August he was back in England, carrying out two raids on banks in west London. In January 1959 Hume staged a third raid, this time on a bank in Zurich, and killed a cabdriver while trying to get away. He was arrested at the scene. Hume was sentenced to life imprisonment for murdering the taxi-man. Dame (as she became) Rebecca West said she'd never accepted that Hume was the killer of Stanley Setty. Her lengthy and detailed essay* Mr Setty and Mr Hume *was published in 1955. "Of course," she explained in 1974, "I knew that Hume had confessed to the murder of Setty before my essay was published . . . He started confessing very soon after he got into prison, and continued to produce confessions at intervals for years, but I think there was a definite reason not to take them seriously . . ." In 1976, Hume was repatriated to Britain as insane and sent to Broadmoor. He was released in 1988, and moved to a hospital for low-risk patients in west London.* He died in 1998.

A KENT MURDER MYSTERY

(Caroline Luard, 1908)

T. C. H. Jacobs

The murder of Caroline Luard on a summer's afternoon in 1908 is still a puzzle some ninety years later. Mrs Luard was fifty-eight and well-to-do. She was the wife of Major-General Charles Luard, with whom she had lived blamelessly (it seems) at a large house called Ightham Knoll in a quiet part of Kent, the county known as the Garden of England. The couple had taken a walk together that afternoon, but Mrs Luard had turned back, saying she had a guest coming to tea. The General said he walked on alone as far as the golf club. Returning home, he found the guest still waiting for her tea, but no sign of his wife. Retracing his walk, he discovered her body near the spot where they'd parted. Mrs Luard had been shot in the head at point-blank range. It wasn't long before the General himself became the object of suspicion. Tongues wagged and anonymous letters were sent to his home. Depressed, the General killed himself by throwing himself under a train, and although the police investigation carried on, no one was ever charged with Mrs Luard's murder. T.C.H. Jacobs was one of several pen-names of Jacques Pendower (1899–1976), one of the most prolific and versatile of writers. He produced more than 180 mystery novels, westerns, romances, and contributed scores of short stories, serials and articles to newspapers and magazines as well as a number of plays for BBC Radio. Pendower was a founding member and former chairman of the Crime Writers Association. Somehow, he also managed (until he was fifty) to hold down a real job

*in the civil service as an investigating officer for the Inland Revenue.
While it is hard to see how he had any free time, Pendower listed his
hobbies as golf, rifle shooting and driving a fast car.*

It was not until the year 1906 that the services of Scotland Yard
were first made available to the provincial police. In that year the
Home Secretary, realizing the unsatisfactory state of affairs, issued
a circular letter to the Chief Constables of county and borough
police forces announcing an important scheme for the investigation
of murder throughout the country.

This scheme provided for the loaning of experienced Chief
Inspectors of Scotland Yard for temporary service in difficult
cases of murder and other major crimes. The Chief Constables
were invited to apply for assistance whenever it was thought
desirable. The Home Secretary could only invite co-operation.
He had no power to order it as the State has no direct control
over any police force in the country.

The suggestion met with a mixed reception, but on the whole
it was welcomed. The provincial constabulary had no detectives
at all and relied on the uniformed police to investigate all crimes,
however grave and complicated the nature.

The numerous errors and failures of these officers with little or no
knowledge or experience of the intricacies of criminal investigation
had prompted the Home Secretary to issue his circular letter. It
was never intended, as some Chief Constables seemed to think,
that the CID officers should be rivals to the local men. Their
function was to be solely that of an expert to assist and advise.

Since that time the scientific investigation of crime has developed
enormously. Today every police force has its own staff of trained
detectives capable of investigating successfully any type of crime.

At first, calls for Scotland Yard aid were slow in coming, but
by 1908 the value of the expert assistant was beginning to be
appreciated.

It was in that year that there occurred a murder mystery that
is still the topic of argument and discussion in Kent. The Chief
Constable, Colonel Warde, wasted no time in asking for CID
help, and Chief Inspector Scott and Detective Sergeant Savage
were detailed for the investigation. The fact that Colonel Warde
was a close personal friend of the murdered woman and her

husband may have prompted him in his immediate request for expert aid. He was particularly anxious to do all in his power to solve the ugly mystery.

Major General Charles Edward Luard was descended from a celebrated Huguenot family who first settled in England in 1685. His ancestors in long succession had served with distinction in the British Army and his own son was a serving officer. He himself had retired after thirty years' service with the Royal Engineers.

On his retirement he had bought Ightham Knoll, a large, redbrick manor house situated between the villages of Seal and Ightham on the Maidstone road. His wife, who was ten years his junior, was the daughter of a Cumberland landed gentleman.

They were a devoted couple and their married life was one of complete happiness. They were often seen walking arm-in-arm through the lovely woods and lanes which surrounded their house, and with them always their faithful companion, an Irish terrier, a somewhat aggressive animal well known locally for his fighting qualities.

The General lived the life of a country gentleman, but he took a great interest in local affairs, too. He was a member of the Kent County Council and patron of a number of sports clubs. He was regarded by the local people as a kind and considerate gentleman, a tall, erect man with remarkable vigour for his years.

At about two-thirty p.m., 2 August 1908, the General and Mrs Luard, accompanied by the Irish terrier, set out for a walk. One of their favourite strolls was through the Fish Pond Woods on the estate of another landowner, Mr Horace Wilkinson, with whom they were very friendly. By taking a short cut across the meadows they entered the woods by a private path winding its way to the Wildernesse golf course at Godden Green, some three miles distant from their house.

In the heart of these woods, about five hundred yards from the main road, was a summer-house belonging to Mr Wilkinson and known as "La Casa". On frequent occasions during the summer months they had taken tea together in this secluded retreat, and it was to this summer-house that Mrs Luard intended walking when she set out with her husband. She was going as far as that and then return home by the same route. The General was walking on to the golf club at Godden Green.

Mrs Luard had invited the wife of a local solicitor, Mrs Stewart, to take tea with her and so she was anxious to return early to the manor house.

The General and Mrs Luard were walking for half an hour together before they parted company at a point beyond "La Casa". She walked back along the bridle-path in the direction of the summer-house and her husband went on to the golf club. The time when they parted was about three o'clock.

The Irish terrier accompanied the General, running freely through the woods on either side of the path, hunting rabbits. They arrived on the golf greens about three twenty-five p.m. where the General spoke to a labourer named King. He reached the club house at three-thirty, where the steward, Harry Kent, gave him his bag of clubs which had been left in his care the last time the General had played golf.

King saw the General a few minutes later returning across the greens carrying his clubs.

The General did not return the way he had come but walked on the road as being much quicker than the woodland path. Here he was overtaken by the Rev. A. B. Cotton of Shipbourne, who offered him a lift in his car. At first the General refused, but finally accepted and with his dog was driven by the parson to the gates of Ightham Knoll, arriving at four-thirty p.m.

His wife's guest, Mrs Stewart, was waiting when he went into the house and he was surprised to learn that his wife had not yet returned. He offered his apologies to the lady and told her that his wife must have been delayed, but would certainly return shortly as she had expressly stated that Mrs Stewart had been invited to tea and she must not be late home.

After waiting some time they decided to have tea and not wait any longer. The General was uneasy about his wife and immediately after tea said that he must go and look for her. Mrs Stewart asked to go with him as she had business with Mrs Luard. To this the General agreed and they set out together. But not meeting Mrs Luard by the time they reached the woods the visitor said she must return home as she herself had a visitor who was due at five-fifteen p.m.

With growing anxiety the General walked on alone, following the bridle-path which led towards "La Casa" deep in the wood, the same path which he had taken with his wife some two and a half hours previously.

As he came within sight of the summer-house he observed his wife stretched face downwards on the floor of the veranda. He ran towards her, thinking that she must have fainted. But when he came up to her he saw the pool of blood on the floor and the extensive bloodstains on her face and head.

A brief examination showed him that she was dead. Her right-hand glove was in place, but the glove from the left hand had obviously been wrenched off and lay turned inside out on the grass. Three valuable rings were missing. In addition, the pocket of her dress had been cut out and her purse stolen. Her hat was lying several yards away.

General Luard was so shocked that he stood regarding his dead wife with helpless astonishment. Plainly she had been murdered and robbed, an unthinkable thing in this quiet backwater of rural Kent.

Greatly distressed, he left the body just as he had found it and hurried through the woods to the Wilkinson stables nearly a mile away. There he saw the butler, Herbert Harding, and the time was five fifty-five p.m. He told Harding what he had discovered and the two men went back to the summer-house. Harding then returned to summon the police and a doctor.

Dr Mansfield, of Sevenoaks, arrived ahead of the police. The gravity of the case was obvious, and the doctor took careful notes and measurements. The dead woman was lying at full length upon the veranda, her right cheek against the floor. Her head was twelve inches from the steps and was in an extensive pool of blood. Behind the right ear was a bullet hole and another over her left temple, two separate shots from a small-calibre revolver. Powder burns showed that the shots had been fired at very close range.

There were heavy bruises on the right cheek, nose and chin. On the left hand were three abrasions on the ring finger and more abrasions on the middle finger, all caused by rings having been dragged with brutal violence from the fingers.

The doctor examined the hat, one of white straw trimmed with a black silk ribbon. He observed a deep dent and some crushing of the straw. This dent corresponded with the position of an effusion of blood on the top of the dead woman's head.

Considering the position of the body and the wounds, Dr Mansfield concluded that Mrs Luard had been sitting or standing on the veranda when she was struck from behind with a heavy stick, club or some such blunt instrument. While still more or less erect she had then been shot twice through the head, the second shot probably as she turned in falling.

When the body was later examined by another doctor the latter disagreed about the cause of the head wound. He thought that it was not the result of blows, but was caused in falling against one of the stone pillars of the veranda. Considering the actual position of the wound and the fact that her hat was found some distance away, this is not likely. He did agree with Dr Mansfield that the bullet wounds could not have been self-inflicted. It was a crime of murder and a very brutal one at that.

The last person known to have seen Mrs Luard alive was her husband, and when the Scotland Yard men began their investigations one of the first things they did, as in all murder cases, was to take a statement from him.

General Luard was shocked and distressed, heart-broken with grief because his affection for his wife had been deep and sincere. Nevertheless, he was a man of strong military discipline and able to control his emotions. He sat down in his library and wrote out a very detailed statement of his movements. The fact that he was a close personal friend of the Chief Constable and a man of wealth and position made no difference to the detectives. They had a duty to do and they did it without regard to the General's standing.

His grief did impress them as being genuine, but it could have been remorse, and they retained an open mind on his innocence. They tested his statement, checking on the time element, a very important factor in the case.

Two independent witnesses, who were at different points in the Fish Pond Woods, stated that they had heard shots at three-fifteen p.m. exactly. One said he heard two shots, the other three shots. At the time both witnesses were roughly 400 yards from the summer-house. Experiments were carried out by the police to test the possibility of shots being heard in woodland at that distance and it was found that they could have been heard quite clearly over a much greater distance.

So three-fifteen p.m. was almost certainly the time when Mrs Luard had been murdered.

At three-twenty p.m., five minutes after the shots had been heard, the General was seen by a brewer's manager, Thomas Durrant, at Hall Farm, a considerable distance from the summer-house, walking in the direction of the golf course. Both the General and the dog appeared to be perfectly normal.

The evidences of the labourer, King, and the steward, Kent, were taken and proved that General Luard had reached the links at three twenty-five p.m. The evidence of the Rev. A. B. Cotton was that the General, when he picked him up, looked hot and tired, but otherwise looked normal and he chatted quite naturally, certainly not like a man with a murder on his conscience.

The route which the General had taken from his home to the golf club was walked over at a normal walking pace by Superintendent Taylor of the Kent Constabulary and another officer. The journey occupied sixty-one minutes. The time from the summer-house to the golf club was thirty minutes, the exact time taken by the General. So that his statement of times taken was checked and found correct.

The evidence of three independent witnesses appeared to put the General above suspicion. But he was the last person known to have seen his wife alive and it would not be wise to let the time element alone prove his innocence. The police wanted something more absolutely conclusive if they could get it.

The Irish terrier was known to be a very intelligent animal with a keen sense of smell and sound. He was accustomed to give warning of any strangers around. If a stranger had attacked Mrs Luard it was thought highly probable that the dog would have detected his presence in the neighbourhood. Yet he had given no sign, according to the General's statement.

The more the detectives investigated the more convinced they became that the person who had murdered Mrs Luard was no stranger to her. They discounted the possibility that some casual tramp or hop-picker was the assassin, basing their belief on the ease with which the murderer had apparently been able to approach her. Why, too, had she been at the summer-house at three-fifteen p.m., when from the time her husband declared he had left her she should have been at least as far as the edge of the wood and probably in the meadows? She had expressly stated that she had to hurry home to be in time for her visitor to tea.

It seemed to suggest that she waited at the summer-house for some reason. One possibility was that she had an appointment there unknown to her husband.

There was the question of motive to consider, another matter of vital importance in a murder investigation. There seemed not the slightest shred of motive as far as her husband was concerned. All the evidence pointed to the fact that he loved and respected his wife to a quite unusual degree. He was not a man given to sudden tempers. He was as fit as a man of his age could possibly hope to be, sound in body and mind. So that the question of sudden homicidal impulse did not arise. On the day of the tragedy they had seemed to the servants to be in a particularly happy frame of mind and gone off arm-in-arm for that last fatal stroll in the woods.

The General's finances were in excellent order, so that there were no monetary worries preying on his mind. He stood to gain no monetary benefit by her death. As far as motive was concerned there was none which the detectives could find.

The question of the revolver was another matter to be settled. No revolver was left behind at the scene of the crime, nor did the General carry firearms. A search of his house failed to find the weapon, or any cartridges to fit such a revolver.

The most thorough searches and widespread enquiries, extending even to London, failed to furnish the slightest thing of assistance to the police. All the while they were convinced that this was not some chance encounter with an armed bandit, but a carefully planned and skilfully carried out murder.

Yet there was the undeniable fact that nobody could have known beforehand which route the General and Mrs Luard were going to take, because they did not make up their minds until after they had left Ightham Knoll. But who had suggested the route which they did take? The General thought he had, but he was not sure. If Mrs Luard had had that secret appointment at the summer-house she could easily have suggested casually that they walked that way and it was not likely that her husband would recall afterwards who had made the actual suggestion, especially with the mental stress caused by the murder agitating his mind.

General Luard could furnish no suggestion as to any person who might hate his wife enough to murder her. He could recall nothing in their lives that could possibly have caused any person to entertain feelings of revenge, jealousy or hate against either of them. His wife, he declared, had often walked home alone along that particular route.

As far as the police were concerned General Luard was eliminated as a suspect. Even if he had run all the way from the summer-house to Hall Farm, where he was seen at three-twenty p.m., he could not have done it in five minutes. Even if that evidence of time was wrong, he could not have covered the distance to the golf course in ten minutes. The man who had seen him at Hall Farm stated positively that he was walking at a normal pace. The time element proved that General Luard was innocent of his wife's murder.

Weeks of intensive investigations yielded absolutely nothing.

Every line petered out, every suggestion proved valueless. The murder was a mystery which could not be solved.

The inquest, opened in the dining-room at Ightham Knoll, was resumed in the local inn. It brought to light nothing not already known. The General could not say why his wife should have taken so long to reach the summer-house or why she was still there at three-fifteen p.m. He did say that it was quicker to walk across the veranda of "La Casa" than go round by the path, and his wife would probably have done that. That might account for her actual presence on the veranda, but not the time she was there, unless she had felt tired and sat down to rest, not very likely in view of her haste to be home in time for her visitor.

But if the police were absolutely satisfied that the General was an innocent man, some members of the public were not. Dozens of anonymous and scurrilous letters poured into Ightham Knoll accusing the General of murdering his wife and abusing him in vile terms.

Already heart-broken by the dreadful tragedy, the General became distracted by these horrible accusations. Friends tried to comfort him and one, Colonel Warde, M P, a relative of the Chief Constable, took him away from his tragic house and brought him to Barnham Court, the Warde residence near Maidstone, to stay for a while.

On the night of 17 September, General Luard told his host that he was going to Southampton the following day to meet his son, Captain Luard, returning from South Africa. In the morning the General was up before most of the household. The butler brought him tea as he sat writing a letter in the library. When the butler had gone General Luard drank the tea, put the letter on the table and walked out of the house. He crossed the park to a gate opening on to the main road, crossed the road and took a footpath leading to the railway line. Concealed behind a clump of bushes he waited until he heard a train approaching and then dashed out and flung himself across the line. The engine and coaches passed over his body before the driver could pull up.

His letter was read at the inquest. It was as follows:

My dear Warde,

I am sorry to have to return your kindness and long friendship in this way, but I am satisfied it is best to join her in the second life at once as I can be of no further use to anyone in future in this world, of which I am tired and in which I do not wish to live any longer. I thought that my strength was sufficient to bear up against the horrible imputations and terrible letters which I have received since that awful crime was committed and which robbed me of my happiness. And so it was for long and the goodness, kindness and sympathy of so many friends kept me going. But somehow in the last day or two something seems to have snapped. The strength has left me and I care for nothing except to join her again. So good-bye, my dear friend, to both of us.

Yours very affectionately,
C. E. Luard.

P.S.—I shall be somewhere on the line of railway.

The Coroner was scathing in his comments on the evil and ignorant minds which had framed those malicious anonymous letters which had driven an honourable gentleman and gallant soldier to take his own life.

He made it absolutely clear that General Luard could not possibly have been responsible for the murder. The police, he declared, had done all they could to bring the criminal to justice, but their task had been rendered more difficult by the absence of motive, the isolated spot in which the murder was committed and the fact that darkness had set in before the police arrived on the scene.

It will be noted that the Coroner did not suggest robbery as the motive. Robbery was the obvious motive, but was it too obvious? Would a ruffian, in such desperate haste that he had dragged the rings from the dead hand with such brutal violence that he had torn the flesh of the fingers, waste the time and trouble to cut out a dress pocket to steal the purse it contained? Why not put his hand in the pocket and take the purse, surely a more simple action, but not one which would leave any visual evidence to deceive the police?

That cut-out pocket was alien to the murder pattern. Was it that little mistake which all murderers who try to be too clever make and which usually is their undoing?

If robbery was merely a blind, what then was the motive for this foul crime? The most extensive investigation failed to answer that vital question.

And so the murder at Ightham Knoll went on the records as an unsolved crime. It remains to this day as great a mystery as ever. Was it, as the police so firmly believed, a carefully planned, premeditated murder carried out with extraordinary skill and good luck by a person well known to the dead woman? Or was it the chance assassination by some casual tramp roaming the woods? No prison breaks or asylum escapes had taken place that year. No tramps had been seen in the neighbourhood. The gamekeepers and estate workers had seen no strangers for days.

Tramps do not carry revolvers, or expect to meet wealthy ladies in such isolated spots as the heart of Fish Pond Woods. But there is always the exception in everything. This may have been one. Only the murderer himself knows the answer, and it is unlikely now that the mystery will ever be solved.

ACKNOWLEDGEMENTS AND SOURCES

The editor would like to thank the following people and organizations for their kind permission to reprint the following:

Mrs Betty Allsop for Kenneth Allsop, *The Short, Sweet Martyrdom of Jake Lingle* from *The Bootleggers* (Hutchinson 1961); Campbell Thomson & McLaughlin for Eric Ambler, *Dr John Bodkin Adams* © 1999 Eric Ambler from *The Ability to Kill* (Bodley Head 1961); The Estate of the late Christianna Brand and A.M. Heath for Christianna Brand, *Murder Hath Charms* from *Brand X* (Michael Joseph 1974, © Christianna Brand); Judith Cook for *True Lies* from *The Weekend Guardian* (17 September 1994); Solo Syndication Ltd for John Edwards, *Fools and Horses* (*Daily Mail*, 12 March 1994); Orbis Publishing for Daniel Farson, *The Case of the Salmon Sandwiches* from *Unsolved* (1984); Paul Foot for *The A6 Murder Case* from *London Review of Books* (11 December 1997); Jonathan Goodman for *A Coincidence of Corpses* from *The Railway Murders* (Allison & Busby 1984); J.A. Harding and David Evans for F. Tennyson Jesse, *Checkmate*; The Trustees of the Estate of the late Edgar Lustgarten for *Florence Maybrick* from *Verdict in Dispute* (Allan Wingate 1949); *Esquire* Magazine © Hearst Communications,

Inc. for Morris Markey, *Who Killed Joe Elwell?* (October 1950); Brian Masters for *Evidence by Entrapment*; Russell Miller for *The Obsession with the Black Dahlia* from Black Dahlia Website; Mrs Sheena Ellis for William Roughead, *The Secret of Ireland's Eye* from *Famous Crimes* (Faber 1935); Tom Smith-Hughes for Jack Smith-Hughes, *Temptation and the Elder* from *Eight Studies in Justice* (Cassell 1953); Philip Sugden for *Jack the Ripper*; Mrs Kathleen Symons for Julian Symons, *Death of a Millionaire* from *A Reasonable Doubt* (Cresset Press 1960); Viking-Penguin for James Thurber, *A Sort of Genius* from *Vintage Thurber* (Hamish Hamilton 1963); David Wallechinsky for Irving Wallace, *The Real Marie Roget* from *The Fabulous Originals* (Longmans 1955); Express Syndication for Rebecca West, *The Man Who Contracted Out of Humanity*, from *Evening Standard* (27 January 1950); Orbis Publishing for Colin Wilson, *The Zodiac Murders* from *Unsolved* (1984); Robinson Publishing for Kirk Wilson, *The Dumb Blonde Who Knew Too Much* from *Investigating Murder* (1993); and Viking Penguin, a division of Penguin Putnam Inc. for Alexander Woollcott, *The Mystery of the Hansom Cab* from *While Rome Burns* © 1943, renewed by Joseph P. Hennessey 1962.

Every effort has been made to trace the original copyright holders of the following, without success; the editor and publishers would be pleased to hear from any claimants to legal copyright of:
George A. Birmingham, *Mistress and Maid* from *Murder Most Foul* (Chatto & Windus 1929); Douglas G. Browne & E. V. Tullett, *The Murder of Margery Wren* from *Bernard Spilsbury: His Life and Cases* (Harrap 1952); Dorothy Dunbar, *And to Hell with Burgundy* from *Blood in the Parlor* (A.S. Barnes 1962); Nina Warner Hooke and Gil Thomas, *The Camden Town Murder* from *Marshall Hall* (Arthur Barker 1966); Sydney Horler, *The Hoop-la Murder Trial* from *Malefactors' Row* (Robert Hale 1940); T.C.H. Jacobs, *A Kent Murder Mystery* from *Cavalcade of Murder* (Stanley Paul 1955); Guy B.H. Logan, *California's Worst Crime* from *Great Murder Mysteries* (Stanley Paul 1928); Elliott O'Donnell, *What Became of Martin Guerre* from *Strange Disappearances* (The Bodley Head 1927); Sir Edward Parry, *The Mystery of Merstham Tunnel* (Ernest Benn 1924); Edmund Pearson, *The Death of Bella Wright* from *More Studies in Murder* (Smith & Haas 1936); Damon Runyon, *Arnold Rothstein's Final Payoff* from *New York American* (1929);

Louis Stark, *A Case that Rocked the World* from *We Saw It Happen* (Simon & Schuster 1938); and C.J.S. Thompson, *The Mystery of the Poisoned Partridges* from *Poison Mysteries Unsolved* (Hutchinson 1937).